35.

Sam Castellani, MD
May '92

Jake Bernstein

TIMING SIGNALS IN THE FUTURES MARKET

The Trader's Definitive Guide To Buy/Sell Indicators

PROBUS PUBLISHING COMPANY
Chicago, Illinois
Cambridge, England

ISBN 1-55738-155-0

Printed in the United States of America

EB

1   2   3   4   5   6   7   8   9   0

Contents

Acknowledgments

Special thanks to the following:

CQG Inc. for permission to reproduce charts from their outstanding quotation software, System I;

Jerry Becker of Commodity Research Bureau Commodity Perspective for permission to use their excellent futures charts;

Larry Williams for his input, ideas, creativity and inspiration through the years;

Ralph Rieves of Business One Irwin for permission to quote;

Bruce Babcock for permission to quote from his book the Business One Irwin Guide to Futures Trading;

Michael Steinberg, my literary agent for tolerating my chronic tardiness;

Bethany Stubbe at Probus for succeeding in accomplishing what others have failed to do; getting my book to press in spite of me;

And to all would be readers who have been patiently waiting through the numerous delays.

Jake Bernstein

1

The Problems

TRADERS, SYSTEMS, EMOTIONS: THE NATURE OF FUTURES TRADING

Today's futures trader lives in a world of ever-growing technological advancement, complex economics, an unstable international situation, highly competitive markets and a tomorrow which, at times, seems more uncertain, unpredictable and unstable than ever before. Advances in computer hardware and software continue to grow at a virtually exponential pace. At no time in the history of futures trading has there been as many tools, techniques, programs, systems or methods available to the futures trader, all designed and developed with essentially one purpose in mind—to increase the probability of success.

Although the cost of computer hardware, software and historical data has been prohibitive in the past, this is no longer the case. Affordable state-of-the-art equipment and analytical programs are available for as little as several thousand dollars. This will buy more than mere entry-level processing ability. With computers and programs so affordable, and with historical futures and stock data also readily available at a reasonable price, it would seem that virtually every serious futures trader would be trading more successfully, generating more profits and avoiding the many pitfalls which have heretofore been the bane of the trader's existence. Yet it has become increasingly and sadly clear that this is, indeed, not the case. As a matter of fact, it seems that if we examine the lot of the futures trader from a distance, things have not improved much at all!

It has been said that well over 80 percent of all futures traders lose money. In my estimation this figure is likely a conservative one. What's wrong with this picture? How could it be that with such powerful technology and programs at our disposal, so many traders still lose? While it may seem at first blush that this is an incongruous situation, the fact is that a good understanding of the futures markets leads inexorably to a logical, rational and simple explanation. As even the novice futures trader knows, one of the distinguishing characteristics of the futures markets is that *there is a winner for every loser.* New money can only come into the futures game from new players or through current players adding more to the pool. In a sense, the futures market is a cause-and-effect system. Every dollar made by one trader is a dollar which has been lost by another trader. This is the painful and cold truth of futures trading. Every time you profit you are doing so, to a certain extent, at the expense of another trader or competitor. Every time you lose, you lose to another trader.

While we all know these facts, we frequently tend to forget them. Yet, in remembering the "jungle law" of futures trading, we find an answer to the seemingly paradoxical problem posed earlier. Clearly, the lot of the average futures trader has *not* improved significantly in spite of recent hardware and software advances because the game has become more competitive! There is still a winner for every loser. Only a few scenarios are possible in such a situation:

• If a higher percentage of traders wins, and the size of the dollar pool remains relatively fixed, then each of the winners will win less. In other words, the "jackpot" will be divided among more traders, each receiving less for his or her efforts

• If the size of the dollar pool increases, then there will be more money for the very small percentage of winners; or if the percentage of winners also increases, there will be only slightly more money for the larger number of winners

• As the game's strategies (i.e., trading systems) become more sophisticated, the odds of newcomers being successful will decrease. Veteran traders will be quick to pounce upon the new entrants.

• In a system which provides relatively similar tools to all traders, the small group of winners will advance at about the same pace. Hence, the net effect will be nil. If, for example, I begin using a more effective trading system and if others implement better performing systems, then we will all be upgraded and the differential between systems will be narrowed. Consider the following analogy. If you are walking and an automobile moving at the rate of 45 miles per hour passes you, its speed will seem significant. If, however, you are also in an automobile, but moving at the rate of 35 miles per hour, the speed of the other vehicle will only be 10 miles per hour faster than your speed—the differential is narrowed. And so it is in the area of systems trading in the futures markets.

Consider also the fact that as trading systems become more sophisticated, more able to take advantage of aberrations in the marketplace, the markets will become more efficient. Traders will be able to recognize opportunities more quickly and more frequently than they have in the past. This will result in a smoother operation of the market machinery. Ultimately, opportunities for profit may become less frequent and they may not last as long, as the markets become more "efficient."

Perhaps the most important variables are those which cannot be totally computerized. Has there been any appreciable or quantifiable improvement in trader discipline? Has the average trader learned how to control his or her emotions? I have observed that virtually no progress has been made in these areas. A good majority of market losses are not system-related but rather are the clear result of trader error, lack of discipline, or emotional response. It may be sad, but it is also true that these facts of trading life will never change. Human beings will always be subject to fear, greed, impulsivity, lack of good judgment, and other frailties which are often counterproductive to the task of making profits in the futures markets. As long as a majority of traders' losses are attributable to these characteristically human qualities, it is unlikely that technology and advanced software will have a positive impact on overall trading results. Hence, it may seem fruitless to develop bigger and better trading systems in the absence of improvements in trader discipline.[1]

As you can see from the points I've just raised, technological and software progress are not the salvations they may seem to be. The mere development of faster "number crunching" computers to research complex trading systems and theories, and /or the development of artificial intelligence (AI) computer techniques, do not *ipso facto* guarantee that there will be fewer losers in the futures markets. If traders and investors followed their systems and theories, the markets would be considerably more efficient, there would be more winners than there are now and the profits would be more evenly distributed among winners as opposed to being severely skewed. The current push toward better systems, faster computers and highly optimized trading systems may be illusory. The advantage to traders may soon reach the point of diminishing returns, if it has not already done so.

By now you may be wondering why I have emphasized these points in a book which is dedicated almost exclusively to the examination of timing signals in the futures markets. My reason is twofold:

1. To remind you that trading system and timing signal research is meaningless in the absence of trader discipline and self-control. And,

2. To remimd you that the human element is the weakest link in the trading chain.

Finally, the markets will become more competitive. As trading systems, methods and technology improve, more traders may be able to participate in the potential profits. Yet unless a significant influx of new capital enters the pool of the markets, there will be less profits per trader if the percentage of successful traders increases.

---

[1]The issues of trader psychology, discipline and self-control have already been given considerable attention in my books *Beyond the Investor's Quotient* (New York, John Wiley & Sons 1988) and *The Investor's Quotient* (New York, John Wiley & Sons, 1988).

MARKET MYTH AND REALITY

There is yet another problem which must be examined. Every field of endeavor has its attendant set of unique characteristics. Among these are included methods, procedures, jargon, and a collection of folklore and myth. Beliefs which may have been born in adversity tend to persist and, with the passage of time, they frequently acquire a reality of their own. Futures traders, for example, have for many years held numerous trading myths near and dear. Can you think of some beliefs you have about the futures markets which have been handed down to you from other traders? Do you have expectations about the behavior of markets based on certain indicators? Do you accept these expectations on faith, or do you have conclusive statistical evidence that they are valid? How often have you or other traders expressed expectations based upon reasoning such as:

"Yes, today's report was very bearish, but if the market can't close lower tomorrow in spite of this bearish report, then we may be starting a new bull market."

"This market won't top until the public turns very bullish."

"Precious metals decline when stocks move higher and they rally when stocks move lower."

"If interest rates go down, then the stock market will go up."

"The market is so severely oversold that it's almost certain to turn higher any day now."

"Prices have closed lower seven days in succession now. It's almost certain that they'll close higher today."

"In a bull market buy reactions to support and in a bear market sell rallies to resistance."

"It's hard to make money and avoid losing it back in a trendless market."

"Buy on the full moon and sell on the new moon."

"A market will eventually 'fill' all of its price gaps."

"New highs beget new lows and new lows beget new highs."

"Buy markets that are making new highs and sell markets that are making new lows."

"The trend is your friend."

I've found that traders in general are a rather "superstitious" lot. By this I mean that futures traders take solace in pithy beliefs which may not have any basis in reality. It is a well-known fact that many futures pit brokers have their "lucky" ties, shirts, jackets or other talismans. But such behavior is not unique to futures traders. Consider the athlete who follows a rigid practice ritual or pre-competition routine in the belief that it improves performance or increases the probability of success. The why's and wherefore's of such behavior are not difficult to understand. As long as the future is uncertain there will always exist the opportunity to take refuge in expectations and/or beliefs which give comfort, whether they are valid or not. The aborigine with a headache visits the witch doctor for treatment. The witch doctor performs a ceremony. The patient feels better. Whether or not the cause of the headache is gone, the symptoms have been relieved!

Behavioral psychologist B. F. Skinner has demonstrated the development and existence of what he termed "superstitious" behavior in laboratory animals. He was able to create such behaviors by subjecting experimental animal subjects to stimulus and response conditions which, in layman's terms, were "uncertain," or unpredictable. While I am not attempting to anthropomorphize, I think that there are, indeed, many similarities between superstitious behavior in animals and faulty belief systems in human beings. My point, however, is that many futures traders—myself included—have certain expectations about the markets which may not be grounded in fact but which have developed from years of exposure to untested ideas, indicators and methods, some of which may have been valid in the past, some which may have face validity and some which may be partially correct. Perhaps some of these ideas will strike home if we examine Skinnerian learning theory in greater detail.

Skinner's theories can help us understand how and why market myths and folklore develop and persist. The elementary concepts of operant conditioning explain the metamorphosis of such beliefs as well as their longevity. The tenacity with which investors and speculators often cling to market myths which have no statistical validity can only be explained in terms of what Skinner termed intermittent reinforcement. Consider the following simple explanation for the persistence of market myths and folklore in Skinnerian (i.e., behavioral learning) terms:

> *Behavior followed by positive consequence tends to increase in frequency. Hence, if a trader followed a given signal or indicator and showed a profit as a result, the specific behavior of following this signal or indicator would be prone to increase.*

Skinner also noted that if positive consequences follow a given behavior intermittently (i.e., not on a one-for-one basis), the given behavior may be acquired (learned) more slowly. However, it will be more resistant to change—either forgetting, or what Skinner called "extinction"—and it will be relearned or revived more quickly than if it had been rewarded each and every time by a positive outcome.

Hence, traders who are intermittently rewarded, or who have intermittent positive experiences with a given timing signal or "rule," are likely to cling to the given indicator with considerable conviction and tenacity.

Assume now that a group of investors or traders experiences the same set of conditions at about the same time. You now have the makings of a market myth. Consider the following example:

A well-known trader of yesteryear notes in his memoirs that he has made considerable money by following a certain set of market parameters. Let's assume that the signal is a key reversal (KR). The trader attributes many of his profits to buying on days following a key reversals to the upside (KR+) and selling on days following key reversals to the downside (KR−). Remember that a KR is defined as a day in which prices trade both above and below their previous daily range. A key reversal up (KR+) is a KR day which closes above the

Figure 1.1:   Key Reversal Up (KR+)

A KR+ occurs when prices move above and below the previous daily high and low, then close above the previous daily close.

Figure 1.2:   Key Reversal Down (KR–)

A KR– occurs when prices move above and below the previous daily high and low and then close below the previous daily close.

previous daily close; a KR− is a KR day which closes below the previous daily close (see Figures 1-1 and 1-2 for diagrammatic representation of KR's).

Attracted by the success of our legendary trader, other traders seeking to learn his secrets read his memoirs. They are prompted to watch and/or trade the KR signals. At times they will profit from their KR signals; at other times they will not. This sets up the necessary conditions for the type of strong learning I've described earlier. This type of learning is very hard to unlearn. The longer the intermittent results continue, the more resistant the behavior (i.e., use of KR signal) will become to forgetting or unlearning. And the longer it continues to be followed without clear-cut testing, the more likely it is to acquire the status of a myth. And the longer it remains a myth, the more of a following it will acquire.

Today, however, it is possible to test thoroughly timing signals, indicators and trading systems. We are able, with the right software and data, to subject indicators, whether they have acquired mythological status or not, to extensive testing in order to arrive at a valid conclusion regarding their efficacy. This is one of the goals I have pursued in this book. I am sure you'll find that many icons have fallen and I hope that as a consequence your results will improve markedly. However, I will also show you that some market myths *do have validity under the right circumstances. In other words, I will show you that there are some very specific ways in which indicators can be improved by the application of simple filters and concomitant indicators.*

TRICKS WITH STATISTICS

Archimedes, who among other things is credited with the invention of the lever, said "Give me where to stand and I will move the earth." The contemporary equivalent of this expression is, "Give me enough statistics and I can prove anything." While statistics are absolutely necessary in the sciences and in other analytical methodoligies, there are many ways, unfortunately, in which statistics can be misleading. Recently, for example, there have been many advertisements touting particular trading systems as highly effective or profitable. The promoters of these systems may claim, for example, that their system has "...made money 85 percent of the time in stock index futures." At first blush the statistic is certainly an amazing one. Yet, without a more detailed explanation of this number, it is totally meaningless. A system may have made money in five of the last six years. This is an attractive performance statistic, but it is meaningless unless the results are based on a sufficiently lengthy data history.

The promoter of such a system may counter this criticism with other statistics noting that there were, on average, sixteen trades per year using this system, and that of the ninety-six trades over the six-year period (sixteen trades times six years equals ninety-six trades), sixty were profitable. This, he claims, is a more meaningful statistic. It is not. Possibly fifty-three of the sixty winning trades were small winners, but a mere seven were large winners. The statistics are again misleading unless additional questions are asked and unless additional information is available.

DRAWDOWN

Another consideration in system development and indicator analysis is the issue of drawdown. How bad did things get? That is, how large were the losses which accumulated during the declining portion of this system's history? Clearly, a system which suffered an 80 percent drawdown before getting back on track is one which would also have resulted in a total lack of confidence on behalf of its users. The average speculator would have abandoned such a system or indicator long before it turned profitable again.

TREND

Another factor which must be examined in testing a system, method or timing indicator is the direction of the trend. Consider a system which shows a very promising hypothetical or even real-time track record during a run of successive years in a bullish market. Upon examination it will likely be found that a majority of the trades and signals generated by this system were on the long side. What will happen to the system when the long-term trend changes? We don't know! It may never have been subjected to such a test. And what will happen to this system or method when the markets begin to move sideways, generating a multiplicity of "false" signals?

This is why it is important to gather all available information about system performance. And this is why it is especially important to back-test systems and signals for as long as possible and/or in as many different market climates as possible. When you consider the fact that many systems which have been offered to the public since the 1980's were back-tested to the late 1970's or early 1980's, you may begin to wonder (as I often do) whether any of them will continue to work in the future regardless how well they tested.
do) whether any of them will continue to work in the future regardless how well they tested.

As you can see, the issue of system and signal testing is multifaceted. While it may appear a relatively simple matter to conceive of and test systems, it is an entirely different matter to analyze their hypothetical performance statistics, to determine their validity and to offer an opinion regarding their future performance. Yet the limitations and problems discussed in this chapter should not act as deterrents to the formulation, analysis and testing of systems, signals and timing indicators. My experience as a trader since the late 1960's has taught me many lessons. I have learned very well that success in futures trading depends upon a combination of the following elements, a synthesis of which will help avoid many of the problems outlined in this chapter:

Discipline and self-control—these form the backbone or structure of every successful trading system;

Extensive historical testing of signals, systems and indicators in many different types of markets;

The ability to translate research into pragmatic (i.e., real-time) application; and

The ability to fine-tune systems or change them entirely as the markets become more competitive.

This book provides a variety of directions, analyses and suggestions for extensively testing market signals and indicators. I feel that the ideas and insights I offer in the following pages will prove very valuable to those who decide to join the current trend toward trading system development. Moreover, I hope that my work can help dispel some of the myths while it helps confirm or validate indicators which have either not been subjected to rigorous testing or which have been accepted as valid based on nothing more than good faith.

2

Objectives and Working Definitions

Shortly after I started trading futures I realized that in order to arrive at a systematic approach to the markets, considerable historical research was necessary. It was obvious to me that computers were ideal for this application. In 1968, however, computer technology was not readily available to the general public. The cost of historical futures data was prohibitive to most traders. It was not until the early 1970's that I was able to acquire the data and computer time necessary to begin back-testing some of my ideas.
some of my ideas.

My studies took me in many directions. I examined price patterns, volume relationships, open interest and all of their interrelationships. During those days the most popular trading systems were based on moving average concepts which had been introduced in the 1950's by Richard Donchian. Traditional chart technical analysis a la Edwards and McGee was also widely followed by many traders. While moving averages were relatively simple to track and test by computer, chart formations and patterns were not readily amenable to the type of algorithms required by computers. Hence, I was relegated to testing only those indicators and signals which could be operationally defined and expressed. After considerable testing I realized that there were numerous limitations to my work.

To begin with, my data history was severely limited. I had only several years worth of history. Furthermore, I was restricted to borrowed computer time and lacked the services of a full-time programmer. Also, I continued to labor under the misconception that I needed to know more about economics. The net result of these limitations was to inhibit both the volume and intensity of research I so passionately hoped to complete. When finances finally permitted, I bought a state-of-the-art computer system. I also acquired many years of cash historical data—literally hundreds of years worth—until I had accumulated what I feel is today one of the lengthiest historical databases in the futures industry. This proved to be both a blessing and a curse in one expensive package.

When I began my testing I observed a most peculiar phenomenon. While many of the indicators and systems I tested seemed very profitable at first, the more I tested them, the more they regressed to the mean. In other words, the farther back I went with my testing, the less effective the indicators were. It appeared that every timing signal or system had its good times and its bad times. Sometimes the profitable stretches were more than enough to overcome the periods of poor performance (i.e., drawdown). In other cases the periods of losses were so extended and severe that in spite of very large profits during other periods, the indicators were net losers. And what was even more interesting—even shocking—was the fact that many indicators which tested as virtually useless were being touted by traders, system developers and market "gurus" as effective. But I couldn't blame them for their ignorance. After all, they had tunnel vision. They were looking at a limited data history; at a period of time during which virtually every indicator or system worked well; at a picture which was not entirely representative of all market climates and conditions.

In other words, I realized that while some systems and indicators tested well in certain market conditions, they did not fare well during other market conditions. It has long been known that most trading systems and indicators do well in trending markets, but that they lose money in sideways or "whipsaw" markets. A good majority of systems research is directed at limiting losses during sideways markets while attempting to maximize profits during trending markets.

Following my many years of research into market timing, indicators, systems, cycles, seasonals and more, I reached the following:

There are many different timing signals, all of which may be considered effective at various times, but none of which can be considered effective in all markets and at all times.

Timing signals which are effective for market entry are not necessarily equally effective for market exit.

Some timing signals which have been considered reliable by traders for many years are in fact no more effective than the proverbial "random walk."

Some timing signals are virtually useless as stand-alone entry or exit techniques; however, they can be extremely effective in combination with other signals. Such synergism can be very important in developing and designing effective trading systems.

Specific money management techniques for maximizing performance are exceptionally important. While effective money management is often considered to encompass such things as limiting risk and allocating account capital according to strict guidelines, it is even more important to know when to maximize on trades in order to make the most of signals and systems when they are experiencing a winning streak.

The performance of such techniques as seasonals, cycles and day-of-week patterns may be significantly enhanced by the addition of specific timing signals or combinations of timing signals.

This book aims to achieve the following goals:

1. To examine numerous technical indicators and timing signals in a thorough, organized and extensive fashion using a vast historical database.

2. To determine if given indicators and signals are more effective in certain types of markets than they are in other types of markets.

3. To determine if certain timing indicators heretofore considered effective are in fact effective when viewed from a lengthy historical perspective.

4. To test various heretofore untested timing indicators.

5. To provide suggestions regarding optimum application of various indicators.

6. To provide extensive performance statistics.

7. To provide suggestions for optimizing market entry and exit based on the test results.

7. To provide suggestions for optimizing market entry and exit based on the test results.

8. To suggest future directions for research.
may be more effective than the performance of any one of the indicators by itself.

9. To suggest future directions for research.

Bear in mind that it is not my purpose to test and evaluate currently popular trading systems. Other publications can provide such information; their drawback, however, is that their tests are frequently limited in the length of their data history. The publishers of these reports often accept the historical performance statistics of the system developer and pick up their monitoring from the point at which they began following the given system. Furthermore, as I pointed out earlier, many contemporary systems are back-tested for a period from as little as three years to as many as fifteen years. Few are back-tested to the 1960's or earlier. And with good reason! Many systems just don't hold up when tested that far back.

The question which must then be pondered by the system developer is whether on not to ignore the historical data or to start again from scratch in order to develop a new system. While some may consider this a philosophical issue, I consider it an ethical and pragmatic issue. I maintain that if a system or indicator is used for the purpose of trading, then it must show its ability to perform in all types of markets and at all times. The system must be "intelligent" enough to know when to stay out of the market and when to stay in the market. At the very least it must have the ability to hold its own during periods of whipsaw and it must have the ability to capture big moves when the markets are trending.

As I indicated earlier, I do not purport to provide within these pages the ultimate test of every system or indicator currently in use. To do so would take considerably more time and much more space than is possible in this already large volume. I do not single out any one system by name or any one indicator by name. Rather, I provide an unbiased report of specific timing indicators based on massive research and detailed examination of a vast historical database.

While you may disagree with some of my methods and procedures, I can assure you that they have been designed in order to reflect the realities of trading as closely as possible. We know that to present any indicator or system in its optimal light is to engage in unrealistic representation. All systems are subject to the deteriorating influences of slippage, to the ubiquitous cost of commissions, and to the vagaries of trends.

A Few Words About Optimization

In the last few years system developers have embarked in a new and, I feel, a risky direction. They've moved more and more in the direction of optimization, or curve-fitting. There are two strongly opposed schools of thought regarding optimization. Proponents of each have made strong supportive claims for their positions. Consider the following observations made by Bruce Babcock in his book *The Dow Jones-Irwin Guide to Tading Systems* (Dow Jones-Irwin, 1990):

> If the computer examined the last five years of data in ten individual markets and found the best acceleration factor to use in each month for each market, it would create 12 different sets of rules for each market, or a total of 120 separate rule-sets in all. You could still consider it as one system, however. The historical profits for the 120-rule-set system would be far higher than the profits for the original (Wilder system), which had only one set of rules for all the markets.
>
> If you had to guess which system would be more likely to be profitable in the future, would you select the more complicated system merely because it showed the most profits historically? . . . The correct answer is no. *A curve-fitted system is, by its very method of creation, guaranteed to be profitable on the historical data used to create it. This says little about its likely profitability in the future.*
>
> If you were in commodity trading dreamland, you could create a system without any reference to historical data and then find that it was wildly profitable in every market during every time period you tested it. Then, unfortunately, you would wake up and have to face reality, where this does not happen. When dealing with the complexities of mathematical trading systems, there are usually many parameters you can change. The only way to know not to maximize the effectiveness of your system is to test it historically, using different values for the changeable parameters. Thus, some optimization is required. *If you over-optimize, however, you end up with a highly curve-fitted system that will probably not be reliable in the future.*
>
> When doing historical testing, it is essential to remember what the goal is. It is not to create a system that generated the most hypothetical profits trading in the past. It is to create a system that will generate the most profits

trading in the future. The future is the only arena where you can make real money.

As far as I'm concerned, the jury is still out on the issue of optimization. However, I lean in the direction of non-optimized or minimally optimized systems. I feel that they more closely represent reality than do curve-fitted systems. None of the indicators examined in this book were optimized. In other words, they were tested "as is," without being altered to fit the data.

PROCEDURES AND DEFINITIONS

In order to understand what I have done and to best translate my results into real time, you will need to know a few important facts about my methods and procedures.

The Database

In order to subject the indicators and systems selected to extensive testing, I have employed a very lengthy historical database. In most cases indicators have been back-tested to the mid-1960's. In some cases I have also tested on a "spot check" basis contracts dating as far back as the 1920's.

Type of Data

Many systems are back-tested using "continuous data." The purpose of using this type of data is to avoid the problems associated with contract switchovers and the frequently large price differentials which exist between an expiring contract month and the next tradeable contract month. Continuous data is altered for the purpose of testing in order that the system being tested need not close out a position at the end of a contract only to be faced with the problem of when to enter the next contract month. Those who employ the continuous data approach claim that the alterations made do not misrepresent what actual results might have been.

I maintain, however, that a system should be tested in the way that a trader would trade it. In real life a trader can't trade a continuous contract: he or she is faced with the situation of being forced to exit a position in order to avoid delivery, and is furthermore faced with the next decision, which is when to enter the next contract month. These are *real-life* decisions—they don't disappear with the use of continuous data. I have, therefore, used continuous data files only minimally. My procedure was to use two or three active contract months for each market. Signals were only tested during the active portion of each contract month. Testing was stopped on the last day of the month prior to the delivery period and exit was forced on that date if a signal was still in effect. No new position was taken until the next signal occurred in the subsequent contract month. I feel that this procedure is more representative of real market conditions than is a continuous data file.
ditions than is a continuous data file.

Signals and timing indicators were tested using various methods and procedures. Initial tests were completed on a Data General Eclipse MV mini-computer. Programming was in Fortran 77.

The first step in my testing procedure was to determine the signals and indicators to be tested. These were then programmed. A pretest was then performed on a representative database which consisted of different types of markets (described later on) such as bull markets, bear markets, whipsaw markets and so on. Signals which showed some degree of positive results were then subjected to a thorough test which involved examination of their performance during two to three contract months for every year for each market as far back as 1967.

Indicators were also tested using using Bill Cruz's excellent analytical software, System Writer Plus (SWP). I noted earlier that it is now possible for the average investor to buy highly effective computer hardware and software at an affordable price. System Writer Plus is just one example of the powerful software which investors and traders can use to test their ideas, systems and methods.

By applying further testing to our timing indicators and signals using SWP, I was able to examine them in a trading-oriented environment inasmuch as specific strategies and alternatives were used. Signals which might have initially tested as marginal were enhanced by the application of filters, combined signals, stop losses and various exit indicators. This is where SWP does its best work, and I took full advantage of it.

Let me repeat here that it is not the intention of this book to provide a list of infallible trading systems, indicators, methods and/or signals. There are literally hundreds of possible combinations of timing signals and indicators. To effectively examine every one of these would take literally thousands of hours. It is my hope that you will save valuable time, as well as money, by focusing your attention on some of the indicators and signals I've already tested so thoroughly. I suggest that you use the findings of this study as your starting point for further research into trading systems, timing signals and trend indicators.

Indicators and Signals Tested

Numerous indicators and signals were tested. Each indicator and its precise test conditions are described in detail when its results are reported. In addition an algorithm, a diagrammatic representation, and several chart examples are provided for each indicator (where relevant).

The indicators and signals were derived from the following sources:

1. My own observations and theories which were derived from my years of experience in the futures market.

2. Some indicators and methods were derived from market folklore. In other words I gathered a variety of market adages and, where possible, translated them into trading algorithms for the purpose of testing.

3. Some timing indicators, signals and systems were prompted by the current literature. Reports from different market publications, articles, books and so on were taken as the starting point for various indicators which I tested. I took particular interest in testing indicators or signals for which highly positive claims were made.

Unfortunately, most of these did not stand the test of time. Since I do not wish to cast aspersions on the work of other analysts, no names are mentioned in connection with negative results. In some cases I found that ideas or indicators which I felt had potential or which actually back-tested profitably in my previous work were not as effective when subjected to more lengthy analysis, while in other instances some of my indicators performed better than expected.

Markets and Contracts Tested

In order to thoroughly test the selected indicators and signals I departed from some of the procedures usually employed in testing signals, indicators and trading systems. Rather than use five or ten years of data, I tested back to 1967. I felt that it would be instructive to examine indicators and signals in different types of markets. Consequently, I divided all markets tested into a variety of categories depending upon their trend characteristics. Furthermore, I did not "curve-fit" any of the tests. I merely back-tested the indicators without then retesting a modified version of the indicator(s) in order to see if they would have produced different results.

Several examples of each market category are given below. To a certain extent my selections were subjective. I am certain that there will be some disagreement with my choices; however, I expect that for the most part I have placed markets in their appropriate categories. Finally, remember that two or three contract months of every market for every year back to 1967 were included in the database.

Some signals and indicators perform differently in different types of markets. In order to quantify their performance I categorize every single contract month for every market. All contract months were carefully studied in order to classify them into specific categories according to trend. Here are the categories, their definitions and a chart example of each condition. Remember that the purpose of making these distinctions was to ascertain how different signals acted in different markets. The KR+ (Key Reversal Up) signal, for example, was tested first on all files and then on the specific market categories. This allowed us to answer such questions as: how did KR+ signals fare in sideways markets; how did they fare in bull markets only; and how did they perform in choppy bull markets?

Bull Markets   A bull market for the purposes of this study is defined as a market which trends higher, with few sizeable corrections during the time frame studied. Remember that our study period did not cover the entire contract length. Generally we did not evaluate signals for the first 100 days of each contract, and we stopped the analysis at the end of the month prior to the delivery month. Figures 2-1, 2-2 and 2-3 show the closing prices charts for three representative bull markets. Note that prices and dates have been "stripped off" in order to increase the plotting speed of the charts (since I analyzed so many markets, and since the analyses were all computer-generated, I spent as little time as possible on graphics). Remember that I did not consider the last approximately 30 days of each contract as part of the analysis.

Bear Markets   These are markets which trend generally lower during the analysis period, with few significant interruptions or corrections in trend. Figures 2-4 through 2-6 illustrate several of the bear markets used in my analyses.

Choppy Bull Markets   These are markets which move higher, but irregularly. They tend to exhibit significant corrections within their uptrends, which make them difficult markets for trend-following systems to trade. Figures 2-7 through 2-9 show a number of choppy bull markets.

Choppy Bear Markets   These are markets which trend lower, but irregularly and with significant upside corrections. Figures 2-10 through 2-12 show some of the choppy bear markets which were used in my analyses.

Figure 2.1: Bull Market—July 1972 Soybean Meal

7207SM

Figure 2.2: Bull Market—December 1977—Swiss Franc

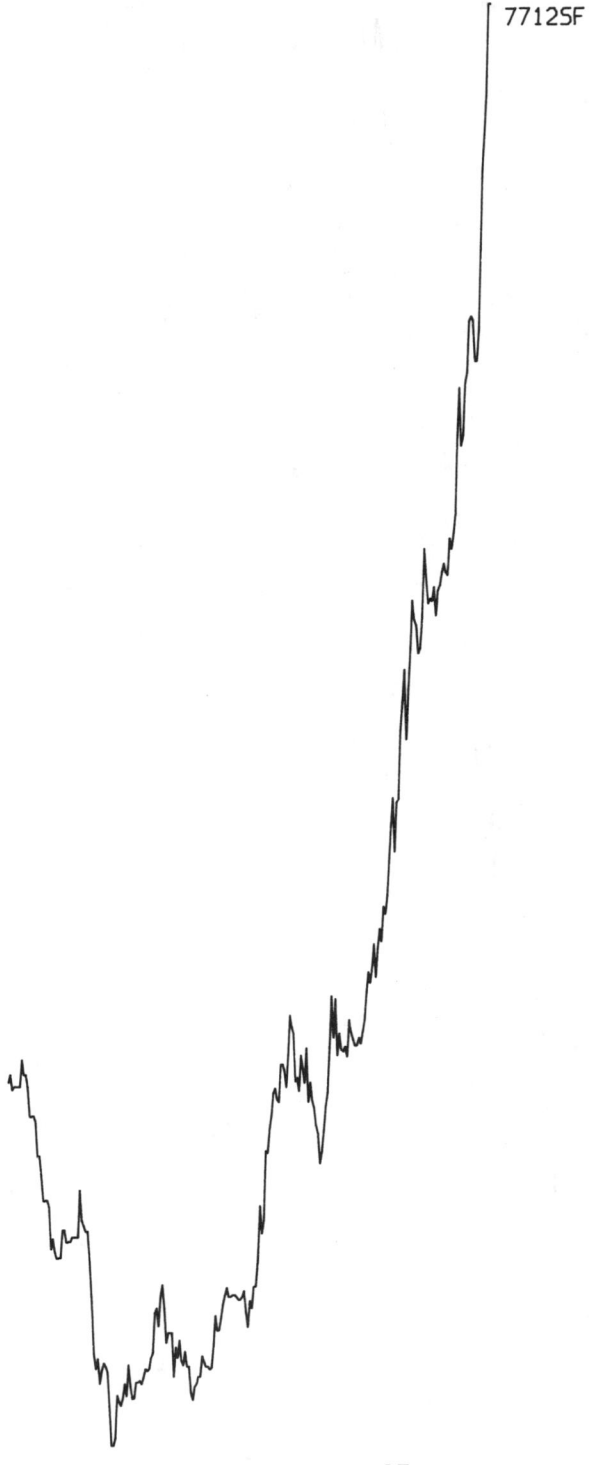

7712SF

Figure 2.3: Bull Market—June 1987—British Pound

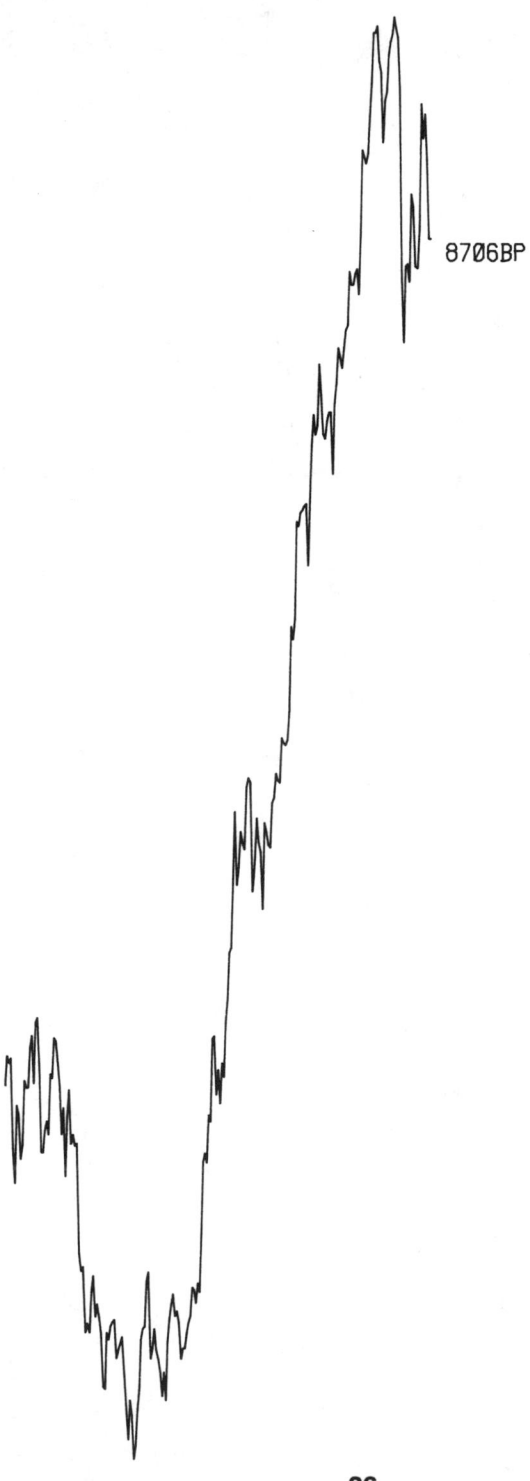

8706BP

26

Figure 2.4:   Bear Market—July 1968—Wheat

6807W

27

Figure 2.5:   Bear Market—October 1984—Sugar

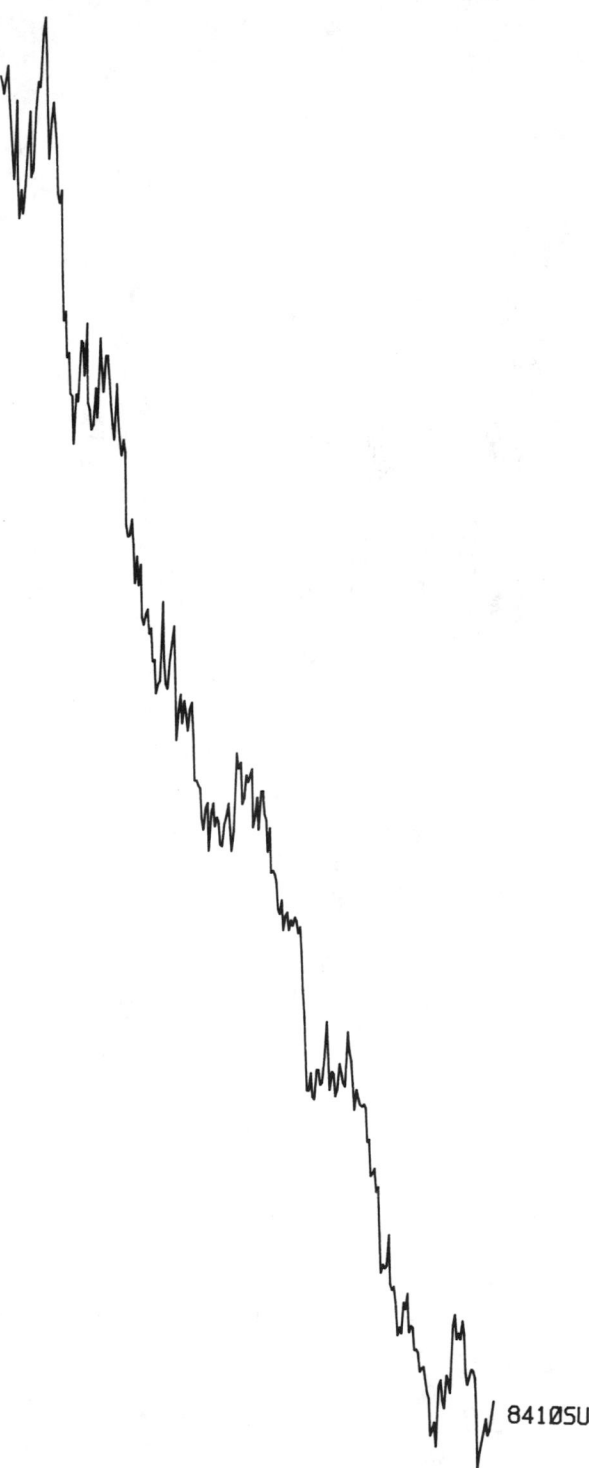

8410SU

Figure 2.6:   Bear Market—December 1984—Swiss Franc

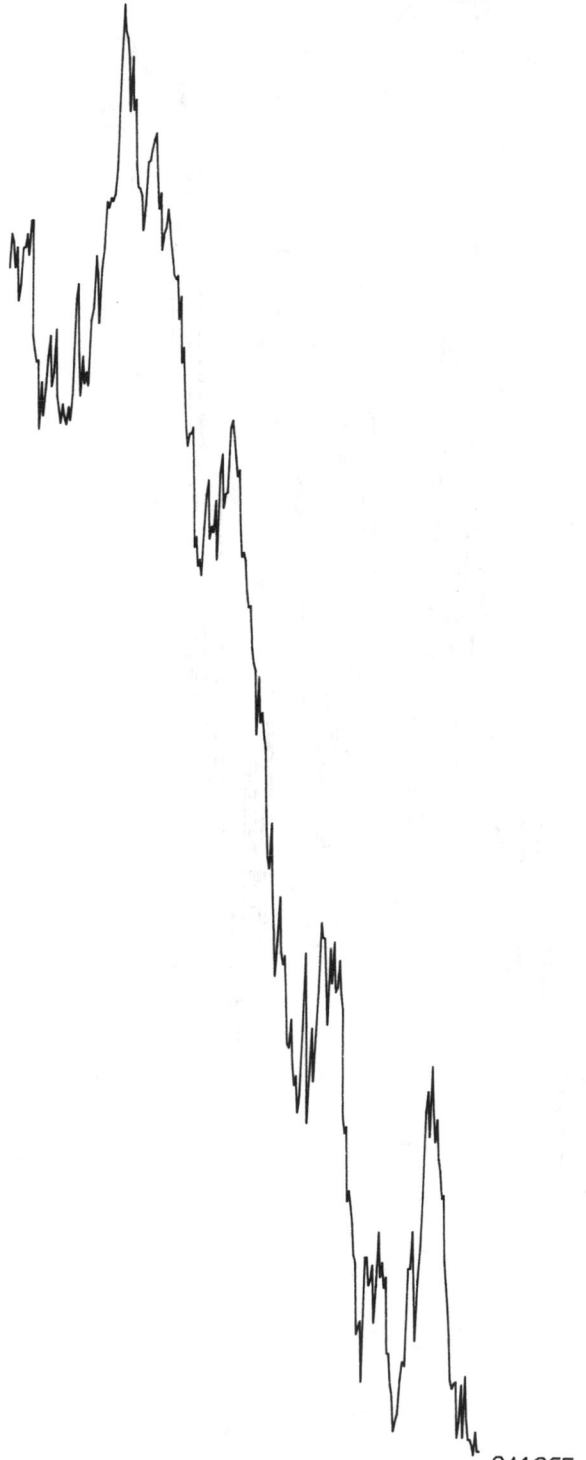

8412SF

Figure 2.7:   Choppy Bull Market—July 1970—Wheat

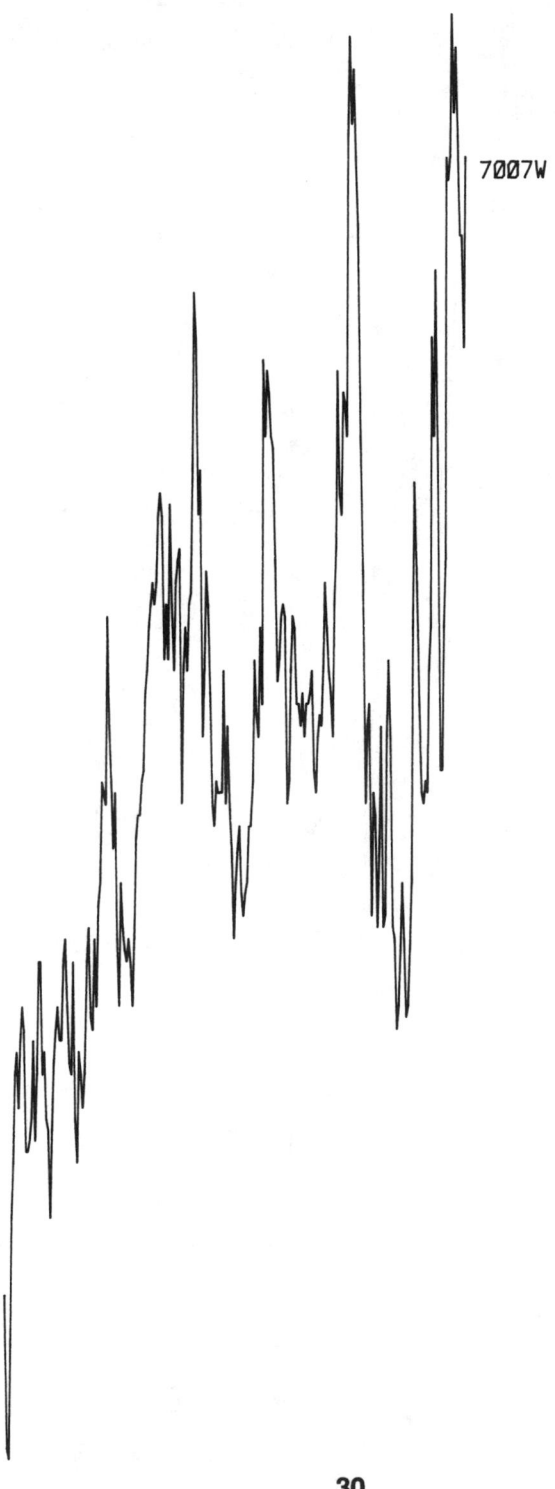

7007W

Figure 2.8: Choppy Bull Market—December 1986—Swiss Franc

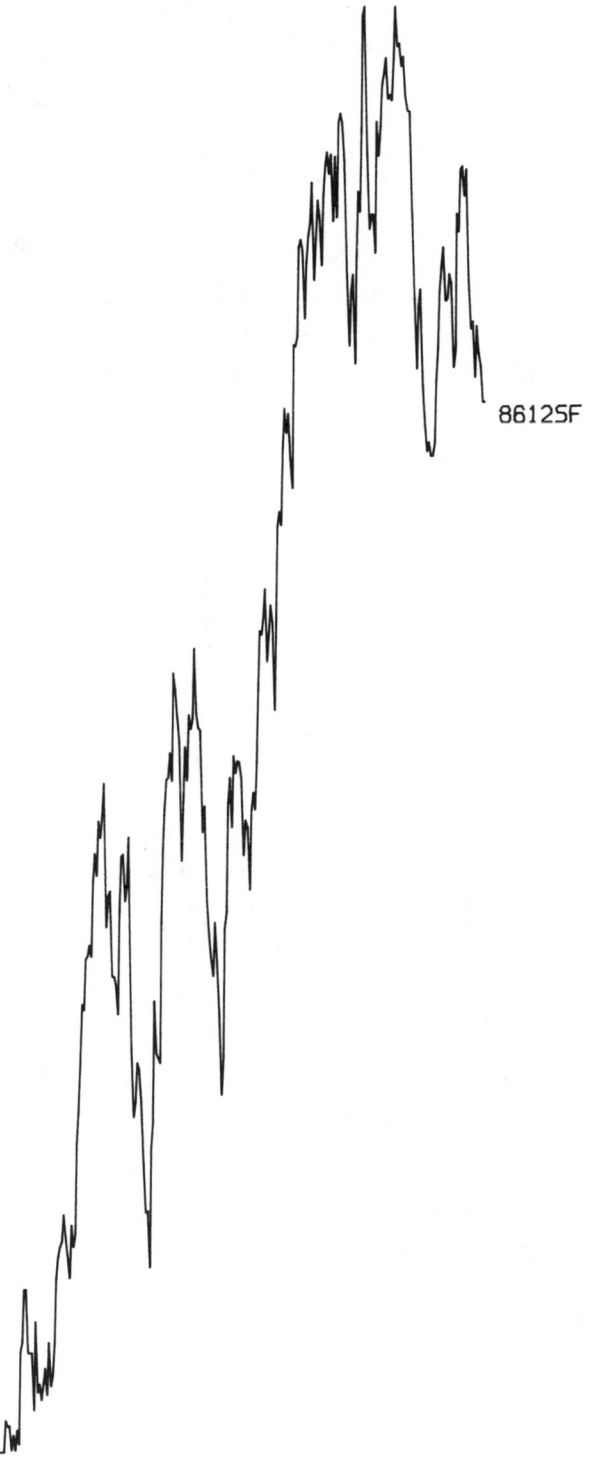

8612SF

Figure 2.9:   Choppy Bull Market—October 1988—Sugar

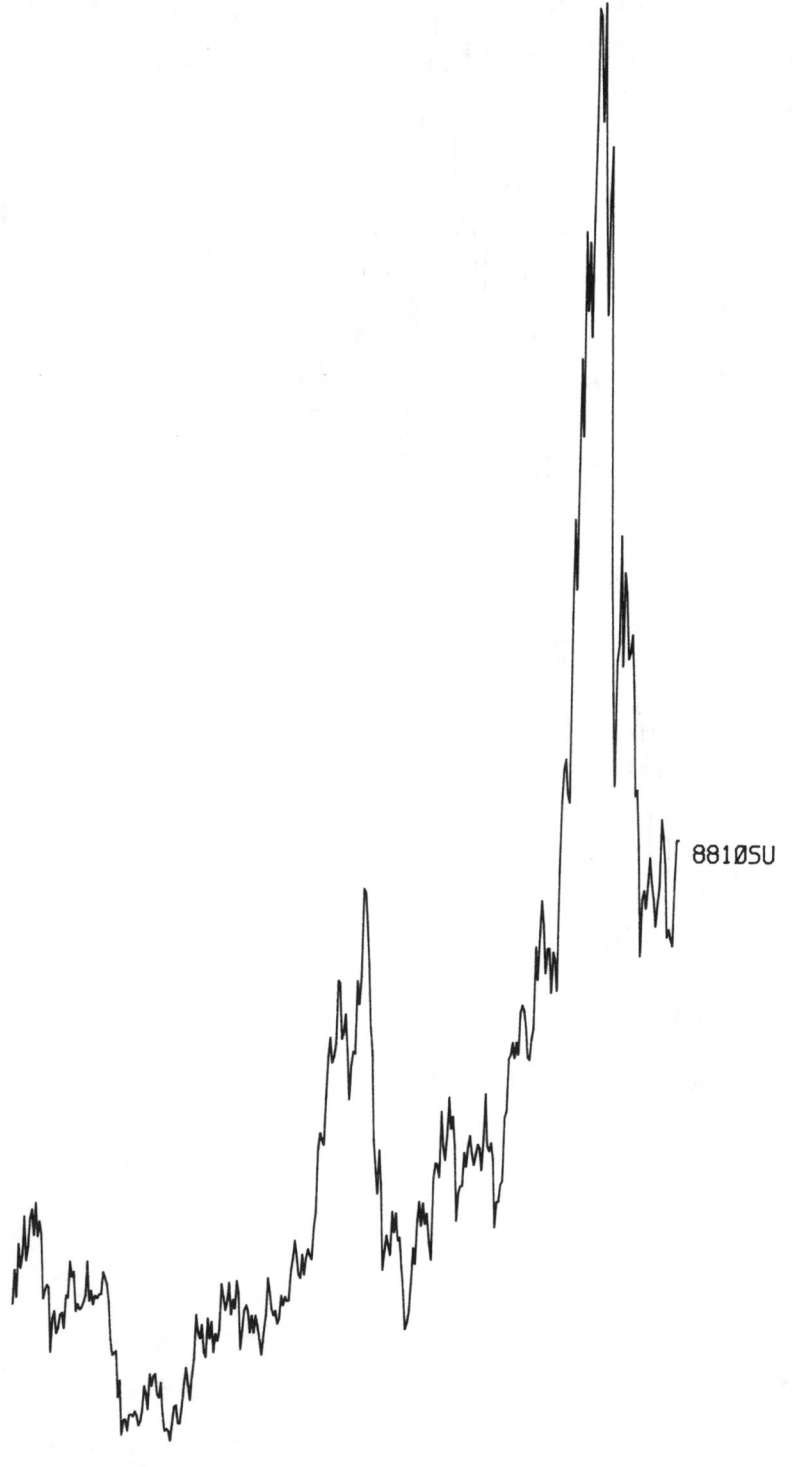

8810SU

Figure 2.10: Choppy Bear Market—April 1972—Platinum

7204PL

Figure 2.11: Choppy Bear Market—July 1976—Wheat

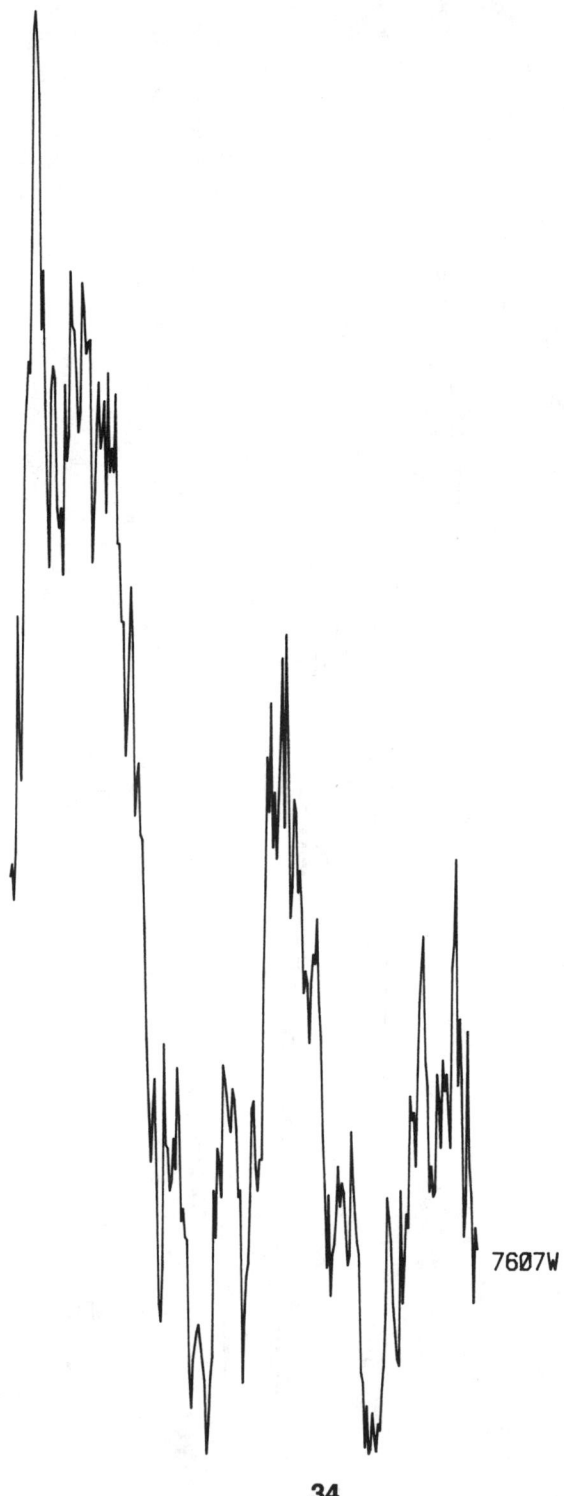

7607W

Figure 2.12: Choppy Bear Market—November 1986—Soybeans

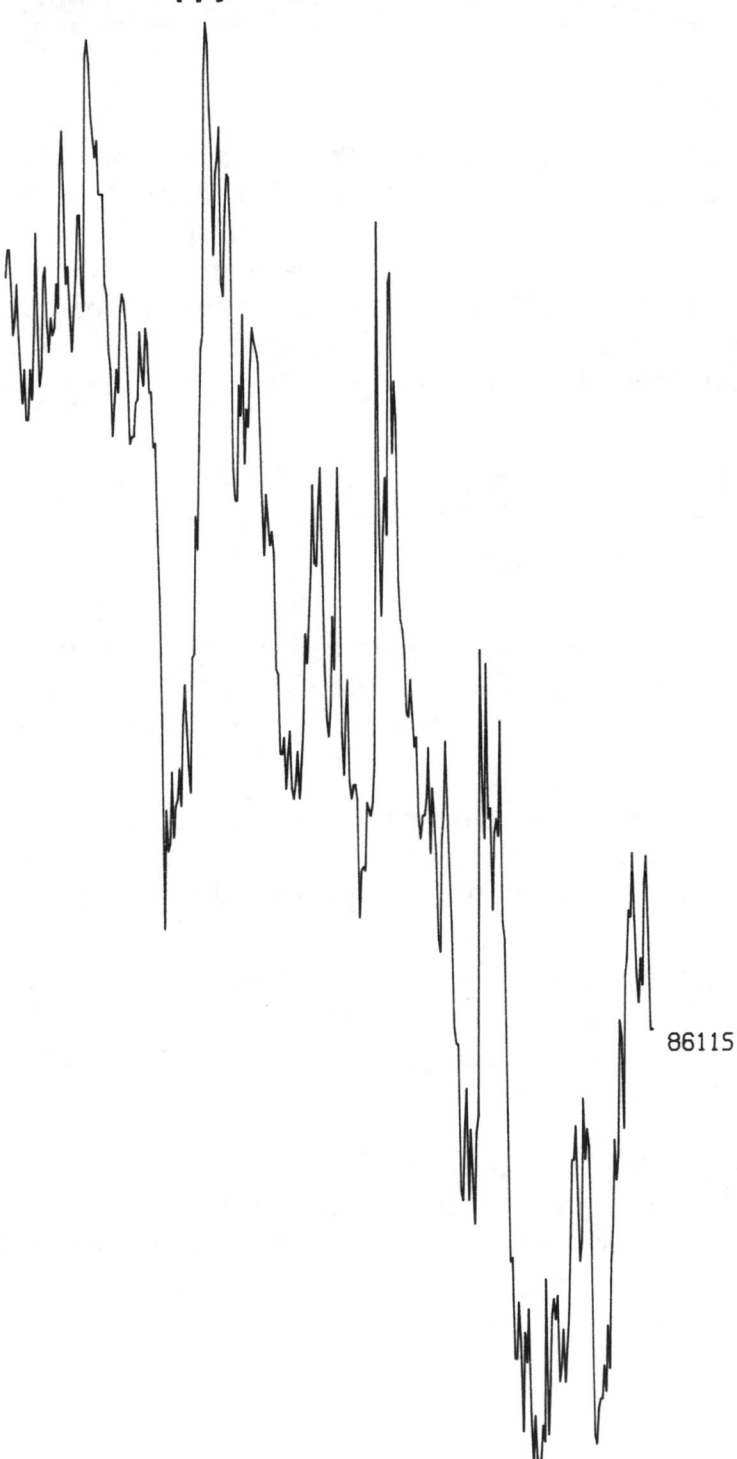

86115

Whipsaw and Sideways Markets   These markets are charac-
terized by either their lack of continuous trend or relatively sideways
markets. Some whipsaw markets show large up and down movements, while others are very tame by comparison. They share the
common characteristic of numerous up and down moves which
usually but not always take the market nowhere. Figures 2-13
through 2-15 show some of the whipsaw markets used in my
analyses.

Bear/Bull Markets   These markets are those which begin with
a pronounced bearish trend, but change to a pronounced bullish
trend. See Figures 2-16 through 2-18.

Bull/Bear Markets   These markets begin with a distinct bull
trend but change direction and turn into clearly bearish markets.
Some bull/bear markets are shown in Figures 2-19 through 2-21.

Bear/Bull/Bear Markets   These markets begin with a distinct
downtrend, turn bullish and then turn bearish again. Examples of
bear/bull/bear markets are shown in Figures 2-22 through 2-24.

Bull/Bear/Bull Markets   These markets begin with a bullish
trend, turn bearish and then turn bullish again. Examples of bull/
bear/bull markets used in my analyses are shown in Figures 2-25
through 2-27.

For a look at all of the markets by category used in my data sample, see Appendix I. As I have earlier stated, you may disagree with
some of the choices I have made, but for the most part I think that
there will be little controversy about my evaluations.

Figure 2.13: Whipsaw or Sideways Market—April 1969—Platinum

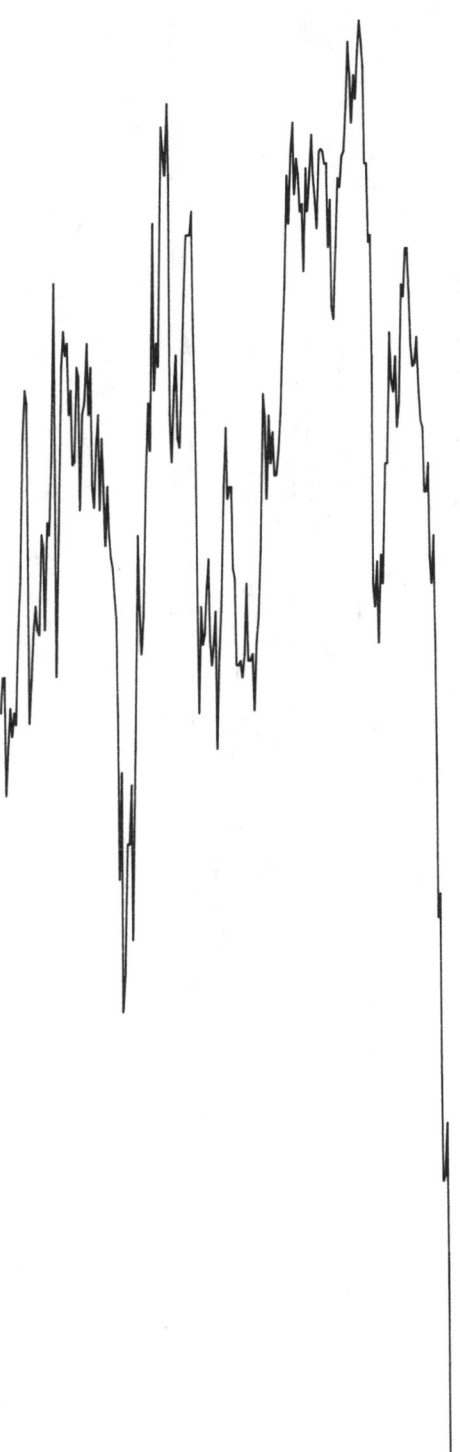

6904PL

Figure 2.14: Whipsaw or Sideways Market—July 1972—Wheat

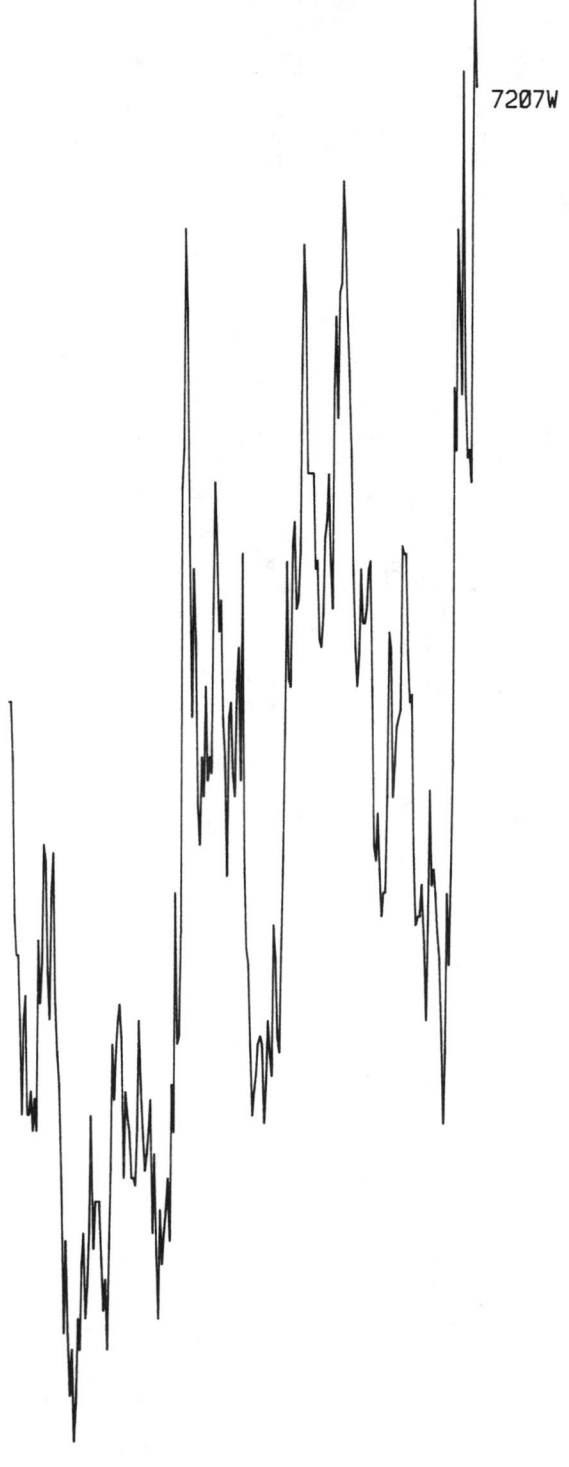

7207W

Figure 2.15: Whipsaw or Sideways Market—December 1983—Wheat

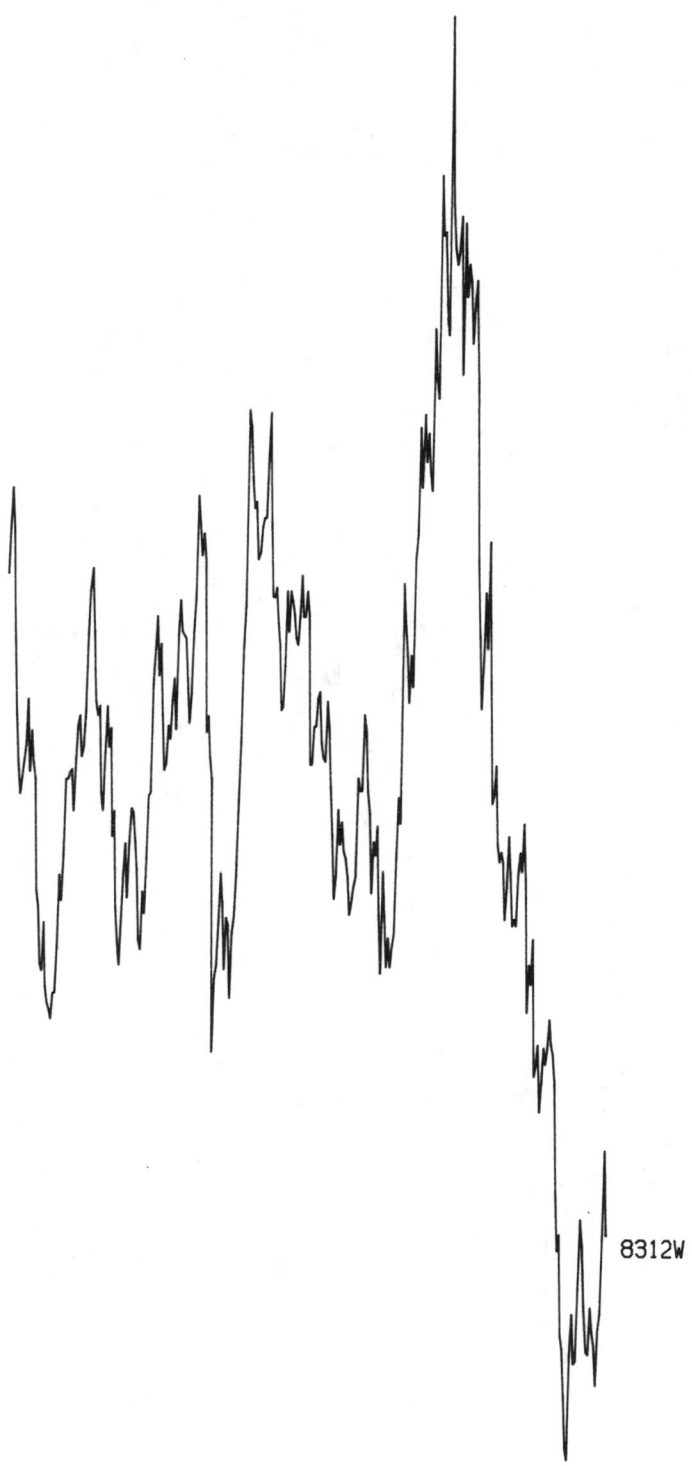

8312W

Figure 2.16: Bear/Bull Market—December 1968—Copper

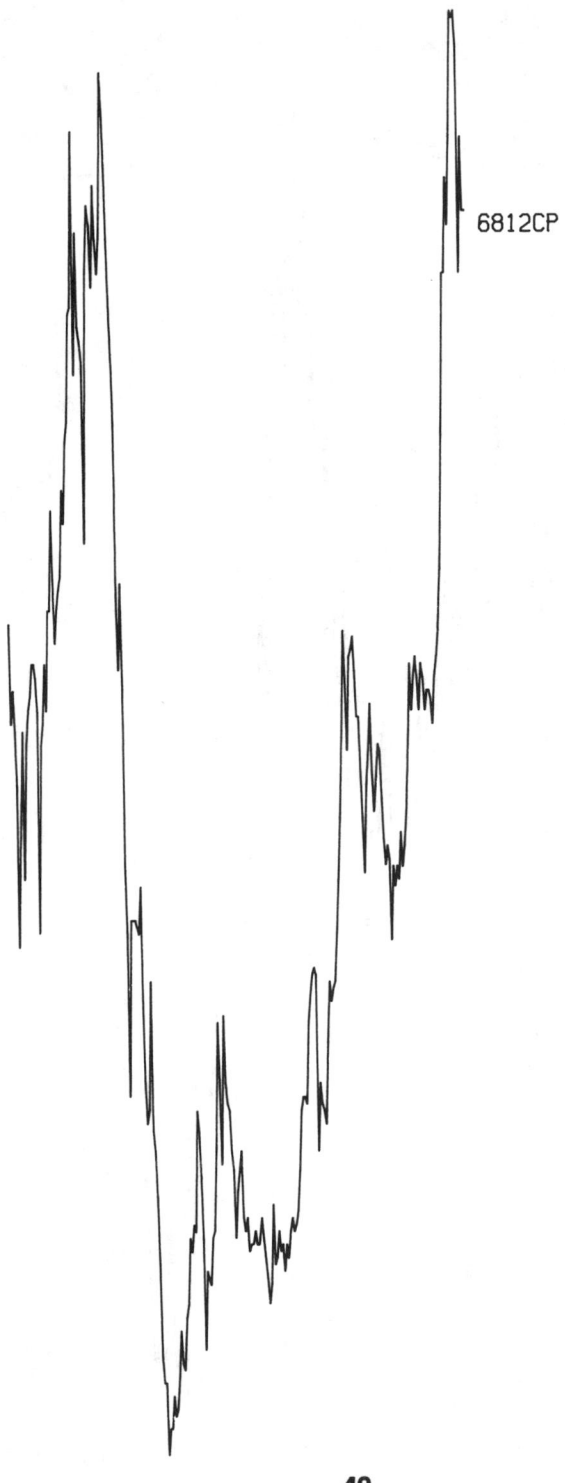

6812CP

Figure 2.17: Bear/Bull Market—July 1979—Corn

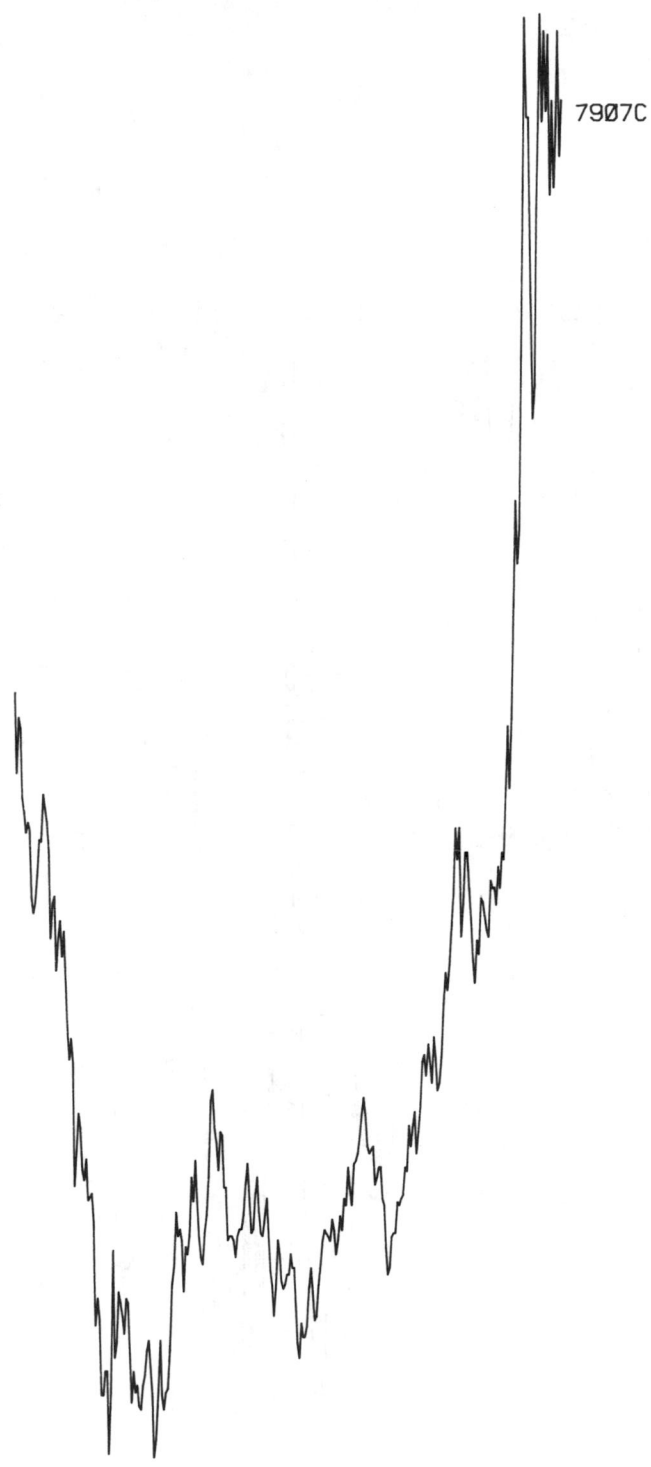

7907C

Figure 2.18: Bear/Bull Market—July 1986—Wheat

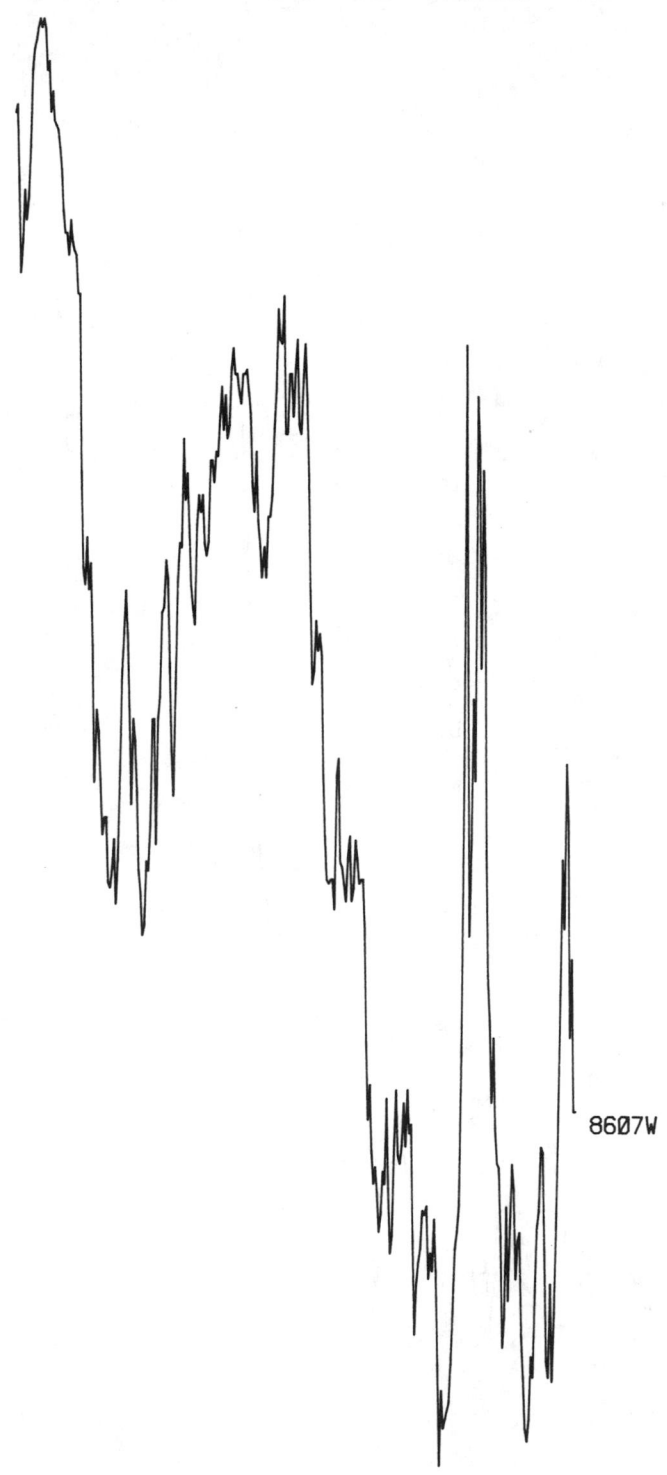

8607W

Figure 2.19: Bull/Bear Market—July 1969—Wheat

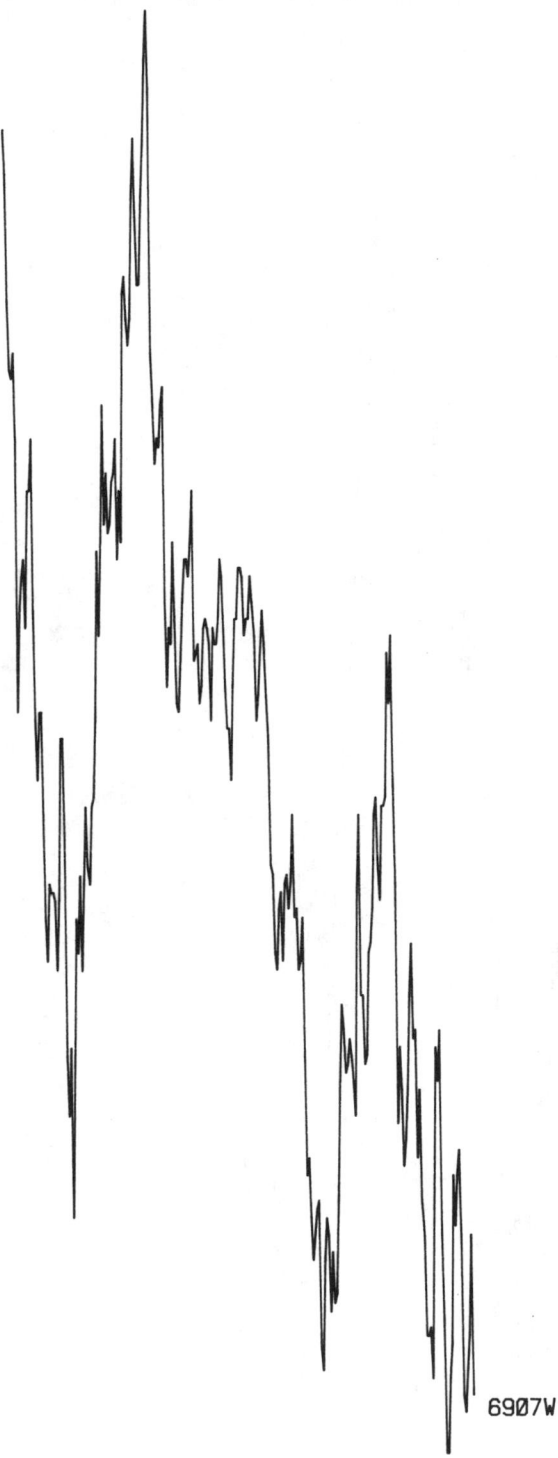

6907W

Figure 2.20: Bull/Bear Market—July 1974—Wheat

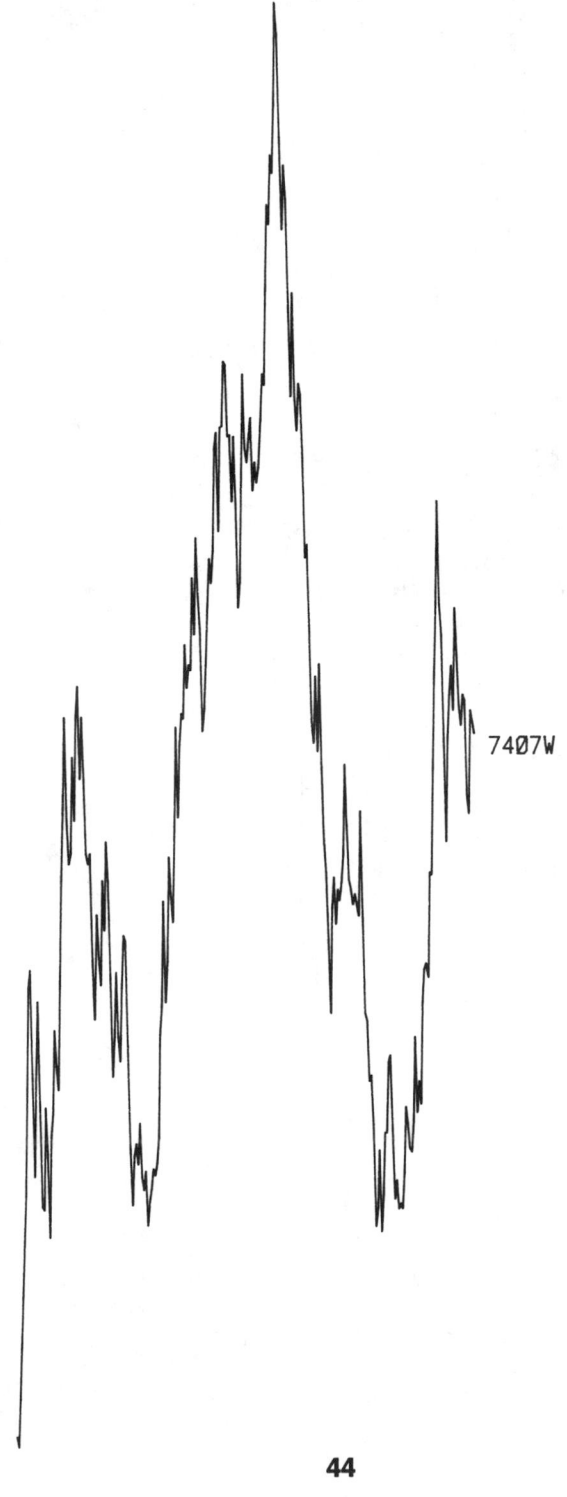

7407W

Figure 2.21: Bull/Bear Market—October 1983—Platinum

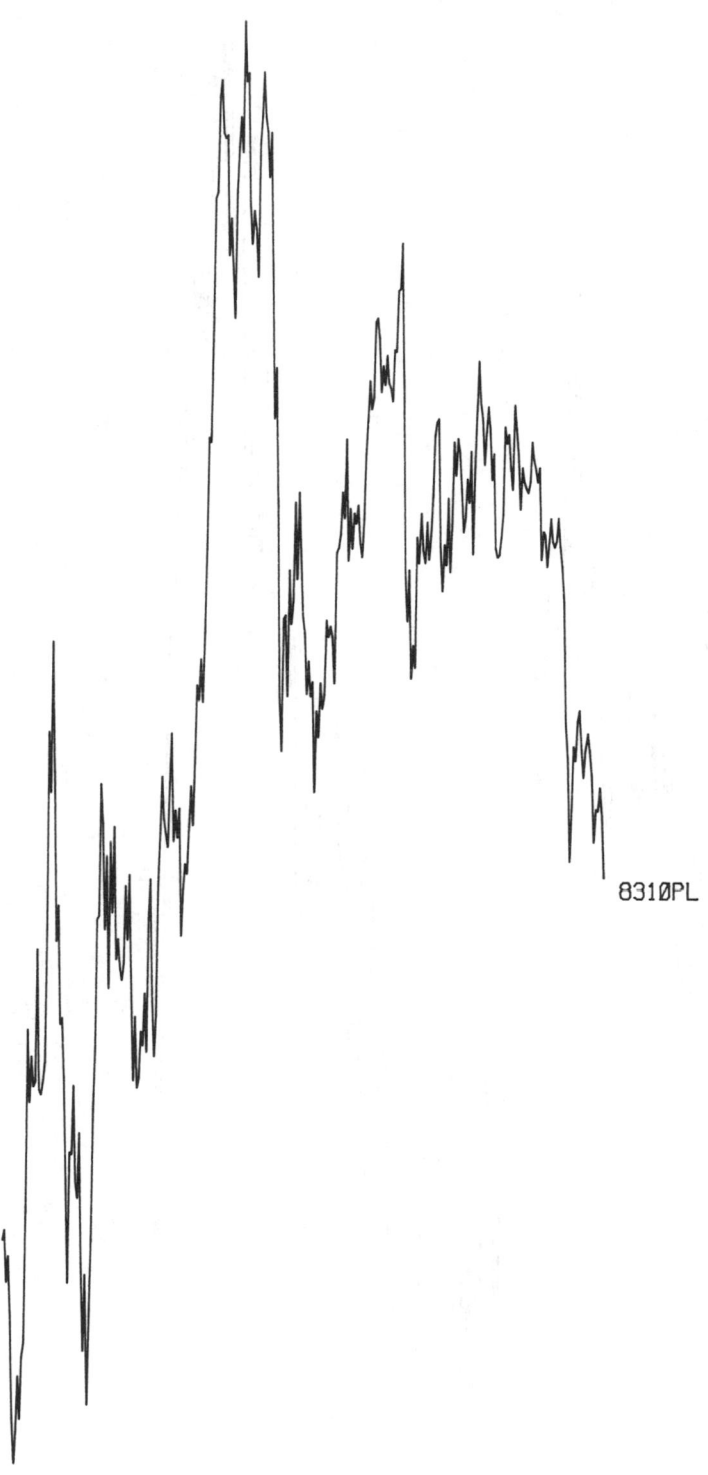

8310PL

Figure 2.22: Bear/Bull/Bear Market—December 1980—Wheat

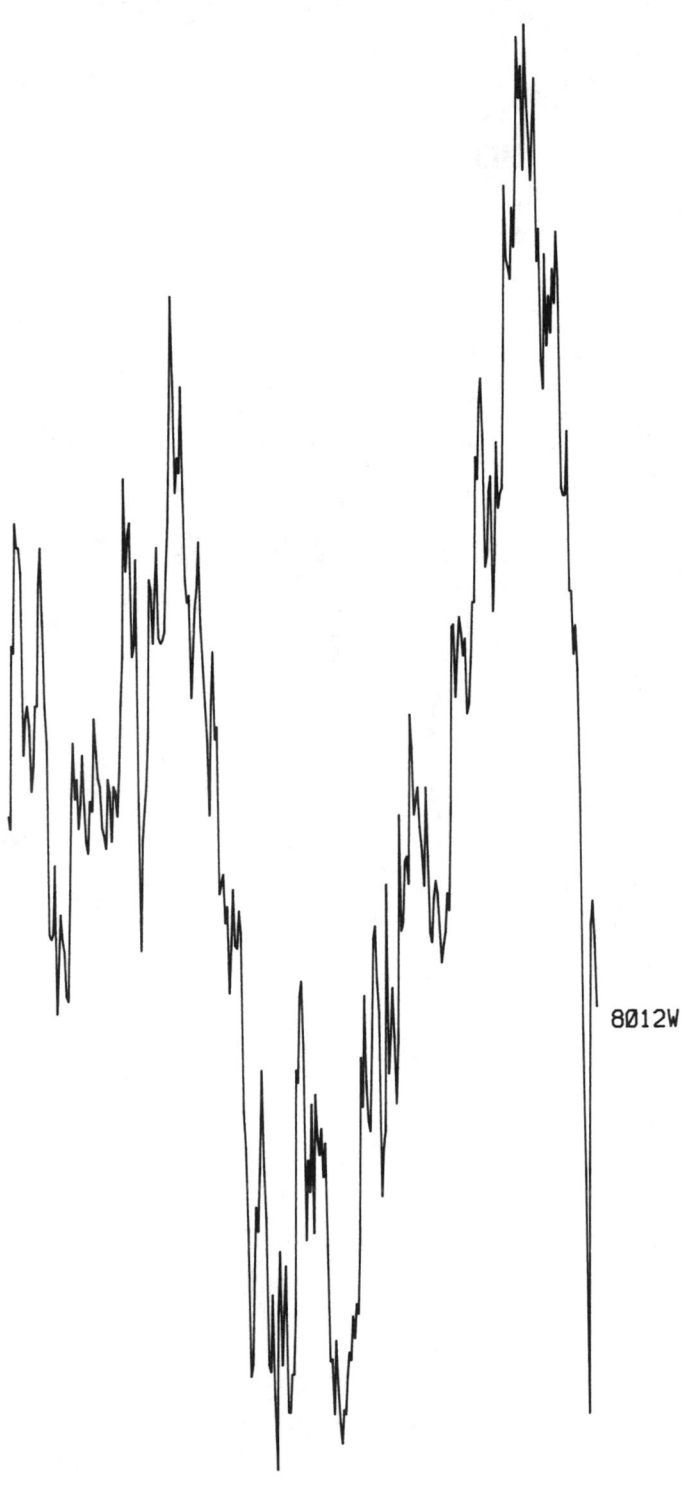

8012W

Figure 2.23: Bear/Bull/Bear Market—July 1985—Pork Bellies

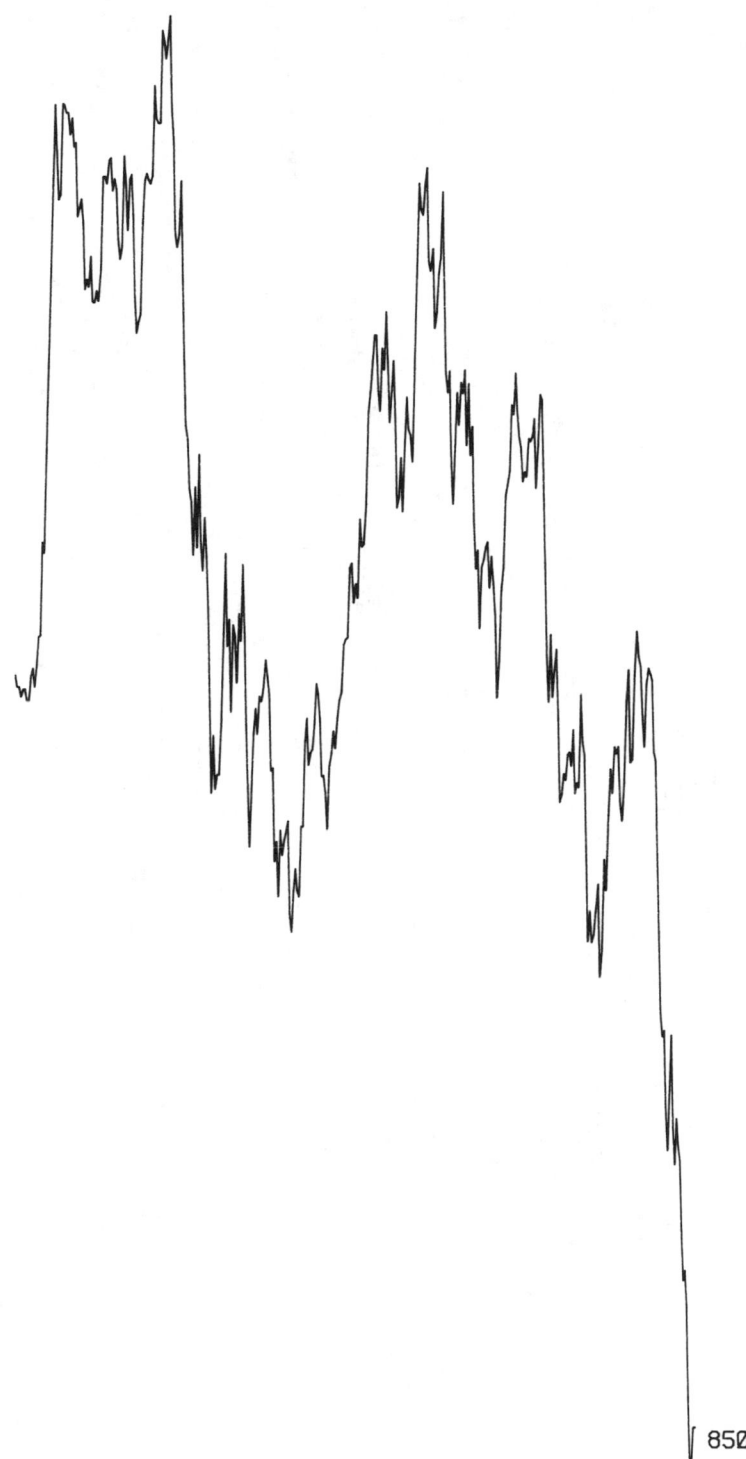

8507PB

Figure 2.24: Bear/Bull/Bear Market—December 1987—Live Hogs

8712LH

Figure 2.25: Bull/Bear/Bull Market—November 1974—Orange Juice

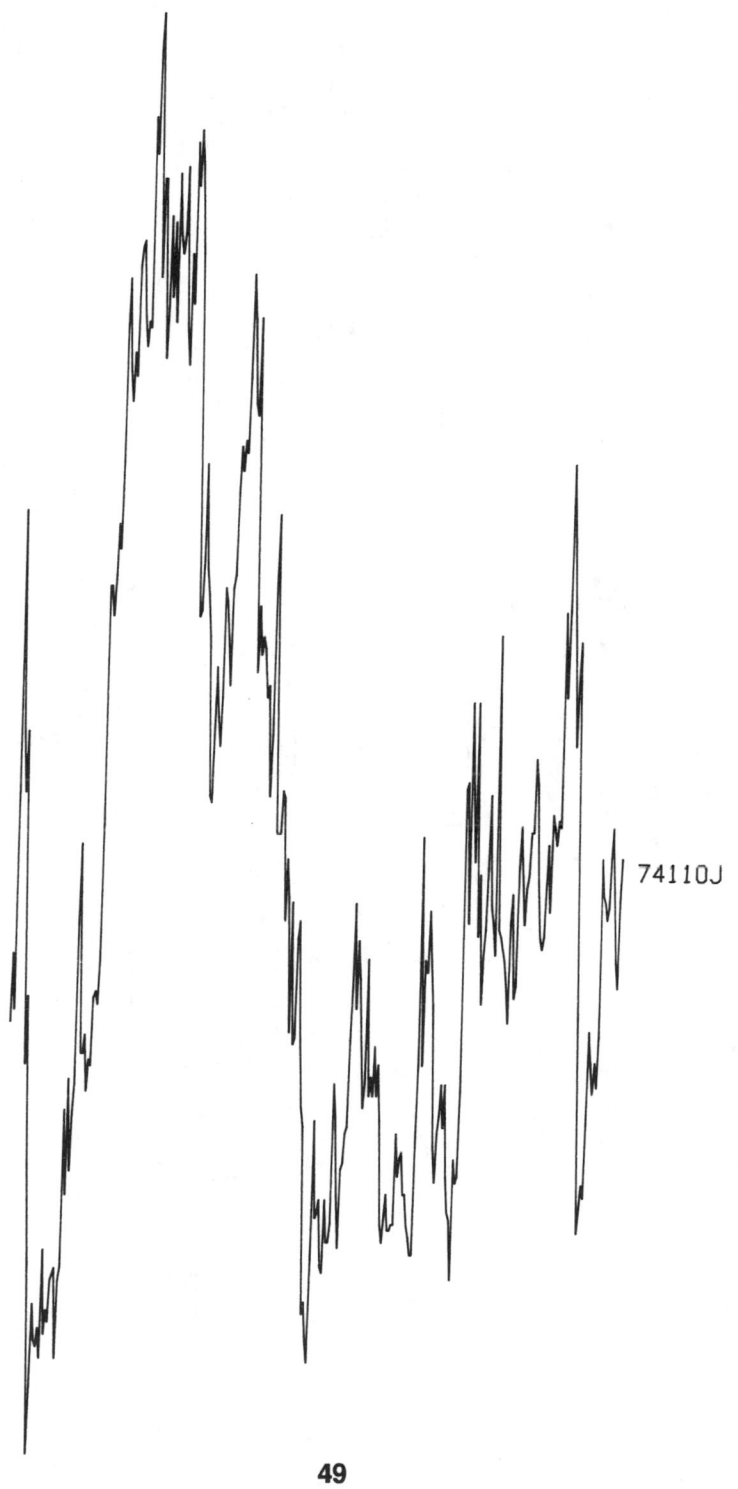

74110J

Figure 2.26: Bull/Bear/Bull Market—December 1984—Live Hogs

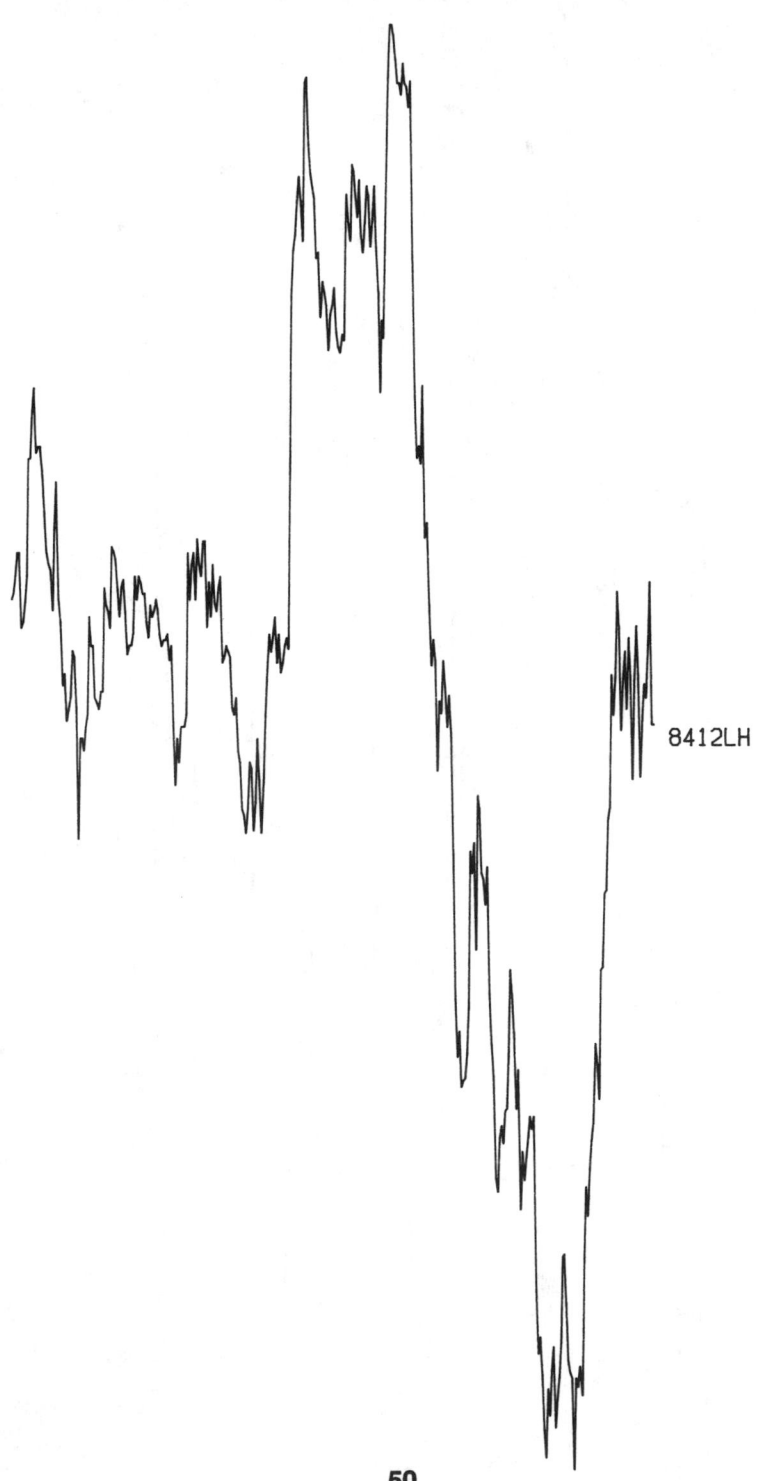

8412LH

Figure 2.27: Bull/Bear/Bull Market—December 1985—Cocoa

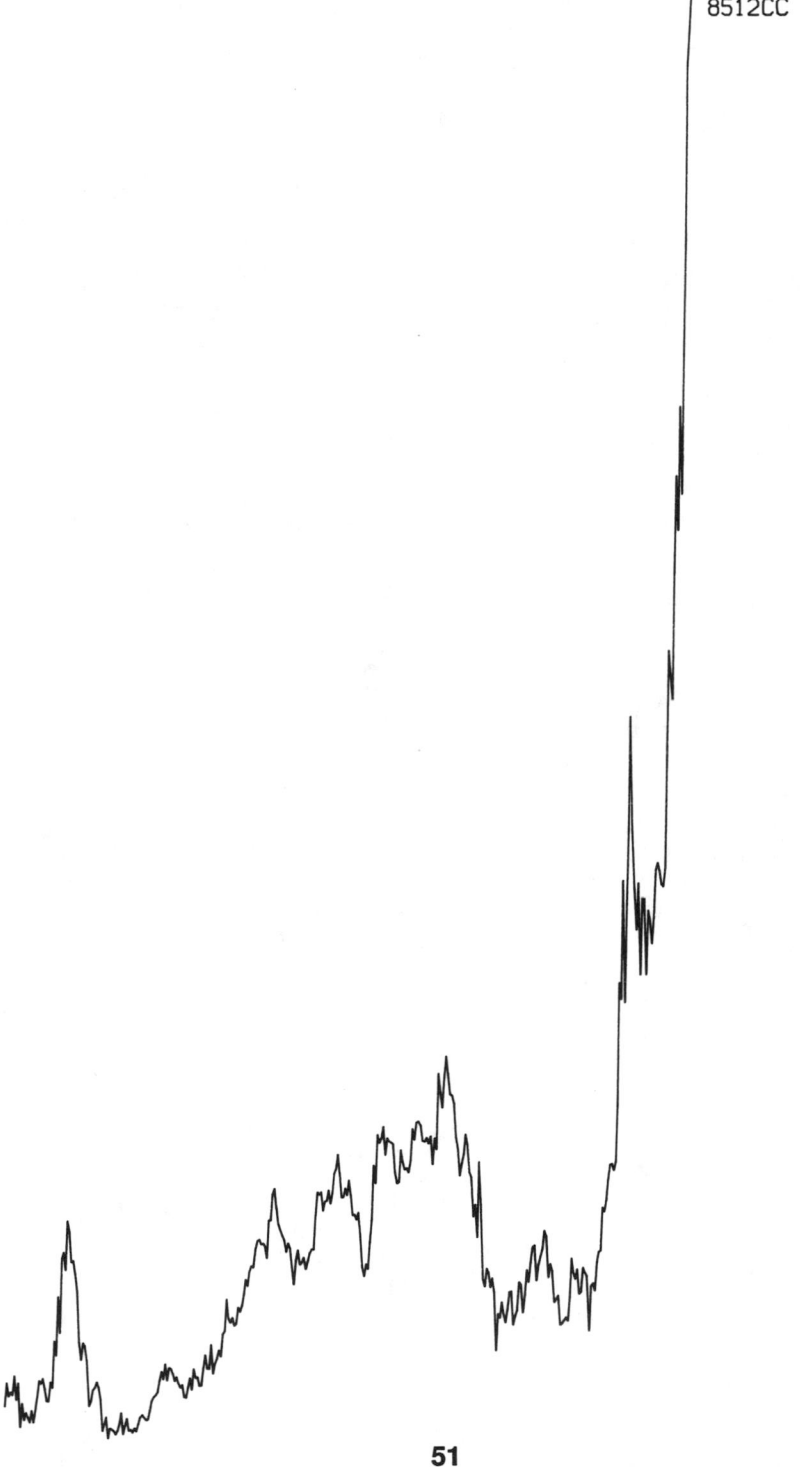

8512CC

3

Price Bar Signals

SIMPLE ONE-DAY UPSIDE REVERSALS (R+)

We begin with the most simple signals. Whether you've been trading futures for a considerable period of time or whether you're a newcomer, you most likely have heard of reversals. Through the years, technical traders have come to place considerable faith in the meaning of price reversals. For the most part traders feel (as opposed to *know*) that a reversal up is usually a bullish sign and that higher prices are likely to follow, whereas they feel that a reversal down is usually a bearish sign.

The diagram below shows a simple one-day reversal to the upside (R+). A reversal day is defined as :

A day during which prices fall below their previous daily low and close higher than their previous daily close.

The algorithm for a reversal day up (R+) is:

$$R+ = L2 < L1 \text{ and } C2 > C1$$

where:

    L2 = low of day 2;
    L1 = low of day 1;
    C2 = close of day 2; and
    C1 = 1 close of day 1.

    As I noted earlier, R+ signals are among the most well known of all price bar signals. Market folklore has always considered them important. What do my studies reveal? Figure 3-1 shows several R+ and R− signals. Figure 3-2 shows the performance of R+ signals over the entire historical database regardless of market trend. The statistical table in Figure 3-2 includes explanatory information which will help you understand it. In testing R+ and many other signals, we examined closing price data for the day following the signal and for ten consecutive days after the day the signal was generated. The tabular reading shows the percentage of time the price closed up or down on each of the ten days following the signal day, as well as the total number of signals over the length of the data history. Figures 3-3 through 3-11 show the performance of R+ and R− signals in the various market categories I've selected. You will note that the performance tables show the percentage of time the price closed higher on the day following the upside reversal and for the next ten trading days. This was done to determine if the effect of a simple one-day upside reversal could be observed for a longer period of time than just the day following its occurrence.

SIMPLE ONE-DAY DOWNSIDE REVERSALS (R−)

Simple one-day downside reversals are the exact opposite of R+ signals. The diagram below shows a simple one-day reversal to the downside (R−). The exact definition of an R− is:

A day during which prices trade above their previous daily high but close below their previous daily close.

The algorithm for a reversal day down (R−) is:

$$R- = H2 > H1 \text{ and } C2 < C1$$

where:

H2 = high of day 2;
H1 = high of day 1;
C2 = close of day 2; and
C1 = close day 1.

Examples of R+ and R− signals are shown in Figure 3-1.

Explanation and Interpretation of Results: Reversals

The statistical results for simple one-day upside and downside reversals revealed some interesting facts.

The fact that simple one-day up and down reversal signals have only limited validity when examined according to my criteria does not mean that they have only minimal validity when employed with money management principles as a trading system. Such an application seeks to improve signal reliability in conjunction with a system which limits losses and lets profits run. As I have pointed out previously—and as all veteran traders know—an effective money management approach can make random signals profitable and a poor money management approach can turn otherwise valid signals and indicators into losers.

The row headings of the statistical tables are defined as follows:

Close + = number of cases of up close after signal

Close − = number of cases of down close after signal

No Chng = number of cases showing no change after signal

%+ = percent of cases up close after signal

%− = percent of cases down close after signal

%NC = percent of cases of no change after signal

Each column in the table stands for one additional day following the signal. The first column, therefore, shows the results for the first day following the signal. The last column shows the results for the tenth day following the signal. Please make certain you understand how to read the tables, as they apply to many of the other indicators I will discuss in this chapter.

If you examine the results of Figures 3.3 through 3.11 you will find the following:

In bull markets R+ signals appear to have some degree of predictive validity about seven to nine days from the R+ signal (i.e., 62.1 percent, 63.7 percent and 63.7 percent higher than on day one after reversal). These figures are somewhat small, but they may have validity when examined in connection with risk management methods.

An interesting incongruity in connection with R− (reversal down) signals is that they appear to be more reliable in bull markets than do R+ signals in bull markets, showing from 62.2 percent through 64.4 percent from seven to ten days after the signal.

Choppy bull market results for R+ and R− signals are shown in Figure 3.4. As you can see, the results are not impressive, suggesting that choppy markets do not facilitate the performance of reversal signals.

Bear market reversal results are shown in Figure 3.5. They showed virtually no predictive validity.

Choppy bear markets showed equally poor results for reversal signal accuracy. See Figures 3.6.

Bull/bear market and **Bear/bull market** results using reversal signals were equally meaningless (i.e., random). See Figures 3.7 and 3.8.

Bull/bear/bull and **Bear/bull/bear market** results are shown in Figures 3.9 and 3.10. Clearly, the results here also showed random behavior.

Whipsaw market results for reversals are shown in Figure 3.11. As with all other market categories with the exception of bull markets, the results here suggested random behavior.

Figure 3.1: R+ and R− Signals

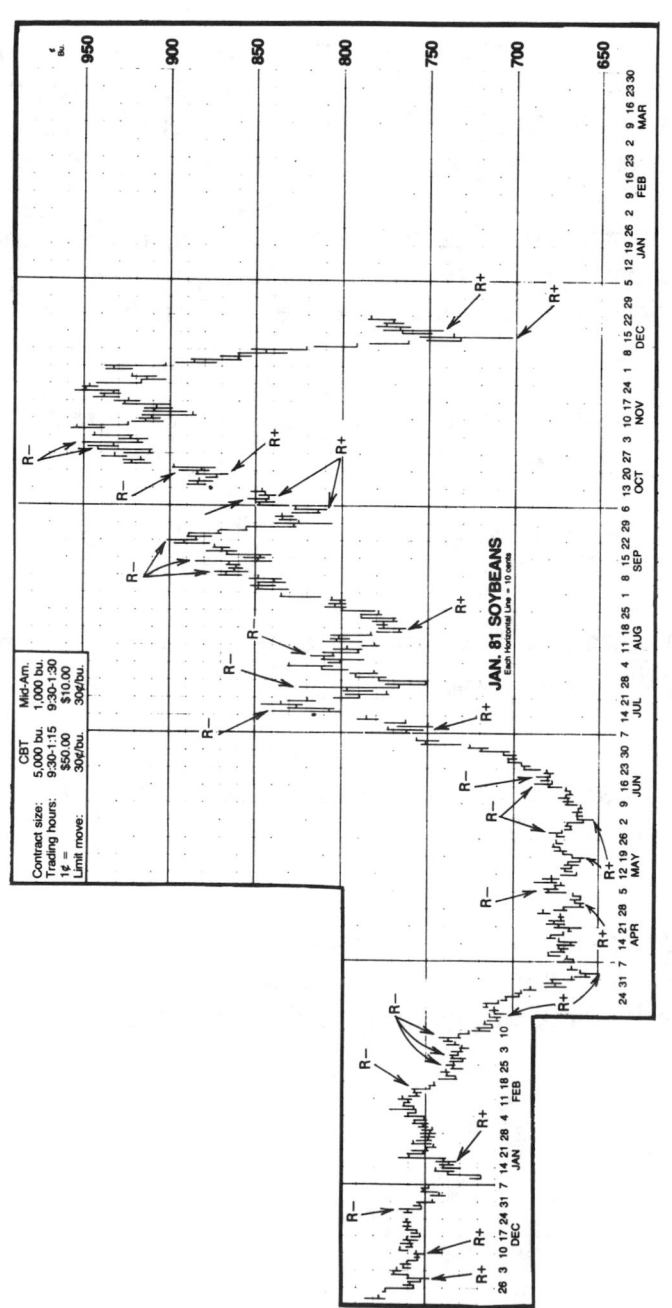

Chart reprinted with permission of Commodity Price Charts, 219 Parkade, Cedar Falls, IA 50613.

Figure 3.2:

Total net profit	$6,093.75	Gross loss	-189,031.25
Gross profit	$195,125.00		
Total # of trades	195	Percent profitable	38%
Number winning trades	75	Number losing trades	120
Largest winning trade	$15,931.25	Largest losing trade	$-5,037.50
Average winning trade	$2,601.67	Average losing trade	$-1,575.26
Ratio avg win/avg loss	1.65	Avg trade (win & loss)	$31.25
Max consecutive winners	4	Max consecutive losers	8
Avg # bars in winners	25	Avg # bars in losers	10
Max closed-out drawdown	$-35,662.50	Max intra-day drawdown	$-36,718.75
Profit factor	1.03	Max # of contracts held	1
Account size required	$39,718.75	Return on account	15%

Figure 3.3: R+ and R– Signal Accuracy: Bull Markets

REPORT TOTAL * * * * *

SIMPLE 1-DAY REVERSALS UP: 512 SIGNALS

	1	2	3	4	5	6	7	8	9	10
Close+	275	305	313	305	308	310	318	326	326	307
Close–	219	184	178	181	178	166	151	144	139	155
No Chng	14	13	8	10	6	7	9	7	7	5
%+	53.7	59.6	61.1	59.6	60.2	60.5	62.1	63.7	63.7	60.0
%–	42.8	35.9	34.8	35.4	34.8	32.4	29.5	28.1	27.1	30.3
%NC	2.7	2.5	1.6	2.0	1.2	1.4	1.8	1.4	1.4	1.0

SIMPLE 1-DAY REVERSALS DOWN: 519 SIGNALS

	1	2	3	4	5	6	7	8	9	10
Close+	269	279	295	315	320	320	323	328	337	334
Close–	217	211	203	177	171	167	164	149	140	139
No Chng	25	20	9	11	5	7	3	6	4	5
%+	51.8	53.8	56.8	60.7	61.7	61.7	62.2	63.2	64.9	64.4
%–	41.8	40.7	39.1	34.1	32.9	32.2	31.6	28.7	27.0	26.8
%NC	4.8	3.9	1.7	2.1	1.0	1.3	.6	1.2	.8	1.0

Days After Signal

%NC = 5 of Days No Change

Figure 3.4: R+ and R− Signal Accuracy: Choppy Bull Markets

```
REPORT TOTAL  *  *  *  *  *

  SIMPLE 1-DAY REVERSALS UP:       896 SIGNALS
Close+    476   491   480   480   472   469   477   475   476   471
Close-    393   378   384   386   382   377   369   370   358   362
No Chng    21    15     9     5    11    11     8     3     6     4
%+       53.1  54.8  53.6  53.6  52.7  52.3  53.2  53.0  53.1  52.6
%-       43.9  42.2  42.9  43.1  42.6  42.1  41.2  41.3  40.0  40.4
%NC       2.3   1.7   1.0    .6   1.2   1.2    .9    .3    .7    .4

  SIMPLE 1-DAY REVERSALS DOWN:      938 SIGNALS
Close+    492   518   520   510   493   503   499   488   476   463
Close-    413   398   393   393   399   387   379   385   392   391
No Chng    23     8     9    10    10     5    10     6     6     8
%+       52.5  55.2  55.4  54.4  52.6  53.6  53.2  52.0  50.7  49.4
%-       44.0  42.4  41.9  41.9  42.5  41.3  40.4  41.0  41.8  41.7
%NC       2.5    .9   1.0   1.1   1.1    .5   1.1    .6    .6    .9
```

Figure 3.5: R+ and R– Signal Accuracy: Bear Markets

```
REPORT TOTAL * * * * *
```

SIMPLE 1-DAY REVERSALS UP: 663 SIGNALS

Close+	321	287	276	279	271	258	243	230	208	206
Close-	317	343	354	352	355	366	374	379	396	391
No Chng	22	21	16	10	11	7	7	7	7	9
%+	48.4	43.3	41.6	42.1	40.9	38.9	36.7	34.7	31.4	31.1
%-	47.8	51.7	53.4	53.1	53.5	55.2	56.4	57.2	59.7	59.0
%NC	3.3	3.2	2.4	1.5	1.7	1.1	1.1	1.1	1.1	1.4

SIMPLE 1-DAY REVERSALS DOWN: 573 SIGNALS

Close+	242	237	228	222	218	217	185	195	180	170
Close-	300	309	313	321	320	323	350	343	346	352
No Chng	24	16	16	10	10	4	6	2	7	4
%+	42.2	41.4	39.8	38.7	38.0	37.9	32.3	34.0	31.4	29.7
%-	52.4	53.9	54.6	56.0	55.8	56.4	61.1	59.9	60.4	61.4
%NC	4.2	2.8	2.8	1.7	1.7	.7	1.0	.3	1.2	.7

Figure 3.6: R+ and R− Signal Accuracy: Choppy Bear Markets

REPORT TOTAL * * * * *

SIMPLE 1-DAY REVERSALS UP: 520 SIGNALS

Close+	249	223	215	221	208	196	195	192	180	190
Close-	252	282	292	279	293	295	299	297	302	298
No Chng	16	10	6	9	6	11	4	5	4	6
%+	47.9	42.9	41.3	42.5	40.0	37.7	37.5	36.9	34.6	34.6
%-	48.5	54.2	56.2	53.7	56.3	56.7	57.5	57.1	58.1	57.3
%NC	3.1	1.9	1.2	1.7	1.2	2.1	.8	1.0	.8	1.2

SIMPLE 1-DAY REVERSALS DOWN: 502 SIGNALS

Close+	209	209	210	196	191	187	181	178	171	173
Close-	276	275	273	288	285	290	285	288	294	292
No Chng	12	11	8	2	6	1	6	4	3	2
%+	41.6	41.6	41.8	39.0	38.0	37.3	36.1	35.5	34.1	34.5
%-	55.0	54.8	54.4	57.4	56.8	57.8	56.8	57.4	58.6	58.2
%NC	2.4	2.2	1.6	.4	1.2	.2	1.2	.8	.6	.4

Figure 3.7: R+ and R– Signal Accuracy: Bull/Bear Markets

REPORT TOTAL * * * * *

SIMPLE 1-DAY REVERSALS UP: 845 SIGNALS

Close+	401	356	358	359	357	338	334	336	314	322
Close-	432	462	456	452	455	463	467	460	466	461
No Chng	8	13	10	10	4	11	5	3	12	6
%+	47.5	42.1	42.4	42.5	42.2	40.0	39.5	39.8	37.2	38.1
%-	51.1	54.7	54.0	53.5	53.8	54.8	55.3	54.4	55.1	54.6
%NC	.9	1.5	1.2	1.2	.5	1.3	.6	.4	1.4	.7

SIMPLE 1-DAY REVERSALS DOWN: 794 SIGNALS

Close+	362	362	363	335	317	308	312	310	301	290
Close-	406	405	409	417	434	434	434	435	432	440
No Chng	18	15	4	10	7	10	5	2	12	7
%+	45.6	45.6	45.7	42.2	39.9	38.8	39.3	39.0	37.9	36.5
%-	51.1	51.0	51.5	52.5	54.7	54.7	54.7	54.8	54.4	55.4
%NC	2.3	1.9	.5	1.3	.9	1.3	.6	.3	1.5	.9

Figure 3.8: R+ and R− Signal Accuracy: Bear/Bull Markets

```
REPORT TOTAL  *  *  *  *  *

SIMPLE 1-DAY REVERSALS UP:      998 SIGNALS
Close+    532   563   547   561   556   558   579   571   582   585
Close-    418   400   416   405   397   388   363   352   349   339
No Cnng    43    22    19    11    15    11    11    19     8     5
%+       53.3  56.4  54.8  56.2  55.7  55.9  59.0  57.2  58.3  58.6
%-       41.9  40.1  41.7  40.6  39.8  38.9  36.4  35.3  35.0  34.0
%NC       4.3   2.2   1.9   1.1   1.5   1.1   1.1   1.9    .8    .5

SIMPLE 1-DAY REVERSALS DOWN:    979 SIGNALS
Close+    502   530   544   519   538   561   542   564   553   552
Close-    429   417   395   410   387   360   366   346   353   346
No Cnng    36    14    17    19    12    11    16    10     6     9
%+       51.3  54.1  55.6  53.0  55.0  57.3  55.4  57.6  56.5  56.4
%-       43.8  42.6  40.3  41.9  39.5  36.8  37.4  35.3  36.1  35.3
%NC       3.7   1.4   1.7   1.9   1.2   1.1   1.6   1.0    .6    .9
```

Figure 3.9: R+ and R− Signal Accuracy: Bear/Bull/Bear Markets

REPORT TOTAL * * * * *

SIMPLE 1-DAY REVERSALS UP: 152 SIGNALS

Close+	87	82	77	72	76	71	73	73	73	73
Close-	63	67	70	73	70	73	69	70	67	67
No Chng	1	1	0	2	0	1	1	0	2	0
%+	57.2	53.9	50.7	47.4	50.0	46.7	48.0	48.0	48.0	48.0
%-	41.4	44.1	46.1	48.0	46.1	48.0	45.4	46.1	44.1	44.1
%NC	.7	.7	.0	1.3	.0	.7	.7	.0	1.3	.0

SIMPLE 1-DAY REVERSALS DOWN: 144 SIGNALS

Close+	71	71	73	66	68	67	67	64	63	67
Close-	72	70	68	75	72	72	71	74	74	70
No Chng	1	2	1	1	2	1	1	0	1	0
%+	49.3	49.3	50.7	45.8	47.2	46.5	46.5	44.4	43.7	46.5
%-	50.0	48.6	47.2	52.1	50.0	50.0	49.3	51.4	51.4	48.6
%NC	.7	1.4	.7	.7	1.4	.7	.7	.0	.7	.0

Figure 3.10: R+ and R– Signal Accuracy: Bull/Bear/Bull Markets

REPORT TOTAL * * * * *

SIMPLE 1-DAY REVERSALS UP: 193 SIGNALS

Close+	107	98	103	102	108	98	94	99	100	96
Close-	84	92	87	85	76	85	89	82	80	80
No Chng	2	3	2	1	4	1	1	1	2	3
%+	55.4	50.8	53.4	52.8	56.0	50.8	48.7	51.3	51.8	49.7
%-	43.5	47.7	45.1	44.0	39.4	44.0	46.1	42.5	41.5	41.5
%NC	1.0	1.6	1.0	.5	2.1	.5	.5	.5	1.0	1.6

SIMPLE 1-DAY REVERSALS DOWN: 210 SIGNALS

Close+	108	115	118	116	116	120	111	111	104	110
Close-	95	89	86	88	83	80	85	83	84	81
No Chng	6	2	1	1	2	1	2	0	4	1
%+	51.4	54.8	56.2	55.2	55.2	57.1	52.9	52.9	49.5	52.4
%-	45.2	42.4	41.0	41.9	39.5	38.1	40.5	39.5	40.0	38.6
%NC	2.9	1.0	.5	.5	1.0	.5	1.0	.0	1.9	.5

Figure 3.11: R+ and R− Signal Accuracy: Whipsaw Markets

```
REPORT TOTAL  * * * * *

SIMPLE 1-DAY REVERSALS UP:     747 SIGNALS

Close+    366   343   340      353   356   344      351   349   341   340
Close-    358   375   382      366   359   367      357   351   353   344
No Chng    17    19    12        8     9     6        8     6     7     9
%+       49.0  45.9  45.5     47.3  47.7  46.1     47.0  46.7  45.6  45.5
%-       47.9  50.2  51.1     49.0  48.1  49.1     47.8  47.0  47.3  46.1
%NC       2.3   2.5   1.6      1.1   1.2    .8      1.1    .8    .9   1.2


SIMPLE 1-DAY REVERSALS DOWN:    722 SIGNALS

Close+    359   368   368      358   355   341      342   338   337   335
Close-    332   328   321      330   329   341      328   330   329   324
No Chng    25    15    14       10     7     8       11     9     3     5
%+       49.7  51.0  51.0     49.6  49.2  47.2     47.4  46.8  46.7  46.4
%-       46.0  45.4  44.5     45.7  45.6  47.2     45.4  45.7  45.6  44.9
%NC       3.5   2.1   1.9      1.4   1.0   1.1      1.5   1.2    .4    .7
```

The results of my extensive R+/R− analysis were clearly disappointing. They confirmed that simple one day up and down reversal signals were, when used alone, not valid indicators when used without considering trend. The tabular presentation of results by market category suggests that in bull markets (see figure 3-3) there has been a tendency for R+ signals to show some predictive validity from 5-10 days following their occurrence. But R− also seem to work in bull trends. This indicates once again the importance of trend vs. timing signals. And in bear markets (see Figure 3.5) R+ and R− signals actually appear to have a reverse effect from 5-10 days following their occurrence. In other words, in the case of R+ signals the 5-10 day trend is lower in bear markets as is also the case in bear markets. This is, of course understandable inasmuch as trend is the single most important factor. Results were mixed in other types of trends suggesting again that R+ and R− signals yield essentially random results when examined on an extensive data base. The general SWP findings support these conclusions.

KEY REVERSALS UP (KR+)

A KR+ signal is essentially similar to an R+ signal with the exception that on the reversal day both the high and the low of the previous day are exceeded. The diagram below shows a one-day key reversal to the upside (KR+). A KR+ is defined as follows:

A day on which the high and low of the previous day are exceeded and on which the closing price is greater than the closing price of the day before.

Figure 3.12: R+/R– Performance Using SYSTEM WRITER PLUS: Cotton

```
---------------- COTTON #2          06/89 - All trades ------------
Test #       1 of    1                          Space bar to toggle display

Total net profit          $-8,255.00
Gross profit           $240,115.00   Gross loss                   -248,370.00

Total # of trades            684     Percent profitable                  38%
Number winning trades        266     Number losing trades                418

Largest winning trade    $13,325.00  Largest losing trade         $-6,085.00
Average winning trade       $902.69  Average losing trade         $ -594.19
Ratio avg win/avg loss         1.52  Avg trade (win & loss)        $-12.07

Max consecutive winners        8     Max consecutive losers               15
Avg # bars in winners          7     Avg # bars in losers                  5

Max closed-out drawdown  $-41,240.00 Max intra-day drawdown     $-41,275.00
Profit factor                  0.97  Max # of contracts held               1
Account size required    $44,275.00  Return on account                  -18%
```

Figure 3.13: R+/R– Performance Using SYSTEM WRITER PLUS: Pork Bellies

```
---------------- PORK BELLIES        06/89 - All trades ------------
Test #       1 of    1                          Space bar to toggle display

Total net profit         $-56,304.00
Gross profit           $349,636.00   Gross loss                   -405,940.00

Total # of trades            924     Percent profitable                  39%
Number winning trades        364     Number losing trades                560

Largest winning trade     $7,790.00  Largest losing trade         $-5,270.00
Average winning trade       $960.54  Average losing trade         $ -724.89
Ratio avg win/avg loss         1.33  Avg trade (win & loss)        $-60.94

Max consecutive winners        7     Max consecutive losers               14
Avg # bars in winners          6     Avg # bars in losers                  4

Max closed-out drawdown  $-65,080.00 Max intra-day drawdown     $-65,502.00
Profit factor                  0.86  Max # of contracts held               1
Account size required    $68,502.00  Return on account                  -82%
```

Figure 3.14: R+/R– Performance Using SYSTEM WRITER PLUS: Copper

```
------------- COPPER              06/89 - All trades ----------------------
Test #      1 of     1                          Space bar to toggle display

Total net profit         $-26,475.00
Gross profit             $159,562.50  Gross loss                  -186,037.50

Total # of trades               531   Percent profitable                  40%
Number winning trades           216   Number losing trades                315

Largest winning trade     $6,400.00   Largest losing trade        $-8,200.00
Average winning trade       $738.72   Average losing trade        $ -590.60
Ratio avg win/avg loss         1.25   Avg trade (win & loss)         $-49.86

Max consecutive winners           6   Max consecutive losers               11
Avg # bars in winners             8   Avg # bars in losers                  7

Max closed-out drawdown  $-49,262.50  Max intra-day drawdown     $-49,262.50
Profit factor                  0.86   Max # of contracts held               1
Account size required    $52,262.50   Return on account                  -50%
```

Figure 3.15: R+/R– Performance Using SYSTEM WRITER PLUS: S&P Index

```
------------- S&P INDEX           06/89 - All trades ----------------------
Test #      1 of     1                          Space bar to toggle display

Total net profit         $-99,550.00
Gross profit             $245,900.00  Gross loss                  -345,450.00

Total # of trades               324   Percent profitable                  39%
Number winning trades           129   Number losing trades                195

Largest winning trade     $9,275.00   Largest losing trade       $-39,875.00
Average winning trade     $1,906.20   Average losing trade       $-1,771.54
Ratio avg win/avg loss         1.08   Avg trade (win & loss)        $ -307.25

Max consecutive winners           6   Max consecutive losers                8
Avg # bars in winners             6   Avg # bars in losers                  4

Max closed-out drawdown -106,125.00   Max intra-day drawdown    -106,975.00
Profit factor                  0.71   Max # of contracts held               1
Account size required    $109,975.00  Return on account                  -90%
```

Figure 3.16: R+/R– Performance Using SYSTEM WRITER PLUS: Japanese Yen

```
――――――――――― JAPANESE YEN        06/89 – All trades ―――――――
Test #       1 of    1                          Space bar to toggle display

Total net profit          $29,075.00
Gross profit             $159,275.00  Gross loss                 –130,200.00

Total # of trades               262   Percent profitable                 41%
Number winning trades           108   Number losing trades               154

Largest winning trade     $7,050.00   Largest losing trade        $–4,062.50
Average winning trade     $1,474.77   Average losing trade        $  –845.45
Ratio avg win/avg loss         1.74   Avg trade (win & loss)        $110.97

Max consecutive winners           4   Max consecutive losers               7
Avg # bars in winners            15   Avg # bars in losers                 9

Max closed-out drawdown  $–19,475.00  Max intra-day drawdown      $–19,475.00
Profit factor                  1.22   Max # of contracts held              1
Account size required    $22,475.00   Return on account                  129%
```

The algorithm for a KR+ day is:

$$KR+ = H2 > H1 \text{ and } L2 < L1 \text{ and } C2 > C1$$

where:

KR+ = key reversal up;
H2 = high day 2;
H1 = high day 1;
L2 = low day 2;
L1 = low day 1;
C2 = close day 2; and
C1 = close day 1.

Figure 3-17 shows some KR+ and KR– signals and Figures 3-18 through 3-27 show KR+ and KR– performance in the different market categories.

Figure 3.17: KR+ and KR− Signals in December 1991 T-Bonds

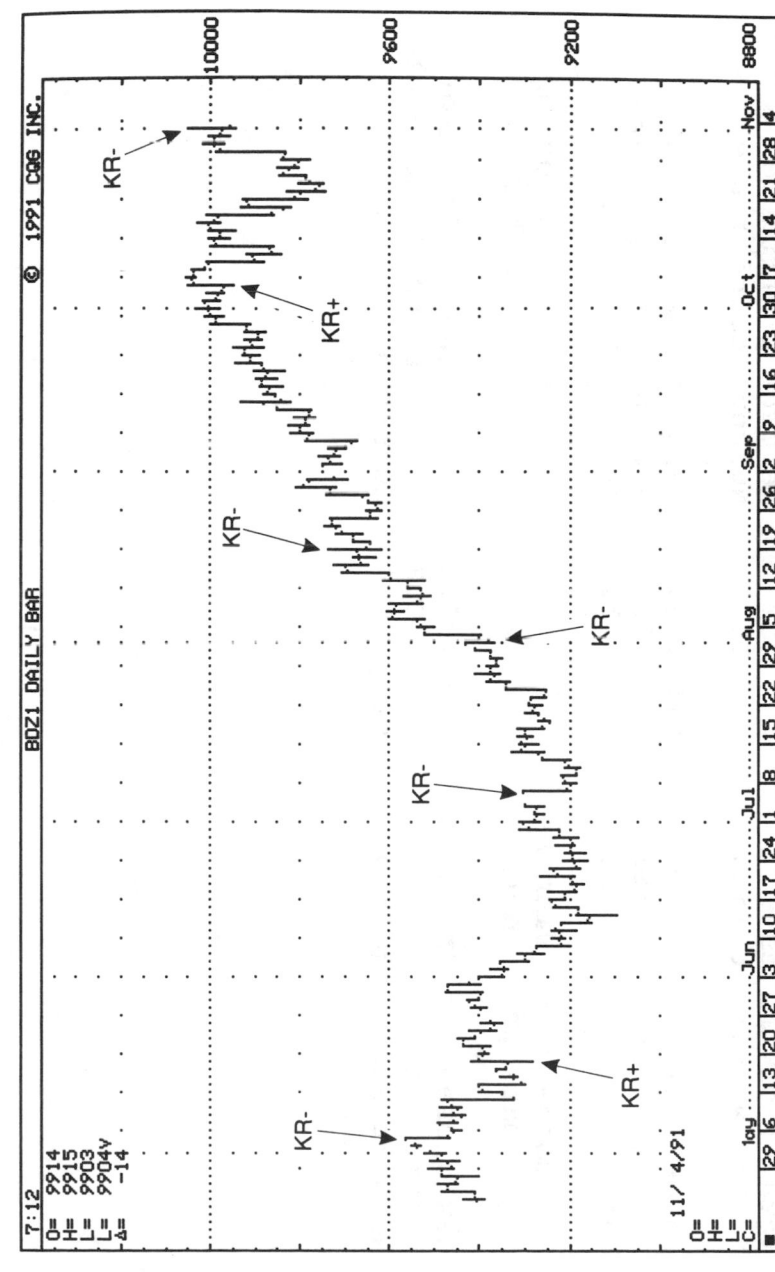

Figure 3.18:

Total net profit	$-32,585.00	Gross loss	-181,205.00
Gross profit	$148,620.00		
Total # of trades	351	Percent profitable	32%
Number winning trades	113	Number losing trades	238
Largest winning trade	$16,125.00	Largest losing trade	$-5,345.00
Average winning trade	$1,315.22	Average losing trade	$ -761.37
Ratio avg win/avg loss	1.73	Avg trade (win & loss)	$-92.83
Max consecutive winners	3	Max consecutive losers	13
Avg # bars in winners	20	Avg # bars in losers	8
Max closed-out drawdown	$-39,795.00	Max intra-day drawdown	$-39,910.00
Profit factor	0.82	Max # of contracts held	1
Account size required	$42,910.00	Return on account	-75%

Figure 3.19: KR+ and KR− Signal Results: Bull Markets

REPORT TOTAL * * * * *

KEY REVERSALS UP: 206 SIGNALS

Close+	110	122	130	130	133	133	135	141	138	127
Close−	87	73	65	64	62	56	52	49	49	56
No Chng	6	4	3	4	2	3	4	1	2	3
%+	53.4	59.2	63.1	63.1	64.6	64.6	65.5	68.4	67.0	61.7
%−	42.2	35.4	31.6	31.1	30.1	27.2	25.2	23.8	23.8	27.2
%NC	2.9	1.9	1.5	1.9	1.0	1.5	1.9	.5	1.0	1.5

KEY REVERSALS DOWN: 175 SIGNALS

Close+	90	94	98	95	104	105	104	103	109	108
Close−	74	72	69	66	58	56	56	50	43	44
No Chng	9	7	4	7	2	3	0	2	2	2
%+	51.4	53.7	56.0	54.3	59.4	60.0	59.4	58.9	62.3	61.7
%−	42.3	41.1	39.4	37.7	33.1	32.0	32.0	28.6	24.6	25.1
%NC	5.1	4.0	2.3	4.0	1.1	1.7	.0	1.1	1.1	1.1

Figure 3.20: KR+ and KR– Signal Results: Choppy Bull Markets

REPORT TOTAL * * * * *

KEY REVERSALS UP: 338 SIGNALS

Close+	156	172	176	171	176	181	186	190	190	183
Close-	173	158	152	157	149	139	132	130	127	132
No Chng	6	4	3	3	3	4	4	1	2	2
%+	46.2	50.9	52.1	50.6	52.1	53.6	55.0	56.2	56.2	54.1
%-	51.2	46.7	45.0	46.4	44.1	41.1	39.1	38.5	37.6	39.1
%NC	1.8	1.2	.9	.9	.9	1.2	1.2	.3	.6	.6

KEY REVERSALS DOWN: 349 SIGNALS

Close+	181	184	181	178	179	192	189	175	165	156
Close-	157	158	161	156	155	138	135	147	157	161
No Chng	7	2	2	6	3	2	4	3	1	3
%+	51.9	52.7	51.9	51.0	51.3	55.0	54.2	50.1	47.3	44.7
%-	45.0	45.3	46.1	44.7	44.4	39.5	38.7	42.1	45.0	46.1
%NC	2.0	.6	.6	1.7	.9	.6	1.1	.9	.3	.9

Figure 3.21: KR+ and KR– Signal Results: Bear Markets

```
REPORT TOTAL  * * * * *

          KEY REVERSALS UP:   226 SIGNALS
Close+    110    96    93   102    94    93    93    85    75    72
Close-    108   121   124   115   119   123   119   125   134   132
No Chng     6     5     4     2     5     1     1     2     2     4
%+       48.7  42.5  41.2  45.1  41.6  41.2  41.2  37.6  33.2  31.9
%-       47.8  53.5  54.9  50.9  52.7  54.4  52.7  55.3  59.3  58.4
%NC       2.7   2.2   1.8    .9   2.2    .4    .4    .9    .9   1.8

          KEY REVERSALS DOWN:  215 SIGNALS
Close+     86    87    80    79    77    80    70    72    62    56
Close-    120   119   124   123   124   120   128   127   133   140
No Chng     7     6     5     5     3     1     3     2     4     1
%+       40.0  40.5  37.2  36.7  35.8  37.2  32.6  33.5  28.8  26.0
%-       55.8  55.3  57.7  57.2  57.7  55.8  59.5  59.1  61.9  65.1
%NC       3.3   2.8   2.3   2.3   1.4    .5   1.4    .9   1.9    .5
```

Figure 3.22: KR+ and KR– Signal Results: Choppy Bear Markets

```
REPORT TOTAL * * * * *
```

KEY REVERSALS UP: 196 SIGNALS

Close+	99	85	89	90	81	75	75	81	67	68
Close-	91	105	104	99	109	113	114	107	116	113
No Chng	5	4	1	4	3	4	1	0	3	4
%+	50.5	43.4	45.4	45.9	41.3	38.3	38.3	41.3	34.2	34.7
%-	46.4	53.6	53.1	50.5	55.6	57.7	58.2	54.6	59.2	57.7
%NC	2.6	2.0	.5	2.0	1.5	2.0	.5	.0	1.5	2.0

KEY REVERSALS DOWN: 199 SIGNALS

Close+	76	83	79	72	67	69	67	61	62	59
Close-	112	103	112	119	119	117	113	118	116	119
No Chng	7	7	2	0	3	0	2	1	1	1
%+	38.2	41.7	39.7	36.2	33.7	34.7	33.7	30.7	31.2	29.6
%-	56.3	51.8	56.3	59.8	59.8	58.8	56.8	59.3	58.3	59.8
%NC	3.5	3.5	1.0	.0	1.5	.0	1.0	.5	.5	.5

Figure 3.23: KR+ and KR− Signal Results: Bull/Bear Markets

```
REPORT TOTAL * * * * *

              KEY REVERSALS UP:      345 SIGNALS
Close+     163   148   144   147   142   143   137   141   133   141
Close-     179   186   188   184   187   185   191   184   184   178
No Chng      2     5     4     4     3     3     2     0     6     2
%+        47.2  42.9  41.7  42.6  41.2  41.4  39.7  40.9  38.6  40.9
%-        51.9  53.9  54.5  53.3  54.2  53.6  55.4  53.3  53.3  51.6
%NC         .6   1.4   1.2   1.2    .9    .9    .6    .0   1.7    .6

              KEY REVERSALS DOWN:    326 SIGNALS
Close+     144   146   137   123   114   121   118   119   117   110
Close-     172   169   178   184   193   179   184   183   176   185
No Chng      7     5     2     3     2     5     2     0     9     3
%+        44.2  44.8  42.0  37.7  35.0  37.1  36.2  36.5  35.9  33.7
%-        52.8  51.8  54.6  56.4  59.2  54.9  56.4  56.1  54.0  56.7
%NC        2.1   1.5    .6    .9    .6   1.5    .6    .0   2.8    .9
```

Figure 3.24: KR+ and KR– Signal Results: Bear/Bull Markets

REPORT TOTAL   *   *   *   *   *

KEY REVERSALS UP: 362 SIGNALS

Close+	196	213	212	203	202	215	226	213	217	220
Close-	150	134	141	148	149	130	118	123	124	120
No Chng	14	12	5	5	3	5	3	8	3	2
%+	54.1	58.8	58.6	56.1	55.8	59.4	62.4	58.8	59.9	60.8
%-	41.4	37.0	39.0	40.9	41.2	35.9	32.6	34.0	34.3	33.1
%NC	3.9	3.3	1.4	1.4	.8	1.4	.8	2.2	.8	.6

KEY REVERSALS DOWN: 337 SIGNALS

Close+	162	173	184	163	168	180	172	179	176	171
Close-	153	147	138	151	144	126	131	124	125	127
No Chng	13	5	2	6	2	4	6	3	2	3
%+	48.1	51.3	54.6	48.4	49.9	53.4	51.0	53.1	52.2	50.7
%-	45.4	43.6	40.9	44.8	42.7	37.4	38.9	36.8	37.1	37.7
%NC	3.9	1.5	.6	1.8	.6	1.2	1.8	.9	.6	.9

Figure 3.25: KR+ and KR– Signal Results: Bear/Bull/Bear Markets

```
REPORT TOTAL  * * * * *        50  SIGNALS           65  SIGNALS
```

KEY REVERSALS UP:

	REPORT TOTAL			50 SIGNALS			65 SIGNALS		
Close+	29	28	27	27	27	28	26	27	26
Close-	21	22	21	20	20	18	21	18	20
No Chng	0	0	0	1	0	1	0	2	0
%+	58.0	56.0	54.0	54.0	54.0	56.0	52.0	54.0	52.0
%-	42.0	44.0	42.0	40.0	40.0	36.0	42.0	36.0	40.0
%NC	.0	.0	.0	2.0	.0	2.0	.0	4.0	.0

KEY REVERSALS DOWN:

	REPORT TOTAL			50 SIGNALS			65 SIGNALS		
Close+	34	41	39	33	35	35	32	30	31
Close-	30	23	26	31	29	28	31	33	32
No Chng	1	1	0	1	1	1	0	0	0
%+	52.3	63.1	60.0	50.8	53.8	53.8	49.2	46.2	47.7
%-	46.2	35.4	40.0	47.7	44.6	43.1	47.7	50.8	49.2
%NC	1.5	1.5	.0	1.5	1.5	1.5	.0	.0	.0

Figure 3.26: KR+ and KR− Signal Results: Bull/Bear/Bull Markets

```
REPORT TOTAL  * * * * *

          KEY REVERSALS UP :          81  SIGNALS
Close+    46    39    39    41    43    37    34    42    47    42
Close-    33    42    41    36    34    38    41    33    29    32
No Chng    2     0     0     1     1     1     1     1     0     0
%+      56.8  48.1  48.1  50.6  53.1  45.7  42.0  51.9  58.0  51.9
%-      40.7  51.9  50.6  44.4  42.0  46.9  50.6  40.7  35.8  39.5
%NC      2.5    .0    .0   1.2   1.2   1.2   1.2   1.2    .0    .0

          KEY REVERSALS DOWN :         80  SIGNALS
Close+    41    40    40    40    42    42    39    39    36    38
Close-    37    36    36    36    34    34    36    35    37    34
No Chng    1     1     1     1     0     0     0     0     0     1
%+      51.2  50.0  50.0  50.0  52.5  52.5  48.7  48.7  45.0  47.5
%-      46.2  45.0  45.0  45.0  42.5  42.5  45.0  43.7  46.2  42.5
%NC      1.3   1.3   1.3   1.3    .0    .0    .0    .0    .0   1.3
```

Figure 3.27: KR+ and KR− Signal Results: Whipsaw Markets

REPORT TOTAL * * * * *

KEY REVERSALS UP: 296 SIGNALS

Close+	142	135	136	141	146	137	146	140	140	142
Close−	149	153	154	145	140	144	138	139	139	135
No Chng	4	6	2	2	1	4	1	1	1	1
%+	48.0	45.6	45.9	47.6	49.3	46.3	49.3	47.3	47.3	48.0
%−	50.3	51.7	52.0	49.0	47.3	48.6	46.6	47.0	47.0	45.6
%NC	1.4	2.0	.7	.7	.3	1.4	.3	.3	.3	.3

KEY REVERSALS DOWN: 239 SIGNALS

Close+	120	123	120	113	112	112	105	107	101	101
Close−	105	105	104	114	104	111	111	110	118	115
No Chng	8	4	7	3	3	3	7	5	1	2
%+	50.2	51.5	50.2	47.3	50.2	46.9	43.9	44.8	42.3	42.3
%−	43.9	43.9	43.5	47.7	43.5	46.4	46.4	46.0	49.4	48.1
%NC	3.3	1.7	2.9	1.3	1.3	1.3	2.9	2.1	.4	.8

KEY REVERSAL DOWN (KR−)

KR− signals are essentially similar to R− signals except for the fact that on the reversal day down prices exceed both their high and low prices of the previous day. The diagram below shows a one-day key reversal to the downside (KR−). A KR− is defined as follows:

A day on which prices exceed both their high and low the previous day and on which price closes lower than price for the previous day.

The algorithm for KR− is:

$$KR- = H2 > H1; L2 < L1; \text{ and } C2 < C1$$

where:

KR− = key reversal down;
H2 = high day 2;
H1 = high day 1;
L2 = low day 2;
L1 = low day 1;
C2 = close day 2; and
C1 = close day 1.

However, when subjected to a more intensive examination using SWP and money management rules, the results of daily KR+ and KR− signals were more positive. Figures 3-28 through 3-32 show the SWP results on the five markets I've previously selected as good test cases. An examination of the results shows them to be quite good, even taking $100 per trade slippage and commission. The popular belief that key reversal signals are somehow particularly meaningful appears to have little or no validity when such signals are not filtered with other indicators such as cycles, or with money management rules.

Even if we use a high/low variation for the SWP test of key reversal signals, the results are not improved. By a high/low variation I mean filtering a KR+ signal and buying only on the close of trading on the day of the KR+ signal if the close is greater than the high of the day previous to the KR+, or selling on a KR− signal if the close on the day of the KR− signal is lower than the low of the day before the KR− signal. These results are shown in Figures 3-33 through 3-37.

Explanation and Interpretation of Results

Key reversal up and down signals (KR+ and KR−) were tested according to the same parameters as were R+ and R− signals. I examined closings for up to ten days subsequent to the KR signals. As you can see from Figures 3-18 through 3-27, the results were interesting but not impressive. There was a slightly better predictive tendency for these signals as opposed to simple upside and/or downside signals, but certainly nothing to get too excited about. Best results were again noted in bull markets.

As I've pointed out previously, this does *not mean* that the use of key reversal signals will not prove profitable when used with money management principles. I have previously shown that key reversal signals do have validity as weekly and monthly signals, and in conjunction with cycle highs and lows.[1]

[1] See Jake Bernstein, *The Analysis and Forecasting of Long-Term Trends*, Probus Publishing, 1988.

Figure 3.28: SYSTEM WRITER PLUS Test of KR+ and KR– Signals, High/Low Breakout: Japanese Yen

```
------------------ JAPANESE YEN          06/89 - All trades ----------------
  Test #        1 of    1                       Space bar to toggle display
------------------------------------------------------------------------------
  Total net profit           $25,712.50
  Gross profit               $86,650.00  Gross loss               $-60,937.50

  Total # of trades               106    Percent profitable            41%
  Number winning trades            44    Number losing trades           62

  Largest winning trade       $6,212.50  Largest losing trade     $-1,862.50
  Average winning trade       $1,969.32  Average losing trade     $  -982.86
  Ratio avg win/avg loss           2.00  Avg trade (win & loss)     $242.57

  Max consecutive winners           4    Max consecutive losers          6
  Avg # bars in winners            19    Avg # bars in losers            7

  Max closed-out drawdown     $-7,562.50  Max intra-day drawdown   $-8,062.50
  Profit factor                    1.42  Max # of contracts held         1
  Account size required       $11,062.50  Return on account            232%
```

Figure 3.29: SYSTEM WRITER PLUS Test of KR+ and KR– Signals with $100 Slippage and Commission: Pork Bellies

```
------------------ PORK BELLIES          06/89 - All trades ----------------
  Test #        1 of    1                       Space bar to toggle display
------------------------------------------------------------------------------
  Total net profit           $-48,486.00
  Gross profit              $202,788.00  Gross loss               -251,274.00

  Total # of trades               447    Percent profitable            38%
  Number winning trades           170    Number losing trades          277

  Largest winning trade       $6,898.00  Largest losing trade     $-1,762.00
  Average winning trade       $1,192.87  Average losing trade     $  -907.13
  Ratio avg win/avg loss           1.31  Avg trade (win & loss)   $  -108.47

  Max consecutive winners           4    Max consecutive losers          8
  Avg # bars in winners            10    Avg # bars in losers            4

  Max closed-out drawdown    $-63,228.00  Max intra-day drawdown  $-63,608.00
  Profit factor                    0.81  Max # of contracts held         1
  Account size required       $66,608.00  Return on account           -72%
```

Figure 3.30: SYSTEM WRITER PLUS Test of KR+ and KR– Signals with $100 Slippage and Commission: Cotton

```
------------------ COTTON #2        06/89 - All trades -------------
Test #        1 of      1                      Space bar to toggle display

Total net profit          $-50,000.00
Gross profit              $118,295.00  Gross loss              -168,295.00

Total # of trades              297    Percent profitable              37%
Number winning trades          111    Number losing trades            186

Largest winning trade     $4,975.00   Largest losing trade      $-2,150.00
Average winning trade     $1,065.72   Average losing trade      $ -904.81
Ratio avg win/avg loss         1.18   Avg trade (win & loss)    $ -168.35

Max consecutive winners          5    Max consecutive losers           15
Avg # bars in winners           11    Avg # bars in losers              5

Max closed-out drawdown   $-61,680.00  Max intra-day drawdown   $-61,680.00
Profit factor                  0.70   Max # of contracts held           1
Account size required     $64,680.00   Return on account              -77%
```

Figure 3.31: SYSTEM WRITER PLUS Test of KR+ and KR– Signals, High/Low Breakout: S&P

```
------------------ S&P INDEX        06/89 - All trades -------------
Test #        1 of      1                      Space bar to toggle display

Total net profit          $-57,675.00
Gross profit              $53,750.00   Gross loss              -111,425.00

Total # of trades              108    Percent profitable              31%
Number winning trades           34    Number losing trades             74

Largest winning trade     $8,450.00   Largest losing trade      $-8,750.00
Average winning trade     $1,580.88   Average losing trade      $-1,505.74
Ratio avg win/avg loss         1.05   Avg trade (win & loss)    $ -534.03

Max consecutive winners          4    Max consecutive losers            6
Avg # bars in winners            5    Avg # bars in losers              1

Max closed-out drawdown   $-59,625.00  Max intra-day drawdown   $-59,625.00
Profit factor                  0.48   Max # of contracts held           1
Account size required     $62,625.00   Return on account              -92%
```

Figure 3.32: SYSTEM WRITER PLUS Test of KR+ and KR– Signals with $100 Slippage and Commission: Copper

```
───────────── COPPER                06/89 – All trades ─────────────
Test #        1 of      1                   Space bar to toggle display

Total net profit           $-7,075.00
Gross profit            $102,862.50   Gross loss               -109,937.50

Total # of trades              252    Percent profitable               45%
Number winning trades          114    Number losing trades             138

Largest winning trade    $5,300.00    Largest losing trade      $-1,800.00
Average winning trade      $902.30    Average losing trade      $ -796.65
Ratio avg win/avg loss        1.13    Avg trade (win & loss)     $-28.08

Max consecutive winners          8    Max consecutive losers             6
Avg # bars in winners           16    Avg # bars in losers               9

Max closed-out drawdown  $-16,000.00  Max intra-day drawdown    $-16,062.50
Profit factor                 0.94    Max # of contracts held            1
Account size required    $19,062.50   Return on account                -37%
```

Figure 3.33: SYSTEM WRITER PLUS Test of KR+ and KR– Signals, High/Low Breakout: Yen

```
Total net profit           $56,862.50
Gross profit            $192,450.00   Gross loss               -135,587.50

Total # of trades              247    Percent profitable               38%
Number winning trades           96    Number losing trades             151

Largest winning trade    $7,387.50    Largest losing trade      $-2,512.50
Average winning trade    $2,004.69    Average losing trade      $ -897.93
Ratio avg win/avg loss        2.23    Avg trade (win & loss)      $230.21

Max consecutive winners          4    Max consecutive losers             8
Avg # bars in winners           22    Avg # bars in losers               7

Max closed-out drawdown  $-14,162.50  Max intra-day drawdown    $-14,687.50
Profit factor                 1.42    Max # of contracts held            1
Account size required    $17,687.50   Return on account               321%
```

Figure 3.34: SYSTEM WRITER PLUS Test of KR+ and KR– Signals, High/Low Breakout: Pork Bellies

```
------------------- PORK BELLIES        06/89 - All trades -------------
Test #       1 of    1                          Space bar to toggle display

Total net profit        $-24,138.00
Gross profit           $165,714.00  Gross loss                 -189,852.00

Total # of trades             327   Percent profitable                 38%
Number winning trades         127   Number losing trades              200

Largest winning trade    $6,898.00  Largest losing trade       $-1,830.00
Average winning trade    $1,304.83  Average losing trade       $  -949.26
Ratio avg win/avg loss        1.37  Avg trade (win & loss)      $-73.82

Max consecutive winners         4   Max consecutive losers             7
Avg # bars in winners          12   Avg # bars in losers               5

Max closed-out drawdown $-42,672.00 Max intra-day drawdown     $-42,784.00
Profit factor                 0.87  Max # of contracts held            1
Account size required   $45,784.00  Return on account                 -52%
```

Figure 3.35: SYSTEM WRITER PLUS Test of KR+ and KR– Signals, High/Low Breakout: Copper

```
Total net profit        $-58,525.00
Gross profit           $246,575.00  Gross loss                 -305,100.00

Total # of trades             263   Percent profitable                 29%
Number winning trades          77   Number losing trades              186

Largest winning trade   $32,700.00  Largest losing trade       $-9,425.00
Average winning trade    $3,202.27  Average losing trade       $-1,640.32
Ratio avg win/avg loss        1.95  Avg trade (win & loss)     $ -222.53

Max consecutive winners         3   Max consecutive losers             9
Avg # bars in winners          14   Avg # bars in losers               3

Max closed-out drawdown $-70,700.00 Max intra-day drawdown     $-71,000.00
Profit factor                 0.81  Max # of contracts held            1
Account size required   $74,000.00  Return on account                 -79%
```

Figure 3.36: SYSTEM WRITER PLUS Test of KR+ and KR– Signals, High/Low Breakout: Cotton

```
————————————— COTTON #2          06/89 – All trades —————————————
Test #        1 of    1                        Space bar to toggle display

Total net profit           $-17,930.00
Gross profit               $111,395.00   Gross loss                 -129,325.00

Total # of trades                  221   Percent profitable                 39%
Number winning trades               88   Number losing trades               133

Largest winning trade        $4,975.00   Largest losing trade       $-2,150.00
Average winning trade        $1,265.85   Average losing trade        $ -972.37
Ratio avg win/avg loss            1.30   Avg trade (win & loss)        $-81.13

Max consecutive winners              9   Max consecutive losers               9
Avg # bars in winners               14   Avg # bars in losers                 5

Max closed-out drawdown    $-36,520.00   Max intra-day drawdown     $-37,005.00
Profit factor                     0.86   Max # of contracts held              1
Account size required      $40,005.00    Return on account                 -44%
```

Figure 3.37: SYSTEM WRITER PLUS Test of KR+ and KR– Signals, High/Low Breakout: S&P Index

```
————————————— COPPER             06/89 – All trades —————————————
Test #        1 of    1                        Space bar to toggle display

Total net profit            $-7,175.00
Gross profit               $80,087.50    Gross loss                 $-87,262.50

Total # of trades                  184   Percent profitable                 42%
Number winning trades               79   Number losing trades               105

Largest winning trade        $5,450.00   Largest losing trade       $-1,800.00
Average winning trade        $1,013.77   Average losing trade        $ -831.07
Ratio avg win/avg loss            1.22   Avg trade (win & loss)        $-38.99

Max consecutive winners              9   Max consecutive losers              13
Avg # bars in winners               19   Avg # bars in losers                11

Max closed-out drawdown    $-25,925.00   Max intra-day drawdown     $-27,100.00
Profit factor                     0.92   Max # of contracts held              1
Account size required      $30,100.00    Return on account                 -23%
```

90

KEY OPEN REVERSALS

This category of signal is a variation on the theme of KR signals, with the stipulation that a buy signal must also show a closing price above the opening price of the previous day and a sell signal must also show a closing price below the opening of the previous day. The algorithm for a KRO+ buy signal is:

$$KRO+ = H2 > H1; L2 < L1; C2 > C1; C2 > O1$$

where:

H1 = high day 1;
H2 = high day 2;
C2 = close day 2;
C1 = close day 1; and
O1 = open day 1.

The KRO− sell signal algorithm is:

$$KRO- = H2 > H1; L2 < L1; C2 < C1; C2 < O1$$

where:

H1 = high day 1;
H2 = high day 2;
C2 = close day 2;
C1 = close day 1; and
O1 = open day 1.

Diagramatically these signals appear as follows:

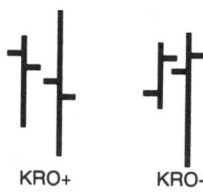

KRO+   KRO-

The KRO+ and KRO− signals were tested using the ten-day forward procedure employed in previous test models. Figures 3-38 through 3-46 show the results on my different market categories as well as the overall performance.

Figure 3.38: Key Open Reversals: Bull Markets

REPORT TOTAL * * * * *

KEY OPEN REVERSALS UP: 181 SIGNALS

Close+	98	108	116	115	115	115	117	122	119	108
Close-	76	62	57	57	56	52	48	45	46	53
No Chng	4	4	1	2	2	2	3	1	1	2
%+	54.1	59.7	64.1	63.5	63.5	63.5	64.6	67.4	65.7	59.7
%-	42.0	34.3	31.5	31.5	30.9	28.7	26.5	24.9	25.4	29.3
%NC	2.2	2.2	.6	1.1	1.1	1.1	1.7	.6	.6	1.1

KEY OPEN REVERSALS DOWN: 147 SIGNALS

Close+	76	78	82	80	88	93	91	90	94	94
Close-	61	61	58	54	47	42	43	39	33	33
No Chng	8	6	3	6	2	2	0	1	2	2
%+	51.7	53.1	55.8	54.4	59.9	63.3	61.9	61.2	63.9	63.9
%-	41.5	41.5	39.5	36.7	32.0	28.6	29.3	26.5	22.4	22.4
%NC	5.4	4.1	2.0	4.1	1.4	1.4	.0	.7	1.4	1.4

REPORT TOTAL * * * * *

KEY OPEN REVERSALS UP: 312 SIGNALS

Close+	142	157	156	154	157	161	169	173	173	169
Close-	162	147	146	149	142	134	125	124	121	124
No Chng	5	4	3	2	3	4	4	1	2	1
%+	45.5	50.3	50.0	49.4	50.3	51.6	54.2	55.4	55.4	54.2
%-	51.9	47.1	46.8	47.8	45.5	42.9	40.1	39.7	38.8	39.7
%NC	1.6	1.3	1.0	.6	1.0	1.3	1.3	.3	.6	.3

KEY OPEN REVERSALS DOWN: 289 SIGNALS

Close+	152	154	146	146	142	153	151	138	133	130
Close-	128	131	139	133	135	121	117	128	133	132
No Chng	7	1	1	4	3	2	4	3	1	3
%+	52.6	53.3	50.5	50.5	49.1	52.9	52.2	47.8	46.0	45.0
%-	44.3	45.3	48.1	46.0	46.7	41.9	40.5	44.3	46.0	45.7
%NC	2.4	.3	.3	1.4	1.0	.7	1.4	1.0	.3	1.0

Figure 3.40: Key Open Reversals: Bear Markets

```
REPORT TOTAL  * * * * *
```

KEY OPEN REVERSALS UP: 188 SIGNALS

Close+	87	78	74	83	80	77	77	70	64	61
Close-	93	101	106	96	98	103	99	105	110	109
No Chng	6	5	3	2	3	1	1	2	2	3
%+	46.3	41.5	39.4	44.1	42.6	41.0	41.0	37.2	34.0	32.4
%-	49.5	53.7	56.4	51.1	52.1	54.8	52.7	55.9	58.5	58.0
%NC	3.2	2.7	1.6	1.1	1.6	.5	.5	1.1	1.1	1.6

KEY OPEN REVERSALS DOWN: 189 SIGNALS

Close+	74	70	69	69	66	69	61	63	56	49
Close-	106	110	109	109	110	105	111	111	114	124
No Chng	7	6	5	3	2	1	3	1	4	0
%+	39.2	37.0	36.5	36.5	34.9	36.5	32.3	33.3	29.6	25.9
%-	56.1	58.2	57.7	57.7	58.2	55.6	58.7	58.7	60.3	65.6
%NC	3.7	3.2	2.6	1.6	1.1	.5	1.6	.5	2.1	.0

Figure 3.41: Key Open Reversals: Choppy Bear Markets

```
REPORT TOTAL  * * * * *
```

KEY OPEN REVERSALS UP: 165 SIGNALS

Close+	81	73	76	78	70	67	64	71	58	59
Close-	78	88	87	82	91	92	96	88	97	95
No Chng	5	2	0	3	2	4	1	0	2	2
%+	49.1	44.2	46.1	47.3	42.4	40.6	38.8	43.0	35.2	35.8
%-	47.3	53.3	52.7	49.7	55.2	55.8	58.2	53.3	58.8	57.6
%NC	3.0	1.2	.0	1.8	1.2	2.4	.6	.0	1.2	1.2

KEY OPEN REVERSALS DOWN: 173 SIGNALS

Close+	67	71	64	61	57	58	54	50	52	49
Close-	96	92	102	105	104	104	102	105	102	105
No Chng	6	5	2	0	3	0	2	1	1	1
%+	38.7	41.0	37.0	35.3	32.9	33.5	31.2	28.9	30.1	28.3
%-	55.5	53.2	59.0	60.7	60.1	60.1	59.0	60.7	59.0	60.7
%NC	3.5	2.9	1.2	.0	1.7	.0	1.2	.6	.6	.6

Figure 3.42: Key Open Reversals: Bull/Bear Markets

```
REPORT TOTAL  *  *  *  *  *

         KEY OPEN REVERSALS UP:     301 SIGNALS
Close+   141  126  122  120  126  124  120  123  116  122
Close-   157  166  166  166  163  161  166  161  161  157
No Chng    2    3    4    2    2    3    2    0    5    1
%+      46.8 41.9 40.5 39.9 41.9 41.2 39.9 40.9 38.5 40.5
%-      52.2 55.1 55.1 55.1 54.2 53.5 55.1 53.5 53.5 52.2
%NC       .7  1.0  1.3   .7   .7  1.0   .7   .0  1.7   .3

         KEY OPEN REVERSALS DOWN:   292 SIGNALS
Close+   130  134  127  115  109  114  114  111  108  101
Close-   153  148  155  160  167  157  159  161  156  164
No Chng    7    5    2    3    2    4    1    0    8    3
%+      44.5 45.9 43.5 39.4 37.3 39.0 39.0 38.0 37.0 34.6
%-      52.4 50.7 53.1 54.8 57.2 53.8 54.5 55.1 53.4 56.2
%NC      2.4  1.7   .7  1.0   .7  1.4   .3   .0  2.7  1.0
```

Figure 3.43: Key Open Reversals: Bear/Bull Markets

```
REPORT TOTAL  *  *  *  *  *
```

KEY OPEN REVERSALS UP: 325 SIGNALS

Close+	177	196	196	190	186	199	204	195	199	202
Close-	134	116	120	125	129	110	106	108	109	105
No Chng	12	10	5	4	3	5	3	8	3	2
%+	54.5	60.3	60.3	58.5	57.2	61.2	62.8	60.0	61.2	62.2
%-	41.2	35.7	36.9	38.5	39.7	33.8	32.6	33.2	33.5	32.3
%NC	3.7	3.1	1.5	1.2	.9	1.5	.9	2.5	.9	.6

KEY OPEN REVERSALS DOWN: 303 SIGNALS

Close+	149	159	167	149	151	162	155	162	158	152
Close-	138	130	124	136	131	114	118	113	113	117
No Chng	10	5	2	4	2	4	6	1	2	3
%+	49.2	52.5	55.1	49.2	49.8	53.5	51.2	53.5	52.1	50.2
%-	45.5	42.9	40.9	44.9	43.2	37.6	38.9	37.3	37.3	38.6
%NC	3.3	1.7	.7	1.3	.7	1.3	2.0	.3	.7	1.0

Figure 3.44: Key Open Reversals: Bear/Bull/Bear Markets

REPORT TOTAL * * * * *

KEY OPEN REVERSALS UP: 43 SIGNALS

Close+	24	26	24	25	25	23	23	21	24	22
Close-	19	17	17	15	15	16	17	19	15	17
No Chng	0	0	0	1	1	1	0	0	1	0
%+	55.8	60.5	55.8	58.1	58.1	53.5	53.5	48.8	55.8	51.2
%-	44.2	39.5	39.5	34.9	34.9	37.2	39.5	44.2	34.9	39.5
%NC	.0	.0	.0	2.3	2.3	2.3	.0	.0	2.3	.0

KEY OPEN REVERSALS DOWN: 53 SIGNALS

Close+	31	34	31	28	30	28	29	27	24	25
Close-	21	18	22	24	23	23	22	24	27	26
No Chng	1	1	0	1	0	1	1	0	0	0
%+	58.5	64.2	58.5	52.8	56.6	52.8	54.7	50.9	45.3	47.2
%-	39.6	34.0	41.5	45.3	43.4	43.4	41.5	45.3	50.9	49.1
%NC	1.9	1.9	.0	1.9	.0	1.9	1.9	.0	.0	.0

Figure 3.45: Key Open Reversals: Bull/Bear/Bull Markets

REPORT TOTAL * * * * *

KEY OPEN REVERSALS UP: 71 SIGNALS

Close+	39	36	34	34	38	32	31	39	43	39
Close-	30	35	36	33	30	34	35	28	24	27
No Chng	2	0	0	1	0	1	1	0	0	0
%+	54.9	50.7	47.9	47.9	53.5	45.1	43.7	54.9	60.6	54.9
%-	42.3	49.3	50.7	46.5	42.3	47.9	49.3	39.4	33.8	38.0
%NC	2.8	.0	.0	1.4	.0	1.4	1.4	.0	.0	.0

KEY OPEN REVERSALS DOWN: 74 SIGNALS

Close+	37	37	37	37	40	40	38	38	35	37
Close-	36	34	34	34	31	31	32	31	33	30
No Chng	1	1	1	1	0	0	0	0	0	1
%+	50.0	50.0	50.0	50.0	54.1	54.1	51.4	51.4	47.3	50.0
%-	48.6	45.9	45.9	45.9	41.9	41.9	43.2	41.9	44.6	40.5
%NC	1.4	1.4	1.4	1.4	.0	.0	.0	.0	.0	1.4

Figure 3.46: Key Open Reversals: Whipsaw Markets

REPORT TOTAL * * * * *

KEY OPEN REVERSALS UP: 259 SIGNALS

Close+	122	117	119	122	129	117	124	120	119	122
Close-	134	134	134	127	120	127	123	122	123	119
No Chng	2	6	2	2	1	4	1	1	1	1
%+	47.1	45.2	45.9	47.1	49.8	45.2	47.9	46.3	45.9	47.1
%-	51.7	51.7	51.7	49.0	46.3	49.0	47.5	47.1	47.5	45.9
%NC	.8	2.3	.8	.8	.4	1.5	.4	.4	.4	.4

KEY OPEN REVERSALS DOWN: 205 SIGNALS

Close+	102	103	104	95	104	98	92	93	86	86
Close-	90	92	87	99	90	93	93	92	101	99
No Chng	8	4	7	3	1	3	6	5	1	1
%+	49.8	50.2	50.7	46.3	50.7	47.8	44.9	45.4	42.0	42.0
%-	43.9	44.9	42.4	48.3	43.9	45.4	45.4	44.9	49.3	48.3
%NC	3.9	2.0	3.4	1.5	.5	1.5	2.9	2.4	.5	.5

Explanation and Interpretation of Results

The results suggest that using the opening price as an additional filter for KR signals improves statistical reliability, but only slightly. The "acid test" of course is the more comprehensive test using SWP. These results are shown in Figures 3-47 through 3-51 on my five-market test file.

In addition to the price bar signals already discussed, I tested many others, some which I felt had validity and others which have been bandied about in the futures literature as reliable timing indicators. Results were similarly unimpressive.

CONCLUSIONS

The use of price bar signals as tested, without additional confirming indicators or risk management procedures is not a viable methodology. When used with trends these indicators and signals have some potential, however, additional analyses are necessary.

Figure 3.47: KRO+ and KRO– Signal Results on SYSTEM WRITER PLUS: Pork Bellies

Total net profit	$31,525.00	Gross loss	-134,737.50
Gross profit	$166,262.50		
Total # of trades	276	Percent profitable	40%
Number winning trades	112	Number losing trades	164
Largest winning trade	$7,125.00	Largest losing trade	$-2,400.00
Average winning trade	$1,484.49	Average losing trade	$ -821.57
Ratio avg win/avg loss	1.81	Avg trade (win & loss)	$114.22
Max consecutive winners	5	Max consecutive losers	9
Avg # bars in winners	21	Avg # bars in losers	7
Max closed-out drawdown	$-14,150.00	Max intra-day drawdown	$-14,412.50
Profit factor	1.23	Max # of contracts held	1
Account size required	$17,412.50	Return on account	181%

Figure 3.48: KRO+ and KRO– Signal Results on SYSTEM WRITER PLUS: Copper

Total net profit	$9,262.50		
Gross profit	$212,100.00	Gross loss	-202,837.50
Total # of trades	306	Percent profitable	35%
Number winning trades	109	Number losing trades	197
Largest winning trade	$8,187.50	Largest losing trade	$-3,187.50
Average winning trade	$1,945.87	Average losing trade	$-1,029.63
Ratio avg win/avg loss	1.89	Avg trade (win & loss)	$30.27
Max consecutive winners	4	Max consecutive losers	13
Avg # bars in winners	20	Avg # bars in losers	7
Max closed-out drawdown	$-19,450.00	Max intra-day drawdown	$-19,625.00
Profit factor	1.05	Max # of contracts held	1
Account size required	$22,625.00	Return on account	40%

Figure 3.49: KRO+ and KRO– Signal Results on SYSTEM WRITER PLUS: Japanese Yen

Total net profit	$28,087.50		
Gross profit	$315,881.25	Gross loss	-287,793.75
Total # of trades	357	Percent profitable	35%
Number winning trades	125	Number losing trades	232
Largest winning trade	$12,556.25	Largest losing trade	$-4,131.25
Average winning trade	$2,527.05	Average losing trade	$-1,240.49
Ratio avg win/avg loss	2.04	Avg trade (win & loss)	$78.68
Max consecutive winners	4	Max consecutive losers	9
Avg # bars in winners	18	Avg # bars in losers	5
Max closed-out drawdown	$-57,437.50	Max intra-day drawdown	$-57,437.50
Profit factor	1.10	Max # of contracts held	1
Account size required	$60,437.50	Return on account	46%

Figure 3.50: KRO+ and KRO– Signal Results on SYSTEM WRITER PLUS: S&P Index

Total net profit	$56,870.00		
Gross profit	$231,900.00	Gross loss	-175,030.00
Total # of trades	290	Percent profitable	39%
Number winning trades	114	Number losing trades	176
Largest winning trade	$26,940.00	Largest losing trade	$-4,850.00
Average winning trade	$2,034.21	Average losing trade	$ -994.49
Ratio avg win/avg loss	2.05	Avg trade (win.& loss)	$196.10
Max consecutive winners	5	Max consecutive losers	9
Avg # bars in winners	20	Avg # bars in losers	7
Max closed-out drawdown	$-18,300.00	Max intra-day drawdown	$-18,850.00
Profit factor	1.32	Max # of contracts held	1
Account size required	$21,850.00	Return on account	260%

Figure 3.51: KRO+ and KRO— Signal Results on SYSTEM WRITER PLUS: Cotton

Total net profit	$-37,990.00		
Gross profit	$71,530.00	Gross loss	-109,520.00
Total # of trades	218	Percent profitable	33%
Number winning trades	72	Number losing trades	146
Largest winning trade	$7,040.00	Largest losing trade	$-1,970.00
Average winning trade	$993.47	Average losing trade	$ -750.14
Ratio avg win/avg loss	1.32	Avg trade (win & loss)	$ -174.27
Max consecutive winners	3	Max consecutive losers	10
Avg # bars in winners	18	Avg # bars in losers	7
Max closed-out drawdown	$-44,520.00	Max intra-day drawdown	$-45,280.00
Profit factor	0.65	Max # of contracts held	1
Account size required	$48,280.00	Return on account	-78%

4

Moving Average Signals

Trading systems based on moving averages have been favored by futures traders since their introduction in the 1950's by Richard Donchian. While the popularity of such systems seems to grow with each passing, there are some serious questions as to their efficacy. Bruce Babcock, in his excellent book, *Trading Systems*, has reviewed a number of popular trading systems, including moving averages. He sums up his testing of one moving average system as follows:

> ... On average the system lost money, although it was profitable in six of the nine markets. Overall performance was dragged down by the horrendous results in the S&P 500. Even in the profitable markets the drawdown was usually large in relation to the cumulative profit.... [page 114]

And he also notes:

> Over the years, traders have tried various ways to improve moving-average performance by refining the calculation. This has resulted in exponentially smoothed, linear-weighted and step-weighted moving-average systems. These refinements have not made an appreciable difference in performance. [page 115]

As you can see, Babcock is less than thrilled with the results of moving-average systems based on his experience. Yet it is important to point out that he back-tested the indicated moving-average combinations in selected markets for only a five-year period. Hence, it is possible to conclude that Babcock did not give moving averages a fair test. I have, therefore, employed a variety of moving averages to a lengthier test across virtually all active markets. There is no doubt that Babcock's major conclusions regarding large drawdowns and whipsaws are valid. Yet, for the avid systems trader dedicated to moving averages, the information which can be gleaned from the present extensive study may prove invaluable.

THE LOGIC OF MOVING-AVERAGE SYSTEMS

The paradigm of moving-average systems is a simple one indeed. Since a moving average is the smoothed result of a data series, it tends to make its up and down movements more slowly than does the data from which it is derived. The longer a moving average, the slower it changes direction and the less responsive it is to up and down moves within the raw data. The use of moving averages is not restricted to stock and futures trading. The idea of using moving averages, in fact, was borrowed from the physical sciences and economics.

By applying moving-average smoothing to raw price data it is possible to eliminate much of the "noise" or randomness from the data series and to follow price trends for a good majority of their moves. This feature of moving averages is both the blessing and the bane of such systems. While they tend to work well when there are longlasting trends, they tend to work poorly when trends are short-lived. There are, however, so many different combinations of moving averages and so many variations on the moving average theme that it would not be fair to make a blanket statement about either the merits or limitations of such systems without a comprehensive test. The fact remains that many of today's successful money management programs are based on moving averages in one form or another.

Furthermore, it is very possible to use signals based on moving averages for trade entry and another set of indicators or rules for exit, thereby filtering out many of the whipsaws. It is also possible to filter the entry signals using a variety of rules. In doing so, however, one must take caution to avoid over-optimization which may, in the end, lead to a system that will look good when subjected to hypothetical back-testing but which may not perform well in the future.

DUAL MOVING-AVERAGE INDICATORS

With the above caveats in mind, let's move on to the tests and analyses. My first test examined dual moving-average crossovers. I have dispensed with an examination of single moving-average systems inasmuch as they tend to have low accuracy rates, and are subject to merciless drawdowns and considerable whipsaws. The present test examines dual moving average crossovers according to the following model:

MA 1 = Shorter Moving Average

MA 2 = Longer Moving Average

If MA 1 > MA 2, Buy (or exit short position and go long)

If MA 1 < MA 2, Sell (or exit long position and go short)

The above conditions were applied in an "always in the market" fashion except for exits forced by contract termination per our test rules discussed earlier. Figure 4-1 illustrates a number of typical buy and sell signals using this approach using a five-day/twenty-day MA combination.

In order to subject the dual moving-average approach to as thorough a test as possible, numerous combinations of MAs were used. The starting point for this study was three days for MA I (the shorter MA) and five days for MA 2. The longest MA I examined was thirty-five days and the longest MA 2 examined was fifty-five days. In other words, I first tested the results of a three and five combination; then a three and six then a three and seven, a three and eight . . . and so on through three and fifty-five. Then we began with a four and six, a four and seven, a four and eight and so on. Literally hundreds

Figure 4.1: 5- and 20-Day Moving Average Buy/Sell Signals

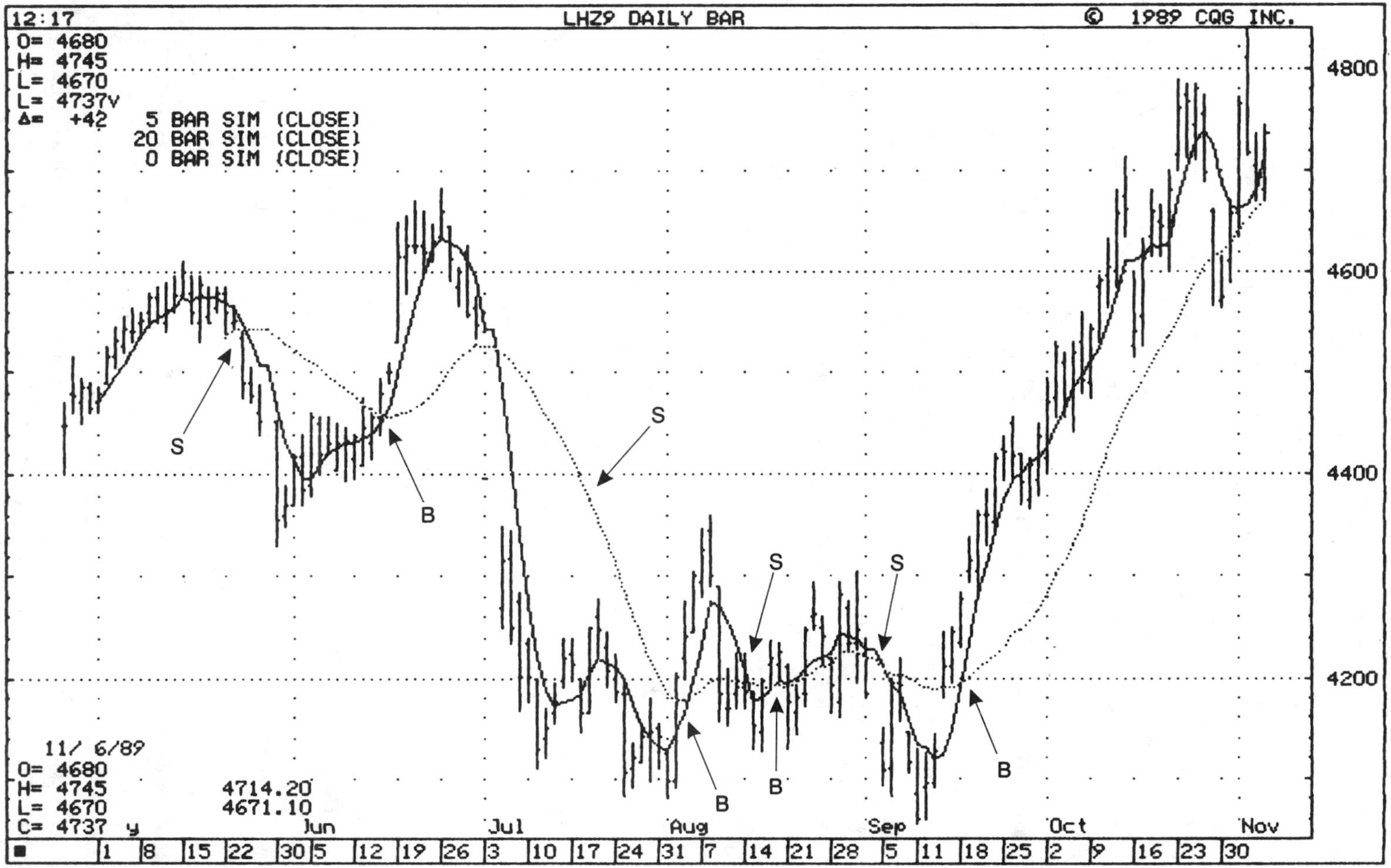

of combinations of dual moving averages were tested. While this has been done before, I know of no other study which has examined as many combinations on as long a data history. Nor do I know of any study which then classified the results by market type (i.e., bull market performance, bear market performance, whipsaw perform- ance, etc).

The results of my testing were voluminous. In fact, an entire book could have been written on this test alone. Here I will provide only the highlights (see Figures 4-2 through 4-6).

Bruce Babcock, in *Trading Systems*, reporting his five-year M.A. test results using selected markets (see Figure 4-7) noted that the performance was not particularly impressive. Remember, how- ever, that his test was limited to a five-year period and to selected markets. My test of the 4-, 9- and 18-day MA combination covered a much longer time span and many more markets.

TRIPLE MOVING AVERAGES

Another variation on the moving average theme is to use three mov- ing averages. This approach can be represented as follows:

MA 1 = Shortest Moving Average

MA 2 = Mid-Length Moving Average

MA 3 = Longest Moving Average

If MA 1 and MA 2 > MA 3, Buy (or exit short position and go long)

If MA 1 and MA 2 < MA 3, Sell (or exit long and go short)

Figure 4-2: Results of Dual Moving Average System, Eurodollar: 5- and 33-Day M.A; $75 Shippage and Commission; $2,500 Initial Stop Loss; $2,300 Trailing Stop Loss

Performance Summary: All Trades

Total net profit	$ 21425.00	Open position P/L	$ 300.00
Gross profit	$ 51450.00	Gross loss	$ -30025.00
Total # of trades	89	Percent profitable	36%
Number winning trades	32	Number losing trades	57
Largest winning trade	$ 8100.00	Largest losing trade	$ -1800.00
Average winning trade	$ 1607.81	Average losing trade	$ -526.75
Ratio avg win/avg loss	3.05	Avg trade(win & loss)	$ 240.73
Max consecutive winners	3	Max consecutive losers	9
Avg # bars in winners	41	Avg # bars in losers	13
Max intraday drawdown	$ -7525.00		
Profit factor	1.71	Max # contracts held	1
Account size required	$ 10525.00	Return on account	204%

Performance Summary: Long Trades

Total net profit	$ 25875.00	Open position P/L	$ 300.00
Gross profit	$ 37000.00	Gross loss	$ -11125.00
Total # of trades	44	Percent profitable	43%
Number winning trades	19	Number losing trades	25
Largest winning trade	$ 8100.00	Largest losing trade	$ -1100.00
Average winning trade	$ 1947.37	Average losing trade	$ -445.00
Ratio avg win/avg loss	4.38	Avg trade(win & loss)	$ 588.07
Max consecutive winners	3	Max consecutive losers	4
Avg # bars in winners	41	Avg # bars in losers	14
Max intraday drawdown	$ -2725.00		
Profit factor	3.33	Max # contracts held	1
Account size required	$ 5725.00	Return on account	452%

Performance Summary: Short Trades

Total net profit	$ -4450.00	Open position P/L	$ 0.00
Gross profit	$ 14450.00	Gross loss	$ -18900.00
Total # of trades	45	Percent profitable	29%
Number winning trades	13	Number losing trades	32
Largest winning trade	$ 2925.00	Largest losing trade	$ -1800.00
Average winning trade	$ 1111.54	Average losing trade	$ -590.63
Ratio avg win/avg loss	1.88	Avg trade(win & loss)	$ -98.89
Max consecutive winners	5	Max consecutive losers	8
Avg # bars in winners	42	Avg # bars in losers	12
Max intraday drawdown	$ -8675.00		
Profit factor	0.76	Max # contracts held	1
Account size required	$ 8675.00	Return on account	-51%

Figure 4-3: Results of Dual Moving Average System, Swiss Franc: 5- and 45-Day MA; $175 Shippage and Commission; $3,500 Stop Loss; $2,800 Trailing Stop Loss

```
                    Performance Summary:   All Trades

Total net profit       $   32800.00    Open position P/L      $      275.00
Gross profit           $  122275.00    Gross loss             $   -89475.00

Total # of trades             117      Percent profitable            40%
Number winning trades          47      Number losing trades           70

Largest winning trade  $    9650.00    Largest losing trade   $    -4650.00
Average winning trade  $    2601.60    Average losing trade   $    -1278.21
Ratio avg win/avg loss        2.04     Avg trade(win & loss)  $      280.34

Max consecutive winners         3      Max consecutive losers          6
Avg # bars in winners          47      Avg # bars in losers            9

Max intraday drawdown  $  -16025.00
Profit factor                 1.37     Max # contracts held            1
Account size required  $   19025.00    Return on account             172%


                    Performance Summary:   Long Trades

Total net profit       $   13650.00    Open position P/L      $      275.00
Gross profit           $   60362.50    Gross loss             $   -46712.50

Total # of trades              58      Percent profitable            38%
Number winning trades          22      Number losing trades           36

Largest winning trade  $    9650.00    Largest losing trade   $    -2950.00
Average winning trade  $    2743.75    Average losing trade   $    -1297.57
Ratio avg win/avg loss        2.11     Avg trade(win & loss)  $      235.34

Max consecutive winners         3      Max consecutive losers          6
Avg # bars in winners          43      Avg # bars in losers            9

Max intraday drawdown  $  -18962.50
Profit factor                 1.29     Max # contracts held            1
Account size required  $   18962.50    Return on account              72%


                    Performance Summary:   Short Trades

Total net profit       $   19150.00    Open position P/L      $        0.00
Gross profit           $   61912.50    Gross loss             $   -42762.50

Total # of trades              59      Percent profitable            42%
Number winning trades          25      Number losing trades           34

Largest winning trade  $    9137.50    Largest losing trade   $    -4650.00
Average winning trade  $    2476.50    Average losing trade   $    -1257.72
Ratio avg win/avg loss        1.97     Avg trade(win & loss)  $      324.58

Max consecutive winners         6      Max consecutive losers         14
Avg # bars in winners          49      Avg # bars in losers           10

Max intraday drawdown  $  -22425.00
Profit factor                 1.45     Max # contracts held            1
Account size required  $   25425.00    Return on account              75%
```

113

Figure 4-4: Results of Dual Moving Average System, Crude Oil: 14- and 54-Day MA (Same Parameters as Figure 4-3)

```
                   Performance Summary:  All Trades

Total net profit        $   27465.00    Open position P/L     $       0.00
Gross profit            $   46940.00    Gross loss            $  -19475.00

Total # of trades              37       Percent profitable           49%
Number winning trades          18       Number losing trades          19

Largest winning trade   $    9995.00    Largest losing trade  $   -3885.00
Average winning trade   $    2607.78    Average losing trade  $   -1025.00
Ratio avg win/avg loss          2.54    Avg trade(win & loss) $     742.30

Max consecutive winners         4       Max consecutive losers         6
Avg # bars in winners          68       Avg # bars in losers          18

Max intraday drawdown   $   -5575.00
Profit factor                   2.41    Max # contracts held           1
Account size required   $    8575.00    Return on account           320%


                   Performance Summary:  Long Trades

Total net profit        $   25980.00    Open position P/L     $       0.00
Gross profit            $   31850.00    Gross loss            $   -5870.00

Total # of trades              18       Percent profitable           56%
Number winning trades          10       Number losing trades           8

Largest winning trade   $    9995.00    Largest losing trade  $   -1405.00
Average winning trade   $    3185.00    Average losing trade  $    -733.75
Ratio avg win/avg loss          4.34    Avg trade(win & loss) $    1443.33

Max consecutive winners         5       Max consecutive losers         3
Avg # bars in winners          74       Avg # bars in losers          22

Max intraday drawdown   $   -2760.00
Profit factor                   5.43    Max # contracts held           1
Account size required   $    5760.00    Return on account           451%


                   Performance Summary:  Short Trades

Total net profit        $    1485.00    Open position P/L     $       0.00
Gross profit            $   15090.00    Gross loss            $  -13605.00

Total # of trades              19       Percent profitable           42%
Number winning trades           8       Number losing trades          11

Largest winning trade   $    3805.00    Largest losing trade  $   -3885.00
Average winning trade   $    1886.25    Average losing trade  $   -1236.82
Ratio avg win/avg loss          1.53    Avg trade(win & loss) $      78.16

Max consecutive winners         2       Max consecutive losers         4
Avg # bars in winners          60       Avg # bars in losers          14

Max intraday drawdown   $   -5525.00
Profit factor                   1.11    Max # contracts held           1
Account size required   $    8525.00    Return on account            17%
```

Figure 4-5: Results of Dual Moving Average System, Japanese Yen: 14- and 54-Day MA (Same Parameters as Figure 4-3)

```
                    Performance Summary:   All Trades

Total net profit      $   64725.00    Open position P/L     $       0.00
Gross profit          $   94575.00    Gross loss            $  -29850.00

Total # of trades            63       Percent profitable            52%
Number winning trades        33       Number losing trades          30

Largest winning trade $   10137.50    Largest losing trade  $   -2650.00
Average winning trade $    2865.91    Average losing trade  $    -995.00
Ratio avg win/avg loss       2.88     Avg trade(win & loss) $    1027.38

Max consecutive winners       6       Max consecutive losers         5
Avg # bars in winners        49       Avg # bars in losers          20

Max intraday drawdown $   -6612.50
Profit factor                3.17     Max # contracts held           1
Account size required $    6612.50    Return on account            979%


                    Performance Summary:   Long Trades

Total net profit      $   29712.50    Open position P/L     $       0.00
Gross profit          $   44075.00    Gross loss            $  -14362.50

Total # of trades            31       Percent profitable            52%
Number winning trades        16       Number losing trades          15

Largest winning trade $   10137.50    Largest losing trade  $   -2362.50
Average winning trade $    2754.69    Average losing trade  $    -957.50
Ratio avg win/avg loss       2.88     Avg trade(win & loss) $     958.47

Max consecutive winners       5       Max consecutive losers         3
Avg # bars in winners        44       Avg # bars in losers          18

Max intraday drawdown $   -8025.00
Profit factor                3.07     Max # contracts held           1
Account size required $   11025.00    Return on account            270%


                    Performance Summary:   Short Trades

Total net profit      $   35012.50    Open position P/L     $       0.00
Gross profit          $   50500.00    Gross loss            $  -15487.50

Total # of trades            32       Percent profitable            53%
Number winning trades        17       Number losing trades          15

Largest winning trade $    9350.00    Largest losing trade  $   -2650.00
Average winning trade $    2970.59    Average losing trade  $   -1032.50
Ratio avg win/avg loss       2.88     Avg trade(win & loss) $    1094.14

Max consecutive winners       5       Max consecutive losers         5
Avg # bars in winners        55       Avg # bars in losers          22

Max intraday drawdown $   -5350.00
Profit factor                3.26     Max # contracts held           1
Account size required $    8350.00    Return on account            419%
```

115

Figure 4-6: Results of Dual Moving Average System, Coffee: 14- and 54-Day MA (Same Parameters as Figure 4-3)

```
                    Performance Summary:  All Trades

Total net profit       $  65270.00    Open position P/L      $       0.00
Gross profit           $ 157895.00    Gross loss             $  -92625.00

Total # of trades             98      Percent profitable             44%
Number winning trades         43      Number losing trades           55

Largest winning trade  $  14145.00    Largest losing trade   $   -2695.00
Average winning trade  $   3671.98    Average losing trade   $   -1684.09
Ratio avg win/avg loss       2.18     Avg trade(win & loss)  $     666.02

Max consecutive winners        6      Max consecutive losers          4
Avg # bars in winners          6      Avg # bars in losers            3

Max intraday drawdown  $ -20190.00
Profit factor                1.70     Max # contracts held            1
Account size required  $  20190.00    Return on account            323%

                    Performance Summary:  Long Trades

Total net profit       $  51155.00    Open position P/L      $       0.00
Gross profit           $  89170.00    Gross loss             $  -38015.00

Total # of trades             49      Percent profitable             53%
Number winning trades         26      Number losing trades           23

Largest winning trade  $  12325.00    Largest losing trade   $   -2575.00
Average winning trade  $   3429.62    Average losing trade   $   -1652.83
Ratio avg win/avg loss       2.08     Avg trade(win & loss)  $    1043.98

Max consecutive winners        3      Max consecutive losers          3
Avg # bars in winners          6      Avg # bars in losers            2

Max intraday drawdown  $  -6110.00
Profit factor                2.35     Max # contracts held            1
Account size required  $   6110.00    Return on account            837%

                    Performance Summary:  Short Trades

Total net profit       $  14115.00    Open position P/L      $       0.00
Gross profit           $  68725.00    Gross loss             $  -54610.00

Total # of trades             49      Percent profitable             35%
Number winning trades         17      Number losing trades           32

Largest winning trade  $  14145.00    Largest losing trade   $   -2695.00
Average winning trade  $   4042.65    Average losing trade   $   -1706.56
Ratio avg win/avg loss       2.37     Avg trade(win & loss)  $     288.06

Max consecutive winners        6      Max consecutive losers          6
Avg # bars in winners          6      Avg # bars in losers            3

Max intraday drawdown  $ -23905.00
Profit factor                1.26     Max # contracts held            1
Account size required  $  23905.00    Return on account             59%
```

Figure 4.7: Babcock's Performance Report of 4-, 9-, and 18-Day Moving Average

	S&P 500	T-Bonds	Euro dollars	Swiss Francs	Japanese Yen	Comex Gold	Heating Oil	Soy beans	Sugar	Live Cattle	Average
Number of Closed Trades	67	56	58	58	52	58	46	60	59	52	57
Number of Profitable Trades	20	21	22	22	26	19	12	22	20	13	20
Percent Profitable	30%	37%	38%	38%	50%	33%	26%	37%	34%	25%	35%
Total Profit or Loss	-75,650	16,440	14,775	4,763	34,625	13,920	-605	3,338	-3,147	-13,200	-474
Average Profitable Trade	3,179	3,404	1,794	2,088	2,241	2,415	3,086	1,676	1,108	1,060	2,206
Average Losing Trade	-2,962	-1,572	-686	-1,144	-910	-820	-1,106	-883	-648	-692	-1,190
Maximum Drawdown	-80,375	-15,619	-7,425	-12,050	-4,638	-11,520	-17,535	-12,000	-6,328	-15,344	-18,283
Average Profit Per Trade	-1,129	294	255	82	666	240	-13	56	-53	-254	-8

Source: Bruce Babcock, *Trading Systems*. Homewood, IL: (Dow-Jones Irwin, 1989. Figure 8-4, p. 116).

Figures 4-8 and 4-9 illustrate several buy and sell signals using this approach. Note that this method yields fewer signals than does the dual MA technique, since a triple MA approach tends to minimize whipsaws. The shortest MA (MA1) is used as a short-term filter since no MA signal is taken unless both MA1 and MA2 are above MA3 or below it.

As you can well imagine, the possible number of combinations for three MAs is immense. To devote the system to a test of all possible three MA combinations would have been too time consuming. However, I tested significant combinations, beginning with the very popular 4-day, 9-day and 18-day. The results should give you a good idea about performance.

Performance of 4-Day, 9-Day and 18-Day MA in Bull Markets

Our bull market sample consisted of thirty-nine classic bull markets from 1967 through 1988. The results were very positive and not at all in agreement with Babcock's findings. But this is understandable given the significant differences between his test and mine. Overall performance was impressive for the bull market sample, even allowing for slippage and commission. Paradoxically, however, buy signals in bull market turned in a net loss while sell signals in bull markets were profitable. The results are summarized in Figure 4-10.

Performance of 4-Day, 9-Day and 18-Day MA in Bear Markets

The next 4-day, 9-day and 18-day MA system was on the sample of fifty classic bear markets. Overall performance here was better than the results for bull markets. This is understandable inasmuch as bear markets usually move down faster than bull markets move up, and bear markets tend to trend better. Results are summarized in Figure 4-11.

Figure 4.8: Signals Using Triple Moving Average System: 9-, 18- and 36-Day

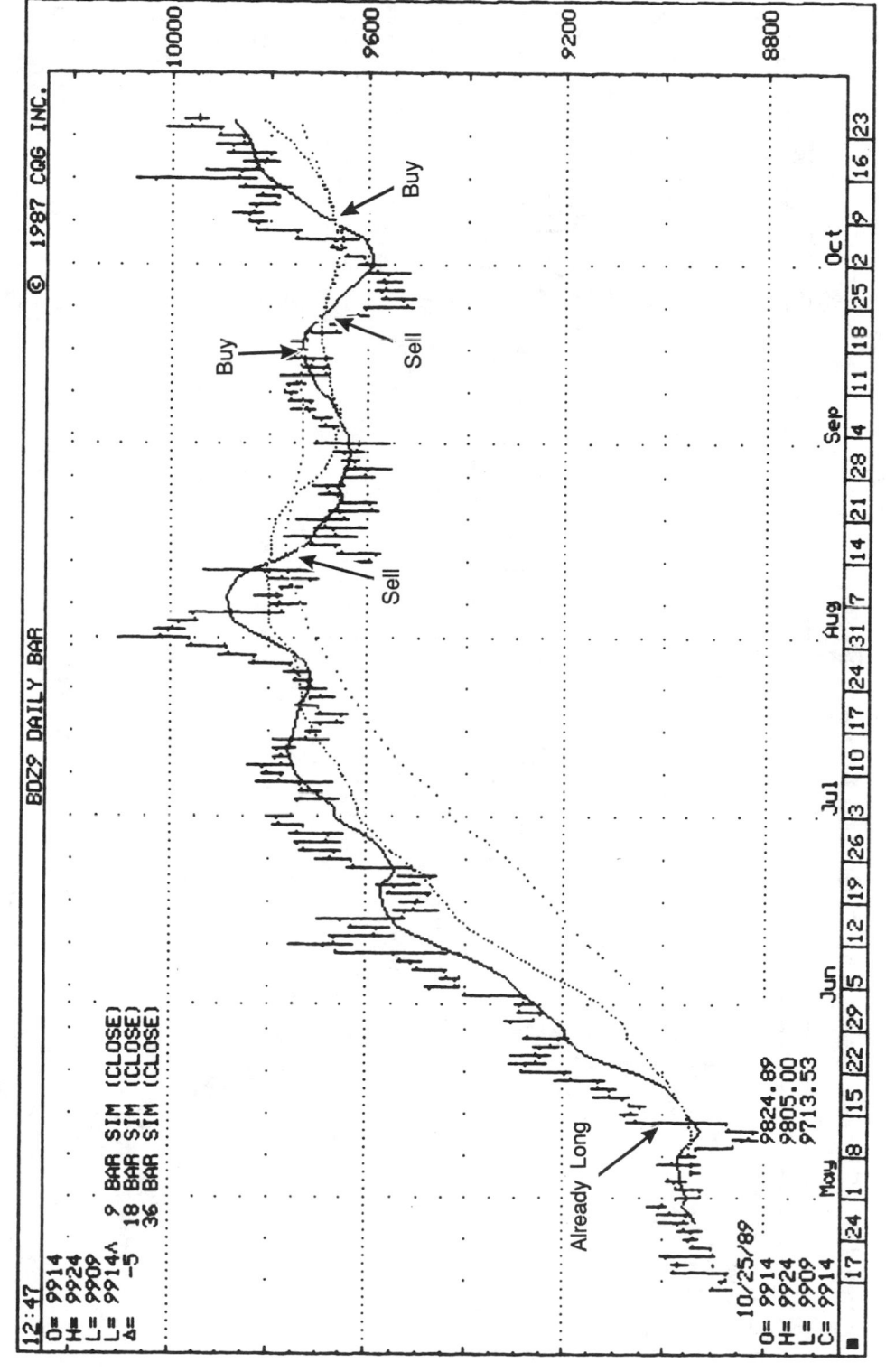

Figure 4.9: Signals Using Triple Moving Average System

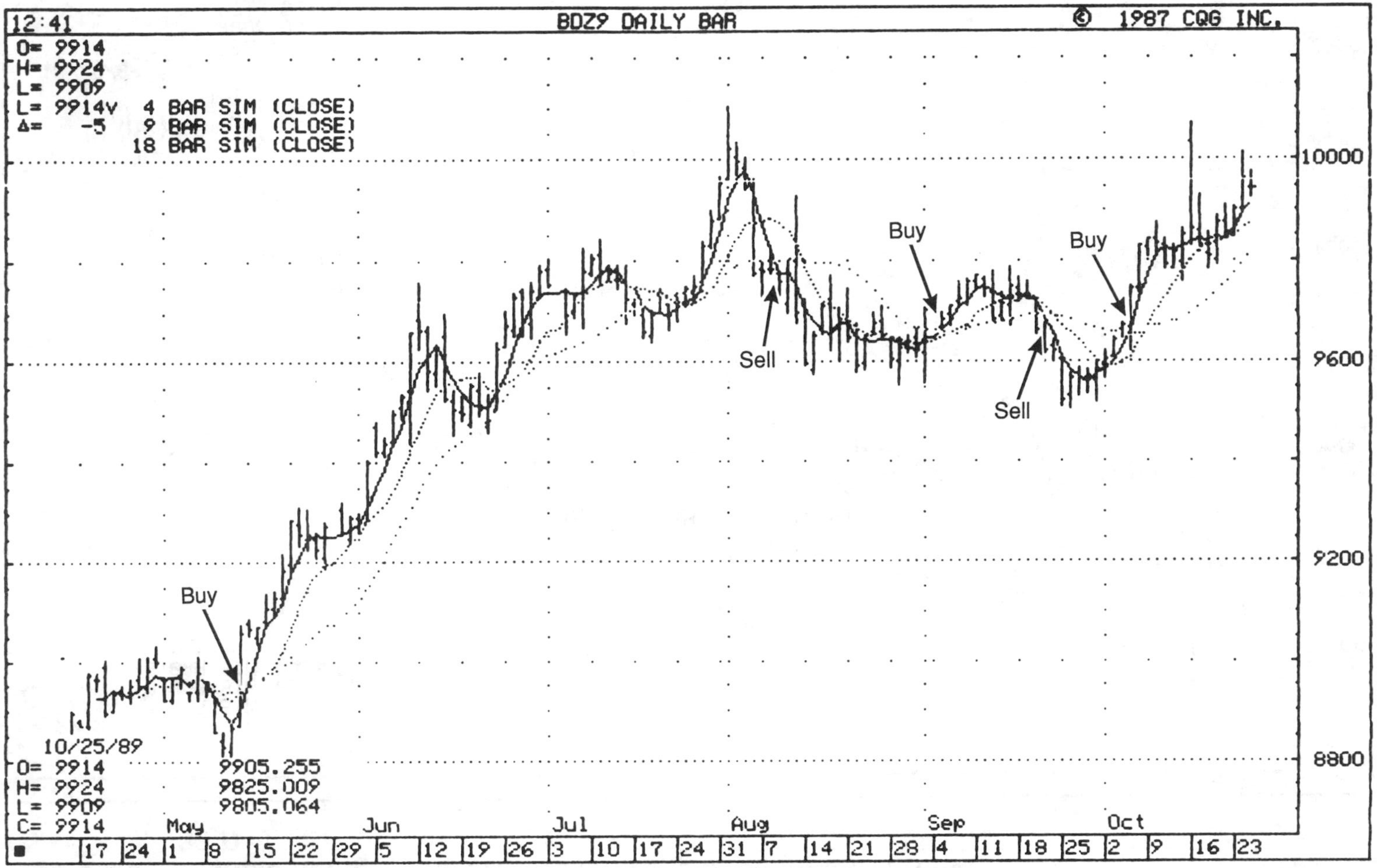

Figure 4.10: Performance of 4-, 9-, 18-Day MA in Bull Markets

BUY SIGNALS

Total Number of Signals	% Signals Profitable	Average Trade $ +/-	Total Profit/Loss $ +/-
1305	20	($506.38)	($660,824.69)

SELL SIGNALS

Total Number of Signals	% Signals Profitable	Average Trade $ +/-	Total Profit/Loss $ +/-
1335	51.84	$872.87	$1,165,287.00

TOTAL SIGNALS

Total Number of Signals	% Signals Profitable	Average Trade $ +/-	Total Profit/Loss $ +/-
2640	36.1	$191.08	$504,462.56

Figure 4.11: Performance of 4-, 9-, 18-Day MA in Bear Markets

BUY SIGNALS

Total Number of Signals	% Signals Profitable	Average Trade $ +/-	Total Profit/Loss $ +/-
1766	49.32	$673.97	$1,190,238.00

SELL SIGNALS

Total Number of Signals	% Signals Profitable	Average Trade $ +/-	Total Profit/Loss $ +/-
1751	21.42	($506.43)	($886,763.94)

TOTAL SIGNALS

Total Number of Signals	% Signals Profitable	Average Trade $ +/-	Total Profit/Loss $ +/-
3517	35.43	$86.29	$303,474.37

Performance of 4-Day, 9-Day and 18-Day MA in Bull/Bear Markets

I then checked the performance of the 4-day, 9-day and 18 day MA system in fifty-seven bull/bear markets. As you will recall, these are markets which made the transition from strong bull market to strong bear market. It is most interesting to note that overall performance here was more evenly distributed. In other words, not only was the system profitable overall, but profits were split about evenly among buy and sell signals, which we would expect. Overall performance is summarized in Figure 4-12.

Performance of 4-Day, 9-Day and 18-Day MA in Bear/Bull Markets

Then I next checked performance of the 4-day, 9-day and 18-day MA system in seventy-three bear/bull markets. These are markets which made the transition from bearish to bullish. Again, results were profitable and fairly evenly distributed, with an average profit for the buy and the sell signals. The results here and in bull/bear markets are very encouraging inasmuch as they suggest that profits are possible even in markets which make the transition from bullish to bearish or vice-versa. The results for this test are shown in Figure 4-13.

Performance of 4-Day, 9-Day and 18-Day MA in Choppy Bull Markets

This test was an important one. It has long been maintained that moving averages tend to do poorly in choppy markets. While this may be true for "whipsaw" markets, it may not necessarily be true for what I have defined as "choppy" bull markets. In fact the test proved that even in choppy markets a profit can be generated; however, the overall results are not impressive. They are summarized in Figure 4-14.

Figure 4.12: Performance of 4-, 9-, 18-Day MA in Bull/Bear Markets

BUY SIGNALS

Total Number of Signals	% Signals Profitable	Average Trade $ +/-	Total Profit/Loss $ +/-
1602	38.83	$234.35	$375,424.75

SELL SIGNALS

Total Number of Signals	% Signals Profitable	Average Trade $ +/-	Total Profit/Loss $ +/-
1629	34.56	$312.12	$508,444.81

TOTAL SIGNALS

Total Number of Signals	% Signals Profitable	Average Trade $ +/-	Total Profit/Loss $ +/-
3231	36.68	$273.56	$883,869.56

Figure 4.13: Performance of 4-, 9-, 18-Day MA in Bear/Bull Markets

BUY SIGNALS

Total Number of Signals	% Signals Profitable	Average Trade $ +/-	Total Profit/Loss $ +/-
1591	36.64	$50.91	$81,000.44

SELL SIGNALS

Total Number of Signals	% Signals Profitable	Average Trade $ +/-	Total Profit/Loss $ +/-
1620	36.85	$226.87	$367,535.00

TOTAL SIGNALS

Total Number of Signals	% Signals Profitable	Average Trade $ +/-	Total Profit/Loss $ +/-
3211	36.75	$139.69	$448,535.44

Figure 4.14: Performance of 4-, 9-, 18-Day MA in Choppy Bull Markets

		BUY SIGNALS	
Total Number of Signals	% Signals Profitable	Average Trade $ +/-	Total Profit/Loss $ +/-
1065	23.66	($719.00)	($765,740.19)

		SELL SIGNALS	
Total Number of Signals	% Signals Profitable	Average Trade $ +/-	Total Profit/Loss $ +/-
1088	47.06	$1,018.10	$1,107,690.00

		TOTAL SIGNALS	
Total Number of Signals	% Signals Profitable	Average Trade $ +/-	Total Profit/Loss $ +/-
2153	35.49	$158.82	$341,949.37

Performance of 4-Day, 9-Day and 18-Day MA in Choppy Bear Markets

Performance of the 4-day, 9-day and 18-day MA system in choppy bear markets was not as good as it was in trending markets or in bull/bear and bear/bull markets, but it was still profitable. Performance clearly was diminished, as can be seen from the results in Figure 4-15.

Performance of 4-Day, 9-Day and 18-Day MA in Whipsaw Markets

While it may be a matter of opinion as to what constitutes a "whipsaw" market, there is no doubt in my mind that the sample of fifty-two "whipsaw" markets I selected represent some of the most difficult and treacherous markets known to traders. In fact, the results demonstrate that the 4-day, 9-day and 18-day system does not produce profits in such markets. Overall results as shown in Figure 4-16 are negative. There is, therefore, considerable evidence to support the longstanding conclusion that moving-average systems tend to lose money in non-trending markets.

Performance of 4-Day, 9-Day and 18-Day MA in Bull/Bear/Bull Markets

Another category I tested consisted of fifteen markets which moved from bullish to bearish and then back to bullish again. While there were only fifteen such markets, the results were marginally profitable. This suggests again that the presence of trends, even though they may change, is a positive consideration in the 4-day, 9-day and 18-day MA approach. Results of this test are shown in Figure 4-17.

Figure 4.15: Performance of 4-, 9-, 18-Day MA in Choppy Bear Markets

		BUY SIGNALS	
Total Number of Signals	% Signals Profitable	Average Trade $ +/-	Total Profit/Loss $ +/-
792	46.59	$320.89	$254,148.25

		SELL SIGNALS	
Total Number of Signals	% Signals Profitable	Average Trade $ +/-	Total Profit/Loss $ +/-
785	24.71	($361.87)	($284,065.25)

		TOTAL SIGNALS	
Total Number of Signals	% Signals Profitable	Average Trade $ +/-	Total Profit/Loss $ +/-
1577	35.7	($18.97)	($29,916.98)

Figure 4.16: Performance of 4-, 9-, 18-Day MA in Whipsaw Markets

BUY SIGNALS

Total Number of Signals	% Signals Profitable	Average Trade $ +/-	Total Profit/Loss $ +/-
1030	36.89	$5.78	$5,956.50

SELL SIGNALS

Total Number of Signals	% Signals Profitable	Average Trade $ +/-	Total Profit/Loss $ +/-
1028	35.12	($80.12)	($82,361.81)

TOTAL SIGNALS

Total Number of Signals	% Signals Profitable	Average Trade $ +/-	Total Profit/Loss $ +/-
2058	36.01	($37.13)	($76,405.31)

Figure 4.17: Performance of 4-, 9-, 18-Day MA in Bull/Bear/Bull Markets

BUY SIGNALS

Total Number of Signals	% Signals Profitable	Average Trade $ +/-	Total Profit/Loss $ +/-
465	28.39	($139.72)	($64,970.98)

SELL SIGNALS

Total Number of Signals	% Signals Profitable	Average Trade $ +/-	Total Profit/Loss $ +/-
472	40.68	$456.98	$215,693.81

TOTAL SIGNALS

Total Number of Signals	% Signals Profitable	Average Trade $ +/-	Total Profit/Loss $ +/-
937	34.58	$160.86	$150,722.81

Performance of 4-Day, 9-Day and 18-Day MA in Bear/Bull/Bear Markets

I also examined ten markets which moved from bearish to bullish and back to bearish. Performance was impressive, with profits generated for buy and sell signals. The fact that at least 66 percent of the trends were bearish suggests that bear trends tend to produce better overall results. However, let's not forget that only ten such markets were tested and that this may not be a sufficiently large sample for conclusive results. Figure 4-18 shows my findings.

Figure 4-19 shows Triple MA 4-Day, 9-Day and 18-Day *overall* test results.

VALIDATION OF RESULTS USING SYSTEM WRITER PLUS (SWP)

In order to validate the test results in a more global fashion I tested the 4-day, 9-day and 18-day MA method on SWP. The test rules were as described earlier and no optimization was used. In order to more realistically reflect actual market conditions and show the system's worst-case performance I deducted $100 slippage and commission for each trade. Markets tested were live cattle, cocoa, pork bellies, copper, cotton, coffee, orange juice, platinum, silver, soybeans, soybean meal, sugar, wheat, Swiss Franc, gold, TBonds, Japanese Yen, heating oil, Eurodollar, S&P Index and Crude Oil. Even without optimization or filtering of trades the results were impressive. Figures 4-20 through 4-41 summarize the market-by-market performance of this method. As you can see, some markets were losers, but many were large winners. Furthermore, drawdown was rather large in some cases, and there is some question as to whether an individual acually would have been able to trade this approach given the drawdown. Yet with some minor optimization and filtering, this method appears to have good potential.

Figure 4.18: Performance of 4-, 9-, 18-Day MA in Bear/Bull/Bear Markets

BUY SIGNALS

Total Number of Signals	% Signals Profitable	Average Trade $ +/-	Total Profit/Loss $ +/-
394	39.85	$311.19	$122,610.31

SELL SIGNALS

Total Number of Signals	% Signals Profitable	Average Trade $ +/-	Total Profit/Loss $ +/-
381	31.23	$35.89	$13,673.91

TOTAL SIGNALS

Total Number of Signals	% Signals Profitable	Average Trade $ +/-	Total Profit/Loss $ +/-
775	35.61	$175.85	$136,284.25

Figure 4.19: Triple MA—4-, 9-, 18-Day MA Overall Test Results

BUY SIGNALS

Total Number of Signals	% Signals Profitable	Average Trade $ +/-	Total Profit/Loss $ +/-
10010	36.23	$53.73	$537,842.69

SELL SIGNALS

Total Number of Signals	% Signals Profitable	Average Trade $ +/-	Total Profit/Loss $ +/-
10089	35.73	$210.64	$2,125,133.00

TOTAL SIGNALS

Total Number of Signals	% Signals Profitable	Average Trade $ +/-	Total Profit/Loss $ +/-
20099	35.98	$132.49	$2,662,976.00

Figure 4.20: 4-, 9-, 18-MA: Live Cattle

```
                        Performance Summary:  All Trades

Total net profit        $ -10480.00    Open position P/L      $     196.00
Gross profit            $  75608.00    Gross loss             $ -86088.00

Total # of trades            177       Percent profitable           33%
Number winning trades         59       Number losing trades        118

Largest winning trade   $   6148.00    Largest losing trade   $  -1916.00
Average winning trade   $   1281.49    Average losing trade   $   -729.56
Ratio avg win/avg loss       1.76      Avg trade(win & loss)  $    -59.21

Max consecutive winners        4       Max consecutive losers         9
Avg # bars in winners         37       Avg # bars in losers          13

Max intraday drawdown   $ -22628.00
Profit factor                0.88      Max # contracts held           1
Account size required   $  25628.00    Return on account           -41%
```

Figure 4.21: 4-, 9-, 18-MA: Cocoa

```
                        Performance Summary:  All Trades

Total net profit        $ -12343.00    Open position P/L      $      -6.00
Gross profit            $   3611.00    Gross loss             $ -15954.00

Total # of trades            119       Percent profitable           18%
Number winning trades         21       Number losing trades         98

Largest winning trade   $    538.00    Largest losing trade   $   -385.00
Average winning trade   $    171.95    Average losing trade   $   -162.80
Ratio avg win/avg loss       1.06      Avg trade(win & loss)  $   -103.72

Max consecutive winners        2       Max consecutive losers        17
Avg # bars in winners         53       Avg # bars in losers          17

Max intraday drawdown   $ -12678.00
Profit factor                0.23      Max # contracts held           1
Account size required   $  15678.00    Return on account           -79%
```

Figure 4.22: 4-, 9-, 18-MA: Coffee

Total net profit	$ 542780.00	Open position P/L	$ 5650.00
Gross profit	$1122850.00	Gross loss	$-580070.00
Total # of trades	191	Percent profitable	39%
Number winning trades	74	Number losing trades	117
Largest winning trade	$ 190610.00	Largest losing trade	$ -33450.00
Average winning trade	$ 15173.65	Average losing trade	$ -4957.86
Ratio avg win/avg loss	3.06	Avg trade(win & loss)	$ 2841.78
Max consecutive winners	4	Max consecutive losers	12
Avg # bars in winners	37	Avg # bars in losers	14
Max intraday drawdown	$ -91410.00		
Profit factor	1.94	Max # contracts held	1
Account size required	$ 94410.00	Return on account	575%

Figure 4.23: 4-, 9-, 18-MA: Copper

Performance Summary: All Trades

Total net profit	$ -17125.00	Open position P/L	$ 1975.00
Gross profit	$ 114987.50	Gross loss	$-132112.50
Total # of trades	176	Percent profitable	36%
Number winning trades	64	Number losing trades	112
Largest winning trade	$ 11075.00	Largest losing trade	$ -5925.00
Average winning trade	$ 1796.68	Average losing trade	$ -1179.58
Ratio avg win/avg loss	1.52	Avg trade(win & loss)	$ -97.30
Max consecutive winners	4	Max consecutive losers	7
Avg # bars in winners	41	Avg # bars in losers	15
Max intraday drawdown	$ -42662.50		
Profit factor	0.87	Max # contracts held	1
Account size required	$ 45662.50	Return on account	-38%

Figure 4.24: 4-, 9-, 18-MA: Cotton

```
Total net profit          $  -6620.00   Open position P/L       $    244.00
Gross profit              $  31423.00   Gross loss              $ -38043.00

Total # of trades              190      Percent profitable           30%
Number winning trades           57      Number losing trades         133

Largest winning trade     $   3672.00   Largest losing trade    $   -667.00
Average winning trade     $    551.28   Average losing trade    $   -286.04
Ratio avg win/avg loss          1.93    Avg trade(win & loss)   $    -34.84

Max consecutive winners          4      Max consecutive losers        12
Avg # bars in winners           46      Avg # bars in losers          15

Max intraday drawdown     $ -15763.00
Profit factor                   0.83    Max # contracts held           1
Account size required     $  18763.00   Return on account           -35%
```

Figure 4.25: 4-, 9-, 18-MA: NY Light Crude Oil

```
                      Performance Summary:  All Trades

Total net profit          $  29590.00   Open position P/L       $    340.00
Gross profit              $  70920.00   Gross loss              $ -41330.00

Total # of trades               68      Percent profitable           47%
Number winning trades           32      Number losing trades          36

Largest winning trade     $  14140.00   Largest losing trade    $  -5640.00
Average winning trade     $   2216.25   Average losing trade    $  -1148.06
Ratio avg win/avg loss          1.93    Avg trade(win & loss)   $    435.15

Max consecutive winners          3      Max consecutive losers         5
Avg # bars in winners           44      Avg # bars in losers          14

Max intraday drawdown     $ -15190.00
Profit factor                   1.72    Max # contracts held           1
Account size required     $  18190.00   Return on account           163%
```

Figure 4.26: 4-, 9-, 18-MA: Eurodollar

Total net profit	$ 7575.00	Open position P/L	$ 250.00
Gross profit	$ 52950.00	Gross loss	$ -45375.00
Total # of trades	98	Percent profitable	36%
Number winning trades	35	Number losing trades	63
Largest winning trade	$ 7525.00	Largest losing trade	$ -3550.00
Average winning trade	$ 1512.86	Average losing trade	$ -720.24
Ratio avg win/avg loss	2.10	Avg trade(win & loss)	$ 77.30
Max consecutive winners	3	Max consecutive losers	8
Avg # bars in winners	39	Avg # bars in losers	14
Max intraday drawdown	$ -13275.00		
Profit factor	1.17	Max # contracts held	1
Account size required	$ 16275.00	Return on account	47%

Figure 4.27: 4-, 9-, 18-MA: COMEX Gold

Total net profit	$ 86200.00	Open position P/L	$ 1470.00
Gross profit	$ 172300.00	Gross loss	$ -86100.00
Total # of trades	162	Percent profitable	40%
Number winning trades	64	Number losing trades	98
Largest winning trade	$ 24470.00	Largest losing trade	$ -4740.00
Average winning trade	$ 2692.19	Average losing trade	$ -878.57
Ratio avg win/avg loss	3.06	Avg trade(win & loss)	$ 532.10
Max consecutive winners	4	Max consecutive losers	10
Avg # bars in winners	39	Avg # bars in losers	15
Max intraday drawdown	$ -18750.00		
Profit factor	2.00	Max # contracts held	1
Account size required	$ 21750.00	Return on account	396%

Figure 4.28: 4-, 9-, 18-MA: NY Heating Oil

```
Total net profit        $    41979.77   Open position P/L       $      399.00
Gross profit            $   137238.78   Gross loss              $   -95259.01

Total # of trades              127      Percent profitable             41%
Number winning trades           52      Number losing trades           75

Largest winning trade   $    13512.20   Largest losing trade    $    -4052.20
Average winning trade   $     2639.21   Average losing trade    $    -1270.12
Ratio avg win/avg loss        2.08      Avg trade(win & loss)   $      330.55

Max consecutive winners          4      Max consecutive losers           6
Avg # bars in winners           38      Avg # bars in losers            13

Max intraday drawdown   $   -13641.00
Profit factor                  1.44     Max # contracts held             1
Account size required   $    16641.00   Return on account             252%
```

Figure 4.29: 4-, 9-, 18-MA: Japanese Yen

```
Total net profit        $   122662.50   Open position P/L       $      600.00
Gross profit            $   195512.50   Gross loss              $   -72850.00

Total # of trades              127      Percent profitable             49%
Number winning trades           62      Number losing trades           65

Largest winning trade   $    12587.50   Largest losing trade    $    -3787.50
Average winning trade   $     3153.43   Average losing trade    $    -1120.77
Ratio avg win/avg loss        2.81      Avg trade(win & loss)   $      965.85

Max consecutive winners          6      Max consecutive losers           5
Avg # bars in winners           42      Avg # bars in losers            15

Max intraday drawdown   $   -13987.50
Profit factor                  2.68     Max # contracts held             1
Account size required   $    16987.50   Return on account             722%
```

Figure 4.30: 4-, 9-, 18-MA: Lumber

```
Total net profit        $ -21681.80   Open position P/L      $     109.20
Gross profit            $   6761.20   Gross loss             $ -28443.00

Total # of trades              217    Percent profitable            18%
Number winning trades           38    Number losing trades         179

Largest winning trade   $    880.20   Largest losing trade   $   -404.20
Average winning trade   $    177.93   Average losing trade   $   -158.90
Ratio avg win/avg loss         1.12   Avg trade(win & loss)  $    -99.92

Max consecutive winners          3    Max consecutive losers        23
Avg # bars in winners           44    Avg # bars in losers          16

Max intraday drawdown   $ -21837.10
Profit factor                  0.24   Max # contracts held           1
Account size required   $  21837.10   Return on account            -99%
```

Figure 4.31: 4-, 9-, 18-MA: Orange Juice

```
Total net profit        $   6895.00   Open position P/L      $    -600.00
Gross profit            $  64245.00   Gross loss             $ -57350.00

Total # of trades              192    Percent profitable            32%
Number winning trades           62    Number losing trades         130

Largest winning trade   $   6450.00   Largest losing trade   $  -2725.00
Average winning trade   $   1036.21   Average losing trade   $   -441.15
Ratio avg win/avg loss         2.35   Avg trade(win & loss)  $     35.91

Max consecutive winners          6    Max consecutive losers         9
Avg # bars in winners           43    Avg # bars in losers          15

Max intraday drawdown   $ -13360.00
Profit factor                  1.12   Max # contracts held           1
Account size required   $  13360.00   Return on account            52%
```

Figure 4.32: 4-, 9-, 18-MA: Platinum

```
Total net profit        $ -15565.00   Open position P/L      $       -5.00
Gross profit            $ 114360.00   Gross loss             $-129925.00

Total # of trades            212      Percent profitable            34%
Number winning trades         72      Number losing trades          140

Largest winning trade   $  18730.00   Largest losing trade   $ -16100.00
Average winning trade   $   1588.33   Average losing trade   $   -928.04
Ratio avg win/avg loss         1.71   Avg trade(win & loss)  $    -73.42

Max consecutive winners        4      Max consecutive losers          8
Avg # bars in winners         37      Avg # bars in losers           14

Max intraday drawdown   $ -28865.00
Profit factor                  0.88   Max # contracts held            1
Account size required   $  31865.00   Return on account            -49%
```

Figure 4.33: 4-, 9-, 18-MA: Pork Bellies

```
Total net profit        $ -41284.00   Open position P/L      $     -980.00
Gross profit            $ 201180.00   Gross loss             $-242464.00

Total # of trades            265      Percent profitable            35%
Number winning trades         94      Number losing trades          171

Largest winning trade   $  14236.00   Largest losing trade   $  -4520.00
Average winning trade   $   2140.21   Average losing trade   $  -1417.92
Ratio avg win/avg loss         1.51   Avg trade(win & loss)  $   -155.79

Max consecutive winners        4      Max consecutive losers         10
Avg # bars in winners         33      Avg # bars in losers           14

Max intraday drawdown   $ -48000.00
Profit factor                  0.83   Max # contracts held            1
Account size required   $  51000.00   Return on account            -81%
```

Figure 4.34: 4-, 9-, 18-MA: S&P Index

```
Total net profit        $ -93050.00    Open position P/L        $    3925.00
Gross profit            $ 162700.00    Gross loss               $-255750.00

Total # of trades             115      Percent profitable             33%
Number winning trades          38      Number losing trades           77

Largest winning trade   $   31050.00   Largest losing trade     $  -10900.00
Average winning trade   $    4281.58   Average losing trade     $   -3321.43
Ratio avg win/avg loss         1.29    Avg trade(win & loss)    $    -809.13

Max consecutive winners         3      Max consecutive losers          7
Avg # bars in winners          30      Avg # bars in losers           13

Max intraday drawdown   $-103350.00
Profit factor                 0.64     Max # contracts held            1
Account size required   $ 106350.00    Return on account             -87%
```

Figure 4.35: 4-, 9-, 18-MA: COMEX Silver

```
Total net profit        $ 211305.00    Open position P/L        $     845.00
Gross profit            $ 427820.00    Gross loss               $-216515.00

Total # of trades             226      Percent profitable             32%
Number winning trades          72      Number losing trades          154

Largest winning trade   $   97800.00   Largest losing trade     $  -11125.00
Average winning trade   $    5941.94   Average losing trade     $   -1405.94
Ratio avg win/avg loss         4.23    Avg trade(win & loss)    $     934.98

Max consecutive winners         3      Max consecutive losers         13
Avg # bars in winners          37      Avg # bars in losers           14

Max intraday drawdown   $  -36450.00
Profit factor                 1.98     Max # contracts held            1
Account size required   $   39450.00   Return on account             536%
```

Figure 4.36: 4-, 9-, 18-MA: Soybeans

```
Total net profit        $   -8386.00    Open position P/L       $     -36.00
Gross profit            $   33264.00    Gross loss              $ -41650.00

Total # of trades              246      Percent profitable             27%
Number winning trades           67      Number losing trades          179

Largest winning trade   $    3022.00    Largest losing trade    $  -2460.00
Average winning trade   $     496.48    Average losing trade    $   -232.68
Ratio avg win/avg loss          2.13    Avg trade(win & loss)   $    -34.09

Max consecutive winners          6      Max consecutive losers          18
Avg # bars in winners           42      Avg # bars in losers            15

Max intraday drawdown   $  -15034.00
Profit factor                   0.80    Max # contracts held             1
Account size required   $   18034.00    Return on account             -47%
```

Figure 4.37: 4-, 9-, 18-MA: Soybean Meal

```
Total net profit        $  629400.00    Open position P/L       $   10900.00
Gross profit            $ 1601200.00    Gross loss              $ -971800.00

Total # of trades              246      Percent profitable             36%
Number winning trades           88      Number losing trades          158

Largest winning trade   $  165100.00    Largest losing trade    $ -72100.00
Average winning trade   $   18195.45    Average losing trade    $  -6150.63
Ratio avg win/avg loss          2.96    Avg trade(win & loss)   $   2558.54

Max consecutive winners          3      Max consecutive losers          10
Avg # bars in winners           38      Avg # bars in losers            14

Max intraday drawdown   $ -127800.00
Profit factor                   1.65    Max # contracts held             1
Account size required   $  127800.00    Return on account             492%
```

Figure 4.38: 4-, 9-, 18-MA: Sugar

```
Total net profit        $ -11632.00    Open position P/L       $      97.00
Gross profit            $  12770.00    Gross loss              $ -24402.00

Total # of trades            202       Percent profitable            19%
Number winning trades         39       Number losing trades         163

Largest winning trade   $   1977.00    Largest losing trade    $    -806.00
Average winning trade   $    327.44    Average losing trade    $    -149.71
Ratio avg win/avg loss         2.19    Avg trade(win & loss)   $     -57.58

Max consecutive winners        3       Max consecutive losers        21
Avg # bars in winners         53       Avg # bars in losers          17

Max intraday drawdown   $ -12052.00
Profit factor                  0.52    Max # contracts held           1
Account size required   $  15052.00    Return on account           -77%
```

Figure 4.39: 4-, 9-, 18-MA: Swiss Franc

```
Total net profit        $  58262.50    Open position P/L       $   2250.00
Gross profit            $ 184350.00    Gross loss              $-126087.50

Total # of trades            171       Percent profitable            46%
Number winning trades         78       Number losing trades          93

Largest winning trade   $  13675.00    Largest losing trade    $   -5800.00
Average winning trade   $   2363.46    Average losing trade    $   -1355.78
Ratio avg win/avg loss         1.74    Avg trade(win & loss)   $     340.72

Max consecutive winners        4       Max consecutive losers         5
Avg # bars in winners         37       Avg # bars in losers          12

Max intraday drawdown   $ -14100.00
Profit factor                  1.46    Max # contracts held           1
Account size required   $  17100.00    Return on account           341%
```

Figure 4.40: 4-, 9-, 18-MA: T-Bonds

```
Total net profit         $ -14555.00    Open position P/L      $      12.00
Gross profit             $   2497.00    Gross loss             $ -17052.00

Total # of trades              151      Percent profitable           12%
Number winning trades           18      Number losing trades        133

Largest winning trade    $    424.00    Largest losing trade   $   -270.00
Average winning trade    $    138.72    Average losing trade   $   -128.21
Ratio avg win/avg loss         1.08     Avg trade(win & loss)  $    -96.39

Max consecutive winners          2      Max consecutive losers        18
Avg # bars in winners           58      Avg # bars in losers          17

Max intraday drawdown    $ -14570.00
Profit factor                  0.15     Max # contracts held           1
Account size required    $  17570.00    Return on account           -83%
```

Figure 4.41: 4-, 9-, 18-MA: CBT Wheat

```
Total net profit         $ -17846.00    Open position P/L      $      18.00
Gross profit             $  13106.00    Gross loss             $ -30952.00

Total # of trades              236      Percent profitable           22%
Number winning trades           51      Number losing trades        185

Largest winning trade    $   1656.00    Largest losing trade   $   -584.00
Average winning trade    $    256.98    Average losing trade   $   -167.31
Ratio avg win/avg loss         1.54     Avg trade(win & loss)  $    -75.62

Max consecutive winners          3      Max consecutive losers        14
Avg # bars in winners           45      Avg # bars in losers          17

Max intraday drawdown    $ -17846.00
Profit factor                  0.42     Max # contracts held           1
Account size required    $  17846.00    Return on account          -100%
```

THE 9-DAY, 18-DAY AND 36-DAY MOVING-AVERAGE APPROACH

Another popular combination of moving averages is the 9-day, 18-day and 36-day MA approach. The rules here are very simple. As long as the 9-day and 18-day moving averages are greater than the 36-day moving average, the system is long, but when the 9-day and 18-day moving averages become less than the 36-day moving average, the system goes into a sell mode. Figure 4-42 illustrates the basic approach. Inasmuch as the MAs used in this approach are longer, fewer signals will be generated than with the previously examined 4-day, 9-day and 18-day MA method.

Performance of 9-Day, 18-Day and 36-Day MA in Bull Markets

My bull market test revealed excellent overall results, with the average trade quite large. There were fewer trades generated. Frequently four to six signals were generated per contract. This cut down on slippage and commission and resulted in a higher average profit per trade. Results are shown in Figure 4-43.

Performance of 9-Day, 18-Day and 36-Day MA in Bear Markets

The next test of this combination was on my sample of bear markets. The results indicated that performance was clearly superior for sell signals in bear markets and overall performance was most impressive. Buy signals in bear markets produced an overall loss, while sell signals produced an overall profit. This clearly supports the practice of following sell signals in bear markets and buy signals in bull markets. Results of this study are shown in Figure 4-44.

Performance of 9-Day, 18-Day and 36-Day MA in Choppy Bull Markets

I then tested the 9-day, 18-day and 36-day combination on my choppy bull market sample. The results were not nearly as impressive as those for bull or bear markets. Apparently choppy bull markets are not as reliable as markets with less back and forth movement. Results are shown in Figure 4-45.

Figure 4.42: Signals Using Triple Moving Average System: 9-, 18-, and 36-Day

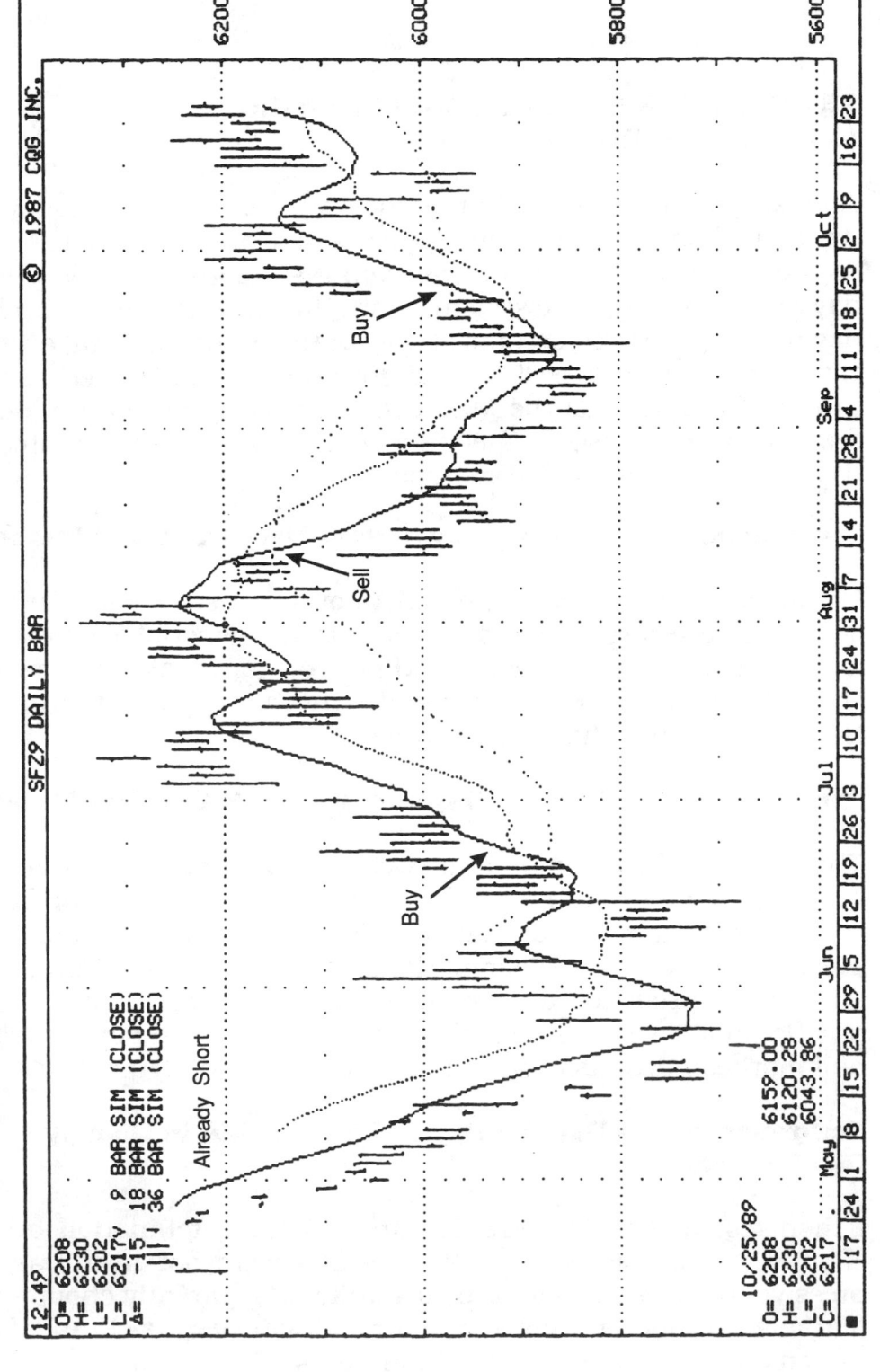

Figure 4.43: Performance of 9-, 18-, and 36-Day MA in Bull Markets

BUY SIGNALS

Total Number of Signals	% Signals Profitable	Average Trade $ +/-	Total Profit/Loss $ +/-
643	15.71	($750.65)	($482,669.37)

SELL SIGNALS

Total Number of Signals	% Signals Profitable	Average Trade $ +/-	Total Profit/Loss $ +/-
694	49.57	$1,613.71	$1,119,918.00

TOTAL SIGNALS

Total Number of Signals	% Signals Profitable	Average Trade $ +/-	Total Profit/Loss $ +/-
1337	33.28	$476.63	$637,248.13

Figure 4.44: Performance of 9-, 18-, and 36-Day MA in Bear Markets

BUY SIGNALS

Total Number of Signals	% Signals Profitable	Average Trade $ +/-	Total Profit/Loss $ +/-
902	53.99	$1,323.86	$1,194,120.00

SELL SIGNALS

Total Number of Signals	% Signals Profitable	Average Trade $ +/-	Total Profit/Loss $ +/-
859	14.9	($784.41)	($673,805.37)

TOTAL SIGNALS

Total Number of Signals	% Signals Profitable	Average Trade $ +/-	Total Profit/Loss $ +/-
1761	34.92	$295.47	$520,314.94

Figure 4.45: Performance of 9-, 18-, and 36-Day MA in Choppy Bull Markets

BUY SIGNALS

Total Number of Signals	% Signals Profitable	Average Trade $ +/-	Total Profit/Loss $ +/-
430	46.51	$680.56	$292,639.25

SELL SIGNALS

Total Number of Signals	% Signals Profitable	Average Trade $ +/-	Total Profit/Loss $ +/-
410	16.34	($614.81)	($252,073.69)

TOTAL SIGNALS

Total Number of Signals	% Signals Profitable	Average Trade $ +/-	Total Profit/Loss $ +/-
840	31.79	$48.29	$40,565.55

Performance of 9-Day, 18-Day and 36-Day MA in Choppy Bear Markets

The performance of this system in choppy bull markets was essentially similar to its performance in choppy bear markets. The results were less than impressive, showing an overall loss, as can be seen in Figure 4-46.

It seems that this combination of moving averages works best in markets which are not "choppy." If this is true, then we should see very poor results in the "whipsaw" market sample.

Performance of 9-Day, 18-Day and 36-Day MA in Bull/Bear Markets

I also examined this approach in bull/bear markets. The results were positive. This lent further support to the conclusion that trending markets as opposed to choppy or whipsaw markets are best suited to the triple moving-average approach. As you can see from the results in Figure 4-47, the overall performance was quite impressive.

Performance of 9-Day 18-Day and 36-Day MA in Bear/Bull Markets

On the basis of performance in bull/bear markets, we would expect the results for bear/bull markets to be essentially similar. As a matter of fact, this did prove to be the case. Performance of this method in bear/bull markets was impressive, with buy and sell signals turning in an average profit per trade and a healthy overall profit. The results are shown in Figure 4-48.

Performance of 9-Day, 18-Day and 36-Day MA in Bull/Bear/Bull Markets

I would also expect that this method would work well in bull/bear/bull markets inasmuch as the trends are quite clear regardless of the transition. The results of my test revealed that this was true. While the total number of markets tested was relatively small, the results were positive, as you can clearly see from Figure 4-49.

Figure 4.46: Performance of 9-, 18-, and 36-Day MA in Choppy Bear Markets

BUY SIGNALS

Total Number of Signals	% Signals Profitable	Average Trade $ +/-	Total Profit/Loss $ +/-
562	19.57	($1,420.54)	($798,343.44)

SELL SIGNALS

Total Number of Signals	% Signals Profitable	Average Trade $ +/-	Total Profit/Loss $ +/-
592	47.64	$1,495.66	$885,430.44

TOTAL SIGNALS

Total Number of Signals	% Signals Profitable	Average Trade $ +/-	Total Profit/Loss $ +/-
1154	33.97	$75.47	$87,087.00

Figure 4.47: Performance of 9-, 18-, and 36-Day MA in Bull/Bear Markets

BUY SIGNALS

Total Number of Signals	% Signals Profitable	Average Trade $ +/-	Total Profit/Loss $ +/-
809	39.31	$577.58	$467,261.19

SELL SIGNALS

Total Number of Signals	% Signals Profitable	Average Trade $ +/-	Total Profit/Loss $ +/-
812	30.17	$283.25	$229,998.56

TOTAL SIGNALS

Total Number of Signals	% Signals Profitable	Average Trade $ +/-	Total Profit/Loss $ +/-
1621	34.73	$430.14	$697,259.75

Figure 4.48: Performance of 9-, 18-, and 36-Day MA in Bear/Bull Markets

BUY SIGNALS

Total Number of Signals	% Signals Profitable	Average Trade $ +/-	Total Profit/Loss $ +/-
798	35.71	$78.26	$62,454.14

SELL SIGNALS

Total Number of Signals	% Signals Profitable	Average Trade $ +/-	Total Profit/Loss $ +/-
815	40.37	$598.91	$488,107.50

TOTAL SIGNALS

Total Number of Signals	% Signals Profitable	Average Trade $ +/-	Total Profit/Loss $ +/-
1613	38.07	$341.33	$550,561.69

Figure 4.49: Performance of 9-, 18-, and 36-Day MA in Bull/Bear/Bull Markets

BUY SIGNALS

Total Number of Signals	% Signals Profitable	Average Trade $ +/-	Total Profit/Loss $ +/-
218	31.65	($30.49)	($6,647.07)

SELL SIGNALS

Total Number of Signals	% Signals Profitable	Average Trade $ +/-	Total Profit/Loss $ +/-
242	47.93	$990.06	$239,594.50

TOTAL SIGNALS

Total Number of Signals	% Signals Profitable	Average Trade $ +/-	Total Profit/Loss $ +/-
460	40.22	$506.41	$232,947.44

Performance of 9-Day, 18-Day and 36-Day MA in Bear/Bull/Bear Markets

I would expect performance here to be about the same as it was for bull/bear/bull markets. It was in fact better, and positive for both buy and sell signals. This is additional confirmation of the general contention that trending markets tend to produce positive results for MA systems. Results are shown in Figure 4-50.

Performance of 9-Day, 18-Day and 36-Day MA's in Whipsaw Markets

The final test category was in whipsaw markets. We would expect the system to be a net loser in this type of market if our working theory is correct. The test results were very clearly in support of our expectation. Both the buy and sell signals under this approach proved to be losers. Results are shown in Figure 4-51.

TEST RESULTS USING SYSTEM WRITER PLUS (SWP)

In order to validate the test results in a more global fashion, I tested the 9-day, 18-day, and 36-day MA method on SWP. The test rules were as described earlier and no optimization was used. In order to more realistically reflect actual market conditions and show the systems worst-case performance we deducted $100 slippage and commission for each trade. Markets tested were live cattle, cocoa, pork bellies, copper, cotton, coffee, orange juice, platinum, silver, soybeans, soybean meal, sugar, wheat, Swiss Francs, gold, TBonds, Japanese Yen, heating oil, Eurodollar, S&P Index and Crude Oil. Even without optimization or filtering of trades the results were impressive. Figures 4-43 through 4-51 summarize the market-by-market performance of this method. As you can see, some markets were losers, but many markets were large winners. Furthermore, drawdown was rather large in some cases and there is some question as to whether an individual would have actually been able to trade this approach given the drawdown. Yet with some minor optimization and filtering, this method appears to have good potential. Overall test results for the 9-day, 18-day, and 36-day MA method are shown in Figures 4-52 through 4-73.

Figure 4.50: Performance of 9-, 18-, and 36-Day MA in Bear/Bull/Bear Markets

BUY SIGNALS

Total Number of Signals	% Signals Profitable	Average Trade $ +/-	Total Profit/Loss $ +/-
211	38.86	$364.25	$292,639.25

SELL SIGNALS

Total Number of Signals	% Signals Profitable	Average Trade $ +/-	Total Profit/Loss $ +/-
198	32.83	$25.75	$5,097.55

TOTAL SIGNALS

Total Number of Signals	% Signals Profitable	Average Trade $ +/-	Total Profit/Loss $ +/-
409	35.94	$200.38	$81,954.69

Figure 4.51: Performance of 9-, 18-, and 36-Day MA in Whipsaw Markets

BUY SIGNALS

Total Number of Signals	% Signals Profitable	Average Trade $ +/-	Total Profit/Loss $ +/-
569	30.58	($288.92)	($164,397.56)

SELL SIGNALS

Total Number of Signals	% Signals Profitable	Average Trade $ +/-	Total Profit/Loss $ +/-
550	28.18	($384.35)	($211,393.31)

TOTAL SIGNALS

Total Number of Signals	% Signals Profitable	Average Trade $ +/-	Total Profit/Loss $ +/-
1119	29.4	($335.83)	($375,790.87)

Figure 4.52: 9-,18-, 36-MA: Live Cattle

```
Total net profit       $    6456.00   Open position P/L    $    1536.00
Gross profit           $   63244.00   Gross loss           $  -56788.00

Total # of trades              82     Percent profitable          34%
Number winning trades          28     Number losing trades        54

Largest winning trade  $    7340.00   Largest losing trade  $  -2860.00
Average winning trade  $    2258.71   Average losing trade  $  -1051.63
Ratio avg win/avg loss        2.15    Avg trade(win & loss) $     78.73

Max consecutive winners         4     Max consecutive losers        7
Avg # bars in winners          81     Avg # bars in losers         25

Max intraday drawdown  $  -10124.00
Profit factor                 1.11    Max # contracts held          1
Account size required  $   13124.00   Return on account           49%
```

Figure 4.53: 9-,18-, 36-MA: Cocoa

```
Total net profit       $   -7410.00   Open position P/L    $      38.00
Gross profit           $    2297.00   Gross loss           $   -9707.00

Total # of trades              73     Percent profitable          19%
Number winning trades          14     Number losing trades        59

Largest winning trade  $     705.00   Largest losing trade  $   -393.00
Average winning trade  $     164.07   Average losing trade  $   -164.53
Ratio avg win/avg loss        1.00    Avg trade(win & loss) $    -101.51

Max consecutive winners         2     Max consecutive losers       16
Avg # bars in winners          76     Avg # bars in losers         28

Max intraday drawdown  $   -8104.00
Profit factor                 0.24    Max # contracts held          1
Account size required  $   11104.00   Return on account          -67%
```

Figure 4.54: 9-,18-, 36-MA: Coffee

```
Total net profit        $ 286990.00   Open position P/L        $    3550.00
Gross profit            $ 816390.00   Gross loss               $-529400.00

Total # of trades              111    Percent profitable              37%
Number winning trades           41    Number losing trades            70

Largest winning trade   $ 149620.00   Largest losing trade     $ -37350.00
Average winning trade   $  19911.95   Average losing trade     $  -7562.86
Ratio avg win/avg loss        2.63    Avg trade(win & loss)    $   2585.50

Max consecutive winners          3    Max consecutive losers           7
Avg # bars in winners           67    Avg # bars in losers            22

Max intraday drawdown   $-111110.00
Profit factor                 1.54    Max # contracts held             1
Account size required   $ 114110.00   Return on account             252%
```

Figure 4.55: 9-,18-, 36-MA: Copper

```
Total net profit        $  34462.50   Open position P/L        $    1700.00
Gross profit            $ 104212.50   Gross loss               $ -69750.00

Total # of trades              106    Percent profitable              36%
Number winning trades           38    Number losing trades            68

Largest winning trade   $  13750.00   Largest losing trade     $  -5325.00
Average winning trade   $   2742.43   Average losing trade     $  -1025.74
Ratio avg win/avg loss        2.67    Avg trade(win & loss)    $    325.12

Max consecutive winners          3    Max consecutive losers          12
Avg # bars in winners           69    Avg # bars in losers            24

Max intraday drawdown   $ -20512.50
Profit factor                 1.49    Max # contracts held             1
Account size required   $  23512.50   Return on account             147%
```

Figure 4.56: 9-,18-, 36-MA: Cotton

```
Total net profit        $    3996.00    Open position P/L       $      831.00
Gross profit            $   26071.00    Gross loss              $  -22075.00

Total # of trades              98       Percent profitable             37%
Number winning trades          36       Number losing trades           62

Largest winning trade   $    4973.00    Largest losing trade    $   -1207.00
Average winning trade   $     724.19    Average losing trade    $    -356.05
Ratio avg win/avg loss         2.03     Avg trade(win & loss)   $      40.78

Max consecutive winners         4       Max consecutive losers          5
Avg # bars in winners          82       Avg # bars in losers           25

Max intraday drawdown   $   -6100.00
Profit factor                  1.18     Max # contracts held            1
Account size required   $    9100.00    Return on account              44%
```

Figure 4.57: 9-,18-, 36-MA: NY Light Crude Oil

```
Total net profit        $   46670.00    Open position P/L       $     6990.00
Gross profit            $   60970.00    Gross loss              $   -14300.00

Total # of trades              35       Percent profitable             54%
Number winning trades          19       Number losing trades           16

Largest winning trade   $   13740.00    Largest losing trade    $    -1970.00
Average winning trade   $    3208.95    Average losing trade    $     -893.75
Ratio avg win/avg loss         3.59     Avg trade(win & loss)   $     1333.43

Max consecutive winners         3       Max consecutive losers          3
Avg # bars in winners          77       Avg # bars in losers           25

Max intraday drawdown   $   -3640.00
Profit factor                  4.26     Max # contracts held            1
Account size required   $    6640.00    Return on account             703%
```

Figure 4.58: 9-,18-, 36-MA: Eurodollar

```
Total net profit          $  13750.00    Open position P/L       $     425.00
Gross profit              $  48700.00    Gross loss              $ -34950.00

Total # of trades                51      Percent profitable             37%
Number winning trades            19      Number losing trades           32

Largest winning trade     $  16200.00    Largest losing trade    $  -2375.00
Average winning trade     $   2563.16    Average losing trade    $  -1092.19
Ratio avg win/avg loss          2.35     Avg trade(win & loss)   $    269.61

Max consecutive winners           3      Max consecutive losers          4
Avg # bars in winners            75      Avg # bars in losers           24

Max intraday drawdown     $  -7575.00
Profit factor                   1.39     Max # contracts held            1
Account size required     $  10575.00    Return on account            130%
```

Figure 4.59: 9-,18-, 36-MA: COMEX Gold

```
Total net profit          $  61300.00    Open position P/L       $  -3080.00
Gross profit              $ 142090.00    Gross loss              $ -80790.00

Total # of trades                94      Percent profitable             39%
Number winning trades            37      Number losing trades           57

Largest winning trade     $  20900.00    Largest losing trade    $  -4350.00
Average winning trade     $   3840.27    Average losing trade    $  -1417.37
Ratio avg win/avg loss          2.71     Avg trade(win & loss)   $    652.13

Max consecutive winners           3      Max consecutive losers          8
Avg # bars in winners            68      Avg # bars in losers           26

Max intraday drawdown     $ -25100.00
Profit factor                   1.76     Max # contracts held            1
Account size required     $  28100.00    Return on account            218%
```

Figure 4.60: 9-,18-, 36-MA: NY Heating Oil

```
Total net profit         $   67474.01    Open position P/L      $    8572.20
Gross profit             $   95206.80    Gross loss             $  -27732.80

Total # of trades                59      Percent profitable             56%
Number winning trades            33      Number losing trades           26

Largest winning trade    $   12663.80    Largest losing trade   $   -3497.80
Average winning trade    $    2885.05    Average losing trade   $   -1066.65
Ratio avg win/avg loss         2.70      Avg trade(win & loss)  $    1143.63

Max consecutive winners           5      Max consecutive losers          6
Avg # bars in winners            62      Avg # bars in losers           33

Max intraday drawdown    $   -8525.60
Profit factor                  3.43      Max # contracts held            1
Account size required    $   11525.60    Return on account            585%
```

Figure 4.61: 9-,18-, 36-MA: Japanese Yen

```
Total net profit         $   78525.00    Open position P/L      $        0.00
Gross profit             $  142825.00    Gross loss             $   -64300.00

Total # of trades                76      Percent profitable             50%
Number winning trades            38      Number losing trades           38

Largest winning trade    $   12637.50    Largest losing trade   $   -6375.00
Average winning trade    $    3758.55    Average losing trade   $   -1692.11
Ratio avg win/avg loss         2.22      Avg trade(win & loss)  $    1033.22

Max consecutive winners           6      Max consecutive losers          3
Avg # bars in winners            68      Avg # bars in losers           25

Max intraday drawdown    $   -7912.50
Profit factor                  2.22      Max # contracts held            1
Account size required    $    7912.50    Return on account            992%
```

Figure 4.62: 9-,18-, 36-MA: Lumber

```
Total net profit          $   -7553.60   Open position P/L        $       -3.90
Gross profit              $    7334.90   Gross loss               $  -14888.50

Total # of trades                 111    Percent profitable               26%
Number winning trades              29    Number losing trades             82

Largest winning trade     $     820.40   Largest losing trade     $    -478.30
Average winning trade     $     252.93   Average losing trade     $    -181.57
Ratio avg win/avg loss            1.39   Avg trade(win & loss)    $     -68.05

Max consecutive winners             3    Max consecutive losers            8
Avg # bars in winners              78    Avg # bars in losers             28

Max intraday drawdown     $   -7876.80
Profit factor                    0.49    Max # contracts held              1
Account size required     $   10876.80   Return on account              -69%
```

Figure 4.63: 9-,18-, 36-MA: Orange Juice

```
Total net profit          $  -17285.00   Open position P/L        $      535.00
Gross profit              $   51355.00   Gross loss               $  -68640.00

Total # of trades                 115    Percent profitable               28%
Number winning trades              32    Number losing trades             83

Largest winning trade     $    7405.00   Largest losing trade     $   -3110.00
Average winning trade     $    1604.84   Average losing trade     $    -826.99
Ratio avg win/avg loss            1.94   Avg trade(win & loss)    $    -150.30

Max consecutive winners             3    Max consecutive losers            9
Avg # bars in winners              82    Avg # bars in losers             23

Max intraday drawdown     $  -28760.00
Profit factor                    0.75    Max # contracts held              1
Account size required     $   31760.00   Return on account              -54%
```

Figure 4.64: 9-,18-, 36-MA: Platinum

```
Total net profit        $   10545.00    Open position P/L      $    1720.00
Gross profit            $   83140.00    Gross loss             $  -72595.00

Total # of trades              110      Percent profitable            35%
Number winning trades           38      Number losing trades          72

Largest winning trade   $    9725.00    Largest losing trade   $   -2940.00
Average winning trade   $    2187.89    Average losing trade   $   -1008.26
Ratio avg win/avg loss          2.17    Avg trade(win & loss)  $      95.86

Max consecutive winners          3      Max consecutive losers         7
Avg # bars in winners           69      Avg # bars in losers          27

Max intraday drawdown   $  -15195.00
Profit factor                   1.15    Max # contracts held           1
Account size required   $   18195.00    Return on account            58%
```

Figure 4.65: 9-,18-, 36-MA: Pork Bellies

```
Total net profit        $  -68940.00    Open position P/L      $   -1316.00
Gross profit            $  132340.00    Gross loss             $ -201280.00

Total # of trades              148      Percent profitable            31%
Number winning trades           46      Number losing trades         102

Largest winning trade   $   12400.00    Largest losing trade   $   -5932.00
Average winning trade   $    2876.96    Average losing trade   $   -1973.33
Ratio avg win/avg loss          1.46    Avg trade(win & loss)  $    -465.81

Max consecutive winners          3      Max consecutive losers        10
Avg # bars in winners           66      Avg # bars in losers          24

Max intraday drawdown   $  -74860.00
Profit factor                   0.66    Max # contracts held           1
Account size required   $   77860.00    Return on account           -89%
```

Figure 4.66: 9-,18-, 36-MA: S&P Index

```
Total net profit        $ -16875.00    Open position P/L       $ -15150.00
Gross profit            $ 155600.00    Gross loss              $-172475.00

Total # of trades              58      Percent profitable             34%
Number winning trades          20      Number losing trades           38

Largest winning trade   $  35875.00    Largest losing trade    $ -12475.00
Average winning trade   $   7780.00    Average losing trade    $  -4538.82
Ratio avg win/avg loss        1.71     Avg trade(win & loss)   $   -290.95

Max consecutive winners         3      Max consecutive losers          8
Avg # bars in winners          59      Avg # bars in losers           26

Max intraday drawdown   $ -57150.00
Profit factor                 0.90     Max # contracts held            1
Account size required   $  60150.00    Return on account            -28%
```

Figure 4.67: 9-,18-, 36-MA: COMEX Silver

```
Total net profit        $ 196995.00    Open position P/L       $    -170.00
Gross profit            $ 374110.00    Gross loss              $-177115.00

Total # of trades             138      Percent profitable             32%
Number winning trades          44      Number losing trades           94

Largest winning trade   $  93300.00    Largest losing trade    $ -15825.00
Average winning trade   $   8502.50    Average losing trade    $  -1884.20
Ratio avg win/avg loss        4.51     Avg trade(win & loss)   $   1427.50

Max consecutive winners         3      Max consecutive losers          9
Avg # bars in winners          62      Avg # bars in losers           23

Max intraday drawdown   $ -34085.00
Profit factor                 2.11     Max # contracts held            1
Account size required   $  37085.00    Return on account            531%
```

Figure 4.68: 9-,18-, 36-MA: Soybeans

```
Total net profit         $  -3348.00    Open position P/L        $     632.00
Gross profit             $  27576.00    Gross loss               $ -30924.00

Total # of trades              140      Percent profitable             29%
Number winning trades           41      Number losing trades           99

Largest winning trade    $   2600.00    Largest losing trade     $  -1424.00
Average winning trade    $    672.59    Average losing trade     $   -312.36
Ratio avg win/avg loss         2.15     Avg trade(win & loss)    $    -23.91

Max consecutive winners          4      Max consecutive losers         18
Avg # bars in winners           71      Avg # bars in losers           26

Max intraday drawdown    $ -12070.00
Profit factor                  0.89     Max # contracts held            1
Account size required    $  15070.00    Return on account            -22%
```

Figure 4.69: 9-,18-, 36-MA: Soybean Meal

```
Total net profit         $ 521200.00    Open position P/L        $  24600.00
Gross profit             $1162500.00    Gross loss               $-641300.00

Total # of trades              132      Percent profitable             42%
Number winning trades           56      Number losing trades           76

Largest winning trade    $ 110900.00    Largest losing trade     $ -51700.00
Average winning trade    $  20758.93    Average losing trade     $  -8438.16
Ratio avg win/avg loss         2.46     Avg trade(win & loss)    $   3948.48

Max consecutive winners          5      Max consecutive losers          5
Avg # bars in winners           67      Avg # bars in losers           22

Max intraday drawdown    $-126600.00
Profit factor                  1.81     Max # contracts held            1
Account size required    $ 129600.00    Return on account            402%
```

Figure 4.70: 9-,18-, 36-MA: Sugar

```
Total net profit         $  50500.00    Open position P/L        $    -450.00
Gross profit             $ 142237.50    Gross loss               $ -91737.50

Total # of trades               91      Percent profitable             48%
Number winning trades           44      Number losing trades           47

Largest winning trade    $  12725.00    Largest losing trade     $  -6650.00
Average winning trade    $   3232.67    Average losing trade     $  -1951.86
Ratio avg win/avg loss         1.66     Avg trade(win & loss)    $    554.95

Max consecutive winners          4      Max consecutive losers          5
Avg # bars in winners           66      Avg # bars in losers           23

Max intraday drawdown    $ -20175.00
Profit factor                  1.55     Max # contracts held            1
Account size required    $  23175.00    Return on account             218%
```

Figure 4.71: 9-,18-, 36-MA: Swiss Franc

```
Total net profit         $  -1476.00    Open position P/L        $      91.00
Gross profit             $  11821.00    Gross loss               $ -13297.00

Total # of trades              107      Percent profitable             24%
Number winning trades           26      Number losing trades           81

Largest winning trade    $   2230.00    Largest losing trade     $   -506.00
Average winning trade    $    454.65    Average losing trade     $   -164.16
Ratio avg win/avg loss         2.77     Avg trade(win & loss)    $    -13.79

Max consecutive winners          2      Max consecutive losers         12
Avg # bars in winners           90      Avg # bars in losers           30

Max intraday drawdown    $  -5397.00
Profit factor                  0.89     Max # contracts held            1
Account size required    $   8397.00    Return on account             -18%
```

Figure 4.72: 9-,18-, 36-MA: T-Bonds

```
Total net profit        $  -6553.00   Open position P/L      $     -67.00
Gross profit            $   2634.00   Gross loss             $  -9187.00

Total # of trades             79      Percent profitable           20%
Number winning trades         16      Number losing trades          63

Largest winning trade   $    634.00   Largest losing trade   $    -295.00
Average winning trade   $    164.63   Average losing trade   $    -145.83
Ratio avg win/avg loss        1.13    Avg trade(win & loss)  $     -82.95

Max consecutive winners        3      Max consecutive losers        12
Avg # bars in winners         87      Avg # bars in losers          31

Max intraday drawdown   $  -6657.00
Profit factor                 0.29    Max # contracts held           1
Account size required   $   9657.00   Return on account           -68%
```

Figure 4.73: 9-,18-, 36-MA: CBT Wheat

```
                      Performance Summary:  All Trades

Total net profit        $ -12486.00   Open position P/L      $     828.00
Gross profit            $   8710.00   Gross loss             $ -21196.00

Total # of trades            132      Percent profitable           20%
Number winning trades         26      Number losing trades         106

Largest winning trade   $   1008.00   Largest losing trade   $    -686.00
Average winning trade   $    335.00   Average losing trade   $    -199.96
Ratio avg win/avg loss        1.68    Avg trade(win & loss)  $     -94.59

Max consecutive winners        3      Max consecutive losers        28
Avg # bars in winners         80      Avg # bars in losers          30

Max intraday drawdown   $ -13108.00
Profit factor                 0.41    Max # contracts held           1
Account size required   $  16108.00   Return on account           -78%
```

The 9-day, 18-day and 36-day MA method appears to be more effective than the 4-day, 9-day, 18-day method: some markets showed significantly better results. Crude oil, for example, which showed a maximum drawdown of over $10,000 on the 4-day,9-day, 18-day method, showed higher net profits and only an approximate $2,450 maximum drawdown on the 9-day, 18-day, 36-day MA approach. In addition, the percentage of profitable trades jumped sharply. The S&P Index went from a net loser under the 4-day, 9-day, 18-day method to a net winner in the 9-day, 18-day, 36-day condition. But examine the results for yourself and be the judge.

THE 14-DAY, 28-DAY AND 54-DAY MOVING AVERAGE SYSTEM

A long-term approach to moving averages should lead to fewer signals and a large per trade profit. Accordingly, I also tested the 14-day, 28-day, and 54-day moving-average approach. The trading rules here are similar to those of the previous triple moving-average systems I have examined, but the MA periods are longer. A buy signal is generated when the 14-day and 28-day MAs are greater than the 54-day MA, and a sell signal is generated when the 14-day and 28-day MAs are less than the 54-day MA. Figure 4-74 illustrates the signals. Now let's examine the historical performance of this approach by market categories.

The 14-Day, 28-Day and 54-Day MA System in Bull Markets

Results of this approach in bull markets were generally as anticipated. Only three to four signals were generated for each market due to the length of the moving averages, and the overall profit per signal was considerably greater. Results for bull markets alone were most impressive, with a large profit per trade and only approximately 105 trades for the entire bull market data file. In many cases there were no signals whatsoever. I consider this to be an asset rather than a liability. In other words, the ability of a trading system to keep a trader out of certain markets is not necessarily a bad feature. Figure 4-75 shows the results for bull markets using this MA combination.

Figure 4.74: Signals Using Triple Moving Average System: 14-, 28-, and 54-Day

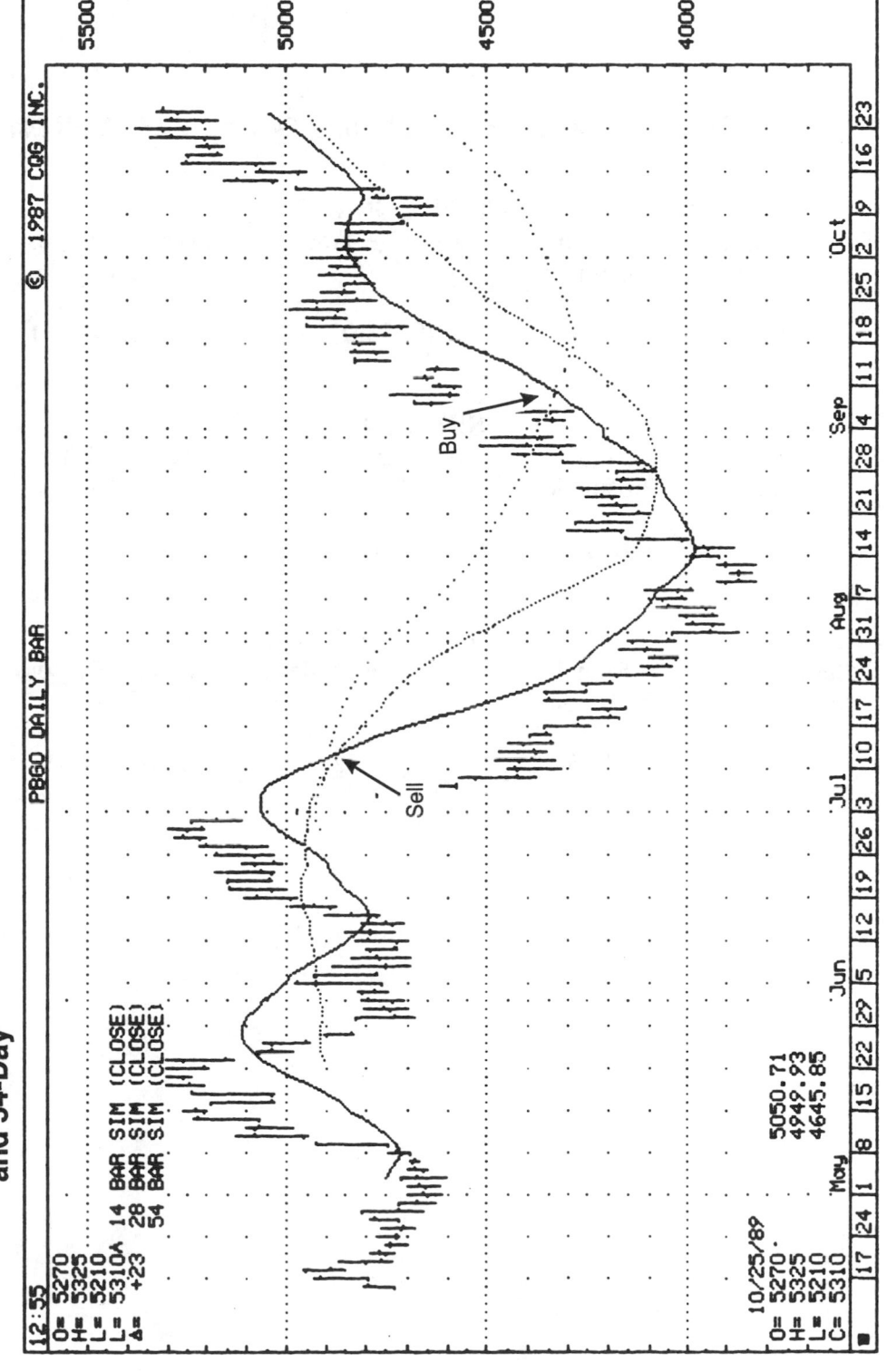

Figure 4.75: Performance of 14-, 28-, and 54-Day MA in Bull Markets

BUY SIGNALS

Total Number of Signals	% Signals Profitable	Average Trade $ +/-	Total Profit/Loss $ +/-
360	15.56	($933.03)	($335,891.94)

SELL SIGNALS

Total Number of Signals	% Signals Profitable	Average Trade $ +/-	Total Profit/Loss $ +/-
407	48.16	$2,239.97	$910,852.75

TOTAL SIGNALS

Total Number of Signals	% Signals Profitable	Average Trade $ +/-	Total Profit/Loss $ +/-
767	32.86	$749.62	$574,960.81

The 14-Day, 28-Day and 54-Day MA System in Bear Markets

Results of this approach in bear markets should also be profitable if the system performs well in trending markets. The test results illustrate that this was indeed the case. In most cases there were only two to five signals per contract, and the average profit per trade was larger than that of shorter term moving averages. See Figure 4-76.

The 14-Day, 28-Day and 54-Day MA System in Choppy Bear Markets

This combination of MAs did not fare well in choppy bear markets. Although there were not many signals per contract, the overall results showed a loss. Clearly, this suggests that longer MAs are more dependent upon trending markets than shorter term MAs. If this is true, then we should also expect to see poor results in choppy bull markets. Performance of the 14-day, 28-day and 54-day MA system in choppy bear markets is shown in Figure 4-77.

The 14-Day, 28-Day and 54-Day MA System in Choppy Bull Markets

The choppy bull market test did not reveal an overall loss. While it showed a net profit, the bottom line results were not impressive, still suggesting that the long-term MAs may be more dependent upon a strongly trending market than are the shorter-term MAs. Clearly, the issue of selecting an optimum MA combination becomes one of balancing several variables such as number of trades, profit per trade, drawdown and market trend. Results of the 14-day, 28-day, and 54-day MA system in choppy bull markets is shown in Figure 4-78.

Figure 4.76: Performance of 14-, 28-, and 54-Day MA in Bear Markets

BUY SIGNALS

Total Number of Signals	% Signals Profitable	Average Trade $ +/-	Total Profit/Loss $ +/-
553	51.72	$1,756.95	$971,592.44

SELL SIGNALS

Total Number of Signals	% Signals Profitable	Average Trade $ +/-	Total Profit/Loss $ +/-
483	15.94	($1,120.92)	($541,403.31)

TOTAL SIGNALS

Total Number of Signals	% Signals Profitable	Average Trade $ +/-	Total Profit/Loss $ +/-
1036	35.04	$415.24	$430,189.12

Figure 4.77: Performance of 14-, 28-, and 54-Day MA in Choppy Bear Markets

BUY SIGNALS

Total Number of Signals	% Signals Profitable	Average Trade $ +/-	Total Profit/Loss $ +/-
286	46.5	$957.63	$273,882.56

SELL SIGNALS

Total Number of Signals	% Signals Profitable	Average Trade $ +/-	Total Profit/Loss $ +/-
254	11.42	($803.46)	($204,079.94)

TOTAL SIGNALS

Total Number of Signals	% Signals Profitable	Average Trade $ +/-	Total Profit/Loss $ +/-
540	30	$129.26	$69,802.63

Figure 4.78: Performance of 14-, 28-, and 54-Day MA in Choppy Bull Markets

BUY SIGNALS

Total Number of Signals	% Signals Profitable	Average Trade $ +/-	Total Profit/Loss $ +/-
363	15.98	($1,946.28)	($706,499.44)

SELL SIGNALS

Total Number of Signals	% Signals Profitable	Average Trade $ +/-	Total Profit/Loss $ +/-
398	47.99	$2,217.58	$882,596.44

TOTAL SIGNALS

Total Number of Signals	% Signals Profitable	Average Trade $ +/-	Total Profit/Loss $ +/-
761	32.72	$231.40	$176,097.00

The 14-Day, 28-Day and 54-Day MA System in Bull/Bear Markets

If previous experience with the triple MA is any guide, then we ought to expect performance in bull/bear markets to be positive. It was. As you can see from the results in Figure 4-79, an overall profit was generated, along with a reasonably low number of trades. We should expect essentially similar performance in the bear/bull market category.

The 14-Day, 28-Day and 54-Day MA System in Bear/Bull Markets

Expectations for performance of this approach in bear/bull markets were verified as the system test turned in an overall profit and a reasonably small number of trades per market. Again, we have an indication that trend is a more important consideration than trend change when it comes to the performance of longer term triple MA systems. Figure 4-80 shows the results of this test.

The 14-Day, 28-Day and 54-Day MA System in Bull/Bear/Bull Markets

Based on previous findings we would expect performance of this MA combination to be positive in the bull/bear/bull market category. An examination of the summary in Figure 4-81 shows this, in fact, to have been the case. Again we have evidence that trend is very important, more important in fact than trend change. Traders often express concern about how MA systems perform in markets which change trend. This did not appear to be a cause for concern. Rather, it was the "integrity" of trend that was important.

Figure 4.79: Performance of 14-, 28-, and 54-Day MA in Bull/Bear Markets

BUY SIGNALS

Total Number of Signals	% Signals Profitable	Average Trade $ +/-	Total Profit/Loss $ +/-
528	45.45	$966.95	$510,548.75

SELL SIGNALS

Total Number of Signals	% Signals Profitable	Average Trade $ +/-	Total Profit/Loss $ +/-
524	26.34	$233.58	$122,397.44

TOTAL SIGNALS

Total Number of Signals	% Signals Profitable	Average Trade $ +/-	Total Profit/Loss $ +/-
1052	35.93	$601.66	$632,946.25

Figure 4.80: Performance of 14-, 28-, and 54-Day MA in Bear/Bull Markets

BUY SIGNALS

Total Number of Signals	% Signals Profitable	Average Trade $ +/-	Total Profit/Loss $ +/-
507	29.59	$19.52	$9,895.07

SELL SIGNALS

Total Number of Signals	% Signals Profitable	Average Trade $ +/-	Total Profit/Loss $ +/-
520	46.35	$1,049.50	$545,738.87

TOTAL SIGNALS

Total Number of Signals	% Signals Profitable	Average Trade $ +/-	Total Profit/Loss $ +/-
1027	38.07	$541.03	$555,633.94

Figure 4.81: Performance of 14-, 28-, and 54-Day MA in Bull/Bear/Bull Markets

BUY SIGNALS

Total Number of Signals	% Signals Profitable	Average Trade $ +/-	Total Profit/Loss $ +/-
122	31.15	($11.03)	($1,345.79)

SELL SIGNALS

Total Number of Signals	% Signals Profitable	Average Trade $ +/-	Total Profit/Loss $ +/-
154	45.45	$1,297.96	$199,886.37

TOTAL SIGNALS

Total Number of Signals	% Signals Profitable	Average Trade $ +/-	Total Profit/Loss $ +/-
276	39.13	$719.35	$198,540.56

14-Day, 28-Day and 54-Day MA System in
Bear/Bull/Bear Markets

We would expect performance in this category also to yield positive results. In other words, if trend is the single most important consideration in system performance, then the bear/bull/bear category should yield profitable results. It did. The results are shown in Figure 4-82.

The 14-Day, 28-Day and 54-Day MA System in
Whipsaw Markets

Finally, the whipsaw market category should show overall losses if our expectations are correct. Once again, the results were verified by testing, as you can see in Figure 4-83. Clearly, this is the final and most important piece of evidence supporting the conclusion that trending markets are very important in the profitable performance of MA systems.

TEST RESULTS USING SYSTEM WRITER PLUS (SWP)

In order to validate the test results in a more global fashion, I tested the 14-day, 28-day, 54-day MA method on SWP. The test rules were as described earlier, and no optimization was used. In order to more realistically reflect actual market conditions and show the system's worst-case performance, we deducted $100 slippage and commission for each trade. Markets tested were live cattle, cocoa, pork bellies, copper, cotton, coffee, orange juice, platinum, silver, soybeans, soybean meal, sugar, wheat, Swiss Francs, gold, TBonds, Japanese Yen, heating oil, Eurodollar, S&P Index and Crude Oil. Even without optimization or filtering of trades the results were impressive. Figures 4-75 through 4-83 summarize the market-by-market performance of this method. As you can see, some markets were losers, but many markets were large winners. Furthermore, drawdown was rather large in some cases and there is some question as to whether an individual would have actually been able to trade this approach given the drawdown. Yet with some minor optimization and filtering, this method appears to have good potential. Overall test results for the 14-day, 28-day, 54-day MA method are shown in Figures 4-84 through 4-105.

Figure 4.82: Performance of 14-, 28-, and 54-Day MA in Bear/Bull/Bear Markets

BUY SIGNALS

Total Number of Signals	% Signals Profitable	Average Trade $ +/-	Total Profit/Loss $ +/-
144	38.89	$395.88	$57,006.37

SELL SIGNALS

Total Number of Signals	% Signals Profitable	Average Trade $ +/-	Total Profit/Loss $ +/-
116	39.66	$271.61	$31,506.51

TOTAL SIGNALS

Total Number of Signals	% Signals Profitable	Average Trade $ +/-	Total Profit/Loss $ +/-
260	39.23	$340.43	$88,512.88

Figure 4.83: Performance of 14-, 28-, and 54-Day MA in Whipsaw Markets

BUY SIGNALS

Total Number of Signals	% Signals Profitable	Average Trade $ +/-	Total Profit/Loss $ +/-
400	25.75	($363.39)	($145,356.12)

SELL SIGNALS

Total Number of Signals	% Signals Profitable	Average Trade $ +/-	Total Profit/Loss $ +/-
390	23.08	($502.40)	($195,934.44)

TOTAL SIGNALS

Total Number of Signals	% Signals Profitable	Average Trade $ +/-	Total Profit/Loss $ +/-
790	24.43	($432.01)	($341,290.56)

Figure 4.84: 14-, 28-, 54-MA: Live Cattle

```
Total net profit        $  12640.00    Open position P/L       $   5940.00
Gross profit            $  51944.00    Gross loss              $ -39304.00

Total # of trades             51       Percent profitable           41%
Number winning trades         21       Number losing trades         30

Largest winning trade   $   7372.00    Largest losing trade    $  -2972.00
Average winning trade   $   2473.52    Average losing trade    $  -1310.13
Ratio avg win/avg loss       1.89      Avg trade(win & loss)   $    247.84

Max consecutive winners       3        Max consecutive losers        4
Avg # bars in winners        104       Avg # bars in losers         41

Max intraday drawdown   $  -9688.00
Profit factor                1.32      Max # contracts held          1
Account size required   $  12688.00    Return on account          100%
```

Figure 4.85: 14-, 28-, 54-MA: Cocoa

```
Total net profit        $  -6499.00    Open position P/L       $    140.00
Gross profit            $   1821.00    Gross loss              $  -8320.00

Total # of trades             48       Percent profitable           21%
Number winning trades         10       Number losing trades         38

Largest winning trade   $    770.00    Largest losing trade    $   -426.00
Average winning trade   $    182.10    Average losing trade    $   -218.95
Ratio avg win/avg loss       0.83      Avg trade(win & loss)   $   -135.40

Max consecutive winners       2        Max consecutive losers       12
Avg # bars in winners        105       Avg # bars in losers         42

Max intraday drawdown   $  -7368.00
Profit factor                0.22      Max # contracts held          1
Account size required   $  10368.00    Return on account          -63%
```

Figure 4.86: 14-, 28-, 54-MA: Coffee

```
Total net profit       $ 405700.00    Open position P/L      $  14000.00
Gross profit           $ 787660.00    Gross loss             $-381960.00

Total # of trades             68      Percent profitable            44%
Number winning trades         30      Number losing trades          38

Largest winning trade  $ 153650.00    Largest losing trade   $ -35650.00
Average winning trade  $  26255.33    Average losing trade   $ -10051.58
Ratio avg win/avg loss       2.61     Avg trade(win & loss)  $   5966.18

Max consecutive winners        3      Max consecutive losers         6
Avg # bars in winners         97      Avg # bars in losers          34

Max intraday drawdown  $-107720.00
Profit factor                2.06     Max # contracts held           1
Account size required  $ 110720.00    Return on account           366%
```

Figure 4.87: 14-, 28-, 54-MA: Copper

```
Total net profit       $  25850.00    Open position P/L      $   1700.00
Gross profit           $  92362.50    Gross loss             $ -66512.50

Total # of trades             74      Percent profitable            30%
Number winning trades         22      Number losing trades          52

Largest winning trade  $  15862.50    Largest losing trade   $  -3925.00
Average winning trade  $   4198.30    Average losing trade   $  -1279.09
Ratio avg win/avg loss       3.28     Avg trade(win & loss)  $    349.32

Max consecutive winners        3      Max consecutive losers        10
Avg # bars in winners        115      Avg # bars in losers          33

Max intraday drawdown  $ -23662.50
Profit factor                1.39     Max # contracts held           1
Account size required  $  26662.50    Return on account            97%
```

Figure 4.88: 14-, 28-, 54-MA: Cotton

```
Total net profit          $    5664.00    Open position P/L         $     637.00
Gross profit              $   25379.00    Gross loss                $  -19715.00

Total # of trades                 76      Percent profitable               39%
Number winning trades             30      Number losing trades             46

Largest winning trade     $    4750.00    Largest losing trade      $   -1303.00
Average winning trade     $     845.97    Average losing trade      $    -428.59
Ratio avg win/avg loss           1.97     Avg trade(win & loss)     $      74.53

Max consecutive winners           4       Max consecutive losers            6
Avg # bars in winners           102       Avg # bars in losers             31

Max intraday drawdown     $   -5956.00
Profit factor                    1.29     Max # contracts held              1
Account size required     $    8956.00    Return on account                63%
```

Figure 4.89: 14-, 28-, 54-MA: NY Light Crude Oil

```
Total net profit          $   26740.00    Open position P/L         $    6210.00
Gross profit              $   49110.00    Gross loss                $  -22370.00

Total # of trades                 31      Percent profitable               52%
Number winning trades             16      Number losing trades             15

Largest winning trade     $   10350.00    Largest losing trade      $   -3710.00
Average winning trade     $    3069.38    Average losing trade      $   -1491.33
Ratio avg win/avg loss           2.06     Avg trade(win & loss)     $     862.58

Max consecutive winners           3       Max consecutive losers            4
Avg # bars in winners            93       Avg # bars in losers             25

Max intraday drawdown     $  -14180.00
Profit factor                    2.20     Max # contracts held              1
Account size required     $   14180.00    Return on account               189%
```

Figure 4.90: 14-, 28-, 54-MA: Eurodollar

```
Total net profit        $  12375.00    Open position P/L       $     350.00
Gross profit            $  40900.00    Gross loss              $ -28525.00

Total # of trades             32       Percent profitable             44%
Number winning trades         14       Number losing trades           18

Largest winning trade   $  16200.00    Largest losing trade    $  -6925.00
Average winning trade   $   2921.43    Average losing trade    $  -1584.72
Ratio avg win/avg loss         1.84    Avg trade(win & loss)   $    386.72

Max consecutive winners        3       Max consecutive losers          5
Avg # bars in winners        104       Avg # bars in losers           40

Max intraday drawdown   $ -11525.00
Profit factor                  1.43    Max # contracts held            1
Account size required   $  14525.00    Return on account             85%
```

Figure 4.91: 14-, 28-, 54-MA: COMEX Gold

```
Total net profit        $  47080.00    Open position P/L       $  -3080.00
Gross profit            $ 116270.00    Gross loss              $ -69190.00

Total # of trades             61       Percent profitable             39%
Number winning trades         24       Number losing trades           37

Largest winning trade   $  26450.00    Largest losing trade    $  -8170.00
Average winning trade   $   4844.58    Average losing trade    $  -1870.00
Ratio avg win/avg loss         2.59    Avg trade(win & loss)   $    771.80

Max consecutive winners        3       Max consecutive losers          8
Avg # bars in winners        109       Avg # bars in losers           36

Max intraday drawdown   $ -18130.00
Profit factor                  1.68    Max # contracts held            1
Account size required   $  21130.00    Return on account            223%
```

Figure 4.92: 14-, 28-, 54-MA: NY Heating Oil

```
Total net profit         $   9720.21   Open position P/L      $   6245.40
Gross profit             $  57367.00   Gross loss             $ -47646.79

Total # of trades               49     Percent profitable           41%
Number winning trades           20     Number losing trades         29

Largest winning trade    $   9761.60   Largest losing trade   $  -9886.00
Average winning trade    $   2868.35   Average losing trade   $  -1642.99
Ratio avg win/avg loss          1.75   Avg trade(win & loss)  $    198.37

Max consecutive winners          4     Max consecutive losers        4
Avg # bars in winners            86    Avg # bars in losers         40

Max intraday drawdown    $ -13204.00
Profit factor                   1.20   Max # contracts held          1
Account size required    $  16204.00   Return on account            60%
```

Figure 4.93: 14-, 28-, 54-MA: Japanese Yen

```
Total net profit         $  44412.50   Open position P/L      $  -1325.00
Gross profit             $ 106225.00   Gross loss             $ -61812.50

Total # of trades               47     Percent profitable           47%
Number winning trades           22     Number losing trades         25

Largest winning trade    $  21437.50   Largest losing trade   $  -5775.00
Average winning trade    $   4828.41   Average losing trade   $  -2472.50
Ratio avg win/avg loss          1.95   Avg trade(win & loss)  $    944.95

Max consecutive winners          3     Max consecutive losers        6
Avg # bars in winners           118    Avg # bars in losers         36

Max intraday drawdown    $ -19625.00
Profit factor                   1.72   Max # contracts held          1
Account size required    $  22625.00   Return on account           196%
```

Figure 4.94: 14-, 28-, 54-MA: Lumber

```
Total net profit         $   -4115.20    Open position P/L        $     566.80
Gross profit             $    6115.80    Gross loss               $  -10231.00

Total # of trades                71      Percent profitable              27%
Number winning trades            19      Number losing trades            52

Largest winning trade    $     867.20    Largest losing trade     $    -527.70
Average winning trade    $     321.88    Average losing trade     $    -196.75
Ratio avg win/avg loss          1.64     Avg trade(win & loss)    $     -57.96

Max consecutive winners          4       Max consecutive losers          16
Avg # bars in winners          113       Avg # bars in losers            43

Max intraday drawdown    $   -4115.20
Profit factor                   0.60     Max # contracts held             1
Account size required    $    4115.20    Return on account             -100%
```

Figure 4.95: 14-, 28-, 54-MA: Orange Juice

```
Total net profit         $    4525.00    Open position P/L        $    -940.00
Gross profit             $   41235.00    Gross loss               $  -36710.00

Total # of trades                74      Percent profitable              39%
Number winning trades            29      Number losing trades            45

Largest winning trade    $    7555.00    Largest losing trade     $   -3030.00
Average winning trade    $    1421.90    Average losing trade     $    -815.78
Ratio avg win/avg loss          1.74     Avg trade(win & loss)    $      61.15

Max consecutive winners          4       Max consecutive losers           8
Avg # bars in winners          100       Avg # bars in losers            37

Max intraday drawdown    $  -17580.00
Profit factor                   1.12     Max # contracts held             1
Account size required    $   20580.00    Return on account              22%
```

Figure 4.96: 14-, 28-, 54-MA: Platinum

```
Total net profit        $  26450.00   Open position P/L       $   4220.00
Gross profit            $  82345.00   Gross loss              $ -55895.00

Total # of trades             70      Percent profitable            34%
Number winning trades         24      Number losing trades          46

Largest winning trade   $   9920.00   Largest losing trade    $  -4110.00
Average winning trade   $   3431.04   Average losing trade    $  -1215.11
Ratio avg win/avg loss        2.82    Avg trade(win & loss)   $    377.86

Max consecutive winners        3      Max consecutive losers         7
Avg # bars in winners        119      Avg # bars in losers          35

Max intraday drawdown   $ -15085.00
Profit factor                 1.47    Max # contracts held           1
Account size required   $  18085.00   Return on account           146%
```

Figure 4.97: 14-, 28-, 54-MA: Pork Bellies

```
Total net profit        $   5988.00   Open position P/L       $  -1520.00
Gross profit            $ 112624.00   Gross loss              $-106636.00

Total # of trades             90      Percent profitable            39%
Number winning trades         35      Number losing trades          55

Largest winning trade   $  12020.00   Largest losing trade    $  -7020.00
Average winning trade   $   3217.83   Average losing trade    $  -1938.84
Ratio avg win/avg loss        1.66    Avg trade(win & loss)   $     66.53

Max consecutive winners        3      Max consecutive losers        10
Avg # bars in winners         99      Avg # bars in losers          36

Max intraday drawdown   $ -33420.00
Profit factor                 1.06    Max # contracts held           1
Account size required   $  36420.00   Return on account            16%
```

Figure 4.98: 14-, 28-, 54-MA: S&P Index

```
Total net profit        $  44175.00    Open position P/L       $  11275.00
Gross profit            $ 165500.00    Gross loss              $-121325.00

Total # of trades             36       Percent profitable           28%
Number winning trades         10       Number losing trades         26

Largest winning trade   $  42875.00    Largest losing trade    $ -11450.00
Average winning trade   $  16550.00    Average losing trade    $  -4666.35
Ratio avg win/avg loss        3.55     Avg trade(win & loss)   $   1227.08

Max consecutive winners        3       Max consecutive losers         6
Avg # bars in winners        121       Avg # bars in losers          34

Max intraday drawdown   $ -39925.00
Profit factor                 1.36     Max # contracts held           1
Account size required   $  39925.00    Return on account           111%
```

Figure 4.99: 14-, 28-, 54-MA: COMEX Silver

```
Total net profit        $ 201180.00    Open position P/L       $   6160.00
Gross profit            $ 333115.00    Gross loss              $-131935.00

Total # of trades             74       Percent profitable           42%
Number winning trades         31       Number losing trades         43

Largest winning trade   $  98340.00    Largest losing trade    $ -24300.00
Average winning trade   $  10745.65    Average losing trade    $  -3068.26
Ratio avg win/avg loss        3.50     Avg trade(win & loss)   $   2718.65

Max consecutive winners        3       Max consecutive losers         6
Avg # bars in winners        110       Avg # bars in losers          31

Max intraday drawdown   $ -43700.00
Profit factor                 2.52     Max # contracts held           1
Account size required   $  46700.00    Return on account           431%
```

Figure 4.100: 14-, 28-, 54-MA: Soybeans

```
Total net profit      $    3906.00   Open position P/L     $     640.00
Gross profit          $   22770.00   Gross loss            $  -18864.00

Total # of trades            88      Percent profitable          41%
Number winning trades        36      Number losing trades        52

Largest winning trade $    4120.00   Largest losing trade  $   -1592.00
Average winning trade $     632.50   Average losing trade  $    -362.77
Ratio avg win/avg loss       1.74    Avg trade(win & loss) $      44.39

Max consecutive winners       5      Max consecutive losers        5
Avg # bars in winners        98      Avg # bars in losers         37

Max intraday drawdown $   -3412.00
Profit factor                1.21    Max # contracts held          1
Account size required $    6412.00   Return on account           61%
```

Figure 4.101: 14-, 28-, 54-MA: Soybean Meal

```
Total net profit      $  498900.00   Open position P/L     $   22400.00
Gross profit          $ 1125200.00   Gross loss            $ -626300.00

Total # of trades            89      Percent profitable          42%
Number winning trades        37      Number losing trades        52

Largest winning trade $  148400.00   Largest losing trade  $  -61100.00
Average winning trade $   30410.81   Average losing trade  $  -12044.23
Ratio avg win/avg loss       2.52    Avg trade(win & loss) $    5605.62

Max consecutive winners       4      Max consecutive losers        4
Avg # bars in winners        97      Avg # bars in losers         35

Max intraday drawdown $ -125600.00
Profit factor                1.80    Max # contracts held          1
Account size required $  128600.00   Return on account          388%
```

Figure 4.102: 14-, 28-, 54-MA: Sugar

```
Total net profit        $    3429.00   Open position P/L       $     531.00
Gross profit            $   11580.00   Gross loss              $   -8151.00

Total # of trades              61      Percent profitable            25%
Number winning trades          15      Number losing trades          46

Largest winning trade   $    4084.00   Largest losing trade    $   -1079.00
Average winning trade   $     772.00   Average losing trade    $    -177.20
Ratio avg win/avg loss         4.36    Avg trade(win & loss)   $      56.21

Max consecutive winners         2      Max consecutive losers        10
Avg # bars in winners         153      Avg # bars in losers          50

Max intraday drawdown   $   -2801.00
Profit factor                  1.42    Max # contracts held           1
Account size required   $    5801.00   Return on account             59%
```

Figure 4.103: 14-, 28-, 54-MA: Swiss Franc

```
Total net profit        $   73525.00   Open position P/L       $   -3687.50
Gross profit            $  131062.50   Gross loss              $  -57537.50

Total # of trades              47      Percent profitable            47%
Number winning trades          22      Number losing trades          25

Largest winning trade   $   17625.00   Largest losing trade    $   -5725.00
Average winning trade   $    5957.39   Average losing trade    $   -2301.50
Ratio avg win/avg loss         2.59    Avg trade(win & loss)   $    1564.36

Max consecutive winners         5      Max consecutive losers         5
Avg # bars in winners         137      Avg # bars in losers          36

Max intraday drawdown   $  -17837.50
Profit factor                  2.28    Max # contracts held           1
Account size required   $   20837.50   Return on account            353%
```

Figure 4.104: 14-, 28-, 54-MA: T-Bonds

```
Total net profit        $   -4248.00   Open position P/L       $     172.00
Gross profit            $    1819.00   Gross loss              $   -6067.00

Total # of trades                53    Percent profitable              19%
Number winning trades            10    Number losing trades            43

Largest winning trade   $     695.00   Largest losing trade    $    -297.00
Average winning trade   $     181.90   Average losing trade    $    -141.09
Ratio avg win/avg loss         1.29    Avg trade(win & loss)   $     -80.15

Max consecutive winners           2    Max consecutive losers          15
Avg # bars in winners           106    Avg # bars in losers            51

Max intraday drawdown   $   -4282.00
Profit factor                  0.30    Max # contracts held             1
Account size required   $    7282.00   Return on account             -58%
```

Figure 4.105: 14-, 28-, 54-MA: CBT Wheat

```
Total net profit        $   -8128.00   Open position P/L       $     844.00
Gross profit            $    7368.00   Gross loss              $  -15496.00

Total # of trades                90    Percent profitable              23%
Number winning trades            21    Number losing trades            69

Largest winning trade   $    1882.00   Largest losing trade    $    -720.00
Average winning trade   $     350.86   Average losing trade    $    -224.58
Ratio avg win/avg loss         1.56    Avg trade(win & loss)   $     -90.31

Max consecutive winners           3    Max consecutive losers          14
Avg # bars in winners           106    Avg # bars in losers            44

Max intraday drawdown   $   -8854.00
Profit factor                  0.48    Max # contracts held             1
Account size required   $   11854.00   Return on account             -69%
```

RESULTS OF TRIPLE MOVING-AVERAGE STUDIES

My tests of the triple MA approach lead to the following conclusions:

1. The triple MA approach is an effective method which has yielded profitable results in back-testing.

2. The importance of trend was verified as a significant factor in the profitable performance of triple MA systems.

3. The systems did well in bull markets, bear markets, choppy bull and bear markets and markets which made transitions from bullish to bearish or from bearish to bullish. The systems also performed well in markets which had three distinct bullish or bearish patterns.

4. Clearly, the importance of avoiding "whipsaw" markets was verified, however, it was also demonstrated that trend changes and choppy trending markets did not pose serious drawbacks to the overall performance of triple MA systems.

5. The expectation that buy signals would perform best in bull markets and sell signals best in bear markets was also verified. This suggests that a method or methods for filtering signals by market category could yield very positive results. In other words, a technique for following buy signals in bull market only and sell signals in bear markets only should be investigated.

6. Accordingly, it behooves the trader to develop, formulate, test and apply a method or methods to filter out "whipsaw" markets. Whether this can actually be achieved is still debatable.
yet be answered.

7. Traders should seriously consider their method(s) for dealing with contract switches. Simply closing out a trade when a contract is near expiration or prior to the first delivery notice day and not reinstating a position may significantly diminish performance. A good technique might be to roll into the next active contract month upon liquidation of the current position until an signal opposite from the current one is generated.

5

Day-of-Week Studies

Some traders feel that certain days of the week are more important than others. For many years I have heard traders claim that Tuesdays are important days for price reversals; that a strong close on Friday often brings an up-move the coming Monday; that a weak close on Friday brings a lower market on the coming Monday; and so on. In addition, many traders feel that certain closing price patterns are important—for example, they assert that four days of higher closes in succession tend to be followed by a lower close on the fifth day. As romantic as these ideas may seem, and as reliable as they may be over the short run, I have often asked myself if they can pass the test of time when subjected to lengthy historical examination. This chapter evaluates a number of different approaches to such patterns.

PRE-HOLIDAY BEHAVIOR

In my 1989 book, *Seasonal Concepts in Futures Trading*, I noted that :

> *price behavior prior to important holidays, and fundamental events such as discount rate cuts, elections, etc. Merrill clearly showed that prices for the Dow Jones Industrial Average had some very definite tendencies before*

*and after legal and religious holidays. Figure 5-1 shows
some of the relationships he discovered using statistics
spanning the period from January 1897 through December 1983. You can see that Merrill used a lengthy data
sample in order to validate his theory to a large sample.*

Such "daily" seasonality is not unique to commodity
prices. In fact, Arthur A. Merrill, is his classic book *The
Behavior of Prices on Wall Street,* gave many examples of
price behavior prior to important holidays, events and so
forth. I have already quoted from the work of Art Merrill,
who clearly showed that prices for the Dow Jones Industrial
Average had some very definite tendencies before and after
legal and religious holidays. Figure 5-1 shows some of the
relationships he discovered using statistics spanning the
period from January 1897 through December 1983. You
can see that Merrill used a lengthy data sample in order to
subject his theory to a valid test.

Note that the abbreviation HS stands for highly significant, PS for probably significant and S for significant.
These abbreviations are associated with different levels of
statistical confidence or reliability. The HS or highly significant readings are those which have a one in a thousand
times probability of being a chance event. In other words,
these are particularly significant results!

It is quite clear to me from Merrill's studies that pre-holiday
behavior is a statistically valid phenomenon in the Dow Jones Industrial Average. While it may not be strictly valid to extrapolate
from these findings and conclude that futures prices also show
statistically reliable pre-holiday behavior, my studies suggest that
there is compelling initial evidence that such patterns indeed do
exist. The present chapter will examine a variety of patterns related
to either date or day of week.

I must point out at the outset that there is considerably less
futures data at our disposal than there is stock market data. Most
contemporary market analyses track ten to fifteen years' worth of
data. In other words, they study the performance of their parameters

Figure 5.1: Holiday Behavior

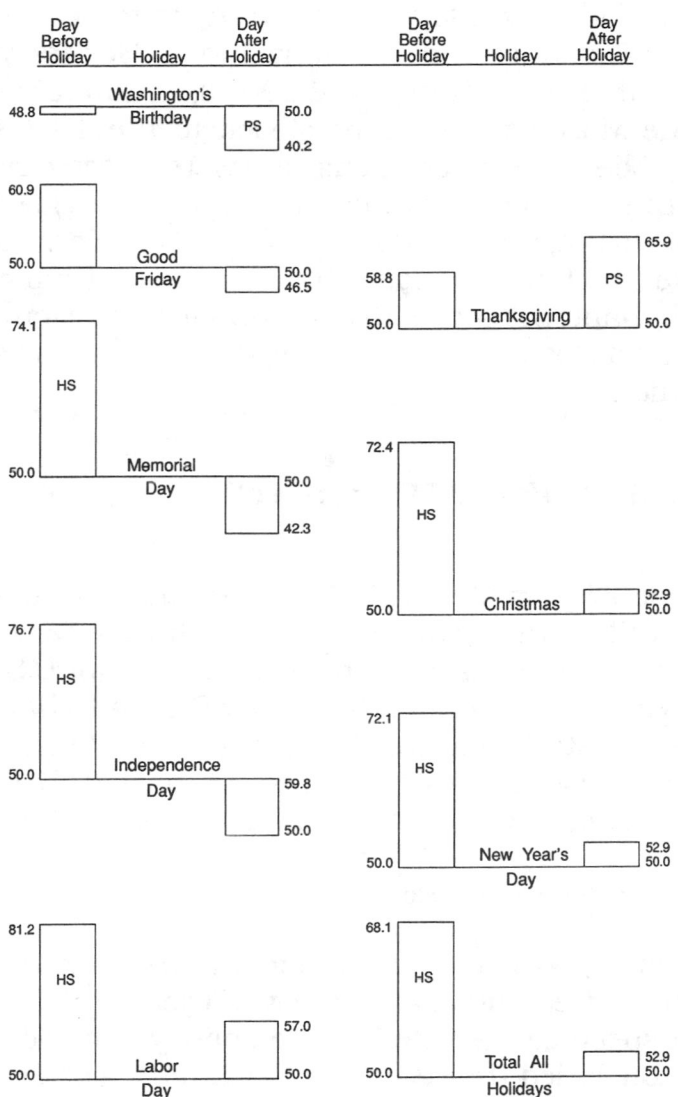

Jan. 1897- Dec. 1983
(Percent of Years in Which the D-J Industrials
Posted an Increase for the Day - -)

197

over the period from roughly the mid-to early-1970 s through to the present. As you know, I have attempted to include as much data as possible in my studies. While futures contracts traded at the Chicago Mercantile Exchange and the International Monetary Mart are tracked back to their inception in the 1960 s, a number of Chicago Board of Trade Markets are studied back to the 1920 s (with a hiatus during the 1940 s when exchanges were closed due to World War II). While this is still not as much data history as a good statistician would like to see, I feel that it is sufficient to allow us to reach some tentative conclusions about the patterns and indicators examined in this chapter. A good starting point for this excursion is to study daily market closing tendencies by date, in a fashion similar to Merrill's technique.

DAILY MARKET PROBABILITY STUDIES

As I noted previously, Art Merrill, in *The Behavior of Prices on Wall Street*,[1] statistically demonstrated a tendency for the Dow Jones Industrial Average to close higher on days prior to major U.S. holidays such as New Years Day, Veterans Day, Labor Day and Thanksgiving. In some cases the statistical reliability of this tendency indicated that such an event could occur by chance only once in 10,000 times. This clearly validated the pre-holiday behavior of stock averages.

[2]Analysis Press, Chappaqua NY, 1980.

My research supports the conclusion that there are similar patterns in futures prices and that, moreover, there are also patterns which are not specifically related to pre-holiday behavior. In other words, I have concluded that there are certain days of the calendar year as well as certain strings of days (that is, several days in succession) which have in the past shown a tendency for up or down closings a majority of the time. *Although these findings are restricted to the length of my data history, their persistence suggests the presence of reliable calendar day tendencies.* Such tendencies are, to a certain extent, manifestations of seasonal price behavior.

We know that seasonality is an important variable in all data series, particularly those related to economic phenomena. Economists and statisticians regularly filter out seasonal factors in order to obtain what they feel is a more reliable and valid indication of secular trends. This is, indeed, a valid procedure in the search for long-term trend and cyclical patterns. Yet, as I have demonstrated in my previous studies, seasonal price behavior can be a valuable tool for futures traders as well as investors. The knowledge that prices in certain markets move in certain directions at given times of the year can be used as an adjunct to trading systems, or in combination with timing indicators, as a trading system unto itself.[3]

[3]I have already published the following studies and/or texts which demonstrate the existence and evaluate the reliability of seasonal patterns in cash, futures and futures spreads: *Seasonal Cash Charts* (1977-1990 Editions) and *Seasonal Futures Charts* (1977-1990 Editions); both available from MBH, P.O. Box 353, Winnetka, IL, 60093. *Seasonal Concepts in Futures Trading* (New York, John Wiley & Sons).

In order to determine whether there are significant calendar date patterns in closing futures prices, I developed my Daily Market Probability Studies, which examined closing price tendencies on a daily basis and provided data as follows for each market analyzed:

1. Percent of time prices have closed up or down for each calendar day.

2. Ranking of percent reliability for each day.

3. Average percent size of up or down move for each day.

4. Suggestions for using the above statistics.

The daily market probability statistics which are shown in this chapter provide the information in items 1-3 listed above. Each market and contract month has a separate listing which begins approximately six months prior to contract expiration and ends at approximately contract expiration. Due to limitations of space I have not been able to provide listings for all contract months of all markets; however, those I have provided will give you a good idea of what my daily market probability studies have shown.

EXPLANATION OF PRINTOUTS/PRECAUTIONS
AND LIMITATIONS

Figure 5-2 explains the data listed on each of the daily market probability study printouts. Please review the following additional ex-
planatory notes:

1. Percent of time up or down readings are based on the
amount of data analyzed for each of the printouts. The data lengths
are as follows:

a) grains, soybean complex, meats, cotton, silver and copper,
early to mid-1960 s through 1988;

b) all others from start of futures trading through 1988.

2. Note that for markets such as S&P and TBonds the number
of years of data history is limited and, as a consequence, percent
readings are not as reliable as they might be for markets which have
longer histories. Remember this when you use the daily market
probability statistics in your trading program(s).

3. *These figures do not constitute a trading system.* They are
merely historical listings which may or may not be of assistance in
your own trading program or analytical methodology.

4. Stop losses should be used regardless of how high a given
percent reading may be. Risk management is an integral aspect of
successful futures trading.

5. The "+" and "−" signs in the far left column are inter-
preted as:

a) + = up close 60-70 percent of the time;

b) ++ = up close 71-79 percent of the time;

c) +++ = up close 80 percent of the time or more;

d) − = down close 60-70 percent of the time;

e) −− = down close 71-79 percent of the time;

f) −−− = down close 80 percent of the time or more.

Figure 5.2: Daily Market Probability Statistics

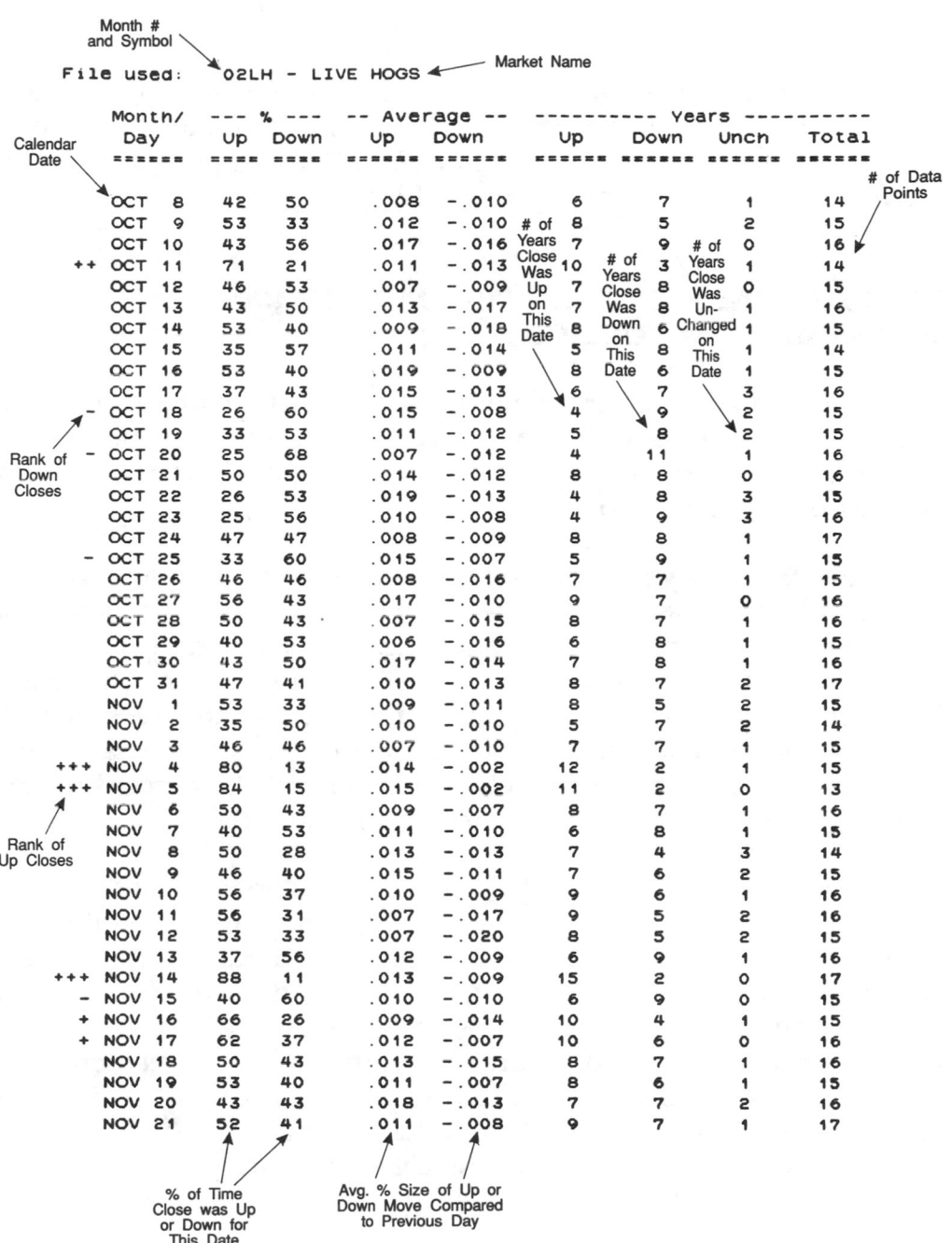

Month #
and Symbol

File used: 02LH - LIVE HOGS ◄─── Market Name

Calendar Date	Month/ Day	--- % --- Up	Down	-- Average -- Up	Down	---------- Years ---------- Up	Down	Unch	Total
	OCT 8	42	50	.008	-.010	6	7	1	14
	OCT 9	53	33	.012	-.010	8	5	2	15
	OCT 10	43	56	.017	-.016	7	9	0	16
++	OCT 11	71	21	.011	-.013	10	3	1	14
	OCT 12	46	53	.007	-.009	7	8	0	15
	OCT 13	43	50	.013	-.017	7	8	1	16
	OCT 14	53	40	.009	-.018	8	6	1	15
	OCT 15	35	57	.011	-.014	5	8	1	14
	OCT 16	53	40	.019	-.009	8	6	1	15
	OCT 17	37	43	.015	-.013	6	7	3	16
-	OCT 18	26	60	.015	-.008	4	9	2	15
-	OCT 19	33	53	.011	-.012	5	8	2	15
-	OCT 20	25	68	.007	-.012	4	11	1	16
	OCT 21	50	50	.014	-.012	8	8	0	16
	OCT 22	26	53	.019	-.013	4	8	3	15
	OCT 23	25	56	.010	-.008	4	9	3	16
	OCT 24	47	47	.008	-.009	8	8	1	17
-	OCT 25	33	60	.015	-.007	5	9	1	15
	OCT 26	46	46	.008	-.016	7	7	1	15
	OCT 27	56	43	.017	-.010	9	7	0	16
	OCT 28	50	43	.007	-.015	8	7	1	16
	OCT 29	40	53	.006	-.016	6	8	1	15
	OCT 30	43	50	.017	-.014	7	8	1	16
	OCT 31	47	41	.010	-.013	8	7	2	17
	NOV 1	53	33	.009	-.011	8	5	2	15
	NOV 2	35	50	.010	-.010	5	7	2	14
	NOV 3	46	46	.007	-.010	7	7	1	15
+++	NOV 4	80	13	.014	-.002	12	2	1	15
+++	NOV 5	84	15	.015	-.002	11	2	0	13
	NOV 6	50	43	.009	-.007	8	7	1	16
	NOV 7	40	53	.011	-.010	6	8	1	15
	NOV 8	50	28	.013	-.013	7	4	3	14
	NOV 9	46	40	.015	-.011	7	6	2	15
	NOV 10	56	37	.010	-.009	9	6	1	16
	NOV 11	56	31	.007	-.017	9	5	2	16
	NOV 12	53	33	.007	-.020	8	5	2	15
	NOV 13	37	56	.012	-.009	6	9	1	16
+++	NOV 14	88	11	.013	-.009	15	2	0	17
-	NOV 15	40	60	.010	-.010	6	9	0	15
+	NOV 16	66	26	.009	-.014	10	4	1	15
+	NOV 17	62	37	.012	-.007	10	6	0	16
	NOV 18	50	43	.013	-.015	8	7	1	16
	NOV 19	53	40	.011	-.007	8	6	1	15
	NOV 20	43	43	.018	-.013	7	7	2	16
	NOV 21	52	41	.011	-.008	9	7	1	17

# of Data
Points

# of Years Close Was Up on This Date

# of Years Close Was Down on This Date

# of Years Close Was Un-Changed on This Date

Rank of Down Closes

Rank of Up Closes

% of Time Close was Up or Down for This Date

Avg. % Size of Up or Down Move Compared to Previous Day

Figures 5-3 through 5-10 show listings for various markets. Please refer to the above explanations for instructions regarding their interpretation and application. Additional suggestions for application of such data are provided below.

SUGGESTIONS FOR USING THE DAILY MARKET PROBABILITY STATISTICS

If you feel, as I do, that daily market probabilities constitute a valid approach to the isolation of repetitive patterns in the futures market, then consider the following ways in which they may be used as part of a trading program.

As a filter to your trading signals. Assume that your trading system has signalled a short sale. When you examine the daily listings for the given market you notice that the next three trading days have shown a high percent of time closing up for the day. This might lead you to filter the short signal. You might wait for the system to give a second sell signal before taking action. As an alternative, you might pass on the trade entirely, particularly if the percent of time readings are very high (i.e., 80 percent or higher).

As a confirming indicator to your trading signals. An adaptation of application #1 is to use the daily percent readings as a confirming indicator with your trading signals. Simply stated, this means that when your signals are to go long and when they are in agreement with strong percent of time up readings, then you will go long. When your signals are to go short, and when they are in agreement with strong percent of time down readings, you will go short. Finally, if there are no strong percent up or down readings, you will either take no action or you will trade exclusively with your signals.

Figure 5.3: Daily Market Probability Statistics

File used: 07S   - SOYBEANS

	Month/ Day	Up	Down	Up	Down	Up	Down	Unch	Total
		--- % ---		-- Average --		---------- Years ----------			
+	FEB 1	68	31	.066	-.028	11	5	0	16
	FEB 2	58	41	.098	-.057	10	7	0	17
	FEB 3	52	47	.099	-.081	9	8	0	17
	FEB 4	47	47	.065	-.082	8	8	0	17
	FEB 5	41	58	.087	-.057	7	10	0	17
	FEB 6	43	50	.093	-.051	7	8	1	16
	FEB 7	46	46	.107	-.041	7	7	1	15
-	FEB 8	37	62	.090	-.077	6	10	0	16
-	FEB 9	29	64	.095	-.076	5	11	1	17
	FEB 10	47	47	.062	-.074	8	8	1	17
	FEB 11	58	35	.063	-.060	10	6	1	17
-	FEB 12	40	60	.075	-.139	6	9	0	15
	FEB 13	50	50	.085	-.086	8	8	0	16
	FEB 14	53	46	.116	-.059	8	7	0	15
	FEB 15	46	53	.095	-.072	6	7	0	13
	FEB 16	57	35	.057	-.073	8	5	1	14
+++	FEB 17	80	20	.083	-.040	12	3	0	15
	FEB 18	42	57	.071	-.086	6	8	0	14
	FEB 19	46	53	.071	-.091	7	8	0	15
+	FEB 20	64	28	.075	-.110	9	4	1	14
-	FEB 21	27	63	.112	-.054	3	7	1	11
-	FEB 22	30	69	.150	-.076	4	9	0	13
	FEB 23	43	43	.136	-.058	7	7	2	16
	FEB 24	47	52	.042	-.070	8	9	0	17
	FEB 25	41	52	.092	-.097	7	9	1	17
-	FEB 26	35	64	.093	-.088	6	11	0	17
	FEB 27	50	50	.053	-.103	8	8	0	16
-	FEB 28	40	60	.054	-.134	6	9	0	15
+	FEB 29	60	40	.131	-.028	3	2	0	5
+	MAR 1	68	25	.126	-.040	11	4	1	16
+	MAR 2	62	37	.084	-.146	10	6	0	16
+	MAR 3	64	29	.090	-.080	11	5	1	17
	MAR 4	41	58	.056	-.078	7	10	0	17
	MAR 5	52	41	.092	-.066	9	7	1	17
++	MAR 6	75	25	.106	-.049	12	4	0	16
	MAR 7	50	43	.092	-.067	8	7	1	16
	MAR 8	43	56	.108	-.118	7	9	0	16

Figure 5.3:   *(Continued)*

File used: 07S - SOYBEANS

Month/Day	--- % --- Up	Down	-- Average -- Up	Down	---------- Years ---------- Up	Down	Unch	Total
++ MAR 9	70	29	.072	-.087	12	5	0	17
- MAR 10	33	61	.032	-.104	6	11	1	18
MAR 11	50	44	.089	-.044	9	8	1	18
MAR 12	58	35	.086	-.121	10	6	1	17
MAR 13	43	50	.104	-.111	7	8	1	16
MAR 14	52	41	.074	-.111	9	7	1	17
MAR 15	52	47	.097	-.090	9	8	0	17
MAR 16	47	47	.072	-.094	8	8	1	17
++ MAR 17	77	22	.127	-.090	14	4	0	18
+ MAR 18	61	38	.076	-.111	11	7	0	18
MAR 19	58	41	.067	-.063	10	7	0	17
- MAR 20	31	68	.082	-.087	5	11	0	16
MAR 21	47	52	.125	-.055	8	9	0	17
MAR 22	41	58	.072	-.037	7	10	0	17
MAR 23	41	52	.144	-.062	7	9	1	17
MAR 24	56	43	.081	-.038	9	7	0	16
MAR 25	38	55	.071	-.075	7	10	1	18
MAR 26	47	52	.084	-.073	8	9	0	17
- MAR 27	40	60	.101	-.115	6	9	0	15
MAR 28	53	46	.063	-.069	8	7	0	15
- MAR 29	35	64	.077	-.098	6	11	0	17
MAR 30	41	52	.066	-.100	7	9	1	17
++ MAR 31	75	25	.105	-.090	12	4	0	16
APR 1	50	50	.101	-.105	8	8	0	16
APR 2	41	58	.121	-.098	7	10	0	17
APR 3	37	56	.106	-.151	6	9	1	16
+ APR 4	66	26	.131	-.121	10	4	1	15
+ APR 5	68	31	.092	-.152	11	5	0	16
APR 6	58	35	.084	-.073	10	6	1	17
+ APR 7	66	33	.105	-.073	12	6	0	18
++ APR 8	75	18	.070	-.122	12	3	1	16
APR 9	57	42	.133	-.069	8	6	0	14
APR 10	37	56	.034	-.129	6	9	1	16
++ APR 11	70	29	.059	-.095	12	5	0	17
- APR 12	40	60	.188	-.089	6	9	0	15
APR 13	50	43	.065	-.130	8	7	1	16
APR 14	44	50	.079	-.078	8	9	1	18
+ APR 15	61	38	.100	-.095	11	7	0	18
APR 16	53	40	.066	-.059	8	6	1	15
APR 17	50	50	.048	-.074	7	7	0	14
APR 18	58	41	.079	-.088	10	7	0	17
+ APR 19	64	29	.065	-.061	11	5	1	17
+ APR 20	66	26	.066	-.120	10	4	1	15
APR 21	33	55	.096	-.049	6	10	2	18
APR 22	44	50	.083	-.073	8	9	1	18

204

Figure 5.3: *(Continued)*

File used: 07S   - SOYBEANS

	Month/ Day	--- % --- Up	 Down	-- Average -- Up	 Down	---------- Years ---------- Up	 Down	 Unch	 Total
	APR 23	41	58	.087	-.092	7	10	0	17
	APR 24	50	43	.086	-.070	8	7	1	16
	APR 25	52	41	.132	-.067	9	7	1	17
--	APR 26	29	70	.159	-.118	5	12	0	17
--	APR 27	29	70	.113	-.106	5	12	0	17
++	APR 28	72	22	.051	-.212	13	4	1	18
	APR 29	44	55	.155	-.083	8	10	0	18
	APR 30	52	47	.117	-.072	9	8	0	17
	MAY 1	37	56	.072	-.075	6	9	1	16
	MAY 2	43	43	.139	-.068	7	7	2	16
-	MAY 3	35	64	.131	-.059	6	11	0	17
	MAY 4	58	29	.054	-.145	10	5	2	17
	MAY 5	55	44	.090	-.111	10	8	0	18
-	MAY 6	33	61	.066	-.106	6	11	1	18
	MAY 7	47	47	.119	-.074	8	8	1	17
++	MAY 8	75	25	.092	-.087	12	4	0	16
+++	MAY 9	82	17	.082	-.104	14	3	0	17
++	MAY 10	76	23	.085	-.089	13	4	0	17
+	MAY 11	64	35	.100	-.140	11	6	0	17
	MAY 12	38	55	.079	-.100	7	10	1	18
+	MAY 13	66	33	.099	-.068	12	6	0	18
+	MAY 14	64	35	.100	-.046	11	6	0	17
	MAY 15	43	56	.091	-.076	7	9	0	16
	MAY 16	47	41	.138	-.054	8	7	2	17
-	MAY 17	35	64	.069	-.096	6	11	0	17
	MAY 18	58	41	.110	-.105	10	7	0	17
	MAY 19	55	44	.050	-.085	10	8	0	18
+	MAY 20	61	38	.080	-.109	11	7	0	18
	MAY 21	52	47	.117	-.077	9	8	0	17
	MAY 22	50	50	.059	-.045	8	8	0	16
+	MAY 23	64	35	.078	-.119	11	6	0	17
	MAY 24	41	58	.219	-.063	7	10	0	17
	MAY 25	53	46	.142	-.113	8	7	0	15
-	MAY 26	40	60	.091	-.073	6	9	0	15
+	MAY 27	62	37	.089	-.141	10	6	0	16
--	MAY 28	28	71	.022	-.069	4	10	0	14
	MAY 29	38	53	.163	-.070	5	7	1	13
-	MAY 30	40	60	.156	-.067	4	6	0	10
+	MAY 31	61	38	.167	-.108	8	5	0	13
	JUN 1	58	41	.137	-.110	10	7	0	17
	JUN 2	38	55	.081	-.145	7	10	1	18
	JUN 3	55	38	.105	-.114	10	7	1	18
+	JUN 4	64	35	.120	-.055	11	6	0	17
+	JUN 5	62	37	.063	-.080	10	6	0	16
	JUN 6	47	52	.122	-.153	8	9	0	17

205

Figure 5.3: *(Concluded)*

File used: 07S   - SOYBEANS

Month/Day	--- % --- Up	Down	-- Average -- Up	Down	---------- Years ---------- Up	Down	Unch	Total
JUN 7	58	41	.118	-.264	10	7	0	17
JUN 8	47	52	.144	-.150	8	9	0	17
JUN 9	55	38	.103	-.099	10	7	1	18
JUN 10	44	55	.111	-.072	8	10	0	18
+ JUN 11	64	35	.216	-.062	11	6	0	17
- JUN 12	31	68	.120	-.045	5	11	0	16
JUN 13	47	47	.069	-.107	8	8	1	17
- JUN 14	35	64	.124	-.218	6	11	0	17
JUN 15	58	41	.197	-.112	10	7	0	17
JUN 16	52	47	.093	-.090	9	8	0	17
-- JUN 17	17	70	.158	-.124	3	12	2	17
JUN 18	58	41	.143	-.124	10	7	0	17
JUN 19	50	50	.082	-.078	8	8	0	16
+ JUN 20	62	37	.138	-.062	10	6	0	16
+ JUN 21	66	33	.149	-.148	10	5	0	15
+ JUN 22	62	37	.130	-.232	10	6	0	16
JUN 23	41	58	.181	-.076	7	10	0	17
JUN 24	47	52	.146	-.061	8	9	0	17
JUN 25	41	52	.092	-.144	7	9	1	17
JUN 26	37	56	.097	-.165	6	9	1	16
- JUN 27	37	62	.139	-.141	6	10	0	16
- JUN 28	33	60	.058	-.101	5	9	1	15
- JUN 29	37	62	.130	-.207	6	10	0	16
+ JUN 30	64	35	.107	-.117	11	6	0	17
JUL 1	52	47	.144	-.120	9	8	0	17
++ JUL 2	70	29	.137	-.218	12	5	0	17
+ JUL 3	61	23	.147	-.434	8	3	2	13
+ JUL 5	66	33	.145	-.451	8	4	0	12
- JUL 6	37	62	.190	-.219	6	10	0	16
JUL 7	35	47	.097	-.171	6	8	3	17
JUL 8	52	47	.207	-.124	9	8	0	17
JUL 9	58	41	.099	-.122	10	7	0	17
JUL 10	50	50	.199	-.125	8	8	0	16
JUL 11	43	56	.223	-.113	7	9	0	16
+ JUL 12	62	37	.203	-.182	10	6	0	16
JUL 13	56	43	.286	-.106	9	7	0	16
JUL 14	52	41	.173	-.187	9	7	1	17
+ JUL 15	64	35	.094	-.105	11	6	0	17
JUL 16	52	47	.258	-.101	9	8	0	17
+ JUL 17	62	37	.166	-.095	10	6	0	16
JUL 18	43	43	.158	-.171	7	7	2	16
- JUL 19	37	62	.296	-.096	6	10	0	16
JUL 20	50	50	.203	-.227	8	8	0	16
+ JUL 21	60	40	.126	-.141	6	4	0	10
+ JUL 22	60	40	.060	-.132	6	4	0	10

Figure 5.4: Daily Market Probability Statistics

File used: 07W   - WHEAT

	Month/ Day	% Up	% Down	Average Up	Average Down	Years Up	Years Down	Years Unch	Years Total
+	FEB 1	68	31	.084	-.046	11	5	0	16
	FEB 2	52	35	.091	-.034	9	6	2	17
	FEB 3	58	35	.065	-.059	10	6	1	17
	FEB 4	58	35	.095	-.120	10	6	1	17
	FEB 5	35	52	.065	-.081	6	9	2	17
	FEB 6	43	56	.054	-.096	7	9	0	16
	FEB 7	53	46	.078	-.098	8	7	0	15
	FEB 8	43	56	.060	-.074	7	9	0	16
	FEB 9	35	52	.125	-.073	6	9	2	17
	FEB 10	58	41	.099	-.054	10	7	0	17
	FEB 11	58	29	.087	-.061	10	5	2	17
-	FEB 12	26	60	.215	-.078	4	9	2	15
--	FEB 13	25	75	.043	-.081	4	12	0	16
-	FEB 14	33	60	.122	-.106	5	9	1	15
	FEB 15	53	30	.112	-.039	7	4	2	13
	FEB 16	57	42	.107	-.039	8	6	0	14
	FEB 17	53	46	.100	-.028	8	7	0	15
--	FEB 18	21	78	.152	-.111	3	11	0	14
-	FEB 19	33	66	.115	-.093	5	10	0	15
	FEB 20	57	42	.147	-.045	8	6	0	14
	FEB 21	54	36	.152	-.079	6	4	1	11
-	FEB 22	38	61	.160	-.083	5	8	0	13
-	FEB 23	31	68	.091	-.103	5	11	0	16
	FEB 24	52	47	.068	-.057	9	8	0	17
	FEB 25	35	58	.130	-.091	6	10	1	17
	FEB 26	41	58	.040	-.118	7	10	0	17
-	FEB 27	37	62	.099	-.105	6	10	0	16
	FEB 28	40	53	.080	-.209	6	8	1	15
---	FEB 29	20	80	.136	-.045	1	4	0	5
+	MAR 1	68	31	.119	-.082	11	5	0	16
	MAR 2	43	50	.073	-.200	7	8	1	16
	MAR 3	58	35	.058	-.050	10	6	1	17
	MAR 4	58	35	.083	-.103	10	6	1	17
	MAR 5	52	47	.077	-.099	9	8	0	17
	MAR 6	56	37	.088	-.107	9	6	1	16
	MAR 7	56	31	.128	-.069	9	5	2	16
--	MAR 8	25	75	.067	-.125	4	12	0	16

Figure 5.4: *(Continued)*

File used: 07W - WHEAT

	Month/ Day	% Up	% Down	Average Up	Average Down	Years Up	Years Down	Unch	Total
	MAR 9	50	43	.088	-.087	8	7	1	16
	MAR 10	41	52	.041	-.119	7	9	1	17
	MAR 11	35	58	.103	-.081	6	10	1	17
-	MAR 12	29	64	.095	-.107	5	11	1	17
-	MAR 13	37	62	.120	-.066	6	10	0	16
+	MAR 14	62	31	.090	-.126	10	5	1	16
+	MAR 15	62	31	.087	-.140	10	5	1	16
-	MAR 16	25	62	.093	-.065	4	10	2	16
	MAR 17	52	35	.158	-.106	9	6	2	17
	MAR 18	58	35	.073	-.082	10	6	1	17
	MAR 19	47	52	.050	-.087	8	9	0	17
---	MAR 20	18	81	.027	-.126	3	13	0	16
	MAR 21	56	43	.073	-.118	9	7	0	16
+	MAR 22	68	31	.121	-.109	11	5	0	16
	MAR 23	56	43	.079	-.079	9	7	0	16
	MAR 24	40	46	.079	-.070	6	7	2	15
	MAR 25	41	58	.055	-.109	7	10	0	17
	MAR 26	52	47	.094	-.123	9	8	0	17
	MAR 27	53	46	.154	-.132	8	7	0	15
--	MAR 28	21	71	.036	-.112	3	10	1	14
	MAR 29	37	50	.050	-.126	6	8	2	16
	MAR 30	56	37	.131	-.068	9	6	1	16
	MAR 31	50	50	.129	-.115	7	7	0	14
	APR 1	46	53	.080	-.091	7	8	0	15
++	APR 2	70	29	.094	-.127	12	5	0	17
-	APR 3	37	62	.151	-.079	6	10	0	16
+++	APR 4	85	14	.102	-.092	12	2	0	14
+	APR 5	60	33	.080	-.192	9	5	1	15
	APR 6	56	43	.067	-.064	9	7	0	16
	APR 7	47	52	.122	-.087	8	9	0	17
+	APR 8	62	37	.089	-.041	10	6	0	16
--	APR 9	21	78	.223	-.040	3	11	0	14
	APR 10	43	56	.050	-.151	7	9	0	16
	APR 11	56	43	.059	-.133	9	7	0	16
	APR 12	35	57	.131	-.129	5	8	1	14
-	APR 13	33	66	.068	-.100	5	10	0	15
	APR 14	52	47	.103	-.056	9	8	0	17
	APR 15	58	41	.124	-.101	10	7	0	17
+	APR 16	60	33	.113	-.124	9	5	1	15
-	APR 17	35	64	.087	-.109	5	9	0	14
--	APR 18	25	75	.038	-.069	4	12	0	16
	APR 19	43	56	.056	-.080	7	9	0	16
	APR 20	50	50	.047	-.060	7	7	0	14
	APR 21	52	47	.088	-.084	9	8	0	17
	APR 22	35	58	.080	-.074	6	10	1	17

208

Figure 5.4: *(Continued)*

File used: 07W - WHEAT

Month/ Day	--- % --- Up	Down	-- Average -- Up	Down	---------- Years ---------- Up	Down	Unch	Total
APR 23	41	58	.127	-.099	7	10	0	17
+ APR 24	62	37	.090	-.148	10	6	0	16
+ APR 25	62	37	.165	-.116	10	6	0	16
- APR 26	25	68	.061	-.112	4	11	1	16
APR 27	43	50	.083	-.111	7	8	1	16
APR 28	52	47	.108	-.106	9	8	0	17
APR 29	41	52	.110	-.133	7	9	1	17
APR 30	47	47	.156	-.074	8	8	1	17
- MAY 1	31	68	.073	-.165	5	11	0	16
MAY 2	53	40	.102	-.192	8	6	1	15
- MAY 3	31	68	.076	-.096	5	11	0	16
MAY 4	56	43	.089	-.097	9	7	0	16
MAY 5	41	58	.143	-.119	7	10	0	17
+ MAY 6	64	29	.072	-.194	11	5	1	17
MAY 7	58	41	.085	-.073	10	7	0	17
+ MAY 8	62	31	.158	-.086	10	5	1	16
MAY 9	43	50	.077	-.111	7	8	1	16
MAY 10	50	50	.085	-.068	8	8	0	16
MAY 11	43	50	.174	-.093	7	8	1	16
MAY 12	41	52	.119	-.140	7	9	1	17
MAY 13	52	47	.159	-.049	9	8	0	17
MAY 14	35	58	.114	-.062	6	10	1	17
MAY 15	56	37	.143	-.133	9	6	1	16
- MAY 16	31	62	.124	-.094	5	10	1	16
MAY 17	41	58	.085	-.116	7	10	0	17
+ MAY 18	64	29	.108	-.155	11	5	1	17
MAY 19	50	50	.176	-.068	9	9	0	18
- MAY 20	27	61	.045	-.112	5	11	2	18
MAY 21	58	41	.140	-.079	10	7	0	17
MAY 22	56	43	.086	-.090	9	7	0	16
MAY 23	52	41	.100	-.069	9	7	1	17
MAY 24	41	58	.170	-.067	7	10	0	17
- MAY 25	33	66	.187	-.127	5	10	0	15
MAY 26	46	46	.081	-.100	7	7	1	15
MAY 27	50	50	.101	-.095	8	8	0	16
-- MAY 28	21	78	.080	-.091	3	11	0	14
- MAY 29	30	69	.232	-.103	4	9	0	13
MAY 30	50	50	.082	-.114	5	5	0	10
MAY 31	38	53	.141	-.154	5	7	1	13
JUN 1	52	47	.071	-.099	9	8	0	17
-- JUN 2	27	72	.092	-.103	5	13	0	18
JUN 3	50	50	.118	-.061	9	9	0	18
JUN 4	52	47	.117	-.074	9	8	0	17
JUN 5	56	43	.141	-.104	9	7	0	16
- JUN 6	35	64	.194	-.121	6	11	0	17

209

Figure 5.4: *(Concluded)*

File used: 07W   - WHEAT

Month/ Day	--- % --- Up	Down	-- Average -- Up	Down	---------- Years ---------- Up	Down	Unch	Total
JUN 7	35	58	.108	-.115	6	10	1	17
JUN 8	52	47	.111	-.106	9	8	0	17
+ JUN 9	66	33	.081	-.139	12	6	0	18
JUN 10	50	44	.110	-.089	9	8	1	18
++ JUN 11	70	29	.168	-.122	12	5	0	17
JUN 12	43	56	.134	-.141	7	9	0	16
JUN 13	47	52	.119	-.062	8	9	0	17
- JUN 14	35	64	.152	-.094	6	11	0	17
JUN 15	52	41	.172	-.127	9	7	1	17
JUN 16	58	41	.148	-.094	10	7	0	17
JUN 17	23	58	.302	-.074	4	10	3	17
JUN 18	41	58	.044	-.083	7	10	0	17
JUN 19	43	43	.149	-.079	7	7	2	16
+ JUN 20	62	37	.210	-.114	10	6	0	16
JUN 21	50	50	.180	-.101	8	8	0	16
- JUN 22	31	68	.139	-.099	5	11	0	16
JUN 23	52	47	.152	-.103	9	8	0	17
JUN 24	41	58	.166	-.082	7	10	0	17
JUN 25	47	52	.101	-.202	8	9	0	17
--- JUN 26	18	81	.087	-.103	3	13	0	16
--- JUN 27	18	81	.281	-.122	3	13	0	16
JUN 28	43	56	.044	-.192	7	9	0	16
- JUN 29	37	62	.136	-.127	6	10	0	16
JUN 30	35	58	.091	-.078	6	10	1	17
JUL 1	52	41	.196	-.163	9	7	1	17
JUL 2	58	35	.162	-.064	10	6	1	17
+ JUL 3	69	30	.141	-.084	9	4	0	13
JUL 5	41	58	.212	-.134	5	7	0	12
+ JUL 6	68	31	.136	-.162	11	5	0	16
-- JUL 7	29	70	.089	-.126	5	12	0	17
JUL 8	52	47	.247	-.073	9	8	0	17
JUL 9	41	58	.126	-.165	7	10	0	17
JUL 10	52	47	.097	-.112	9	8	0	17
JUL 11	56	43	.187	-.091	9	7	0	16
- JUL 12	33	66	.128	-.159	5	10	0	15
+ JUL 13	68	31	.100	-.086	11	5	0	16
JUL 14	52	47	.195	-.115	9	8	0	17
JUL 15	41	58	.100	-.130	7	10	0	17
JUL 16	58	41	.141	-.156	10	7	0	17
JUL 17	35	58	.092	-.125	6	10	1	17
JUL 18	56	37	.152	-.176	9	6	1	16
JUL 19	53	40	.103	-.119	8	6	1	15
JUL 20	37	50	.167	-.068	6	8	2	16
JUL 21	54	45	.158	-.148	6	5	0	11
JUL 22	50	50	.116	-.106	5	5	0	10

Figure 5.5: Daily Market Probability Statistics

File used: 07NY - COTTON

```
------------------------------------------------------------
:   (c) Copyright      MBH Commodity Advisors, Inc.         :
:         Reproduction strictly prohibited by law           :
:         without prior written permission of MBH.          :
------------------------------------------------------------
```

Month/ Day	--- % --- Up	Down	-- Average -- Up	Down	---------- Years ---------- Up	Down	Unch	Total
FEB 1	45	54	.010	-.005	5	6	0	11
FEB 2	45	54	.013	-.007	5	6	0	11
FEB 3	53	46	.007	-.005	7	6	0	13
FEB 4	57	42	.011	-.007	8	6	0	14
-- FEB 5	28	71	.006	-.010	4	10	0	14
--- FEB 6	14	85	.011	-.014	2	12	0	14
FEB 7	41	50	.010	-.005	5	6	1	12
FEB 8	54	45	.012	-.005	6	5	0	11
- FEB 9	33	66	.017	-.011	4	8	0	12
FEB 10	41	58	.013	-.004	5	7	0	12
FEB 11	50	42	.010	-.005	7	6	1	14
FEB 12	46	53	.008	-.007	6	7	0	13
FEB 13	42	57	.011	-.018	6	8	0	14
+ FEB 14	63	36	.014	-.011	7	4	0	11
FEB 15	44	55	.009	-.013	4	5	0	9
++ FEB 16	77	22	.004	-.006	7	2	0	9
FEB 17	45	45	.017	-.008	5	5	1	11
FEB 18	45	45	.014	-.010	5	5	1	11
-- FEB 19	23	76	.011	-.015	3	10	0	13
+++ FEB 20	83	16	.015	-.003	10	2	0	12
FEB 21	44	55	.013	-.007	4	5	0	9
-- FEB 22	20	70	.016	-.013	2	7	1	10
+ FEB 23	63	36	.006	-.011	7	4	0	11
FEB 24	46	46	.005	-.008	6	6	1	13
FEB 25	50	50	.009	-.008	7	7	0	14
FEB 26	50	50	.007	-.007	7	7	0	14
FEB 27	42	57	.007	-.008	6	8	0	14
FEB 28	41	58	.012	-.008	5	7	0	12
++ FEB 29	75	25	.005	-.003	3	1	0	4
MAR 1	54	36	.009	-.005	6	4	1	11
+ MAR 2	63	36	.009	-.012	7	4	0	11
- MAR 3	38	61	.007	-.008	5	8	0	13
-- MAR 4	26	73	.009	-.007	4	11	0	15
- MAR 5	35	64	.006	-.005	5	9	0	14
- MAR 6	38	61	.009	-.010	5	8	0	13
MAR 7	46	53	.006	-.010	6	7	0	13
MAR 8	45	54	.011	-.007	5	6	0	11

Figure 5.5: *(Continued)*

File used: 07NY - COTTON

	Month/ Day	--- % --- Up	Down	-- Average -- Up	Down	--------- Years --------- Up	Down	Unch	Total
	MAR 9	36	54	.007	-.006	4	6	1	11
	MAR 10	46	46	.005	-.012	6	6	1	13
+	MAR 11	66	33	.009	-.008	10	5	0	15
+	MAR 12	64	35	.007	-.012	9	5	0	14
	MAR 13	46	53	.008	-.013	6	7	0	13
	MAR 14	46	38	.008	-.004	6	5	2	13
	MAR 15	54	45	.008	-.008	6	5	0	11
---	MAR 16	18	81	.010	-.009	2	9	0	11
+	MAR 17	61	38	.010	-.006	8	5	0	13
-	MAR 18	40	60	.013	-.010	6	9	0	15
+	MAR 19	64	28	.013	-.004	9	4	1	14
+	MAR 20	69	23	.010	-.007	9	3	1	13
++	MAR 21	76	23	.009	-.004	10	3	0	13
-	MAR 22	36	63	.012	-.007	4	7	0	11
	MAR 23	54	45	.004	-.011	6	5	0	11
+	MAR 24	66	33	.005	-.007	8	4	0	12
-	MAR 25	33	66	.003	-.016	5	10	0	15
	MAR 26	42	50	.008	-.008	6	7	1	14
	MAR 27	33	58	.009	-.010	4	7	1	12
+	MAR 28	66	33	.012	-.010	8	4	0	12
+	MAR 29	66	33	.006	-.006	8	4	0	12
	MAR 30	33	58	.005	-.006	4	7	1	12
	MAR 31	46	53	.011	-.008	6	7	0	13
	APR 1	53	46	.009	-.015	7	6	0	13
	APR 2	57	42	.007	-.016	8	6	0	14
-	APR 3	35	64	.013	-.011	5	9	0	14
	APR 4	33	58	.008	-.009	4	7	1	12
	APR 5	54	45	.005	-.009	6	5	0	11
	APR 6	50	33	.008	-.007	6	4	2	12
+	APR 7	64	35	.006	-.007	9	5	0	14
	APR 8	57	42	.004	-.011	8	6	0	14
++	APR 9	75	25	.008	-.010	9	3	0	12
	APR 10	50	50	.014	-.005	7	7	0	14
-	APR 11	28	64	.016	-.006	4	9	1	14
	APR 12	40	50	.010	-.009	4	5	1	10
--	APR 13	18	72	.020	-.006	2	8	1	11
	APR 14	57	42	.008	-.007	8	6	0	14
-	APR 15	33	66	.009	-.011	5	10	0	15
+	APR 16	61	38	.011	-.004	8	5	0	13
	APR 17	41	50	.007	-.011	5	6	1	12
	APR 18	42	50	.011	-.008	6	7	1	14
	APR 19	41	50	.013	-.008	5	6	1	12
-	APR 20	36	63	.003	-.006	4	7	0	11
	APR 21	35	57	.011	-.011	5	8	1	14
-	APR 22	40	60	.014	-.006	6	9	0	15

Figure 5.5: *(Continued)*

File used: 07NY - COTTON

Month/ Day	--- % --- Up	Down	-- Average -- Up	Down	---------- Years ---------- Up	Down	Unch	Total
+ APR 23	64	35	.008	-.008	9	5	0	14
+ APR 24	64	35	.008	-.007	9	5	0	14
APR 25	35	57	.009	-.007	5	8	1	14
++ APR 26	75	16	.009	-.005	9	2	1	12
APR 27	41	50	.005	-.007	5	6	1	12
APR 28	57	35	.006	-.006	8	5	1	14
++ APR 29	73	26	.007	-.004	11	4	0	15
APR 30	50	42	.012	-.006	7	6	1	14
MAY 1	50	42	.009	-.014	7	6	1	14
MAY 2	42	50	.009	-.011	6	7	1	14
- MAY 3	25	66	.008	-.005	3	8	1	12
MAY 4	33	58	.004	-.008	4	7	1	12
MAY 5	42	50	.009	-.004	6	7	1	14
MAY 6	53	46	.008	-.010	8	7	0	15
+ MAY 7	64	28	.011	-.015	9	4	1	14
MAY 8	42	50	.016	-.003	6	7	1	14
++ MAY 9	78	14	.011	-.015	11	2	1	14
MAY 10	33	58	.007	-.006	4	7	1	12
MAY 11	41	50	.009	-.010	5	6	1	12
MAY 12	57	42	.006	-.006	8	6	0	14
+ MAY 13	60	40	.008	-.013	9	6	0	15
-- MAY 14	28	71	.013	-.013	4	10	0	14
- MAY 15	35	64	.008	-.008	5	9	0	14
++ MAY 16	71	21	.012	-.009	10	3	1	14
MAY 17	41	50	.009	-.009	5	6	1	12
MAY 18	41	50	.006	-.011	5	6	1	12
MAY 19	42	50	.008	-.008	6	7	1	14
+ MAY 20	60	40	.008	-.015	9	6	0	15
MAY 21	50	42	.015	-.004	7	6	1	14
-- MAY 22	28	71	.016	-.011	4	10	0	14
--- MAY 23	7	85	.002	-.011	1	12	1	14
- MAY 24	25	66	.009	-.007	3	8	1	12
- MAY 25	30	60	.009	-.006	3	6	1	10
MAY 26	54	36	.011	-.008	6	4	1	11
- MAY 27	38	61	.010	-.013	5	8	0	13
MAY 28	58	41	.006	-.014	7	5	0	12
+ MAY 29	66	25	.012	-.009	8	3	1	12
-- MAY 30	25	75	.013	-.008	2	6	0	8
MAY 31	55	33	.018	-.005	5	3	1	9
- JUN 1	25	66	.013	-.012	3	8	1	12
JUN 2	28	57	.005	-.011	4	8	2	14
++ JUN 3	73	26	.008	-.005	11	4	0	15
JUN 4	57	42	.019	-.009	8	6	0	14
JUN 5	50	42	.011	-.007	7	6	1	14
JUN 6	57	35	.009	-.006	8	5	1	14

213

Figure 5.5: *(Concluded)*

File used: 07NY - COTTON

Month/Day	% Up	% Down	Average Up	Average Down	Years Up	Years Down	Years Unch	Years Total
JUN 7	50	41	.013	-.004	6	5	1	12
JUN 8	33	58	.012	-.017	4	7	1	12
JUN 9	57	35	.012	-.008	8	5	1	14
JUN 10	46	53	.007	-.008	7	8	0	15
JUN 11	42	57	.014	-.011	6	8	0	14
JUN 12	57	35	.009	-.012	8	5	1	14
JUN 13	42	50	.007	-.009	6	7	1	14
JUN 14	41	50	.010	-.017	5	6	1	12
JUN 15	58	33	.013	-.019	7	4	1	12
+ JUN 16	69	30	.014	-.015	9	4	0	13
JUN 17	50	50	.009	-.009	7	7	0	14
JUN 18	42	57	.016	-.006	6	8	0	14
-- JUN 19	21	71	.014	-.009	3	10	1	14
JUN 20	53	46	.011	-.004	7	6	0	13
+ JUN 21	63	36	.018	-.020	7	4	0	11
JUN 22	45	54	.004	-.010	5	6	0	11
JUN 23	46	53	.007	-.008	6	7	0	13
++ JUN 24	71	28	.026	-.021	10	4	0	14
JUN 25	42	57	.020	-.013	6	8	0	14
JUN 26	35	57	.013	-.008	5	8	1	14
-- JUN 27	15	76	.006	-.016	2	10	1	13
-- JUN 28	18	72	.017	-.011	2	8	1	11
JUN 29	45	36	.015	-.007	5	4	2	11
+ JUN 30	69	15	.018	-.016	9	2	2	13
JUL 1	42	57	.031	-.011	6	8	0	14
+ JUL 2	64	35	.011	-.012	9	5	0	14
+ JUL 3	66	33	.009	-.009	6	3	0	9
JUL 5	57	28	.019	-.020	4	2	1	7
JUL 6	45	27	.011	-.017	5	3	3	11
JUL 7	41	50	.008	-.031	5	6	1	12
- JUL 8	36	63	.009	-.012	4	7	0	11
- JUL 9	27	63	.008	-.014	3	7	1	11

Figure 5.6: Daily Market Probability Statistics

File used: 12SF - SWISS FRANC

```
------------------------------------------------------------
:    (c) Copyright       MBH Commodity Advisors, Inc.    :
:         Reproduction strictly prohibited by law        :
:         without prior written permission of MBH.       :
------------------------------------------------------------
```

	Month/ Day	--- % --- Up	Down	-- Average -- Up	Down	--------- Years --------- Up	Down	Unch	Total
	JUL 1	36	54	.363	-.512	4	6	1	11
+	JUL 2	60	40	.125	-.806	6	4	0	10
+++	JUL 3	85	14	.608	-1.061	6	1	0	7
	JUL 5	42	57	1.101	-.632	3	4	0	7
---	JUL 6	20	80	.183	-.699	2	8	0	10
	JUL 7	45	54	.493	-.589	5	6	0	11
	JUL 8	54	45	.373	-.568	6	5	0	11
+	JUL 9	60	40	.724	-.248	6	4	0	10
-	JUL 10	33	66	.982	-.353	3	6	0	9
	JUL 11	40	50	.478	-.622	4	5	1	10
	JUL 12	55	44	.635	-.443	5	4	0	9
	JUL 13	40	50	.359	-.307	4	5	1	10
-	JUL 14	40	60	.421	-.328	4	6	0	10
-	JUL 15	36	63	.866	-.545	4	7	0	11
+++	JUL 16	80	20	.761	-.591	8	2	0	10
--	JUL 17	22	77	1.093	-.841	2	7	0	9
	JUL 18	50	50	.661	-.711	5	5	0	10
	JUL 19	44	44	.723	-.556	4	4	1	9
	JUL 20	50	40	.629	-.436	5	4	1	10
++	JUL 21	72	27	.477	-.379	8	3	0	11
	JUL 22	54	45	.461	-.460	6	5	0	11
	JUL 23	50	50	.479	-.411	5	5	0	10
	JUL 24	55	44	.277	-.227	5	4	0	9
--	JUL 25	30	70	.690	-.422	3	7	0	10
-	JUL 26	33	66	.683	-.495	3	6	0	9
-	JUL 27	40	60	.202	-.418	4	6	0	10
	JUL 28	45	54	.846	-1.175	5	6	0	11
-	JUL 29	27	63	.231	-.612	3	7	1	11
+	JUL 30	60	40	.226	-1.030	6	4	0	10
	JUL 31	55	44	.866	-.606	5	4	0	9
+	AUG 1	60	40	.382	-.623	6	4	0	10
+	AUG 2	66	33	.907	-.222	6	3	0	9
---	AUG 3	20	80	.800	-.610	2	8	0	10
	AUG 4	45	54	.747	-.613	5	6	0	11
	AUG 5	45	54	.583	-.628	5	6	0	11
---	AUG 6	20	80	.653	-.769	2	8	0	10
-	AUG 7	33	66	.329	-.719	3	6	0	9

215

Figure 5.6:   (Continued)

File used: 12SF - SWISS FRANC

	Month/ Day	Up	Down	Up	Down	Up	Down	Uncn	Total
		--- % ---		-- Average --		---------- Years ----------			
	AUG 8	50	50	.667	-.461	5	5	0	10
	AUG 9	55	44	.559	-.534	5	4	0	9
-	AUG 10	40	60	.544	-.481	4	6	0	10
++	AUG 11	72	27	.643	-.205	8	3	0	11
+	AUG 12	63	36	.496	-.496	7	4	0	11
	AUG 13	50	50	.554	-.605	5	5	0	10
+	AUG 14	66	33	.840	-.482	6	3	0	9
-	AUG 15	40	60	1.554	-.272	4	6	0	10
--	AUG 16	22	77	.182	-.424	2	7	0	9
+	AUG 17	60	40	.545	-.569	6	4	0	10
	AUG 18	54	45	.601	-.667	6	5	0	11
+++	AUG 19	81	18	.573	-.366	9	2	0	11
	AUG 20	50	50	.423	-.582	5	5	0	10
	AUG 21	44	55	1.181	-.385	4	5	0	9
	AUG 22	50	50	.575	-.501	5	5	0	10
	AUG 23	55	44	.409	-.432	5	4	0	9
	AUG 24	50	40	.909	-.754	5	4	1	10
---	AUG 25	18	81	.631	-.667	2	9	0	11
+	AUG 26	63	36	.566	-.903	7	4	0	11
-	AUG 27	40	60	.578	-.744	4	6	0	10
+	AUG 28	66	33	.417	-.717	6	3	0	9
-	AUG 29	40	60	.867	-.503	4	6	0	10
	AUG 30	55	44	.444	-.760	5	4	0	9
-	AUG 31	30	60	.625	-.391	3	6	1	10
++	SEP 1	75	25	.402	-.397	6	2	0	8
+++	SEP 2	80	20	.664	-.532	8	2	0	10
++	SEP 3	75	25	.381	-1.072	6	2	0	8
--	SEP 4	25	75	.435	-.599	2	6	0	8
--	SEP 5	28	71	.725	-.727	2	5	0	7
	SEP 6	42	57	.497	-.526	3	4	0	7
-	SEP 7	37	62	.318	-.703	3	5	0	8
-	SEP 8	27	63	.321	-.514	3	7	1	11
-	SEP 9	36	63	.582	-.314	4	7	0	11
	SEP 10	40	50	.412	-.284	4	5	1	10
	SEP 11	44	55	.495	-.647	4	5	0	9
	SEP 12	50	50	.729	-.354	5	5	0	10
	SEP 13	33	55	.952	-.344	3	5	1	9
	SEP 14	50	50	.455	-.637	5	5	0	10
+	SEP 15	60	40	.473	-.106	6	4	0	10
+	SEP 16	60	40	.652	-.373	6	4	0	10
+	SEP 17	60	40	.487	-.824	6	4	0	10
+	SEP 18	66	33	.870	-.434	6	3	0	9
+	SEP 19	66	33	.326	-.230	6	3	0	9
+	SEP 20	62	37	1.292	-.781	5	3	0	8
++	SEP 21	77	22	.996	-.283	7	2	0	9

216

Figure 5.6: *(Continued)*

File used: 12SF - SWISS FRANC

	Month/ Day	--- % --- Up	Down	-- Average -- Up	Down	---------- Years ---------- Up	Down	Unch	Total
-	SEP 22	40	60	.575	-1.097	4	6	0	10
	SEP 23	50	50	1.215	-.718	5	5	0	10
++	SEP 24	70	20	.234	-.160	7	2	1	10
	SEP 25	33	55	.841	-.546	3	5	1	9
	SEP 26	55	44	.223	-.664	5	4	0	9
++	SEP 27	75	25	.489	-.788	6	2	0	8
	SEP 28	55	44	.380	-.703	5	4	0	9
	SEP 29	50	50	.582	-.570	5	5	0	10
	SEP 30	50	50	.264	-.372	5	5	0	10
+++	OCT 1	80	20	.935	-.175	8	2	0	10
-	OCT 2	33	66	1.332	-.848	3	6	0	9
	OCT 3	55	44	.591	-.605	5	4	0	9
--	OCT 4	25	75	.261	-.568	2	6	0	8
++	OCT 5	77	22	.514	-.343	7	2	0	9
+	OCT 6	60	30	.273	-.427	6	3	1	10
+	OCT 7	60	40	.843	-.474	6	4	0	10
	OCT 8	50	50	.454	-.822	5	5	0	10
+	OCT 9	66	33	.644	-.563	6	3	0	9
	OCT 10	55	33	.647	-.498	5	3	1	9
-	OCT 11	37	62	1.758	-.742	3	5	0	8
-	OCT 12	33	66	.372	-.486	3	6	0	9
+	OCT 13	60	40	.479	-.538	6	4	0	10
-	OCT 14	40	60	.692	-.701	4	6	0	10
	OCT 15	50	50	.298	-.596	5	5	0	10
	OCT 16	55	44	.513	-.660	5	4	0	9
++	OCT 17	77	22	.486	-.672	7	2	0	9
+	OCT 18	62	37	.451	-.160	5	3	0	8
	OCT 19	44	55	.511	-.971	4	5	0	9
	OCT 20	50	50	.603	-.723	5	5	0	10
--	OCT 21	30	70	.323	-.454	3	7	0	10
	OCT 22	50	50	.353	-.254	5	5	0	10
--	OCT 23	22	77	2.018	-.523	2	7	0	9
	OCT 24	33	55	.501	-.693	3	5	1	9
-	OCT 25	37	62	.833	-.446	3	5	0	8
	OCT 26	55	44	.464	-.747	5	4	0	9
-	OCT 27	40	60	.585	-.733	4	6	0	10
+	OCT 28	60	40	.745	-.135	6	4	0	10
	OCT 29	50	50	.807	-.506	5	5	0	10
	OCT 30	55	44	1.002	-.748	5	4	0	9
	OCT 31	44	55	.761	-.705	4	5	0	9
+	NOV 1	62	37	.877	-.669	5	3	0	8
	NOV 2	50	37	1.092	-.998	4	3	1	8
-	NOV 3	40	60	.424	-.854	4	6	0	10
-	NOV 4	33	66	.199	-.421	3	6	0	9
--	NOV 5	30	70	.698	-.626	3	7	0	10

Figure 5.6: *(Concluded)*

File used: 12SF - SWISS FRANC

	Month/ Day	--- % --- Up	Down	-- Average -- Up	Down	---------- Years ---------- Up	Down	Unch	Total
	NOV 6	55	33	.524	-1.753	5	3	1	9
	NOV 7	50	50	.448	-.481	4	4	0	8
	NOV 8	50	50	.603	-.481	4	4	0	8
	NOV 9	55	44	.715	-.397	5	4	0	9
+	NOV 10	60	40	.762	-.573	6	4	0	10
	NOV 11	40	40	.508	-.718	4	4	2	10
+	NOV 12	60	40	.677	-.884	6	4	0	10
	NOV 13	44	55	.397	-.497	4	5	0	9
	NOV 14	55	33	.415	-.209	5	3	1	9
	NOV 15	50	50	.183	-.755	4	4	0	8
-	NOV 16	33	66	.572	-.966	3	6	0	9
---	NOV 17	10	90	1.473	-.637	1	9	0	10
+++	NOV 18	80	20	.438	-.299	8	2	0	10
++	NOV 19	70	30	.294	-.954	7	3	0	10
-	NOV 20	33	66	.101	-.679	3	6	0	9
-	NOV 21	33	66	.897	-.582	3	6	0	9
+	NOV 22	66	16	.536	-.523	4	1	1	6
	NOV 23	50	50	.356	-.435	4	4	0	8
	NOV 24	57	42	.843	-.269	4	3	0	7
+++	NOV 25	85	14	:640	-.080	6	1	0	7
-	NOV 26	37	62	.449	-.398	3	5	0	8
	NOV 27	50	50	.889	-.412	3	3	0	6
	NOV 28	50	50	.614	-.398	4	4	0	8
++	NOV 29	75	25	.588	-.503	6	2	0	8
	NOV 30	55	44	.824	-.486	5	4	0	9
	DEC 1	50	50	.251	-.607	5	5	0	10
	DEC 2	50	50	.355	-.414	5	5	0	10
+	DEC 3	60	40	.493	-.548	6	4	0	10
	DEC 4	44	55	.870	-.753	4	5	0	9
--	DEC 5	22	77	.450	-.583	2	7	0	9
+	DEC 6	62	37	.614	-.488	5	3	0	8
--	DEC 7	22	77	.112	-.495	2	7	0	9
	DEC 8	50	50	.455	-.836	5	5	0	10
-	DEC 9	30	60	.093	-.646	3	6	1	10
-	DEC 10	40	60	.855	-.457	4	6	0	10
	DEC 11	44	44	.314	-.409	4	4	1	9
-	DEC 12	33	66	.558	-.246	3	6	0	9
-	DEC 13	25	62	.626	-.332	2	5	1	8
++	DEC 14	71	28	.671	-.773	5	2	0	7
-	DEC 15	33	66	.904	-.227	2	4	0	6
-	DEC 16	33	66	.558	-.256	1	2	0	3
---	DEC 17	0	100	.000	-.207	0	2	0	2
+++	DEC 18	100	0	1.803	.000	1	0	0	1
+++	DEC 19	100	0	.703	.000	2	0	0	2

218

Figure 5.7: Daily Market Probability Statistics

File used: 12TB - T BILLS (90)

	Month/ Day	--- % --- Up	 Down	-- Average -- Up	 Down	--------- Years --------- Up	 Down	 Unch	 Total
	JUL 1	55	44	.101	-.147	5	4	0	9
++	JUL 2	77	22	.056	-.103	7	2	0	9
+++	JUL 3	83	16	.143	-.120	5	1	0	6
-	JUL 5	33	66	.244	-.180	2	4	0	6
+++	JUL 6	100	0	.063	.000	9	0	0	9
--	JUL 7	22	77	.149	-.213	2	7	0	9
	JUL 8	44	44	.296	-.132	4	4	1	9
	JUL 9	44	55	.173	-.106	4	5	0	9
--	JUL 10	25	75	.290	-.069	2	6	0	8
	JUL 11	50	50	.087	-.163	4	4	0	8
+	JUL 12	62	25	.061	-.089	5	2	1	8
--	JUL 13	22	77	.145	-.069	2	7	0	9
+	JUL 14	62	25	.052	-.091	5	2	1	8
+	JUL 15	66	33	.181	-.111	6	3	0	9
	JUL 16	44	55	.228	-.180	4	5	0	9
++	JUL 17	75	25	.044	-.142	6	2	0	8
	JUL 18	37	50	.099	-.124	3	4	1	8
+	JUL 19	62	25	.028	-.049	5	2	1	8
	JUL 20	44	55	.104	-.198	4	5	0	9
	JUL 21	44	44	.059	-.203	4	4	1	9
--	JUL 22	22	77	.228	-.092	2	7	0	9
	JUL 23	55	44	.125	-.086	5	4	0	9
-	JUL 24	37	62	.164	-.108	3	5	0	8
+++	JUL 25	87	12	.103	-.022	7	1	0	8
	JUL 26	50	37	.050	-.157	4	3	1	8
	JUL 27	22	55	.145	-.119	2	5	2	9
---	JUL 28	11	88	.130	-.141	1	8	0	9
	JUL 29	44	44	.069	-.055	4	4	1	9
	JUL 30	55	44	.145	-.131	5	4	0	9
+	JUL 31	62	37	.065	-.160	5	3	0	8
	AUG 1	37	25	.051	-.078	3	2	3	8
+	AUG 2	62	37	.140	-.084	5	3	0	8
	AUG 3	44	55	.114	-.239	4	5	0	9
+	AUG 4	66	33	.080	-.085	6	3	0	9
	AUG 5	44	55	.089	-.065	4	5	0	9
	AUG 6	44	55	.111	-.094	4	5	0	9
+	AUG 7	62	12	.085	-.035	5	1	2	8

Figure 5.7: *(Continued)*

File used: 12TB - T BILLS (90)

Month/ Day		--- % --- Up	Down	-- Average -- Up	Down	---------- Years ---------- Up	Down	Unch	Total
+	AUG 8	62	37	.069	-.128	5	3	0	8
++	AUG 9	75	25	.109	-.146	6	2	0	8
-	AUG 10	22	66	.208	-.110	2	6	1	9
+	AUG 11	66	33	.091	-.109	6	3	0	9
++	AUG 12	77	22	.116	-.172	7	2	0	9
	AUG 13	55	33	.104	-.056	5	3	1	9
	AUG 14	37	50	.063	-.139	3	4	1	8
	AUG 15	12	50	.234	-.060	1	4	3	8
+++	AUG 16	87	12	.122	-.194	7	1	0	8
+	AUG 17	66	22	.130	-.055	6	2	1	9
-	AUG 18	22	66	.111	-.192	2	6	1	9
	AUG 19	55	33	.093	-.106	5	3	1	9
	AUG 20	44	44	.041	-.047	4	4	1	9
	AUG 21	50	50	.076	-.174	4	4	0	8
-	AUG 22	37	62	.141	-.029	3	5	0	8
-	AUG 23	37	62	.103	-.091	3	5	0	8
	AUG 24	44	55	.094	-.192	4	5	0	9
	AUG 25	55	44	.045	-.219	5	4	0	9
	AUG 26	33	33	.055	-.043	3	3	3	9
--	AUG 27	22	77	.155	-.214	2	7	0	9
-	AUG 28	37	62	.080	-.142	3	5	0	8
+	AUG 29	62	37	.201	-.128	5	3	0	8
+	AUG 30	62	37	.050	-.086	5	3	0	8
-	AUG 31	33	66	.062	-.144	3	6	0	9
--	SEP 1	28	71	.168	-.042	2	5	0	7
	SEP 2	37	50	.226	-.103	3	4	1	8
++	SEP 3	71	28	.115	-.106	5	2	0	7
--	SEP 4	28	71	.100	-.128	2	5	0	7
---	SEP 5	16	83	.054	-.103	1	5	0	6
+	SEP 6	66	33	.072	-.168	4	2	0	6
	SEP 7	42	57	.125	-.068	3	4	0	7
---	SEP 8	11	88	.101	-.125	1	8	0	9
	SEP 9	55	33	.132	-.142	5	3	1	9
++	SEP 10	77	22	.189	-.346	7	2	0	9
-	SEP 11	37	62	.326	-.129	3	5	0	8
	SEP 12	37	37	.092	-.070	3	3	2	8
	SEP 13	50	50	.180	-.052	4	4	0	8
	SEP 14	55	44	.135	-.071	5	4	0	9
-	SEP 15	33	66	.074	-.139	3	6	0	9
++	SEP 16	77	11	.082	-.104	7	1	1	9
++	SEP 17	77	22	.113	-.022	7	2	0	9
	SEP 18	50	50	.111	-.073	4	4	0	8
	SEP 19	50	25	.206	-.016	4	2	2	8
	SEP 20	50	50	.205	-.078	4	4	0	8
	SEP 21	44	44	.256	-.041	4	4	1	9

Figure 5.7: *(Continued)*

File used: 12TB - T BILLS (90)

	Month/ Day	--- % --- Up	 Down	-- Average -- Up	 Down	---------- Years ---------- Up	 Down	 Unch	 Total
-	SEP 22	33	66	.065	-.302	3	6	0	9
	SEP 23	44	55	.095	-.036	4	5	0	9
	SEP 24	44	55	.107	-.099	4	5	0	9
	SEP 25	50	50	.052	-.262	4	4	0	8
-	SEP 26	37	62	.081	-.180	3	5	0	8
+	SEP 27	62	37	.074	-.135	5	3	0	8
	SEP 28	55	44	.190	-.069	5	4	0	9
-	SEP 29	22	66	.044	-.157	2	6	1	9
+	SEP 30	66	33	.122	-.153	6	3	0	9
	OCT 1	44	44	.141	-.090	4	4	1	9
	OCT 2	50	50	.206	-.057	4	4	0	8
+	OCT 3	62	37	.204	-.091	5	3	0	8
	OCT 4	50	50	.041	-.252	4	4	0	8
-	OCT 5	33	66	.230	-.097	3	6	0	9
	OCT 6	44	33	.262	-.054	4	3	2	9
	OCT 7	44	55	.206	-.055	4	5	0	9
	OCT 8	33	55	.110	-.172	3	5	1	9
	OCT 9	37	50	.316	-.171	3	4	1	8
--	OCT 10	25	75	.060	-.094	2	6	0	8
++	OCT 11	75	25	.169	-.115	6	2	0	8
+	OCT 12	66	22	.147	-.130	6	2	1	9
	OCT 13	44	55	.095	-.141	4	5	0	9
	OCT 14	44	33	.151	-.223	4	3	2	9
	OCT 15	44	55	.071	-.173	4	5	0	9
	OCT 16	37	50	.093	-.170	3	4	1	8
	OCT 17	50	50	.127	-.149	4	4	0	8
+	OCT 18	62	25	.107	-.299	5	2	1	8
	OCT 19	55	44	.212	-.193	5	4	0	9
-	OCT 20	33	66	.486	-.080	3	6	0	9
	OCT 21	44	44	.053	-.102	4	4	1	9
	OCT 22	55	44	.086	-.269	5	4	0	9
	OCT 23	50	50	.189	-.137	4	4	0	8
+	OCT 24	62	37	.160	-.101	5	3	0	8
-	OCT 25	37	62	.073	-.103	3	5	0	8
+	OCT 26	66	33	.175	-.213	6	3	0	9
	OCT 27	44	44	.032	-.269	4	4	1	9
	OCT 28	44	55	.102	-.069	4	5	0	9
++	OCT 29	77	22	.120	-.108	7	2	0	9
+	OCT 30	62	37	.210	-.208	5	3	0	8
-	OCT 31	37	62	.048	-.150	3	5	0	8
++	NOV 1	75	12	.160	-.330	6	1	1	8
-	NOV 2	37	62	.080	-.118	3	5	0	8
	NOV 3	33	44	.163	-.127	3	4	2	9
	NOV 4	50	37	.065	-.087	4	3	1	8
-	NOV 5	33	66	.204	-.088	3	6	0	9

Figure 5.7: *(Concluded)*

File used: 12TB – T BILLS (90)

	Month/ Day	--- % ---		-- Average --		---------- Years ----------			
		Up	Down	Up	Down	Up	Down	Unch	Total
	NOV 6	37	50	.204	-.122	3	4	1	8
	NOV 7	57	42	.203	-.150	4	3	0	7
	NOV 8	50	50	.100	-.076	4	4	0	8
++	NOV 9	77	22	.206	-.090	7	2	0	9
	NOV 10	55	44	.096	-.143	5	4	0	9
	NOV 11	44	55	.305	-.075	4	5	0	9
	NOV 12	55	33	.160	-.107	5	3	1	9
--	NOV 13	25	75	.060	-.146	2	6	0	8
	NOV 14	50	50	.147	-.186	4	4	0	8
-	NOV 15	37	62	.139	-.030	3	5	0	8
	NOV 16	55	44	.078	-.139	5	4	0	9
-	NOV 17	22	66	.129	-.166	2	6	1	9
++	NOV 18	77	11	.240	-.011	7	1	1	9
++	NOV 19	77	22	.098	-.073	7	2	0	9
	NOV 20	37	50	.041	-.104	3	4	1	8
	NOV 21	50	50	.085	-.172	4	4	0	8
+	NOV 22	66	16	.063	-.011	4	1	1	6
	NOV 23	37	50	.183	-.161	3	4	1	8
+	NOV 24	66	16	.250	-.074	4	1	1	6
	NOV 25	50	33	.041	-.032	3	2	1	6
	NOV 26	42	42	.259	-.112	3	3	1	7
-	NOV 27	33	66	.022	-.118	2	4	0	6
---	NOV 28	14	85	.110	-.173	1	6	0	7
+	NOV 29	62	12	.079	-.294	5	1	2	8
	NOV 30	33	44	.104	-.231	3	4	2	9
	DEC 1	44	55	.052	-.146	4	5	0	9
	DEC 2	55	44	.097	-.174	5	4	0	9
++	DEC 3	77	11	.129	-.248	7	1	1	9
	DEC 4	50	37	.198	-.114	4	3	1	8
	DEC 5	25	50	.049	-.221	2	4	2	8
	DEC 6	37	50	.048	-.054	3	4	1	8
--	DEC 7	11	77	.087	-.169	1	7	1	9
--	DEC 8	22	77	.033	-.138	2	7	0	9
+	DEC 9	66	33	.036	-.373	6	3	0	9
-	DEC 10	22	66	.069	-.179	2	6	1	9
	DEC 11	50	50	.060	-.212	4	4	0	8
++	DEC 12	75	12	.159	-.489	6	1	1	8
+	DEC 13	62	37	.066	-.058	5	3	0	8
+	DEC 14	66	33	.150	-.026	6	3	0	9
	DEC 15	44	44	.105	-.131	4	4	1	9
	DEC 16	44	44	.051	-.111	4	4	1	9
	DEC 17	50	50	.147	-.119	4	4	0	8
-	DEC 18	40	60	.306	-.103	2	3	0	5
	DEC 19	40	20	.074	-.022	2	1	2	5
	DEC 20	40	40	.048	-.088	2	2	1	5

222

Figure 5.8: Daily Market Probability Statistics

File used: 01PL - PLATINUM

	Month/ Day	Up	Down	Up	Down	Up	Down	Unch	Total
		--- % ---		-- Average --		---------- Years ----------			
	AUG 1	57	42	.179	-.211	8	6	0	14
-	AUG 2	38	61	.166	-.227	5	8	0	13
	AUG 3	41	58	.106	-.203	5	7	0	12
++	AUG 4	76	15	.130	-.104	10	2	1	13
--	AUG 5	21	78	.043	-.179	3	11	0	14
-	AUG 6	40	60	.105	-.138	6	9	0	15
	AUG 7	57	35	.164	-.065	8	5	1	14
-	AUG 8	35	64	.184	-.186	5	9	0	14
	AUG 9	38	53	.195	-.192	5	7	1	13
	AUG 10	50	50	.171	-.125	6	6	0	12
++	AUG 11	76	23	.154	-.130	10	3	0	13
	AUG 12	42	42	.113	-.109	6	6	2	14
	AUG 13	53	46	.181	-.166	8	7	0	15
++	AUG 14	78	21	.161	-.201	11	3	0	14
	AUG 15	42	57	.152	-.086	6	8	0	14
	AUG 16	58	41	.223	-.109	7	5	0	12
+	AUG 17	63	36	.107	-.148	7	4	0	11
+	AUG 18	69	30	.161	-.111	9	4	0	13
++	AUG 19	71	21	.211	-.052	10	3	1	14
	AUG 20	46	53	.221	-.175	7	8	0	15
	AUG 21	57	42	.156	-.172	8	6	0	14
	AUG 22	50	50	.188	-.139	7	7	0	14
+	AUG 23	69	30	.203	-.100	9	4	0	13
-	AUG 24	33	66	.095	-.133	4	8	0	12
-	AUG 25	30	69	.091	-.088	4	9	0	13
+	AUG 26	64	35	.146	-.194	9	5	0	14
	AUG 27	40	53	.081	-.162	6	8	1	15
+	AUG 28	64	35	.144	-.148	9	5	0	14
	AUG 29	28	50	.231	-.154	4	7	3	14
	AUG 30	46	46	.091	-.063	6	6	1	13
---	AUG 31	16	83	.033	-.064	2	10	0	12
	SEP 1	55	44	.091	-.067	5	4	0	9
++	SEP 2	72	27	.214	-.281	8	3	0	11
	SEP 3	58	41	.239	-.254	7	5	0	12
	SEP 4	58	41	.116	-.186	7	5	0	12
	SEP 5	58	41	.159	-.085	7	5	0	12
-	SEP 6	40	60	.056	-.176	4	6	0	10

Figure 5.8: *(Continued)*

File used: 01PL - PLATINUM

	Month/ Day	--- % --- Up	Down	-- Average -- Up	Down	---------- Years ---------- Up	Down	Unch	Total
--	SEP 7	10	70	.269	-.147	1	7	2	10
-	SEP 8	30	69	.250	-.117	4	9	0	13
	SEP 9	50	50	.063	-.213	7	7	0	14
+	SEP 10	60	40	.114	-.272	9	6	0	15
-	SEP 11	21	64	.145	-.181	3	9	2	14
--	SEP 12	21	71	.078	-.127	3	10	1	14
+	SEP 13	61	30	.131	-.067	8	4	1	13
	SEP 14	50	50	.080	-.195	6	6	0	12
	SEP 15	53	46	.082	-.128	7	6	0	13
	SEP 16	50	42	.089	-.098	7	6	1	14
	SEP 17	46	53	.116	-.251	7	8	0	15
-	SEP 18	35	64	.128	-.159	5	9	0	14
+++	SEP 19	100	0	.143	.000	14	0	0	14
+	SEP 20	69	30	.137	-.168	9	4	0	13
++	SEP 21	75	16	.284	-.156	9	2	1	12
	SEP 22	46	53	.228	-.136	6	7	0	13
	SEP 23	50	50	.179	-.055	7	7	0	14
-	SEP 24	40	60	.207	-.166	6	9	0	15
	SEP 25	42	57	.161	-.116	6	8	0	14
	SEP 26	50	50	.148	-.142	7	7	0	14
-	SEP 27	38	61	.061	-.080	5	8	0	13
	SEP 28	41	58	.141	-.086	5	7	0	12
-	SEP 29	30	61	.087	-.278	4	8	1	13
--	SEP 30	21	78	.202	-.176	3	11	0	14
++	OCT 1	73	26	.146	-.104	11	4	0	15
	OCT 2	50	50	.142	-.102	7	7	0	14
+	OCT 3	64	35	.148	-.195	9	5	0	14
-	OCT 4	30	69	.116	-.130	4	9	0	13
	OCT 5	41	50	.182	-.115	5	6	1	12
	OCT 6	46	53	.181	-.081	6	7	0	13
	OCT 7	50	50	.171	-.187	7	7	0	14
-	OCT 8	35	64	.171	-.146	5	9	0	14
	OCT 9	42	50	.172	-.190	6	7	1	14
++	OCT 10	78	21	.120	-.166	11	3	0	14
-	OCT 11	38	61	.234	-.217	5	8	0	13
+	OCT 12	66	33	.156	-.140	8	4	0	12
	OCT 13	53	46	.190	-.106	7	6	0	13
	OCT 14	57	42	.078	-.181	8	6	0	14
-	OCT 15	33	66	.151	-.139	5	10	0	15
	OCT 16	57	42	.094	-.111	8	6	0	14
+	OCT 17	64	35	.095	-.114	9	5	0	14
+	OCT 18	61	38	.172	-.088	8	5	0	13
	OCT 19	50	41	.049	-.240	6	5	1	12
	OCT 20	53	46	.186	-.118	7	6	0	13
	OCT 21	42	50	.128	-.091	6	7	1	14

Figure 5.8: *(Continued)*

File used: 01PL - PLATINUM

Month/ Day	--- % --- Up	 Down	-- Average -- Up	 Down	---------- Years ---------- Up	 Down	 Unch	 Total
OCT 22	42	50	.168	-.077	6	7	1	14
OCT 23	35	57	.061	-.136	5	8	1	14
OCT 24	42	57	.185	-.099	6	8	0	14
- OCT 25	30	69	.118	-.199	4	9	0	13
OCT 26	41	58	.111	-.196	5	7	0	12
OCT 27	46	53	.162	-.114	6	7	0	13
OCT 28	42	57	.150	-.079	6	8	0	14
- OCT 29	40	60	.067	-.198	6	9	0	15
OCT 30	42	57	.167	-.178	6	8	0	14
OCT 31	50	42	.176	-.187	7	6	1	14
+ NOV 1	61	38	.134	-.124	8	5	0	13
-- NOV 2	30	70	.221	-.135	3	7	0	10
NOV 3	58	41	.111	-.167	7	5	0	12
++ NOV 4	76	23	.113	-.245	10	3	0	13
NOV 5	53	46	.172	-.282	7	6	0	13
NOV 6	42	42	.273	-.169	6	6	2	14
NOV 7	50	50	.173	-.139	6	6	0	12
+ NOV 8	61	30	.127	-.258	8	4	1	13
NOV 9	58	41	.150	-.120	7	5	0	12
NOV 10	46	53	.153	-.200	6	7	0	13
- NOV 11	28	64	.118	-.150	4	9	1	14
+ NOV 12	60	40	.113	-.181	9	6	0	15
-- NOV 13	21	71	.046	-.126	3	10	1	14
NOV 14	42	57	.084	-.181	6	8	0	14
- NOV 15	38	61	.154	-.170	5	8	0	13
+ NOV 16	66	25	.136	-.238	8	3	1	12
NOV 17	53	38	.141	-.241	7	5	1	13
NOV 18	42	57	.166	-.155	6	8	0	14
+ NOV 19	66	33	.150	-.189	10	5	0	15
++ NOV 20	78	21	.103	-.044	11	3	0	14
NOV 21	50	50	.156	-.199	7	7	0	14
++ NOV 22	70	20	.182	-.307	7	2	1	10
NOV 23	55	44	.095	-.070	5	4	0	9
- NOV 24	40	60	.180	-.189	4	6	0	10
+++ NOV 25	80	20	.075	-.043	8	2	0	10
NOV 26	46	53	.157	-.231	6	7	0	13
NOV 27	55	44	.124	-.135	5	4	0	9
+ NOV 28	60	40	.263	-.120	6	4	0	10
+ NOV 29	66	25	.135	-.058	8	3	1	12
NOV 30	58	41	.118	-.053	7	5	0	12
DEC 1	46	53	.150	-.079	6	7	0	13
DEC 2	50	42	.064	-.151	7	6	1	14
DEC 3	53	46	.130	-.131	8	7	0	15
DEC 4	57	42	.083	-.174	8	6	0	14
DEC 5	50	50	.070	-.076	7	7	0	14

Figure 5.8: *(Concluded)*

File used: 01PL - PLATINUM

	Month/ Day	Up	Down	Up	Down	Up	Down	Unch	Total
		--- % ---		-- Average --		---------- Years ----------			
+	DEC 6	61	38	.114	-.065	8	5	0	13
+	DEC 7	66	33	.098	-.114	8	4	0	12
-	DEC 8	30	61	.102	-.171	4	8	1	13
-	DEC 9	28	64	.076	-.179	4	9	1	14
	DEC 10	46	53	.084	-.130	7	8	0	15
	DEC 11	57	35	.096	-.229	8	5	1	14
	DEC 12	42	57	.149	-.097	6	8	0	14
+	DEC 13	61	38	.084	-.192	8	5	0	13
	DEC 14	50	50	.081	-.207	6	6	0	12
+	DEC 15	61	38	.144	-.136	8	5	0	13
	DEC 16	42	57	.081	-.086	6	8	0	14
	DEC 17	46	46	.137	-.125	7	7	1	15
	DEC 18	57	42	.146	-.056	8	6	0	14
+	DEC 19	64	35	.147	-.070	9	5	0	14
	DEC 20	46	53	.118	-.111	6	7	0	13
	DEC 21	41	50	.194	-.063	5	6	1	12
+++	DEC 22	84	15	.108	-.144	11	2	0	13
	DEC 23	42	50	.136	-.127	6	7	1	14
	DEC 24	50	37	.098	-.052	4	3	1	8
++	DEC 26	75	25	.167	-.060	6	2	0	8
+	DEC 27	69	30	.121	-.105	9	4	0	13
-	DEC 28	27	63	.085	-.084	3	7	1	11
+	DEC 29	61	38	.090	-.071	8	5	0	13
--	DEC 30	21	71	.096	-.155	3	10	1	14
-	DEC 31	33	66	.186	-.126	3	6	0	9
--	JAN 3	25	75	.097	-.054	2	6	0	8
-	JAN 4	40	60	.168	-.181	4	6	0	10
+	JAN 5	60	40	.156	-.079	6	4	0	10
	JAN 6	50	50	.167	-.080	7	7	0	14
	JAN 7	53	46	.134	-.198	8	7	0	15
	JAN 8	57	42	.086	-.203	8	6	0	14
	JAN 9	42	50	.242	-.103	6	7	1	14
--	JAN 10	28	71	.175	-.098	4	10	0	14
	JAN 11	53	46	.190	-.134	7	6	0	13
	JAN 12	42	57	.144	-.173	6	8	0	14
	JAN 13	50	50	.034	-.107	7	7	0	14
++	JAN 14	73	26	.232	-.075	11	4	0	15
	JAN 15	57	42	.262	-.303	4	3	0	7
++	JAN 16	71	28	.151	-.097	5	2	0	7
+	JAN 17	66	33	.185	-.089	4	2	0	6
-	JAN 18	40	60	.118	-.056	2	3	0	5
+	JAN 19	66	33	.148	-.251	4	2	0	6
+	JAN 20	66	33	.088	-.278	4	2	0	6
---	JAN 21	14	85	.147	-.100	1	6	0	7
	JAN 22	42	57	.117	-.411	3	4	0	7

Figure 5.9: Daily Market Probability Statistics

File used:　　03SU - SUGAR

Month/Day	--- % --- Up	Down	-- Average -- Up	Down	---------- Years ---------- Up	Down	Unch	Total
OCT 1	46	53	.027	-.010	6	7	0	13
OCT 2	38	46	.033	-.014	5	6	2	13
+ OCT 3	69	23	.016	-.016	9	3	1	13
- OCT 4	30	61	.018	-.023	4	8	1	13
+ OCT 5	64	28	.025	-.014	9	4	1	14
OCT 6	53	46	.020	-.011	8	7	0	15
OCT 7	50	50	.015	-.011	7	7	0	14
OCT 8	50	41	.013	-.014	6	5	1	12
++ OCT 9	72	18	.016	-.008	8	2	1	11
+ OCT 10	66	33	.020	-.015	8	4	0	12
OCT 11	45	54	.039	-.024	5	6	0	11
OCT 12	45	54	.015	-.015	5	6	0	11
+ OCT 13	61	38	.015	-.017	8	5	0	13
- OCT 14	30	61	.010	-.022	4	8	1	13
OCT 15	46	53	.020	-.013	6	7	0	13
++ OCT 16	76	23	.026	-.023	10	3	0	13
- OCT 17	23	69	.017	-.017	3	9	1	13
OCT 18	46	53	.019	-.015	6	7	0	13
-- OCT 19	21	78	.018	-.022	3	11	0	14
OCT 20	53	40	.022	-.022	8	6	1	15
++ OCT 21	78	21	.014	-.022	11	3	0	14
OCT 22	50	41	.030	-.010	6	5	1	12
++ OCT 23	75	25	.016	-.021	9	3	0	12
OCT 24	46	46	.030	-.030	6	6	1	13
OCT 25	41	41	.029	-.021	5	5	2	12
OCT 26	50	50	.013	-.013	7	7	0	14
OCT 27	53	40	.014	-.022	8	6	1	15
OCT 28	50	42	.024	-.019	7	6	1	14
OCT 29	53	46	.026	-.013	7	6	0	13
+ OCT 30	61	38	.023	-.016	8	5	0	13
OCT 31	46	53	.013	-.015	6	7	0	13
NOV 1	53	38	.022	-.014	7	5	1	13
-- NOV 2	27	72	.031	-.013	3	8	0	11
NOV 3	35	50	.026	-.006	5	7	2	14
+ NOV 4	63	36	.020	-.017	7	4	0	11
NOV 5	54	45	.015	-.012	6	5	0	11
+ NOV 6	66	33	.017	-.023	8	4	0	12

Figure 5.9:   *(Continued)*

File used: 03SU - SUGAR

	Month/ Day	--- % --- Up	Down	-- Average -- Up	Down	---------- Years ---------- Up	Down	Unch	Total
++	NOV 7	70	30	.017	-.016	7	3	0	10
	NOV 8	54	45	.014	-.018	6	5	0	11
	NOV 9	57	42	.020	-.017	8	6	0	14
	NOV 10	40	53	.024	-.024	6	8	1	15
---	NOV 11	16	83	.003	-.026	1	5	0	6
+	NOV 12	61	30	.020	-.028	8	4	1	13
-	NOV 13	30	61	.017	-.022	4	8	1	13
	NOV 14	53	38	.031	-.023	7	5	1	13
	NOV 15	46	38	.025	-.017	6	5	2	13
	NOV 16	50	42	.023	-.009	7	6	1	14
-	NOV 17	40	60	.009	-.018	6	9	0	15
	NOV 18	50	50	.021	-.008	7	7	0	14
	NOV 19	46	53	.019	-.011	6	7	0	13
	NOV 20	53	46	.014	-.019	7	6	0	13
-	NOV 21	33	66	.032	-.015	4	8	0	12
	NOV 22	45	45	.016	-.025	5	5	1	11
	NOV 23	45	54	.014	-.019	5	6	0	11
	NOV 24	41	58	.022	-.019	5	7	0	12
--	NOV 25	27	72	.039	-.015	3	8	0	11
+	NOV 26	60	40	.018	-.029	6	4	0	10
	NOV 27	44	55	.020	-.027	4	5	0	9
	NOV 28	45	45	.021	-.017	5	5	1	11
+	NOV 29	61	30	.016	-.031	8	4	1	13
	NOV 30	57	42	.019	-.010	8	6	0	14
-	DEC 1	26	66	.023	-.024	4	10	1	15
--	DEC 2	21	78	.016	-.016	3	11	0	14
-	DEC 3	30	61	.010	-.014	4	8	1	13
	DEC 4	38	53	.025	-.019	5	7	1	13
	DEC 5	53	46	.016	-.018	7	6	0	13
	DEC 6	46	53	.031	-.017	6	7	0	13
	DEC 7	57	42	.021	-.014	8	6	0	14
-	DEC 8	40	60	.011	-.021	6	9	0	15
	DEC 9	42	57	.009	-.017	6	8	0	14
	DEC 10	46	53	.023	-.023	6	7	0	13
+	DEC 11	61	30	.024	-.042	8	4	1	13
	DEC 12	30	53	.027	-.022	4	7	2	13
-	DEC 13	38	61	.027	-.019	5	8	0	13
	DEC 14	57	42	.020	-.008	8	6	0	14
+	DEC 15	66	33	.035	-.011	10	5	0	15
	DEC 16	35	57	.017	-.015	5	8	1	14
	DEC 17	53	38	.041	-.019	7	5	1	13
	DEC 18	53	38	.014	-.015	7	5	1	13
+	DEC 19	61	23	.013	-.020	8	3	2	13
+	DEC 20	61	38	.021	-.025	8	5	0	13
++	DEC 21	71	28	.011	-.017	10	4	0	14

Figure 5.9: *(Continued)*

File used: 03SU - SUGAR

Month/ Day	--- % --- Up	Down	-- Average -- Up	Down	--------- Years --------- Up	Down	Unch	Total
DEC 22	42	42	.025	-.013	6	6	2	14
DEC 23	42	50	.033	-.016	6	7	1	14
- DEC 24	33	66	.017	-.009	2	4	0	6
DEC 26	50	33	.030	-.014	3	2	1	6
- DEC 27	38	61	.016	-.022	5	8	0	13
DEC 28	53	38	.012	-.019	7	5	1	13
DEC 29	46	53	.021	-.022	7	8	0	15
DEC 30	50	50	.021	-.014	7	7	0	14
+ DEC 31	60	20	.021	-.034	6	2	2	10
JAN 3	42	57	.008	-.027	3	4	0	7
JAN 4	41	41	.021	-.033	5	5	2	12
JAN 5	46	53	.025	-.015	6	7	0	13
JAN 6	53	46	.017	-.027	8	7	0	15
- JAN 7	28	64	.014	-.020	4	9	1	14
JAN 8	46	46	.017	-.028	6	6	1	13
JAN 9	46	53	.028	-.021	6	7	0	13
+ JAN 10	64	35	.026	-.016	9	5	0	14
JAN 11	53	40	.027	-.026	8	6	1	15
JAN 12	56	43	.021	-.029	9	7	0	16
+ JAN 13	66	33	.026	-.022	10	5	0	15
+++ JAN 14	85	14	.024	-.021	12	2	0	14
JAN 15	46	53	.026	-.020	6	7	0	13
JAN 16	30	53	.020	-.025	4	7	2	13
+ JAN 17	64	28	.026	-.013	9	4	1	14
JAN 18	50	50	.015	-.018	7	7	0	14
JAN 19	56	43	.022	-.019	9	7	0	16
+ JAN 20	64	35	.015	-.019	9	5	0	14
+ JAN 21	64	35	.024	-.022	9	5	0	14
- JAN 22	30	69	.028	-.017	4	9	0	13
++ JAN 23	76	23	.031	-.032	10	3	0	13
JAN 24	57	42	.019	-.032	8	6	0	14
+ JAN 25	64	35	.025	-.020	9	5	0	14
+ JAN 26	68	31	.017	-.020	11	5	0	16
JAN 27	53	46	.024	-.017	8	7	0	15
-- JAN 28	28	71	.027	-.029	4	10	0	14
JAN 29	30	53	.047	-.025	4	7	2	13
+ JAN 30	69	30	.014	-.017	9	4	0	13
JAN 31	42	50	.025	-.015	6	7	1	14
FEB 1	53	46	.020	-.028	8	7	0	15
FEB 2	50	37	.022	-.020	8	6	2	16
- FEB 3	26	66	.016	-.022	4	10	1	15
FEB 4	50	50	.018	-.023	7	7	0	14
FEB 5	38	53	.025	-.027	5	7	1	13
- FEB 6	30	61	.046	-.026	4	8	1	13
FEB 7	38	53	.024	-.022	5	7	1	13

229

Figure 5.9: *(Concluded)*

File used: 03SU - SUGAR

	Month/ Day	Up	Down	Up	Down	Up	Down	Unch	Total
		--- % ---		-- Average --		---------- Years ----------			
	======	====	====	======	======	======	======	======	======
	FEB 8	46	53	.030	-.025	7	8	0	15
	FEB 9	43	50	.016	-.028	7	8	1	16
	FEB 10	57	35	.027	-.022	8	5	1	14
++	FEB 11	78	14	.027	-.023	11	2	1	14
--	FEB 12	25	75	.004	-.026	1	3	0	4
--	FEB 13	27	72	.060	-.027	3	8	0	11
--	FEB 14	21	71	.013	-.022	3	10	1	14
	FEB 15	50	50	.014	-.012	5	5	0	10
	FEB 16	50	50	.021	-.019	5	5	0	10
---	FEB 17	20	80	.007	-.022	2	8	0	10
	FEB 18	44	44	.018	-.005	4	4	1	9
-	FEB 19	37	62	.058	-.044	3	5	0	8
++	FEB 20	71	28	.037	-.017	5	2	0	7
+++	FEB 21	85	14	.031	-.037	6	1	0	7
--	FEB 22	25	75	.009	-.044	3	9	0	12
	FEB 23	50	50	.009	-.025	6	6	0	12
	FEB 24	45	45	.025	-.024	5	5	1	11
---	FEB 25	18	81	.032	-.035	2	9	0	11
---	FEB 26	20	80	.050	-.024	2	8	0	10
--	FEB 27	11	77	.034	-.038	1	7	1	9
	FEB 28	50	50	.023	-.033	5	5	0	10
++	FEB 29	75	25	.053	-.061	3	1	0	4

Figure 5.10: Daily Market Probability Statistics

	Month/ Day	--- % --- Up	 Down	-- Average -- Up	 Down	---------- Years ---------- Up	 Down	 Unch	 Total
+	OCT 1	62	37	.014	-.015	10	6	0	16
	OCT 2	37	56	.015	-.017	6	9	1	16
	OCT 3	43	56	.012	-.014	7	9	0	16
+	OCT 4	60	40	.009	-.012	9	6	0	15
	OCT 5	46	53	.014	-.010	7	8	0	15
+	OCT 6	62	37	.010	-.011	10	6	0	16
+	OCT 7	62	37	.015	-.009	10	6	0	16
--	OCT 8	26	73	.009	-.015	4	11	0	15
	OCT 9	46	53	.014	-.011	7	8	0	15
	OCT 10	43	56	.008	-.020	7	9	0	16
	OCT 11	42	42	.011	-.018	6	6	2	14
	OCT 12	41	58	.020	-.009	5	7	0	12
	OCT 13	42	50	.017	-.011	6	7	1	14
	OCT 14	53	46	.013	-.005	8	7	0	15
	OCT 15	43	50	.011	-.016	7	8	1	16
	OCT 16	43	56	.010	-.020	7	9	0	16
	OCT 17	43	50	.010	-.011	7	8	1	16
	OCT 18	46	46	.010	-.009	7	7	1	15
--	OCT 19	26	73	.013	-.015	4	11	0	15
	OCT 20	56	43	.009	-.025	9	7	0	16
	OCT 21	56	43	.012	-.007	9	7	0	16
-	OCT 22	40	60	.013	-.010	6	9	0	15
+++	OCT 23	80	20	.015	-.012	12	3	0	15
-	OCT 24	31	62	.013	-.008	5	10	1	16
	OCT 25	50	50	.016	-.016	7	7	0	14
	OCT 26	40	53	.009	-.016	6	8	1	15
	OCT 27	56	43	.010	-.009	9	7	0	16
	OCT 28	50	50	.008	-.007	8	8	0	16
	OCT 29	56	43	.009	-.011	9	7	0	16
+++	OCT 30	81	18	.012	-.006	13	3	0	16
+	OCT 31	62	37	.020	-.010	10	6	0	16
	NOV 1	53	46	.012	-.011	8	7	0	15
	NOV 2	50	33	.019	-.004	6	4	2	12
	NOV 3	53	40	.007	-.010	8	6	1	15
	NOV 4	53	38	.013	-.009	7	5	1	13
	NOV 5	57	42	.010	-.007	8	6	0	14
	NOV 6	53	40	.023	-.008	8	6	1	15

Figure 5.10: *(Continued)*

File used: 03CP - COPPER

	Month/ Day	--- % --- Up	Down	-- Average -- Up	Down	---------- Years ---------- Up	Down	Unch	Total
	======	====	====	======	======	======	======	======	======
-	NOV 7	30	69	.007	-.012	4	9	0	13
	NOV 8	57	42	.012	-.014	8	6	0	14
+	NOV 9	60	40	.011	-.014	9	6	0	15
-	NOV 10	25	68	.017	-.009	4	11	1	16
	NOV 11	50	50	.006	-.014	5	5	0	10
+	NOV 12	62	37	.010	-.014	10	6	0	16
	NOV 13	43	50	.005	-.011	7	8	1	16
-	NOV 14	37	62	.012	-.009	6	10	0	16
	NOV 15	53	46	.010	-.012	8	7	0	15
	NOV 16	46	53	.010	-.011	7	8	0	15
	NOV 17	56	43	.005	-.009	9	7	0	16
	NOV 18	56	43	.011	-.011	9	7	0	16
	NOV 19	43	50	.012	-.016	7	8	1	16
-	NOV 20	25	62	.011	-.006	4	10	2	16
	NOV 21	56	31	.009	-.014	9	5	2	16
+ +	NOV 22	75	25	.008	-.020	9	3	0	12
	NOV 23	41	58	.013	-.012	5	7	0	12
+	NOV 24	61	38	.012	-.014	8	5	0	13
	NOV 25	38	53	.015	-.008	5	7	1	13
	NOV 26	53	46	.009	-.017	7	6	0	13
	NOV 27	50	50	.019	-.014	6	6	0	12
	NOV 28	53	46	.016	-.012	7	6	0	13
+	NOV 29	66	33	.011	-.012	10	5	0	15
+	NOV 30	60	33	.016	-.024	9	5	1	15
	DEC 1	50	43	.013	-.010	8	7	1	16
	DEC 2	31	56	.012	-.014	5	9	2	16
	DEC 3	50	50	.010	-.009	8	8	0	16
	DEC 4	50	50	.012	-.020	8	8	0	16
	DEC 5	56	37	.014	-.011	9	6	1	16
	DEC 6	53	40	.010	-.018	8	6	1	15
	DEC 7	46	46	.025	-.011	7	7	1	15
	DEC 8	50	50	.010	-.013	8	8	0	16
	DEC 9	37	56	.006	-.016	6	9	1	16
	DEC 10	56	43	.013	-.015	9	7	0	16
+++	DEC 11	81	18	.015	-.026	13	3	0	16
-	DEC 12	25	68	.013	-.009	4	11	1	16
-	DEC 13	20	66	.005	-.014	3	10	2	15
	DEC 14	33	53	.017	-.009	5	8	2	15
	DEC 15	50	43	.009	-.010	8	7	1	16
+	DEC 16	68	31	.013	-.008	11	5	0	16
	DEC 17	43	56	.014	-.012	7	9	0	16
+	DEC 18	62	37	.012	-.012	10	6	0	16
	DEC 19	50	50	.009	-.007	8	8	0	16
	DEC 20	53	40	.009	-.006	8	6	1	15
	DEC 21	53	46	.014	-.012	8	7	0	15

232

Figure 5.10: *(Continued)*

File used: 03CP - COPPER

	Month/ Day	--- % --- Up	Down	-- Average -- Up	Down	---------- Years ---------- Up	Down	Unch	Total
+	DEC 22	62	37	.005	-.008	10	6	0	16
	DEC 23	43	50	.013	-.004	7	8	1	16
+++	DEC 24	88	11	.011	-.014	8	1	0	9
+++	DEC 26	88	11	.013	-.008	8	1	0	9
+	DEC 27	60	40	.015	-.005	9	6	0	15
	DEC 28	50	42	.009	-.009	7	6	1	14
	DEC 29	43	56	.011	-.011	7	9	0	16
	DEC 30	50	43	.008	-.017	8	7	1	16
+	DEC 31	61	38	.011	-.012	8	5	0	13
++	JAN 3	77	11	.013	-.016	7	1	1	9
-	JAN 4	30	69	.010	-.011	4	9	0	13
	JAN 5	43	50	.016	-.013	7	8	1	16
--	JAN 6	17	76	.007	-.016	3	13	1	17
	JAN 7	35	58	.019	-.013	6	10	1	17
	JAN 8	43	56	.007	-.010	7	9	0	16
	JAN 9	50	43	.015	-.012	8	7	1	16
	JAN 10	56	43	.014	-.009	9	7	0	16
	JAN 11	43	50	.020	-.012	7	8	1	16
	JAN 12	58	41	.009	-.014	10	7	0	17
	JAN 13	35	58	.012	-.016	6	10	1	17
+++	JAN 14	88	11	.011	-.019	15	2	0	17
-	JAN 15	31	68	.013	-.010	5	11	0	16
-	JAN 16	37	62	.014	-.011	6	10	0	16
+	JAN 17	68	25	.016	-.007	11	4	1	16
+	JAN 18	66	26	.015	-.010	10	4	1	15
	JAN 19	52	47	.013	-.013	9	8	0	17
	JAN 20	50	50	.007	-.018	8	8	0	16
	JAN 21	47	52	.021	-.009	8	9	0	17
-	JAN 22	18	68	.019	-.017	3	11	2	16
-	JAN 23	37	62	.008	-.014	6	10	0	16
+	JAN 24	68	31	.016	-.015	11	5	0	16
	JAN 25	53	46	.021	-.015	8	7	0	15
	JAN 26	58	41	.012	-.009	10	7	0	17
++	JAN 27	70	29	.014	-.017	12	5	0	17
	JAN 28	47	52	.018	-.012	8	9	0	17
	JAN 29	50	50	.016	-.014	8	8	0	16
++	JAN 30	75	25	.008	-.008	12	4	0	16
	JAN 31	56	37	.019	-.012	9	6	1	16
+	FEB 1	62	31	.013	-.020	10	5	1	16
	FEB 2	41	58	.015	-.007	7	10	0	17
	FEB 3	52	47	.012	-.010	9	8	0	17
+	FEB 4	64	35	.008	-.017	11	6	0	17
	FEB 5	56	31	.015	-.010	9	5	2	16
	FEB 6	31	56	.013	-.011	5	9	2	16
	FEB 7	46	53	.014	-.012	7	8	0	15

233

Figure 5.10: *(Concluded)*

File used: 03CP - COPPER

Month/ Day	--- % --- Up	Down	-- Average -- Up	Down	---------- Years ---------- Up	Down	Unch	Total
FEB 8	50	50	.015	-.009	8	8	0	16
-- FEB 9	29	70	.013	-.009	5	12	0	17
+ FEB 10	62	37	.013	-.009	10	6	0	16
FEB 11	52	47	.012	-.006	9	8	0	17
+ FEB 12	66	22	.009	-.007	6	2	1	9
FEB 13	53	46	.018	-.009	8	7	0	15
+ FEB 14	62	31	.015	-.006	10	5	1	16
+ FEB 15	61	38	.017	-.017	8	5	0	13
FEB 16	57	35	.015	-.006	8	5	1	14
FEB 17	46	53	.009	-.011	7	8	0	15
FEB 18	57	21	.009	-.023	8	3	3	14
FEB 19	42	57	.015	-.013	6	8	0	14
FEB 20	50	50	.020	-.016	7	7	0	14
FEB 21	58	33	.017	-.010	7	4	1	12
+ FEB 22	61	38	.016	-.028	8	5	0	13
- FEB 23	37	62	.009	-.018	6	10	0	16
FEB 24	35	58	.016	-.007	6	10	1	17
- FEB 25	35	64	.015	-.014	6	11	0	17
FEB 26	56	43	.016	-.020	9	7	0	16
++ FEB 27	75	25	.013	-.014	12	4	0	16
FEB 28	56	43	.013	-.025	9	7	0	16
- FEB 29	40	60	.027	-.008	2	3	0	5
+ MAR 1	68	31	.020	-.010	11	5	0	16
MAR 2	37	56	.016	-.018	6	9	1	16
MAR 3	41	58	.012	-.011	7	10	0	17
++ MAR 4	76	23	.016	-.020	13	4	0	17
+ MAR 5	62	37	.012	-.017	10	6	0	16
MAR 6	50	31	.019	-.017	8	5	3	16
MAR 7	47	52	.017	-.011	8	9	0	17
MAR 8	50	50	.011	-.017	8	8	0	16
MAR 9	50	50	.012	-.012	8	8	0	16
MAR 10	58	29	.012	-.025	10	5	2	17
MAR 11	47	52	.022	-.009	8	9	0	17
- MAR 12	31	62	.016	-.012	5	10	1	16
+ MAR 13	62	31	.009	-.021	10	5	1	16
MAR 14	58	35	.017	-.008	10	6	1	17
MAR 15	53	40	.008	-.013	8	6	1	15
MAR 16	43	56	.021	-.006	7	9	0	16
MAR 17	58	35	.011	-.017	10	6	1	17
MAR 18	58	35	.017	-.011	10	6	1	17
+ MAR 19	68	31	.018	-.007	11	5	0	16
MAR 20	56	31	.014	-.019	9	5	2	16
MAR 21	54	45	.013	-.020	6	5	0	11
MAR 22	45	54	.009	-.014	5	6	0	11
++ MAR 23	72	27	.019	-.013	8	3	0	11

234

As a trading system. The market probability readings can be developed into a trading system. This requires developing the following elements and incorporating them into an operational plan:

a) timing indicators;

b) risk management considerations; and

c) precise entry and exit procedures.

Consider the following approach as a further suggestion for developing a trading system based on the percent readings. Trades will only be made when percent reading for a given day is 75 percent or higher, up or down. Toward the end of the previous trading day you will begin to watch intra-day timing indicators (i.e., moving averages, oscillators and stochastics). When these indicators turn in the same direction as the percent reading for the next day or several days, you will enter the market consistent with the direction of the expected move. You will exit when the timing indicators turn in the opposite direction at the end of the day (or days) of strong percentage reading(s), or at a predetermined stop loss or objective which is determined by another method of analysis.

The above, being only a suggestion, must be developed in considerable detail and must be thoroughly tested if it is to have any merit.

As an indicator of more significant seasonal movement. By examining the daily percentage readings over blocks of time (for example, weekly or monthly), you can ascertain probable seasonal movement for the given block of time. December and February live hog futures, for example, show a large number of percentage of time up closes for the month of November. The conclusion is that November has often been a bullish month for live hog futures. This information might not only be valuable to position traders, but should prove especially valuable to hedgers, producers and commercial interests.

To isolate possible seasonal spread situations. This application is also particularly suited to hedgers, commercial interests and more experienced traders. By examining the percentage of time up/

down readings during similar periods of time for different contract months of the same market, or for the same contract months of different but related markets (i.e., July corn and July wheat), one can determine the historical tendency of prices on a relative basis. Assume for example that during a given month July corn futures have shown only a few plus readings with a majority of minus readings, but that July wheat futures have shown very few minus readings with a majority of plus readings. In such a situation the spread—long July wheat, short July corn—appears to have merit from a seasonal standpoint. There are many such situations both on an intra-and inter-market basis.

Trade only the highest readings. You may wish to scan the data for the highest percent up and down readings, trading the markets consistent with these readings. Look for the "+ + +" or "– – –" notations in the left-hand margin for each of the listings. These figures note the largest percent of time readings and are likely to be the most reliable readings.

Trade only high percentage of time strings. One might reasonably argue that taken by itself, any one day of high percentage of time up or down readings could be a random or chance event. In order to minimize the possibility of this being the case, one might ignore such days and, as a more reliable alternative, focus only on strings of days having high percentage readings in the same direction. As an example, note the strings taken from actual statistics for the given markets (Figure 5-11). Strings, or successive days of high readings in a given direction, are more likely to be statistically valid than are single days.

Figure 5.11: Daily Market Probability Printout Sample

File used: 12CO - COCOA

	Month/Day	% Up	% Down	Average Up	Average Down
-	OCT 29	31	68	.015	-.012
	OCT 30	43	50	.016	-.013
+++	OCT 31	81	18	.016	-.022
+	NOV 1	66	33	.011	-.018
++	NOV 2	75	25	.013	-.016
	NOV 3	46	53	.021	-.012
	NOV 4	46	53	.016	-.013
	NOV 5	50	50	.011	-.014
-	NOV 6	40	60	.018	-.013
+	NOV 7	69	30	.006	-.008
+++	NOV 8	84	15	.017	-.006
+	NOV 9	60	33	.011	-.008
	NOV 10	50	50	.014	-.018
+	NOV 11	62	37	.012	-.010
-	NOV 12	31	68	.027	-.014
	NOV 13	56	43	.009	-.015
	NOV 14	43	56	.014	-.021
	NOV 15	46	53	.017	-.012
--	NOV 16	26	73	.016	-.013
--	NOV 17	25	75	.003	-.012
--	NOV 18	18	81	.011	-.012

File used: 07C - CORN

	Month/Day	% Up	% Down	Average Up	Average Down
-	JUN 7	35	57	.202	-.112
-	JUN 8	23	76	.063	-.081
	JUN 9	53	46	.096	-.056
	JUN 10	30	53	.169	-.087
	JUN 11	46	38	.140	-.075
	JUN 12	50	50	.107	-.075
	JUN 13	40	40	.054	-.071
-	JUN 14	14	71	.308	-.105
	JUN 15	46	53	.174	-.117
	JUN 16	58	41	.107	-.050
	JUN 17	50	50	.104	-.121
	JUN 18	38	53	.145	-.080
+	JUN 19	64	28	.134	-.051
	JUN 20	57	42	.138	-.058
	JUN 21	46	53	.242	-.092
+	JUN 22	66	33	.097	-.192
	JUN 23	41	50	.109	-.090
	JUN 24	33	50	.185	-.050
-	JUN 25	30	61	.090	-.160
--	JUN 26	21	71	.082	-.104
--	JUN 27	28	71	.086	-.127
--	JUN 28	15	76	.091	-.148

Pre-holiday or pre-report behavior. Pre-holiday or pre-report behavior can be evaluated by using the daily market probability studies. Examine markets for their percentage readings on days before major holidays or other significant days (Labor Day, Christmas, Fourth of July, New Year, Jewish New Year, election days, key government report days and so on). You are likely to be pleasantly surprised by what you find!

Other patterns. Other patterns may be found by close examination of the data. I will leave these to your study and imagination.

A Few Words About The Data History

As mentioned previously, the data history I employed is quite extensive. Yet in spite of the length and scope of our data history, *the reliability of the percentage of time up and down readings is limited by the length of the database.* In some cases, for example, the data history is relatively brief. Hence, there will be many high percentage of time up and down readings for markets with limited data history. In such cases the reliability of readings is questionable even if there are high readings, and in spite of the fact that there may be fairly long strings of high readings.

Remember that statistical reliability is a function of time or data length. The more lengthy the data history, the more statistically valid will be the results. Don't draw strong conclusions in markets which have brief data histories.

Note also that the far right-hand column for each printout shows the actual number of data points for each calendar day. You will note that although the history length may cover twenty-four years, the number shown in this column may only be sixteen or fifteen years. Remember that there are two weekend days in each week, and therefore statistics for these days are not available. This is why the numbers in the far right-hand column are lower than the total number of years evaluated.

As you know, futures trading is not a certain thing. There is always the risk of loss as well as the potential for profit. Past performance of the daily market probability readings is not indicative of future performance. I caution all readers to take great care when using these statistics in trading programs. Remember, however, that in spite of the limitations which must be placed on the applications of this data, this does not negate the value and potential which the daily market probability studies can have in the overall area of market analysis and trading system development.

SEASONALITY AND DAILY MARKET PROBABILITY STUDIES

When I began my career in the futures industry, seasonality was neither popular nor well understood. While many traders were familiar with the highly seasonal behavior of the then-active Shell Egg futures market, few traders recognized the fact that seasonality is a major force in virtually every market. Although W. D. Gann had spent considerable time and effort researching and writing about seasonal behavior, traders are, unfortunately, more interested in his technical work than they are in his conclusions regarding seasonality in the various markets (stocks and futures). Yet the lack of interest afforded seasonality does not diminish its importance and/or influence in the markets.

In 1977, Williams and Noseworthy published *Sure Thing Commodity Trading*,[4] which was based exclusively on seasonal price patterns and repetition. Their study brought seasonality to the forefront as a viable and necessary method of price analysis, not only in the agricultural markets but in all futures markets. Their book has become a classic. It will always rank the high on list of recommended reading for futures traders.

Art Merrill's revolutionary work, *The Behavior of Prices on Wall Street*, statistically demonstrated the existence of seasonality in the stock market. In my seminars and lectures throughout the world I am always amazed by the few responses I get when I ask for a show of hands from those who have read Merrill's book or who are familiar

---

[4]Larry R. Williams and Michelle Noseworthy, *Sure Thing Commodity Trading* (Brightwater, NY: Windsor Books, 1977).

with his work. This suggests to me that there are not many traders who are familiar with the concepts of seasonality or who use them in their trading or analyses. From the viewpoint of contrary opinion this probably means that the concepts have considerable value.

Whether the daily market probability studies I have just discussed are seasonals or whether they are merely market patterns is not a significant consideration. The fact remains that my work, as well as the research of those cited in this chapter, has demonstrated the existence of calendar-based repetitive patterns which can, I feel, be used to the advantage of futures traders, commercial interests, hedgers and investors.

DAY-OF-WEEK ANALYSIS

A variation on the theme of daily market probabilities by calendar date is the examination of daily closing patterns according to the actual day of the week. For example some traders have felt that lower closes on Monday through Thursday have significance for Friday's closing, or that a lower close on Friday may signal a lower close on Monday. Accordingly, I subjected this approach to rigorous study by market. Figures 5-12 through 5.34 show:

a) contract symbols and years tested (two contracts per market);

b) the pattern(s) tested; and

c) result of test.

d) the % listings which follow the closing pattern(s) show the percentage of time price closed up on the indicated date.

Figure 5.12: Day of Week Closing Patterns for Live Cattle

MON	TUE	WED	06LC ---- THU ---- 12LC		TOT
+	+	+	52%	53%	53%
+	+	−	52%	51%	51%
+	−	+	55%	50%	52%
+	−	−	52%	58%	55%
−	+	+	46%	53%	49%
−	+	−	49%	49%	49%
−	−	+	51%	47%	49%
−	−	−	63%	49%	56%

MON	TUE	WED	THU	06LC ---- FRI ---- 12LC		TOT
+	+	+	+	64%	62%	63%
+	+	+	−	69%	51%	60%
+	+	−	+	47%	47%	47%
+	+	−	−	55%	55%	55%
+	−	+	+	63%	65%	64%
+	−	+	−	41%	49%	45%
+	−	−	+	57%	52%	55%
+	−	−	−	41%	50%	45%
−	+	+	+	56%	55%	56%
−	+	+	−	45%	40%	42%
−	+	−	+	53%	52%	52%
−	+	−	−	42%	57%	49%
−	−	+	+	40%	40%	40%
−	−	+	−	46%	47%	47%
−	−	−	+	44%	46%	45%
−	−	−	−	45%	31%	38%

WED	THU	FRI	06LC ---- MON ---- 12LC		TOT
+	+	+	54%	60%	57%
+	+	−	48%	63%	56%
+	−	+	50%	57%	53%
+	−	−	53%	44%	48%
−	+	+	48%	46%	47%
−	+	−	47%	43%	45%
−	−	+	49%	52%	50%
−	−	−	41%	34%	38%

FRI	06LC ---- MON ---- 12LC		TOT
+	51%	54%	53%
−	49%	46%	47%

Figure 5.13: Day of Week Closing Patterns for Live Hogs

MON	TUE	WED	06LH ---- THU	12LH ----	TOT
+	+	+	52%	48%	50%
+	+	−	53%	55%	54%
+	−	+	45%	52%	48%
+	−	−	48%	47%	47%
−	+	+	44%	36%	40%
−	+	−	52%	51%	51%
−	−	+	48%	42%	45%
−	−	−	48%	54%	51%

MON	TUE	WED	THU	06LH ---- FRI	12LH ----	TOT
+	+	+	+	58%	56%	57%
+	+	+	−	48%	50%	49%
+	+	−	+	50%	53%	51%
+	+	−	−	56%	54%	55%
+	−	+	+	53%	41%	47%
+	−	+	−	60%	52%	56%
+	−	−	+	54%	41%	47%
+	−	−	−	43%	53%	48%
−	+	+	+	41%	45%	43%
−	+	+	−	38%	40%	39%
−	+	−	+	39%	45%	42%
−	+	−	−	42%	49%	45%
−	−	+	+	53%	49%	51%
−	−	+	−	48%	43%	45%
−	−	−	+	38%	36%	37%
−	−	−	−	36%	38%	37%

WED	THU	FRI	06LH ---- MON	12LH ----	TOT
+	+	+	59%	54%	56%
+	+	−	48%	57%	53%
+	−	+	47%	48%	48%
+	−	−	59%	52%	55%
−	+	+	47%	50%	48%
−	+	−	45%	44%	45%
−	−	+	54%	46%	50%
−	−	−	46%	48%	47%

FRI	06LH ---- MON	12LH ----	TOT
+	52%	50%	51%
−	48%	53%	50%

Figure 5.14: Day of Week Closing Patterns for Pork Bellies

MON	TUE	WED	02PB ---- THU ----	07PB	TOT
+	+	+	48%	43%	45%
+	+	−	55%	52%	54%
+	−	+	47%	44%	45%
+	−	−	48%	55%	52%
−	+	+	43%	45%	44%
−	+	−	56%	52%	54%
−	−	+	61%	55%	58%
−	−	−	71%	66%	68%

MON	TUE	WED	THU	02PB ---- FRI ----	07PB	TOT
+	+	+	+	61%	63%	62%
+	+	+	−	51%	65%	58%
+	+	−	+	46%	45%	45%
+	+	−	−	54%	56%	55%
+	−	+	+	55%	54%	55%
+	−	+	−	47%	50%	49%
+	−	−	+	44%	48%	46%
+	−	−	−	56%	47%	52%
−	+	+	+	64%	46%	55%
−	+	+	−	43%	41%	42%
−	+	−	+	52%	54%	53%
−	+	−	−	53%	44%	48%
−	−	+	+	34%	33%	33%
−	−	+	−	57%	47%	52%
−	−	−	+	38%	51%	44%
−	−	−	−	53%	53%	53%

WED	THU	FRI	02PB ---- MON ----	07PB	TOT
+	+	+	56%	57%	57%
+	+	−	50%	48%	49%
+	−	+	46%	52%	49%
+	−	−	51%	47%	49%
−	+	+	51%	45%	48%
−	+	−	46%	44%	45%
−	−	+	44%	45%	44%
−	−	−	48%	47%	47%

FRI	02PB ---- MON ----	07PB	TOT
+	50%	51%	50%
−	48%	46%	47%

243

Figure 5.15: Day of Week Closing Patterns for Corn

MON	TUE	WED	07C	12C	TOT
			---- THU ----		
+	+	+	35%	36%	35%
+	+	−	49%	43%	46%
+	−	+	46%	53%	50%
+	−	−	39%	45%	42%
−	+	+	48%	38%	43%
−	+	−	42%	47%	45%
−	−	+	50%	43%	46%
−	−	−	44%	49%	46%

MON	TUE	WED	THU	07C	12C	TOT
				---- FRI ----		
+	+	+	+	69%	46%	57%
+	+	+	−	46%	52%	49%
+	+	−	+	50%	52%	51%
+	+	−	−	36%	41%	38%
+	−	+	+	54%	46%	50%
+	−	+	−	50%	43%	46%
+	−	−	+	60%	45%	53%
+	−	−	−	50%	48%	49%
−	+	+	+	38%	47%	42%
−	+	+	−	46%	47%	46%
−	+	−	+	48%	45%	47%
−	+	−	−	42%	51%	47%
−	−	+	+	36%	36%	36%
−	−	+	−	38%	44%	41%
−	−	−	+	54%	50%	52%
−	−	−	−	42%	52%	47%

WED	THU	FRI	07C	12C	TOT
			---- MON ----		
+	+	+	43%	48%	46%
+	+	−	40%	43%	42%
+	−	+	56%	51%	53%
+	−	−	46%	42%	44%
−	+	+	44%	38%	41%
−	+	−	40%	42%	41%
−	−	+	39%	49%	44%
−	−	−	48%	46%	47%

FRI	07C	12C	TOT
	---- MON ----		
+	46%	48%	47%
−	45%	43%	44%

244

Figure 5.16: Day of Week Closing Patterns for Soybean Oil

MON	TUE	WED	07BO ---- THU ----	12BO	TOT
+	+	+	48%	51%	49%
+	+	−	54%	50%	52%
+	−	+	38%	46%	42%
+	−	−	54%	58%	56%
−	+	+	42%	37%	39%
−	+	−	48%	55%	51%
−	−	+	49%	53%	51%
−	−	−	51%	45%	48%

MON	TUE	WED	THU	07BO ---- FRI ----	12BO	TOT
+	+	+	+	50%	50%	50%
+	+	+	−	57%	57%	57%
+	+	−	+	46%	48%	47%
+	+	−	−	41%	41%	41%
+	−	+	+	56%	38%	47%
+	−	+	−	53%	43%	48%
+	−	−	+	61%	60%	61%
+	−	−	−	45%	45%	45%
−	+	+	+	44%	44%	44%
−	+	+	−	37%	47%	42%
−	+	−	+	49%	46%	47%
−	+	−	−	40%	59%	49%
−	−	+	+	41%	46%	43%
−	−	+	−	45%	40%	43%
−	−	−	+	45%	45%	45%
−	−	−	−	48%	47%	47%

WED	THU	FRI	07BO ---- MON ----	12BO	TOT
+	+	+	54%	53%	53%
+	+	−	45%	46%	46%
+	−	+	51%	53%	52%
+	−	−	35%	39%	37%
−	+	+	52%	44%	48%
−	+	−	41%	41%	41%
−	−	+	37%	45%	41%
−	−	−	41%	37%	39%

FRI	07BO ---- MON ----	12BO	TOT
+	49%	49%	49%
−	39%	40%	39%

245

Figure 5.17: Day of Week Closing Patterns for Wheat

MON	TUE	WED	07W ---- THU	12W ----	TOT
+	+	+	35%	31%	33%
+	+	−	44%	44%	44%
+	−	+	48%	50%	49%
+	−	−	44%	50%	47%
−	+	+	47%	44%	46%
−	+	−	45%	45%	45%
−	−	+	52%	54%	53%
−	−	−	53%	45%	49%

MON	TUE	WED	THU	07W ---- FRI	12W ----	TOT
+	+	+	+	56%	58%	57%
+	+	+	−	46%	55%	50%
+	+	−	+	56%	68%	62%
+	+	−	−	42%	45%	44%
+	−	+	+	49%	55%	52%
+	−	+	−	33%	24%	28%
+	−	−	+	52%	55%	53%
+	−	−	−	50%	47%	48%
−	+	+	+	46%	39%	43%
−	+	+	−	45%	42%	43%
−	+	−	+	45%	45%	45%
−	+	−	−	39%	51%	45%
−	−	+	+	39%	45%	42%
−	−	+	−	45%	49%	47%
−	−	−	+	53%	59%	56%
−	−	−	−	50%	53%	52%

WED	THU	FRI	07W ---- MON	12W ----	TOT
+	+	+	49%	46%	47%
+	+	−	40%	43%	41%
+	−	+	50%	46%	48%
+	−	−	40%	46%	43%
−	+	+	41%	40%	40%
−	+	−	44%	42%	43%
−	−	+	52%	54%	53%
−	−	−	44%	44%	44%

FRI	07W ---- MON	12W ----	TOT
+	48%	46%	47%
−	41%	43%	42%

246

Figure 5.18: Day of Week Closing Patterns for Soybean Meal

MON	TUE	WED	07SM ---- THU	12SM ----	TOT
+	+	+	42%	46%	44%
+	+	−	47%	50%	49%
+	−	+	54%	45%	49%
+	−	−	53%	50%	51%
−	+	+	43%	46%	44%
−	+	−	53%	46%	49%
−	−	+	49%	48%	48%
−	−	−	49%	47%	48%

MON	TUE	WED	THU	07SM ---- FRI	12SM ----	TOT
+	+	+	+	54%	62%	58%
+	+	+	−	60%	55%	57%
+	+	−	+	38%	44%	41%
+	+	−	−	40%	48%	44%
+	−	+	+	60%	53%	56%
+	−	+	−	44%	45%	44%
+	−	−	+	58%	61%	60%
+	−	−	−	48%	43%	45%
−	+	+	+	53%	46%	49%
−	+	+	−	57%	52%	54%
−	+	−	+	44%	38%	41%
−	+	−	−	49%	44%	46%
−	−	+	+	34%	45%	40%
−	−	+	−	36%	55%	46%
−	−	−	+	53%	51%	52%
−	−	−	−	50%	51%	51%

WED	THU	FRI	07SM ---- MON	12SM ----	TOT
+	+	+	52%	44%	48%
+	+	−	44%	43%	43%
+	−	+	43%	48%	46%
+	−	−	34%	40%	37%
−	+	+	38%	34%	36%
−	+	−	40%	30%	35%
−	−	+	44%	37%	41%
−	−	−	34%	36%	35%

FRI	07SM ---- MON	12SM ----	TOT
+	44%	42%	43%
−	40%	38%	39%

Figure 5.19: Day of Week Closing Patterns for Soybeans

MON	TUE	WED	07S ---- THU	11S ----	TOT
+	+	+	48%	47%	48%
+	+	−	59%	52%	55%
+	−	+	47%	50%	49%
+	−	−	64%	60%	62%
−	+	+	44%	46%	45%
−	+	−	58%	50%	54%
−	−	+	46%	53%	49%
−	−	−	47%	59%	53%

MON	TUE	WED	THU	07S ---- FRI	11S ----	TOT
+	+	+	+	58%	58%	58%
+	+	+	−	56%	46%	51%
+	+	−	+	53%	58%	56%
+	+	−	−	46%	51%	48%
+	−	+	+	58%	49%	53%
+	−	+	−	48%	43%	46%
+	−	−	+	52%	46%	49%
+	−	−	−	46%	39%	42%
−	+	+	+	46%	42%	44%
−	+	+	−	46%	48%	47%
−	+	−	+	47%	52%	49%
−	+	−	−	51%	54%	52%
−	−	+	+	47%	49%	48%
−	−	+	−	53%	55%	54%
−	−	−	+	52%	54%	53%
−	−	−	−	43%	40%	41%

WED	THU	FRI	07S ---- MON	11S ----	TOT
+	+	+	52%	52%	52%
+	+	−	49%	43%	46%
+	−	+	46%	40%	43%
+	−	−	46%	44%	45%
−	+	+	32%	36%	34%
−	+	−	38%	34%	36%
−	−	+	47%	39%	43%
−	−	−	41%	43%	42%

FRI	07S ---- MON	11S ----	TOT
+	44%	42%	43%
−	42%	41%	42%

Figure 5.20: Day of Week Closing Patterns for Oats

MON	TUE	WED	070 ---- THU	120 ----	TOT
+	+	+	49%	47%	48%
+	+	−	44%	43%	43%
+	−	+	47%	40%	43%
+	−	−	40%	48%	44%
−	+	+	49%	47%	48%
−	+	−	48%	43%	45%
−	−	+	50%	49%	49%
−	−	−	48%	43%	45%

MON	TUE	WED	THU	070 ---- FRI	120 ----	TOT
+	+	+	+	43%	56%	50%
+	+	+	−	53%	47%	50%
+	+	−	+	47%	48%	47%
+	+	−	−	46%	48%	47%
+	−	+	+	55%	62%	59%
+	−	+	−	51%	46%	48%
+	−	−	+	55%	56%	55%
+	−	−	−	40%	43%	41%
−	+	+	+	38%	47%	43%
−	+	+	−	54%	48%	51%
−	+	−	+	50%	51%	50%
−	+	−	−	33%	47%	40%
−	−	+	+	42%	46%	44%
−	−	+	−	48%	61%	54%
−	−	−	+	52%	35%	44%
−	−	−	−	58%	53%	55%

WED	THU	FRI	070 ---- MON	120 ----	TOT
+	+	+	43%	45%	44%
+	+	−	38%	36%	37%
+	−	+	48%	48%	48%
+	−	−	42%	42%	42%
−	+	+	44%	42%	43%
−	+	−	40%	39%	39%
−	−	+	47%	43%	45%
−	−	−	41%	36%	38%

FRI	070 ---- MON	120 ----	TOT
+	46%	44%	45%
−	40%	39%	40%

Figure 5.21: Day of Week Closing Patterns for Sugar

MON	TUE	WED	07SU ---- THU ----	10SU	TOT
+	+	+	44%	47%	45%
+	+	−	51%	44%	47%
+	−	+	45%	45%	45%
+	−	−	56%	53%	55%
−	+	+	50%	48%	49%
−	+	−	58%	62%	60%
−	−	+	46%	48%	47%
−	−	−	47%	51%	49%

MON	TUE	WED	THU	07SU ---- FRI ----	10SU	TOT
+	+	+	+	62%	57%	60%
+	+	+	−	58%	59%	58%
+	+	−	+	73%	67%	70%
+	+	−	−	63%	57%	60%
+	−	+	+	54%	51%	52%
+	−	+	−	41%	59%	50%
+	−	−	+	55%	56%	56%
+	−	−	−	50%	40%	45%
−	+	+	+	44%	56%	50%
−	+	+	−	52%	55%	54%
−	+	−	+	57%	49%	53%
−	+	−	−	44%	48%	46%
−	−	+	+	44%	41%	43%
−	−	+	−	44%	38%	41%
−	−	−	+	50%	40%	45%
−	−	−	−	52%	59%	56%

WED	THU	FRI	07SU ---- MON ----	10SU	TOT
+	+	+	47%	41%	44%
+	+	−	43%	42%	43%
+	−	+	42%	40%	41%
+	−	−	45%	51%	48%
−	+	+	49%	49%	49%
−	+	−	45%	44%	45%
−	−	+	44%	47%	46%
−	−	−	38%	46%	42%

FRI	07SU ---- MON ----	10SU	TOT
+	45%	43%	44%
−	44%	46%	45%

Figure 5.22: Day of Week Closing Patterns for Cocoa

MON	TUE	WED	07CO ---- THU	12CO ----	TOT
+	+	+	43%	42%	42%
+	+	−	54%	52%	53%
+	−	+	45%	47%	46%
+	−	−	56%	50%	53%
−	+	+	47%	47%	47%
−	+	−	51%	51%	51%
−	−	+	52%	54%	53%
−	−	−	50%	53%	51%

MON	TUE	WED	THU	07CO ---- FRI	12CO ----	TOT
+	+	+	+	46%	51%	48%
+	+	+	−	54%	38%	46%
+	+	−	+	54%	58%	56%
+	+	−	−	55%	59%	57%
+	−	+	+	50%	46%	48%
+	−	+	−	48%	43%	46%
+	−	−	+	52%	48%	50%
+	−	−	−	56%	57%	56%
−	+	+	+	46%	51%	49%
−	+	+	−	54%	56%	55%
−	+	−	+	53%	61%	57%
−	+	−	−	65%	69%	67%
−	−	+	+	53%	50%	51%
−	−	+	−	48%	51%	49%
−	−	−	+	58%	60%	59%
−	−	−	−	53%	54%	53%

WED	THU	FRI	07CO ---- MON	12CO ----	TOT
+	+	+	52%	54%	53%
+	+	−	48%	42%	45%
+	−	+	53%	54%	54%
+	−	−	40%	45%	42%
−	+	+	50%	50%	50%
−	+	−	46%	50%	48%
−	−	+	48%	44%	46%
−	−	−	43%	50%	47%

FRI	07CO ---- MON	12CO ----	TOT
+	50%	50%	50%
−	44%	47%	46%

251

Figure 5.23: Day of Week Closing Patterns for Coffee

MON	TUE	WED	07CC THU 12CC		TOT
+	+	+	52%	60%	56%
+	+	−	57%	53%	55%
+	−	+	57%	45%	51%
+	−	−	59%	56%	58%
−	+	+	58%	58%	58%
−	+	−	57%	49%	53%
−	−	+	55%	55%	55%
−	−	−	47%	57%	52%

MON	TUE	WED	THU	07CC FRI 12CC		TOT
+	+	+	+	52%	65%	59%
+	+	+	−	54%	50%	52%
+	+	−	+	50%	64%	57%
+	+	−	−	33%	39%	36%
+	−	+	+	53%	59%	56%
+	−	+	−	44%	55%	49%
+	−	−	+	53%	65%	59%
+	−	−	−	44%	56%	50%
−	+	+	+	60%	53%	57%
−	+	+	−	35%	53%	44%
−	+	−	+	64%	44%	54%
−	+	−	−	44%	51%	47%
−	−	+	+	50%	53%	51%
−	−	+	−	48%	44%	46%
−	−	−	+	60%	52%	56%
−	−	−	−	43%	27%	35%

WED	THU	FRI	07CC MON 12CC		TOT
+	+	+	56%	55%	56%
+	+	−	50%	56%	53%
+	−	+	51%	46%	48%
+	−	−	38%	40%	39%
−	+	+	55%	49%	52%
−	+	−	32%	43%	38%
−	−	+	46%	51%	49%
−	−	−	41%	41%	41%

FRI	07CC MON 12CC		TOT
+	52%	50%	51%
−	40%	44%	42%

Figure 5.24: Day of Week Closing Patterns for Orange Juice

MON	TUE	WED	07OJ ---- THU	11OJ	TOT
+	+	+	46%	45%	46%
+	+	-	46%	50%	48%
+	-	+	44%	38%	41%
+	-	-	45%	52%	48%
-	+	+	43%	41%	42%
-	+	-	43%	47%	45%
-	-	+	50%	49%	49%
-	-	-	56%	51%	54%

MON	TUE	WED	THU	07OJ ---- FRI	11OJ	TOT
+	+	+	+	53%	56%	54%
+	+	+	-	43%	48%	45%
+	+	-	+	64%	55%	59%
+	+	-	-	53%	46%	50%
+	-	+	+	50%	54%	52%
+	-	+	-	52%	48%	50%
+	-	-	+	46%	52%	49%
+	-	-	-	50%	62%	56%
-	+	+	+	44%	50%	47%
-	+	+	-	59%	52%	55%
-	+	-	+	44%	45%	45%
-	+	-	-	59%	43%	51%
-	-	+	+	36%	46%	41%
-	-	+	-	55%	54%	55%
-	-	-	+	58%	47%	52%
-	-	-	-	61%	61%	61%

WED	THU	FRI	07OJ ---- MON	11OJ	TOT
+	+	+	50%	51%	51%
+	+	-	48%	45%	46%
+	-	+	51%	54%	52%
+	-	-	49%	47%	48%
-	+	+	53%	58%	55%
-	+	-	44%	47%	45%
-	-	+	50%	48%	49%
-	-	-	51%	47%	49%

FRI	07OJ ---- MON	11OJ	TOT
+	53%	55%	54%
-	48%	48%	48%

Figure 5.25: Day of Week Closing Patterns for Copper

MON	TUE	WED	07CP ---- THU 12CP ----		TOT
			07CP	12CP	
			THU		TOT
+	+	+	44%	42%	43%
+	+	−	46%	47%	47%
+	−	+	51%	56%	54%
+	−	−	60%	55%	57%
−	+	+	38%	40%	39%
−	+	−	49%	47%	48%
−	−	+	45%	49%	47%
−	−	−	61%	58%	59%

MON	TUE	WED	THU	07CP FRI	12CP	TOT
+	+	+	+	53%	41%	47%
+	+	+	−	70%	64%	67%
+	+	−	+	50%	56%	53%
+	+	−	−	70%	68%	69%
+	−	+	+	45%	54%	50%
+	−	+	−	52%	54%	53%
+	−	−	+	39%	39%	39%
+	−	−	−	52%	49%	50%
−	+	+	+	43%	51%	47%
−	+	+	−	56%	60%	58%
−	+	−	+	50%	51%	50%
−	+	−	−	70%	67%	69%
−	−	+	+	43%	43%	43%
−	−	+	−	55%	53%	54%
−	−	−	+	50%	48%	49%
−	−	−	−	66%	64%	65%

WED	THU	FRI	07CP MON	12CP	TOT
+	+	+	36%	39%	37%
+	+	−	44%	41%	43%
+	−	+	45%	43%	44%
+	−	−	52%	48%	50%
−	+	+	35%	37%	36%
−	+	−	38%	39%	38%
−	−	+	39%	40%	40%
−	−	−	38%	38%	38%

FRI	07CP MON	12CP	TOT
+	40%	41%	40%
−	43%	42%	43%

254

Figure 5.26: Day of Week Closing Patterns for Gold

MON	TUE	WED	06GC THU	12GC	TOT
+	+	+	39%	36%	37%
+	+	−	50%	52%	51%
+	−	+	30%	31%	30%
+	−	−	41%	43%	42%
−	+	+	40%	43%	41%
−	+	−	61%	63%	62%
−	−	+	46%	42%	44%
−	−	−	58%	57%	57%

MON	TUE	WED	THU	06GC FRI	12GC	TOT
+	+	+	+	50%	41%	45%
+	+	+	−	68%	67%	68%
+	+	−	+	40%	41%	41%
+	+	−	−	69%	66%	67%
+	−	+	+	57%	56%	56%
+	−	+	−	54%	49%	52%
+	−	−	+	41%	47%	44%
+	−	−	−	51%	50%	50%
−	+	+	+	36%	42%	39%
−	+	+	−	61%	58%	59%
−	+	−	+	45%	47%	46%
−	+	−	−	52%	52%	52%
−	−	+	+	38%	39%	38%
−	−	+	−	50%	51%	51%
−	−	−	+	56%	52%	54%
−	−	−	−	51%	60%	55%

WED	THU	FRI	06GC MON	12GC	TOT
+	+	+	41%	40%	40%
+	+	−	50%	54%	52%
+	−	+	51%	48%	49%
+	−	−	52%	51%	52%
−	+	+	50%	47%	49%
−	+	−	48%	48%	48%
−	−	+	42%	46%	44%
−	−	−	31%	36%	33%

FRI	06GC MON	12GC	TOT
+	48%	47%	47%
−	46%	48%	47%

255

Figure 5.27: Day of Week Closing Patterns for Lumber

MON	TUE	WED	01LB ---- THU 07LB		TOT
			01LB	07LB	
+	+	+	60%	58%	59%
+	+	−	55%	47%	51%
+	−	+	64%	60%	62%
+	−	−	53%	55%	54%
−	+	+	48%	51%	50%
−	+	−	48%	52%	50%
−	−	+	55%	57%	56%
−	−	−	47%	53%	50%

MON	TUE	WED	THU	01LB ---- FRI 07LB		TOT
				01LB	07LB	
+	+	+	+	56%	39%	48%
+	+	+	−	40%	69%	54%
+	+	−	+	63%	69%	66%
+	+	−	−	44%	65%	55%
+	−	+	+	40%	55%	48%
+	−	+	−	42%	50%	46%
+	−	−	+	55%	52%	54%
+	−	−	−	43%	54%	48%
−	+	+	+	37%	39%	38%
−	+	+	−	46%	60%	53%
−	+	−	+	65%	51%	58%
−	+	−	−	35%	65%	50%
−	−	+	+	53%	48%	50%
−	−	+	−	46%	45%	45%
−	−	−	+	44%	28%	36%
−	−	−	−	44%	46%	45%

WED	THU	FRI	01LB ---- MON 07LB		TOT
			01LB	07LB	
+	+	+	53%	44%	48%
+	+	−	35%	41%	38%
+	−	+	47%	50%	48%
+	−	−	51%	50%	50%
−	+	+	47%	50%	49%
−	+	−	41%	40%	40%
−	−	+	44%	47%	46%
−	−	−	36%	38%	37%

FRI	01LB ---- MON 07LB		TOT
	01LB	07LB	
+	47%	48%	47%
−	39%	39%	39%

Figure 5.28: Day of Week Closing Patterns for Cotton

MON	TUE	WED	07NY ---- THU 12NY ----		TOT
			07NY	12NY	
+	+	+	45%	40%	43%
+	+	−	43%	44%	43%
+	−	+	52%	53%	52%
+	−	−	51%	52%	51%
−	+	+	46%	47%	47%
−	+	−	41%	49%	45%
−	−	+	43%	41%	42%
−	−	−	55%	53%	54%

MON	TUE	WED	THU	07NY ---- FRI	12NY ----	TOT
				07NY	12NY	
+	+	+	+	53%	46%	50%
+	+	+	−	63%	54%	58%
+	+	−	+	69%	73%	71%
+	+	−	−	54%	62%	58%
+	−	+	+	48%	54%	51%
+	−	+	−	54%	55%	54%
+	−	−	+	61%	49%	55%
+	−	−	−	57%	57%	57%
−	+	+	+	48%	41%	45%
−	+	+	−	43%	44%	43%
−	+	−	+	46%	50%	48%
−	+	−	−	53%	51%	52%
−	−	+	+	61%	43%	52%
−	−	+	−	56%	47%	52%
−	−	−	+	54%	59%	56%
−	−	−	−	47%	43%	45%

WED	THU	FRI	07NY ---- MON	12NY ----	TOT
			07NY	12NY	
+	+	+	49%	56%	53%
+	+	−	47%	49%	48%
+	−	+	50%	44%	47%
+	−	−	43%	44%	43%
−	+	+	50%	47%	49%
−	+	−	33%	43%	38%
−	−	+	59%	49%	54%
−	−	−	36%	43%	40%

FRI	07NY ---- MON	12NY ----	TOT
	07NY	12NY	
+	51%	50%	50%
−	41%	44%	43%

257

Figure 5.29: Day of Week Closing Patterns for Treasury Bonds

MON	TUE	WED	06TR THU	12TR	TOT
+	+	+	43%	40%	42%
+	+	−	41%	43%	42%
+	−	+	51%	52%	52%
+	−	−	58%	56%	57%
−	+	+	48%	55%	52%
−	+	−	40%	40%	40%
−	−	+	55%	52%	53%
−	−	−	48%	44%	46%

MON	TUE	WED	THU	06TR FRI	12TR	TOT
+	+	+	+	44%	41%	43%
+	+	+	−	42%	42%	42%
+	+	−	+	50%	43%	46%
+	+	−	−	44%	47%	45%
+	−	+	+	45%	47%	46%
+	−	+	−	47%	46%	47%
+	−	−	+	54%	54%	54%
+	−	−	−	45%	38%	42%
−	+	+	+	49%	48%	48%
−	+	+	−	41%	39%	40%
−	+	−	+	47%	53%	50%
−	+	−	−	47%	44%	45%
−	−	+	+	40%	39%	39%
−	−	+	−	43%	47%	45%
−	−	−	+	68%	69%	69%
−	−	−	−	34%	37%	36%

WED	THU	FRI	06TR MON	12TR	TOT
+	+	+	44%	46%	45%
+	+	−	50%	50%	50%
+	−	+	46%	40%	43%
+	−	−	47%	51%	49%
−	+	+	48%	51%	50%
−	+	−	39%	35%	37%
−	−	+	39%	43%	41%
−	−	−	35%	37%	36%

FRI	06TR MON	12TR	TOT
+	43%	43%	43%
−	42%	43%	42%

258

Figure 5.30: Day of Week Closing Patterns for Treasury Bills

MON	TUE	WED	06TB THU	12TB	TOT
+	+	+	44%	46%	45%
+	+	−	38%	46%	42%
+	−	+	53%	48%	51%
+	−	−	43%	53%	48%
−	+	+	54%	57%	56%
−	+	−	47%	42%	44%
−	−	+	50%	48%	49%
−	−	−	44%	46%	45%

MON	TUE	WED	THU	06TB FRI	12TB	TOT
+	+	+	+	65%	72%	68%
+	+	+	−	44%	38%	41%
+	+	−	+	57%	50%	54%
+	+	−	−	59%	45%	52%
+	−	+	+	35%	43%	39%
+	−	+	−	38%	44%	41%
+	−	−	+	69%	57%	63%
+	−	−	−	40%	47%	43%
−	+	+	+	50%	48%	49%
−	+	+	−	42%	36%	39%
−	+	−	+	37%	53%	45%
−	+	−	−	37%	37%	37%
−	−	+	+	58%	64%	61%
−	−	+	−	32%	42%	37%
−	−	−	+	55%	51%	53%
−	−	−	−	41%	41%	41%

WED	THU	FRI	06TB MON	12TB	TOT
+	+	+	49%	51%	50%
+	+	−	40%	40%	40%
+	−	+	57%	47%	52%
+	−	−	43%	42%	43%
−	+	+	48%	48%	48%
−	+	−	51%	50%	50%
−	−	+	39%	43%	41%
−	−	−	49%	48%	48%

FRI	06TB MON	12TB	TOT
+	48%	47%	48%
−	45%	44%	45%

259

Figure 5.31: Day of Week Closing Patterns for Swiss Franc

MON	TUE	WED	06SF ---- THU ----	12SF	TOT
+	+	+	43%	47%	45%
+	+	−	45%	53%	49%
+	−	+	40%	48%	44%
+	−	−	43%	44%	43%
−	+	+	45%	48%	46%
−	+	−	56%	52%	54%
−	−	+	34%	35%	35%
−	−	−	36%	31%	34%

MON	TUE	WED	THU	06SF ---- FRI ----	12SF	TOT
+	+	+	+	66%	66%	66%
+	+	+	−	68%	56%	62%
+	+	−	+	50%	58%	54%
+	+	−	−	38%	32%	35%
+	−	+	+	62%	53%	58%
+	−	+	−	35%	38%	37%
+	−	−	+	58%	45%	51%
+	−	−	−	35%	45%	40%
−	+	+	+	53%	68%	60%
−	+	+	−	27%	36%	32%
−	+	−	+	50%	47%	48%
−	+	−	−	33%	29%	31%
−	−	+	+	40%	45%	43%
−	−	+	−	27%	29%	28%
−	−	−	+	19%	57%	38%
−	−	−	−	35%	33%	34%

WED	THU	FRI	06SF ---- MON ----	12SF	TOT
+	+	+	48%	56%	52%
+	+	−	45%	50%	47%
+	−	+	51%	39%	45%
+	−	−	42%	46%	44%
−	+	+	45%	49%	47%
−	+	−	46%	39%	42%
−	−	+	42%	46%	44%
−	−	−	40%	38%	39%

FRI	06SF ---- MON ----	12SF	TOT
+	48%	49%	48%
−	45%	43%	44%

Figure 5.32: Day of Week Closing Patterns for Japanese Yen

MON	TUE	WED	06JY ---- THU 12JY ----		TOT
+	+	+	40%	42%	41%
+	+	-	44%	55%	49%
+	-	+	62%	59%	61%
+	-	-	32%	36%	34%
-	+	+	50%	43%	47%
-	+	-	43%	44%	44%
-	-	+	41%	43%	42%
-	-	-	42%	40%	41%

MON	TUE	WED	THU	06JY ---- FRI 12JY ----		TOT
+	+	+	+	53%	61%	57%
+	+	+	-	50%	56%	53%
+	+	-	+	38%	44%	41%
+	+	-	-	50%	52%	51%
+	-	+	+	50%	48%	49%
+	-	+	-	40%	46%	43%
+	-	-	+	23%	33%	28%
+	-	-	-	50%	45%	47%
-	+	+	+	55%	59%	57%
-	+	+	-	34%	39%	37%
-	+	-	+	46%	35%	41%
-	+	-	-	51%	54%	52%
-	-	+	+	45%	57%	51%
-	-	+	-	41%	45%	43%
-	-	-	+	37%	40%	39%
-	-	-	-	21%	25%	23%

WED	THU	FRI	06JY ---- MON 12JY ----		TOT
+	+	+	68%	63%	66%
+	+	-	42%	51%	46%
+	-	+	53%	56%	54%
+	-	-	41%	53%	47%
-	+	+	55%	58%	57%
-	+	-	35%	27%	31%
-	-	+	54%	48%	51%
-	-	-	38%	38%	38%

FRI	06JY ---- MON 12JY ----		TOT
+	59%	56%	57%
-	40%	45%	42%

261

Figure 5.33: Day of Week Closing Patterns for British Pound

MON	TUE	WED	06BP ---- THU	12BP ----	TOT
+	+	+	42%	45%	43%
+	+	−	60%	55%	57%
+	−	+	44%	48%	46%
+	−	−	37%	43%	40%
−	+	+	46%	44%	45%
−	+	−	42%	50%	46%
−	−	+	38%	37%	37%
−	−	−	36%	46%	41%

MON	TUE	WED	THU	06BP ---- FRI	12BP ----	TOT
+	+	+	+	65%	62%	63%
+	+	+	−	38%	47%	42%
+	+	−	+	44%	47%	45%
+	+	−	−	38%	37%	37%
+	−	+	+	48%	39%	43%
+	−	+	−	42%	43%	43%
+	−	−	+	62%	53%	58%
+	−	−	−	40%	42%	41%
−	+	+	+	48%	44%	46%
−	+	+	−	51%	40%	46%
−	+	−	+	46%	47%	46%
−	+	−	−	30%	42%	36%
−	−	+	+	41%	46%	44%
−	−	+	−	53%	48%	50%
−	−	−	+	50%	56%	53%
−	−	−	−	35%	46%	41%

WED	THU	FRI	06BP ---- MON	12BP ----	TOT
+	+	+	66%	64%	65%
+	+	−	45%	53%	49%
+	−	+	39%	48%	44%
+	−	−	47%	55%	51%
−	+	+	53%	50%	51%
−	+	−	31%	41%	36%
−	−	+	52%	59%	55%
−	−	−	37%	44%	41%

FRI	06BP ---- MON	12BP ----	TOT
+	51%	54%	52%
−	43%	48%	45%

Figure 5.34: Day of Week Closing Patterns for Platinum

MON	TUE	WED	04PL ----	THU	10PL ----	TOT
+	+	+	39%		45%	42%
+	+	--	46%		46%	46%
+	--	+	39%		39%	39%
+	--	--	45%		46%	46%
--	+	+	46%		47%	47%
--	+	--	50%		52%	51%
--	--	+	40%		43%	42%
--	--	--	50%		52%	51%

MON	TUE	WED	THU	04PL ----	FRI	10PL ----	TOT
+	+	+	+	54%		53%	54%
+	+	+	--	51%		47%	49%
+	+	--	+	38%		47%	42%
+	+	--	--	64%		57%	60%
+	--	+	+	53%		50%	51%
+	--	+	--	47%		ᴜ3%	45%
+	--	--	+	48%		50%	49%
+	--	--	--	42%		50%	46%
--	+	+	+	44%		48%	46%
--	+	+	--	60%		54%	57%
--	+	--	+	52%		57%	55%
--	+	--	--	45%		52%	49%
--	--	+	+	62%		48%	55%
--	--	+	--	62%		63%	62%
--	--	--	+	52%		48%	50%
--	--	--	--	54%		61%	58%

WED	THU	FRI	04PL ----	MON	10PL ----	TOT
+	+	+	55%		55%	55%
+	+	--	44%		50%	47%
+	--	+	53%		42%	47%
+	--	--	41%		45%	43%
--	+	+	52%		45%	49%
--	+	--	48%		43%	46%
--	--	+	46%		52%	49%
--	--	--	41%		38%	40%

FRI	04PL ----	MON	10PL ----	TOT
+	52%		49%	50%
--	44%		44%	44%

6

Seasonal Timing Signals

KEY DATE SEASONAL ANALYSIS

What is seasonality? Since before the days of W .D. Gann, futures traders have known and employed seasonal futures tendencies in their trading. Gann popularized the notion of seasonal price behavior. However, even today, many years after his seasonal studies, traders are still not entirely convinced that these repetitive patterns can be an asset to trading programs. Perhaps this is because a majority of traders do not understand seasonals and their considerable importance in the futures and stock markets. Let's begin with a simple definition of seasonality:

> *Seasonality is the tendency for prices or economic data to move in certain directions during certain times of the year; patterns which are often repetitive and, therefore, relatively predictable.*

Given this definition, we can easily understand that the price of corn might move lower during harvest when producers bring their crop to market. We can also understand that cattle prices might move higher during the winter months as animals are stressed due to cold weather. Certainly one of the most obvious seasonals is the tendency for orange juice futures prices to move higher during the frost and freeze season. Yet, strangely enough, the OJ seasonal is not nearly as reliable as are other seasonal patterns and tendencies. In fact, there are many more reliable seasonals in such markets as copper or lumber. The fact is that seasonality is not merely a function of weather. It is rather a function of intra-year supply and demand factors which tend to follow essentially similar patterns during given times of the calendar year.

This, to many traders, is the most surprising aspect of seasonals. They feel, erroneously, that seasonality and the effects of weather on prices are one and the same thing. Actually, the effect of weather on prices is just one aspect of seasonality. There are many other factors which influence prices on a relatively regular intra-year basis, such as supply, demand, consumption, production, availability of transportation, advance purchases, hedging and so on. Some or all of these in combination with weather factors can exert a marked and repetitive effect on the price of virtually any market.

Seasonal price behavior is not limited to the agricultural commodity markets: it exists in virtually all markets, with varying degrees of intensity and regularity.

Seasonal price tendencies can be found in the cash and futures markets both. I have demonstrated the existence of cash and futures seasonal tendencies in numerous published studies and books since the 1970 s.[1]

There are two general categories of seasonal price tendencies. They are related to one another. Seasonal cash tendencies are determined by studying and analyzing the cash markets. Seasonal futures tendencies are determined by studying and analyzing the futures markets. Figures 6-1 and 6-2 show monthly cash seasonal price tendencies in wheat and stock prices. Figures 6-3 and 6-4 show weekly futures seasonal tendencies in copper and live cattle prices. As you can see, there are distinct patterns, some of which can be traced back many years.

[1]*How to Profit from Seasonal Commodity Spreads* (New York, John Wiley & Sons, 1983); *Seasonal Cash Charts* and *Seasonal Futures Charts* (New York, John Wiley & Sons, 1991); *Seasonal Concepts in Futures Trading* (New York, John Wiley & Sons, 1989); and *Jake Bernstein's Seasonal Futures Spreads* (New York, John Wiley & Sons, 1990). In addition, there have been various seasonal studies and publications by others.

Figure 6.1: The Cash Seasonal Tendency in Wheat, 1862–1990

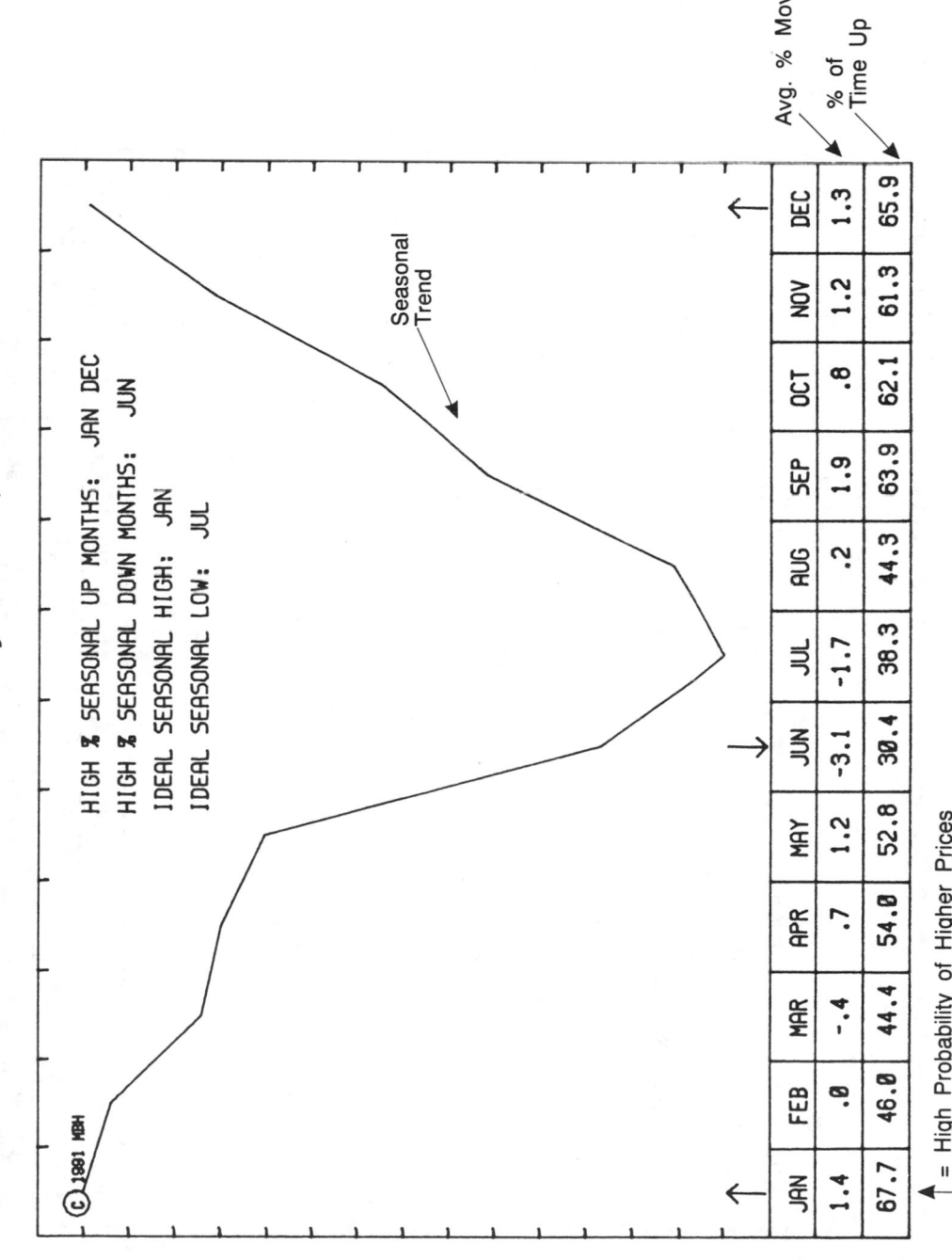

© 1991 MBH

HIGH % SEASONAL UP MONTHS: JAN DEC
HIGH % SEASONAL DOWN MONTHS: JUN
IDEAL SEASONAL HIGH: JAN
IDEAL SEASONAL LOW: JUL

Seasonal
Trend

Avg. % Move

% of
Time Up

	JAN	FEB	MAR	APR	MAY	JUN	JUL	AUG	SEP	OCT	NOV	DEC
Avg. % Move	1.4	.0	-.4	.7	1.2	-3.1	-1.7	.2	1.9	.8	1.2	1.3
% of Time Up	67.7	46.0	44.4	54.0	52.8	30.4	38.3	44.3	63.9	62.1	61.3	65.9

← = High Probability of Higher Prices
→ = High Probability of Lower Prices

Figure 6.2: Standard 14-Period Stochastic Crossover Signals: Buy and Sell on %K and %D crossovers

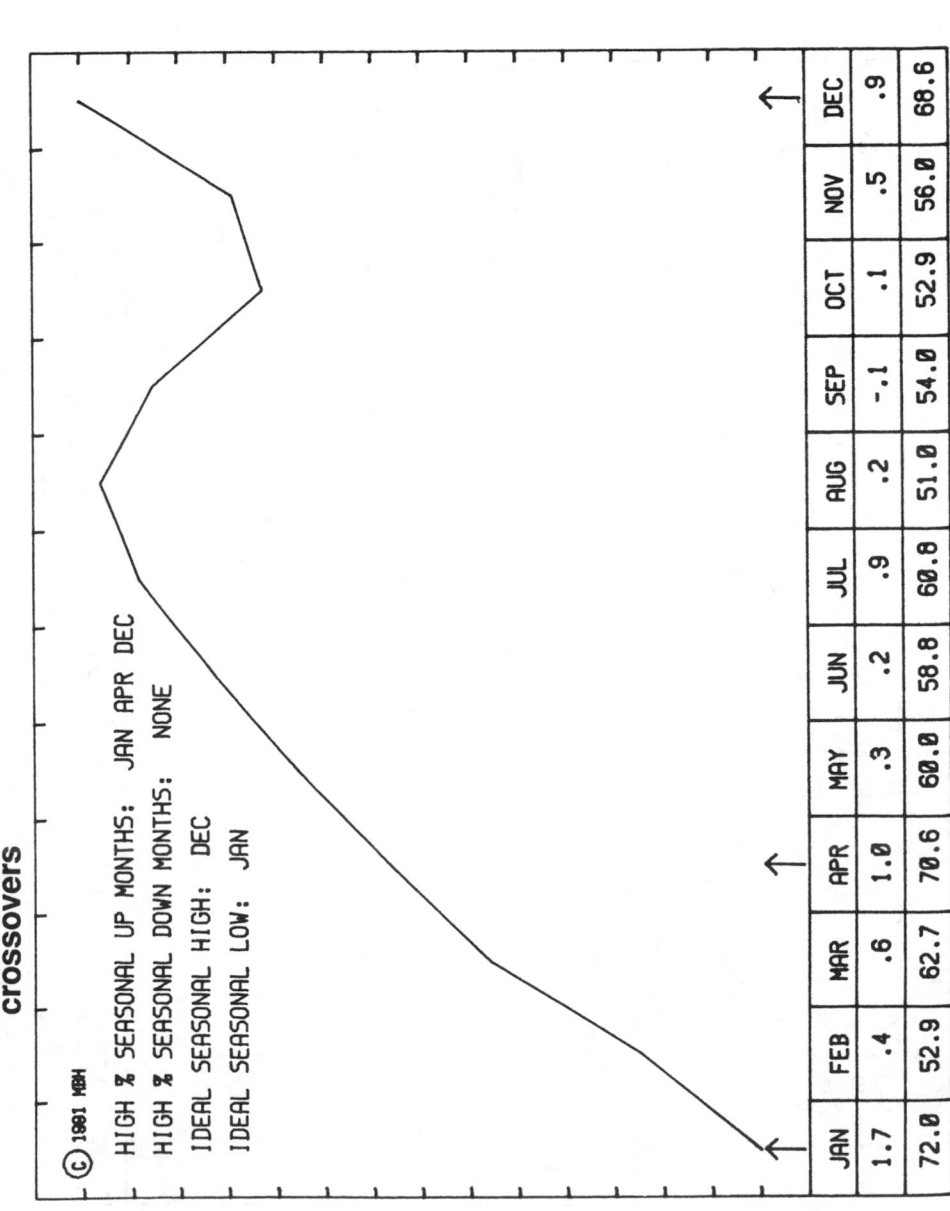

© 1981 MBH

HIGH % SEASONAL UP MONTHS: JAN APR DEC
HIGH % SEASONAL DOWN MONTHS: NONE
IDEAL SEASONAL HIGH: DEC
IDEAL SEASONAL LOW: JAN

JAN	FEB	MAR	APR	MAY	JUN	JUL	AUG	SEP	OCT	NOV	DEC
1.7	.4	.6	1.0	.3	.2	.9	.2	-.1	.1	.5	.9
72.0	52.9	62.7	70.6	60.0	58.8	60.8	51.0	54.0	52.9	56.0	68.6

Figure 6.3: Weekly Seasonal Futures Tendency: Copper

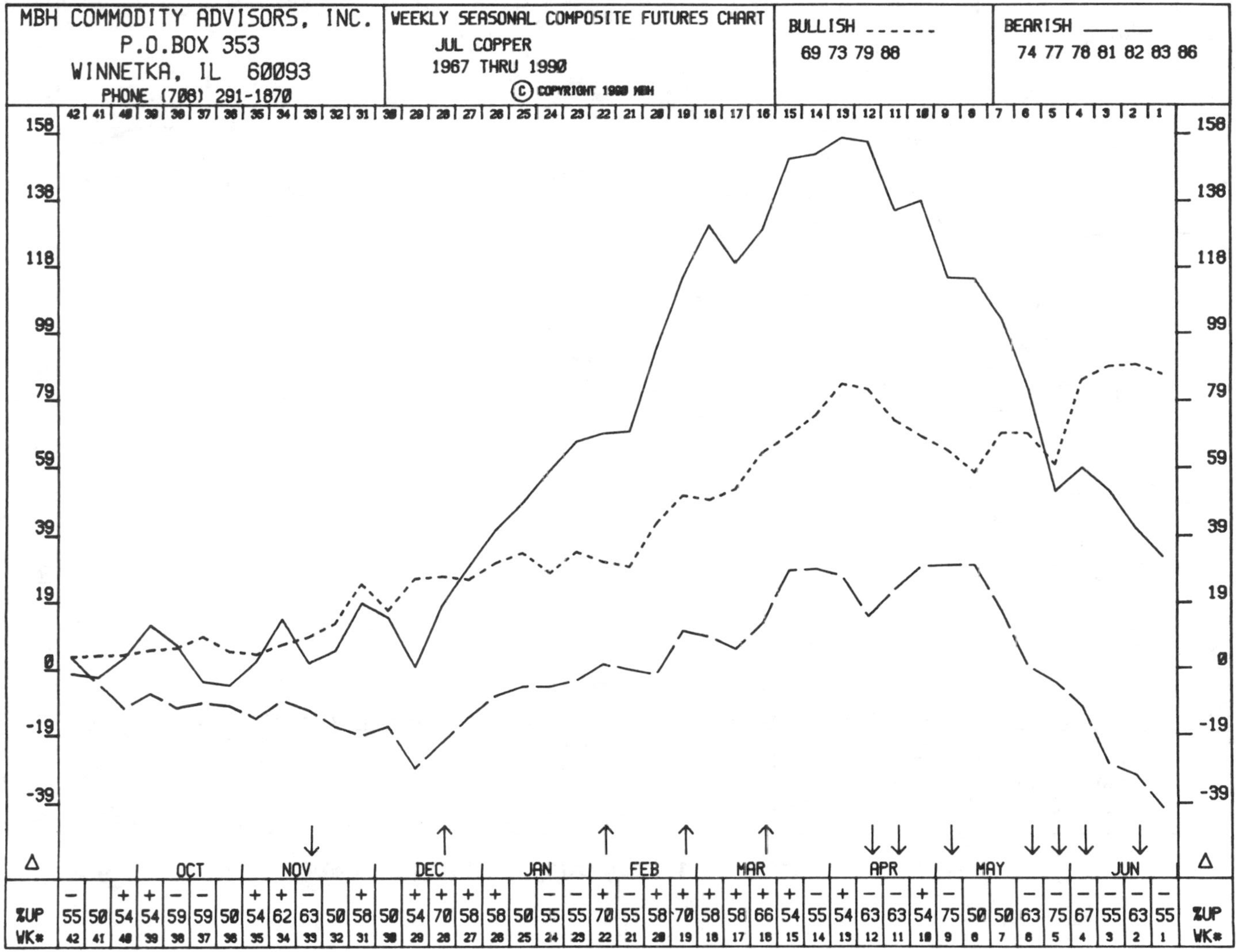

Figure 6.4: Weekly Seasonal Futures Tendency: Live Cattle

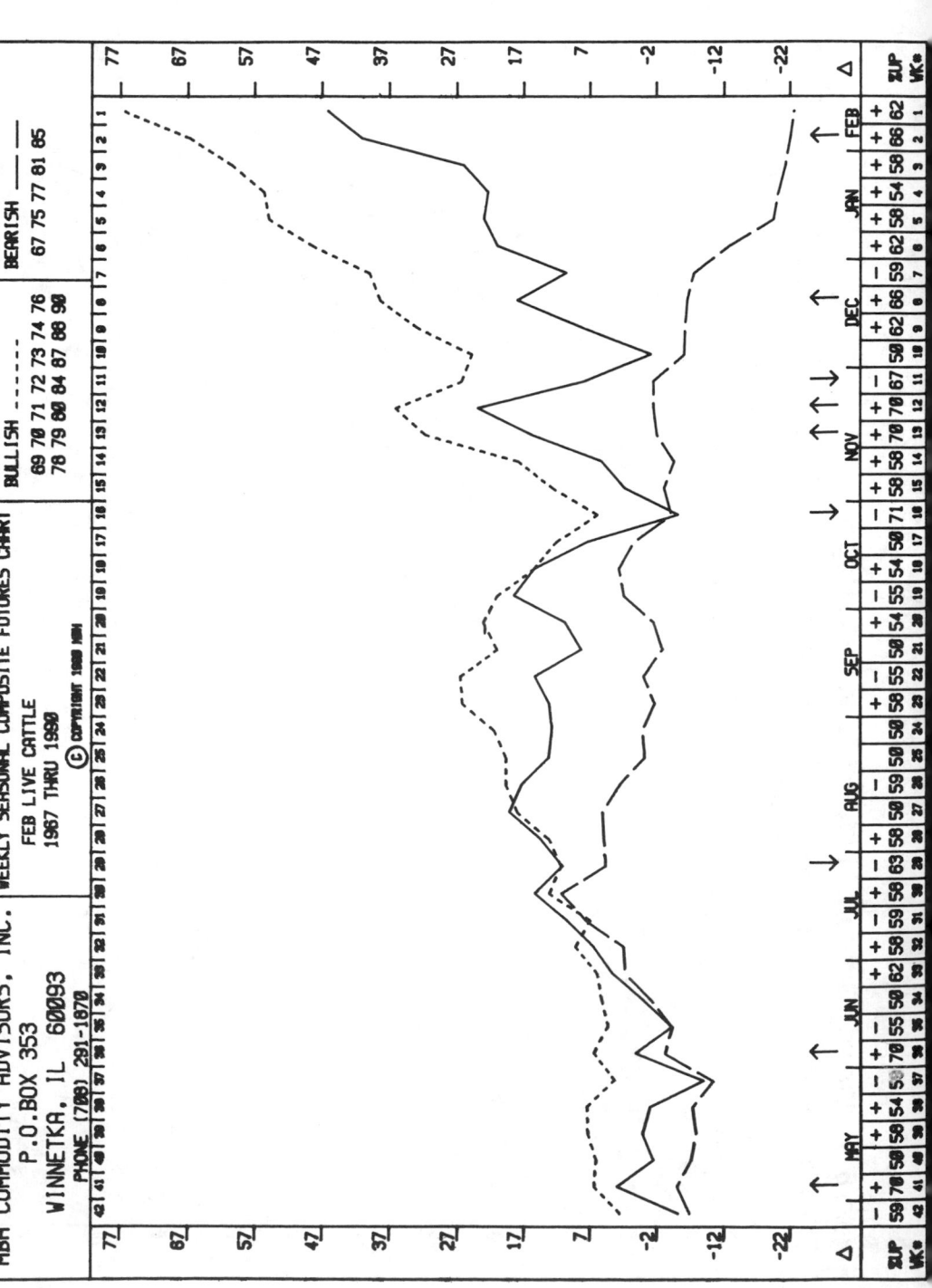

Although it may be reasonably concluded that seasonals can and will change over time, the fact remains that there are general and specific patterns which have lasted for many years and which should persist in the future. Cash and futures tend to move together, each affecting the other. The futures trader, however, is primarily concerned with *futures seasonal tendencies*, which relate more directly to the specific aspects of futures trading.

In addition to the existence of seasonality in cash and futures markets, there are also reliable seasonal patterns and tendencies in futures spreads. These tendencies were examined in my book *How to Profit from Seasonal Commodity Spreads* (New York, John Wiley & Sons, 1983). (This book is presently out of print and has been replaced by *Jake Bernstein's Seasonal Futures Spreads*, (New York, John Wiley & Sons, 1990.) After considerable research I have concluded that there are highly reliable seasonal spread patterns; patterns which may, in fact, be more reliable than those found in either net long or short futures positions. This is not surprising to me inasmuch as there are numerous technical and fundamental factors which make the likelihood of highly reliable spread seasonals more probable. Figure 6-5 shows one such spread, the long June/short October live cattle spread. It is one of the most historically reliable and repetitive of all spreads.

In addition to the cash, futures and spread seasonal parameters discussed previously, seasonals can also be viewed from varying time frames or perspectives. Earlier we examined cash monthly seasonal charts and futures weekly seasonal charts. Seasonals may also be studied on a daily basis. Art Merrill's work employed a daily time frame in order to determine the existence of strong closing price tendencies the day prior to U.S. legal holidays (such as Thanksgiving, Labor Day and Christmas). Hence, there are three time frames from which seasonals may be viewed: monthly, weekly and daily.

The shortest period for which I have extensively examined seasonal price behavior is the daily time frame. Although I have also investigated intra-day and time-of-day patterns, my work here has

Figure 6.5: Seasonal Spread Composite Chart—June Live Cattle/ October Live Cattle, 1967–1988

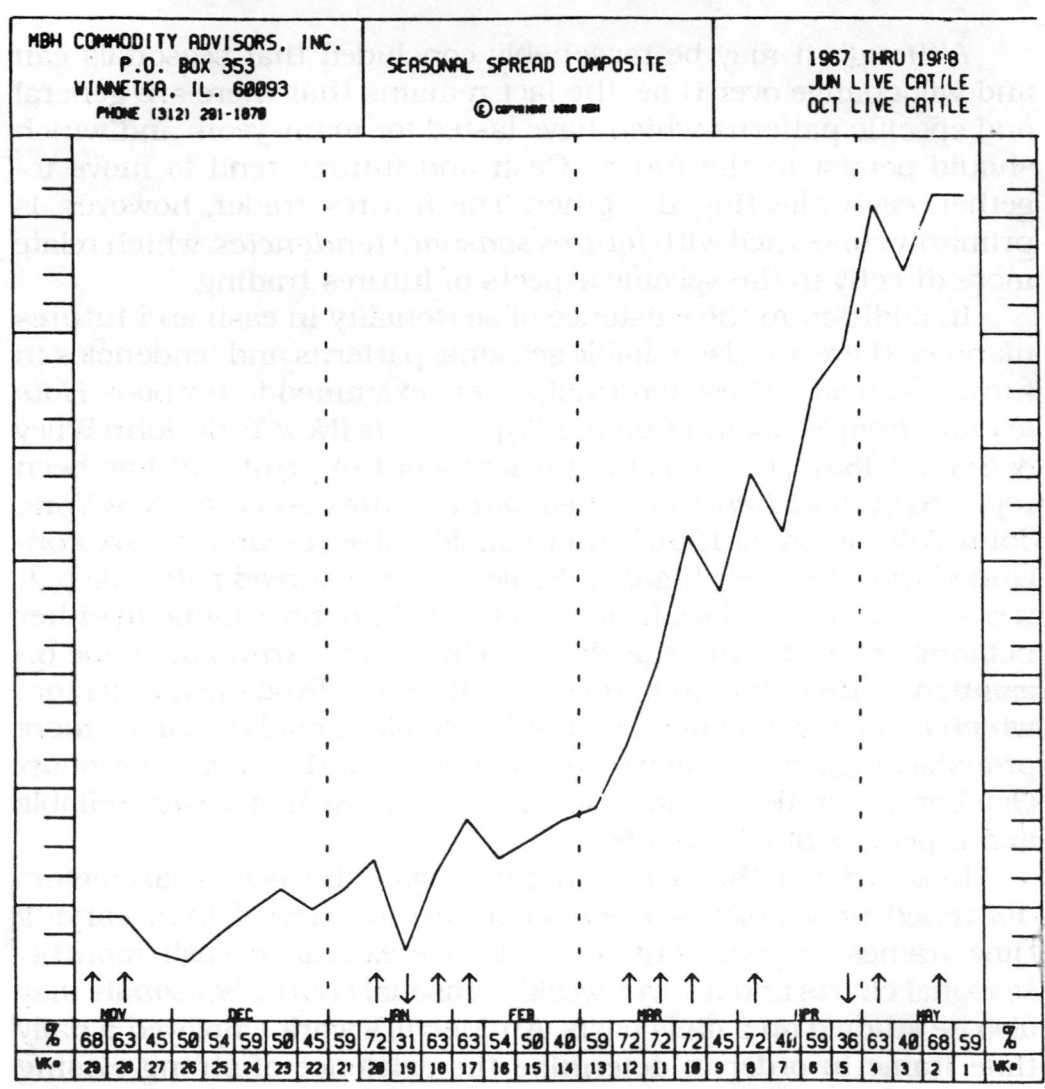

MBH COMMODITY ADVISORS, INC. P.O. BOX 353 WINNETKA, IL. 60093 PHONE (312) 291-1870	SEASONAL SPREAD COMPOSITE © COPYRIGHT 1988 MBH	1967 THRU 1988 JUN LIVE CATTLE OCT LIVE CATTLE

%	68	63	45	50	54	59	50	45	59	72	31	63	63	54	50	40	59	72	72	72	45	72	40	59	36	63	40	68	59	%
WK•	29	28	27	26	25	24	23	22	21	20	19	18	17	16	15	14	13	12	11	10	9	8	7	6	5	4	3	2	1	WK•

272

not been as exhaustive as it has been with monthly, weekly and daily periods. My Critical Time of Day (CTOD) indicator is a type of intraday "seasonal" tendency. It would, however, be more appropriately termed a "diurnal" or daily pattern as opposed to a strictly seasonal pattern. Chronobiologists have discovered many highly repetitive and important diurnal patterns in human and animal biological systems; patterns which can have a marked effect on such things as behavior and the efficacy of therapeutic drugs. It is highly likely that diurnal activity also exists in futures and stock prices. My CTOD indicator is a variant of diurnal behavior.[2]

As you can see from these figures, there have indeed been specific dates and strings of dates during which prices have been prone to move up or down a high percentage of the time for the period of years studied. This, of course, does not imply that history will always repeat itself. Were this true, there would be no markets, no traders, no risk and no reward. The fact of the matter, is as well known, is that there is always risk of loss in futures trading and that signals, whether derived from trading systems, indicators and combinations of indicators and/or fundamentals, won't always work. Economic science has not yet mastered flawless forecasting. There will always be intangibles which affect the functioning of any system, method, indicator or approach to futures trading. Losses are an inherent feature—even a necessary feature—of the whole system. We all profess to know this, yet there is a small (perhaps not so small) part of us that wants to believe in perfection. Many traders fantasize about "perfect systems," and this is perhaps why many unscrupulous operators and system developers have been able to sell what appear to be "near perfect" trading systems, when in fact their systems have proven to be far from perfect.

---

[2]For a specific discussion of CTOD parameters and signals see my book, *Short-Term Trading in Futures* (Chicago, IL, Probus Publishing, 1988).

Figure 6-6: Key Date Seasonal Tendency in January Heating Oil: Buy Mode

CONTRACT	-----ENTRY-----		-----EXIT-----		PROFIT	% PROFIT	ACCUM
	--DATE--	-PRICE-	--DATE--	-PRICE-	LOSS(-)	LOSS(-)	TOTAL
========	========	=======	========	=======	========	=========	=======
8001HO	9/ 4/79	83.50	9/27/79	90.00	6.50	7.78	6.50
8101HO	9/ 2/80	81.44	9/29/80	83.32	1.88	2.31	8.38
8201HO	9/ 1/81	97.97	9/28/81	98.65	.68	.69	9.06
8301HO	9/ 1/82	96.31	9/27/82	101.28	4.97	5.16	14.03
8401HO	9/ 1/83	86.13	9/27/83	86.54	.41	.48	14.44
8501HO	9/ 4/84	81.65	9/27/84	84.98	3.33	4.08	17.77
8601HO	9/ 3/85	79.90	9/27/85	82.77	2.87	3.59	20.64
8701HO	9/ 2/86	48.79	9/ 9/86	44.94	-3.85	-7.89	16.79
8801HO	9/ 1/87	54.22	9/28/87	54.82	.60	1.11	17.39
8901HO	9/ 1/88	45.09	9/ 9/88	42.69	-2.40	-5.32	14.99
9001HO	9/ 1/89	54.65	9/27/89	58.54	3.89	7.12	18.88
9101HO	9/ 4/90	81.54	9/27/90	104.63	22.99	28.16	41.87

TRADE SUMMARY
=============

| # POSITIVE: 10 | # NEGATIVE: 2 | # UNCH: 0 | # TOTAL: 12 |
| AVERAGE PROFIT: 4.81 (6.05%) | AVERAGE LOSS: -3.12 (-6.61%) |
| % TRADES PROFITABLE: 83.33 |

Figure 6-7: Key Date Seasonal Tendency in March T-Bond Futures: Sell Short Mode

CONTRACT	-----ENTRY-----		------EXIT------		PROFIT	% PROFIT	ACCUM
	--DATE--	-PRICE-	--DATE--	-PRICE-	LOSS(-)	LOSS(-)	TOTAL
========	========	======	========	======	========	========	======
7803TR	12/27/77	99.02	1/ 9/78	97.06	1.96	1.98	1.96
7903TR	12/26/78	90.07	1/ 8/79	90.00	.07	.08	2.03
8003TR	12/26/79	81.02	1/ 8/80	80.08	.94	1.16	2.97
8103TR	12/24/80	72.01	1/ 8/81	71.06	.95	1.32	3.92
8203TR	12/24/81	61.03	1/ 8/82	59.05	1.98	3.24	5.90
8303TR	12/27/82	77.01	1/10/83	76.05	.96	1.25	6.86
8403TR	12/27/83	70.04	1/ 9/84	70.04	.00	.00	6.86
8503TR	12/24/84	72.05	1/ 8/85	71.07	.98	1.36	7.84
8603TR	12/24/85	84.25	1/ 8/86	84.11	.14	.17	7.98
8703TR	12/24/86	100.12	1/ 8/87	101.04	-.92	-.92	7.06
8803TR	12/24/87	88.68	1/ 8/88	86.31	2.37	2.67	9.43
8903TR	12/27/88	89.14	1/ 9/89	88.25	.89	1.00	10.32
9003TR	12/26/89	98.12	1/ 8/90	97.19	.93	.95	11.25
9103TR	12/24/90	94.22	1/ 8/91	94.20	.02	.02	11.27

TRADE SUMMARY
===============

POSITIVE: 12   # NEGATIVE: 1   # UNCH: 1   # TOTAL: 14
AVERAGE PROFIT: 1.02 (1.27%)   AVERAGE LOSS: -.92 (-.92%)
% TRADES PROFITABLE: 85.71

Here's our working definition of a "key date trade" (KDT):

A key date trade is a futures market trade initiated on a specific date (or the next business day if the market is closed on the key date) and exited on a specific date (or the next business day if the market is closed on the key date) or exited at a predetermined stop loss.

KDT may also be defined as:

A specific set of market instructions defining market, contract month, buy or sell direction, entry and exit date as well as stop loss level.

Now that we've looked at the theory and concepts of KDT's, let's look at a sample KDT generated by my computer studies. The listing below shows the following KDT:

BUY JULY SOYBEAN MEAL ON THE CLOSE OF TRADING JUNE 8th WITH A 4 PERCENT STOP LOSS CLOSE ONLY. EXIT ON THE CLOSE OF TRADING JUNE 16th IF THE TRADE HAS NOT BEEN STOPPED OUT.

As you can see from the accompanying KDT's (Figures 6-6 through 6-12), there is considerable information which may be derived from the Key Date Listings. Each key date listing provides the following information:

1. Market and contract month to enter

2. Buy or sell short

3. Entry date

4. Exit date

5. Specific stop loss

6. Total number of years tested

7. Average percentage correct

8. Average profitable trade

9. Average losing trade

10. Average trade

11. Profit/loss ratio

12. Cumulative profit

14. Maximum drawdown per trade

As you can readily see, the information for each and every KDT is specific as well comprehensive.

The process of finding KDTs is essentially simple: however, it requires an exceptionally large historical database as well as a considerable amount of computer time. To have run our KDT analysis on all futures markets, for all contract months, for up to sixty years in some markets, would have been unfeasible on a microcomputer system. My KDT statistics were run on a Data General MV Eclipse™ minicomputer.

A KDT search performs hypothetical buys and sells for every possible combination of dates over the entire range of years for every market and every contract month. In other words, the KDT search tells us what the results would have been both for buying and for selling short using every combination of calendar days for every market and delivery month. The total number of combinations for only one contract of one market runs into the thousands!

The KDT search also tests various stop loss parameters in order to determine which stop loss would have produced the best overall results. In checking stop losses I attempt to determine a maximum acceptable drawdown level per year tested for each market and contract month.

To a given extent this could be considered optimization, but it is not optimization in its strictest sense. We are not "curve-fitting" our system parameters or rules; rather, we are testing already hypothetically profitable trades in order to determine which stop losses would have yielded the best results. Once this process has been completed for long-side trades, it is repeated for short-side trades.

Once all trades and stops have been generated, I visually examine all of the KDTs, selecting only those with the greatest reliability and historically validated profit potential.
the statistics for these trades prior to their inclusion as *bona fide* KDTs.

Keep in mind these two limitations of key trading dates:

1. The single greatest limitation in using closing prices is that in real-time trading, entry or exit at the given price might not have been possible.

2. Another limitation is that the stop loss for each KDT is based on the closing. In the case of a locked limit up or down move, exit or entry may not be possible.

Some current key date trades are shown in Figures 6-6 through 6-12. As you can see, they have shown a high probability of success and accuracy. However, I must remind you that statistics are limited and that even the most reliable seasonal key date trade has only approximately thirty repetitions.

Figure 6.8: Key Date Seasonal Timing in December Corn

```
                         SHORT Dec Corn ON THE CLOSE 10/11
                WITH A 4% STOP LOSS CLOSE ONLY, OR EXIT ON CLOSE 10/23

Entry Date:              10/11          Exit Date:              10/23
Positive Trades:            18          Negative Trades:            6
Starting Year:            1967          Ending Year:             1990
% Positive Trades:       75.00          % Negative Trades:      25.00
Average Gain:             5.64          Average Loss:           -4.85
Average Trade:            3.02          Profit/Loss Ratio:       3.49
Years Analyzed:             24          Cumulative $:       $3618.50
Maximum Drawdown:     -$375.00          Calculated Stop:         0.00
```

Figure 6.9: Key Date Seasonal Timing in November Soybeans

```
                       LONG Nov Soy Beans ON THE CLOSE 09/01
                WITH A 3% STOP LOSS CLOSE ONLY, OR EXIT ON CLOSE 09/05

Entry Date:              09/01          Exit Date:              09/05
Positive Trades:            19          Negative Trades:            5
Starting Year:            1967          Ending Year:             1990
% Positive Trades:       79.17          % Negative Trades:      20.83
Average Gain:            12.16          Average Loss:          -12.10
Average Trade:            7.10          Profit/Loss Ratio:       3.82
Years Analyzed:             24          Cumulative $:       $8525.00
Maximum Drawdown: -$1200.00            Calculated Stop:         0.00
```

Figure 6.10: Key Date Seasonal Timing in December Wheat

```
                    LONG Dec Wheat ON THE CLOSE 09/01
         WITH A 5% STOP LOSS CLOSE ONLY, OR EXIT ON CLOSE 10/24

Entry Date:            09/01        Exit Date:            10/24
Positive Trades:          18        Negative Trades:          6
Starting Year:          1967        Ending Year:_          1990
% Positive Trades:     75.00        % Negative Trades:    25.00
Average Gain:          18.01        Average Loss:        -20.94
Average Trade:          8.27        Profit/Loss Ratio:     2.58
Years Analyzed:           24        Cumulative $:     $9924.50
Maximum Drawdown: -$2012.50         Calculated Stop:       0.00
```

Figure 6.11: Key Date Seasonal Timing in December Gold

```
                    LONG Dec Gold ON THE CLOSE 09/01
         WITH A 3% STOP LOSS CLOSE ONLY, OR EXIT ON CLOSE 09/21

Entry Date:            09/01        Exit Date:            09/21
Positive Trades:          12        Negative Trades:          4
Starting Year:          1975        Ending Year:           1990
% Positive Trades:     75.00        % Negative Trades:    25.00
Average Gain:          22.88        Average Loss:         -9.18
Average Trade:         14.86        Profit/Loss Ratio:     7.48
Years Analyzed:           16        Cumulative $:    $23780.00
Maximum Drawdown: -$1370.00         Calculated Stop:       0.00
```

Figure 6.12: Key Date Seasonal Timing in December Swiss Franc

```
                   LONG Dec Swiss Franc ON THE CLOSE 08/08
         WITH A 2% STOP LOSS CLOSE ONLY, OR EXIT ON CLOSE 08/31

Entry Date:            08/08        Exit Date:            08/31
Positive Trades:          12        Negative Trades:          4
Starting Year:          1975        Ending Year:           1990
% Positive Trades:     75.00        % Negative Trades:    25.00
Average Gain:           0.85        Average Loss:         -0.71
Average Trade:          0.46        Profit/Loss Ratio:     3.61
Years Analyzed:           16        Cumulative $:     $9200.00
Maximum Drawdown: -$2200.00         Calculated Stop:       0.00
```

7

Stochastics

When I first met George Lane, the "father" of stochastics, he was wearing leather cowboy boots, a ten-gallon hat and a wide belt with a shiny metal buckle. He completed his striking appearance with a handsome grey moustache and beard. His "wild west" dress and iconoclastic style were refreshing. Yet anyone who has spent some time with George knows that although stochastics can be used to the considerable advantage of the trader, this indicator is by no means a panacea for the myriad timing problems facing the trader. My research strongly suggests that the best application of stochastics is in combination with other timing indicators or as a filter. Yet there are some specific applications which do appear to have potential. In order to remove as much of the art and stick as closely to the science as possible, I have subjected stochastics to rigorous computer testing.

I must admit that stochastics is one of the most attractive indicators I have ever seen. It has considerable "sex appeal," for want of a better phrase. Many traders have fallen in love with stochastics, and many have quickly come to realize that it is, as I have said, not a market deity—it is just another indicator, albeit a very good one. The performance of the stochastics indicator (SI) can be dramatically improved when it is used in conjunction with other timing signals and indicators.

The formula for calculating SI is as follows:

$$\%K = 100 \times [(C - Lp)/(Hp - Lp)]$$

where:

      C = today's close;
      Lp = the lowest low of the time period chosen; and
      Hp = the highest high of the time period chosen.

There are two stochastics lines or values, %K and %D. %D is a three-period moving average of %K. There are "fast" and "slow" versions of stochastics, the "slow" version being a smoothed derivative of the fast SI. Those who are interested in learning considerably more about SI should contact Dr. Lane at Investment Educators.

Bruce Babcock has observed and explained the similarities and differences between SI, Welles Wilder's Relative Strength Index (RSI), and Larry Williams' %R. In addition, Babcock provided an excellent comparison of SI signals and RSI signals, as shown in Figure 7-1.

There are perhaps as many applications of the SI as there are traders. It seems that virtually every SI devotee has his or her own pet use for this versatile indicator. Hence, I was not able to examine every application. Here are some of the SI applications I did check.

STOCHASTIC CONDITION #1.

My first study concentrated on crosses of %K and %D as buy and sell signals, as illustrated in Figure 7.2. I tested several SI lengths (9-day, 14-day and 21-day) on my historical database. The results are shown in Figures 7-3 through 7-5.

An analysis of the results follows.

Figure 7.1:   Daily Chart of S&P 500 with Assorted RSI and Stochastic Oscillators (September 1988 Contract)

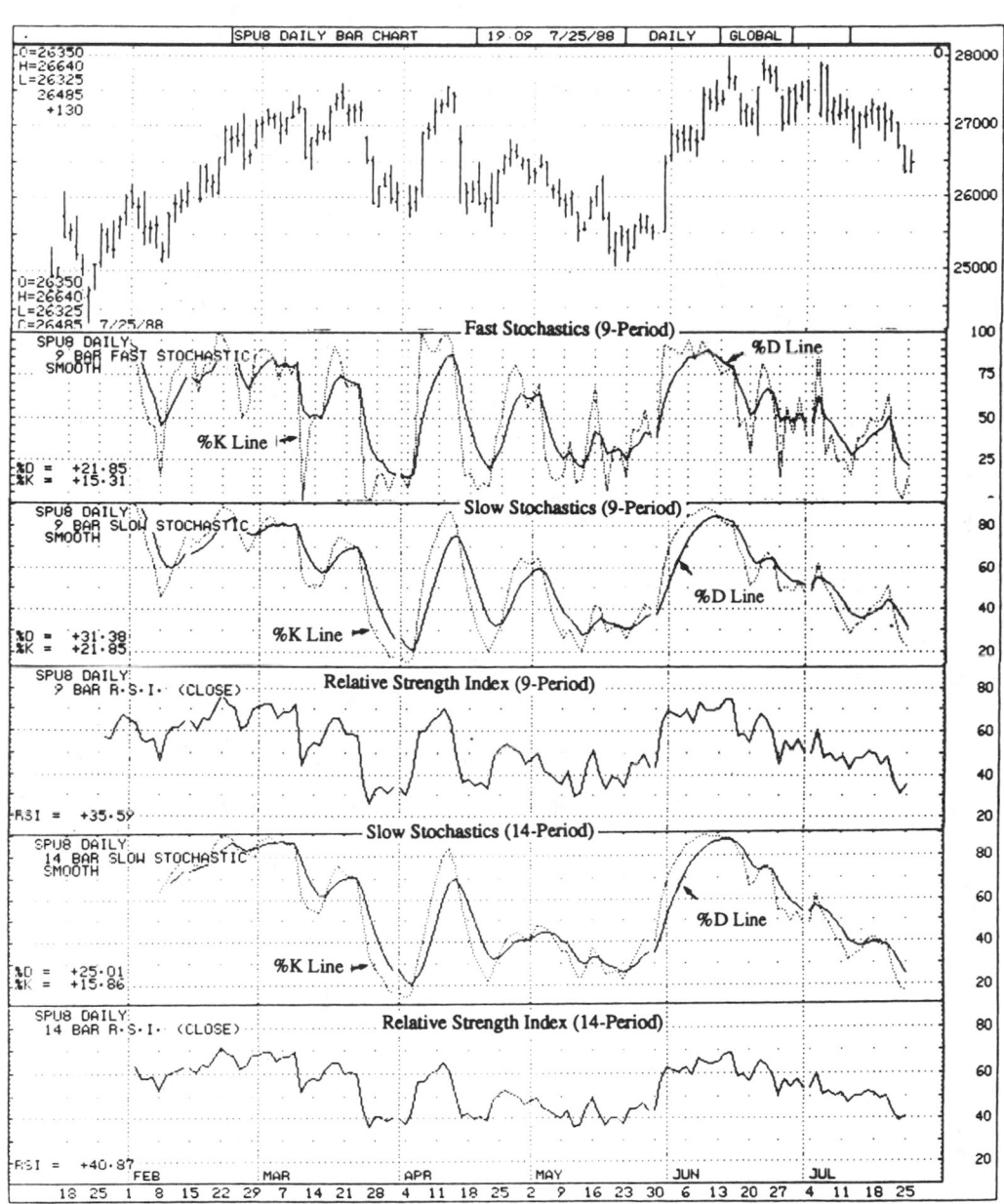

Source: Babcock, Bruce, *The Dow Jones-Irwin Guide to Trading Systems* (Homewood, IL: Dow Jones-Irwin, 1989).

Figure 7.2: Standard 14-Period Stochastic Crossover Signals

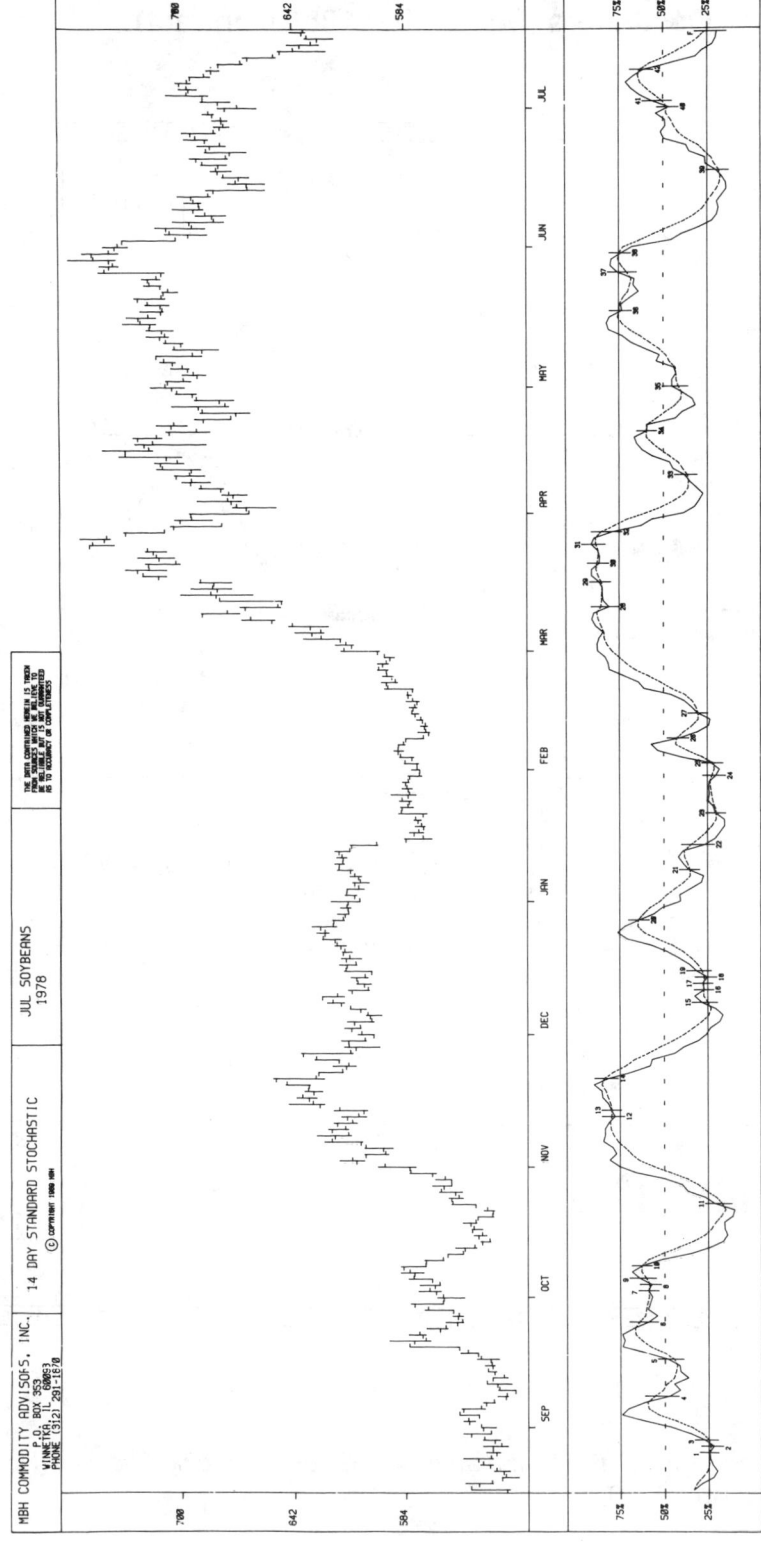

Figure 7.3: 9-Day Standard Stochastic Crossover Results

	BUY				SELL				TOTAL		
	#	PROF	AVG $	TOT $	#	PROF	AVG $	TOT $	#	PROF	AVG $	TOT $
BULL	2539	-594.12	-111.57	-283271.87	2558	5054.64	357.60	914735.31	5097	4460.53	123.89	631463.44
BEAR	3261	4700.55	226.49	738599.87	3249	-2606.03	-200.43	-651193.81	6510	2094.52	13.43	87406.06
BUBE	3801	1215.54	44.79	170241.25	3806	2630.30	107.79	410234.06	7607	3845.84	76.31	580475.31
BEBU	3553	779.94	-9.69	-34421.82	3536	766.75	28.13	99453.50	7089	1546.70	9.17	65031.68
BUBEBU	650	-347.11	-36.57	-23770.54	653	77.71	97.86	63901.37	1303	-269.40	30.80	40130.83
BEBUBE	744	311.18	126.66	94233.56	755	171.66	2.84	2146.92	1499	482.84	64.30	96380.50
CHOPBU	2995	-1105.17	-81.51	-244129.94	3004	3375.52	150.06	450791.00	5999	2270.35	34.45	206661.06
CHOPBE	1888	1954.06	153.83	290462.37	1899	-643.37	-57.19	-108594.56	3787	1310.69	48.01	181831.81
WHIP	2353	666.39	75.58	177848.00	2343	291.59	44.50	104259.50	4696	957.98	60.07	282107.50
	21784	7581.26	40.66	885754.88	21803	9118.77	58.97	1285733.29	43587	16700.05	49.82	2171488.19

Figure 7.4: 14-Day Standard Stochastic Crossover Results

	BUY				SELL				TOTAL		
	#	PROF	AVG $	TOT $	#	PROF	AVG $	TOT $	#	PROF	AVG $	TOT $
BULL	2340	-1038.25	-163.26	-382031.44	2343	4645.41	347.48	814147.88	4683	3607.16	92.27	432116.44
BEAR	2919	4933.82	265.21	774148.62	2917	-2361.92	-207.93	-606521.69	5836	2571.90	28.72	167626.94
BUBE	3399	1243.15	63.58	216099.56	3412	2214.51	120.20	410131.50	6811	3457.66	91.94	626231.06
BEBU	3218	671.39	-9.96	-32057.07	3214	721.47	32.20	103477.44	6432	1392.86	11.10	71420.38
BUBEBU	578	-264.09	-30.22	-17464.45	584	133.76	119.41	69737.44	1162	-130.33	44.99	52272.99
BEBUBE	682	260.81	133.79	91243.75	696	219.35	1.89	1315.78	1378	480.16	67.17	92559.56
CHOPBU	2721	-1068.90	-96.37	-262222.56	2723	3352.50	154.58	420929.12	5444	2283.60	29.15	158706.56
CHOPBE	1717	1643.70	165.09	283455.37	1728	-958.96	-66.13	-114265.12	3445	684.74	49.11	169190.25
WHIP	2102	601.38	77.27	162422.19	2108	268.29	38.16	80431.50	4210	869.68	57.68	242853.69
	19676	6983.01	42.37	833593.97	19725	8234.41	59.79	1179383.85	39401	15217.43	51.09	2012977.87

*The "Prof" column indicates total profit or loss in "points" before conversion to dollars

The "#" column indicates total number of trades

Figure 7.5: 21-Day Standard Stochastic Crossover Results

		BUY				SELL				TOTAL		
	#	PROF	AVG $	TOT $	#	PROF	AVG $	TOT $	#	PROF	AVG $	TOT $
BULL	2203	-806.22	-182.44	-401916.81	2218	4858.93	354.76	786866.19	4421	4052.72	87.07	384949.37
BEAR	2680	4629.48	313.83	841076.94	2672	-2398.26	-187.93	-502159.06	5352	2231.22	63.33	338917.87
BUBE	3203	1781.39	76.09	243705.44	3198	2612.03	122.46	391621.44	6401	4393.42	99.25	635326.87
BEBU	3004	732.42	5.20	15605.88	2999	775.21	57.27	171756.25	6003	1507.63	31.21	187362.12
BUBEBU	558	-195.03	-34.38	-19184.24	561	204.24	122.57	68763.38	1119	9.21	44.31	49579.14
BEBUBE	625	180.39	114.99	71871.00	640	123.62	-23.78	-15220.88	1265	304.01	44.78	56650.12
CHOPBU	2591	-1226.99	-121.37	-314480.06	2589	3340.13	144.16	373233.00	5180	2113.14	11.34	58752.94
CHOPBE	1597	1820.33	178.65	285308.56	1607	-905.05	-72.73	-116880.75	3204	915.28	52.57	168427.81
WHIP	1957	665.98	74.72	146225.31	1961	355.33	39.09	76658.63	3918	1021.31	56.89	222883.94
	18418	7581.75	47.14	868212.02	18445	8966.18	66.94	1234638.20	36863	16547.94	57.05	2102850.18

Performance of SI in Bull Markets

Our bull market sample consisted of thirty-nine classic bull markets from 1967 through 1988. The results showed that SI was an inconsistent performer, even in classic bull markets. While some markets produced excellent profits, other markets showed considerable trading with net losses. If slippage and commissions of $100 per trade are also considered in the overall results, then they are clearly unimpressive. Remember that no filters or other optimizing tools were used in order to reduce the number of trades or the number of losing trades. The best overall results were noted for the 21 day SI, while the 90 day SI weas best in bull markets.

Performance of SI in Bear Markets

The SI results in bear markets were also unimpressive. In fact, they were bad. Given the large number of trades and the relatively low dollar profit per trade, it appeared that SI was not a good timing signal when used in the fashion prescribed. Do note, however, its good performance for buy signals in bear markets.

Performance of SI in Bull/Bear Markets

I then checked the performance of SI in fifty-seven bull/bear markets. As you will recall, these are markets which made the transition from strong bull market to strong bear market. Again, results were poor.

Performance of SI in Choppy Bull Markets

This test was an important one. It has long been maintained that trend following systems tend to do poorly in choppy markets. While this may be true for "whipsaw" markets, it may not necessarily be true for what I have defined as "choppy" bull markets. Results here were also poor in all three SI lengths.

Performance of SI in Choppy Bear Markets

Performance of the SI system in choppy bear markets was also as expected, showing minimal success and a large number of trades.

Performance of SI in Whipsaw Markets

While it may be a matter of opinion as to what constitutes a "whipsaw" market, there is no doubt in my mind that the sample of fifty-two "whipsaw" markets I selected represent some of the most difficult and treacherous markets known to traders. In fact, my results demonstrate that the SI system does not produce profits in such markets.

Performance of SI in Bull/Bear/Bull Markets

Another category I tested consisted of fifteen markets which moved from bullish to bearish and then back to bullish again. While there were only fifteen such markets, the results were still poor.

Performance of SI in Bear/Bull/Bear Markets

I then tested the performance of the SI crossover in bear/bull/bear markets. In other words, I examined the ten markets which moved from bearish to bullish and then back to bearish. Performance was unimpressive. While only ten markets were tested, the overall results were just as poor as for most other categories.

STOCHASTIC CONDITION #2

The second SI condition I studied was: a buy signal, if SI closed 25 percent or greater after first being below 25; and a sell if SI closed 75 percent or lower after being above 75 percent. This condition is illustrated in Figure 7-6. The results of my test by market category are shown in Figures 7-7 through 7-9. An analysis of my results follows.

Figure 7.6: Buy and Sell Signals Using Stochastics

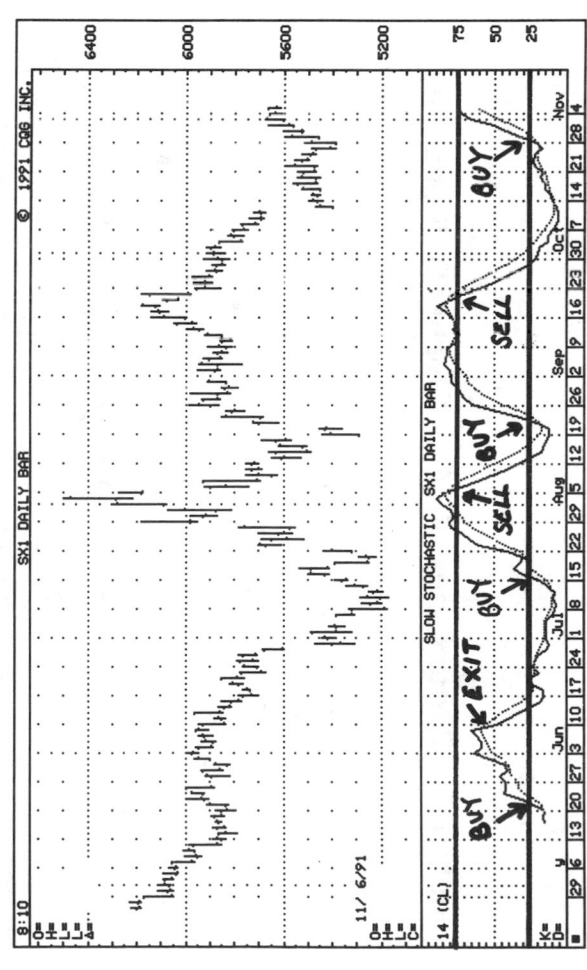

Figure 7.7: Performance of 75/25 Stochastic Signals by Market Category: 9-Day

	BUY				SELL				TOTAL		
#	PROF	AVG $	TOT $	#	PROF	AVG $	TOT $	#	PROF	AVG $	TOT $
1664	-1229.11	-286.76	-477138.81	1673	4297.31	430.83	720773.69	3337	2968.20	73.01	243634.87
2116	3977.10	386.11	817016.50	2119	-3393.51	-267.15	-566093.62	4235	483.58	59.25	250922.87
2462	827.31	-2.13	-5241.30	2455	2032.15	76.26	137528.12	4921	2859.46	37.04	182286.81
2356	223.38	14.16	33365.13	2351	353.39	75.91	178469.25	4707	676.77	45.00	211834.44
116	-90.26	-12.53	-5211.55	417	248.05	173.30	74349.38	933	151.65	33.00	69137.81
496	142.16	167.92	83290.19	507	-38.37	-24.68	-12513.26	1003	103.79	70.57	70776.94
1996	-1653.03	-178.55	-356750.94	1992	2785.46	167.29	333336.44	3990	1086.93	-5.89	-23514.50
1278	1325.96	162.10	207153.37	1278	-1350.37	-164.22	-209371.25	2556	-24.41	-1.06	-2712.87
1562	435.00	43.71	68275.38	1562	167.79	4.59	7166.10	3124	602.79	24.15	75441.50
14346	3606.91	25.42	364763.00	14358	5101.39	49.66	713044.87	28706	9908.79	37.55	1077803.00

Figure 7.8: Performance of 75/25 Stochastic Signals by Market Category: 14-Day

	BUY				SELL				TOTAL		
	#	PROF	AVG $	TOT $	#	PROF	AVG $	TOT $	#	PROF	AVG $	TOT $
BULL	1332	-1382.41	-333.25	-443882.94	1347	4252.00	562.19	757272.37	2679	2869.59	116.98	313389.44
BEAR	1706	4198.18	476.70	813247.25	1709	-2964.34	-316.81	-541433.50	3415	1233.84	79.59	271813.75
BUBE	1999	830.11	61.58	123094.56	1983	1601.06	126.43	250720.56	3982	2431.17	93.88	373815.12
BEBU	1937	264.44	-63.08	-122183.62	1942	386.37	12.93	25117.27	3879	650.81	-25.02	-97066.38
BUBEBU	329	-14.48	-62.53	-20699.77	333	363.75	182.96	60926.01	662	349.26	60.46	40026.24
BEBUBE	415	191.52	195.69	81211.25	420	50.65	-13.53	-5684.29	835	242.17	90.45	75526.94
CHOP3U	1599	-1112.32	-183.51	-293425.50	1539	3297.17	238.52	381393.75	3198	2184.85	27.51	87968.25
CHOP3E	1037	1540.29	228.21	236650.87	1050	-1116.01	-154.65	-162380.69	2087	424.28	35.59	74270.19
WHIP	1266	490.93	91.88	116321.62	1277	204.99	30.54	38998.06	2543	695.92	61.08	155319.69
	11620	5006.26	42.18	490133.75	11650	6075.64	69.03	804929.50	23280	11081.90	55.63	1295063.00

Figure 7.9: Performance of 75/25 Stochastic Signals by Market Category: 21-Day

21 DAY 75/25 STOCHASTIC

	BUY				SELL				TOTAL		
	#	PROF	AVG $	TOT $	#	PROF	AVG $	TOT $	#	PROF	AVG $	TOT $
BULL	1025	-1257.33	-372.00	-381297.12	1034	4355.35	775.84	802221.50	2059	3096.02	204.43	420924.37
BEAR	1343	3436.02	528.99	710438.63	1358	-3185.48	-431.42	-595369.50	2701	300.54	46.12	124569.19
BUBE	1676	1172.79	57.03	95584.93	1653	1706.20	127.02	209962.37	3329	2878.99	91.78	305547.25
BEBU	1538	338.81	-66.87	-102846.69	1551	480.99	33.96	60425.69	3089	819.80	-13.73	-42421.00
BUBEBU	276	-5.77	-84.14	-23223.05	276	371.36	218.17	60214.49	552	366.19	67.01	36991.43
BEBUBE	329	227.16	247.00	91263.75	340	117.63	-5.84	-1985.10	669	344.79	118.50	79278.63
CHOP3U	1345	-1952.22	-226.62	-304809.75	1354	2517.07	262.20	365019.12	2599	524.84	18.60	50209.38
CHOP3E	847	1369.42	249.79	211572.62	856	-1127.63	-192.41	-165089.87	1705	241.79	27.26	46483.75
WHIP	1072	387.12	75.41	80838.00	1013	42.90	2.90	3139.94	2155	430.02	38.97	83977.94
	9451	3725.00	38.89	367521.31	9507	5276.99	77.63	738039.62	18958	9002.98	58.32	1105561.00

Performance of 75/25 SI Crossovers in Bull Markets

Our bull market sample consisted of thirty-nine classic bull markets from 1967 through 1988. The results show that on an overall basis the 9-, 14-, and 21-period SI signals were profitable in bull markets, but only marginally so when looking at the average trade size. If we deduct $75 for slippage and commission for each trade, then the results look quite poor. As an interesting point of information, the sell trades were considerably more profitable in bull markets than were the buy trades! This approach could have good potential.

Performance of 75/25 SI Crossovers in Bear Markets

Bear market results for SI on all three lengths were less impressive than bull market results. Buy signals worked better than did sell signals.

Performance of 75/25 SI Crossovers in Bull/Bear Markets

I then checked the performance of the in fifty-seven bull/bear markets. Results were marginal.

Performance of 75/25 SI Crossovers in Bear/Bull Markets

I next checked the performance of the 75/25 SI system in seventy-three bear/bull markets. The results for this test revealed an overall losing performance.

Performance of 75/25 SI Crossovers in Choppy Bull Markets

This test was an important one. It has long been maintained that moving averages tend to do poorly in choppy markets. While this may be true for "whipsaw" markets, it may not necessarily be true for what I have defined as "choppy" bull markets. Bottom line performance was minimally profitable, but definitely negative when considering slippage and commission.

Performance of 75/25 SI Crossovers in Choppy Bear Markets

Performance of the 75/25 SI crossover system in choppy bear markets was also poor, as can be seen from the test results.

Performance of 75/25 SI Crossovers in Whipsaw Markets

While it may be a matter of opinion as to what constitutes a "whipsaw" market, there is no doubt in my mind that the sample of fifty-two "whipsaw" markets I selected represent some of the most difficult and treacherous markets known to traders. In fact, the results demonstrate that the 75/25 system performs poorly here, but not as poorly as other types of markets.

Performance of 75/25 SI Crossovers in Bull/Bear/Bull Markets

Another category I tested consisted of fifteen markets which moved from bullish to bearish, and then back to bullish again. While there were only fifteen such markets, the results were not impressive.

Performance of 75/25 SI Crossovers in Bear/Bull/Bear Markets

I then tested performance of the SI in bear/bull/bear markets, examining the ten markets which moved from bearish to bullish and back to bearish. Performance was unimpressive. However, note that only ten markets only were tested, and this may not be a sufficiently large sample for conclusive results.

STOCHASTIC CONDITION #3

A third and final condition I studied was POP indicators, which I introduced a number of years ago and which are discussed in my book, *Short-Term Trading in Futures*.[1] Here is a brief explanation of the SI POP as discussed therein:

> This interesting new application of stochastics may well become one of the most potent short-term trend indicators I've ever developed. The POP technique triggers long entry when a market becomes overbought on stochastic (75 percent and above). When a market becomes oversold on stochastic (25 percent or lower), POP goes short. This approcah is contrary to what many analysts advocate, yet it makes sense because it should keep you in the strong moves. [Figures 7-10, 7-11 amd 7-12 further illustrate the Stochastic POP Method.] These charts merely show the raw signals on a number of timeframes. *When combined with the trading rules I've developed, the POP achieves its true greatness!*
>
> As soon as %K and %D rise above 75 percent on a closing basis, you go long. You stay long until the two lines cross. It doesn't take much for %D and %K to cross when the market is overbought—it occurs as soon as a market shows even a sight amount of weakness. When this happens, don't sell short; just liquidate your long. Each entry and exit is "at the market." Indicators are calculated on a closing basis. The optimal time period I've found for the POP is the thirty-minute segment. There also appears to be good potential on five-minute charts, but research remains to be done on this. SI POP also has potential on hourly, daily and weekly data. Remember that you cannot enter or exit a POP trade until

[1]Bernstein, J., *Short-Term Trading in Futures* (Chicago, IL: Probus Publishing Company, 1987).

Figure 7.10

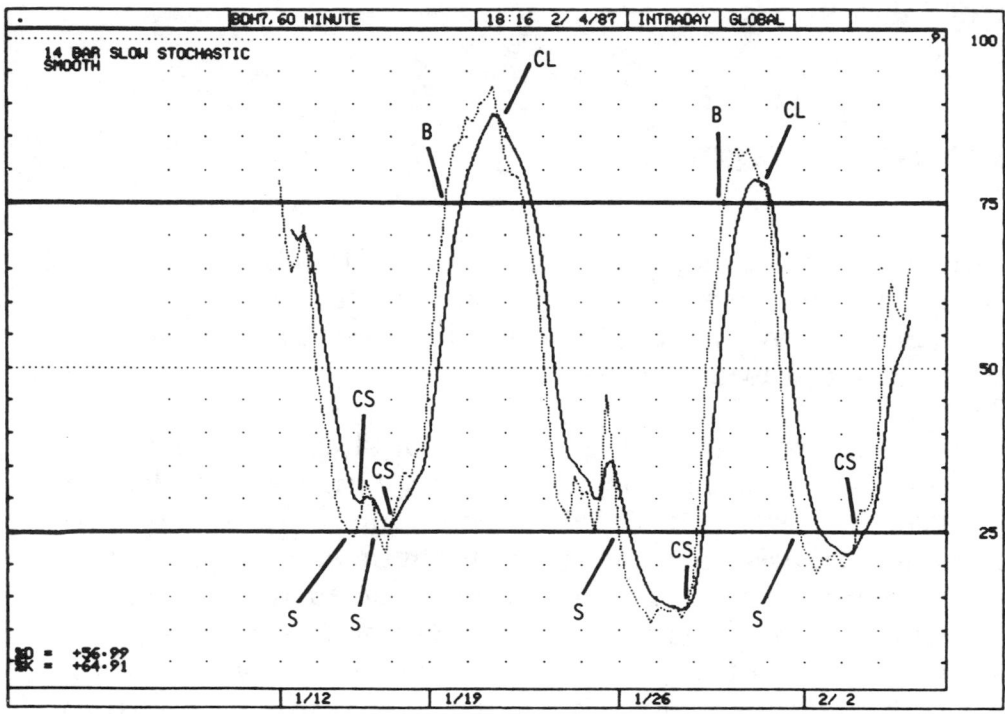

Figure 7.11

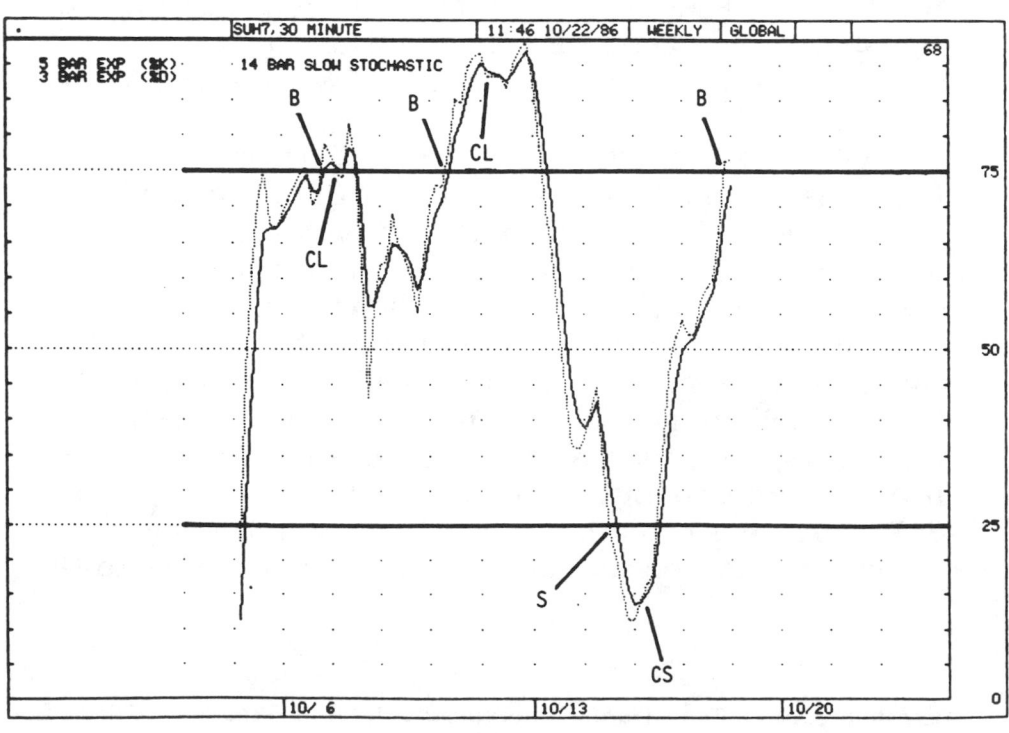

Figure 7.12

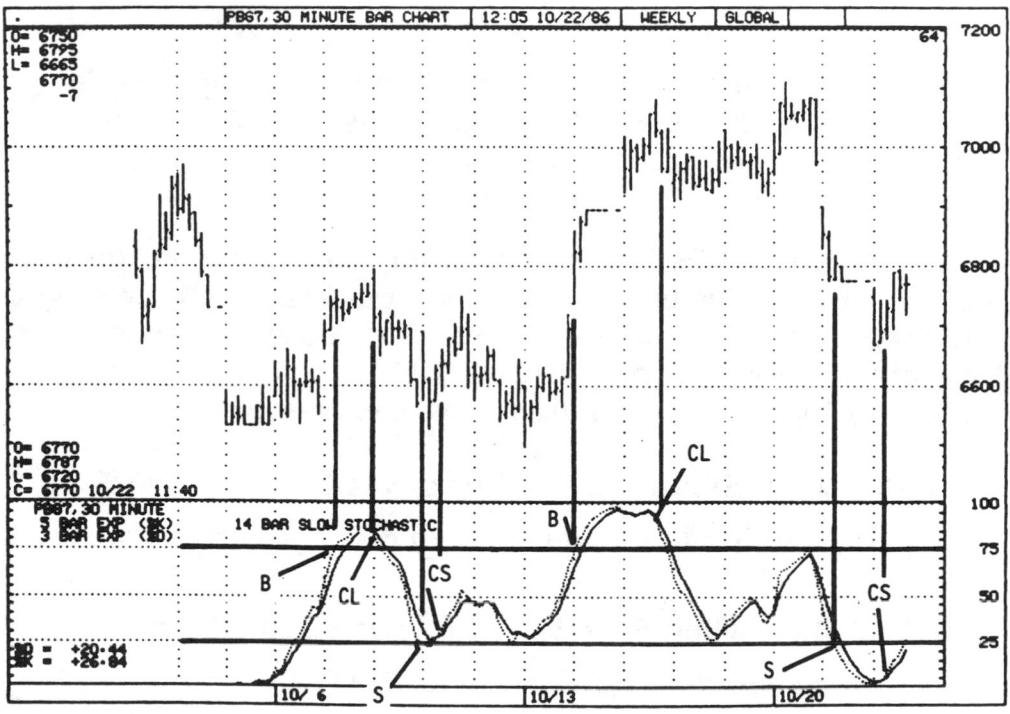

the time segment you are using has been completed. In other words, the POP is not calculated on a tic-by-tic basis, but on the basis of the time segment you are tracking (i.e., hourly, half-hourly, five-minute).

As you can see, the POP is a somewhat contrary indicator inasmuch as it generates buy signals when markets are "overbought" and sell signals when markets are "oversold," based on the commonplace interpretation of these terms.

These different POP conditions were examined:

1. Buy when SI closes at 75% or greater.

2. Close out long and go flat when SI values cross on closing basis.

3. Sell short when SI is 25% or less on closing basis.

4. Cover short and go flat when SI values cross on closing basis.

I studied the results of using various POP trigger values and 9-, 14-, and 21-day stochastic lengths. The results of all approaches are shown in Figures 7-13 through 7-21.

Figure 7.13: 9-Day 75/25 Stochastic Indicator: Pop Results

	BUY				SELL				TOTAL		
	#	PROF	AVG $	TOT $	#	PROF	AVG $	TOT $	#	PROF	AVG $	TOT $
BULL	1246	2410.40	412.56	514055.37	740	66.83	-172.38	-127562.88	1986	2477.23	194.61	386492.50
BEAR	946	-861.76	-137.16	-129754.13	1659	2018.05	139.31	231121.62	2605	1156.28	38.91	101367.50
BUBE	1483	1533.86	162.03	240293.31	1533	906.97	60.99	93502.50	3016	2440.83	110.68	333795.81
BEBU	1407	414.83	80.54	113325.69	1481	88.66	-51.18	-75803.44	2888	503.49	12.99	37522.25
BUBEBU	269	221.63	115.89	31173.59	247	-97.18	-30.39	-7505.11	516	124.45	45.87	23668.47
BEBUBE	278	-56.25	-32.68	-9086.16	325	161.12	178.54	58024.08	603	104.87	81.16	48937.92
CHOPBU	1413	1350.24	118.65	167653.00	985	-871.83	-107.46	-105847.69	2398	478.41	25.77	61805.31
CHOPBE	616	-291.43	-16.67	-10271.30	954	663.42	92.36	88107.81	1570	371.99	49.58	77836.50
WHIP	953	-9.89	25.25	24060.74	1012	143.99	9.57	9682.23	1965	134.10	17.17	33742.98
	8611	4711.63	109.33	941450.11	8936	3080.03	18.32	163719.12	17547	7791.65	62.98	1105169.24

Figure 7.14: 14-Day 75/25 Stochastic Indicator: Pop Results

	BUY				SELL				TOTAL		
	#	PROF	AVG $	TOT $	#	PROF	AVG $	TOT $	#	PROF	AVG $	TOT $
BULL	1021	2732.91	462.46	472176.19	582	-144.21	-190.39	-110809.75	1603	2588.70	225.43	361366.44
BEAR	752	-859.70	-194.48	-146251.56	1360	2037.84	179.60	244249.37	2112	1178.14	46.40	97997.81
BUBE	1217	1625.19	234.22	285041.56	1260	1132.45	121.68	153312.00	2477	2757.64	176.97	438353.56
BEBU	1151	587.75	56.55	65092.36	1185	418.22	6.45	7646.82	2336	1005.97	31.14	72739.19
BUBEBU	207	243.23	200.93	41591.91	195	-48.43	17.91	3493.35	402	194.80	112.15	45085.26
BEBUBE	241	-79.16	-80.48	-19394.67	282	296.37	118.05	33290.11	523	217.21	26.57	13895.43
CHOPBU	1145	1288.62	175.29	200711.75	838	-672.91	-143.39	-120157.06	1983	615.71	40.62	80554.69
CHOPBE	528	-187.95	-32.03	-16914.09	777	623.44	104.10	80887.37	1305	435.49	49.02	63973.29
WHIP	756	81.19	59.78	45193.63	860	113.60	7.17	6163.88	1616	194.79	31.78	51357.51
	7018	5432.08	132.12	927247.08	7339	3756.37	40.62	298076.09	14357	9188.45	85.35	1225323.18

Figure 7.15: 21-Day 75/25 Stochastic Indicator: Pop Results

		BUY				SELL				TOTAL		
	#	PROF	AVG $	TOT $	#	PROF	AVG $	TOT $	#	PROF	AVG $	TOT $
BULL	804	2273.13	446.16	358710.50	446	54.42	-138.23	-61649.16	1250	2327.55	237.65	297061.37
BEAR	550	-300.82	-140.33	-77182.94	1065	1483.57	145.50	154955.37	1615	1182.75	48.16	77772.44
BUBE	991	1485.88	189.90	188194.06	1032	855.75	138.15	142575.50	2023	2341.63	163.50	330769.56
BEBU	940	538.12	99.37	93411.75	949	305.45	13.81	13101.15	1889	843.57	56.39	106512.87
BUBEBU	177	180.04	247.85	43868.87	147	-132.07	-26.22	-3854.44	324	47.97	123.50	40014.43
BEBUBE	178	-4.04	-25.13	-4472.62	227	97.34	42.61	9672.43	405	93.30	12.84	5199.81
CHOPBU	961	1118.31	157.91	151755.19	689	-766.99	-143.42	-98819.38	1650	351.32	32.08	52935.81
CHOPBE	399	-285.65	-86.83	-34645.74	659	601.35	109.83	72375.69	1058	315.70	35.66	37729.95
WHIP	635	-57.14	44.32	28145.63	722	55.95	7.46	5383.40	1357	-1.19	24.71	33529.02
	5635	4947.83	132.70	747784.70	5936	2554.77	39.38	233740.56	11571	7502.60	84.83	981525.26

Figure 7.16: 9-Day 65/35 Stochastic Indicator: Pop Results

		BUY				SELL				TOTAL		
	#	PROF	AVG $	TOT $	#	PROF	AVG $	TOT $	#	PROF	AVG $	TOT $
BULL	1299	2447.11	410.64	533414.87	979	-125.55	-105.41	-103199.31	2278	2321.56	188.86	430215.56
BEAR	1301	-1342.64	-155.77	-202655.25	1699	2525.29	208.86	354858.19	3000	1182.65	50.73	152202.94
BUBE	1772	1255.98	164.66	291779.00	1801	710.88	98.22	176892.37	3573	1966.86	131.17	468671.37
BEBU	1645	569.04	117.54	193348.37	1683	434.45	-11.13	-18730.59	3328	1003.49	52.47	174617.81
BUBEBU	305	202.70	96.54	29443.37	281	-268.51	-35.99	-10113.52	586	-65.81	32.99	19329.84
BEBUBE	332	2.56	-35.91	-11923.11	366	233.22	145.16	53128.16	698	235.78	59.03	41205.05
CHOPBU	1528	1440.53	151.98	232218.87	1296	-1053.36	-97.14	-125899.37	2824	387.17	37.65	106319.50
CHOPBE	826	-321.10	-28.96	-23920.97	1034	892.06	118.69	122729.56	1860	570.96	53.12	98808.56
WHIP	1155	-28.62	22.15	25581.75	1148	436.76	80.72	92663.88	2303	408.14	51.34	118245.62
	10163	4225.56	105.02	1067286.90	10287	3785.24	52.72	542329.37	20450	8010.80	78.71	1609616.25

Figure 7.17: 14-Day 65/35 Stochastic Indicator: Pop Results

	BUY				SELL				TOTAL		
	#	PROF	AVG $	TOT $	#	PROF	AVG $	TOT $	#	PROF	AVG $	TOT $
BULL	936	2508.60	529.96	496042.06	724	-61.38	-174.66	-126455.69	1660	2447.22	222.64	369586.37
BEAR	921	-859.51	-129.15	-118951.00	1247	2685.27	254.85	317799.69	2168	1825.76	91.72	198848.69
BUBE	1294	1305.80	189.42	245110.12	1372	1069.61	163.93	224907.69	2666	2375.41	176.30	470017.81
BEBU	1208	394.77	102.60	123936.12	1231	709.31	19.04	23443.12	2439	1104.08	60.43	147379.25
BUBEBU	220	331.21	179.39	39465.97	202	-93.98	41.20	8321.62	422	237.23	113.24	47787.59
BEBUBE	258	22.13	1.73	445.16	259	317.28	196.73	50952.20	517	339.41	99.41	51397.36
CHOPBU	1153	1733.48	207.42	239149.56	994	-625.71	-124.31	-123560.37	2147	1107.77	53.84	115589.19
CHOPBE	622	-223.56	12.13	7542.58	772	914.00	177.81	137272.00	1394	690.44	103.88	144814.56
WHIP	855	71.27	62.05	53050.92	897	370.08	45.54	40853.37	1752	441.35	53.60	93904.31
	7467	5284.19	145.41	1085791.49	7698	5284.48	71.91	553533.63	15165	10568.67	108.10	1639325.13

Figure 7.18: 21-Day 65/35 Stochastic Indicator: Pop Results

	BUY				SELL				TOTAL		
	#	PROF	AVG $	TOT $	#	PROF	AVG $	TOT $	#	PROF	AVG $	TOT $
BULL	719	2199.88	405.31	291416.87	510	-218.87	-237.88	-121319.62	1229	1981.01	138.40	170097.25
BEAR	671	-522.53	-137.50	-92265.56	939	1799.55	234.47	220163.19	1610	1277.02	79.44	127897.62
BUBE	982	1203.65	175.35	172193.44	1026	1278.30	227.58	233499.44	2008	2481.95	202.04	405692.87
BEBU	905	567.12	172.22	155861.12	914	692.16	2.87	2627.13	1819	1259.28	87.13	158488.25
BUBEBU	168	312.50	314.56	52846.72	153	-55.52	-8.00	-1224.22	321	256.98	160.82	51622.50
BEBUBE	197	63.26	13.40	2639.03	216	102.66	35.45	7657.87	413	165.92	24.93	10296.90
CHOPBU	899	1422.32	181.09	162796.81	756	-746.87	-130.59	-98727.44	1655	675.45	38.71	64069.38
CHOPBE	460	-538.30	-69.64	-32034.23	579	408.42	95.83	55487.01	1039	-129.88	22.57	23452.77
WHIP	665	-91.82	95.89	63765.66	722	207.56	64.47	46548.67	1387	115.74	79.53	110314.31
	5666	4616.08	137.17	777219.86	5815	3467.39	59.28	344712.03	11481	8083.47	97.72	1121931.85

Figure 7.19: 9-Day 80/20 Stochastic Indicator: Pop Results

	BUY				SELL				TOTAL			
	#	PROF	AVG $	TOT $	#	PROF	AVG $	TOT $	#	PROF	AVG $	TOT $
BULL	1165	2352.26	425.59	495816.31	586	89.55	-180.64	-105855.87	1751	2441.81	222.71	389960.44
BEAR	723	-626.33	-184.88	-133668.12	1548	1258.72	119.50	184982.87	2271	632.39	22.60	51314.75
BUBE	1278	2091.24	235.76	301299.81	1299	667.69	21.70	28190.93	2577	2758.93	127.86	329490.75
BEBU	1207	353.00	25.69	31004.82	1266	135.59	-2.88	-3639.87	2473	488.59	11.07	27364.95
BUBEBU	215	219.98	162.86	35015.39	209	-87.51	-27.01	-5645.14	424	132.47	69.27	29370.25
BEBUBE	241	191.90	17.14	4130.04	292	33.52	123.97	36199.95	533	225.42	75.67	40329.99
CHOPBU	1292	953.46	124.45	160790.19	778	-830.60	-122.39	-95216.81	2070	122.86	31.68	65573.38
CHOPBE	475	-100.71	-69.98	-33241.45	841	314.52	46.16	38817.48	1316	213.81	4.24	5576.03
WHIP	757	42.70	43.79	33148.08	833	80.15	-12.30	-10241.99	1590	122.85	14.41	22906.09
	7353	5477.50	121.62	894295.07	7652	1661.63	8.83	67591.55	15005	7139.13	64.10	961886.63

Figure 7.20: 14-Day 80/20 Stochastic Indicator: Pop Results

	BUY				SELL				TOTAL			
	#	PROF	AVG $	TOT $	#	PROF	AVG $	TOT $	#	PROF	AVG $	TOT $
BULL	1026	2401.91	396.58	406888.75	487	-214.54	-202.79	-98760.06	1513	2187.37	203.65	308128.69
BEAR	612	-522.30	-157.54	-96411.88	1343	1559.80	132.66	178167.50	1955	1037.50	41.82	81755.63
BUBE	1129	1165.67	187.45	211632.31	1147	812.04	99.74	114396.06	2276	1977.71	143.25	326028.37
BEBU	1047	631.79	104.45	109361.37	1121	234.10	-7.25	-8131.48	2168	865.89	46.69	101229.87
BUBEBU	202	247.24	196.06	39605.09	188	-37.51	-7.68	-1443.46	390	209.73	97.85	38161.62
BEBUBE	206	-50.16	-61.71	-12712.72	268	178.13	119.49	32024.50	474	127.97	40.74	19311.79
CHOPBU	1134	1339.77	149.89	169972.44	702	-538.64	-168.71	-118435.25	1836	801.13	28.07	51537.19
CHOPBE	433	-293.36	-92.21	-39926.86	766	220.15	60.84	46606.02	1199	-73.21	5.57	6679.16
WHIP	684	-71.03	-2.03	-1389.50	769	85.14	-26.45	-20339.20	1453	14.11	-14.95	-21728.70
	6473	4849.53	121.58	787019.00	6791	2298.67	18.27	124084.63	13264	7148.20	68.69	911103.62

Figure 7.21: 21-Day 80/20 Stochastic Indicator: Pop Results

	BUY				SELL				TOTAL			
	#	PROF	AVG $	TOT $	#	PROF	AVG $	TOT $	#	PROF	AVG $	TOT $
BULL	877	2542.52	421.69	369817.87	378	3.51	-142.74	-53954.95	1255	2546.03	251.68	315862.94
BEAR	484	-555.40	-122.74	-59404.93	1146	1311.78	102.19	117105.94	1630	756.38	35.40	57701.01
BUBE	947	1544.43	229.96	217768.44	1022	1208.93	170.68	174430.00	1969	2753.36	199.19	392198.44
BEBU	927	409.83	65.97	61155.11	929	291.61	-.53	-496.99	1856	701.44	32.68	60658.12
BUBEBU	186	319.09	240.66	44762.84	151	-45.04	13.03	1966.85	337	274.05	138.66	46729.69
BEBUBE	169	-36.10	-20.19	-3412.40	219	108.39	76.15	16677.02	388	72.29	34.19	13264.52
CHOPBU	997	1077.31	110.47	110137.62	600	-856.96	-170.11	-102064.50	1597	220.35	5.06	8073.13
CHOPBE	362	-197.68	-128.02	-46344.35	669	247.27	37.45	25056.85	1031	49.59	-20.65	-21287.50
WHIP	586	48.07	19.26	11286.34	660	-19.22	-42.95	-28347.24	1246	28.85	-13.69	-17060.90
	5535	5152.07	127.51	705766.45	5774	2250.27	26.04	150372.98	11309	7402.34	75.70	856139.45

Results of the SI POP Test

As you can readily observe, the SI POP using 14 day SI with 65% and 35% cutoff yielded the best results of all SI applications tested. This method appears to have good potential when used judiciously. My recent research shows that SI performs best when used with four traditional timing indicators.*

X*Stochastic Fantastic; published by MBH, PO Box 353, Winnetka, IL 60093.

8

Is Closing Price
Direction Random?

As futures traders, we are committed to a never ending search for more profitable trading systems, more reliable timing indicators and more effective trading techniques, a search in which we have left virtually no stone unturned. One of the more basic approaches which has been investigated through the years is that of closing pattern studies. From time to time various studies of this nature appear on the trading scene.

Larry Williams has given closing patterns considerable attention. His 1989 book, *The Definitive Guide to Futures Trading— Volume I*, discussed many different types of price patterns as well as opening and closing price relationships. He claims to have found a number of patterns which show good promise and potential as trading tools.

Clearly, the closing price pattern concept is very simple to understand, and it is equally simple to employ in futures trading. All it amounts to is a study and application of closing patterns. In other words, we ask such questions as, "If a market closes up on the day five days in a row, how often has it closed up or down on the sixth day?" In examining closing patterns we make an assumption about the future based on past behavior. This is, of course, the underlying tenet of virtually all futures research. We assume that if a given pattern has occurred a given number of times in the past, then it is likely to be repeated in the future. Enter the proverbial "coin toss" issue. If a tossed coin turns up heads ten times in a row, are we statistically justified in expecting heads on the next toss, or are we justified in expecting tails? As a matter of fact, we are not justified in expecting either one. Each toss is independent of the previous toss, assuming that the coin is not biased or otherwise flawed.

Those who subscribe to the random walk theory of market behavior would argue that the same is true of market closing prices. Does the fact that a market has closed higher ten days in a row make it more likely that the eleventh close will be higher? Or does it mean that there is a greater probability of a lower close the next day? My work shows that in terms of overall market behavior the random walk conclusion is probably well justified. Yet, in spite of the obvious conclusion, various statistics continue to be manipulated by systems researchers. While I do not claim that individuals who engage in such pursuits are attempting to deceive the public, I do feel strongly that their conclusions are not valid inasmuch as they are based on limited historical data.

My extensive research, some of which I am about to describe, tells a very different story than the one told by various analysts. While we may have been led to believe that closing pattern relationships and expectations are valid, my work shows that *if studied back to the 1960s, there are very few overall statistically valid or predictable closing price patterns* (of those I examined).

Remember that while this may be true for closing patterns only, such patterns as those studied by Larry Williams and others involve more than just closing price patterns. They deal with closings and openings. I plan to subject their findings to the "acid test" next. The results which follow are based on my study of 504 patterns in most of the futures markets from 1991, as far back as the mid-to-late 1960s. Only the active portion of each contract month for every market was analyzed.

As an example, the pattern +++− was studied from 1967 through 1991 for all active markets. Over 22,400 cases were recorded. The result? The closing price on the next day was up 49 percent of the time and down 46 percent of the time. In other words, it's clearly a random event!

You may now argue that the example just cited was too simple. We need to examine a longer pattern; that is, one covering a longer number of days. Consider, then, the following pattern: +++++++.

In other words, seven consecutive closes up in a row. How often was the next day up or down? It was 48 percent of the time up and 47 percent of the time down! And 2,064 cases were studied. The patterns I studied and the statistics I generated are shown herein. While some of the markets themselves showed significant readings, the overall results suggest random behavior.

But there may still be a way of achieving useful results from market patterns. This can be done by developing risk management strategies for each pattern. My next study examined closing patterns in bull markets, bear markets, whipsaw markets and so on. And thereafter I studied closing patterns and opening/closing relationships. I suggest you take closing price patterns with a grain of salt when it comes to their use as timing indicators or trading signals.

There is an understandable relationship between the length of a closing pattern and the number of times it occurred in our database: the longer the pattern, the less often it occurred. Yet even the longest patterns had several thousand occurrences. As you can see from examining the results, the longer the pattern, the greater the frequency of those occurring over 60 percent of the time. See Figure 8-1 for daily closing direction patterns and their results.

Another finding, and one which deserves considerable attention, is the fact that if all patterns are averaged across markets, then we have a clear regression to the mean. In other words, the net effect is no better than chance. This clearly supports the random walk conclusion. While it may be true that a $+++++++++(-)$ pattern has occurred 89 percent of the time in soybeans, it is also true that the total number of cases for this pattern in soybeans was only twenty-three, hardly enough to support the conclusion that this pattern is statistically valid.

How then can we salvage what seems to be a good idea? One way a might be to break patterns down for further study by underlying trend. The question is, "How often have certain patterns occurred during certain types of markets?" We might ask, therefore, "How often has a $++--++--+$ pattern occurred in bull markets? In bear markets? In choppy bull markets?" In order to answer these questions we need to return to our historical database and repeat the same study using the previously determined market categories. Figures 8-2 through 8-10 show the results. As you can see, there are some high percentages to be found, so check the printouts carefully!

Finally, my more recent findings suggest that while daily closing patterns may not be reliable, intraday closing patterns are highly reliable in certain markets. This area requires intense study.

Figure 8.1: Daily Closing Pattern Percentages: All Markets

		BO	BP	C	CC	CD	CL	CO	CP	FC	GC	HO	JY	LB	LC	LH	NY	O	OJ	FB	PL	S	SF	SV	SM	SP	SU	TB	TR	W	T%	T#	-------- 65% -------
--	(+)	49	50	47	49	44	44	54	56	50	54	44	47	49	51	53	51	49	52	52	53	53	46	52	49	54	52	46	49	51	50	95156	
--	(-)	46	44	46	48	47	50	43	40	44	43	50	47	45	44	42	45	44	43	45	44	43	48	45	45	43	44	47	43	44	45	84595	
-+	(+)	49	46	49	53	49	52	51	49	49	45	51	48	49	49	48	50	49	52	48	46	49	45	48	50	48	46	50	46	52	49	98324	
-+	(-)	46	48	45	44	43	42	46	47	45	52	44	48	46	45	46	46	43	43	49	50	47	49	48	44	49	50	43	48	44	46	93462	
+-	(+)	47	46	46	48	43	42	48	48	49	55	46	45	45	50	50	48	45	48	49	52	50	46	53	45	57	47	44	46	44	48	96793	
+-	(-)	48	47	49	48	48	52	49	47	45	42	50	50	50	45	44	48	48	47	48	45	46	48	43	48	40	49	49	48	51	47	95053	
++	(+)	45	48	41	50	46	49	46	42	49	41	46	46	45	47	46	46	44	46	45	47	44	47	46	45	47	43	50	44	44	45	90195	
++	(-)	51	46	54	47	46	45	52	54	45	56	50	49	50	47	48	50	48	49	52	50	52	48	50	50	50	54	43	49	52	50	98990	
---	(+)	50	53	50	50	44	41	55	55	51	54	45	50	48	51	55	52	5·	53	53	53	53	46	52	51	59	51	47	47	53	51	43193	
---	(-)	46	41	44	48	48	54	42	42	45	44	50	44	46	45	41	44	42	42	45	44	43	48	45	43	39	45	46	46	42	45	38053	
--+	(+)	50	47	49	52	51	50	50	48	48	45	49	44	48	49	48	49	50	52	49	46	51	43	45	52	50	46	49	46	54	49	46930	
--+	(-)	45	45	45	45	43	44	46	48	46	52	47	52	47	46	46	47	42	43	48	50	46	51	51	43	47	49	44	47	42	46	44586	
-+-	(+)	46	46	45	48	42	40	49	48	48	55	43	44	44	50	50	48	46	48	49	52	50	45	51	45	60	46	45	45	43	48	44922	
-+-	(-)	50	49	49	49	51	54	48	48	47	41	53	52	51	44	45	48	47	48	48	45	46	49	45	49	36	49	48	48	52	48	44850	
-++	(+)	45	48	42	50	49	45	46	42	48	42	46	44	46	47	46	48	45	46	44	48	43	46	43	43	45	43	49	45	45	45	44670	
-++	(-)	51	47	53	47	44	49	52	54	46	55	50	52	49	47	49	49	47	49	53	49	53	50	52	51	51	53	44	48	51	50	49879	
+--	(+)	50	47	45	49	46	47	54	57	51	54	44	46	50	53	52	49	47	51	51	53	54	46	52	48	52	53	45	52	49	50	48227	
+--	(-)	46	48	49	48	47	46	43	39	44	43	51	49	45	43	44	47	46	44	46	44	43	48	44	46	45	43	49	41	46	45	42899	
+-+	(+)	48	45	49	53	48	55	51	49	49	45	54	53	50	49	49	50	48	52	47	46	48	47	49	48	47	46	52	44	49	49	47625	
+-+	(-)	47	50	45	44	44	40	47	47	45	53	42	44	45	45	45	46	45	44	50	51	48	48	47	46	51	50	41	50	47	47	45665	
++-	(+)	49	48	46	49	46	44	48	49	51	54	48	47	46	50	50	48	44	48	49	51	50	46	56	46	53	47	44	48	45	49	48423	
++-	(-)	47	45	48	48	46	50	50	47	44	43	48	49	49	45	45	48	49	47	48	45	46	48	41	48	44	49	49	47	50	47	46650	
+++	(+)	45	49	40	50	43	53	45	43	50	40	46	48	44	48	47	44	44	46	47	46	45	49	49	46	49	42	50	43	43	46	41750	
+++	(-)	51	45	55	47	51	41	52	52	45	57	50	48	52	47	48	52	49	50	50	51	51	46	48	49	48	55	43	51	52	50	45129	
----	(+)	51	54	47	50	50	39	54	55	48	57	43	51	48	52	52	52	55	50	52	51	53	50	50	51	60	52	47	54	54	51	19473	
----	(-)	45	41	46	48	44	55	43	43	48	41	52	44	47	44	44	43	39	43	45	47	43	46	48	43	38	44	45	39	41	45	17161	
---+	(+)	49	47	48	52	48	44	50	51	47	45	41	46	45	48	45	51	48	50	48	49	49	44	43	49	50	43	48	47	53	48	20781	
---+	(-)	47	47	45	45	46	51	47	44	47	53	55	51	51	47	50	46	44	45	50	48	47	50	54	45	47	52	45	47	42	48	20820	
--+-	(+)	46	50	46	49	41	42	49	52	49	59	47	45	45	51	47	49	48	48	48	53	50	46	52	47	64	47	43	46	48	49	21874	
--+-	(-)	49	47	48	48	53	51	48	45	47	37	49	51	51	44	47	48	44	48	49	44	46	49	43	47	32	49	52	46	48	47	20963	
--++	(+)	45	49	44	49	46	43	46	42	49	41	46	42	46	45	42	48	45	43	41	48	45	43	42	42	50	42	49	41	45	44	20988	
--++	(-)	50	46	51	49	47	51	52	54	46	56	51	53	49	49	53	48	47	51	56	49	52	54	53	52	48	54	46	51	52	51	24136	
-+--	(+)	50	47	49	49	44	45	56	59	50	51	43	42	48	53	49	46	48	51	50	51	53	44	51	46	54	52	42	53	51	50	22563	
-+--	(-)	45	48	45	48	49	48	41	37	44	45	54	53	47	44	47	51	45	44	47	46	44	49	45	47	42	43	52	39	44	45	20502	
-+-+	(+)	49	46	49	52	43	52	53	48	52	47	51	49	50	51	50	51	48	49	50	48	49	45	50	49	48	47	49	46	49	49	22260	
-+-+	(-)	47	50	45	44	47	45	45	48	44	51	46	48	45	44	45	45	46	46	48	48	47	51	46	45	49	50	45	49	47	47	21137	
-++-	(+)	50	46	44	44	45	43	45	48	51	57	45	44	48	49	48	44	45	47	46	53	50	44	57	47	53	48	43	48	46	48	24195	
-++-	(-)	46	47	51	53	48	52	51	47	45	40	51	51	47	47	47	51	48	48	51	43	47	51	40	47	44	48	50	47	49	47	23778	
-+++	(+)	44	46	42	49	48	52	45	41	49	41	44	47	41	48	45	43	44	43	46	49	46	49	45	46	51	39	48	42	43	45	20246	
-+++	(-)	52	49	54	49	47	42	52	53	46	55	53	49	54	47	50	53	49	53	51	49	50	47	52	49	46	57	45	52	52	51	22824	
+---	(+)	48	53	52	49	41	45	56	54	53	51	49	51	48	50	58	52	48	55	53	55	53	44	54	51	59	51	45	42	52	51	22093	
+---	(-)	48	41	42	48	51	51	41	42	43	46	46	43	46	45	38	44	44	40	44	41	44	50	43	44	38	45	48	51	43	44	19193	
+--+	(+)	52	48	50	53	55	56	51	45	49	45	57	41	52	50	50	49	52	54	51	44	51	42	47	56	50	49	51	46	54	50	24375	
+--+	(-)	44	44	44	44	40	38	46	51	45	53	40	54	43	45	44	48	41	41	46	53	45	53	49	40	46	46	44	47	42	45	22125	
+-+-	(+)	45	42	43	46	44	37	49	44	47	53	37	43	43	50	53	48	44	47	50	50	50	45	50	43	56	47	48	45	39	47	21584	
+-+-	(-)	51	52	51	51	50	58	48	51	48	44	59	53	51	44	42	48	49	48	47	47	46	50	47	51	40	49	43	50	57	49	22383	
+-++	(+)	44	46	39	52	52	49	45	42	47	43	45	45	45	49	50	47	48	50	47	47	41	49	44	44	41	45	50	48	44	46	21958	
+-++	(-)	52	48	56	45	40	47	52	55	47	55	50	51	49	46	45	49	46	46	51	50	55	47	52	51	55	52	42	47	51	50	24000	
++--	(+)	50	48	42	48	47	50	52	56	53	57	46	50	52	52	54	53	46	51	53	55	55	49	53	50	50	54	47	49	48	51	24001	
++--	(-)	46	47	51	49	45	44	45	41	43	40	49	44	43	42	41	44	46	44	44	42	41	47	44	45	46	42	47	43	47	44	20794	
++-+	(+)	48	45	48	54	53	57	49	51	47	42	58	56	50	48	49	50	48	53	45	44	48	48	49	46	45	45	54	43	50	49	23736	
++-+	(-)	48	50	46	43	43	36	49	46	47	54	38	40	45	47	46	46	44	42	53	53	49	47	49	48	53	51	38	51	47	47	22960	
+++-	(+)	47	50	50	52	48	47	50	50	52	49	51	50	44	52	52	52	43	49	53	50	51	48	55	45	52	46	44	48	46	49	22406	
+++-	(-)	48	44	45	45	44	48	48	47	44	48	45	45	51	43	43	44	50	46	44	47	46	46	41	49	45	50	48	48	50	46	21039	

T% = Total % close in direction shown

T# = Total number of cases

65% = Markets where closing pattern occurred 65% of the time or more

Figure 8.1: Continued

	(±)	BO	BP	C	CC	CD	CL	CO	CP	FC	GC	HO	JY	LB	LC	LH	NY	O	OJ	PB	PL	S	SF	SV	SM	SP	SU	TB	TR	W	T%	T#	
+ + + + +	(+)	46	51	39	52	38	53	46	43	50	39	49	47	47	47	49	49	42	49	48	44	44	47	54	47	47	46	53	46	45	47	19826	
+ + + + +	(−)	51	43	56	45	57	42	51	52	45	59	47	47	49	48	46	52	51	47	49	53	53	47	43	51	49	51	40	49	51	49	20505	
− − − − −	(+)	51	61	50	49	51	41	56	53	50	61	41	55	48	51	51	53	56	53	52	54	52	51	46	50	52	48	61	56	56	51	8873	SP
− − − − −	(−)	44	36	44	49	42	46	46	38	42	46	52	40	40	46	43	44	38	46	47	44	48	47	41	46	44	42	44	32	39	44	7629	
− − − − +	(+)	51	50	42	51	46	44	52	46	48	52	58	40	55	46	48	48	47	46	51	49	48	48	55	53	50	53	42	52	57	47	9238	
− − − − +	(−)	43	44	50	51	46	54	43	46	47	38	52	57	50	49	49	54	43	43	49	48	48	48	41	42	65	53	50	42	39	49	9522	
− − − + −	(+)	51	50	47	54	43	46	51	51	46	51	58	57	53	45	49	48	46	52	50	46	52	52	45	48	66	49	49	44	49	48	10091	SP
− − − + −	(−)	43	54	43	46	51	51	46	51	51	38	51	45	46	47	51	43	43	41	46	49	43	40	45	47	29	49	49	49	47	47	9918	
− − + − −	(+)	52	52	48	43	50	47	44	36	51	38	44	50	53	53	46	47	44	48	49	45	43	52	45	47	45	41	48	40	44	43	8996	
− − + − −	(−)	44	51	43	48	39	44	44	44	45	62	49	45	42	45	42	47	43	41	53	52	57	40	56	55	29	55	45	56	53	43	11017	
− − + − +	(+)	51	48	49	52	40	49	56	56	41	45	41	49	49	56	47	45	50	53	51	49	51	46	52	51	58	51	46	56	51	50	10579	
− − + − +	(−)	52	47	49	52	53	46	41	55	46	47	55	47	47	47	48	53	42	47	47	48	45	47	52	52	48	51	36	45	53	53	9605	
− − + + −	(+)	43	48	46	44	53	49	56	42	46	44	44	56	45	43	45	43	45	49	47	48	51	50	46	45	46	45	42	45	43	50	11046	
− − + + −	(−)	51	54	54	41	47	50	43	47	44	50	55	44	50	50	47	46	45	43	51	46	48	43	60	52	50	49	43	45	42	46	10084	
− − + + +	(+)	51	46	49	48	47	42	52	52	52	57	47	44	41	48	47	41	42	39	51	51	40	49	35	49	50	52	48	43	41	48	11732	
− − + + +	(−)	51	48	48	48	41	57	50	53	43	51	50	45	54	54	48	48	39	47	51	43	44	46	45	49	47	52	53	48	42	47	11497	
− + − − −	(+)	54	39	57	49	36	47	41	41	50	55	55	52	52	48	47	54	51	51	57	57	52	51	44	51	60	46	49	50	42	44	9397	
− + − − −	(−)	45	53	51	49	36	47	56	47	51	50	50	44	54	56	58	43	52	54	53	52	52	42	54	53	63	53	47	54	55	52	10893	
− + − − +	(+)	50	40	43	49	56	49	41	41	50	47	47	40	49	49	38	40	41	45	40	41	40	53	49	36	34	44	60	49	40	44	10599	
− + − − +	(−)	53	48	55	57	61	43	53	48	50	51	50	46	51	49	49	52	52	50	45	38	53	40	58	43	44	44	49	58	59	50	11412	
− + − + −	(+)	43	42	40	61	41	36	48	56	47	42	39	39	43	43	45	43	49	45	47	53	47	50	49	36	57	47	38	47	41	45	10340	
− + − + −	(−)	50	45	43	44	34	58	46	48	50	43	38	57	54	44	54	50	49	47	53	47	55	45	47	44	39	44	59	50	37	46	9716	
− + + − −	(+)	53	48	55	56	47	49	49	54	43	50	47	46	51	48	45	52	54	53	47	52	46	46	50	50	50	43	54	47	54	50	10636	
− + + − −	(−)	43	39	40	34	36	41	41	42	51	39	47	55	39	47	38	47	46	46	47	45	42	55	46	43	39	52	39	50	48	46	10259	
− + + − +	(+)	41	53	39	48	52	32	48	48	53	42	51	59	49	41	49	51	48	51	55	49	55	42	48	50	48	54	54	47	58	45	11275	
− + + − +	(−)	55	42	55	50	40	48	55	47	53	55	50	50	50	47	41	53	54	54	52	57	53	48	44	57	61	52	45	50	48	50	12043	
− + + + −	(+)	46	50	40	48	46	47	52	54	45	39	55	54	52	46	41	47	49	47	40	44	46	48	44	40	43	43	50	42	37	45	10850	
− + + + −	(−)	50	53	48	46	51	47	44	54	51	39	52	42	45	50	52	53	43	46	53	41	47	51	50	60	46	44	59	50	48	48	11719	
− + + + +	(+)	48	39	52	51	40	41	50	43	53	41	41	54	52	46	52	48	43	47	44	55	47	51	47	53	52	42	34	43	48	48	11661	
− + + + +	(−)	47	56	46	50	55	49	47	54	52	52	56	47	45	50	51	49	45	51	55	52	50	50	56	49	57	49	41	48	41	49	11321	
+ − − − −	(+)	50	42	43	45	45	41	47	50	49	46	47	52	54	42	48	45	51	42	45	43	47	47	41	44	40	47	52	48	48	46	10695	
+ − − − −	(−)	45	59	32	51	52	36	55	54	53	64	48	51	45	49	49	45	54	53	43	52	50	53	55	45	43	50	53	44	46	46	9409	
+ − − − +	(+)	46	37	61	46	50	54	47	43	44	50	55	39	50	47	47	53	41	54	40	45	47	44	45	45	54	57	36	45	54	50	10173	
+ − − − +	(−)	52	49	45	52	50	57	44	48	50	44	46	57	50	53	53	44	54	50	52	49	54	48	48	52	40	52	48	49	52	51	9766	
+ − − + −	(+)	44	44	48	45	54	48	48	44	50	44	46	46	47	44	44	44	40	44	45	48	42	48	44	52	36	44	47	45	44	45	8806	
+ − − + −	(−)	53	50	48	54	52	46	53	48	47	44	52	51	50	48	52	48	43	49	48	48	46	53	41	44	45	52	46	50	52	49	10828	
+ − + − −	(+)	50	45	54	54	42	52	48	47	47	47	52	46	47	50	51	50	43	41	49	48	46	53	55	51	63	46	50	50	51	47	10517	
+ − + − −	(−)	43	50	43	52	54	54	47	43	48	54	58	51	46	43	48	48	48	49	49	48	55	42	41	43	47	38	47	38	53	46	10992	
+ − + − +	(+)	43	58	47	43	50	42	46	56	43	40	47	47	45	44	50	50	48	51	49	44	48	47	44	42	34	48	55	47	53	48	10307	
+ − + − +	(−)	47	39	48	53	56	46	49	52	41	47	44	40	40	49	49	47	48	48	49	52	53	48	45	54	53	42	48	42	46	46	11195	
+ − + + −	(+)	46	48	46	50	55	48	42	47	53	55	52	45	51	42	46	42	44	49	46	52	46	51	53	50	54	55	45	42	46	46	12254	
+ − + + −	(−)	49	47	50	46	51	41	50	54	38	49	45	53	55	46	51	50	48	49	59	49	47	51	47	53	43	42	56	50	50	50	11279	
+ + − − −	(+)	49	48	49	46	44	44	41	32	56	60	41	45	51	53	50	48	48	43	49	44	43	42	47	47	52	42	56	43	44	45	10242	
+ + − − −	(−)	49	48	51	51	53	48	50	51	49	50	51	46	43	44	50	51	48	49	49	53	54	53	53	48	43	54	43	41	50	45	10512	
+ + − − +	(+)	47	48	45	46	49	49	47	51	51	47	44	47	44	48	50	46	46	45	49	44	47	51	48	44	52	54	48	55	45	48	10381	
+ + − + −	(+)	49	48	45	49	42	42	47	44	42	44	56	37	50	46	47	42	48	51	44	44	48	48	48	46	48	50	48	48	43	48	11633	
+ + − + −	(−)	48	45	54	48	47	53	54	51	49	56	39	44	53	49	53	44	47	49	51	51	51	48	45	50	57	43	47	42	53	48	11507	
+ + + − −	(+)	46	50	44	48	43	42	50	48	44	40	47	50	40	47	48	44	45	46	46	50	48	48	45	41	42	48	48	40	49	44	10082	
+ + + − −	(−)	46	48	46	51	40	55	48	47	53	55	52	45	51	46	51	47	47	49	51	50	54	47	53	55	44	55	48	52	46	50	11094	
+ + + − +	(+)	49	53	53	50	46	43	56	53	38	55	51	45	51	46	38	53	47	49	49	53	43	42	42	48	43	53	45	40	50	51	10722	
+ + + − +	(−)	46	49	48	46	44	48	55	60	47	47	44	47	44	43	55	52	52	56	39	44	47	48	42	46	46	46	45	52	55	44	9288	
+ + + + −	(+)	51	49	46	50	49	57	50	52	41	49	49	47	52	51	52	46	52	39	46	45	50	45	48	49	51	51	47	45	55	50	12197	
+ + + + −	(−)	44	45	49	48	48	40	48	47	41	49	49	58	47	42	43	51	41	46	46	47	47	50	48	43	46	48	43	49	41	46	11035	

Figure 8.1: Continued

		BO	BP	C	CC	CD	CL	CO	CP	FC	GC	HO	JY	LB	LC	LH	NY	O	OJ	PB	PL	S	SF	SV	SM	SP	SU	TB	TR	W	T%	T#	
+ + - + -	(+)	45	46	42	50	46	39	50	44	50	54	34	47	43	55	53	51	40	52	53	53	51	44	53	42	56	50	50	43	41	48	11131	
+ + - + -	(-)	52	51	53	47	48	54	48	52	45	43	62	49	44	40	46	49	52	45	44	44	47	43	43	44	37	46	48	51	57	48	11026	
+ + - + -	(-)	47	41	39	56	41	49	48	45	48	43	37	42	44	45	51	47	49	51	47	43	43	43	43	44	60	46	45	42	42	46	10952	
+ + - + -	(-)	50	54	56	42	41	46	49	54	46	56	54	45	45	51	44	47	45	45	50	54	52	52	53	51	60	56	47	49	53	50	11954	
+ + - + -	(+)	50	51	47	48	48	43	52	60	52	56	54	51	41	55	53	52	48	46	56	54	53	52	53	51	41	47	52	52	50	52	11095	
+ + - + -	(+)	45	51	47	50	36	49	44	49	44	43	45	45	42	51	53	42	46	41	41	44	40	44	48	47	43	40	40	51	46	43	9121	
+ + - + -	(+)	45	47	50	43	40	37	40	45	49	41	45	60	49	50	48	52	47	53	43	46	50	54	48	43	41	40	40	42	51	50	11172	
+ + - + -	(-)	47	49	48	47	57	58	54	46	54	52	36	59	44	50	50	53	56	42	55	52	52	47	42	45	56	49	47	51	42	46	10458	
+ + - + -	(-)	44	47	41	50	39	37	44	50	60	36	53	59	44	46	50	44	43	49	52	47	53	44	49	52	49	44	40	47	43	50	10240	
+ + - + -	(+)	49	47	46	44	39	49	48	42	45	41	45	43	49	51	52	53	51	46	47	47	44	42	50	45	48	47	47	50	43	46	9511	
+ + - + -	(+)	51	46	45	47	43	44	48	41	51	51	43	39	47	45	43	44	46	51	50	47	47	44	55	50	48	52	52	41	46	48	9614	
+ + - + -	(+)	46	45	47	54	40	52	41	52	46	58	44	54	50	48	45	51	50	46	52	52	51	52	42	47	44	46	44	55	49	48	3893	PL SP
+ + - + +	(+)	51	50	43	56	41	53	44	53	42	44	53	50	50	40	48	55	56	39	45	66	49	52	49	46	82	49	53	59	52	51	3467	
- - - - -	(-)	46	45	48	47	59	41	61	62	48	58	44	54	35	58	47	55	46	45	51	48	46	51	58	47	17	48	39	32	43	45	4254	
- - - - -	(-)	50	52	47	54	36	35	37	47	40	40	52	47	46	40	48	41	46	45	54	52	52	58	38	46	32	43	55	52	62	48	4301	SP
- - - - +	(+)	42	44	53	57	40	54	60	35	47	53	53	42	35	54	49	47	55	45	52	39	52	44	59	52	67	51	37	38	33	47	4533	
- - - - +	(+)	53	50	39	41	54	48	38	47	53	60	55	59	59	40	41	55	46	51	48	48	46	51	38	52	44	51	40	40	44	47	4622	
- - - + -	(-)	43	41	49	54	44	47	46	44	44	41	37	43	43	44	43	48	43	43	50	49	50	49	51	50	64	52	52	52	52	48	4034	
- - - + -	(+)	52	44	54	44	44	52	42	47	47	58	39	41	53	52	48	49	47	47	45	41	42	52	48	38	30	54	54	57	54	43	4855	
- - - + +	(+)	48	50	47	35	34	58	39	34	55	27	58	58	55	47	46	55	48	48	53	41	56	56	46	50	60	59	43	46	32	46	4416	
- - - + +	(-)	52	45	44	51	58	44	60	47	53	70	39	43	51	57	46	44	47	48	52	50	55	44	51	38	45	45	59	57	55	50	5261	
- - + - -	(-)	48	45	49	53	37	47	49	42	44	35	39	45	45	48	44	52	47	48	45	48	42	56	53	45	60	45	43	59	52	46	4588	
- - + - -	(+)	52	46	44	44	57	49	42	44	35	54	44	49	51	51	42	41	44	44	43	45	50	51	50	51	40	52	54	31	43	46	4974	
- - + - +	(+)	50	47	56	52	50	50	50	52	58	44	53	50	50	39	50	54	43	48	58	56	42	39	47	44	49	52	54	64	56	51	5198	
- - + - +	(-)	51	48	39	48	38	48	46	43	38	44	56	52	54	54	47	52	44	48	44	58	40	51	58	52	55	43	42	27	40	45	5446	
- - + + -	(+)	42	52	48	44	40	45	60	58	47	58	56	37	40	54	50	47	54	48	48	50	50	43	51	52	42	43	52	42	48	47	5208	
- - + + -	(-)	54	49	53	50	42	41	51	36	40	40	43	37	59	40	49	54	47	46	53	41	49	49	44	48	46	41	49	49	42	45	4043	
- - + + +	(+)	41	43	37	44	55	49	54	47	37	62	55	52	44	50	46	43	43	38	49	49	41	49	50	47	52	55	41	49	42	52	4674	
- - + + +	(+)	52	58	58	55	34	54	48	42	48	48	58	44	57	47	49	55	51	57	49	41	47	52	47	50	45	55	44	39	64	50	4855	
- + - - -	(-)	43	54	50	51	34	43	59	39	52	48	39	43	45	48	46	55	42	47	52	50	46	41	50	61	50	45	57	46	32	46	4416	
- + - - +	(+)	54	49	51	54	58	52	38	54	44	48	39	44	42	44	53	52	49	49	50	44	47	52	35	45	52	43	35	57	32	46	5261	
- + - + -	(+)	41	43	40	41	34	55	56	41	50	41	52	57	53	48	43	46	40	43	50	50	50	45	61	46	61	50	44	43	40	46	4910	
- + - + -	(-)	49	54	48	34	34	43	45	50	53	41	47	39	44	57	51	45	50	45	51	45	50	57	37	49	37	46	47	55	43	49	4789	
- + - + +	(+)	49	54	46	59	62	65	53	53	49	49	41	57	55	48	50	47	47	50	46	47	51	48	48	51	61	36	63	56	46	47	5179	
- + + - -	(+)	44	44	36	46	59	53	45	44	38	55	55	49	53	57	48	51	48	45	50	52	53	47	55	50	53	61	30	40	46	50	5529	
- + + - -	(-)	51	48	60	59	57	41	54	54	60	45	38	54	58	45	55	50	45	48	50	52	52	49	56	54	40	52	49	49	45	50	5754	
- + + - +	(+)	47	33	32	45	35	45	50	35	37	53	45	57	48	54	51	50	45	41	44	42	50	44	41	42	71	33	47	51	56	46	5338	
- + + + -	(-)	62	39	45	53	37	63	43	42	44	39	44	41	41	46	46	57	37	52	53	44	55	49	47	46	28	47	40	51	52	45	5712	
- + + + -	(+)	35	55	49	64	56	49	34	51	50	61	53	59	57	41	50	46	43	50	48	45	49	49	53	51	41	43	46	53	44	48	5646	
- + + + +	(+)	58	50	46	56	37	43	47	42	48	56	44	44	35	53	46	51	42	42	49	54	54	47	53	55	32	48	42	50	49	48	5292	
- + + + +	(-)	54	41	52	49	44	37	49	48	42	48	61	53	58	45	51	49	52	52	44	44	50	54	48	60	75	48	54	46	47	48	5225	
+ - - - -	(-)	47	41	41	48	37	38	49	61	49	41	58	59	45	46	48	46	42	39	43	40	44	44	47	35	22	48	41	57	42	47	4409	
+ - - - +	(+)	50	62	33	52	52	37	49	49	60	35	49	45	49	50	49	48	51	43	40	40	52	42	50	56	53	62	60	49	56	50	4694	
+ - - + -	(+)	47	33	62	45	57	55	50	45	41	46	56	48	52	54	51	50	42	47	43	54	52	44	51	52	71	33	47	40	43	51	4724	SP
+ - - + -	(-)	62	39	45	53	37	63	43	42	34	51	39	62	48	41	46	50	37	49	44	45	55	49	47	46	28	43	47	51	52	45	4156	
+ - - + +	(+)	35	55	49	64	56	49	34	51	50	61	53	48	47	53	52	45	46	46	43	57	49	57	53	38	65	43	37	44	50	49	5196	
+ - - + +	(+)	58	50	46	56	37	56	49	42	48	61	44	53	48	55	46	51	52	52	54	58	54	48	55	60	32	48	56	53	46	48	5083	SP
+ - + - -	(-)	50	63	45	44	33	38	47	48	56	44	41	44	41	49	52	58	45	52	47	54	54	54	48	35	57	48	41	48	44	45	4614	
+ - + - +	(+)	46	34	50	51	61	53	47	50	53	40	35	52	58	46	48	49	42	43	47	52	42	44	47	22	48	57	41	39	44	45	5183	
+ - + + -	(-)	47	51	43	50	47	50	50	45	41	52	50	50	52	47	51	47	50	52	56	53	61	44	51	59	52	55	46	51	52	50	5804	SP
+ - + + -	(+)	51	46	47	47	41	48	41	52	50	54	36	41	49	53	49	51	47	48	56	52	44	36	52	51	60	53	40	42	51	51	5411	
- + - + -	(-)	45	47	47	57	46	47	45	32	44	41	59	63	45	43	46	50	47	49	42	44	36	52	45	45	39	42	57	45	45	45	4818	

Figure 8.1: Continued

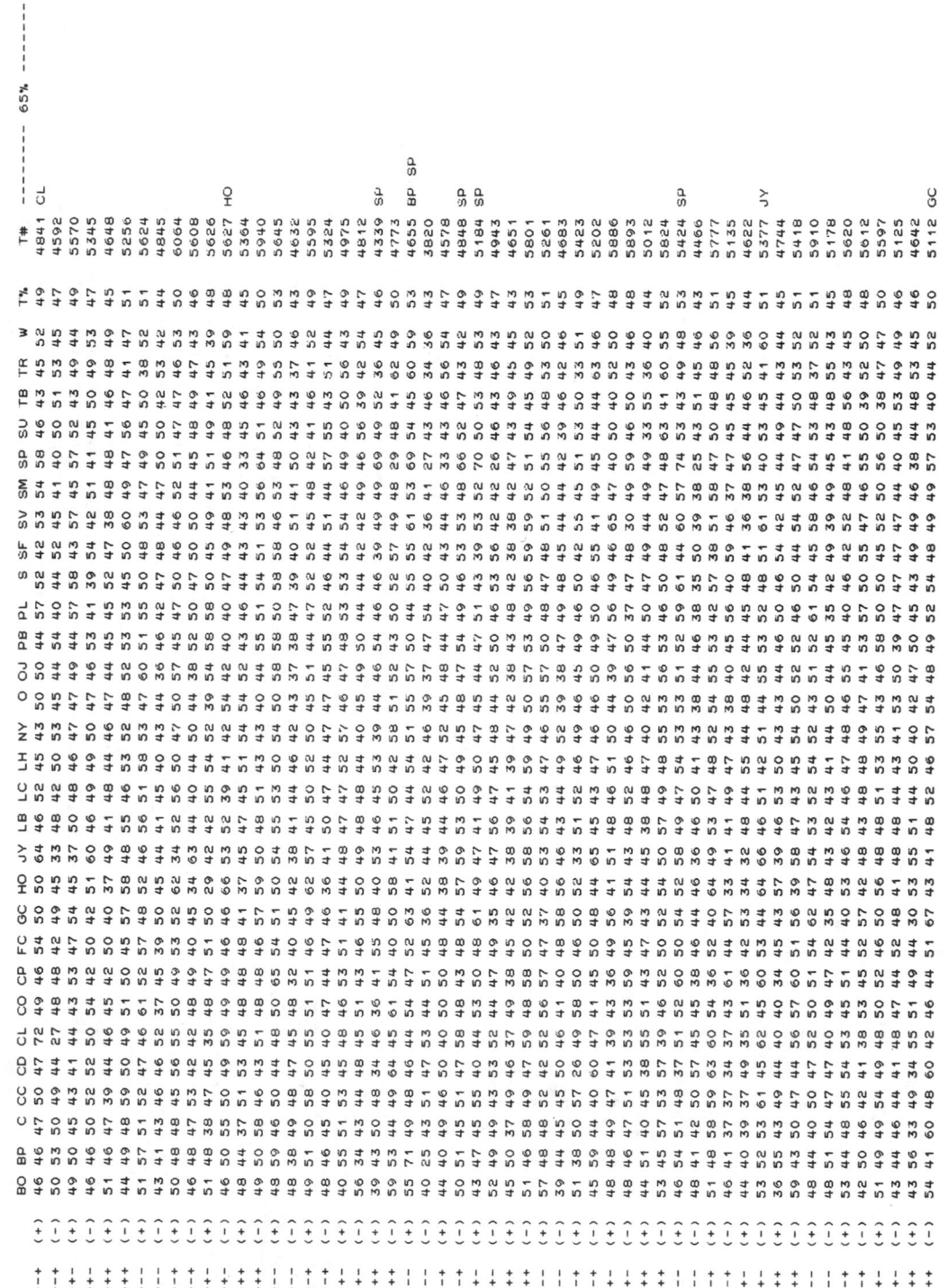

Figure 8.1: Continued

```
                                                                                                      -------- 65% --------
```

	(+-)	BO	BP	C	CC	CD	CL	CO	CP	FC	GC	HO	JY	LB	LC	LH	NV	O	OJ	PB	PL	S	SF	SV	SM	SU	TB	TR	W	T%	T#	
+----	(+-)	43	59	48	50	38	43	52	49	48	48	49	48	53	49	56	54	52	48	52	46	52	50	51	51	53	48	60	58	50	4713	
+--+-	(+-)	53	39	45	48	59	52	45	49	48	50	47	49	43	47	41	41	42	48	45	51	43	45	47	44	53	43	37	38	46	4282	
+--+-	(+-)	50	50	49	55	52	42	47	52	47	50	43	49	43	57	47	46	51	51	42	54	52	45	47	44	46	40	46	51	48	5234	
+---+	(-)	48	46	45	43	42	55	49	52	47	44	54	42	40	48	51	50	41	44	48	55	44	55	54	46	52	37	46	44	47	5121	
+---+	(-)	54	54	49	44	40	36	47	42	52	55	50	49	45	52	48	51	46	52	42	54	55	47	49	46	46	46	48	47	48	5285	
+----	(-)	48	48	44	45	50	58	46	42	52	42	58	37	50	42	40	45	48	46	49	54	42	48	45	49	42	37	47	44	48	5357	
+--++	(+)	43	54	50	52	50	40	46	47	48	48	40	37	51	44	52	52	46	46	39	58	47	45	51	43	50	49	46	48	46	5650	
++--+	(+)	52	43	45	47	41	53	48	54	48	51	55	59	44	50	45	45	48	48	58	40	54	50	43	51	52	47	48	49	50	6105	
++--+	(+)	46	45	52	50	41	58	51	54	48	44	55	49	44	41	52	50	49	48	41	48	47	41	45	53	39	55	52	49	50	5501	
+-+--	(-)	46	52	50	55	41	58	39	33	44	41	54	49	55	50	52	44	49	52	52	41	50	47	48	45	53	53	39	42	46	5122	
+-+--	(-)	48	52	45	46	42	53	51	52	52	52	46	55	51	49	44	45	46	44	56	46	50	54	50	48	44	53	39	39	47	5278	SP
+-+--	(-)	47	50	44	53	46	50	46	33	44	53	52	43	42	50	43	55	41	52	54	48	53	46	44	49	30	59	37	39	49	5485	SP
+-+-+	(-)	49	41	37	43	52	50	49	57	51	60	43	56	51	45	50	36	56	46	48	44	46	50	52	45	47	48	57	57	49	5713	
+-+-+	(-)	59	45	49	50	54	41	52	62	61	53	43	41	53	54	59	43	44	55	49	52	50	50	46	60	58	51	48	42	47	5807	
+-++-	(+)	48	43	57	49	54	35	46	55	52	37	49	50	46	47	46	59	49	41	39	49	54	47	46	38	38	43	48	53	48	5074	
+-++-	(+)	42	44	50	41	64	54	58	42	34	36	47	51	42	45	53	49	39	50	50	42	52	42	52	41	61	48	50	46	46	5074	
+-++-	(+)	43	37	46	57	31	56	57	62	61	60	35	31	55	58	61	56	44	48	39	49	52	46	45	41	54	43	64	53	46	5493	
+-++-	(+)	42	49	50	40	47	51	34	34	34	53	47	50	40	45	53	36	48	53	36	44	50	50	45	54	38	45	45	45	44	4713	
+-+++	(+)	48	43	45	46	46	40	41	55	45	53	41	50	55	49	47	47	49	41	54	52	42	56	48	55	58	48	48	57	44	4069	
+-+++	(+)	43	46	57	64	45	46	40	53	52	60	47	51	51	49	53	50	53	48	43	48	45	42	52	55	51	49	46	57	51	5722	
+-+++	(+)	43	51	42	46	49	51	46	44	43	53	47	42	55	55	53	52	46	41	39	47	50	40	57	42	41	48	50	38	45	5018	
+-+++	(+)	39	44	45	50	42	53	52	45	43	39	47	53	40	41	42	50	42	49	45	50	43	52	49	55	51	57	41	55	45	5118	
++-+-	(+)	58	45	50	60	44	51	48	57	44	38	58	45	47	41	49	49	54	47	49	50	46	51	40	51	44	47	53	43	48	5003	
+++-+	(+)	44	40	41	60	41	43	49	31	47	38	58	52	41	52	46	43	45	52	44	49	42	44	43	48	43	34	46	43	46	5157	
++-++	(+)	53	55	48	49	55	62	66	54	51	55	52	52	54	52	51	50	50	52	56	55	53	44	28	43	54	46	88	43	48	5648	CP
++-+-	(-)	52	44	45	55	55	62	54	54	51	62	50	47	50	57	54	47	48	49	54	54	53	51	70	61	61	45	7	41	48	5054	SV
+++--	(-)	43	53	48	62	53	37	42	42	45	49	49	53	50	37	38	61	54	46	46	54	47	47	29	32	26	54	46	59	49	4125	
+-+--	(-)	49	38	40	36	63	60	57	45	43	60	62	61	54	40	52	34	50	43	57	48	56	37	73	48	37	40	45	37	46	5199	SV
+-+--	(-)	43	50	48	52	52	53	43	43	44	60	35	61	54	55	61	50	44	41	40	48	40	56	43	42	59	60	57	44	50	2002	
+++-+	(+)	51	45	49	48	35	54	55	55	62	45	38	46	52	46	47	44	44	41	54	48	46	50	56	42	30	49	57	51	50	2158	
+++-+	(+)	46	37	46	54	55	50	25	33	36	19	56	46	50	53	36	46	53	56	53	49	49	50	40	40	35	38	35	43	43	1829	
++-+-	(-)	50	61	47	55	65	38	60	60	46	79	31	38	61	40	44	52	43	48	55	56	59	47	61	56	60	49	53	55	53	2293	SP TR
++-+-	(-)	46	43	45	41	33	53	52	43	44	65	51	38	39	55	48	47	44	44	43	42	38	47	45	37	75	45	74	61	46	2165	HO
++-+-	(-)	50	45	37	34	46	40	54	53	50	43	48	57	52	51	54	43	47	48	51	42	49	39	48	52	47	50	31	35	44	2377	CP
+--+-	(+)	43	40	52	41	33	56	49	25	54	43	51	58	53	54	42	51	44	48	45	56	54	55	59	37	52	48	65	61	52	2011	
+--++	(+)	45	52	46	46	33	54	55	39	25	43	60	38	45	43	43	55	44	50	42	42	49	61	36	52	41	48	32	35	44	2429	SP
+--++	(+)	53	56	53	60	46	40	55	39	27	37	60	57	52	50	48	55	42	50	49	43	54	48	39	41	31	40	64	43	47	2278	
--++-	(-)	54	40	44	53	36	43	57	31	38	27	14	49	48	48	52	56	38	50	56	57	47	48	43	61	60	54	57	43	45	1815	
--++-	(-)	36	61	44	65	36	36	70	67	38	55	50	53	44	52	45	41	54	54	56	57	44	33	52	46	48	54	40	56	52	2100	GC
--++-	(-)	57	40	58	53	57	43	31	59	59	74	23	47	55	47	43	57	39	43	53	41	52	44	51	60	60	37	59	63	51	2376	CO CP
--++-	(-)	57	49	43	54	58	54	37	52	42	24	45	73	49	49	61	46	46	39	43	45	53	52	43	50	61	50	44	34	44	2051	
--+-+	(+)	39	53	58	53	57	35	44	52	52	40	32	42	46	45	52	41	46	55	35	40	45	26	68	35	87	45	30	44	48	2416	GC JY SF
--+-+	(+)	46	33	54	46	29	37	46	54	42	40	65	42	46	45	50	52	52	36	55	57	50	51	31	45	45	50	30	43	47	2153	SV SP
--+--	(-)	49	56	39	52	68	77	52	37	54	55	65	53	49	51	44	44	44	62	40	57	41	46	31	49	12	51	69	53	49	2249	CD CL TR

Figure 8.1: Continued

		BO	BP	C	CC	CD	CL	CO	CP	FC	GC	HO	JY	LB	LC	LH	NY	O	OJ	PB	PL	S	SF	SV	SM	SP	SU	TB	TR	W	T%	T#			
--+--++	(+)	41	44	30	35	52	59	41	40	46	44	41	39	52	59	46	42	44	52	48	51	40	48	51	44	36	35	62	55	48	45	2379			
--+--++	(-)	55	50	64	63	40	39	56	58	47	49	58	57	45	40	50	54	51	45	51	46	57	48	59	50	31	62	31	40	50	51	2671	SP		
--+--++	(-)	48	40	45	45	48	62	35	52	53	63	40	48	48	48	42	54	50	50	46	58	57	45	39	45	17	54	48	49	47	51	2655			
--+--++	(-)	47	48	53	52	42	47	42	42	43	35	54	50	48	48	46	42	50	47	39	40	39	50	39	45	77	42	46	45	51	45	2381	SP	CL	JY
--+--++	(-)	40	40	36	51	44	66	51	60	41	38	58	66	47	50	56	39	51	57	51	51	44	46	32	39	42	63	27	48	49	46	2537	CL	JY	
--+--++	(+)	55	57	57	45	53	33	50	38	56	56	60	41	32	41	65	58	57	44	51	65	46	39	74	65	37	47	33	66	50	50	2740	TR		
--+--++	(+)	46	50	57	45	45	29	49	35	46	50	38	50	36	56	43	50	41	53	56	53	51	28	35	21	60	40	40	63	52	48	2274	SV		
--+--++	(-)	50	44	34	51	50	69	49	63	49	40	50	48	56	39	47	53	52	43	43	59	39	51	65	59	37	60	33	45	36	48	2256	CL		
--++-+	(-)	44	72	35	50	37	54	41	27	67	57	43	67	46	53	49	48	53	42	40	38	48	52	43	21	39	59	30	33	45	46	1881	BP	FC	HO
--++-+	(-)	53	25	61	48	58	43	55	71	29	55	31	48	49	48	44	48	49	41	56	58	48	43	44	39	30	66	35	32	62	50	2034	CP	SU	
--++-+	(-)	56	30	48	55	60	29	68	60	44	30	54	44	48	57	54	46	61	55	47	58	52	54	49	52	57	58	47	48	39	52	2313	CO	GC	SP
--++-+	(+)	42	67	47	44	37	63	49	54	50	38	37	53	30	35	42	49	48	43	52	50	40	40	47	40	25	37	46	43	58	44	1964	BP		
--++-+	(+)	63	39	50	64	40	54	46	39	39	54	37	41	53	56	35	47	35	54	52	49	51	41	49	61	49	49	31	57	53	49	2423			
--++-+	(-)	50	61	43	36	33	35	57	69	52	46	55	36	30	52	43	53	46	52	43	59	45	38	33	33	33	55	41	42	40	46	2273			
--++-+	(+)	46	33	50	59	61	52	52	27	44	38	40	53	63	52	46	52	46	44	50	31	56	42	44	57	72	27	56	44	29	49	2441	CP	PL	SP
--++-+	(-)	45	43	46	61	49	44	54	55	53	35	35	43	41	47	49	50	43	44	52	59	47	51	42	38	39	56	66	54	45	46	2283	TB		
--++-+	(-)	49	52	51	50	37	63	50	55	56	56	37	54	54	50	38	46	56	52	62	55	40	55	35	60	48	50	37	43	58	44	2315			
--++-+	(+)	54	51	35	48	47	42	53	52	55	48	33	56	48	50	46	51	44	42	52	55	57	60	48	58	68	51	37	48	55	52	2753	CP	SP	
--++-+	(+)	42	46	63	46	46	52	46	29	68	48	46	33	34	50	50	51	52	43	57	55	39	38	56	48	51	51	48	54	55	51	2528	CP	SP	
--++-+	(-)	52	51	35	48	46	62	52	68	48	48	50	46	63	64	46	55	41	50	43	40	56	44	29	41	62	37	62	43	40	45	2457	CL	JY	SP
--++-+	(+)	52	48	42	46	63	40	52	53	29	50	53	64	64	65	52	39	42	51	56	42	56	56	51	62	67	52	48	54	55	51	2237			
--++-+	(+)	46	51	51	48	48	24	46	68	49	49	45	28	49	43	49	57	55	44	55	55	38	39	41	44	32	45	46	45	41	45	2194			
--++-+	(-)	45	50	56	43	52	37	54	29	52	54	40	39	53	52	50	48	55	50	60	38	43	60	52	52	45	48	46	49	51	49	2732			
--++-+	(+)	48	43	43	34	37	60	63	54	45	40	54	53	43	46	49	55	48	47	39	57	57	63	52	44	40	43	52	44	54	47	2609			
--++-+	(-)	54	47	47	41	46	40	47	37	48	35	35	43	48	54	47	41	43	39	55	39	45	57	38	52	44	45	49	49	46	44	2281			
--++-+	(+)	50	43	46	57	46	56	44	52	52	40	37	54	54	47	57	52	53	50	42	62	50	46	57	56	58	58	50	53	42	52	2779	CO		
--++-+	(+)	50	62	53	51	38	46	67	52	52	44	63	54	44	45	45	45	49	47	62	53	39	43	60	48	60	39	47	43	60	44	2381			
--++-+	(-)	44	35	42	47	56	50	31	44	59	60	58	58	40	48	57	43	48	37	50	43	49	40	56	46	41	55	44	52	34	51	2945	LC		
--++-+	(-)	51	50	45	42	50	47	54	49	60	41	57	24	51	49	50	44	52	38	51	52	44	52	49	51	55	48	49	51	48	46	2650	JY		
--++-+	(-)	46	47	37	53	53	53	47	49	49	51	16	63	56	61	51	51	49	51	56	51	51	45	47	51	45	49	38	48	48	46	2616	PL	SP	
--++-+	(-)	51	47	53	44	43	54	50	40	54	40	71	64	48	34	53	40	43	38	43	56	52	44	38	60	57	16	60	34	46	50	2829	HO		
--++-+	(+)	46	51	56	54	43	45	47	55	40	40	49	48	42	44	44	61	57	54	58	43	41	49	49	54	38	29	55	45	46	46	2642			
--++-+	(-)	48	38	44	43	49	51	55	55	55	47	55	57	55	50	49	35	58	57	59	41	48	53	46	38	38	46	51	53	50	44	2880	SP		
--++-+	(-)	49	48	57	49	49	45	43	45	40	55	37	39	37	49	60	57	60	57	60	59	57	35	38	29	70	55	36	53	48	51	2697	BP	CP	
--++-+	(+)	46	66	47	52	41	67	67	47	51	40	48	48	51	46	45	47	39	57	39	34	41	59	59	42	42	43	50	42	46	44	2324			
--++-+	(-)	50	30	47	52	48	35	45	52	48	50	46	50	53	52	43	45	54	43	42	57	50	35	35	60	38	43	50	50	54	49	2635			
--++-+	(+)	47	48	41	63	47	52	63	44	46	31	47	37	46	39	46	52	45	49	59	43	56	50	56	60	32	40	49	61	46	48	2477			
--++-+	(+)	50	38	52	41	36	48	54	54	48	56	49	53	51	43	39	43	43	49	42	61	47	43	37	37	67	56	39	37	40	48	2248			
--++-+	(+)	38	58	55	52	45	45	36	37	46	52	56	42	48	48	44	45	45	44	53	58	56	56	43	49	56	65	44	51	55	52	2268	SP		
--++-+	(-)	59	58	38	52	72	25	47	41	35	49	49	51	54	51	37	51	49	52	48	64	43	63	50	54	45	41	48	53	44	52	1986	CD		
--++-+	(+)	63	75	52	47	41	39	40	35	40	52	57	54	61	44	54	52	49	42	41	46	51	40	43	42	46	54	57	66	53	62	2292	CD	CO	
--++-+	(-)	32	21	43	52	50	46	41	58	46	40	57	43	43	37	51	43	45	52	52	53	48	29	38	50	56	51	49	51	44	43	2204	BP	CO	
--++-+	(-)	38	43	52	53	55	44	52	37	56	53	54	48	48	47	44	51	46	46	52	43	51	55	43	42	43	48	57	66	42	46	2208	TR		
--++-+	(+)	57	52	41	42	46	46	47	50	53	46	48	34	50	48	54	50	51	48	51	52	46	53	50	42	42	42	50	51	53	50	2375			
--++-+	(-)	45	51	46	44	47	50	44	51	46	31	36	42	48	38	47	54	38	60	50	51	36	40	42	50	44	46	42	33	44	46	2361			
--++-+	(-)	42	55	50	48	44	44	44	41	55	55	49	45	46	42	50	44	42	55	55	46	51	51	45	44	50	44	50	42	44	41	2137			
--++-+	(+)	50	48	46	51	49	50	56	40	50	37	55	50	49	52	61	50	48	60	47	47	39	36	29	50	57	51	49	54	54	49	2912	CP	SV	
--++-+	(-)	57	53	56	52	57	61	57	29	56	57	69	58	57	53	52	53	42	49	58	53	47	58	46	38	69	40	50	54	50	56	2266			
--++-+	(-)	53	42	52	39	33	50	48	37	73	46	58	37	41	45	50	53	52	39	46	49	50	53	44	46	38	51	46	47	47	49	2195	CP	SV	
--++-+	(+)	39	42	44	44	56	61	39	57	48	47	50	56	52	56	50	52	48	48	50	50	49	55	47	50	56	53	56	33	50	46	2712	GC		
--++-+	(-)	57	33	56	42	54	50	48	41	52	39	49	41	43	43	41	49	40	48	48	48	48	62	46	44	44	41	41	63	46	46	2482			

	+/-	BO	BP	C	CC	CD	CL	CO	CP	FC	GC	HO	JY	LB	LC	LH	NY	O	OJ	PB	PL	S	SF	SV	SM	SP	SU	TB	TR	W	T%	T#	
																																	65%
-+--+-+-	(+)	46	51	50	48	45	38	44	33	37	64	43	57	46	45	51	47	38	35	48	66	56	46	69	48	56	50	45	43	52	49	2850	PL SV
-+--+-+-	(−)	50	40	48	49	52	56	52	63	59	30	52	37	49	52	46	48	57	58	49	29	40	50	28	48	43	32	52	53	43	47	2737	
-+--+-++	(−)	41	50	38	41	36	41	52	59	56	56	49	42	59	51	46	52	54	58	50	43	51	47	52	50	47	63	52	35	55	43	2252	
-+--+-++	(+)	56	47	60	57	58	40	44	55	57	42	58	55	59	51	49	46	59	63	46	60	51	47	52	57	47	63	44	69	61	54	2788	TR
-+--+-++	(−)	42	59	60	54	40	55	56	68	56	56	58	39	51	46	54	55	45	50	63	60	38	35	58	57	83	50	34	55	47	54	2595	CP SP
-+--+-++	(+)	51	39	34	44	41	42	29	39	36	48	65	40	50	46	51	59	59	45	46	38	33	59	46	56	56	50	57	39	43	43	2064	
-+-+-+-	(+)	56	35	53	59	50	38	38	60	60	42	36	39	45	48	53	51	38	50	58	48	55	38	55	56	56	50	51	51	59	52	2814	
-+-+-+-	(−)	51	39	34	41	47	43	38	36	36	29	65	40	50	46	56	53	37	58	58	50	38	59	55	56	56	38	43	42	38	45	2432	
-+-+-+-	(+)	42	58	43	38	44	62	51	57	36	36	25	43	50	48	46	51	55	37	44	50	47	39	32	43	62	38	39	42	33	46	2115	
-+-+-+-	(+)	50	44	49	52	37	75	47	56	55	36	75	59	45	45	40	51	39	58	53	50	49	55	65	49	35	58	50	37	60	50	2304	CL HO
-+-+-+-	(−)	47	50	38	44	38	37	38	32	55	39	36	48	46	51	43	43	58	37	45	57	40	40	37	40	45	58	45	41	46	45	2197	
-+-+-++	(−)	43	32	37	48	45	37	38	40	63	57	36	50	45	38	50	50	42	48	51	57	49	57	37	51	46	51	51	41	49	51	2475	
-+-+-++	(+)	54	65	60	46	48	40	49	34	39	62	54	48	64	55	38	50	36	46	52	55	46	34	71	40	65	59	38	30	43	46	2664	SV
-+-+-++	(−)	45	46	38	46	34	45	60	33	45	35	39	49	44	45	40	57	45	42	47	50	34	57	27	43	36	51	42	61	52	48	2476	
-+-+-++	(+)	54	41	49	50	58	47	53	46	46	44	54	53	53	52	46	50	52	43	51	27	43	43	53	46	36	51	36	41	44	51	2672	
-+-++-+	(+)	43	52	45	47	34	45	60	33	47	60	56	42	44	45	46	47	42	43	47	69	53	54	46	49	63	47	42	44	53	51	2729	PL
-+-++-+	(−)	61	60	50	48	61	43	45	46	42	44	36	34	47	46	53	52	54	54	31	50	48	57	62	38	36	52	59	61	52	51	2685	PB
-+-++-+	(−)	35	42	48	43	33	42	50	45	50	44	35	61	50	49	42	40	45	42	40	54	48	50	48	38	44	34	59	57	39	45	2406	
-+-++-+	(+)	42	56	27	43	32	31	42	52	46	71	60	33	62	50	49	52	48	51	57	50	55	55	47	48	40	36	40	53	39	44	2061	
-+-++-+	(−)	42	40	65	51	64	64	45	54	50	53	41	49	50	55	57	56	50	57	43	35	51	56	46	63	59	36	46	59	57	52	2443	GC
-+-++-++	(+)	50	62	46	46	56	40	39	47	45	34	55	52	36	41	54	50	46	44	51	42	43	54	51	50	59	43	49	41	40	50	2449	
-+-++-++	(+)	47	35	47	51	56	49	39	48	49	49	46	53	36	41	42	45	51	53	47	40	42	36	51	49	59	43	49	45	40	46	2249	
-+-++-++	(−)	42	57	47	48	48	50	46	48	47	45	51	49	58	54	45	51	51	51	49	56	45	36	35	58	32	44	56	41	55	49	2749	
-+-++-++	(−)	42	40	48	46	47	44	50	48	45	43	46	46	48	52	54	46	44	51	49	48	41	58	64	48	37	44	38	52	48	47	2683	
-+-++-++	(+)	45	55	51	47	49	34	50	44	45	45	48	47	48	53	46	44	53	43	57	48	52	47	47	46	51	48	37	40	48	49	2649	
-+-++-++	(−)	44	44	50	44	49	61	45	43	50	51	47	51	51	42	41	52	54	43	57	51	58	51	46	46	57	47	57	52	53	47	2762	
-+-++++-	(+)	49	60	51	50	61	40	50	46	50	47	63	54	61	48	48	43	48	48	49	54	44	49	47	46	60	39	56	38	48	47	2846	
-+-+++-	(+)	46	37	44	48	32	64	48	52	46	49	60	57	50	53	54	48	51	51	57	45	47	47	47	48	40	57	40	40	43	49	2992	
-+-+++-	(−)	48	46	65	48	43	55	48	65	50	71	54	32	44	55	52	50	48	44	60	50	48	43	42	38	43	52	39	59	44	48	2735	CP
-+-+++-	(+)	46	50	47	44	56	40	37	32	48	53	45	58	52	52	46	47	50	42	49	52	49	44	50	47	40	53	51	50	48	47	2693	
-+-+++-	(+)	50	41	43	51	33	44	53	35	52	34	50	48	51	49	53	53	55	54	54	46	39	55	45	51	59	46	46	18	38	46	2592	
-+-+++-+	(−)	42	58	42	46	44	48	44	61	46	63	48	47	48	53	54	40	43	52	45	56	52	43	47	36	37	44	65	72	56	50	2847	SP TR
-+-+++-+	(−)	44	55	57	46	55	34	51	44	51	51	54	59	42	54	53	54	51	54	58	51	43	51	42	51	59	48	50	40	56	46	2753	
-+-+++-+	(−)	46	48	45	49	61	48	47	54	50	39	43	69	47	43	42	59	54	50	53	58	43	52	39	54	34	45	61	61	46	50	2975	
-+-+++-+	(−)	45	46	47	46	34	31	50	54	40	38	52	30	46	37	48	40	54	42	57	58	49	43	52	47	45	50	60	58	54	46	2465	SP
-+-+++-+	(+)	52	50	44	48	43	42	49	54	31	47	63	50	61	48	57	51	58	48	49	38	50	44	53	48	36	45	47	41	51	50	2721	
-+-+++++	(+)	43	37	35	57	43	58	47	33	67	48	45	63	44	41	52	53	44	49	54	45	45	38	56	48	50	46	50	54	44	50	2352	FC
-+-+++++	(−)	58	60	41	49	43	68	50	65	51	49	58	69	58	56	52	56	49	47	54	58	60	60	42	50	61	56	42	58	53	45	2121	
-+-+++++	(+)	51	38	55	48	57	64	54	52	47	52	56	58	51	60	61	39	52	54	47	60	43	56	45	48	48	61	55	58	47	52	2936	GC
-+-+++++	(−)	43	58	41	61	32	37	41	43	47	32	41	56	43	35	36	45	39	52	47	38	54	43	45	47	46	48	37	45	48	53	2555	GC
-+++-+-	(−)	48	44	57	47	41	32	51	43	46	51	54	30	46	48	42	56	36	52	52	38	56	51	47	47	54	35	55	36	45	43	2108	
-+++-+-	(−)	49	49	45	61	32	31	49	47	46	58	52	54	50	49	48	44	53	54	57	50	46	43	50	47	54	50	36	58	52	47	2468	CL JY
-+++-++	(+)	49	48	45	45	32	31	42	40	39	39	54	30	46	37	50	50	42	42	54	39	55	64	52	42	55	46	37	32	46	51	2356	
-+++-++	(+)	57	42	62	56	65	65	42	53	40	47	32	73	46	59	50	45	53	53	42	57	43	33	50	42	44	52	54	65	49	45	2442	JY
-+++-++	(−)	40	54	40	42	34	43	47	40	39	39	54	49	49	37	49	47	42	54	42	55	44	42	49	45	34	52	54	32	49	49	2184	
-++++++-	(+)	51	38	49	59	52	53	57	42	46	42	49	49	52	58	48	46	50	47	40	57	54	34	49	53	55	44	51	44	46	49	2137	
-++++++-	(+)	45	57	47	39	43	42	41	46	51	51	43	49	51	47	45	50	50	50	50	50	54	56	28	45	55	52	44	50	49	47	2064	
-+-+---	(−)	45	45	50	54	44	68	40	60	38	58	41	52	50	53	51	47	36	45	37	47	48	50	70	50	0	45	45	88	56	48	1687	CD SP TR
+-+----	(−)	51	50	47	42	29	50	34	37	55	58	54	40	48	46	43	47	45	52	60	47	48	50	50	43100	52	45	46	7	41	48	1660	SV

Figure 8.1: Continued

	+/-	BO	BP	C	CC	CD	CL	CO	CP	FC	GC	HO	JY	LB	LC	LH	NY	O	OJ	PB	PL	S	SF	SV	SM	SP	SU	TB	TR	W	T%	T#		65%
+----+	(+)	47	52	52	62	44	55	56	56	49	49	42	42	34	56	44	61	54	49	45	54	50	57	29	38	26	47	54	46	59	49	1928		
+----++	(-)	49	38	40	36	53	38	34	49	43	49	54	47	52	42	52	34	50	49	52	55	46	37	68	57	73	48	37	45	37	46	1824	SV	SP
+---+	(-)	43	50	50	48	52	58	34	52	43	45	49	43	44	55	61	51	50	43	57	50	43	56	43	42	59	47	40	33	44	46	2002		
+---++	(+)	53	45	46	51	43	43	65	46	51	19	56	53	52	49	36	46	49	49	40	48	49	50	56	56	30	49	60	35	51	50	2158		
+---+++	(+)	45	33	45	43	35	58	43	55	46	56	41	46	36	52	44	44	49	49	41	50	46	42	36	40	35	38	44	42	42	43	1829		
+--+	(-)	50	61	47	55	65	38	56	60	46	79	56	53	61	40	51	52	43	48	55	50	48	47	61	56	60	60	49	53	55	53	2269	GC	
+--++	(-)	48	43	45	58	39	43	59	52	53	65	41	38	65	53	48	35	49	43	40	55	49	53	45	43	75	57	42	74	53	49	2293	SP	TR
+--+++	(-)	46	55	50	39	56	53	40	44	44	28	68	55	58	39	49	62	40	43	56	42	38	42	53	50	25	53	53	16	43	46	2165	HO	
+--++++	(+)	50	53	58	51	54	41	50	74	63	51	51	59	53	51	54	53	47	48	51	42	49	39	48	55	47	57	50	65	61	52	2377	CP	
+-+	(-)	44	45	37	46	33	54	42	25	44	54	42	39	65	48	42	44	44	44	42	49	54	55	41	41	48	41	48	31	35	44	2011		
+-++	(+)	43	40	52	33	46	57	52	56	57	60	65	38	48	50	51	58	51	44	56	55	49	54	59	53	68	45	40	32	53	50	2429	SP	
+-+++	(-)	53	56	47	53	46	40	56	39	42	37	33	57	45	43	55	43	42	50	49	56	43	48	39	41	31	55	50	64	43	47	2278		
+-++++	(-)	44	52	35	53	52	52	55	38	46	27	54	49	58	52	45	55	38	33	48	43	48	52	52	43	35	40	54	57	43	45	1815		
+-+++++	(+)	54	62	45	61	65	60	43	57	52	24	46	58	52	71	56	61	52	46	43	45	57	26	51	60	61	54	40	35	56	52	2100	GC	
++	(+)	39	57	52	45	36	48	70	67	38	74	50	53	44	45	44	57	54	54	56	57	47	44	51	35	30	51	41	35	63	51	2376	CO	CP
+++	(-)	57	40	43	36	47	66	27	31	62	55	32	42	51	46	34	38	39	40	53	40	39	52	43	30	77	42	46	59	34	44	2051		
++++	(+)	56	43	48	45	60	47	46	38	47	60	48	46	23	51	53	61	42	39	45	57	50	51	41	60	51	45	50	59	51	47	2367		
+++++	(+)	39	50	58	53	35	37	52	52	52	58	50	55	73	49	41	38	46	44	62	51	48	65	68	49	37	52	50	30	44	48	2416	GC JY	SF
++++++	(-)	39	33	54	46	46	19	46	54	54	50	32	42	45	51	44	53	55	62	44	58	57	21	87	12	45	59	60	53	51	47	2153	SV	SP
+++++++	(+)	49	56	39	52	68	36	52	42	46	65	65	40	58	51	51	53	52	44	52	49	41	46	45	51	49	51	43	69	53	49	2249	CD CL	TR
+++++++	(+)	41	44	30	35	43	62	41	40	46	43	41	36	52	46	46	42	44	44	52	51	40	48	51	44	36	35	62	55	48	45	2379		
+------+	(+)	50	50	64	63	40	49	56	58	46	49	50	55	45	49	48	51	51	45	45	51	57	48	63	63	39	42	31	40	50	51	2671		
+------++	(+)	48	48	45	43	48	48	62	62	53	63	40	48	48	57	54	54	50	46	58	58	57	45	59	50	17	54	48	47	47	51	2655		
+-----+	(-)	47	48	53	52	52	52	40	42	43	35	54	50	48	46	42	42	50	50	47	39	40	50	39	45	77	42	46	45	51	45	2381	SP	
+-----++	(-)	40	40	48	45	44	66	35	41	48	54	38	66	51	38	46	35	51	39	44	44	52	39	49	33	48	62	47	48	39	46	2537	CL	JY
+-----+++	(-)	57	40	57	53	37	33	46	38	56	60	41	32	50	41	50	58	42	39	52	51	65	55	52	55	37	63	33	66	49	50	2740	TR	
+----+	(+)	46	50	57	46	46	29	50	35	46	58	50	38	38	36	51	46	41	53	56	53	60	28	74	36	60	37	40	63	52	48	2274	SV	
+----++	(-)	50	44	34	51	50	49	63	49	45	50	34	55	49	39	53	47	53	52	45	39	39	65	21	59	39	60	60	33	45	48	2256	CL	
+----+++	(-)	44	72	35	50	37	54	49	40	46	43	67	51	46	53	49	48	49	41	40	38	48	43	44	50	66	30	59	59	36	46	1881	BP FC	HO
+----++++	(+)	53	25	61	48	58	43	55	71	29	55	31	48	49	42	48	48	56	39	56	58	48	49	50	57	35	66	32	32	62	50	2034	CP	SU
+---+	(-)	56	30	48	48	58	60	68	60	67	60	49	44	54	41	57	48	61	55	58	60	44	50	52	75	58	35	47	48	39	52	2313	CO GC	SP
+---++	(-)	42	67	47	44	37	63	29	39	53	30	52	36	48	39	45	35	50	37	48	47	40	42	54	47	25	37	46	43	58	44	1964	BP	
+---+++	(+)	63	50	39	50	64	40	49	54	50	38	37	54	46	50	48	46	48	50	52	41	51	40	49	61	61	49	37	57	53	49	2423		
+---++++	(-)	46	43	48	51	56	35	56	27	44	41	45	29	39	47	50	52	50	44	36	50	42	39	50	49	61	56	45	31	46	46	2273	CP PL	SP
+---+++++	(+)	50	61	50	52	34	46	50	69	44	63	56	41	53	53	54	46	53	53	68	68	47	55	57	44	72	39	48	44	45	49	2441	TB	
+--+	(-)	45	33	59	46	61	52	40	27	48	35	40	38	46	39	42	54	47	44	42	31	42	39	38	39	27	56	66	54	53	46	2283		
+--++	(-)	43	46	51	49	37	46	47	35	44	37	53	35	43	56	38	45	53	43	45	35	49	35	45	33	58	58	45	31	46	44	2315		
+--+++	(+)	49	52	50	45	53	63	46	44	44	60	56	41	49	50	56	41	44	52	55	57	57	50	60	51	51	50	49	57	52	52	2753		
+--++++	(+)	54	51	51	35	43	42	53	68	48	41	33	64	48	52	46	39	52	42	62	55	60	39	56	48	68	51	37	48	55	51	2528	CP	SP
+--+++++	(-)	42	43	56	48	43	52	46	63	48	63	46	68	46	41	50	57	47	52	41	38	55	55	41	63	67	41	62	41	43	45	2237		
+-+	(-)	52	48	40	50	51	76	43	45	50	53	39	72	52	43	46	39	53	50	45	59	56	50	48	52	52	45	48	54	55	49	2457	CL JY	SP
+-++	(+)	46	51	56	48	42	24	55	45	45	55	42	28	46	56	49	57	42	45	52	38	39	45	41	44	32	45	46	45	41	45	2194		
+-+++	(-)	50	43	42	43	37	54	44	48	45	42	54	40	51	52	52	49	39	43	48	52	51	38	38	39	40	52	45	46	46	49	2732		
+-++++	(-)	48	44	51	53	48	56	51	45	48	58	54	58	46	54	50	47	47	39	46	46	51	57	52	44	40	45	46	49	51	47	2609		
+-+++++	(+)	54	47	47	40	40	40	44	37	48	42	57	43	48	50	54	49	41	41	39	51	44	43	38	39	44	38	45	44	54	44	2281		
+-++++++	(+)	43	46	51	57	51	51	52	48	63	63	57	32	45	45	54	57	49	39	53	56	51	56	60	56	83	56	60	47	42	52	2699		
++	(+)	50	62	53	49	38	46	67	62	52	57	45	16	46	52	53	54	53	43	46	50	49	58	48	58	60	46	58	43	60	52	2779	CO	
+++	(+)	46	35	42	53	46	50	40	44	40	38	65	45	49	49	45	41	48	37	48	50	52	47	48	45	47	55	44	52	34	44	2381		
++++	(+)	51	50	45	48	56	54	54	51	51	45	69	51	51	45	51	45	43	59	49	45	45	51	40	40	45	45	48	48	48	51	2945	LC	
+++++	(-)	46	48	50	51	38	48	56	45	55	37	55	45	44	49	47	53	38	58	52	34	37	52	47	51	49	51	46	44	51	49	2650	JY	
++++++	(+)	51	47	57	53	43	51	51	42	42	16	57	51	56	51	44	53	41	40	56	67	52	44	44	16	51	83	46	38	54	46	2616	CP PL	SP
+++++++	(-)	46	51	37	54	54	33	60	44	32	32	37	60	44	51	43	54	57	58	43	41	50	40	49	38	29	58	49	44	46	50	2829	HO	
++++++++	(-)	48	51	38	52	49	51	42	40	55	62	37	38	49	50	45	61	57	40	54	55	48	43	49	49	46	46	55	45	46	46	2642		
+++++++++	(+)	49	48	57	43	45	49	55	55	40	36	60	50	51	51	50	35	36	36	54	55	50	53	46	57	70	51	36	53	50	50	2880	SP	

Figure 8.1: Continued

------- 65% -------

		BO	BP	C	CC	CD	CL	CO	CP	FC	GC	HO	JY	LB	LC	LH	NV	O	OJ	PB	PL	S	SF	SV	SM	SP	SU	TB	TR	W	T%	T#	
+-++++-	(+)	46	66	47	46	35	47	41	67	51	48	51	52	48	54	52	51	50	53	59	62	57	57	39	60	57	51	43	53	48	51	2697	BP CP
+-++++-	(-)	50	30	47	52	60	43	56	31	43	47	45	37	48	43	46	45	43	39	39	34	41	41	59	35	42	43	50	42	46	44	2324	
+-++++-	(-)	50	48	63	50	60	33	51	57	48	47	45	56	48	53	45	52	43	39	39	52	56	41	59	38	50	43	52	50	54	49	2635	
+-++++-	(+)	47	48	41	47	47	63	47	35	46	46	42	42	51	43	39	45	48	42	53	61	42	46	60	51	61	55	40	45	43	46	2477	
+-++++-	(-)	38	62	55	52	45	45	45	52	52	41	39	53	46	40	53	43	43	50	46	58	47	56	60	46	32	40	49	61	40	48	2248	
+-++++-	(-)	58	26	38	45	44	58	54	51	44	58	59	53	45	55	45	45	50	48	67	58	50	43	37	56	48	56	39	48	41	48	2268	SP
+-+++--	(-)	37	38	58	39	25	39	40	37	56	52	41	53	48	37	51	44	39	47	55	44	46	31	49	46	65	45	52	48	41	45	1986	CD
+-+++--	(+)	59	58	57	72	48	41	56	61	40	47	57	42	49	57	44	54	54	51	43	52	52	64	50	51	31	54	42	51	52	52	2292	BP CO
+-+++--	(+)	63	75	50	48	52	35	56	57	47	56	40	53	53	49	52	57	57	56	55	54	54	55	50	57	56	57	48	62	52	53	2204	
+-+++--	(+)	32	21	43	25	52	59	33	32	56	52	34	45	42	48	48	37	32	31	43	58	41	42	41	39	35	41	48	31	34	43	1797	TR
+-+++--	(-)	38	43	41	48	52	39	58	55	44	46	42	48	42	48	50	47	42	35	46	45	47	44	43	44	45	46	57	66	47	46	2208	
+-+++--	(+)	57	52	47	55	53	57	41	48	54	61	54	51	56	50	38	50	50	44	51	54	53	55	29	57	53	54	51	49	44	50	2375	
+-+++--	(+)	57	52	52	45	33	48	40	29	51	64	57	73	41	45	44	38	38	50	55	50	43	63	38	58	58	44	46	47	48	50	2361	
+-+++--	(+)	45	51	47	51	50	41	47	49	47	64	44	57	50	48	50	52	50	52	46	50	43	35	46	44	42	53	56	47	53	46	2543	
+-+++--	(-)	50	48	46	54	44	50	41	40	49	30	34	42	37	38	44	38	45	46	51	48	53	49	49	48	45	42	43	49	44	41	2137	
+-++-+-	(+)	42	55	39	46	57	56	56	67	49	55	61	52	49	52	53	52	48	58	55	47	62	47	52	58	40	51	53	49	53	56	2912	CP SV
+-++-+-	(-)	42	56	52	57	33	57	51	29	46	23	51	47	41	52	42	38	52	58	50	39	53	50	69	38	42	50	41	49	50	47	2266	
+-++-+-	(-)	39	34	44	52	39	48	57	37	57	73	46	53	41	50	43	44	46	50	52	48	42	57	47	50	57	46	53	44	47	50	2195	GC
+-++-+-	(+)	40	64	56	41	54	50	44	44	36	52	57	45	46	41	49	40	40	37	50	48	40	37	42	38	50	44	41	63	46	46	2712	
+-++-+-	(+)	46	51	41	54	45	38	45	33	52	46	52	45	46	41	51	47	40	35	48	48	56	56	69	43	56	41	63	46	38	49	2492	
+-++-+-	(+)	50	40	49	52	56	56	52	63	59	30	57	37	49	52	46	57	57	58	49	29	46	49	28	48	43	56	45	53	46	47	2850	PL SV
+-++-+-	(-)	41	50	38	41	36	48	52	44	39	64	56	37	37	46	51	48	41	38	47	55	47	49	48	46	43	62	45	53	43	43	2737	
+-++-+-	(+)	56	47	60	49	40	54	48	44	56	30	56	55	49	52	46	43	41	58	54	39	50	47	52	50	47	63	44	69	61	54	2252	
+-++-+-	(+)	51	39	34	44	56	59	38	39	42	56	58	58	46	51	54	53	59	45	46	60	53	43	58	57	83	50	55	39	47	54	2788	TR
+-++-+-	(-)	56	53	44	56	40	53	39	57	38	37	65	49	56	51	43	40	38	50	52	38	33	54	40	36	16	46	42	57	43	43	2595	CP SP
+-++-+-	(-)	42	50	43	33	47	54	38	57	36	36	31	45	47	54	49	46	37	37	40	50	41	61	42	38	49	45	39	42	38	42	2064	
+-++-+-	(-)	42	50	49	38	47	56	44	59	36	61	31	49	44	49	46	44	55	38	44	48	43	39	32	43	62	50	43	42	38	45	2814	
+-++-+-	(-)	46	44	52	41	54	50	47	51	52	57	36	48	37	49	46	40	40	41	60	41	49	55	43	48	44	45	39	57	38	46	2432	
+-++-+-	(+)	47	50	49	49	47	75	37	40	39	30	75	59	50	52	56	51	55	38	47	50	49	55	65	43	62	38	39	60	33	46	2115	
+-++-+-	(-)	43	32	37	48	52	37	38	57	54	62	62	48	46	59	51	41	42	50	45	57	49	65	49	58	49	58	50	37	60	50	2304	CL HO
+-++-+-	(+)	54	65	48	45	49	57	38	32	39	35	54	50	45	38	47	53	53	42	45	39	49	40	37	46	45	45	45	41	46	45	2197	
+-++-+-	(+)	45	60	51	50	49	60	45	63	45	35	39	49	50	44	40	45	36	50	54	42	50	56	56	51	46	51	47	55	49	51	2475	
+-++-+-	(+)	50	51	49	54	58	45	45	64	53	60	43	53	53	49	48	50	57	53	51	27	45	34	27	54	36	38	58	61	52	49	2664	SV
+-++-+-	(-)	41	41	50	56	44	47	60	29	47	56	56	42	47	46	53	47	50	51	44	42	45	57	53	46	51	51	54	44	44	46	2476	
+-++-+-	(-)	43	45	47	33	33	60	43	38	60	60	56	42	49	44	54	53	43	41	69	48	54	43	53	48	36	42	44	44	52	49	2672	
+-++-+-	(-)	43	42	65	50	56	48	57	66	47	71	53	33	62	47	57	45	42	55	57	48	52	54	51	47	67	52	50	53	59	51	2729	PL
+-++-+-	(-)	50	40	46	46	47	53	40	32	50	46	49	46	53	55	54	50	41	44	60	35	43	51	48	56	46	61	36	41	52	51	2685	PB
+-++-+-	(-)	62	60	44	33	49	48	45	48	53	53	55	34	49	46	45	43	52	41	31	50	48	50	36	48	44	34	59	56	45	45	2406	
+-++-+-	(+)	47	35	47	41	33	42	45	35	39	53	53	37	62	54	40	57	50	55	55	35	42	58	42	46	53	63	38	44	59	52	2061	
+-++-+-	(+)	53	57	53	49	50	49	46	48	55	46	46	53	58	50	42	45	46	51	47	40	43	36	35	47	58	54	38	39	57	52	2443	GC
+-++-+-	(-)	42	42	48	47	47	34	49	48	38	50	46	46	38	53	51	50	45	45	49	56	46	46	64	54	37	48	40	52	57	46	2449	
+-++-+-	(+)	45	55	51	47	49	60	45	53	45	55	48	51	49	44	53	47	52	43	57	50	54	46	51	54	48	47	57	57	47	49	2249	
+-++-+-	(-)	46	37	44	38	32	48	50	44	54	46	35	42	50	49	54	53	45	42	57	42	49	47	47	46	51	48	48	40	43	47	2749	
+-++-+-	(+)	48	55	51	50	42	52	54	66	48	54	54	54	50	44	51	50	43	41	57	40	48	42	49	49	60	57	57	57	47	47	2683	
+-++-+-	(-)	44	44	42	51	48	59	46	54	49	49	49	51	44	44	50	52	45	57	38	56	48	43	43	42	43	39	57	50	44	49	2649	
+-++-+-	(+)	48	46	56	44	49	57	46	32	45	49	48	51	50	51	46	45	45	48	49	59	49	58	49	50	51	45	51	50	48	49	2762	
+-++-+-	(+)	46	50	47	33	33	48	37	48	50	54	63	52	46	36	46	41	47	62	43	51	47	36	50	50	45	39	50	45	41	48	2846	
+-++-+-	(+)	46	40	57	48	42	40	57	42	49	54	33	59	52	41	50	50	46	47	60	35	52	43	50	50	67	52	51	50	40	49	2992	
+-++-+-	(-)	46	53	44	52	56	54	61	66	47	49	43	44	52	52	46	45	50	45	45	35	56	55	49	51	52	45	50	48	47	48	2735	CP
+-++-+-	(-)	46	54	43	51	33	64	53	35	31	63	33	40	53	46	53	53	55	44	47	51	39	58	39	51	67	52	33	18	38	47	2693	
+-++-+-	(-)	46	58	33	42	50	36	51	41	50	55	43	44	47	43	33	45	33	47	44	46	41	43	49	39	65	52	36	36	49	46	2592	
+-++-+-	(-)	60	58	55	46	50	47	54	54	48	41	54	51	47	54	42	64	53	50	53	50	56	43	50	54	34	45	59	61	46	50	2847	SP TR
+-++-+-	(-)	35	40	58																												2753	

Figure 8.1: Concluded

		BO	BP	C	CC	CD	CL	CO	CP	FC	GC	HO	JV	LB	LC	LH	NV	O	OJ	PB	PL	S	SF	SV	SM	SP	SU	TB	IR	W	T%	T#	------ 65% ------
+++-+++	(+)	45	46	47	52	46	43	49	33	62	51	34	47	36	49	48	45	49	46	48	58	46	49	45	37	74	45	47	36	38	46	2465	SP
+++-++-	(-)	51	44	49	46	34	51	48	63	31	47	63	50	61	48	51	53	42	48	49	38	50	44	53	58	25	50	47	61	57	50	2721	
+++--++	(+)	50	41	48	48	43	50	49	55	67	48	50	44	44	57	55	53	42	54	54	45	49	59	56	41	61	56	46	54	44	50	2352	FC
+++--+-	(-)	47	56	46	49	48	47	50	37	25	50	46	54	50	41	39	40	52	42	43	48	45	37	42	54	30	40	48	41	54	45	2121	
+++---+	(+)	54	48	38	54	45	68	47	39	50	43	51	47	54	49	51	57	36	40	60	57	50	42	39	46	40	38	52	50	60	51	2903	CL
+++----	(-)	40	46	55	45	50	30	50	43	39	56	48	38	41	58	54	59	37	54	37	42	58	43	55	47	57	50	60	54	36	45	2562	
++-++-+	(-)	45	48	43	54	61	48	50	43	50	39	43	50	53	54	41	40	58	42	51	55	40	53	43	48	36	45	26	41	51	46	2697	
++-++--	(-)	52	50	50	44	30	50	47	54	45	48	54	56	37	37	52	44	49	49	54	45	37	38	30	48	50	46	50	38	43	44	2446	
++-+-++	(+)	43	37	35	57	46	55	47	33	43	48	45	63	37	41	52	42	44	47	54	45	37	60	65	47	50	35	42	45	48	44	2477	
++-+-+-	(-)	54	58	60	41	43	38	50	65	51	50	51	32	58	54	43	56	49	47	42	54	58	60	53	47	50	50	42	58	53	52	2936	
++-+--+	(+)	51	38	55	41	61	64	56	54	50	67	56	58	51	60	61	52	39	43	47	60	43	56	53	48	61	55	55	52	47	53	2555	GC
++-+---	(-)	43	58	41	57	37	32	41	43	47	32	41	37	43	35	36	45	56	53	48	38	54	43	45	47	46	35	37	45	48	43	2108	
++--+++	(+)	48	44	47	54	65	66	56	49	48	47	65	69	50	47	39	52	52	52	40	47	50	53	47	48	54	46	59	36	45	49	2468	CL JY
++--++-	(-)	49	49	51	45	32	31	42	49	46	52	32	30	46	48	55	44	42	45	57	50	46	43	52	47	45	50	36	58	52	47	2356	
++--+-+	(+)	57	42	36	56	65	51	55	58	58	52	65	73	46	59	50	52	42	53	54	39	55	64	45	42	55	46	37	32	46	51	2442	JY
++--+--	(-)	40	54	62	40	32	46	42	49	39	47	32	26	49	37	46	45	50	47	42	57	43	33	50	57	44	52	54	65	49	45	2184	
++---++	(+)	51	38	49	59	52	53	57	52	52	48	52	49	46	50	49	47	42	54	47	40	42	42	46	53	34	55	51	44	46	49	2137	
++---+-	(-)	45	57	47	39	43	42	41	46	46	51	43	49	51	47	45	47	50	42	50	57	54	56	49	45	55	44	44	50	49	47	2064	

Figure 8.2: Daily Closing Patterns: Bull Market Samples

------- 65% -------

Pattern	Sign	BO	BP	C	CC	CD	CL	CO	CP	FC	GC	HO	JY	LB	LC	LH	NY	O	OJ	PB	PL	S	SF	SV	SM	SP	SU	TB	TR	W	T%	T#	
- - - - -	(+)	55	52	51	53	0	0	61	61	0	65	0	48	55	58	58	58	56	55	54	53	55	47	0	57	0	56	46	50	52	54	3116	
- - - - +	(-)	43	41	45	46	0	0	35	35	0	33	0	45	34	33	38	34	44	41	46	41	41	46	0	34	0	40	47	46	41	41	2401	
- - - + -	(+)	53	50	49	60	0	0	62	35	0	58	0	58	50	57	51	54	51	54	49	53	55	53	0	57	0	54	56	51	55	54	3781	
- - - + +	(-)	42	42	46	37	0	0	35	41	0	41	0	40	45	36	40	43	40	42	49	45	41	41	0	39	0	44	38	48	39	41	2888	
- - + - -	(+)	49	52	51	48	0	0	52	54	0	62	0	52	44	47	52	47	51	56	53	53	52	52	0	42	0	55	44	50	50	50	3536	
- - + - +	(-)	49	40	44	48	0	0	37	41	0	35	0	44	50	44	40	43	46	46	41	43	43	43	0	50	0	42	48	47	43	45	3140	
- - + + -	(+)	43	51	48	54	0	0	53	42	0	43	0	54	45	53	48	54	48	52	46	51	53	52	0	53	0	49	56	50	48	51	4395	
- - + + +	(+)	52	40	47	43	0	0	44	53	0	55	0	41	47	41	41	44	44	43	43	45	46	45	0	40	0	49	37	47	44	44	3811	
- + - - -	(+)	53	53	51	52	0	0	64	61	0	66	0	58	51	65	58	65	65	51	52	57	57	41	0	59	0	56	50	49	55	54	1304	GC
- + - - +	(+)	46	42	42	46	0	0	35	35	0	33	0	37	36	30	34	42	31	44	44	41	38	53	0	34	0	42	42	48	41	41	1003	
- + - + -	(+)	56	53	48	59	0	0	53	48	0	51	0	57	49	56	57	52	56	52	55	54	53	58	0	59	0	61	55	53	58	54	1704	
- + - + +	(-)	40	40	46	39	0	0	42	47	0	48	0	41	46	38	46	39	39	40	42	48	37	43	0	37	0	38	39	46	37	42	1315	
- + + - -	(+)	48	53	49	44	0	0	60	57	0	63	0	51	46	40	59	51	48	54	52	52	55	52	0	43	0	60	47	50	44	51	1474	
- + + - +	(+)	50	51	46	51	0	0	39	40	0	34	0	48	50	46	36	47	43	47	45	50	41	44	0	50	0	37	47	46	48	51	1289	
- + + + -	(+)	47	48	51	55	0	0	49	42	0	51	0	52	43	58	43	58	52	52	45	54	53	52	0	55	0	43	53	53	50	51	1944	
- + + + +	(-)	50	43	44	42	0	0	47	54	0	48	0	42	50	37	60	41	41	41	53	50	44	46	0	41	0	54	38	43	46	44	1679	
+ - - - -	(+)	57	51	46	53	0	0	58	61	0	63	0	50	60	55	60	60	58	58	55	53	53	53	0	55	0	57	51	61	54	54	1693	
+ - - - +	(-)	40	41	48	46	0	0	36	36	0	34	0	42	33	36	32	35	35	38	40	47	44	42	0	38	0	39	45	49	40	41	1307	
+ - - + -	(+)	52	47	50	63	0	0	65	59	0	61	0	51	52	60	55	55	50	53	44	53	51	54	0	52	0	46	47	48	53	54	1921	
+ - - + +	(-)	43	46	45	35	0	0	34	37	0	38	0	37	46	33	36	46	42	41	43	45	35	39	0	42	0	48	39	49	40	41	1477	
+ - + - -	(+)	48	51	48	46	0	0	62	53	0	63	0	52	46	50	48	56	56	50	60	53	50	51	0	38	0	52	43	50	44	50	1928	
+ - + - +	(+)	49	41	42	47	0	0	57	40	0	35	0	43	48	45	44	44	50	47	36	42	47	44	0	50	0	46	47	52	45	45	1725	
+ - + + -	(+)	38	54	44	55	0	0	34	37	0	38	0	33	50	51	36	51	55	54	54	54	44	53	0	56	0	58	59	47	47	51	2272	
+ - + + +	(-)	57	38	50	43	0	0	42	53	0	63	0	41	45	44	36	48	49	44	54	50	41	44	0	39	0	41	35	50	48	44	1961	
+ + - - -	(+)	60	49	58	51	0	0	84	60	0	50	0	63	46	61	58	50	77	49	70	48	60	35	0	55	0	45	45	52	54	53	535	BP CO O PB
+ + - - +	(+)	39	31	39	47	0	0	15	36	0	50	0	23	46	38	46	22	48	51	23	51	48	23	0	32	0	54	44	44	42	43	434	
+ + - + -	(+)	54	43	60	68	0	0	58	46	0	57	0	57	42	51	37	54	53	55	64	55	64	59	0	60	0	64	51	53	55	54	716	CC
+ + - + +	(-)	45	43	60	30	0	0	37	51	0	68	0	42	57	37	58	45	44	43	55	44	33	38	0	36	0	35	40	46	41	42	555	GC
+ + + - -	(+)	44	50	55	44	0	0	51	60	0	60	0	49	55	58	36	50	48	50	50	52	61	55	0	47	0	65	46	52	51	51	674	
+ + + - +	(-)	53	42	42	52	0	0	48	36	0	39	0	44	58	45	36	57	46	46	38	46	41	41	0	47	0	32	47	42	45	45	595	
+ + + + -	(+)	42	54	52	43	0	0	50	38	0	50	0	55	48	48	48	56	57	49	50	48	53	40	0	47	0	44	50	56	49	50	855	
+ + + + +	(-)	55	36	43	55	0	0	50	59	0	50	0	48	42	36	48	56	43	43	46	56	36	56	0	45	0	52	41	39	45	45	783	
	(+)	61	50	58	60	0	0	66	65	0	68	0	34	62	61	48	56	53	53	50	46	56	50	0	52	0	58	31	50	49	53	689	CO GC
	(-)	34	49	37	44	0	0	29	34	0	26	0	61	37	33	36	37	34	34	43	51	56	43	0	42	0	39	59	46	42	42	541	
	(+)	53	49	52	73	0	0	71	59	0	57	0	48	48	46	41	56	56	51	64	43	53	56	0	48	0	56	33	46	55	55	819	CC CO LC
	(-)	46	43	45	25	0	0	28	35	0	42	0	38	51	17	37	44	22	46	35	43	40	33	0	51	0	45	42	44	44	41	606	
	(+)	54	54	51	45	0	0	62	55	0	62	0	49	44	50	56	56	48	47	59	56	44	55	0	53	0	50	43	43	45	50	848	
	(-)	40	43	43	57	0	0	43	37	0	37	0	55	55	59	36	41	42	42	50	48	43	41	0	40	0	45	48	54	50	45	765	
	(-)	28	50	46	40	0	0	55	43	0	35	0	59	45	54	35	54	54	46	37	49	61	62	0	57	0	54	59	52	55	50	986	BO
	(+)	69	49	47	57	0	0	56	62	0	75	0	50	56	70	66	57	58	53	59	48	35	48	0	37	0	65	54	46	57	55	726	GC LC
	(+)	47	47	46	47	0	0	43	35	0	25	0	37	32	27	28	41	41	38	61	34	38	44	0	38	0	32	39	53	40	40	534	
	(+)	52	50	40	54	0	0	48	49	0	60	0	58	51	62	53	53	50	57	58	48	52	50	0	59	0	61	59	52	61	54	928	
	(-)	57	61	43	54	0	0	45	44	0	60	0	51	42	53	39	53	56	47	48	46	52	46	0	59	0	38	38	47	33	42	711	
	(+)	36	33	50	44	0	0	44	47	0	65	0	48	43	42	60	31	36	39	33	52	58	47	0	39	0	58	50	40	52	44	763	CO
	(+)	53	57	52	44	0	0	67	54	0	65	0	48	38	60	34	38	48	48	44	45	36	48	0	41	0	58	45	50	47	44	646	
	(+)	46	38	50	52	0	0	32	41	0	31	0	51	44	46	34	59	40	37	51	45	50	36	0	55	0	39	45	48	51	53	1021	CC
	(-)	42	51	45	31	0	0	45	52	0	50	0	43	51	30	48	39	40	40	38	43	44	39	0	32	0	54	35	47	43	43	827	
	(-)	55	54	42	49	0	0	53	58	0	62	0	56	59	51	66	64	53	55	68	55	46	56	0	57	0	54	51	50	53	54	938	LH PB
	(+)	44	41	57	50	0	0	64	61	0	64	0	60	58	54	31	31	46	54	27	42	50	41	0	36	0	37	47	47	41	41	714	
	(+)	50	47	47	59	0	0	61	58	0	60	0	58	54	55	53	53	58	57	58	48	52	50	0	56	0	46	55	46	58	54	1043	
	(+)	41	46	47	38	0	0	35	36	0	35	0	38	38	39	33	38	44	42	69	45	50	46	0	38	0	50	34	50	37	42	807	PB
	(+)	40	52	57	55	0	0	67	50	0	63	0	55	50	51	44	56	40	51	60	51	55	55	0	33	0	57	43	56	45	51	1002	CO
	(-)	59	43	40	42	0	0	32	46	0	34	0	39	41	46	48	42	55	46	35	43	42	44	0	59	0	38	48	42	51	45	884	

Figure 8.2: Continued

		BO	BP	C	CC	CD	CL	CO	CP	FC	GC	HO	JY	LB	LC	LH	NY	O	OJ	PB	PL	S	SF	SV	SM	SP	SU	TB	TR	W	T%	T#	-------- 65% -------
++++	(+)	54	55	44	51	0	0	58	40	0	33	0	50	55	43	55	51	40	54	50	45	48	45	0	56	0	66	58	60	50	52	1183	SU
++++	(-)	40	35	52	47	0	0	40	56	0	66	0	48	44	52	36	47	55	41	50	51	47	53	0	39	0	33	37	36	44	44	1008	GC
-----	(+)	60	85	55	50	0	0	100	45	0	75	0	83	42	62	83	40	80	54	75	56	50	31	0	54	0	35	54	50	57	53	231	BP CO GC JY LH O PB
-----	(-)	40	7	38	50	0	0	0	45	0	25	0	16	42	37	16	51	20	42	0	43	50	68	0	36	0	64	38	50	38	43	188	SF
----+	(+)	47	43	62	64	0	0	63	38	0	25	0	39	28	69	50	62	35	52	50	51	61	66	0	52	0	85	58	61	57	55	296	LC SF SU
----+	(-)	52	53	33	32	0	0	36	55	0	75	0	60	71	7	40	37	58	47	50	48	33	33	0	42	0	14	33	38	42	41	224	GC LB
---+-	(+)	40	39	52	56	0	0	55	59	0	72	0	62	41	41	58	41	70	48	55	50	46	50	0	14	0	60	48	37	56	49	272	GC O
---+-	(-)	60	50	47	44	0	0	44	40	0	27	0	37	58	41	41	55	30	51	44	47	53	45	0	80	0	40	48	53	40	47	264	SM
---++	(+)	33	40	60	41	0	0	50	45	0	40	0	50	33	39	54	52	54	46	63	63	41	38	0	45	C	40	51	70	46	49	351	TR
---++	(-)	66	48	39	57	0	0	50	50	0	60	0	46	66	60	45	45	33	48	36	36	58	54	0	54	0	51	38	24	51	47	338	BO LB
--+--	(+)	65	60	54	65	0	0	50	60	0	55	0	47	50	55	40	58	57	67	50	38	68	43	0	46	0	61	42	43	46	53	317	OJ S
--+--	(-)	34	34	41	34	0	0	50	40	0	33	0	47	50	45	33	37	33	32	37	57	25	52	0	53	0	38	51	50	50	42	254	
--+-+	(+)	57	48	67	87	0	0	85	69	0	50	0	58	23	72	52	58	54	54	61	35	65	64	0	60	0	53	60	62	41	58	391	C CC CO CP LC
--+-+	(-)	42	44	32	12	0	0	14	25	0	50	0	41	76	22	36	36	36	42	38	58	25	29	0	39	0	46	37	37	45	37	255	LB
--++-	(+)	50	42	46	40	0	0	64	57	0	58	0	45	50	55	73	64	57	42	64	65	48	52	0	57	0	50	50	34	52	51	405	LH
--++-	(-)	43	46	50	59	0	0	35	35	0	41	0	54	50	37	26	35	23	55	35	31	51	44	0	42	0	50	46	62	45	45	352	
--+++	(+)	36	51	29	63	0	0	64	44	0	33	0	51	56	66	65	50	53	38	35	48	69	70	0	56	0	32	58	34	50	50	432	LC S SF
--+++	(-)	64	41	67	34	0	0	35	51	0	66	0	45	37	33	35	47	46	57	64	48	30	25	0	40	0	67	32	65	48	46	398	C GC SU
-+---	(+)	33	39	45	42	0	0	57	65	0	60	0	62	58	78	54	50	81	55	38	68	60	37	0	69	0	75	43	48	60	54	295	LC O PL SM SU
-+---	(-)	66	60	45	57	0	0	42	30	0	40	0	33	25	14	18	47	12	42	61	32	40	50	0	30	0	25	48	51	40	41	224	BO
-+--+	(+)	66	58	47	76	0	0	75	42	0	61	0	62	50	65	43	61	52	52	50	44	52	53	0	62	0	70	58	55	50	56	390	BO CC CO SU
-+--+	(-)	29	34	47	23	0	0	18	55	0	38	0	37	40	34	50	36	34	47	50	55	42	46	0	37	0	29	38	44	40	40	280	
-+-+-	(+)	50	56	42	26	0	0	63	40	0	66	0	36	35	16	55	55	47	50	63	53	54	36	0	44	0	62	47	50	38	48	294	GC
-+-+-	(-)	50	40	50	66	0	0	36	53	0	33	0	63	50	33	45	44	47	45	36	42	36	63	0	51	0	37	42	50	46	46	280	CC
-+-++	(+)	56	52	43	67	0	0	39	39	0	65	0	36	42	70	37	57	37	58	40	49	41	72	0	64	0	37	52	60	57	52	425	CC LC SF
-+-++	(-)	39	41	50	32	0	0	53	58	0	35	0	56	42	25	59	40	55	40	55	50	58	27	0	28	0	60	38	39	39	44	362	
-++--	(+)	68	54	44	43	0	0	60	52	0	64	0	58	60	47	77	55	47	59	66	61	43	48	0	51	0	50	42	48	48	53	405	BO LH PB
-++--	(-)	31	38	56	54	0	0	39	45	0	35	0	41	30	39	22	41	39	39	25	38	56	48	0	44	0	38	56	48	46	43	332	
-++-+	(+)	50	36	53	55	0	0	66	58	0	60	0	58	37	44	54	55	50	44	31	55	48	36	0	57	0	41	56	48	56	51	432	CO
-++-+	(-)	43	54	36	44	0	0	33	40	0	39	0	41	62	48	38	43	38	52	63	44	48	56	0	39	0	55	40	48	41	45	381	
-+++-	(+)	36	55	48	53	0	0	70	47	0	66	0	42	71	45	50	54	33	48	68	61	52	48	0	38	0	65	53	64	49	52	467	CO GC LB PB
-+++-	(-)	63	44	48	44	0	0	29	52	0	33	0	46	28	51	38	42	66	49	31	35	44	48	0	55	0	28	38	35	47	44	393	O
-++++	(+)	66	52	40	45	0	0	60	30	0	35	0	56	50	41	60	56	38	51	45	43	41	51	0	53	0	62	60	56	56	50	500	BO
-++++	(-)	26	40	53	51	0	0	40	66	0	64	0	40	50	54	35	43	55	43	54	55	53	48	0	40	0	37	34	40	40	45	451	CP
+----	(+)	61	57	59	52	0	0	80	68	0	25	0	57	50	54	37	58	80	44	69	42	66	40	0	56	0	57	39	55	51	53	286	CO CP O PB S
+----	(-)	38	42	40	44	0	0	20	31	0	75	0	38	50	45	50	41	20	53	30	57	33	52	0	30	0	42	49	39	45	43	230	GC
+---+	(+)	57	46	59	70	0	0	53	48	0	33	0	69	50	46	35	46	65	58	62	58	69	51	0	61	0	53	47	45	53	54	398	CC JY S
+---+	(-)	42	42	40	29	0	0	38	51	0	66	0	30	50	50	64	53	34	41	37	41	30	44	0	36	0	46	42	54	42	42	312	GC
+--+-	(+)	42	65	60	37	0	0	52	61	0	50	0	47	42	43	65	51	36	53	66	55	58	61	0	67	0	65	47	63	41	53	382	PB SM
+--+-	(-)	52	30	36	58	0	0	47	35	0	50	0	52	57	47	30	48	54	41	33	44	33	35	0	26	0	30	43	34	54	42	302	
+--++	(+)	48	59	45	47	0	0	55	36	0	55	0	62	56	65	44	61	41	51	41	56	65	39	0	50	0	47	48	45	52	51	478	
+--++	(-)	48	30	50	52	0	0	44	61	0	44	0	33	39	31	48	38	48	40	58	41	34	60	0	41	0	52	44	52	43	44	414	
+-+--	(+)	55	46	59	53	0	0	83	70	0	80	0	29	76	66	60	54	47	59	47	54	47	54	0	61	0	55	18	56	51	53	346	CO CP GC LB LC
+-+--	(-)	35	43	37	46	0	0	8	30	0	20	0	54	23	22	33	45	42	36	52	46	52	38	0	35	0	40	69	43	44	42	271	TB
+-+-+	(+)	52	48	33	59	0	0	64	44	0	61	0	62	71	93	46	46	58	49	66	68	50	56	0	30	0	52	54	42	56	53	407	LB LC PB PL
+-+-+	(-)	47	44	62	37	0	0	36	50	0	38	0	37	28	6	42	50	37	49	33	29	50	40	0	69	0	45	45	57	40	44	337	SM
+-++-	(+)	59	50	54	54	0	0	46	55	0	64	0	51	33	52	43	50	45	51	55	51	41	58	0	54	0	50	32	50	38	49	411	
+-++-	(-)	36	45	38	45	0	0	53	38	0	36	0	45	66	42	53	45	54	45	38	45	58	41	0	36	0	50	52	50	52	46	383	LB
+-+++	(+)	22	51	64	52	0	0	48	41	0	34	0	67	42	53	46	47	59	53	50	50	51	63	0	54	0	58	63	33	38	51	519	JY
+-+++	(-)	74	45	26	45	0	0	51	52	0	61	0	25	57	44	35	51	37	44	50	48	42	34	0	35	0	41	30	61	59	44	457	BO
++---	(+)	54	51	45	56	0	0	56	56	0	80	0	55	58	64	62	64	42	53	33	60	53	58	0	54	0	62	67	44	56	56	403	GC TB
++---	(-)	45	44	48	42	0	0	43	43	0	20	0	41	41	36	37	35	57	41	66	37	37	41	0	41	0	37	29	55	38	40	291	PB
++--+	(+)	50	63	33	38	0	0	28	57	0	58	0	56	54	60	55	48	45	63	66	50	53	40	0	59	0	52	56	50	64	53	500	PB
++--+	(-)	43	34	54	62	0	0	66	38	0	41	0	43	40	39	41	51	40	35	33	47	43	50	0	38	0	47	41	50	32	43	410	CO

Figure 8.2: Continued

Pattern		BO	BP	C	CC	CD	CL	CO	CP	FC	GC	HO	JY	LB	LC	LH	NY	O	OJ	PB	PL	S	SF	SV	SM	SP	SU	TB	TR	W	T%	T#									65%
+ + + + -	(+)	59	62	42	45	0	0	66	61	0	64	0	57	53	41	73	56	44	68	41	53	63	55	0	39	0	54	51	47	40	54	435	CO	LH	OJ					
+ + + + -	(+)	40	32	51	52	0	0	33	35	0	29	0	42	46	55	15	40	30	58	40	46	61	51	0	57	0	43	48	50	50	42	341								
+ + + + -	(+)	40	51	60	66	0	0	58	47	0	41	0	56	38	62	44	60	65	52	40	46	32	51	0	65	0	50	62	43	49	53	561	CC							
+ + + + -	(-)	51	36	37	30	0	0	39	49	0	58	0	36	57	32	44	39	30	41	60	49	48	48	0	32	0	50	31	56	47	42	444								
+ + + + +	(+)	44	60	57	57	0	0	49	61	0	58	0	43	61	55	54	60	30	57	60	47	48	48	0	62	0	60	59	56	47	56	495	CP	NY	PB					
+ + + + -	(-)	45	55	42	57	0	0	43	28	0	61	0	66	38	38	54	25	34	36	30	51	47	36	0	31	0	34	56	47	61	40	353	GC	LB	LH					
+ + + + +	(+)	54	44	57	42	0	0	61	61	0	70	0	53	76	57	77	61	46	61	23	51	47	61	0	55	0	52	56	50	60	56	568								
+ + + + -	(-)	47	44	53	34	0	0	38	35	0	29	0	38	23	40	22	35	36	36	76	45	50	34	0	41	0	44	42	34	50	39	397	PB							
+ + + + +	(+)	42	44	64	57	0	0	65	52	0	57	0	62	35	56	60	58	43	52	54	45	57	53	0	32	0	48	40	45	42	50	506								
+ + + + +	(+)	50	47	35	40	0	0	34	42	0	35	0	35	52	47	60	48	48	45	36	47	40	41	0	59	0	51	52	51	54	45	457								
+ + + + +	(-)	42	56	44	55	0	0	57	44	0	28	0	48	57	52	47	55	35	55	54	55	57	47	0	59	0	69	64	47	47	53	632	SU							
+ + + + +	(-)	52	33	55	44	0	0	40	51	0	71	0	52	42	50	38	50	51	39	50	48	38	62	0	39	0	30	39	33	43	43	513	GC							
- - - - -	(+)	33	100	57	52	0	0	0	40	0	100	0	100	0	66	0	28	66	58	0	75	33	32	0	25	0	45	73	60	50	51	97	BP	GC	JY	LC	LH	O	@@	
- - - - -	(-)	66	0	28	47	0	0	0	83	0	0	0	0	33	33	0	64	0	41	0	25	66	0	0	50	0	54	21	40	40	44	83	BO	S	SF					
- - - - -	(+)	44	58	70	70	0	0	50	80	0	33	0	30	66	40	60	45	25	47	66	42	66	76	0	33	0	66	62	60	53	55	128	C	CC	CP	LB	PB	S	@@	
- - - - -	(-)	55	41	30	23	0	0	50	20	0	66	0	70	33	20	40	54	75	52	33	57	33	23	0	66	0	33	29	40	46	42	98	GC	JY	O	SM				
- - - - -	(+)	41	25	66	50	0	0	50	60	0	33	0	64	40	100	75	70	30	50	64	35	50	50	0	25	0	50	52	42	57	51	115	C	GC	LC	LH	O			
- - - - -	(-)	58	68	33	50	0	0	50	40	0	66	0	35	60	0	25	54	30	40	50	35	50	50	0	62	0	50	47	57	57	47	106	BP							
- - + - +	(+)	36	15	70	29	0	0	57	40	0	0	0	66	50	44	60	61	66	52	66	66	45	25	0	50	0	8	53	77	42	49	146	GC	JY	O	PB	PL	TR		
- - - - -	(-)	63	69	29	70	0	0	42	57	0	0	0	33	50	55	40	38	33	36	33	33	36	50	0	50	0	83	42	22	57	48	144	BP	CC	SF	SU				
- - + - +	(-)	58	50	40	72	0	0	33	81	0	33	0	55	42	57	28	68	33	52	50	47	62	33	0	41	0	33	34	41	38	48	128	CC	CP	NY					
- - + - -	(-)	41	50	63	27	0	0	66	75	0	33	0	33	57	42	31	31	57	50	47	50	37	66	0	58	0	66	57	58	61	47	126	CO	SF	SU					
- - + - +	(-)	50	54	63	92	0	0	66	18	0	62	0	53	83	50	71	57	50	54	60	52	50	37	0	44	0	44	69	83	38	60	162	CO	CP	LC	NY	S	@@		
- - + + -	(+)	25	36	36	7	0	0	0	83	0	37	0	46	100	16	40	28	50	54	20	63	60	66	0	50	0	55	30	16	44	36	98	LB							
- - + + +	(+)	25	58	46	40	0	0	57	83	0	66	0	53	66	64	80	50	50	46	65	65	35	64	0	55	0	35	57	22	43	50	171	CP	GC	LB	LH				
- - + + -	(-)	62	43	46	59	0	0	42	83	0	0	0	46	33	21	20	50	50	21	50	37	50	35	0	44	0	64	77	22	52	46	156	TR							
- - + + +	(+)	25	40	35	56	0	0	42	63	0	33	0	50	66	88	83	57	51	25	42	45	75	75	0	37	0	45	48	34	42	47	168	LC	LH	S	SF				
- - + - -	(-)	75	50	60	43	0	0	57	36	0	0	0	50	11	11	16	38	66	66	57	48	25	25	0	56	0	54	34	65	52	47	168	BO	GC	LB	OJ				
- - + + -	(-)	37	37	60	46	0	0	50	50	0	66	0	55	66	48	75	50	100	41	66	59	50	41	0	60	0	60	48	62	54	42	137	LB	LC	LH	O				
- - + + +	(-)	62	62	30	53	0	0	50	30	0	33	0	44	22	11	0	42	20	41	40	40	50	41	0	40	0	40	52	30	37	42	107	GC	PB	TR					
- - + - -	(+)	66	64	23	72	0	0	57	40	0	80	0	66	55	45	33	60	66	63	50	55	36	80	0	53	0	50	52	30	46	54	172	BO	CC	GC	SF				
- - + + -	(-)	33	61	61	28	0	0	33	36	0	20	0	55	55	34	66	35	41	36	44	44	20	20	0	46	0	50	69	40	40	42	135	LH	TR						
- - + + +	(+)	62	66	40	0	0	0	50	36	0	71	0	30	30	25	28	50	50	54	51	51	60	44	0	54	0	36	50	35	28	47	121	BP	GC	PB					
- - + + -	(-)	37	25	60	75	0	0	63	63	0	28	0	70	50	23	44	41	50	43	41	20	47	85	0	45	0	63	65	64	59	48	122	CC	JY						
- - + + +	(+)	36	30	33	62	0	0	33	51	0	57	0	35	0	76	23	36	50	54	31	31	60	85	0	82	0	21	65	69	69	51	201	LC	SF	SM	TR	W			
- - + + -	(-)	54	30	61	37	0	0	58	44	0	42	0	57	66	15	69	42	16	41	23	23	76	14	0	11	0	71	24	30	30	43	169	LB	LH	O	PL	S	SU		
- - + + +	(-)	64	41	23	34	0	0	42	63	0	80	0	53	37	30	60	56	50	48	50	50	46	47	0	33	0	50	42	50	56	48	170	CO	GC	PB					
- - + + +	(-)	35	50	76	62	0	0	16	36	0	20	0	46	33	40	40	57	73	50	38	48	57	25	0	58	0	37	65	50	43	52	171	O							
- - + + +	(-)	50	76	33	54	0	0	50	37	0	57	0	54	37	53	50	42	20	46	44	42	42	65	0	41	0	56	27	36	55	44	212	O							
- - + - -	(+)	31	62	33	45	0	0	50	62	0	42	0	60	33	53	42	45	46	80	55	51	42	65	0	27	0	63	54	36	46	53	178								
- - + + -	(-)	55	52	47	50	0	0	36	37	0	0	0	60	66	50	76	62	53	43	80	43	16	63	0	66	0	63	72	56	66	54	214	CO	GC	S	TR				
- - + + +	(+)	68	37	77	50	0	0	36	43	0	20	0	58	44	37	66	33	27	27	44	35	47	44	0	56	0	26	41	33	40	43	174	BO	LB	O	SM				
- - + + -	(-)	33	40	22	56	0	0	50	75	0	60	0	46	55	63	33	60	80	43	20	48	33	20	0	40	0	44	40	43	38	42	228	CC	CP	LH	PB	TB			
- - + + +	(+)	100	42	60	50	0	0	50	50	0	0	0	60	66	33	75	57	50	50	85	60	55	46	0	50	0	75	25	64	33	53	192	CP							
- - + + +	(+)	40	55	40	50	0	0	50	69	0	33	0	50	44	27	66	42	50	43	25	43	16	58	0	56	0	33	53	29	58	43	120	BO	CO	PB	S	SU			
- - + + +	(-)	60	37	22	91	0	0	25	50	0	60	0	58	55	66	40	69	52	65	80	44	44	60	0	61	0	55	61	56	61	54	98	GC	LB						
- - + + -	(-)	33	40	22	8	0	0	33	30	0	40	0	50	71	33	33	60	30	20	20	35	55	33	0	38	0	66	40	43	38	42	162	CC	CP	LH	O	PB			
- - + + +	(+)	70	50	50	40	0	0	60	40	0	50	0	62	62	75	75	45	12	58	85	60	33	46	0	50	0	66	25	56	53	53	125	GC	LB	SU					
- - + - +	(-)	20	50	25	34	0	0	33	43	0	60	0	37	50	25	57	35	14	42	42	35	72	43	0	55	0	50	66	30	37	47	148	BP	CO	LH	PB	SU			
- - + - +	(+)	47	35	68	65	0	0	50	56	0	80	0	41	85	42	64	47	16	59	57	60	27	60	0	45	0	64	33	65	56	48	187	JY	LC	S					
- - + - +	(+)	50	46	78	30	0	0	50	68	0	68	0	50	50	50	35	50	50	56	25	55	62	57	0	42	0	54	22	66	41	53	190	C	O						
- - + - -	(-)	50	46	14	70	0	0	0	31	0	20	0	50	14	0	22	52	37	36	75	45	37	42	0	50	0	45	72	33	58	42	151	C	CO	CP	GC	LB	LH	TR	
																																	119	CC	PB	TB					

Figure 8.2: Continued

	±	BO	BP	C	CC	CD	CL	CO	CP	FC	GC	HO	JY	LB	LC	LH	NY	O	OJ	PB	PL	S	SF	SV	SM	SP	SU	TB	TR	W	T%	T#	------ 65% ------
-+-+-+	(+)	80	44	16	100	0	0	57	36	0	70	0	42	100	100	63	26	50	51	85	76	58	50	0	33	0	55	55	50	70	53	158	BO CC LB LC PB @@
-+-+--	(-)	20	55	83	0	0	0	42	54	0	30	0	27	65	14	24	41	48	37	36	60	14	37	0	66	0	38	45	50	30	44	129	C SM GC
-+-+-+	(+)	66	60	50	50	0	0	26	67	0	71	0	41	66	85	43	59	53	37	60	40	50	63	0	71	0	61	28	37	54	50	183	BO CP GC LB SM
-+-+--	(-)	33	40	43	50	0	0	73	25	0	28	0	58	33	14	50	40	46	62	54	40	50	36	0	14	0	38	52	62	45	46	169	CO JY S
-+-++-	(+)	33	47	78	41	0	0	47	42	0	38	0	81	33	52	40	41	50	47	44	69	30	63	0	62	0	53	55	48	31	49	208	C JY W
-+-++-	(-)	66	52	14	55	0	0	60	52	0	61	0	18	66	42	50	58	50	50	62	55	37	37	0	31	0	46	34	44	68	47	202	BO LB W
-+-+++	(+)	71	58	35	67	0	0	66	38	0	80	0	66	66	66	60	72	44	53	0	56	61	46	0	38	0	57	78	57	71	59	197	BO CC CO GC JY LB @@
-+-+++	(-)	28	41	57	33	0	0	33	61	0	20	0	33	33	33	40	27	55	42	100	43	39	53	0	61	0	42	18	42	23	38	128	BP
-+-+++	(+)	66	70	36	31	0	0	35	61	0	66	0	25	58	66	52	58	45	64	62	48	57	46	0	53	0	41	50	42	68	53	218	BO BP GC W
-+-+++	(-)	26	29	54	68	0	0	57	33	0	33	0	41	41	30	47	41	45	33	37	48	42	40	0	40	0	58	50	57	31	43	176	CC
-+-+++	(+)	53	66	36	36	0	0	60	62	0	55	0	33	66	75	48	41	61	41	58	56	42	40	0	33	0	40	20	60	50	51	194	BP LB LH PL
-+-+++	(-)	46	33	54	57	0	0	40	33	0	33	0	66	33	16	48	48	40	38	58	29	33	43	0	66	0	60	80	33	50	45	174	JY SM TB
-+-++-	(+)	53	41	50	50	0	0	70	48	0	57	0	35	66	66	47	62	61	41	16	44	50	40	0	77	0	53	53	40	43	51	221	CO LC SM
-+-++-	(-)	40	58	43	41	0	0	30	45	0	42	0	66	33	33	41	37	30	55	83	50	50	60	0	22	0	46	39	60	47	49	194	LB PB
-+-+++	(+)	47	80	40	63	0	0	50	63	0	62	0	41	50	50	57	70	50	59	60	39	45	64	0	68	0	44	85	50	62	58	227	BP NY SM TB
-+-+++	(-)	52	20	60	36	0	0	50	31	0	37	0	50	50	47	42	22	77	36	40	60	54	35	0	26	0	44	14	45	33	37	148	
-+++-+	(+)	46	57	40	61	0	0	50	70	0	75	0	72	50	53	64	38	22	62	63	51	53	38	0	46	0	47	65	44	64	57	266	CO CP JY LB O
-+++--	(-)	46	42	53	38	0	0	29	25	0	25	0	27	30	40	44	42	22	37	63	51	53	42	0	46	0	52	20	52	32	40	188	
-++++-	(+)	25	68	58	61	0	0	58	50	0	55	0	50	62	57	50	56	52	52	66	48	64	50	0	42	0	44	42	50	38	51	233	BP PB
-++++-	(-)	75	18	41	33	0	0	41	45	0	33	0	35	37	42	70	44	33	57	33	45	35	32	0	47	0	55	48	50	61	43	197	BO LH
-+++++	(+)	20	66	46	61	0	0	50	36	0	40	0	48	75	45	64	38	38	43	40	48	47	37	0	60	0	58	62	76	36	50	252	BP LB TR
-+++++	(-)	80	33	53	38	0	0	44	63	0	60	0	52	25	50	23	61	61	53	60	51	47	63	0	39	0	41	36	17	52	47	235	BO
+----+	(+)	75	83	54	41	0	0	0	50	0	66	0	66	50	50	23	61	42	66	75	64	42	66	0	71	0	16	42	40	57	53	122	BP CO GC JY LH @@
+-----	(-)	25	8	45	52	0	0	75	23	0	33	0	25	50	40	25	38	33	20	42	66	33	30	0	28	0	83	66	60	42	43	101	SF SU
+---+-	(+)	46	37	56	60	0	0	58	69	0	100	0	41	58	83	33	72	55	33	44	64	65	60	0	61	0	0	57	61	62	55	158	CO LC NY SU
+---+-	(-)	53	56	37	40	0	0	25	30	0	0	0	0	100	42	77	35	33	40	55	38	55	40	0	30	0	0	33	38	37	41	119	CP GC LB LH
+---++	(+)	37	63	45	66	0	0	60	58	0	75	0	60	60	42	54	39	62	37	66	42	37	50	0	7	0	61	48	33	70	48	150	CC GC PB W
+---++	(-)	62	27	54	33	0	0	40	41	0	25	0	40	42	57	45	56	37	62	33	53	62	41	0	92	0	38	45	54	29	48	149	SM
+--++-	(+)	18	66	50	51	0	0	57	50	0	0	0	52	57	28	45	50	44	60	62	38	60	57	0	36	0	66	60	45	54	48	194	BP SU
+--++-	(-)	81	25	50	44	0	0	62	42	0	75	0	66	61	71	50	45	55	40	37	62	39	28	0	63	0	26	31	26	41	45	183	BO GC LB LC
+--+++	(+)	72	71	63	64	0	0	62	43	0	66	0	40	54	69	42	50	50	50	50	29	75	58	0	55	0	85	50	46	52	57	173	BO BP GC O OJ S SU
+--+++	(-)	27	14	27	36	0	0	37	57	0	33	0	45	45	54	42	50	50	14	25	62	12	41	0	44	0	14	45	38	41	41	116	BO
+-+++-	(+)	77	40	66	81	0	0	77	70	0	33	0	66	37	70	70	47	50	85	75	36	57	57	0	52	0	60	50	50	46	56	216	BO C CC CO CP JY @@
+-+++-	(-)	22	53	33	18	0	0	22	25	0	66	0	33	62	30	25	42	50	14	25	53	35	33	0	47	0	40	45	40	53	39	151	GC
+-++++	(+)	73	50	63	60	0	0	66	51	0	62	0	44	44	62	40	73	66	38	40	60	57	58	0	61	0	80	62	69	64	53	220	BO LH NY O PB PL
+-++++	(-)	26	53	50	59	0	0	37	40	0	37	0	66	55	37	60	26	33	70	60	28	40	50	0	68	0	45	45	30	40	43	180	JY
++---+	(+)	43	56	18	70	0	0	80	31	0	40	0	52	61	60	53	47	53	44	28	51	63	76	0	72	0	23	67	31	53	52	251	CO SF SM TB
++----	(-)	56	40	81	25	0	0	66	62	0	60	0	44	30	40	46	53	71	48	50	46	36	23	0	28	0	76	32	68	46	46	152	C CC SU TR
++--+-	(+)	28	38	33	40	0	0	43	57	0	33	0	76	33	64	50	62	62	52	40	78	63	58	0	81	0	81	43	61	61	55	150	CO CP GC JY PL SM SU
++--+-	(-)	71	61	58	60	0	0	52	70	0	66	0	15	62	35	40	37	25	42	60	21	36	41	0	18	0	60	38	38	40	40	111	BO
++--++	(+)	75	63	66	62	0	0	50	56	0	55	0	85	66	40	80	55	75	55	58	58	58	50	0	68	0	47	41	47	50	58	201	CC CO JY LC S SM @@
++--++	(-)	27	35	36	17	0	0	47	39	0	44	0	14	33	55	20	46	41	37	44	42	30	42	0	12	0	20	54	47	50	38	138	BO
++-++-	(+)	45	50	41	30	0	0	66	42	0	62	0	61	66	54	46	51	37	50	18	39	52	45	0	66	0	42	53	42	57	50	166	CO LB SU
++-++-	(-)	54	50	47	57	0	0	80	43	0	37	0	44	41	16	50	50	40	47	50	60	33	35	0	25	0	57	46	52	42	45	152	CC SF
++-+++	(+)	75	66	75	66	0	0	43	23	0	69	0	40	50	64	50	62	35	58	41	57	58	58	0	28	0	47	38	43	50	52	213	BO C CC GC
++-+++	(-)	25	25	22	25	0	0	50	76	0	30	0	53	66	35	37	37	53	41	58	42	41	41	0	57	0	52	53	56	42	45	183	CP
+++--+	(+)	75	63	66	62	0	0	50	56	0	55	0	66	66	33	80	55	41	55	41	58	58	42	0	87	0	81	54	69	38	57	220	BO C LB LH OJ SM
+++---	(-)	25	31	33	37	0	0	47	39	0	44	0	37	25	55	20	38	46	23	28	36	58	42	0	12	0	42	54	47	50	42	148	
+++-+-	(+)	61	33	52	57	0	0	80	54	0	62	0	61	50	54	46	51	18	39	20	60	54	45	0	66	0	42	53	42	57	50	206	CO SM
+++-+-	(-)	30	57	35	45	0	0	80	42	0	37	0	38	50	36	38	43	57	57	46	52	28	54	0	25	0	57	46	52	42	43	186	PB
+++-++	(+)	40	50	44	54	0	0	66	48	0	56	0	50	50	54	60	50	41	45	83	56	54	44	0	46	0	69	52	61	44	51	237	CO LB PB SU
+++-++	(-)	60	50	44	42	0	0	33	51	0	43	0	55	50	43	40	52	58	64	16	40	44	44	0	46	0	30	34	38	52	49	207	
++++-+	(+)	83	50	27	50	0	0	76	28	0	33	0	55	50	52	46	52	66	73	31	83	28	58	0	56	0	33	66	57	45	45	255	BO CO SU
++++--	(-)	16	44	63	47	0	0	23	66	0	66	0	40	50	52	47	47	31	31	83	60	54	54	0	34	0	33	41	35	37	47	244	CP GC O PB

Figure 8.2: Continued

±	BO	BP	C	CC	CD	CL	CO	CP	FC	GC	HO	JY	LB	LC	LH	NY	O	OJ	PB	PL	S	SF	SV	SM	SP	SU	TB	TR	W	T%	T#	------ 65% ------
(+)	27	69	62	57	0	0	71	76	0	50	0	66	50	55	33	58	83	46	75	29	58	38	0	61	0	55	50	47	64	55	161	BP CO CP JY O PB
(−)	72	30	37	38	0	0	28	23	0	50	0	33	40	44	50	41	16	53	25	70	41	46	0	23	0	44	35	47	35	41	120	BO PL
(+)	61	33	60	64	0	0	55	35	0	57	0	81	71	62	10	54	55	64	50	50	51	82	0	64	0	66	47	64	48	64	221	JY LB S SU
(−)	38	53	40	35	0	0	44	64	0	62	0	18	28	37	90	45	44	35	48	48	17	50	0	29	0	33	45	64	44	43	174	LH
(−)	46	61	76	38	0	0	50	61	0	42	0	46	22	46	57	52	50	48	40	50	69	71	0	84	0	50	54	65	33	53	220	C S SF SM
(−)	46	38	15	58	0	0	50	33	0	57	0	53	77	60	35	47	50	45	60	50	23	28	0	15	0	43	35	30	61	42	174	LB
(+)	46	66	87	68	0	0	66	60	0	60	0	52	58	31	58	58	55	40	70	70	62	41	0	51	0	55	45	55	58	53	268	BP C CC CO PL
(+)	46	29	12	31	0	0	33	0	0	40	0	41	33	40	57	41	37	47	60	30	37	58	0	74	0	44	50	45	38	42	213	
(+)	55	46	44	63	0	0	75	71	0	80	0	18	66	68	66	65	50	38	50	51	36	35	0	25	0	56	18	50	31	54	185	CO CP GC LB LC LH SM
(−)	22	46	55	36	0	0	12	28	0	20	0	63	33	25	33	34	40	38	50	48	63	35	0	27	0	37	63	50	62	40	139	
(+)	30	48	46	47	0	0	68	54	0	54	0	68	57	91	35	62	54	48	63	63	42	59	0	75	0	45	60	35	46	52	230	CO JY LC
(−)	69	40	46	47	0	0	31	41	0	45	0	31	42	6	65	37	46	52	37	57	57	40	0	72	0	55	39	65	46	44	194	BO SM
(+)	58	48	50	60	0	0	64	43	0	61	0	62	16	69	42	47	25	62	44	44	20	52	0	38	0	35	39	59	33	48	216	LC PB
(−)	33	48	41	40	0	0	35	50	0	38	0	31	83	22	57	47	75	32	16	50	80	47	0	53	0	64	47	40	54	46	206	LB O S
(+)	14	60	55	59	0	0	52	41	0	30	0	60	50	58	63	53	50	38	58	50	56	75	0	31	0	37	68	11	40	52	293	PB SF TB
(−)	78	33	35	38	0	0	48	51	0	61	0	28	50	40	33	48	35	41	25	39	47	31	0	40	0	35	26	88	56	43	241	BO TR
(+)	47	50	62	35	0	0	57	18	0	80	0	50	40	57	63	55	41	55	66	64	46	71	0	62	0	62	56	31	38	53	189	CP GC PB SF
(−)	52	43	31	60	0	0	14	53	0	50	0	53	62	61	53	56	43	63	71	55	38	34	0	31	0	37	40	68	61	43	152	TR
(+)	35	60	25	42	0	0	57	42	0	50	0	69	11	55	44	75	58	44	55	41	42	56	0	59	0	35	61	55	66	53	264	PB W
(−)	57	35	45	57	0	0	71	60	0	71	0	25	55	50	38	60	35	63	41	41	41	63	0	40	0	66	36	45	33	43	215	CO
(+)	66	36	63	45	0	0	28	40	0	28	0	25	75	58	20	60	25	25	58	58	63	40	0	50	0	66	19	57	53	40	224	BO CO GC JY OJ SU TB
(+)	33	36	50	50	0	0	50	38	0	41	0	57	30	50	43	36	35	54	48	40	42	56	0	50	0	44	70	45	53	56	161	LB
(−)	50	34	66	75	0	100	50	61	0	58	0	38	61	33	43	41	69	61	75	48	66	59	0	50	0	55	54	43	65	40	317	C CC O PB S TB
(−)	50	60	33	24	0	0	45	68	0	60	0	62	60	52	70	66	31	66	56	56	22	60	0	40	0	50	25	54	34	40	231	
(+)	42	36	45	51	0	100	40	25	0	60	0	47	62	60	52	26	66	27	51	40	41	34	62	34	0	28	47	56	41	41	255	CP NY O PB SU
(−)	57	63	54	48	0	0	52	55	0	62	0	52	37	30	88	66	27	51	0	40	54	54	0	37	0	61	51	50	52	57	187	
(+)	42	45	45	32	0	0	47	45	0	37	0	43	16	37	11	26	62	32	100	41	45	33	0	63	0	30	34	41	42	38	288	LB LH NY
(−)	60	31	75	51	0	0	70	57	0	60	0	69	83	55	31	60	28	58	40	41	68	46	0	25	0	52	38	50	48	48	195	PB
(−)	40	63	25	48	0	0	29	35	0	40	0	30	66	31	60	39	71	37	40	31	50	29	0	66	0	47	52	52	47	56	250	C CO JY S
(−)	75	48	53	48	0	0	62	41	0	0	0	50	50	47	45	57	57	65	51	48	32	64	0	59	0	73	53	60	60	56	241	LB O SM
(−)	25	35	46	51	0	0	37	50	0	100	0	50	50	52	45	37	41	27	40	48	50	50	0	38	0	26	44	39	34	40	354	BO S SU
(+)	25	75	35	62	0	0	37	0	100	0	0	50	50	51	45	41	27	42	40	50	50	63	0	50	0	66	44	83	75	50	257	GC
(+)	25	0	50	37	0	0	50	50	0	100	0	50	0	52	33	33	57	57	50	50	50	36	0	50	0	33	0	16	25	45	42	LC SU TB TR W
(+)	75	0	50	66	0	0	0	0	0	0	0	50	100	50	100	55	C	40	66	50	50	63	0	50	0	35	57	55	40	60	38	BO
(−)	100	100	25	66	0	0	100	100	0	100	0	0	0	50	33	25	C	0	33	33	100	0	0	50	0	20	35	33	40	36	59	BO BP CC CP LM
(+)	0	0	75	22	0	0	0	0	0	0	0	50	0	0	45	100	C	66	66	50	0	11	0	25	0	35	44	60	36	45	35	GC PL SM
(−)	0	20	100	100	0	100	0	100	0	100	0	71	100	50	100	50	100	48	100	50	100	66	0	50	0	50	25	33	42	53	52	C CC GC JY LB LC
(+)	100	80	50	48	0	0	0	0	0	0	0	28	0	75	33	50	36	36	0	54	0	33	0	25	0	50	46	57	62	45	44	BO BP CO CP PB S
(−)	50	14	71	50	0	100	75	0	0	0	0	33	50	100	66	50	54	50	77	50	30	60	0	100	0	25	58	11	50	52	67	CO CP GC O PL TR
(+)	50	71	28	50	0	100	25	50	0	0	0	66	50	100	40	0	C	45	22	22	50	70	0	50	0	50	29	62	37	44	57	BP JY LC LH SF SM
(−)	71	54	33	83	0	100	50	0	0	0	0	20	33	50	0	66	75	50	33	33	33	25	0	0	0	100	25	37	50	46	49	BO CC NY OJ SU
(+)	28	45	66	16	0	100	50	50	0	0	0	60	0	0	33	33	28	58	66	66	66	75	0	30	0	50	66	37	50	50	53	CO LB
(+)	40	75	66	83	0	0	47	45	0	0	0	33	66	0	75	57	33	40	33	36	63	25	0	57	0	100	66	66	66	59	67	BP C CO LH PB PL
(+)	0	25	16	16	0	100	70	57	0	0	0	0	100	100	50	37	57	58	63	63	50	66	0	60	0	33	33	16	37	38	43	LB LH PB SU
(−)	0	44	60	47	0	100	29	35	0	0	0	33	0	50	0	42	28	50	50	60	50	25	0	60	0	30	66	0	27	48	70	CP JY LB LC PL SF TB
(+)	85	44	40	52	0	0	0	0	0	0	0	66	0	75	50	54	75	50	33	33	50	33	0	40	0	70	33	100	72	46	70	BO CO SU TR W O S SU
(−)	50	50	41	57	0	100	0	66	0	0	0	66	0	100	0	54	25	50	50	50	50	50	0	0	0	25	70	29	50	48	68	CP JY LC LH O S SU
(−)	100	50	50	33	0	0	0	100	0	100	0	33	50	45	33	42	0	50	50	50	45	50	0	70	0	25	46	50	62	53	71	BO GC LB PL TR
(+)	20	42	50	66	0	100	0	0	0	0	0	66	75	66	100	65	100	45	45	45	54	33	0	30	0	50	46	50	37	42	68	CO CP LB LC LH NY
(−)	80	57	33	66	0	0	0	55	0	0	0	33	25	33	33	33	0	45	54	54	66	33	0	70	0	50	66	14	60	55	54	BO CC GC LH NY S
(+)	71	57	25	50	0	0	0	50	0	33	0	40	33	75	75	75	50	50	50	50	40	66	0	57	0	50	66	85	20	42	71	BO CO GC LC LH NY TB
(+)	28	42	75	50	0	0	0	44	0	33	0	28	40	0	23	23	50	50	66	35	0	0	0	42	0	50	22	87	0	44	54	C LB SF TR
(+)	75	50	0	0	0	0	0	33	0	66	0	60	60	100	25	75	50	50	66	0	0	50	0	0	0	20	87	0	37	44	44	BO NY PB TB
(−)	25	50	50	100	0	0	66	66	0	66	0	71	60	100	75	25	50	50	50	57	0	50	0	0	0	80	12100	12100	50	53	52	CC CP GC JY LC LH

Figure 8.2: Continued

		BO	BP	C	CC	CD	CL	CO	CP	FC	GC	HO	JY	LB	LC	LH	NY	O	OJ	PB	PL	S	SF	SV	SM	SP	SU	TB	TR	W	T%	T#	65%			
--+++	(+)	50	50	42	66	0	0	20	45	0	40	0	25	0	80	0	40	37	55	50	37	40	75	0	100	0	25	50	70	71	49	79	CC	LC	SF	SM	TR	W
--+++	(-)	50	42	42	33	0	0	60	54	0	60	0	75	0	20	100	60	62	44	50	62	60	25	0	0	75	38	30	28	48	77	JY	LH	SU
--+++	(-)	70	50	16	26	0	0	60	0	0	60	0	57	0	66	0	50	50	50	53	100	33	0	25	54	33	54	42	66	50	79	BO CO CP GC LC NY
--++-	(-)	30	50	83	68	0	0	100	100	0	100	0	42	100	33	100	33	40	0	100	42	45	66	0	62	22	45	57	33	46	72	C CC LB LH SF
--++-	(+)	25	42	50	53	0	0	75	60	0	50	0	62	25	33	0	44	100	61	0	46	66	27	40	73	60	73	0	50	49	85	CO O S TB
--+-+	(+)	75	57	50	46	0	0	25	40	0	0	0	37	75	55	100	0	38	38	50	53	33	72	60	33	66	13	100	50	47	81	BO LB LH SF TR
--+-+	(+)	16	20	58	40	0	0	75	50	0	100	0	50	0	100	0	50	61	75	70	29	50	100	0	66	75	75	76	36	54	91	CO GC LH PB PL S
--+--	(+)	83	80	41	60	0	0	25	50	0	0	0	37	100	25	100	37	100	38	25	29	0	100	33	25	33	25	23	63	45	76	BO BP LB LC O SF SM
--+--	(-)	84	16	46	60	0	0	66	16	0	0	0	37	100	25	100	58	62	16	44	66	44	66	50	66	0	64	66	33	50	84	BP C CO LB LH PB
--+--	(-)	100	25	28	53	0	0	66	60	0	0	0	62	0	75	0	41	25	83	33	56	55	33	33	33	60	35	33	55	47	79	BO CP LC OJ
--+++	(-)	100	20	66	57	0	0	33	33	0	0	0	25	50	100	0	55	0	28	45	50	50	60	66	0	100	58	90	16	56	60	C CO LC PB SM
--+-+	(+)	80	33	33	42	0	0	66	0	0	0	0	50	50	0	0	44	57	0	37	50	50	40	33	33	0	33	10	83	41	44	BP CP GC LH O
--+-+	(-)	33	33	33	0	0	0	66	33	0	100	0	60	33	25	66	62	33	46	62	37	50	60	44	66	0	20	40	40	38	78	C CC CP GC LH O
--+-+	(+)	66	33	33	0	0	0	33	66	0	100	0	40	66	62	33	55	28	50	25	50	75	16	55	33	100	22	44	50	47	64	CP LB LH PB PL SU
--+--	(+)	80	20	50	28	0	0	50	75	0	100	0	60	33	66	75	60	80	46	25	62	50	60	50	50	0	66	55	57	48	65	CO GC LC O S SU
--+--	(+)	40	33	33	61	0	0	66	25	0	75	0	40	0	100	50	40	33	60	80	80	25	37	14	0	75	54	50	57	52	91	CO GC JY LC NY S SU
--+++	(+)	40	33	66	61	0	0	33	0	0	25	0	0	40	50	66	29	66	34	50	25	66	62	85	25	57	27	25	28	43	74	C O PL SM
--+++	(+)	0	100	100	0	0	0	100	85	0	50	0	28	100	50	0	71	50	60	100	53	100	0	20	80	42	77	22	71	54	66	BP C CO CP LB LH
--+-+	(-)	100	0	0	66	0	0	0	14	0	50	0	57	0	50	25	71	50	40	46	46	0	60	0	16	50	66	77	80	58	53	BO CC NY SM TB W
--+-+	(-)	100	37	0	0	0	0	0	50	0	40	0	66	100	100	0	80	20	75	0	18	33	0	80	77	50	77	80	75	41	71	BO CO JY LB LC LH
--+--	(+)	0	62	100	0	0	0	0	50	0	60	0	33	0	0	20	80	75	53	46	18	25	0	83	0	70	22	20	25	41	50	C NY O SM
--+--	(+)	50	53	50	50	0	0	14	61	0	33	0	62	100	0	44	72	75	38	76	50	66	0	50	0	70	42	42	75	54	92	LB NY O PL SF SU W
--+--	(-)	50	38	50	0	0	0	85	40	0	66	0	37	0	100	33	27	25	61	23	50	33	66	50	33	0	42	57	25	42	72	C CO GC S SU
--+-+	(+)	50	57	71	47	0	0	66	40	0	25	0	60	33	40	66	42	66	33	50	0	66	100	57	0	66	42	43	33	47	95	C CO CO S SU
--+-+	(+)	50	42	14	47	0	0	33	53	0	75	0	0	50	50	66	57	47	47	50	50	0	47	35	0	33	42	56	66	48	96	GC LH PB W
--+--	(+)	100	66	60	31	0	0	100	57	0	100	0	33	33	66	100	57	66	52	60	62	85	55	45	0	50	81	70	66	60	104	BO BP CC CO GC LC
--+--	(-)	0	33	66	33	0	0	80	42	0	0	0	50	66	33	0	42	33	42	50	60	50	0	54	0	50	12	30	10	36	63	LB PB
--+--	(-)	66	20	66	33	0	0	80	37	0	75	0	57	50	60	33	55	68	68	62	62	50	50	66	0	50	66	40	69	58	99	BO BP C CO GC OJ
--++-	(+)	33	20	33	46	0	0	50	0	0	25	0	40	50	33	71	16	26	37	37	14	85	37	33	0	50	33	60	30	39	67	CC LH NY SF TR
--++-	(+)	62	50	25	36	0	0	50	42	0	0	0	75	75	12	71	75	33	57	64	50	50	44	20	0	44	25	100	54	50	90	LB LH NY SF TR
--+--	(+)	37	57	71	63	0	0	0	33	0	66	0	55	50	75	14	16	33	31	35	35	33	30	66	25	58	38	45	45	44	79	GC LC SM TB
--+--	(-)	57	57	71	53	0	0	71	50	0	25	0	66	66	66	14	63	75	60	65	62	58	66	50	50	0	75	71	36	55	118	C CO JY LB LC NY
--+--	(-)	42	50	28	30	0	0	28	33	0	50	0	16	33	33	71	50	30	40	76	15	37	80	21	0	33	26	28	71	40	86	BO LH PB PL SF TR
--+-+	(+)	54	100	30	75	0	0	0	57	0	75	0	33	50	50	66	90	55	75	68	64	100	0	66	0	40	80	50	53	61	107	BP CC LH NY OJ PB
--+-+	(-)	45	0	70	25	0	0	100	42	0	50	0	55	50	33	0	18	22	18	35	25	50	100	60	0	41	61	55	71	32	57	CC CP GC
--+--	(+)	20	60	45	87	0	0	40	100	0	0	0	50	100	0	66	100	11	68	40	35	25	66	75	25	58	38	61	71	57	124	CC CP GC LB LH O
--+--	(+)	60	40	45	12	0	0	60	0	0	14	0	71	80	33	33	36	33	31	65	65	62	33	20	50	0	46	80	28	39	85	
--+--	(-)	33	75	50	58	0	0	42	66	0	66	0	57	50	50	33	38	60	60	65	58	33	66	50	50	100	54	63	75	58	112	BP CP JY LB PB PL
--+--	(-)	66	10	57	41	0	0	57	33	0	28	0	16	66	33	30	33	75	47	26	33	20	60	30	14	62	30	71	16	54	72	BO LH
--+++	(+)	80	81	42	58	0	0	66	66	0	50	0	60	75	42	66	35	37	52	46	26	33	75	57	36	37	70	88	63	51	118	BP LB LC SU TB TR
--+++	(+)	80	18	57	41	0	0	50	66	0	50	0	40	25	33	30	65	62	50	50	62	60	0	42	60	0	25	11	57	45	104	BO CP GC SF
--+-+	(+)	0	87	50	50	0	0	50	0	0	50	0	75	50	100	100	75	28	28	42	42	50	0	75	0	100	40	20	71	54	53	BP JY LC LH NY O
--+-+	(+)	0	12	50	50	0	0	0	66	0	66	0	25	50	0	0	25	71	71	57	57	50	71	25	25	0	46	80	28	42	42	CP OJ SF TR
--+--	(+)	40	16	50	50	0	0	100	33	0	0	0	66	66	0	63	0	75	44	55	55	60	80	50	50	0	54	63	25	54	65	C OJ OJ SF SU
--+--	(-)	60	83	33	50	0	0	33	66	0	66	0	33	66	0	0	75	25	71	55	20	50	20	50	50	100	27	36	75	42	51	BP CP LB LH O W
--+--	(-)	100	0	50	100	0	0	0	0	0	0	0	57	100	0	100	36	0	0	33	33	0	33	0	14	0	62	30	14	41	52	BP CC LH OJ PB SU
--+--	(-)	66	16	50	41	0	0	50	0	0	50	0	42	40	42	66	41	50	50	26	33	66	66	85	0	37	71	16	54	54	67	CO CO LH OJ PB SU
--+++	(-)	80	18	42	58	0	0	0	22	0	0	0	50	75	66	25	50	37	37	46	54	50	60	36	0	75	36	55	63	51	84	C LB LH PB S SU
--+++	(+)	0	50	41	50	0	0	0	77	0	100	0	37	100	66	25	37	44	45	45	40	75	100	0	63	80	54	22	36	45	73	BO CO CP GC LC
--+-+	(+)	0	0	50	41	0	0	0	0	0	0	0	66	33	33	30	36	62	28	42	50	20	50	25	0	0	25	42	50	46	57	BO OJ PB S
--+-+	(-)	40	50	25	66	0	0	0	62	0	50	0	66	66	40	50	63	42	71	57	0	70	0	75	50	0	46	57	50	50	61	CC CO GC JY LB PL SM
--+--	(-)	60	60	33	50	0	0	100	66	0	0	0	33	66	50	100	33	75	25	55	55	100	50	0	0	100	27	36	57	50	85	BO CC OJ SU LH
--+--	(-)	0	71	50	25	0	0	50	25	0	0	0	0	80	33	33	66	25	25	53	40	33	66	50	0	28	66	33	42	40	60	BP GC LB NY SF TB

Figure 8.2: Continued

		BO	BP	C	CC	CD	CL	CO	CP	FC	GC	HO	JY	LB	LC	LH	NY	O	OJ	PB	PL	S	SF	SV	SM	SP	SU	TB	TR	W	T%	T#	65%
-+--++-	(+)	50	33	54	47	0	0	66	55	0	75	0	50	40	50	66	66	55	30	75	75	33	55	0	55	0	50	83	30	77	54	102	CO GC LH NY PB PL
-+--++-	(-)	50	50	45	52	0	0	33	33	0	25	0	50	60	50	33	33	33	69	25	25	66	44	0	44	0	50	16	69	22	44	83	OJ S TR
-+--++-	(+)	33	75	25	81	0	0	0	0	0	50	0	62	60	50	33	59	31	66	66	0	66	55	0	54	0	83	66	66	66	55	103	BP CC CO LB LC PB
-+--++-	(-)	66	25	75	18	0	0	0	57	0	100	0	37	0	30	75	40	100	68	33	0	50	33	0	45	0	83	33	100	33	44	83	BO C LH O OJ SU TR
-+--++	(+)	20	50	50	57	0	0	0	60	0	50	0	66	0	0	50	45	66	45	33	55	33	0	85	0	80	15	50	57	47	56	GC JY O SM SU
-+--++	(-)	80	50	0	42	0	0	0	40	0	50	0	33	0	0	50	54	66	20	69	44	12	83	0	14	0	20	69	50	42	48	58	BO LB PB S SF TB
-+-++	(+)	60	33	63	100	0	0	75	27	0	50	0	80	16	100	50	70	25	47	100	45	80	25	0	83	0	83	50	66	60	54	83	CC CO JY LC NY PB
-+-++	(-)	66	36	0	0	0	0	40	0	0	50	0	20	66	0	50	30	50	52	0	54	20	75	0	16	0	16	50	33	20	41	63	BP LB SF
-+-++	(+)	50	50	50	0	0	0	75	63	0	50	0	50	66	0	50	64	25	50	100	40	40	33	0	12	0	85	33	33	60	50	64	CO CP GC PB SU
-+-++	(-)	50	50	50	0	0	0	33	33	0	0	0	50	66	0	66	35	75	43	0	60	60	66	0	75	0	14	22	44	66	44	57	LH O SF SM W
-+-++	(+)	87	37	50	75	0	0	33	75	0	71	0	33	40	100	42	85	25	50	52	52	42	50	0	0	0	40	18	33	42	47	75	BO CC CP GC LC NY
-+-++	(-)	12	62	50	25	0	0	75	25	0	28	0	66	40	0	57	14	50	47	50	47	57	50	0	75	0	66	72	50	50	50	79	CO JY SM TB TR
-++-++	(+)	66	50	57	57	0	0	54	14	0	50	0	60	100	16	66	33	42	66	50	83	44	50	0	0	0	50	18	40	20	45	84	BO LB LH OJ PL SM
-++-++	(-)	33	50	42	42	0	0	45	85	0	80	0	40	66	100	42	55	57	33	50	16	55	50	0	60	0	50	72	60	40	52	76	CP LC SF TB
-++-++	(+)	66	33	0	57	0	0	25	36	0	20	0	14	75	75	14	53	54	54	75	50	25	62	0	40	0	53	50	50	50	43	95	BO C CO GC JY LC LH
-++-++	(-)	33	55	0	43	0	0	66	60	0	80	0	50	25	25	80	33	60	57	80	56	50	37	0	60	0	46	50	50	45	55	79	LB PB
-++++	(+)	50	50	50	50	0	0	33	62	0	75	0	50	50	0	75	66	25	53	0	37	50	63	0	60	0	41	62	60	62	52	113	CO GC LB LH PB SM SU
-++++	(-)	50	50	50	50	0	0	50	40	0	25	0	50	50	0	25	25	66	46	42	20	43	100	0	40	0	42	62	60	45	42	86	LC NY S
-++++	(+)	75	44	18	58	0	0	50	62	0	40	0	88	50	44	75	53	40	75	20	38	33	35	0	40	0	62	25	22	75	50	104	BO JY LH OJ
-++++	(-)	25	44	72	41	0	0	50	25	0	60	0	11	50	55	25	46	40	25	80	61	55	64	0	50	0	37	75	77	25	47	96	C PB
-+++++	(+)	0	80	50	44	0	0	100	18	0	75	0	66	25	100	50	60	66	33	100	44	72	28	0	60	0	57	52	18	46	57	74	BP CO CP GC JY LB
-+++++	(-)	100	20	50	44	0	0	81	28	0	25	0	33	75	0	50	40	33	66	0	57	27	71	0	40	0	42	81	40	40	39	51	BO OJ TR
-+++++	(+)	0	57	60	52	0	0	83	28	0	75	0	75	75	16	50	69	50	66	33	44	72	28	0	60	0	52	40	81	46	57	113	BO CO GC JY LB LC
-+++++	(-)	0	42	40	47	0	0	16	71	0	25	0	25	25	100	50	30	50	33	66	69	71	71	0	20	0	40	81	40	28	51	79	CP LH SF TR
-+++++	(+)	75	40	66	53	0	0	50	57	0	33	0	71	83	75	37	50	60	42	66	46	62	28	0	50	0	60	50	75	71	54	91	BO C LC S SM
-+++++	(-)	25	60	33	46	0	0	80	23	0	66	0	60	16	25	37	50	40	40	44	53	37	71	0	50	0	57	41	25	26	41	82	GC JY LB PB PL W
+-+++	(+)	30	25	0	14	0	0	20	76	0	33	0	40	50	28	55	25	20	44	60	46	50	50	0	70	0	57	18	60	62	52	119	CO C CO GC LC
+-+++	(-)	16	50	50	63	0	0	75	75	0	66	0	50	66	62	100	75	25	53	57	37	50	30	0	30	0	41	62	60	37	56	90	CP SF
+-+++	(+)	16	50	50	36	0	0	33	35	0	66	0	33	33	25	66	28	34	14	42	55	50	37	0	16	0	60	37	62	50	40	91	BO CP GC LB LH NY SM
+-+++	(-)	50	50	25	28	0	0	66	46	0	40	0	50	33	25	44	58	41	62	50	37	50	30	0	46	0	62	25	22	75	39	68	CP GC LB NY SM
+++++	(+)	100	41	75	71	0	0	33	53	0	60	0	50	66	75	44	41	25	66	40	68	50	76	0	40	0	62	25	77	25	47	93	CO LB LC O PL SF W
+++++	(-)	41	75	71	0	0	0	53	40	0	60	0	50	33	100	44	58	66	33	60	31	83	23	0	60	0	37	75	25	60	50	98	BO CC OJ S TB TR
+++++	(+)	71	50	33	20	0	0	16	28	0	60	0	50	25	25	61	41	66	38	33	33	33	77	0	53	0	25	27	40	63	48	94	BP CC CO LC OJ PB SF
+++++	(-)	28	33	20	66	0	0	50	50	0	50	0	33	75	0	50	30	42	38	22	42	42	85	0	60	0	72	83	36	37	46	90	LB NY O S TR
++++++	(+)	60	66	66	66	0	0	64	47	0	66	0	55	0	37	66	75	75	50	0	86	33	66	0	37	100	87	66	0	10	50	112	CC GC O PL SF SU TB
++++++	(-)	87	20	37	33	0	0	35	47	0	33	0	44	100	0	62	29	25	12	100	13	50	33	0	56	12	26	16	57	80	45	99	BO LB PB TR W
++++++	(+)	50	66	33	75	0	0	33	35	0	66	0	66	42	50	66	38	55	57	0	71	14	47	0	50	0	60	68	37	50	56	84	BP CP GC LC NY PB
++++++	(-)	16	50	44	75	0	0	33	64	0	66	0	66	57	37	33	14	44	42	66	25	50	60	0	16	0	40	26	62	50	43	60	CO CO JY LB LH
++++++	(+)	27	66	66	25	0	0	72	66	0	60	0	40	0	51	66	44	61	66	66	55	33	62	0	60	100	83	27	40	26	59	119	BP LB LC PB PL SU TB
++++++	(-)	63	33	50	57	0	0	18	28	0	33	0	66	33	100	42	30	38	22	33	33	80	40	0	53	100	0	37	33	36	37	98	CO LH S
++++++	(+)	83	25	42	62	0	0	50	50	0	80	0	33	75	25	66	16	45	45	42	42	58	37	0	66	0	50	33	66	66	57	113	BO CP GC JY LC LH
++++++	(-)	16	37	33	47	0	0	64	37	0	33	0	55	33	66	75	29	57	57	42	57	14	40	0	50	0	16	16	16	16	35	66	LB
++++++	(+)	50	66	33	75	0	0	33	35	0	66	0	66	28	50	50	65	85	55	40	45	40	60	0	83	60	60	68	62	50	54	144	CC CO JY O PB SM TB
++++++	(-)	50	33	44	66	0	0	33	64	0	66	0	66	57	50	66	34	14	14	25	55	60	37	0	16	0	40	26	62	50	43	116	C GC
++++++	(+)	33	66	25	25	0	0	20	18	0	50	0	75	66	57	57	61	83	55	66	68	25	60	0	60	100	75	83	37	37	59	117	CP CO JY O PB SU TR
++++++	(-)	66	36	54	59	0	0	71	58	0	60	0	25	33	42	30	16	45	38	22	29	40	37	0	40	0	25	33	33	36	37	74	BO BP LB
++++++	(+)	0	36	50	59	0	0	58	58	0	80	0	88	80	66	66	70	40	66	42	61	58	62	0	66	0	0	50	33	66	57	132	CO GC JY LB LH NY
++++++	(-)	100	54	50	58	0	0	28	41	0	66	0	11	20	46	33	17	50	50	26	33	33	41	0	33	0	75	35	66	16	37	87	BO PB SU TR
++++++	(+)	62	62	42	41	0	0	62	85	0	33	0	84	80	51	50	12	87	36	87	53	75	52	0	30	0	71	33	0	38	52	122	CP CP JY LC S SU
++++++	(+)	37	85	66	47	0	0	37	14	0	66	0	15	66	50	38	36	36	36	66	57	62	30	0	70	0	28	57	100	88	45	106	BP LB O PB SM TR
++++++	(+)	0	42	33	52	0	0	77	50	0	33	0	25	33	55	43	43	22	22	0	42	37	62	0	64	0	20	55	53	11	40	142	BO SF
++++++	(-)	25	0	50	37	0	0	22	50	0	0	0	55	0	0	0	33	20	57	0	50	50	36	0	50	66	66	55	16	75	50	102	GC SF
++++++	(+)	75	0	50	62	0	0	0	0	0	0	0	0	100	0	55	0	0	42	0	50	50	63	0	50	33	33	0	16	25	45	42	LC SU TB TR W
	(-)																															38	BO

Figure 8.2: Continued

		BO	BP	C	CC	CL	CD	CL	CO	CP	FC	GC	HO	JY	LB	LC	LH	NY	O	OJ	PB	PL	S	SV	SM	SP	SU	TB	TR	W	T%	T#	65%
+----+---	(+)	100	100	25	66	0	0	0	0	100	0	0	0	50	50	50	100	75	100	60	0	33	100	0	0	0	80	57	55	40	60	59	BO BP CC CP LB LH
+----+---	(-)	0	0	75	22	0	0	0	0	100	100	0	0	50	50	0	100	25	40	40	0	66	0	0	100	20	35	44	60	36	35	C CC GC PL SM
+----+-+-	(+)	0	20	100	100	0	0	0	0	0	0	100	0	50	0	0	0	50	63	40	0	66	11	0	0	50	25	33	44	60	53	52	C CC GC JY LB LC
+----+-+-	(+)	100	80	71	50	0	0	0	100	75	0	100	0	28	50	33	100	50	36	54	100	66	66	0	25	25	75	58	66	57	52	67	C CO CP GC O PL TR
+----+-+-	(+)	50	14	28	50	0	0	0	0	25	0	0	0	33	50	66	66	40	60	45	50	22	30	0	100	50	29	58	88	37	44	57	BP JY LC LH SF SM
+----+--+	(-)	71	33	33	83	0	0	0	100	50	0	0	0	20	50	0	100	66	75	33	33	50	70	0	80	50	62	11	37	62	46	49	BO CC NY OJ SU
+----+-+-	(-)	28	45	66	16	0	0	0	0	50	0	0	0	60	50	0	0	33	25	25	66	66	25	0	0	100	29	62	50	50	50	53	CC CO LB LH PB PL
+----+-+-	(+)	40	75	83	83	0	0	0	50	100	0	0	0	66	66	0	100	60	57	33	33	66	75	80	0	0	66	66	37	66	59	67	BP C CC CO CP JY
+----+-+-	(+)	60	25	16	16	0	0	0	0	33	0	0	0	33	100	0	0	57	28	58	66	66	75	0	0	33	33	16	33	16	38	43	LB LH PB SU
+----+--+	(+)	0	44	60	47	0	0	0	0	75	0	0	0	66	0	0	50	42	28	58	66	50	66	60	0	30	50	40	28	0	48	70	CP JY LB LC PL SF TB
+----+---	(-)	85	44	40	52	0	0	0	100	66	0	0	0	33	0	0	50	42	0	50	50	33	50	40	0	70	33	100	29	72	48	70	BO CO SU TR W
+----+---	(-)	0	25	41	57	0	0	0	50	66	0	0	0	66	75	25	25	54	75	25	37	66	60	60	0	0	50	29	50	50	46	71	BO GC LB PL TR
+----+-+-	(+)	100	50	58	33	0	0	0	100	0	0	100	0	33	75	66	100	66	0	50	50	66	50	0	60	50	46	66	50	62	53	68	CO CC LB LC LH NY
+----+--+	(-)	20	42	50	33	0	0	0	100	55	0	0	0	66	25	33	0	33	0	45	50	45	33	0	30	50	40	40	50	37	42	54	BO CC GC LC LH NY S
+----+-+-	(+)	71	57	25	50	0	0	0	100	55	0	0	0	40	33	75	100	76	50	50	50	60	40	0	57	50	66	14	60	50	55	71	BO CO GC LC LH NY TB
+----+-+-	(-)	75	50	42	75	0	0	0	0	44	0	0	33	66	66	25	0	23	50	50	66	40	66	0	0	50	22	85	20	0	42	54	C LB SF TR
+----+--+	(+)	28	42	75	50	0	0	0	0	0	0	0	66	28	40	0	25	75	50	66	33	40	0	0	42	50	20	87	0	37	44	44	BO NY PB TB
+----+-+-	(-)	25	50	50	100	0	0	0	33	66	0	0	0	71	60	100	75	25	50	50	57	57	50	100	0	80	12	100	0	50	53	52	CC CP GC JY LC LH
+----+-++	(+)	50	50	42	66	0	0	0	20	45	0	0	0	25	0	80	0	40	37	55	50	37	62	0	100	25	50	70	71	49	79	CC LC SF SM TR W
+----+-+-	(-)	50	42	33	0	0	0	0	60	54	0	0	60	75	20	100	0	62	44	50	62	60	25	0	0	55	38	30	28	0	48	77	JY LH SU
+----+-+-	(+)	70	50	16	26	0	100	0	100	0	0	0	0	57	66	0	66	66	50	53	100	57	54	25	0	55	54	42	42	66	50	79	BO CO CP GC LC NY
+----+--+	(-)	30	83	83	68	0	0	0	0	0	0	0	0	42	33	33	0	33	40	40	0	42	66	62	0	22	45	57	33	33	46	72	C CC LB LH SF
+----+-+-	(+)	42	50	53	0	0	0	0	75	60	0	50	0	62	25	20	100	44	61	46	50	46	27	40	0	75	54	90	16	49	49	85	CO O S TB
+----+-+-	(+)	75	57	50	46	0	0	0	25	40	0	50	0	37	75	55	100	55	38	50	53	53	33	60	0	20	73	0	13	100	47	81	BO LB LH SF TR
+----+-++	(-)	16	20	58	40	0	0	0	75	0	0	0	0	50	0	0	0	23	61	72	75	70	100	0	33	66	75	76	90	36	54	91	CO GC LH PB PL S
+----+-++	(+)	83	80	41	60	0	0	0	25	66	0	0	0	50	100	0	100	37	38	25	29	0	0	80	0	66	35	25	23	63	45	76	BO BP LB LC O SF
+----+-+-	(+)	0	75	71	46	0	0	0	66	14	0	0	0	37	0	25	100	58	16	83	25	37	44	0	50	40	64	66	90	16	50	84	BP C CO LB LH PB
+----+---	(+)	100	25	28	53	0	0	0	33	85	0	0	0	62	0	0	0	41	25	16	44	56	55	0	33	60	35	33	10	83	47	79	BO CP LC OJ
+----+-+-	(+)	20	60	50	28	0	0	0	66	0	0	0	0	50	50	0	66	44	57	0	0	54	50	66	0	0	33	10	60	60	56	60	BO C CO LC PB SM
+----+---	(-)	0	80	33	42	0	0	0	0	66	0	0	0	50	0	0	0	44	71	25	50	54	0	0	0	100	0	40	40	40	38	44	BP CP GC GC
+----+-+-	(+)	33	33	66	100	0	0	0	33	66	0	0	0	40	66	33	25	44	57	50	50	62	50	55	0	22	44	55	44	50	56	78	C CC CP GC LH O
+----+---	(-)	20	60	50	28	0	0	0	50	75	0	0	0	66	33	66	25	60	20	0	0	75	20	0	0	66	54	57	47	50	38	53	BO LB LH PB PL SU
+----+-+-	(+)	80	33	33	38	0	0	0	33	66	0	0	0	60	66	66	75	70	33	60	50	80	66	14	0	66	54	56	66	57	47	64	CP LB LH PB PL O S
+----+-++	(+)	40	33	66	61	0	0	0	0	0	0	75	0	40	0	50	50	29	66	34	50	25	62	0	0	75	27	25	28	28	48	65	BO CC GC LC NY S SU
+----+-++	(-)	0	100	0	0	0	0	0	14	0	0	0	0	28	50	0	0	58	25	60	0	80	40	80	0	57	22	77	25	25	52	91	CO GC JY LC NY S SU
+----+---	(-)	100	37	0	0	0	0	0	14	0	0	0	0	66	100	100	100	80	20	75	28	81	66	16	0	50	77	80	75	75	43	74	C CP O PL SM
+----+-+-	(+)	0	62	0	0	0	0	0	50	0	0	0	0	33	0	0	0	20	53	50	25	18	33	83	0	70	22	20	20	25	41	50	C NY O SM
+----+-+-	(+)	50	50	53	50	0	0	0	14	61	0	0	0	37	0	0	44	72	38	42	50	42	42	0	50	42	42	75	54	54	LB NY O PL SF SU W
+----+---	(-)	50	50	38	50	0	0	0	85	30	0	0	0	60	66	33	33	27	61	16	50	23	50	0	0	30	42	57	25	25	42	72	CO GC LC
+----+-+-	(+)	50	42	71	47	0	0	0	33	53	0	0	0	60	66	0	75	42	47	33	50	50	0	35	0	66	43	43	33	47	95	CC C SU
+----+-+-	(-)	100	66	40	68	0	0	0	0	66	0	40	0	33	33	66	100	57	52	50	50	40	47	45	0	54	56	66	90	60	48	96	GC LH PB W
+----+-++	(+)	66	80	60	31	0	0	0	80	42	0	75	0	50	33	66	33	66	66	60	75	62	85	50	0	66	81	70	30	90	60	63	BO BP CC CO GC LC
+----+-++	(+)	33	20	33	66	0	0	0	50	55	0	0	0	50	0	0	0	44	33	42	50	37	50	54	0	50	12	30	10	69	36	99	BO BP C CO GC OJ
+----+---	(-)	62	50	25	36	0	0	0	50	0	0	0	0	60	0	0	33	33	57	46	50	64	50	20	0	50	33	60	30	39	58	67	CC LH O
+----+--+	(-)	37	50	50	63	0	0	0	71	60	0	25	0	60	25	75	16	75	33	42	100	37	30	80	0	55	25	0	45	54	39	90	LB LH NY SF TR
+----+-+-	(+)	57	50	71	53	0	0	0	28	33	0	0	0	33	66	66	14	63	40	25	75	15	62	78	0	35	68	28	46	44	118	C LC SM TB LH
+----+-+-	(-)	42	50	28	30	0	0	0	33	33	0	0	0	16	33	33	71	27	40	75	37	76	37	80	0	33	26	71	53	40	86	GC LH PB SF TR

Figure 8.2: Continued

Figure 8.2: Concluded

		BO	BP	C	CC	CD	CL	CO	CP	FC	GC	HO	JY	LB	LC	LH	NY	O	OJ	PB	PL	S	SF	SV	SM	SP	SU	TB	TR	W	T%	T#	------- 65% -------
+++-+++	(+)	0	60	50	66	0	0	64	47	0	66	0	55	0	37	50	45	75	50	0	86	33	66	0	37	0	87	66	0	10	50	112	CC GC O PL SF SU TB
++++---	(-)	87	20	37	33	0	0	35	47	0	33	0	44	100	62	37	55	25	50	100	13	50	33	0	56	0	12	26	100	80	45	99	BO LB PB TR W
+++-+--+	(+)	50	66	55	12	0	0	0	85	0	100	0	33	0	75	33	71	42	57	100	71	66	100	0	40	0	100	66	44	37	56	84	BP CP GC LC NY PB
+++-+--	(-)	50	33	44	75	0	0	100	14	0	0	0	66	100	25	66	28	57	42	0	21	16	0	0	40	0	0	33	55	62	40	60	CC CO JY LB LH
+++--+	(+)	27	66	33	42	0	0	33	64	0	40	0	40	0	75	0	36	44	61	66	66	20	44	0	46	0	75	72	60	60	52	119	BP LB LC PB PL SU TB
+++--+-	(+)	63	25	50	57	0	0	66	28	0	60	0	60	0	100	100	63	22	38	33	33	80	44	0	53	0	25	27	40	26	43	98	CO LH S
+++---+	(-)	83	62	62	55	0	0	60	100	0	75	0	66	33	66	75	70	0	87	42	42	85	40	0	50	0	72	83	36	37	60	113	BO CP GC JY LC LH
+++----	(-)	16	37	25	44	0	0	40	0	0	25	0	33	66	33	25	29	12	57	0	57	14	60	0	50	0	18	16	57	37	35	66	LB
++-++++	(+)	50	36	33	75	0	0	33	35	0	33	0	100	28	62	50	65	85	55	75	45	40	62	0	83	0	60	68	37	50	54	144	CC JY O PB SM TB
++-+++-	(-)	50	54	66	25	0	0	58	64	0	66	0	0	57	37	50	34	14	40	25	55	60	37	0	16	0	40	26	62	50	43	116	C GC
++-++-+	(+)	33	0	42	45	0	0	20	72	0	66	0	75	33	54	57	61	83	55	100	64	60	62	0	60	0	100	62	66	63	59	117	CP GC JY O PB SU TR
++-++--	(-)	66	36	50	54	0	0	60	18	0	33	0	25	66	36	42	30	16	45	0	29	40	37	0	40	0	0	37	33	36	37	74	BO BP LB
++-+-++	(+)	0	36	50	59	0	0	71	58	0	80	0	88	80	46	66	70	40	66	0	61	58	62	0	66	0	0	50	66	66	57	132	CO GC JY LB LH NY
++-+-+-	(-)	100	54	50	36	0	0	28	41	0	20	0	11	20	33	33	17	50	26	100	33	41	37	0	33	0	75	35	16	16	37	87	BO PB SU TR
++-+--+	(+)	62	0	57	58	0	0	62	85	0	66	0	84	0	80	50	61	12	63	33	33	75	52	0	30	0	71	33	0	38	52	122	CP GC JY LC S SU
++-+---	(-)	37	85	42	41	0	0	37	14	0	33	0	15	100	20	50	20	87	36	66	53	25	47	0	70	0	28	57	100	53	45	106	BP LB O PB SM TR
++--+++	(+)	100	42	66	47	0	0	77	50	0	0	0	75	66	44	54	50	60	66	100	57	62	30	0	64	0	80	41	46	88	56	142	BO C CO JY LB OJ
++--++-	(-)	0	42	33	52	0	0	22	50	0	100	0	25	33	55	36	43	20	22	0	42	37	70	0	35	0	20	55	53	11	40	102	GC SF

Figure 8.3: Daily Closing Patterns: Bear Market Samples

	BO	BP	C	CC	CD	CL	CO	CP	FC	GC	HO	JY	LB	LC	LH	NY	O	OJ	PB	PL	S	SF	SV	SM	SP	SU	TB	TR	W	T%	T#	
(+)	36	48	41	42	0	0	45	52	0	48	0	44	38	52	36	48	42	48	47	49	44	44	0	44	0	46	43	45	46	46	4439	
(−)	57	44	53	55	0	0	45	52	0	47	0	51	54	36	47	45	47	48	46	48	50	50	0	51	0	50	47	46	48	48	4651	
(+)	47	38	46	48	0	0	46	48	0	39	0	40	47	41	45	48	45	44	46	43	44	41	0	43	0	44	48	40	50	44	3817	
(+)	42	55	49	48	0	0	47	47	0	59	0	56	45	47	48	44	41	44	44	50	54	53	0	52	0	45	45	47	42	51	4398	
(−)	37	41	43	45	0	0	44	45	0	49	0	41	44	48	44	41	44	40	46	50	43	44	0	42	0	41	37	40	42	44	3802	
(+)	55	53	50	52	0	0	53	52	0	46	0	53	49	42	42	52	51	50	51	46	53	49	0	54	0	55	54	51	54	51	4431	
(−)	42	42	39	45	0	0	36	36	0	34	0	37	39	34	35	35	43	40	42	40	42	40	0	38	0	36	50	38	40	40	2816	
(−)	49	49	57	53	0	0	54	60	0	64	0	59	48	52	58	58	48	55	52	55	55	52	0	58	0	62	41	51	56	55	3863	
(+)	34	50	41	44	0	0	55	54	0	51	0	41	38	50	50	49	44	47	46	48	51	47	0	44	0	45	47	43	49	47	2196	
(−)	58	43	51	53	0	0	42	42	0	46	0	54	56	42	49	49	41	47	53	55	51	48	0	51	0	50	47	48	48	48	2255	
(+)	36	38	40	55	0	0	47	47	0	39	0	36	50	40	40	46	46	47	45	43	44	41	0	44	0	41	40	41	53	44	1964	
(−)	51	54	55	42	0	0	49	47	0	59	0	61	44	46	46	45	43	46	52	53	52	51	0	50	0	54	52	50	45	51	2264	
(+)	41	45	45	43	0	0	44	44	0	48	0	38	43	52	52	52	47	47	48	42	47	41	0	40	0	41	41	38	44	44	1941	
(−)	48	51	49	55	0	0	53	52	0	47	0	57	48	59	59	50	51	49	56	48	52	50	0	56	0	60	48	53	52	51	2264	
(+)	38	45	42	44	0	0	45	37	0	35	0	37	39	53	22	35	40	46	45	42	36	43	0	40	0	38	51	39	42	40	1542	
(−)	52	49	53	54	0	0	49	59	0	61	0	59	48	59	59	57	53	48	52	55	57	54	0	56	0	60	40	51	57	55	2097	
(+)	40	47	39	38	0	0	49	52	0	48	0	47	40	44	44	45	37	47	49	50	50	43	0	45	0	46	39	51	44	46	2055	
(+)	53	48	55	58	0	0	47	44	0	48	0	49	52	44	35	51	50	48	49	49	47	52	0	51	0	51	47	40	51	49	2171	
(−)	54	39	44	51	0	0	47	47	0	39	0	37	47	44	50	43	43	41	40	42	42	41	0	44	0	48	59	38	47	44	1681	
(+)	38	56	44	57	0	0	52	47	0	59	0	51	44	50	50	53	40	42	50	55	51	55	0	51	0	48	31	52	49	51	1959	
(+)	30	43	43	47	0	0	43	44	0	50	0	42	47	42	42	40	40	42	53	53	40	46	0	45	0	41	36	43	40	44	1712	
(−)	65	54	50	49	0	0	52	52	0	45	0	51	49	48	48	55	54	51	54	53	54	49	0	51	0	55	57	50	56	51	1985	
(+)	47	39	35	43	0	0	40	37	0	30	0	38	40	44	44	35	34	34	47	42	42	41	0	35	0	33	48	36	38	39	1113	GC SU
(+)	50	51	62	53	0	0	56	59	0	69	0	61	53	50	50	59	42	60	50	55	53	51	0	61	0	66	43	54	58	56	1576	
(−)	42	52	40	44	0	0	58	58	0	55	0	43	39	44	44	37	47	47	50	53	51	51	0	43	0	51	47	52	50	49	1111	
(−)	51	44	54	53	0	0	39	41	0	41	0	53	54	44	44	50	42	45	48	47	46	47	0	51	0	42	45	40	45	46	1057	
(+)	35	36	41	55	0	0	49	47	0	41	0	40	46	38	38	47	42	44	45	41	41	42	0	41	0	43	39	40	49	44	965	
(−)	56	56	51	42	0	0	48	46	0	57	0	58	46	47	47	45	46	50	54	52	50	47	0	52	0	53	52	53	48	51	1123	
(−)	43	52	46	51	0	0	54	49	0	39	0	41	45	48	48	46	36	43	54	44	52	50	0	43	0	39	44	44	49	46	1047	
(+)	48	46	44	43	0	0	54	48	0	39	0	53	47	48	48	53	54	42	46	38	47	52	0	52	0	58	44	48	47	49	1110	
(−)	42	46	44	55	0	0	55	43	0	29	0	57	35	37	16	37	42	42	38	44	41	41	0	38	0	37	36	34	41	39	776	
(+)	50	52	52	55	0	0	55	55	0	67	0	57	51	72	72	53	60	51	53	60	51	56	0	58	0	61	47	56	56	56	1103	GC LH
(−)	32	49	42	43	0	0	50	52	0	45	0	45	35	46	46	45	37	48	40	47	42	42	0	44	0	45	39	56	47	46	1046	
(+)	53	46	53	53	0	0	41	43	0	52	0	52	58	40	40	40	48	52	53	51	53	52	0	35	0	53	52	35	54	49	1123	BO
(−)	66	40	40	35	0	0	47	51	0	41	0	52	50	37	37	40	45	52	44	51	48	36	0	49	0	47	65	54	44	46	902	
(+)	29	57	44	61	0	0	50	45	0	57	0	44	40	59	59	59	48	39	55	45	49	62	0	48	0	52	21	54	44	50	982	
(−)	37	45	37	41	0	0	50	45	0	55	0	48	53	40	40	37	42	41	43	56	37	48	0	49	0	48	35	45	40	45	959	
(+)	56	48	35	46	0	0	41	37	0	32	0	37	30	51	35	31	41	46	41	44	55	41	0	35	0	32	58	42	42	39	1039	
(−)	62	49	35	53	0	0	41	37	0	32	0	37	30	57	57	31	43	66	41	53	44	41	0	35	0	44	28	38	43	39	610	GC OJ
(+)	33	49	61	53	0	0	67	58	0	67	0	66	62	57	57	66	52	45	55	46	53	55	0	61	0	57	44	50	56	56	863	
(+)	17	50	42	46	0	0	55	52	0	46	0	40	41	52	52	51	45	47	42	47	50	46	0	45	0	39	42	35	49	45	992	
(−)	75	44	52	52	0	0	43	42	0	50	0	64	56	42	42	43	49	49	57	50	46	48	0	51	0	59	53	56	45	50	1088	BO
(+)	40	37	37	55	0	0	46	49	0	36	0	32	39	43	43	54	54	48	46	41	40	40	0	49	0	40	41	47	44	44	918	
(−)	46	51	61	43	0	0	52	47	0	61	0	63	39	50	60	44	37	42	51	56	51	56	0	48	0	55	53	47	55	51	1052	
(+)	36	39	45	35	0	0	44	38	0	44	0	30	43	36	36	48	48	53	40	43	41	42	0	35	0	44	28	32	37	41	808	
(−)	52	58	46	63	0	0	54	58	0	54	0	65	51	65	65	48	48	41	55	46	57	49	0	61	0	54	57	63	59	55	1083	
(+)	34	46	40	40	0	0	47	30	0	42	0	32	43	31	31	31	43	52	28	39	46	54	0	42	0	40	44	44	43	41	690	
(−)	57	48	56	50	0	0	49	66	0	56	0	64	43	57	64	64	52	48	53	50	65	54	0	54	0	58	37	48	53	54	863	GC OJ
(−)	43	34	34	35	0	0	53	52	0	43	0	42	52	38	38	44	38	48	48	43	55	53	0	48	0	50	45	45	41	47	914	CP
(+)	53	50	59	62	0	0	53	45	0	43	0	42	47	43	47	38	50	50	49	32	43	45	0	53	0	47	54	54	54	48	933	
(−)	42	36	50	42	0	0	42	45	0	35	0	41	40	41	47	39	43	44	45	65	45	53	0	40	0	46	38	38	41	41	963	
(+)	17	36	49	55	0	0	40	45	0	62	0	56	42	48	47	44	35	47	63	47	52	52	0	43	0	43	36	50	54	53	715	
(+)	78	58	46	42	0	0	57	54	0	54	0	51	55	49	41	57	54	57	36	47	50	51	0	54	0	66	56	54	55	53	843	BO SU

-------- 65% --------

Figure 8.3:   Continued

------- 65% -------

	±	BO	BP	C	CC	CD	CL	CO	CP	FC	GC	HO	JY	LB	LC	LH	NY	O	OJ	PB	PL	S	SF	SV	SM	SP	SU	TB	TR	W	T%	T#	
++++	(+)	34	35	35	41	0	0	38	39	0	26	0	42	58	0	64	45	46	41	54	39	38	44	0	39	0	32	48	36	31	40	447	GC SU
+++	(+)	65	57	65	53	0	0	58	56	0	74	0	57	38	0	28	54	46	51	45	56	56	47	0	58	0	67	44	60	64	56	623	BP CO
--+	(-)	47	66	38	42	0	0	67	58	0	64	0	46	48	0	37	46	51	40	45	50	56	0	0	49	0	41	40	59	54	52	550	BP CO
---	(-)	47	30	55	57	0	0	32	41	0	34	0	53	44	0	37	51	40	44	48	48	38	41	0	44	0	53	50	29	40	44	467	
--+	(+)	28	43	37	48	0	0	55	38	0	45	0	40	39	0	37	53	38	42	47	48	36	46	0	36	0	37	43	42	53	43	484	
---	(-)	60	51	52	48	0	0	40	50	0	52	0	57	0	0	50	53	55	53	52	50	47	43	0	59	0	58	54	54	43	51	568	
--+	(+)	31	48	38	57	0	0	48	49	0	52	0	37	48	0	70	48	37	42	46	52	50	45	0	55	0	44	56	44	44	47	531	LH
--+	(+)	63	48	57	39	0	0	50	32	0	42	0	55	44	0	30	51	51	53	50	44	47	53	0	40	0	54	44	48	52	48	548	
--+	(-)	50	43	48	38	0	0	44	32	0	19	0	51	25	0	39	39	47	46	29	40	29	36	0	45	0	28	47	29	37	37	364	
--+	(+)	42	56	46	59	0	0	55	63	0	75	0	45	66	0	100	51	44	56	70	58	58	58	0	50	0	71	36	64	55	58	565	GC LB LH PB SU
--+	(-)	44	48	42	53	0	0	53	39	0	47	0	54	39	0	42	46	43	56	48	48	42	41	0	48	0	45	36	58	47	47	526	
--+	(+)	50	46	56	40	0	0	42	55	0	48	0	44	55	0	35	53	56	43	40	52	50	48	0	50	0	53	50	34	50	48	538	
--+	(-)	50	46	56	59	0	0	43	53	0	58	0	57	59	0	55	57	60	48	52	50	57	54	0	56	0	57	57	42	57	48	508	BO
--+	(+)	75	34	52	41	0	0	50	57	0	41	0	45	40	0	28	42	34	53	56	41	51	50	0	43	0	42	28	53	41	46	511	LH
--+	(-)	18	61	45	55	0	0	49	40	0	57	0	50	39	0	71	60	60	34	31	56	48	41	0	37	0	49	35	43	40	49	515	
--+	(+)	30	48	44	40	0	0	43	43	0	48	0	57	46	0	55	33	35	35	63	41	48	39	0	59	0	44	45	40	55	39	548	TB
--+	(+)	61	45	50	57	0	0	50	53	0	41	0	45	59	0	38	42	48	48	50	50	54	63	0	47	0	46	66	48	50	56	308	
--+	(-)	54	42	37	48	0	0	39	42	0	78	0	37	46	0	25	60	53	41	39	53	41	45	0	52	0	44	35	43	43	47	439	GC LB LH OJ
--+	(+)	13	43	38	42	0	0	58	64	0	48	0	61	50	0	75	33	54	50	53	36	57	56	0	49	0	46	45	39	50	49	533	
--+	(-)	36	48	52	57	0	0	50	45	0	49	0	50	39	0	35	54	16	66	44	48	43	40	0	33	0	53	50	45	48	56	550	BO
--+	(+)	44	48	48	58	0	0	50	47	0	61	0	64	47	0	45	47	41	41	51	34	38	43	0	49	0	43	75	48	44	47	491	OJ
--+	(-)	33	46	51	38	0	0	37	45	0	37	0	29	38	0	50	43	33	46	39	48	42	38	0	34	0	62	42	44	28	42	509	
+++	(+)	42	41	47	36	0	0	50	51	0	61	0	44	54	0	68	42	44	52	42	34	51	49	0	33	0	47	41	41	50	42	417	LH
+++	(-)	57	57	44	63	0	0	60	47	0	43	0	52	38	0	27	57	56	48	51	58	58	56	0	61	0	58	57	58	67	54	531	JY W
-++	(-)	37	36	50	54	0	0	33	37	0	31	0	36	37	0	35	52	40	38	50	45	30	44	0	36	0	36	16	29	28	41	373	CP JY S
-++	(+)	62	60	65	42	0	0	64	62	0	54	0	54	58	0	80	61	50	57	42	53	60	56	0	57	0	65	63	63	54	55	497	
-++	(-)	33	46	25	46	0	0	45	45	0	31	0	40	25	0	20	38	43	42	50	54	57	44	0	36	0	26	36	36	28	47	493	
-++	(+)	36	50	42	46	0	0	43	25	0	68	0	57	23	0	37	45	36	51	51	46	45	46	0	38	0	73	25	61	69	48	502	C
-++	(-)	56	47	48	61	0	0	53	70	0	48	0	38	59	0	50	42	47	50	52	48	53	38	0	57	0	51	52	45	44	41	394	TB
-++	(+)	42	61	47	35	0	0	54	44	0	63	0	61	36	0	40	48	50	42	46	37	45	51	0	68	0	46	50	54	54	45	519	PL
-++	(-)	28	36	43	61	0	0	55	52	0	40	0	20	50	0	55	33	41	38	37	30	47	46	0	30	0	44	50	37	44	39	344	
-++	(+)	58	48	38	45	0	0	48	65	0	55	0	73	66	0	53	58	38	37	60	62	52	52	0	68	0	44	50	57	44	56	485	
-++	(-)	10	51	41	36	0	0	48	32	0	44	0	36	28	0	40	33	29	30	66	46	38	45	0	30	0	44	53	48	57	41	255	LB LH
-++	(+)	60	60	48	61	0	0	55	65	0	55	0	61	66	0	61	58	69	37	63	46	47	53	0	68	0	44	16	37	44	28	336	BO C GC SU W
-++	(-)	42	46	48	45	0	0	42	42	0	40	0	26	44	0	32	39	64	36	46	50	44	46	0	43	0	44	52	53	48	55	502	
-+-	(+)	57	51	53	36	0	0	33	39	0	57	0	34	57	0	55	61	17	41	52	40	53	41	0	49	0	52	46	28	37	46	549	LB
-+-	(-)	37	36	46	38	0	0	33	37	0	40	0	56	58	0	37	58	37	36	46	53	46	46	0	50	0	64	57	52	49	50	449	
-+-	(+)	66	50	45	54	0	0	64	62	0	58	0	60	25	0	57	45	37	42	46	40	57	38	0	57	0	55	52	45	45	45	504	
-+-	(-)	36	47	42	46	0	0	55	57	0	48	0	40	23	0	37	42	52	48	45	53	45	44	0	44	0	51	45	54	54	49	478	SM
-+-	(+)	56	53	47	61	0	0	43	52	0	55	0	38	59	0	50	48	42	47	52	48	46	52	0	48	0	46	50	51	45	41	519	SM
-+-	(-)	28	29	35	38	0	0	43	44	0	36	0	61	36	0	40	41	33	41	45	37	47	45	0	68	0	35	37	39	54	53	383	
-+-	(+)	57	36	43	61	0	0	54	52	0	55	0	51	50	0	53	38	41	50	60	62	52	46	0	30	0	61	52	52	44	45	490	JY SM
-+-	(-)	33	48	38	48	0	0	42	45	0	40	0	46	54	0	53	57	38	37	30	43	45	47	0	68	0	48	48	57	48	50	493	
-+-	(+)	58	43	38	54	0	0	48	65	0	55	0	61	28	0	50	50	29	62	37	48	50	44	0	43	0	43	83	57	44	42	345	LB PB
-+-	(-)	60	48	61	45	0	0	55	47	0	57	0	73	44	0	40	50	69	69	66	43	36	49	0	49	0	35	30	48	50	54	345	JY OJ TB
+--	(+)	42	46	23	36	0	0	42	52	0	44	0	26	38	0	32	47	64	36	66	36	44	50	0	50	0	64	52	37	42	44	437	CC NY
+--	(-)	57	53	64	40	0	0	52	52	0	58	0	34	57	0	55	50	17	41	63	46	46	53	0	57	0	52	16	57	47	49	409	
+--	(+)	33	51	46	38	0	0	45	45	0	40	0	56	44	0	40	47	37	42	46	40	53	46	0	27	0	21	42	28	49	38	456	
+-+	(+)	66	62	66	61	0	0	52	62	0	58	0	63	57	0	61	53	54	41	52	58	46	41	0	69	0	75	52	45	45	56	265	SM SU
+-+	(-)	33	53	61	50	0	0	50	52	0	40	0	25	36	0	44	58	37	50	46	58	50	52	0	45	0	30	45	52	52	56	387	BO SM SU
+-+	(+)	18	63	46	47	0	0	45	41	0	37	0	68	31	0	57	33	42	41	52	39	46	50	0	47	0	67	45	40	45	51	494	BO JY PB SU
+-+	(-)	38	32	27	50	0	0	42	46	0	37	0	33	66	0	42	40	41	44	42	34	35	41	0	44	0	48	38	35	55	42	395	LB
+-+	(-)	55	57	68	50	0	0	57	50	0	60	0	61	33	0	50	45	60	43	57	65	60	54	0	50	0	48	55	56	44	54	509	C

Figure 8.3: Continued

Code		BO	BP	C	CC	CD	CL	CO	CP	FC	GC	HO	JY	LB	LC	LH	NY	O	OJ	PB	PL	S	SF	SV	SM	SP	SU	TB	TR	W	T%	T#	Notes
+ + - + -	(+ -)	25	36	43	34	0	0	51	33	0	35	0	0	36	0	50	56	44	54	34	46	44	32	0	34	0	38	25	26	46	40	364	
+ + - + -	(- -)	75	60	50	63	0	0	46	62	0	63	0	60	59	0	50	43	51	40	57	46	55	64	0	65	0	58	58	65	52	56	512	BO
+ + - + +	(+ -)	50	42	30	56	0	0	46	34	0	39	0	60	44	0	27	28	45	55	44	52	57	57	0	44	0	41	40	40	34	41	292	
+ + - + -	(- -)	50	52	66	43	0	0	48	60	0	50	0	50	38	0	54	68	40	55	55	52	53	57	0	52	0	54	47	48	64	54	388	C NY
+ + - - +	(+ -)	50	52	57	31	0	0	43	54	0	50	0	51	50	0	66	37	29	40	68	54	46	46	0	50	0	53	32	47	32	46	393	LH PB
+ + - - -	(- -)	50	42	48	65	0	0	46	45	0	46	0	37	45	0	33	48	52	45	31	39	48	53	0	47	0	46	37	43	60	49	414	
+ + - - -	(+ -)	40	38	45	47	0	0	57	36	0	30	0	37	41	0	37	44	52	40	50	58	51	41	0	50	0	52	56	30	37	41	283	
+ + + + -	(- -)	40	57	42	65	0	0	42	58	0	70	0	62	47	0	50	47	52	52	46	58	50	50	0	43	0	38	56	55	61	52	354	GC
+ + + + -	(+ -)	5	34	53	55	0	0	42	35	0	40	0	55	41	0	47	25	46	53	70	54	54	43	0	45	0	24	36	50	43	46	288	PB
+ + + + +	(- -)	88	61	42	44	0	0	46	41	0	70	0	45	58	0	50	52	67	53	30	42	43	43	0	54	0	72	50	49	52	50	317	BO O SU
+ + + + +	(+ -)	33	12	42	34	0	0	22	25	0	7	0	46	50	0	25	25	41	41	58	31	48	46	0	43	0	41	33	29	33	36	163	
- - - + -	(- -)	66	81	57	60	0	0	70	75	0	92	0	53	52	0	25	48	53	54	50	57	60	62	0	50	0	58	62	67	59	59	265	BO BP CO CP GC NY TR
- - - + -	(+ -)	50	61	30	48	0	0	81	73	0	56	0	47	52	0	0	50	53	54	56	57	60	62	0	43	0	30	54	59	60	51	241	CO CP
- - - + +	(- -)	50	40	63	51	0	0	18	26	0	43	0	52	38	0	66	45	38	36	43	42	35	37	0	50	0	63	36	31	36	44	209	LH
- - - + -	(+ -)	31	40	48	62	0	0	38	38	0	39	0	55	27	0	33	38	36	60	64	61	35	47	0	36	0	36	66	45	57	43	241	TB
- - - - +	(- -)	56	54	48	37	0	0	43	57	0	60	0	56	63	0	65	25	55	61	35	61	67	36	0	60	0	54	22	47	37	50	278	LH S
- - - - -	(+ -)	58	55	40	60	0	0	57	52	0	53	0	33	52	0	75	62	40	50	44	43	54	61	0	41	0	39	40	42	31	46	265	LH
- - - - -	(- -)	62	47	44	34	0	0	31	31	0	17	0	52	30	0	0	40	35	26	25	27	33	42	0	33	0	33	50	25	44	34	276	
- + - + -	(+ -)	37	52	44	65	0	0	68	68	0	78	0	47	69	0	103	50	54	54	75	69	52	57	0	57	0	66	40	67	55	61	168	CO CP GC LB LH PB
- + - + -	(- -)	42	52	46	66	0	0	68	68	0	56	0	53	33	0	50	50	50	38	43	51	52	39	0	58	0	48	27	71	52	51	282	CC TR
- + - + -	(+ -)	50	45	53	26	0	0	39	64	0	36	0	43	58	0	65	57	45	40	56	48	50	50	0	41	0	51	54	21	45	45	249	LH
- + - + +	(- -)	85	25	55	45	0	0	48	56	0	40	0	55	53	0	14	45	62	33	40	62	48	37	0	51	0	62	53	51	62	49	263	BO
- + - + -	(+ -)	14	70	38	54	0	0	50	72	0	58	0	52	66	0	85	55	66	35	60	54	35	62	0	42	0	37	23	41	37	47	249	BP LH OJ
- + - - +	(- -)	16	50	44	51	0	0	43	27	0	41	0	41	27	0	37	31	47	50	42	64	33	41	0	43	0	45	22	38	48	48	274	CP LB
- + - - -	(+ -)	66	44	44	51	0	0	50	72	0	92	0	37	36	0	50	68	47	42	57	35	60	58	0	56	0	51	55	54	51	48	272	BO NY
- + - - -	(- -)	42	36	52	52	0	0	38	35	0	46	0	52	46	0	0	0	25	80	25	39	55	39	0	57	0	50	55	42	40	40	149	
- + + + -	(+ -)	42	42	57	47	0	0	57	58	0	92	0	68	42	0	50	35	50	50	75	59	47	50	0	38	0	50	44	47	57	55	202	GC JY OJ PB
- + + + -	(- -)	42	35	33	33	0	0	68	70	0	46	0	44	30	0	50	39	35	50	38	48	47	50	0	51	0	48	54	38	56	47	253	CO CP
- + + + +	(+ -)	88	52	57	66	0	0	50	66	0	51	0	36	69	0	25	65	56	46	61	51	40	44	0	48	0	51	45	54	40	49	263	BO CC LB
- + + + +	(- -)	50	45	57	50	0	0	51	54	0	37	0	62	22	0	33	65	56	70	53	51	40	35	0	35	0	33	37	47	48	45	241	OJ
- + + + +	(+ -)	25	42	42	50	0	0	42	36	0	62	0	63	66	0	33	35	25	17	40	45	59	64	0	64	0	66	50	45	51	49	261	LB SU
- + + - +	(- -)	37	37	36	47	0	0	36	52	0	38	0	37	36	0	50	35	55	42	46	38	37	40	0	40	0	57	50	30	32	42	216	BO
- + + - -	(+ -)	16	44	36	21	0	0	59	43	0	59	0	36	55	0	40	59	37	42	53	51	39	35	0	50	0	42	50	56	67	54	278	TR W
- + + - -	(- -)	0	55	63	78	0	0	57	24	0	46	0	62	38	0	25	37	46	50	71	45	18	34	0	45	0	28	75	43	46	40	207	PB TB
- + + - -	(+ -)	75	63	33	33	0	0	69	61	0	53	0	53	53	0	50	48	75	60	28	54	54	50	0	50	0	71	25	56	45	55	283	BO CC CP S SU
- - + + -	(- -)	37	52	15	62	0	0	39	38	0	46	0	46	46	0	57	31	47	35	33	53	45	50	0	44	0	34	58	48	54	49	255	
- - + + -	(+ -)	50	47	73	62	0	0	39	38	0	40	0	52	46	0	28	47	31	55	33	53	45	50	0	31	0	39	100	41	42	49	269	C
- - + + +	(- -)	25	27	41	15	0	0	32	65	0	41	0	43	57	0	50	35	55	44	54	54	71	46	0	62	0	53	25	15	51	53	221	TB
- - + + -	(+ -)	75	66	63	78	0	0	67	34	0	58	0	43	42	0	52	47	38	50	45	54	41	50	0	62	0	53	58	53	55	53	276	BO BP CC CO
- - + - +	(- -)	75	37	63	36	0	0	24	25	0	39	0	37	46	0	66	38	44	50	48	48	29	42	0	22	0	35	25	15	51	37	166	BO LH
- - + - -	(+ -)	25	56	31	63	0	0	75	75	0	57	0	66	46	0	33	52	52	52	57	52	60	57	0	72	0	60	75	73	46	58	258	CO CP SM TB TR
- - + - -	(- -)	50	16	63	44	0	0	45	52	0	44	0	20	66	0	54	44	44	50	28	48	30	47	0	35	0	31	66	39	30	41	127	LB TB
- - + - -	(+ -)	42	83	44	50	0	0	55	42	0	55	0	80	16	0	45	55	55	50	71	52	60	41	0	64	0	68	33	56	70	55	172	CP JY LH PB SU
+ - - + -	(- -)	50	28	47	50	0	0	55	77	0	58	0	5	0	0	0	52	52	41	33	47	33	45	0	40	0	58	60	30	35	44	242	CP
+ - - + -	(+ -)	50	64	47	50	0	0	47	22	0	37	0	59	88	0	60	52	52	58	66	52	54	28	0	56	0	29	40	65	61	52	288	LB PB
+ - - + +	(- -)	50	40	47	61	0	0	48	57	0	37	0	40	45	0	40	25	52	60	45	51	42	54	0	55	0	50	33	19	45	43	234	
+ - - + -	(+ -)	50	28	47	38	0	0	51	57	0	62	0	48	50	0	28	75	40	41	55	46	57	62	0	37	0	35	25	66	54	53	282	O TR
+ - - - +	(- -)	33	65	61	46	0	0	33	33	0	45	0	51	50	0	57	62	55	50	33	45	50	50	0	32	0	64	36	36	45	45	231	
+ - - - -	(+ -)	66	30	38	53	0	0	55	53	0	49	0	53	50	0	62	55	40	50	66	45	34	47	0	68	0	64	50	51	54	51	260	BO PB SM
+ - - - -	(- -)	50	41	29	55	0	0	34	54	0	40	0	17	37	0	20	40	60	50	37	36	51	47	0	42	0	27	50	46	39	41	203	
+ - + + -	(+ -)	50	54	70	45	0	0	72	54	0	56	0	20	25	0	40	62	40	62	63	44	56	53	0	53	0	72	50	42	56	53	263	C JY SU
+ - + + -	(- -)	0	48	40	40	0	0	43	82	0	47	0	20	0	0	83	36	26	50	35	44	55	51	0	50	0	20	50	41	47	43	231	CP LH
+ - + + +	(+ -)	50	48	46	70	0	0	53	13	0	52	0	79	85	0	16	60	53	50	57	53	41	48	0	46	0	75	50	51	47	52	277	CC JY LB SU

Figure 8.3: Continued

Signs	+/-	BO	BP	C	CC	CD	CL	CO	CP	FC	GC	HO	JY	LB	LC	LH	NY	O	OJ	PB	PL	S	SF	SV	SM	SP	SU	TB	TR	W	T%	T#	------- 65% -------
-+-+-+	(+)	0	38	50	14	0	0	50	40	0	45	0	90	40	0	33	23	38	60	30	53	54	33	0	57	0	40	66	29	56	42	177	JY TB
-+-+-+	(-)	100	61	50	85	0	0	45	55	0	52	0	10	40	0	60	76	53	20	69	46	45	66	0	42	0	59	33	64	33	54	229	BO CC NY PB SF
-+-+-+	(+)	33	52	40	38	0	0	50	41	0	62	0	24	63	0	66	45	57	50	54	65	53	39	0	50	0	51	66	34	43	48	240	LH TB
-+-+-+	(-)	66	41	60	53	0	0	50	52	0	32	0	65	36	0	33	36	41	41	36	39	33	66	0	50	0	44	33	65	33	47	236	TB
-+-+++	(+)	100	44	47	22	0	0	30	33	0	41	0	20	40	0	40	45	46	30	54	60	29	29	0	33	0	33	46	18	57	38	144	BO
-+-+++	(-)	0	55	47	77	0	0	70	66	0	58	0	80	50	0	60	54	38	69	45	60	66	70	0	66	0	60	46	66	39	58	215	CC CO CP JY OJ S
-+-++-	(-)	20	55	63	65	0	0	51	59	0	46	0	11	50	0	60	51	51	53	47	45	60	61	0	37	0	17	37	34	47	45	230	
-+-++-	(-)	70	44	36	36	0	0	42	31	0	50	0	77	50	0	40	44	46	50	90	50	46	48	0	54	0	79	44	60	39	49	248	BO JY PB SU
-+--+-	(-)	42	35	10	31	0	0	44	45	0	41	0	31	66	0	58	50	40	46	40	32	33	36	0	41	0	43	37	50	52	41	206	LB
-+--+-	(+)	57	64	90	68	0	0	63	45	0	55	0	53	63	0	41	46	53	46	67	45	61	64	0	54	0	56	62	39	41	55	276	C CC PL
-+--++	(+)	16	38	28	80	0	0	48	39	0	36	0	40	35	0	28	52	42	63	36	56	40	32	0	20	0	48	0	28	44	39	207	
-+--++	(+)	83	61	64	65	0	0	51	57	0	61	0	50	60	0	71	27	57	36	54	43	60	60	0	80	0	48	50	68	55	57	299	BO LH SM TR
-+--++	(+)	50	50	76	50	0	0	39	38	0	30	0	38	60	0	66	53	27	31	80	47	39	51	0	50	0	39	33	31	33	39	157	C NY
-+-++-	(+)	40	40	23	50	0	0	50	71	0	64	0	41	60	0	42	25	53	44	54	42	53	38	0	44	0	22	41	30	48	48	213	LH PB
-+-++-	(-)	33	45	52	52	0	0	61	63	0	35	0	33	55	0	25	68	22	46	53	61	42	61	0	52	0	53	28	41	33	46	231	LH PB
-+-+-+	(+)	66	54	38	47	0	0	38	47	0	64	0	50	50	0	50	25	55	30	46	57	38	42	0	44	0	38	71	29	63	48	159	NY
-+-+-+	(+)	10	46	61	50	0	0	50	71	0	37	0	41	33	0	42	81	43	57	40	45	50	43	0	50	0	23	20	62	43	42	165	BO JY TB
-+-+-+	(+)	90	46	33	50	0	0	50	28	0	62	0	58	55	0	40	57	46	50	80	42	50	50	0	44	0	76	80	37	53	49	163	CP PB
-+-+-+	(-)	40	16	50	28	0	0	16	26	0	9	0	50	50	100	50	18	43	43	46	27	50	37	0	44	0	66	12	37	46	34	167	BO LB LH SU TB
-+-+-+	(+)	60	83	50	64	0	0	66	73	0	90	0	37	50	0	25	43	57	50	72	50	72	50	0	55	0	33	46	87	50	61	88	SU
-+-+-+	(-)	47	71	46	34	0	0	66	50	0	69	0	46	54	0	66	42	57	50	47	46	60	60	0	58	0	56	27	58	53	54	158	BP CO CP GC NY PL TR
-+-+-+	(+)	47	23	50	65	0	0	33	50	0	27	0	53	54	0	33	57	45	50	52	50	40	39	0	41	0	40	63	30	39	42	298	BP CO GC LH
-+--++	(-)	18	43	27	36	0	0	59	37	0	46	0	40	59	0	40	38	35	45	31	43	48	60	0	34	0	39	30	47	48	39	233	
-+--++	(-)	72	50	54	59	0	0	37	44	0	48	0	61	28	0	40	55	57	45	68	43	46	55	0	60	0	58	53	52	48	51	215	LB
-+--+-	(+)	33	48	31	53	0	0	42	46	0	49	0	41	50	0	66	39	36	36	46	64	48	29	0	44	0	50	50	50	54	48	261	BO PB
-+--+-	(+)	66	51	63	46	0	0	57	53	0	49	0	58	66	0	33	42	50	48	53	44	63	31	0	66	0	54	33	44	64	48	243	LH SM TB
-+--+-	(+)	25	30	50	42	0	0	58	29	0	20	0	53	23	0	0	40	44	38	50	55	34	44	0	20	0	37	66	48	35	43	247	BO SF
-+--++	(+)	75	69	50	53	0	0	41	64	0	73	0	46	61	100	50	55	55	61	63	44	65	65	0	47	0	75	55	51	46	58	176	
-+--++	(+)	50	38	40	40	0	0	42	48	0	62	0	50	50	0	52	52	38	38	50	54	34	30	0	42	0	55	44	41	58	43	262	BO BP GC LH SU
-+-++-	(+)	50	43	55	53	0	0	53	58	0	42	0	46	50	0	37	47	50	22	47	54	64	56	0	41	0	52	45	44	50	51	230	
-+-++-	(-)	25	55	54	20	0	0	46	38	0	57	0	42	57	0	50	40	50	50	63	53	48	59	0	58	0	52	50	29	58	44	267	
-+-++-	(-)	42	50	37	40	0	0	36	16	0	56	0	59	42	0	57	37	50	15	33	51	52	56	0	64	0	57	28	51	36	45	251	CC OJ TR
-+-++-	(+)	57	44	62	60	0	0	56	80	0	40	0	36	75	0	42	14	45	45	66	43	48	39	0	35	0	38	71	46	61	51	218	
-+-++-	(+)	75	33	40	46	0	0	37	45	0	30	0	66	10	0	33	71	28	70	30	51	48	56	0	13	0	42	12	43	43	39	222	
-+-+-+	(-)	25	55	60	55	0	0	58	54	0	69	0	33	90	0	66	71	28	61	65	40	56	60	0	86	0	57	50	53	53	57	250	CP LB OJ PB TB
-+-+-+	(-)	33	44	46	46	0	0	50	42	0	50	0	50	50	0	66	63	52	54	44	44	65	44	0	44	0	45	33	24	44	48	150	CP JY
-+-+-+	(+)	66	54	46	53	0	0	50	57	0	50	0	27	50	0	33	63	50	45	35	63	48	31	0	55	0	54	33	44	64	48	220	GC LB LH NY OJ SM
-+-+-+	(-)	0	54	38	66	0	0	50	42	0	34	0	27	66	0	33	42	50	54	44	44	63	44	0	66	0	35	33	44	64	48	266	
-+-+-+	(+)	100	47	61	27	0	0	40	40	0	61	0	66	66	0	66	47	50	33	55	51	30	55	0	29	0	55	66	48	35	48	265	BO LH TR
-+-+-+	(-)	0	28	28	27	0	0	47	40	0	59	0	75	33	0	90	28	50	54	50	44	60	30	0	25	0	37	21	35	45	43	237	CC LB OJ SM
-+--+-	(+)	100	47	57	72	0	0	40	55	0	38	0	6	12	0	9	44	55	50	50	69	60	38	0	75	0	62	100	42	69	53	238	BO JY LH TB
-+--+-	(+)	50	40	41	36	0	0	47	26	0	36	0	100	71	0	40	55	44	44	12	52	25	56	0	37	0	46	40	33	48	41	189	BO LB LH
-+--++	(+)	44	28	25	46	0	0	34	41	0	64	0	82	28	0	50	76	54	61	30	25	44	45	0	62	0	53	40	62	55	53	233	BO CC JY PL SM TB
-+--++	(+)	55	71	67	53	0	0	54	54	0	26	0	56	37	0	75	48	36	33	66	29	67	45	0	45	0	54	62	27	55	49	143	CC LB
-+--++	(-)	60	60	67	54	0	0	34	50	0	33	0	44	62	60	12	54	36	66	25	56	29	31	0	54	0	45	25	62	42	46	191	CP JY NY PB
-+--++	(+)	60	45	41	54	0	0	34	40	0	33	0	63	18	0	60	47	38	54	50	36	13	31	0	41	0	50	57	45	45	43	225	LH PB PL S
-+--++	(+)	40	45	36	36	0	0	60	53	0	64	0	66	63	0	40	47	44	38	41	68	56	44	0	52	0	45	28	40	41	41	213	BP C OJ
-+--+-	(+)	35	30	41	36	0	0	40	56	0	47	0	53	50	0	50	61	44	54	41	43	68	56	0	52	0	45	28	40	41	55	161	S
-+--+-	(+)	0	35	30	75	0	0	56	50	0	64	0	57	72	50	50	61	44	54	86	35	68	56	0	56	0	25	35	28	41	41	226	JY PL S
-+--+-	(-)	100	40	37	18	0	0	52	43	0	50	0	66	25	100	30	63	30	50	30	43	37	44	0	43	0	66	54	60	67	41	162	BO PB
-+--+-	(+)	33	40	36	40	0	0	47	40	0	26	0	75	66	0	100	71	63	50	66	37	46	57	0	25	0	14	66	28	25	43	211	BO LB SU W
-+--+-	(-)	66	60	63	50	0	0	52	50	0	73	0	25	33	0	0	28	27	50	33	58	53	46	0	75	0	85	11	71	70	53	142	BO GC SM SU TR W

Figure 8.3: Continued

Pattern	±	BO	BP	C	CC	CD	CL	CO	CP	FC	GC	HO	JY	LB	LC	LH	NY	O	OJ	PB	PL	S	SF	SV	SM	SP	SU	TB	TR	W	T%	T#	Notes
+ + − − + −	(+)	31	58	44	40	0	0	0	60	46	0	31	0	36	41	0	10	48	43	42	66	44	44	0	40	0	58	40	71	51	49	244	LH PB TR
+ + − − + −	(−)	56	41	52	54	0	0	39	53	0	65	0	59	58	0	75	0	43	50	33	55	51	55	0	54	0	38	50	28	46	47	235	
+ + − − − +	(−)	50	21	52	60	0	0	37	47	0	32	0	37	66	0	33	50	50	53	66	50	44	50	0	28	0	50	54	58	42	44	191	LB LH PB
+ + − − − −	(−)	50	69	43	34	0	0	59	52	0	67	0	62	33	0	54	40	40	38	33	44	32	66	0	66	0	45	34	57	58	50	215	BP GC SM
+ + − − + +	(+)	60	57	55	30	0	0	40	53	0	64	0	41	42	0	44	45	35	46	53	50	44	17	0	36	0	36	20	40	45	45	228	
+ + − − + +	(+)	20	42	38	69	0	0	60	43	0	24	0	54	42	0	55	54	64	53	45	55	55	55	0	69	0	56	70	42	35	48	245	CC SM TB
+ + − + − −	(+)	28	58	62	53	0	0	54	46	0	39	0	23	42	0	20	23	20	44	10	60	39	42	0	18	0	64	42	24	38	41	163	PB
+ + − + − −	(−)	57	41	37	46	0	0	45	53	0	60	0	76	42	0	71	61	80	33	10	60	47	57	0	81	0	32	42	60	58	54	214	JY O SM
+ + − + − −	(−)	16	55	43	45	0	0	52	50	0	40	0	52	46	0	42	42	22	26	45	34	43	0	37	0	71	42	59	48	46	238	NY SU
+ + − + − −	(−)	66	44	50	50	0	0	44	58	0	58	0	42	53	0	80	50	46	73	60	34	65	53	0	51	0	28	57	29	58	49	253	BO LH OJ PB
+ + − + − +	(+)	100	63	57	46	0	0	39	35	0	25	0	58	37	0	60	44	25	33	44	44	28	31	0	53	0	21	100	33	50	42	155	BO OJ TB
+ + − + − +	(+)	0	36	42	46	0	0	57	52	0	74	0	41	57	0	40	55	75	16	55	52	71	62	0	46	0	78	37	40	50	40	196	GC O S SU
+ + − + + −	(+)	25	20	16	38	0	0	50	39	0	37	0	53	57	0	55	25	36	40	16	52	52	60	0	27	0	45	62	40	53	53	156	
+ + − + + +	(+)	50	70	62	61	0	0	50	39	0	53	0	38	42	0	83	63	41	37	53	56	69	34	0	66	0	12	28	33	29	36	206	BP LH S SM
+ + − + + +	(+)	25	25	9	47	0	0	57	33	0	31	0	50	25	0	33	22	45	54	35	47	56	53	0	20	0	87	71	47	70	56	107	
+ + + − − −	(−)	75	50	47	9	0	0	42	58	0	68	0	50	62	0	50	50	36	40	41	57	31	40	0	73	0	43	41	53	46	42	164	BO C GC NY SM SU
+ + + − − −	(+)	18	68	14	31	0	0	48	10	0	48	0	27	33	0	50	50	36	18	40	36	47	45	0	57	0	56	37	30	53	42	174	BP
+ + + − − +	(−)	36	33	78	68	0	0	51	75	0	51	0	72	66	0	25	54	60	72	60	58	68	52	0	45	0	33	50	27	60	53	222	BO C CC CP JY LB S
+ + + − + −	(−)	54	55	57	22	0	0	37	45	0	67	0	33	27	0	75	45	30	54	42	50	58	45	0	45	0	12	62	66	39	40	168	CC LB
+ + + − + −	(+)	50	33	66	38	0	0	62	23	0	34	0	26	37	0	33	23	45	25	35	47	61	72	0	61	0	87	33	27	48	55	210	GC LH OJ TR
+ + + − + +	(−)	50	58	26	61	0	0	43	71	0	65	0	73	28	0	50	50	54	62	50	39	47	27	0	38	0	45	66	43	21	39	197	CP JY SF SU
+ + + − + +	(+)	50	37	35	60	0	0	15	84	0	46	0	44	57	0	33	66	66	33	50	57	30	21	0	37	0	54	33	56	78	58	110	TB
+ + + + − −	(+)	53	50	72	40	0	0	52	58	0	72	0	55	57	0	66	76	28	55	57	62	37	35	0	56	0	44	36	32	34	46	163	CP LH NY O SF W
+ + + + − −	(+)	46	50	27	84	0	0	47	41	0	22	0	44	20	0	25	60	28	37	42	42	64	57	0	53	0	55	45	52	65	50	148	C GC
+ + + + − +	(−)	37	33	42	50	0	0	51	70	0	26	0	45	57	0	30	22	40	50	44	35	40	50	0	54	0	50	37	26	41	38	160	CC LH O
+ + + + − +	(−)	25	50	45	68	0	0	66	70	0	73	0	54	60	0	50	37	57	50	55	52	75	52	0	42	0	33	50	61	44	48	111	BO
+ + + + + −	(+)	62	45	31	0	0	0	52	50	0	50	0	41	44	0	100	27	42	50	42	33	25	29	0	61	0	16	100	30	44	50	163	CP GC NY
+ + + + + −	(+)	44	66	37	61	0	0	46	53	0	50	0	32	57	0	0	40	42	62	50	61	42	50	0	55	0	57	16	42	66	46	118	JY LH
+ + + + + −	(+)	55	25	58	44	0	0	41	46	0	42	0	30	42	0	100	40	28	40	90	33	25	44	0	33	0	33	66	30	39	32	136	BO BP O
+ + + + + +	(−)	83	76	62	38	0	0	33	53	0	37	0	69	33	0	0	46	42	37	33	60	25	26	0	58	0	37	16	42	66	62	79	
− − − − − −	(+)	66	50	50	62	0	0	66	80	0	50	0	71	55	0	75	60	50	40	50	54	30	57	0	42	0	80	25	61	50	40	66	LH TR
− − − − − −	(+)	62	75	34	47	0	0	72	50	0	30	0	50	75	0	25	44	30	25	42	35	57	35	0	33	0	36	75	56	77	54	88	BO CO CP GC JY SU
− − − − − −	(+)	37	25	50	68	0	0	27	9	0	22	0	53	25	0	50	41	40	75	42	47	64	50	0	38	0	52	0	0	63	44	94	BP CO LB TR
− − − − − −	(+)	25	50	45	31	0	0	43	90	0	26	0	56	30	0	30	77	57	50	55	52	25	50	0	50	0	55	75	16	55	48	105	GC NY OJ TB
− − − − − −	(−)	62	66	68	50	0	0	66	75	0	72	0	50	57	0	100	36	42	62	44	47	75	52	0	57	0	66	66	30	44	47	113	CC CO TB
− − − − − −	(−)	44	41	31	61	0	0	37	50	0	46	0	41	44	0	0	27	42	16	90	52	29	50	0	42	0	33	16	61	44	48	116	CP S
− − − − − −	(+)	66	55	50	50	0	0	58	46	0	66	0	55	57	0	66	40	50	66	66	50	33	50	0	50	0	57	100	50	66	50	139	BP CP LH SU TB
− − − − − −	(+)	16	63	30	50	0	0	50	46	0	68	0	30	44	0	60	36	42	57	42	27	42	73	0	42	0	20	0	42	66	46	130	W
− − − − − −	(+)	33	44	37	46	0	0	50	61	0	53	0	50	66	0	36	42	42	66	50	60	27	52	0	25	0	43	25	25	50	46	151	BP CC GC JY LB LH
− − − − − −	(−)	66	55	12	25	0	0	55	50	0	0	0	50	50	0	33	33	40	60	25	42	42	28	0	42	0	62	60	60	42	39	67	
− − − − − −	(+)	0	37	75	75	0	0	33	50	0	100	0	72	50	0	44	30	60	100	75	66	71	42	0	42	0	37	40	40	57	55	94	C CC GC JY OJ PB SF
− − − − − −	(+)	0	27	58	33	0	0	72	58	0	56	0	53	50	0	100	33	66	33	66	66	31	55	0	20	0	47	83	40	45	46	114	CO CP LH PB PL TB
− − − − − −	(+)	85	63	53	75	0	0	27	25	0	43	0	46	28	0	0	41	40	66	33	33	62	50	0	80	0	52	16	77	50	48	121	BO CC OJ SM TR
− − − − − −	(+)	50	41	53	50	0	0	43	9	0	28	0	12	57	0	0	77	36	22	57	66	37	18	0	28	0	31	66	50	52	41	116	NY OJ PL
− − − − − −	(+)	16	49	46	50	0	0	55	55	0	72	0	87	75	0	50	22	50	36	42	50	31	81	0	71	0	68	66	40	47	53	151	GC JY LB SF SM SU TB
− − − − − −	(−)	100	41	71	50	0	0	35	90	0	35	0	25	50	0	50	63	50	50	62	33	61	55	0	35	0	66	31	31	42	45	113	BO C CP TB
− − − − − −	(−)	0	58	28	41	0	0	57	9	0	61	0	75	50	0	33	63	50	37	44	60	44	44	0	64	0	40	33	68	57	52	131	JY TR

------ 65% ------

Figure 8.3: Continued

±	BO	BP	C	CC	CD	CL	CO	CP	FC	GC	HQ	JY	LB	LC	LH	NY	O	OJ	PB	PL	S	SF	SV	SM	SP	SU	TB	TR	W	T%	T#	65%
(+)	0	33	30	10	0	0	46	21	0	59	0	54	42	0	0	44	40	50	50	47	12	9	0	29	0	29	85	55	56	39	104	TB BP C CC CP LH
(−)	100	66	70	90	0	0	46	71	0	40	0	45	57	0	100	44	60	50	50	52	81	81	0	64	0	70	14	45	39	57	152	BO BP CP LH OJ
(+)	50	75	0	26	0	0	57	88	0	65	0	57	40	0	75	35	50	50	36	36	50	45	0	38	0	50	20	56	50	48	132	BP CP CC O TB
(−)	50	25	100	73	0	0	42	11	0	34	0	42	40	0	0	40	75	33	54	64	50	55	0	53	0	50	80	43	50	49	134	C CC O TB
(−)	100	11	44	15	0	0	50	70	0	34	0	44	58	0	100	57	28	42	62	40	70	50	0	20	0	50	100	12	60	44	122	CP LH S TB
(+)	100	77	44	76	0	0	50	29	0	65	0	44	41	0	0	52	37	57	66	37	56	35	0	37	0	50	75	39	50	50	139	BO BP CC SM TR
(+)	66	16	63	33	0	0	20	10	0	38	0	46	33	0	0	66	22	37	33	62	50	50	0	37	0	28	25	11	63	39	79	BO NY PB
(+)	33	66	27	66	0	0	80	90	0	61	0	53	33	0	0	35	66	62	33	62	30	64	0	62	0	71	75	77	36	57	116	BP CC CO CP O SU
(+)	66	57	28	40	0	0	40	83	0	0	0	33	75	0	0	33	66	57	66	37	28	44	0	25	0	14	60	50	20	42	63	BP CP LB OJ
(−)	33	42	71	60	0	0	60	16	0	100	0	66	0	0	0	44	0	0	50	36	57	33	0	75	0	85	40	37	80	54	81	C GC JY O SM SU
(+)	75	18	43	62	0	0	66	77	0	85	0	46	11	0	100	50	28	33	36	50	44	40	0	35	0	65	25	40	40	47	126	BO CO CP GC LH
(+)	25	81	56	37	0	0	22	0	0	14	0	53	77	0	50	53	66	25	63	41	57	60	0	60	0	60	76	53	53	49	131	BP LB O OJ TR
(−)	25	81	50	50	0	0	57	63	0	47	0	41	75	0	50	55	53	33	28	41	35	29	0	60	0	57	50	33	42	46	118	LB
(+)	0	55	40	50	0	0	42	31	0	52	0	58	25	0	50	44	0	33	0	58	64	64	0	33	0	42	33	58	57	50	127	O OJ PB
(+)	0	22	40	50	0	0	46	50	0	40	0	33	66	0	50	25	42	66	71	58	16	38	0	22	0	31	25	33	50	39	104	OJ
(−)	100	50	33	50	0	0	53	33	0	48	0	66	50	0	50	57	25	16	83	50	66	55	0	77	0	68	50	62	50	57	149	BO C JY O PB SM SU
(−)	50	80	58	25	0	0	44	58	0	46	0	16	50	0	50	30	75	33	12	41	66	40	0	20	0	54	33	40	41	39	96	CC TB
(−)	50	45	28	20	0	0	55	80	0	53	0	75	0	0	100	23	44	33	87	70	57	50	0	45	0	22	66	39	52	45	138	BP JY LH NY OJ PB SM
(−)	0	71	71	80	0	0	50	10	0	47	0	26	0	0	75	76	33	66	42	29	42	57	0	54	0	77	33	53	47	52	127	CP LH PL TB
(+)	0	50	27	22	0	0	30	33	0	69	0	88	80	0	20	23	25	33	26	41	62	57	0	44	0	58	66	25	70	48	145	C CC JY LB W OJ SU
(−)	0	50	72	77	0	0	70	66	0	26	0	11	50	0	80	66	71	14	50	38	61	50	0	61	0	41	33	75	30	50	105	GC JY OJ TB W
(−)	100	50	50	27	0	0	53	30	0	26	0	14	57	0	80	66	75	50	25	32	52	50	0	55	0	41	33	75	30	44	109	BO C CC CO CP LH
(+)	66	40	50	63	0	0	46	0	0	38	0	78	42	0	100	25	62	50	25	32	43	53	0	50	0	45	100	21	30	50	127	LH TB
(−)	66	40	60	63	0	0	36	37	0	43	0	25	40	0	50	16	57	25	50	43	33	25	0	27	0	53	0	78	70	50	143	BO JY TR W
(+)	100	50	37	0	0	0	63	25	0	43	0	75	40	0	50	83	28	75	50	33	33	66	0	72	0	25	44	22	70	38	80	BO W
(+)	100	50	50	100	0	0	66	26	0	56	0	16	66	0	50	16	57	75	50	35	66	66	0	27	0	11	55	61	30	58	120	CC JY NY OJ PL S
(−)	25	62	57	58	0	0	69	69	0	56	0	55	50	0	100	83	28	44	12	35	50	46	0	54	0	88	57	55	33	49	122	CO CP LB LH
(+)	75	37	42	41	0	0	30	23	0	50	0	33	0	0	0	50	60	33	87	58	42	46	0	37	0	66	66	42	52	46	133	BO JY PB SU
(+)	33	44	41	57	0	0	42	47	0	52	0	33	80	0	75	57	57	44	42	50	50	54	0	20	0	42	50	42	48	40	104	LB LH
(−)	66	55	100	66	0	0	57	52	0	24	0	66	50	0	40	14	60	66	25	73	62	28	0	61	0	60	100	23	37	56	144	BO C CC JY O PL
(+)	41	33	33	33	0	0	57	100	0	24	0	50	50	0	55	55	37	50	60	54	60	28	0	14	0	53	0	23	37	36	101	C
(+)	100	58	55	60	0	0	42	100	0	75	0	44	63	0	25	14	62	20	40	45	60	57	0	85	0	53	25	76	62	61	170	BO CP GC SM TR
(+)	100	40	14	66	0	0	66	26	0	4	0	14	62	0	20	16	40	36	60	45	30	46	0	40	0	45	25	25	35	35	79	BO CC CO O
(+)	100	60	85	33	0	0	33	68	0	91	0	55	25	0	40	27	33	60	63	40	69	53	0	40	0	54	50	75	23	60	133	C CP GC S TR
(−)	55	33	33	58	0	0	38	61	0	26	0	55	33	0	100	27	28	30	100	69	62	60	0	62	0	60	52	52	26	47	122	LH PB PL SU
(+)	44	66	58	58	0	0	61	38	0	68	0	33	0	0	50	45	57	30	100	69	37	40	0	20	0	40	50	50	41	64	120	BO C GC LB OJ TB
(−)	33	33	41	57	0	0	57	85	0	30	0	66	53	0	50	71	40	44	33	41	50	54	0	20	0	42	50	32	38	45	75	CP NY
(−)	66	66	50	42	0	0	57	14	0	30	0	62	40	0	63	14	60	33	58	58	41	36	0	27	0	30	50	46	47	50	83	BO BP GC JY PB
(+)	33	50	63	81	0	0	45	66	0	40	0	66	50	0	33	33	48	16	60	61	50	33	0	46	0	35	33	46	40	50	79	CP PB
(+)	100	28	45	58	0	0	60	57	0	53	0	44	63	0	66	66	57	60	83	41	66	56	0	46	0	65	33	53	41	54	89	BO BP LB LH TB W
(+)	100	50	25	57	0	0	56	53	0	52	0	44	45	0	66	36	50	20	64	58	60	30	0	46	0	80	64	45	58	49	140	BO LH TB W
(+)	33	57	75	42	0	0	45	46	0	44	0	55	40	0	33	50	50	36	63	40	60	70	0	27	0	33	20	35	55	49	138	C OJ SF
(−)	37	50	50	36	0	0	43	21	0	20	0	58	60	0	0	40	25	33	33	54	23	33	0	50	0	26	0	0	41	35	84	
(+)	100	62	50	63	0	0	56	73	0	75	0	41	45	0	100	75	33	66	50	29	45	58	0	50	0	36	73	100	58	62	146	BO CP GC LH O OJ
(−)	50	57	42	16	0	0	73	46	0	71	0	64	45	0	50	66	66	66	58	33	76	62	0	72	0	45	50	56	41	42	111	CC PL S
(−)	50	42	57	83	0	0	53	53	0	62	0	35	46	0	50	50	50	37	50	65	68	62	0	64	0	59	50	40	58	54	141	CC PL S
(+)	100	33	33	33	0	0	53	46	0	62	0	43	50	0	0	50	66	33	50	35	41	41	0	50	0	66	50	22	50	51	118	BO LH O S SU
(−)	60	60	45	58	0	0	46	53	0	37	0	50	50	0	0	50	33	33	50	35	58	31	0	50	0	33	50	77	42	47	109	CC TR

Figure 8.3: Continued

	BO	BP	C	CC	CD	CL	CO	CP	FC	GC	HO	JY	LB	LC	LH	NY	O	OJ	PB	PL	S	SF	SV	SM	SP	SU	TB	TR	W	T%	T#	------- 65% -------
-+---++	(+)	50	53	33	33	0	0	36	14	0	45	0	58	50	0	5C	27	50	10	25	60	64	36	0	64	0	61	66	42	43	44	116	TB
-+---++	(-)	38	38	66	66	0	0	63	78	0	50	0	33	50	0	50	63	50	70	75	30	35	54	0	35	0	30	33	57	56	51	135	C CC CP OJ PB
-+---++	(+)	50	30	20	36	0	0	27	64	0	28	0	66	33	0100	11	55	50	50	50	50	43	36	0	90	0	20	33	39	43	38	78	JY LH

Figure 8.3: Continued

	BO	BP	C	CC	CD	CL	CO	CP	FC	GC	HO	JY	LB	LC	LH	NY	O	OJ	PB	PL	S	SF	SV	SM	SP	SU	TB	TR	W	T%	T#	
(+)	25	50	45	68	0	0	66	9	0	0	53	56	0	0	0	54	57	0	44	25	25	29	0	38	0	55	30	55		47	113	CC CO TB
(−)	62	50	45	31	0	0	33	90	0	0	46	43	60	0	0	27	42	50	55	52	75	50	0	61	0	33	16	61	44	48	116	CP S
(+)	44	66	41	55	0	0	40	75	0	0	46	41	57	0	100	60	50	62	33	33	57	50	0	40	0	66	100	57	26	50	139	BP CP LH SU TB
(−)	55	25	58	44	0	0	60	25	0	0	42	52	42	0	0	40	50	37	0	0	42	50	0	55	0	33	16	30	39	46	130	W
(+)	60	22	50	33	0	0	41	50	0	0	0	30	33	0	0	46	28	40	9	33	25	44	0	33	0	37	16	30	39	32	79	
(+)	40	77	41	66	0	0	58	50	0	100	66	69	66	0	0	46	42	40	90	66	62	55	0	58	0	62	66	55	60	62	151	BP CC GC JY LB LH
(−)	40	50	42	75	0	0	62	45	0	66	66	50	28	0	0	66	42	83	33	70	60	66	0	57	0	47	16	81	52	53	148	CC GC NY OJ SF TR
(+)	60	50	57	12	0	0	37	54	0	27	28	50	57	0	100	33	55	16	66	70	40	33	0	42	0	52	66	11	43	43	121	LH PB PL TB
(−)	83	36	70	50	0	0	41	53	0	28	70	70	55	0	33	60	75	42	37	43	44	26	0	50	0	80	50	45	54	48	129	GC C JY
(−)	16	63	30	50	0	0	58	46	0	68	30	44	46	0	66	66	60	57	62	50	50	73	0	42	0	20	25	45	48	48	138	LB OJ PL
(+)	33	44	37	46	0	0	50	61	0	53	53	66	0	0	0	36	42	66	50	68	27	52	0	25	0	43	25	25	50	46	150	BO LH SM
(−)	66	55	62	46	0	0	45	38	0	46	22	50	66	0	0	63	57	33	50	32	63	47	0	75	0	56	50	62	50	50	67	
(+)	40	37	75	75	0	0	33	50	0	0	0	27	50	0	100	33	60	100	75	40	42	71	0	42	0	62	40	40	57	39	94	C CC GC JY OJ PB SF
(−)	27	40	40	25	0	0	72	75	0	56	56	53	57	0	0	41	30	33	66	66	31	50	0	20	0	47	83	40	45	55	114	CO CP LH PB PL TB
(−)	85	63	53	75	0	0	27	25	0	36	0	46	42	0	0	66	75	66	57	66	62	18	0	80	0	52	0	77	50	46	121	BO CC OJ SM TR
(−)	50	41	53	50	0	0	43	44	0	28	28	12	0	0	0	77	36	22	57	37	37	81	0	28	0	31	0	50	52	41	116	NY OJ PL
(+)	16	50	46	50	0	0	50	55	0	72	72	87	75	0	0	22	36	42	42	62	50	81	0	71	0	68	66	40	47	53	151	GC JY LB SF SM SU TB
(+)	100	41	71	58	0	0	35	90	0	35	25	25	50	0	50	60	50	37	33	30	31	55	0	60	0	60	31	42	45	45	113	BO C CP TB
(−)	58	28	28	41	0	0	57	9	0	61	72	75	50	0	33	50	50	50	44	61	62	44	0	64	0	40	33	68	57	52	131	JY TR
(+)	33	30	30	10	0	0	57	21	0	59	0	54	42	0	0	44	60	50	50	52	12	0	0	29	0	29	85	55	56	39	104	TB
(+)	100	66	70	90	0	0	46	71	0	40	0	45	57	0	75	53	12	66	50	35	81	81	0	38	0	70	14	45	39	57	152	BO BP C CC CP LH
(−)	50	75	26	26	0	0	57	88	0	65	34	57	40	0	75	34	75	33	34	64	50	45	0	53	0	50	20	56	50	48	132	BP CP LH OJ
(−)	50	25	100	73	0	0	42	11	0	34	0	42	58	0	100	42	28	42	62	50	50	50	0	60	0	50	80	60	44	49	134	C CC O TB
(−)	0	11	44	15	0	0	50	70	0	28	72	0	41	0	100	57	36	57	37	56	30	42	0	70	0	50	100	12	60	44	122	CP LH S TB
(+)	100	77	44	76	0	0	50	29	0	65	0	44	41	0	0	57	28	57	87	58	45	50	0	70	0	58	66	40	47	50	139	BO BP CC SM TR
(−)	66	16	63	33	0	0	20	10	0	38	0	46	33	0	80	66	22	37	66	37	30	35	0	62	0	41	25	11	63	39	79	BO NY PB
(+)	33	66	27	66	0	0	80	90	0	61	0	53	66	0	0	33	33	62	33	62	30	64	0	25	0	71	75	77	36	57	116	BO C CC CO CP O SU
(+)	66	57	28	40	0	0	60	83	0	0	0	33	75	0	0	55	33	100	50	63	28	44	0	25	0	14	60	50	20	42	63	BO CP LB OJ
(+)	33	42	43	60	0	0	40	16	0	0	0	66	11	0	0	44	60	50	36	36	57	33	0	75	0	85	40	37	40	54	81	C GC JY O SM SU
(−)	75	18	43	62	0	0	66	77	0	14	0	46	77	0	100	50	28	33	63	50	50	60	0	35	0	65	60	23	40	47	126	BO CO CP GC LH
(+)	25	81	56	37	0	0	22	22	0	52	0	53	25	0	50	50	71	66	50	50	44	50	0	64	0	57	60	76	53	49	131	BP LB O OJ TR
(−)	55	50	40	50	0	0	57	31	0	47	0	41	58	0	50	42	25	66	16	60	35	64	0	33	0	42	33	58	57	46	118	O OJ PB
(−)	50	22	50	50	0	0	46	50	0	40	0	33	50	0	50	50	44	100	66	60	50	38	0	22	0	31	25	33	50	50	127	O OJ PB
(+)	50	40	33	50	0	0	53	50	0	46	0	66	66	0	50	57	25	50	16	43	50	55	0	27	0	68	50	33	39	39	104	OJ
(+)	80	20	41	75	0	0	44	58	0	46	0	16	50	0	100	30	55	75	25	54	54	50	0	70	0	45	66	40	41	57	149	BO C JY O PB SM SU
(+)	50	80	58	25	0	0	55	41	0	53	0	75	0	0	75	69	44	75	87	57	57	50	0	70	0	54	33	52	52	39	96	CC TB
(−)	45	28	25	80	0	0	50	58	0	52	0	26	50	0	25	23	33	33	50	42	57	50	0	45	0	22	33	61	45	45	127	CP LH PL TB
(−)	50	50	71	80	0	0	50	10	0	47	0	73	80	0	75	76	33	66	42	29	42	57	0	54	0	77	33	53	47	52	145	C CC JY LB NY OJ SU
(+)	100	50	27	22	0	0	30	33	0	69	0	88	50	0	80	33	25	71	50	61	50	50	0	44	0	58	66	25	70	48	105	GC JY OJ TB W
(+)	100	50	72	77	0	0	70	66	0	26	0	11	50	0	80	66	75	14	50	38	50	50	0	50	0	41	33	75	30	50	109	BO C CC CO CP LH
(−)	33	50	50	27	0	0	53	66	0	61	0	14	57	0	100	62	50	62	25	60	52	38	0	50	0	45	100	21	30	44	127	LH BO JY TR W
(+)	66	40	50	63	0	0	46	60	0	38	0	78	42	0	50	25	37	25	50	32	43	53	0	50	0	50	44	78	70	50	143	BO JY TR W
(−)	100	50	50	63	0	0	36	60	0	56	0	25	40	0	50	16	37	25	50	33	33	53	0	27	0	25	44	22	70	38	80	BO W
(−)	50	50	50	100	0	0	63	69	0	50	0	75	50	0	100	83	44	66	12	66	66	75	0	72	0	75	55	61	30	58	120	CC JY NY OJ PL S
(+)	25	62	57	58	0	0	69	69	0	50	0	16	66	0	100	50	44	40	87	35	42	46	0	27	0	11	42	40	50	49	122	CO CP LB LH
(+)	75	37	42	41	0	0	30	23	0	50	0	66	33	0	75	57	33	66	42	29	54	57	0	54	0	88	57	55	33	45	133	BO JY PB SU
(−)	33	44	0	33	0	0	42	47	0	52	0	12	83	0	75	57	33	44	42	26	25	33	0	30	0	40	0	40	48	40	104	LB LH W
(+)	66	55	100	66	0	0	57	52	0	47	0	75	16	0	25	42	66	55	57	73	62	66	0	61	0	60	60	42	52	56	144	BO C CC JY O PL
(−)	41	33	33	0	0	0	57	0	0	24	0	50	50	0	50	55	37	25	50	30	40	28	0	14	0	53	0	23	37	36	101	
(+)	100	58	55	60	0	0	63	26	0	75	0	50	50	0	60	44	69	50	40	45	60	57	0	85	0	40	0	76	62	61	170	BO CP GC SM TR
(+)	100	14	14	66	0	0	66	26	0	4	0	33	62	0	20	25	62	50	50	44	30	46	0	40	0	45	25	25	42	35	79	BO CC CO S
(−)	60	60	85	33	0	0	33	68	0	91	0	58	33	0	40	62	66	60	50	69	69	53	0	60	0	54	50	75	57	60	133	C CP GC S TR

Figure 8.3: Continued

		BO	BP	C	CC	CD	CL	CO	CP	FC	GC	HO	JY	LB	LC	LH	NY	O	OJ	PB	PL	S	SF	SV	SM	SP	SU	TB	TR	W	T%	T#	65%
+-+++--	(+)	0	55	33	33	0	0	38	61	0	26	0	55	33	0	100	27	28	30	100	69	62	60	0	62	0	75	0	52	26	47	122	LH PB PL SU
+-+++--	(-)	100	44	66	58	0	0	61	38	0	68	0	33	66	0	0	45	57	70	0	30	37	40	0	37	0	25	66	42	52	46	120	BO C GC LB OJ TB
+-+++-+	(+)	33	33	41	57	0	0	57	85	0	30	0	33	50	0	50	71	40	44	33	41	50	54	0	20	0	42	50	50	38	45	75	CP NY
+-+++-+	(-)	66	66	50	42	0	0	42	14	0	69	0	66	50	0	0	14	60	33	66	58	50	45	0	60	0	57	50	0	61	50	83	BO BP GC JY PB
+-++++-	(+)	0	33	50	50	0	0	45	66	0	40	0	50	0	0	0	40	50	50	80	61	50	57	0	55	0	36	0	53	23	45	79	CP PB
+-++++-	(-)	100	66	40	50	0	0	54	33	0	60	0	50	100	0	100	60	40	50	20	30	50	42	0	44	0	63	100	46	71	51	89	BO BP LB LH TB W
+-+++++	(+)	66	14	100	22	0	0	22	18	0	25	0	0	100	0	0	33	25	50	100	25	33	37	0	40	0	60	50	0	11	30	39	BO C LB PB
+-+++++	(-)	33	85	0	66	0	0	66	81	0	75	0	100	0	0	0	66	50	50	0	75	66	62	0	60	0	40	50	100	66	64	82	BP CC CO CP GC JY
++-----	(+)	66	75	27	18	0	0	60	50	0	71	0	37	53	0	66	36	60	85	58	47	60	63	0	72	0	60	50	57	52	56	161	BO BP GC LH OJ SM
++-----	(-)	33	18	63	81	0	0	40	50	0	28	0	62	40	0	33	63	40	14	41	52	40	36	0	27	0	30	50	32	47	41	119	CC
++----+	(+)	0	57	27	41	0	0	60	42	0	40	0	36	0	0	50	33	28	40	16	58	33	43	0	46	0	35	33	46	50	40	98	
++----+	(-)	100	28	45	58	0	0	40	57	0	53	0	63	100	0	0	66	57	40	83	41	66	56	0	46	0	65	33	53	41	54	131	BO LB NY PB S
++---+-	(+)	100	50	25	57	0	0	56	53	0	52	0	44	60	0	66	50	50	20	36	60	39	30	0	63	0	60	80	64	45	49	140	BO LH TB
++---+-	(-)	0	50	75	42	0	0	43	46	0	44	0	55	40	0	33	50	50	80	63	40	60	70	0	27	0	33	20	35	55	49	138	C OJ SF
++---++	(+)	0	37	50	36	0	0	43	21	0	20	0	58	60	0	0	40	25	33	33	54	23	33	0	50	0	26	0	0	41	35	84	
++---++	(-)	100	62	50	63	0	0	56	73	0	75	0	41	20	0	100	60	75	66	66	45	76	55	0	50	0	73	100	100	58	62	146	BO CP GC LH O OJ
++--+--	(+)	50	57	42	16	0	0	62	46	0	34	0	64	50	0	50	40	40	50	37	29	33	37	0	29	0	36	50	56	41	42	111	
++--+--	(-)	50	42	57	83	0	0	25	53	0	62	0	35	50	0	50	60	60	50	50	70	66	62	0	64	0	59	50	40	58	54	141	CC PL S
++--+-+	(+)	100	33	54	33	0	0	53	46	0	62	0	43	50	0	100	50	66	33	50	65	68	41	0	50	0	66	50	22	50	51	118	BO LH O S SU
++--+-+	(-)	0	60	45	66	0	0	46	53	0	37	0	50	50	0	0	50	33	33	50	35	31	58	0	50	0	33	50	77	42	47	109	CC TR
++--++-	(+)	50	53	33	33	0	0	36	14	0	45	0	58	50	0	50	27	50	10	25	60	64	36	0	64	0	61	66	42	43	44	116	TB
++--++-	(-)	50	38	66	66	0	0	63	78	0	50	0	33	50	0	50	63	50	70	75	30	35	54	0	35	0	30	33	57	56	51	135	C CC CP OJ PB
++--+++	(+)	50	30	20	36	0	0	27	64	0	28	0	66	33	0	100	11	55	50	50	46	43	36	0	9	0	20	33	39	43	38	78	JY LH
++--+++	(-)	50	60	80	63	0	0	63	35	0	71	0	33	66	0	0	66	33	50	25	53	56	63	0	90	0	80	33	56	50	57	116	C GC LB NY SM SU
++-+---	(+)	100	50	57	52	0	0	58	66	0	54	0	52	50	0	100	80	50	0	50	60	71	21	0	25	0	44	0	36	55	51	142	BO CP LH NY S
++-+---	(-)	0	50	42	47	0	0	41	33	0	42	0	31	50	0	0	13	50	100	50	39	21	78	0	75	0	55	50	54	33	44	124	OJ SF SM
++-+--+	(+)	0	42	16	57	0	0	50	52	0	36	0	20	0	0	40	33	50	75	60	36	63	53	0	84	0	40	100	55	66	50	117	OJ SM TB W
++-+--+	(-)	0	57	83	42	0	0	50	47	0	60	0	80	0	0	60	55	50	25	40	63	26	46	0	15	0	60	0	44	33	47	110	C JY
++-+-+-	(+)	0	53	37	25	0	0	55	36	0	53	0	0	100	0	88	56	57	50	33	33	40	54	0	33	0	38	0	60	0	47	108	LB LH
++-+-+-	(-)	100	46	50	75	0	0	44	54	0	46	0	100	0	0	11	43	42	50	66	66	60	41	0	66	0	61	100	40	85	51	117	BO CC JY PB PL SM
++-+-++	(+)	0	37	25	50	0	0	30	12	0	46	0	11	100	0	40	20	60	83	0	71	25	33	0	50	0	44	50	44	44	41	73	LB OJ PL
++-+-++	(-)	0	62	62	50	0	0	70	87	0	53	0	77	0	0	40	80	40	16	100	21	58	66	0	50	0	55	0	55	55	54	97	CO CP JY NY PB SF
++-++--	(+)	50	42	41	28	0	0	30	31	0	64	0	47	50	0	100	40	60	20	100	41	64	30	0	33	0	75	50	23	47	45	107	LH PB SU
++-++--	(-)	50	57	41	71	0	0	61	68	0	29	0	52	50	0	0	60	20	80	0	58	35	61	0	66	0	25	50	76	52	52	123	CC CP OJ SM TR
++-++-+	(+)	66	55	50	60	0	0	15	60	0	24	0	28	28	0	75	55	62	66	83	3	28	33	0	33	0	46	75	33	60	38	91	BO LH OJ PB TB
++-++-+	(-)	33	33	50	40	0	0	76	40	0	72	0	71	57	0	25	44	37	33	16	96	71	66	0	58	0	53	25	44	40	58	140	CO GC JY PL S SF
++-+++-	(+)	0	50	33	57	0	0	42	25	0	43	0	0	40	0	33	50	60	22	80	44	37	33	0	58	0	33	33	22	38	39	84	PB
++-+++-	(-)	0	50	66	42	0	0	57	75	0	52	0	87	60	0	66	50	40	66	20	56	62	66	0	41	0	44	66	77	61	58	126	C CP JY LH OJ SF
++-++++	(+)	25	50	22	0	0	0	33	25	0	12	0	50	75	0	100	60	66	25	66	50	25	40	0	40	0	20	50	40	26	37	54	LB LH O PB
++-++++	(-)	75	50	77	50	0	0	66	75	0	87	0	50	25	0	0	40	16	75	33	43	75	60	0	60	0	80	16	60	73	58	84	BO C CO CP GC OJ
+++----	(+)	42	62	41	25	0	0	75	60	0	35	0	35	50	0	100	38	42	50	70	46	50	38	0	30	0	56	0	73	44	49	122	CO LH PB TR
+++----	(-)	57	37	58	62	0	0	25	40	0	57	0	57	50	0	0	53	42	33	30	53	50	53	0	69	0	39	75	26	55	47	117	SM TB
+++---+	(+)	100	30	52	58	0	0	33	52	0	15	0	50	50	0	100	40	37	50	100	16	53	30	0	22	0	60	80	61	45	44	103	BO LH PB TB
+++---+	(-)	0	70	47	41	0	0	66	47	0	84	0	50	50	0	0	46	62	33	0	66	46	46	0	77	0	40	20	38	54	51	119	BP CO GC PL SM
+++--+-	(+)	50	55	57	18	0	0	53	63	0	50	0	42	66	0	60	58	50	50	55	61	43	25	0	7	0	46	40	72	59	48	131	LB TR
+++--+-	(-)	0	44	28	81	0	0	46	36	0	37	0	57	33	0	40	41	50	50	44	38	56	68	0	76	0	53	60	27	31	47	126	CC SF SM
+++--++	(+)	33	80	0	60	0	0	50	62	0	44	0	42	50	0	14	23	16	16	83	27	46	55	0	30	0	80	66	35	41	44	91	BP PB SU TB
+++--++	(-)	66	20	100	40	0	0	50	37	0	55	0	57	16	0	71	53	83	50	16	72	53	44	0	70	0	20	33	35	54	49	101	BO C LH O PL SM
+++-+--	(+)	20	63	44	46	0	0	47	56	0	33	0	50	50	0	20	62	50	0	16	26	38	35	0	41	0	69	100	36	26	40	121	SU TB
+++-+--	(-)	60	36	44	46	0	0	52	43	0	64	0	50	50	0	80	37	50	75	83	69	61	58	0	45	0	30	0	54	68	55	165	LH OJ PB PL W
+++-+-+	(+)	100	57	75	50	0	0	43	27	0	21	0	50	40	0	100	55	33	85	50	35	16	22	0	50	0	23	0	11	35	37	77	BO C LH OJ
+++-+-+	(-)	0	42	25	33	0	0	56	63	0	78	0	50	40	0	0	44	66	14	50	58	83	77	0	50	0	76	0	44	64	58	120	GC O S SF SU
+++-++-	(+)	0	40	15	0	0	0	50	52	0	36	0	62	50	0	25	41	16	60	14	45	21	58	0	22	0	64	40	28	47	38	82	
+++-++-	(-)	50	60	61	100	0	0	50	29	0	52	0	25	50	0	75	58	50	40	71	54	78	33	0	66	0	35	60	71	41	53	113	CC LH PB S SM TR

Figure 8.3: Concluded

		BO	BP	C	CC	CD	CL	CO	CP	FC	GC	HO	JY	LB	LC	LH	NY	O	OJ	PB	PL	S	SF	SV	SM	SP	SU	TB	TR	W	T%	T#	------ 65% ------
+++-+++	(+)	50	25	0	80	0	0	77	41	0	25	0	0	16	0	0	40	28	75	40	45	55	50		12	0	0	0	55	33	39	62	CC CO OJ
+++-+++	(-)	50	50	100	20	0	0	22	50	0	75	0	50	66	0	50	40	57	25	40	45	33	50		0	0	100	50	44	66	54	85	C GC LB SM SU W
+++-+++	(-)	50	10	37		0	0	55	0	0	43	0	50	20	0	100	37	14	41	50	33	16	53		75	0	38	20	69	38	36	85	LH TR
++++---	(-)	100	50	90	62	0	0	45	84	0	56	0	71	80	0	0	66	57	58	50	66	83	46		58	0	61	60	23	61	60	139	BO C CP JY LB PL S
++++--+	(+)	33	20	44	83	0	0	38	41	0	33	0	50	62	0	0	66	66	16	37	27	53	50		53	0	41	25	34	46	41	97	CC NY O
++++--+	(-)	66	70	44	16	0	0	61	52	0	66	0	40	37	0	33	33	83	83	62	72	46	42		46	0	75	80	53	53	54	127	BO BP GC LH OJ PL TB
++++-++	(-)	50	16	50	44	0	0	57	37	0	35	0	0	50	0	0	50	50	50	18	18	60	37		85	0	0	40	80	52	41	68	LH SM TR
++++-++	(+)	50	66	37	55	0	0	42	62	0	65	0	100	50	0	0	50	25	71	81	50	40	62		0	0	40	0	20	42	55	91	BP JY PB PL SU
++++-++	(-)	100	60	54	40	0	0	54	22	0	54	0	25	0	0	0	27	0	0	50	50	25	22		14	0	100	40	0	30	39	62	BO TB
++++-++	(+)	0	60	54	60	0	0	45	77	0	45	0	75	80	0	72	100	50	50	50	50	62	66		50	0	57	100	71	70	58	93	CP JY LB LH NY O
++++-+-	(-)	44	16	83	28	0	0	54	50	0	80	0	57	0	0	0	50	16	50	50	63	37	37		62	0	42	0	33	33	44	75	C GC
++++-++	(+)	55	83	16	71	0	0	45	50	0	20	0	42	100	0	0	50	66	66	50	62	62	62		47	0	61	50	70	66	54	89	BP CC LB LH O TR W
+++++++	(-)	100	50	45	28	0	0	54	40	0	33	0	60	0	0	33	33	33	37	31	31	45	42		62	0	25	100	29	35	40	66	BO OJ TB
++++++-	(+)	0	33	54	71	0	0	45	60	0	66	0	40	50	0	33	50	50	33	62	68	54	28		37	0	50	0	58	64	54	88	CC GC LB PL
+++++++	(+)	0	33	33	50	0	0	50	36	0	66	0	66	50	0	66	66	14	50	50	50	66	66		40	0	50	33	35	37	45	71	JY LH NY S SF
+++++++	(-)	66	70	66	50	0	0	42	63	0	50	0	33	50	0	0	33	85	50	83	50	16	22		60	0	0	33	64	62	50	79	BO BP C O
+++++++	(+)	50	0	66	50	0	0	66	25	0	0	0	20	50	0	0	50	33	33	16	33	50	33		75	0	25	33	100	16	45	40	C CO LH PB SM TR
+++++++	(-)	50	50	33	50	0	0	33	75	0	100	0	80	50	0	100	50	57	33	16	33	50	66		25	0	75	66	0	83	51	45	CP GC JY SF SU TB W

Figure 8.4: Daily Closing Patterns: Choppy Bull Markets

Note (upper right): -------- 65% --------

Pattern	Dir	BO	BP	C	CC	CD	CL	CO	CP	FC	GC	HO	JY	LB	LC	LH	NY	O	OJ	PB	PL	S	SF	SV	SM	SP	SU	TB	TR	W	T%	T#	Note
- -	(+)	54	51	52	53	0	0	54	61	0	63	0	59	54	54	54	57	49	57	53	56	54	50	0	48	0	34	0	55	53	55	3843	
- -	(-)	41	45	42	44	0	0	35	36	0	33	0	53	39	54	55	41	46	39	46	47	43	47	0	39	0	48	0	43	42	41	2860	
- +	(+)	52	52	51	50	0	0	53	50	0	56	0	53	54	49	51	53	55	55	58	47	54	56	0	53	0	48	0	53	55	52	4390	
- +	(-)	45	43	43	46	0	0	54	46	0	41	0	44	46	43	43	45	38	40	40	49	43	42	0	39	0	50	0	46	40	44	3673	
+ -	(+)	49	49	46	53	0	0	54	49	0	56	0	52	46	45	45	48	44	48	53	43	53	62	0	48	0	45	0	54	52	50	4241	
+ -	(-)	47	46	49	42	0	0	43	47	0	40	0	51	48	42	44	46	46	46	51	43	44	32	0	45	0	45	0	44	52	45	3826	
+ +	(+)	48	53	45	45	0	0	47	45	0	45	0	45	45	44	47	47	48	50	47	45	47	46	0	42	0	43	0	47	45	47	4188	
+ +	(-)	49	43	49	52	0	0	44	51	0	51	0	50	50	47	47	51	45	44	53	47	52	52	0	52	0	54	0	51	50	49	4386	
- - -	(+)	53	56	55	51	0	0	58	58	0	71	0	65	57	56	58	61	49	60	51	62	55	55	0	53	0	59	0	58	55	57	1636	GC
- - -	(-)	43	41	38	46	0	0	39	41	0	27	0	45	38	40	39	38	48	37	36	42	36	42	0	42	0	36	0	40	42	40	1140	
- - +	(+)	54	56	53	53	0	0	51	55	0	60	0	55	55	52	52	53	53	54	58	43	58	57	0	59	0	54	0	60	59	54	2104	
- - +	(-)	43	37	40	46	0	0	47	42	0	38	0	50	38	44	42	45	41	40	34	54	40	38	0	45	0	43	0	39	36	42	1623	
- + -	(+)	46	45	42	46	0	0	51	47	0	62	0	51	51	46	45	49	48	50	48	54	53	56	0	51	0	52	0	50	41	49	1821	
- + -	(-)	51	51	52	40	0	0	46	48	0	36	0	57	52	46	43	49	44	45	52	43	42	33	0	42	0	43	0	46	53	46	1719	
- + +	(+)	47	54	46	52	0	0	54	48	0	50	0	51	47	53	48	48	53	53	45	46	47	41	0	45	0	44	0	52	51	49	2156	
- + +	(-)	49	43	48	45	0	0	51	49	0	47	0	46	48	45	53	49	40	39	52	45	46	45	0	46	0	53	0	46	45	47	2097	
+ - -	(+)	56	48	49	55	0	0	52	63	0	61	0	58	53	54	55	55	48	55	54	50	54	42	0	45	0	64	0	52	52	54	2098	
+ - -	(-)	39	48	44	43	0	0	54	34	0	34	0	39	39	44	44	42	36	40	47	47	43	57	0	45	0	34	0	46	41	42	1604	
+ - +	(+)	48	48	48	47	0	0	54	47	0	53	0	60	55	50	46	50	57	54	52	51	52	60	0	48	0	44	0	47	43	50	2142	
+ - +	(-)	47	48	47	47	0	0	45	50	0	42	0	38	39	46	44	42	44	36	45	47	45	40	0	43	0	53	0	52	44	45	1942	
+ + -	(+)	52	53	50	54	0	0	57	51	0	51	0	49	50	51	51	51	52	46	49	53	51	63	0	49	0	48	0	58	43	51	2266	
+ + -	(-)	44	43	46	43	0	0	54	43	0	44	0	60	45	38	45	46	42	46	46	52	46	33	0	44	0	47	0	47	54	45	1978	
+ + +	(+)	48	53	42	39	0	0	54	43	0	39	0	46	43	42	44	43	42	45	47	45	42	50	0	36	0	42	0	41	37	44	1874	
+ + +	(-)	49	49	52	57	0	0	44	54	0	55	0	53	52	51	47	55	50	50	50	54	55	46	0	59	0	57	0	55	58	51	2150	
- - - -	(+)	50	58	51	55	0	0	54	67	0	70	0	83	59	64	56	55	50	59	51	58	55	55	0	56	0	60	0	72	58	51	665	CP GC JY JY SF TR
- - - -	(-)	46	40	42	41	0	0	42	37	0	41	0	16	35	35	38	34	40	40	48	39	39	25	0	34	0	37	0	24	36	38	441	
- - - +	(+)	50	54	51	54	0	0	45	60	0	58	0	41	53	45	47	55	48	48	61	61	61	45	0	55	0	42	0	69	52	52	851	TR
- - - +	(-)	48	41	37	45	0	0	43	37	0	40	0	58	40	53	48	42	43	50	33	47	36	54	0	36	0	54	0	30	41	44	731	
- - + -	(+)	46	52	45	52	0	0	47	50	0	52	0	50	42	45	44	51	44	56	46	46	57	50	0	47	0	55	0	48	49	50	808	CC
- - + -	(-)	51	45	45	26	0	0	51	47	0	46	0	57	53	45	48	48	50	43	53	41	41	37	0	44	0	40	0	50	54	46	757	
- - + +	(+)	46	54	47	50	0	0	53	51	0	50	0	50	50	50	46	50	48	29	40	49	50	50	0	44	0	46	0	47	43	48	1025	
- - + +	(-)	56	48	46	55	0	0	50	62	0	57	0	60	58	53	52	47	56	48	51	54	54	33	0	52	0	66	0	44	51	54	1010	SU
- + - -	(+)	41	50	36	44	0	0	47	35	0	33	0	37	40	44	47	50	36	46	48	42	54	33	0	40	0	31	0	52	44	42	933	SU
- + - -	(-)	45	46	46	52	0	0	39	49	0	59	0	44	53	44	39	42	43	48	54	51	51	64	0	50	0	47	0	53	49	52	736	SF
- + - +	(+)	50	45	49	44	0	0	39	47	0	37	0	35	40	43	39	30	42	50	32	51	47	35	0	35	0	50	0	46	47	44	949	PB
- + - +	(-)	44	58	42	46	0	0	43	41	0	41	0	37	58	57	50	54	43	41	44	53	53	57	0	56	0	51	0	53	43	51	801	
- + + -	(+)	44	40	52	50	0	0	43	45	0	41	0	58	38	47	44	54	48	48	48	46	45	38	0	41	0	45	0	46	45	45	1074	
- + + -	(-)	47	48	45	41	0	0	56	37	0	52	0	50	40	42	44	46	42	42	50	50	36	40	0	42	0	38	0	34	33	45	954	
- + + +	(+)	50	48	52	56	0	0	51	57	0	56	0	48	55	52	56	53	53	53	48	55	51	60	0	56	0	60	0	63	60	53	929	
- + + +	(-)	55	57	57	48	0	0	60	51	0	71	0	62	54	54	61	56	35	65	58	55	44	41	0	48	0	55	0	47	50	56	1148	
+ - - -	(+)	41	40	37	48	0	0	39	48	0	28	0	25	41	44	37	43	61	30	41	33	44	50	0	51	0	33	0	52	48	41	903	GC
+ - - -	(-)	58	53	53	53	0	0	58	53	0	59	0	46	59	59	56	53	57	58	64	56	56	66	0	62	0	36	0	53	64	56	656	
+ - - +	(+)	39	32	44	44	0	0	41	45	0	39	0	46	37	38	37	46	36	34	41	56	42	22	0	36	0	42	0	46	33	40	1192	SF
+ - - +	(-)	45	40	36	44	0	0	53	47	0	69	0	44	41	48	53	47	55	38	50	61	55	62	0	52	0	51	0	51	32	49	850	
+ - + -	(+)	52	55	57	50	0	0	42	46	0	27	0	53	53	46	42	51	34	44	37	43	43	37	0	41	0	44	0	46	64	46	963	GC
+ - + -	(-)	49	42	50	47	0	0	44	52	0	50	0	60	48	54	56	48	48	56	48	49	51	62	0	42	0	55	0	55	48	47	906	
+ - + +	(+)	48	42	50	48	0	0	44	52	0	50	0	53	48	42	41	51	51	60	48	49	51	43	0	49	0	40	0	56	42	47	1064	
+ - + +	(-)	56	47	43	53	0	0	55	46	0	65	0	52	50	50	53	62	60	48	55	58	54	50	0	37	0	63	0	57	54	55	1022	GC
+ + - -	(+)	43	43	53	43	0	0	50	45	0	34	0	39	44	47	48	51	35	46	43	47	43	22	0	53	0	36	0	42	39	41	1098	
+ + - -	(-)	39	47	50	46	0	0	53	31	0	50	0	60	41	47	43	37	55	35	37	43	50	56	0	47	0	40	0	43	55	49	819	
+ + - +	(+)	50	45	50	43	0	0	50	53	0	46	0	37	56	44	47	53	42	40	50	44	47	43	0	49	0	57	0	56	42	47	1112	
+ + - +	(-)	47	49	45	52	0	0	58	45	0	49	0	62	45	57	53	61	51	51	50	51	49	73	0	41	0	44	0	63	44	52	1077	
+ + + -	(+)	53	51	60	59	0	0	58	45	0	49	0	35	50	53	43	36	43	51	43	51	47	49	0	41	0	51	0	63	44	52	1124	SF
+ + + -	(-)	45	43	39	39	0	0	40	52	0	46	0	35	50	38	43	36	42	43	50	43	47	26	0	48	0	51	0	36	52	44	956	

Figure 8.4: Continued

		BO	BP	C	CC	CD	CL	CO	CP	FC	GC	HO	JY	LB	LC	LH	NY	O	OJ	PB	PL	S	SF	SV	SM	SP	SU	TB	TR	W	T%	T#	
++++	(+)	50	56	43	37	0	0	51	46	0	35	0	41	48	43	48	44	36	51	45	51	48	56	0	34	0	48	0	51	44	47	879	
++++	(+)	47	40	51	55	0	0	46	53	0	62	0	55	48	49	48	52	51	45	52	51	48	43	0	57	0	51	0	45	52	49	922	C CP GC JY NY OJ
----	(-)	45	65	67	55	0	0	52	72	0	100	0	63	48	53	42	70	51	45	52	66	48	50	0	7	0	53	0	83	52	60	264	C CP GC JY NY OJ
----	(-)	54	35	32	38	0	0	47	27	0	0	0	0	31	35	42	29	46	30	44	33	37	50	0	7	0	46	0	16	43	38	167	
++++	(+)	42	48	58	54	0	0	50	64	0	40	0	30	51	46	49	50	54	44	73	44	66	50	0	36	0	37	0	77	63	52	348	PH S TR
----	(-)	56	51	35	45	0	0	50	33	0	59	0	70	54	54	46	55	21	56	33	56	33	50	0	30	0	58	0	22	51	45	299	JY
++++	(+)	40	42	45	59	0	0	48	41	0	48	0	44	43	44	48	51	25	41	53	54	61	33	0	68	0	58	0	27	50	47	346	SM
----	(-)	53	53	48	36	0	0	51	58	0	51	0	50	53	50	50	48	62	58	46	40	38	50	0	51	0	41	0	63	35	48	355	
----	(-)	51	54	36	38	0	0	51	51	0	46	0	61	37	53	43	48	22	33	46	52	61	50	0	51	0	50	0	48	60	47	405	
----	(-)	48	43	59	61	0	0	48	48	0	42	0	38	60	42	55	51	72	41	44	57	47	60	0	47	0	50	0	48	39	49	421	O
----	(-)	60	43	58	57	0	0	48	53	0	50	0	65	68	60	48	53	64	33	52	46	50	33	0	47	0	77	0	53	56	55	418	LB SU
----	(-)	38	52	38	42	0	0	46	42	0	34	0	34	53	39	48	46	31	61	47	51	50	66	0	51	0	22	0	46	43	42	319	SF
----	(-)	47	55	46	54	0	0	61	55	0	53	0	62	56	54	51	52	60	48	46	57	40	75	0	55	0	62	0	73	58	53	427	SF TR
----	(-)	50	44	48	45	0	0	36	44	0	41	0	37	34	40	51	45	26	51	53	51	60	25	0	38	0	37	0	26	41	43	353	SF
----	(-)	44	63	45	46	0	0	52	52	0	45	0	27	58	59	52	45	58	55	46	51	46	50	0	60	0	46	0	52	45	50	504	SF
----	(-)	51	36	49	50	0	0	44	42	0	44	0	72	40	37	44	54	47	38	54	48	50	33	0	36	0	50	0	47	52	47	473	JY
----	(-)	44	50	42	46	0	0	61	37	0	46	0	50	38	34	46	39	28	46	41	51	30	50	0	46	0	42	0	33	32	41	427	
++++	(+)	55	47	57	53	0	0	38	51	0	51	0	58	59	58	54	45	66	37	55	67	56	59	0	59	0	56	0	66	59	55	561	O S TR
----	(-)	58	62	45	45	0	0	61	36	0	72	0	73	50	49	65	62	36	60	57	70	58	33	0	71	0	60	0	50	57	57	418	GC JY OJ PL
++++	(+)	39	34	48	54	0	0	36	63	0	28	0	20	47	52	49	37	63	27	44	29	41	66	0	28	0	30	0	52	30	40	298	LB SM W
++++	(+)	59	59	59	59	0	0	58	48	0	48	0	58	66	66	57	58	66	57	53	58	57	33	0	71	0	60	0	52	67	55	520	LB SM SF
----	(-)	37	45	38	40	0	0	41	52	0	47	0	33	32	40	35	58	47	30	42	63	40	66	0	28	0	36	0	47	30	41	386	O
++++	(+)	47	32	32	41	0	0	64	43	0	47	0	20	35	50	50	50	70	46	45	51	56	50	0	52	0	51	0	52	31	46	370	JY
----	(-)	49	56	62	55	0	0	32	50	0	45	0	80	59	61	46	60	40	54	46	44	50	49	0	35	0	44	0	47	62	49	596	
++++	(+)	50	63	42	47	0	0	49	42	0	62	0	44	43	33	37	37	38	59	52	58	50	54	0	58	0	35	0	59	43	49	467	
++++	(+)	55	46	47	38	0	0	40	37	0	60	0	50	47	61	43	47	47	39	47	50	45	50	0	41	0	62	0	50	56	48	457	
++++	(+)	41	46	52	47	0	0	45	28	0	45	0	48	54	33	46	40	70	47	52	38	48	50	0	40	0	36	0	43	30	41	394	
++++	(+)	50	50	52	37	0	0	64	43	0	50	0	50	65	61	46	55	61	58	41	50	48	50	0	45	0	51	0	50	55	48	529	CP
----	(-)	49	56	62	55	0	0	32	50	0	57	0	33	42	56	59	62	47	60	47	47	44	62	0	58	0	64	0	56	40	55	519	
++++	(+)	52	55	56	68	0	0	33	43	0	57	0	61	42	56	37	64	42	54	54	59	45	62	0	34	0	58	0	67	40	52	522	CC TR
++++	(+)	45	42	41	28	0	0	47	43	0	40	0	38	50	38	37	32	42	42	52	37	52	37	0	43	0	58	0	32	58	43	606	BP SF
----	(-)	51	69	35	42	0	0	47	45	0	37	0	36	34	52	44	60	43	45	50	44	47	66	0	40	0	38	0	52	58	45	504	
++++	(+)	48	30	58	53	0	0	50	54	0	65	0	63	34	52	47	60	39	54	50	45	47	33	0	54	0	61	0	41	60	51	421	JY LC O SF TR
----	(-)	53	51	40	54	0	0	53	64	0	55	0	87	55	66	57	62	66	50	44	54	52	83	0	50	0	60	0	68	64	57	473	
----	(-)	40	34	37	45	0	0	43	42	0	38	0	12	38	38	50	35	50	47	25	38	43	0	0	35	0	45	0	26	33	39	375	
++++	(+)	51	63	54	72	0	0	48	52	0	60	0	45	54	57	44	52	46	31	58	47	40	60	0	61	0	45	0	58	64	44	258	
++++	(+)	63	51	37	42	0	0	43	54	0	55	0	55	38	40	48	47	41	50	41	47	38	60	0	61	0	52	0	41	40	51	468	
++++	(+)	48	36	42	52	0	0	42	43	0	42	0	63	56	57	50	47	50	36	58	31	55	50	0	61	0	50	0	42	52	45	403	CC OJ SF
++++	(+)	44	56	56	57	0	0	55	54	0	47	0	45	52	48	44	50	46	20	74	25	45	50	0	61	0	46	0	45	49	47	440	OJ
----	(-)	54	51	61	52	0	0	51	70	0	70	0	54	48	48	50	46	36	61	60	47	57	33	0	61	0	50	0	39	47	54	386	PB
++++	(+)	51	41	61	50	0	0	51	70	0	70	0	53	52	49	59	53	60	34	52	58	40	66	0	61	0	61	0	56	47	54	587	CP GC
----	(-)	42	43	34	47	0	0	57	29	0	63	0	66	45	49	59	42	60	34	84	47	40	66	0	44	0	35	0	40	37	43	563	SF
++++	(+)	44	55	51	50	0	0	48	48	0	63	0	66	52	58	48	59	37	48	15	50	52	40	0	33	0	37	0	60	58	54	492	JY PB SF
----	(-)	42	48	34	47	0	0	57	48	0	34	0	33	50	45	41	59	41	36	47	42	50	66	0	44	0	40	0	50	37	43	389	
++++	(+)	44	55	45	43	0	0	54	48	0	63	0	66	50	56	48	37	42	37	42	41	39	40	0	44	0	37	0	60	58	51	496	JY PB SF
++++	(+)	48	44	39	46	0	0	60	48	0	34	0	43	61	56	37	48	41	41	48	46	52	40	0	33	0	40	0	60	58	44	426	
++++	(+)	62	53	58	50	0	0	58	58	0	58	0	52	34	56	48	57	52	36	42	55	49	53	0	56	0	59	0	45	43	53	544	C GC
----	(-)	35	43	50	41	0	0	39	37	0	37	0	34	41	55	41	52	34	41	54	44	40	33	0	41	0	34	0	45	34	44	449	
++++	(+)	48	48	50	55	0	0	54	36	0	35	0	47	54	48	48	46	60	60	45	50	56	33	0	37	0	63	0	36	43	52	472	O PB SF
----	(-)	54	52	67	51	0	0	60	60	0	69	0	52	54	55	49	50	60	33	39	60	56	50	0	43	0	34	0	43	63	56	554	JY
++++	(+)	41	47	28	44	0	0	40	37	0	30	0	29	37	40	57	50	36	36	39	39	44	50	0	56	0	34	0	56	56	41	460	C GC
++++	(+)	57	67	45	51	0	0	57	60	0	65	0	25	53	62	56	60	70	36	39	45	55	83	0	59	0	61	0	56	61	58	637	BP O PB SF
----	(-)	40	40	52	48	0	0	42	38	0	33	0	70	36	33	38	39	36	36	31	52	44	44	0	40	0	37	0	45	36	39	436	JY

Figure 8.4: Continued

		BO	BP	C	CC	CD	CL	CO	CP	FC	GC	HO	JY	LB	LC	LH	NY	O	OJ	PB	PL	S	SF	SV	SM	SP	SU	TB	TR	W	T%	T#	
+ + + + +	(+)	44	44	40	47	0	0	48	50	0	82	0	53	45	51	56	54	47	46	51	72	54	70		51	0	49	0	50	34	52	560	GC PL SF
+ + + + -	(-)	53	55	53	47	0	0	48	44	0	17	0	46	47	50	39	45	47	46	48	27	43	30		45	0	45	0	46	65	44	481	
+ + + + -	(-)	47	50	51	61	0	0	58	47	0	45	0	45	50	42	39	56	36	57	42	41	45	23		46	0	51	0	52	42	50	556	
+ + + + -	(-)	49	50	44	38	0	0	41	52	0	54	0	54	46	50	38	52	36	39	60	54	53	76		46	0	46	0	47	50	47	529	SF
+ + + + +	(+)	57	51	41	46	0	0	51	64	0	67	0	61	58	50	47	47	66	66	60	57	58	50		23	0	66	0	64	58	56	535	GC OJ SU
+ + + + -	(-)	36	48	53	53	0	0	46	33	0	32	0	46	46	44	50	52	47	30	42	58	54	50		60	0	50	0	35	57	41	395	
+ + + + +	(+)	50	40	46	46	0	0	53	36	0	55	0	65	46	49	50	55	43	55	39	58	54	63		46	0	43	0	43	57	49	559	
+ + + + +	(+)	46	59	48	51	0	0	46	58	0	41	0	30	44	61	44	41	41	52	56	41	43	36		53	0	60	0	56	42	46	525	
+ + + + +	(+)	53	48	63	44	0	0	53	49	0	39	0	63	52	61	46	56	43	52	45	56	55	85		40	0	43	0	56	42	52	481	SF
+ + + + -	(-)	45	44	36	56	0	0	44	49	0	54	0	31	47	36	47	43	38	52	57	47	39	14		50	0	36	0	43	50	44	413	
+ + + + +	(+)	50	46	53	29	0	0	55	41	0	41	0	42	36	45	54	54	26	45	38	48	48	44		50	0	58	0	50	45	48	422	O
+ + + + -	(-)	46	48	41	58	0	0	40	58	0	58	0	50	61	48	54	39	57	39	48	51	51	55		61	0	41	0	48	48	48	422	C CO CP LB NY PB
+ + + + +	(+)	50	57	88	42	0	0	80	66	0	0	0	50	66	60	47	80	50	50	75	83	62	0	100	0	0	41	0	50	40	58	97	C CO S SF SM IR W
+ + + + -	(-)	50	50	11	42	0	0	44	33	0	0	0	0	33	40	34	20	42	55	25	16	62	0	0	0	57	57	0	100	50	39	65	
+ + + + +	(+)	50	69	57	70	0	0	63	62	0	62	0	0	50	41	44	34	50	55	50	50	80	100	0	0	70	50	0	66	56	56	148	BP CC S SF SM TR W
+ + + + -	(-)	55	30	31	30	0	0	36	37	0	37	100	100	41	55	53	50	37	44	30	15	43	0	0	30	50	28	0	33	40	40	108	JY
+ + + + +	(+)	36	33	54	54	0	0	30	46	0	48	0	57	42	40	48	56	22	60	50	76	53	0	0	71	71	50	0	58	48	48	145	PB PL S SM SU
+ + + + -	(-)	52	66	41	36	0	0	69	53	0	61	0	69	50	51	41	57	60	25	40	15	41	0	0	63	50	28	0	25	25	41	142	BP CO O SF
+ + + + +	(+)	53	64	45	46	0	0	76	48	0	55	0	69	57	45	48	62	18	75	60	60	54	0	0	63	99	33	0	42	58	50	174	CO JY OJ SM
+ + + + -	(-)	46	35	45	53	0	0	23	51	0	44	0	33	62	45	48	37	75	12	64	63	36	0	100	0	23	66	0	57	41	47	163	O SF SU
+ + + + +	(+)	48	60	52	50	0	0	55	60	0	64	0	60	82	46	46	66	30	28	40	60	39	0	0	33	66	33	0	42	66	53	190	LB LC SU
- + + + -	(-)	48	60	41	50	0	0	45	30	0	23	0	44	17	33	52	38	64	42	57	41	41	66	0	0	50	33	0	57	33	43	155	SF SM W
- + + + +	(+)	38	58	50	46	0	0	63	60	0	37	0	87	64	53	57	61	50	50	62	50	36	100	0	0	61	57	0	100	64	54	188	JY SF TR
- + + + -	(-)	61	41	50	53	0	0	12	40	0	41	0	21	21	38	33	41	45	57	45	50	45	0	0	38	42	50	0	50	42	42	146	
- + + + -	(-)	50	62	37	37	0	0	43	57	0	56	0	20	57	57	53	45	50	50	37	42	43	66	0	38	63	42	0	50	23	48	203	SF SM
- + + + +	(+)	44	37	55	62	0	0	52	42	0	35	0	80	42	38	46	54	44	69	50	57	60	33	0	80	63	0	0	76	76	48	202	JY W
- + + + -	(-)	52	40	44	40	0	0	52	43	0	45	0	56	62	40	51	52	69	50	50	38	29	100	0	10	0	28	0	41	30	41	168	SF
- + + + +	(+)	45	55	55	60	0	0	47	53	0	54	0	50	31	45	66	47	25	70	50	38	70	0	0	40	60	33	0	58	69	55	224	LC LH OJ W
- + + + +	(+)	57	50	40	83	0	0	55	69	0	69	0	53	53	55	58	55	25	61	61	61	50	50	0	60	50	66	0	53	53	53	171	CC GC
- + + + -	(-)	39	50	53	16	0	0	63	69	0	30	0	25	46	61	51	57	30	50	38	50	52	50	0	44	50	41	0	71	41	44	142	CP O TR
- + + + -	(-)	48	60	41	50	0	0	45	48	0	63	0	60	64	61	52	38	54	57	75	36	43	100	0	62	55	55	0	50	64	55	233	SF
- + + + -	(-)	34	25	43	50	0	0	36	50	0	36	0	33	35	35	37	42	45	42	44	63	56	0	0	37	37	37	0	50	29	41	174	O
- + + + +	(+)	53	66	75	50	0	0	30	60	0	44	0	66	34	9	36	52	0	57	50	57	36	0	0	57	44	50	0	25	35	50	161	BP C JY LB SF TR
- + + + +	(+)	41	66	36	31	0	0	40	53	0	50	0	60	38	56	48	59	44	44	23	61	47	100	0	28	33	44	0	75	64	50	177	BP C JY LB SF TR
- + + + -	(-)	64	40	57	68	0	0	30	46	0	39	0	60	55	51	53	57	69	69	57	57	52	0	0	50	63	33	0	36	50	48	209	SF
- + + + +	(+)	32	40	50	57	0	0	50	53	0	73	0	46	40	54	64	40	63	42	36	61	42	44	100	0	45	60	0	45	56	54	206	CC OJ
- + + + -	(-)	57	41	50	66	0	0	50	86	0	26	0	80	54	45	40	36	50	36	63	68	50	100	0	54	39	60	0	54	36	41	259	CC CP GC PL
- + + + +	(+)	37	58	42	33	0	0	36	50	0	60	0	20	67	52	53	43	57	55	45	31	42	25	0	50	38	61	0	41	63	48	198	SF
- + + + +	(+)	47	42	45	28	0	0	48	41	0	51	0	80	29	45	54	42	52	55	57	56	57	25	0	44	42	25	0	57	36	49	245	JY LB SF
- + + + +	(+)	50	47	54	64	0	0	52	55	0	48	0	20	34	45	59	50	35	44	45	64	54	100	0	26	61	48	0	50	36	46	247	CC SF
- + + + -	(-)	45	60	46	66	0	0	44	66	0	36	0	55	62	56	36	34	54	34	57	43	58	66	0	66	25	67	0	37	57	45	279	CC SM SU
- + + + -	(-)	54	66	39	46	0	0	44	31	0	36	0	33	35	59	35	52	40	35	45	52	29	33	0	23	48	38	0	57	50	45	262	SM SU
- + + + +	(+)	45	33	56	53	0	0	55	68	0	63	0	66	35	40	51	47	20	54	50	50	43	66	0	61	61	61	0	50	50	50	195	BP SF
- + + + -	(-)	67	18	52	16	0	0	58	58	0	57	0	50	50	50	38	40	42	50	57	50	58	0	0	44	44	44	0	60	35	55	215	CP JY
- + + + +	(+)	25	72	47	33	0	0	23	41	0	28	0	0	43	37	57	40	50	50	44	41	40	33	0	28	30	44	0	30	70	41	166	BO CC CO JY SF
- + + + +	(+)	69	55	43	50	0	0	50	35	0	55	0	45	64	54	46	60	50	60	80	55	47	50	0	44	44	44	0	70	25	52	122	BP
- + + + -	(-)	30	35	43	50	0	0	43	64	0	18	0	25	29	61	38	43	36	37	50	47	52	50	0	50	52	44	0	30	70	44	220	BO PB TR
- + + + +	(+)	50	64	60	81	0	0	52	64	0	57	0	75	56	43	54	56	62	50	50	52	44	100	0	50	65	47	0	62	33	55	187	W
- + + + -	(-)	30	35	34	9	0	0	43	30	0	18	0	50	43	38	37	37	37	50	50	45	46	0	0	40	34	47	0	37	66	42	213	CC GC SF
- + + + -	(-)	49	50	57	56	0	0	52	52	0	57	0	50	54	43	43	50	50	50	50	47	46	0	0	50	47	48	0	44	48	48	162	JY W
- + + + +	(+)	44	44	42	37	0	0	50	52	0	42	0	50	39	51	48	43	50	35	72	45	53	100	0	60	65	76	0	55	44	46	254	SF
- + + + +	(+)	44	42	37	43	0	0	44	41	0	42	0	50	56	50	54	56	57	50	50	47	68	53	100	66	34	47	0	44	52	46	243	PB SF
- + + + +	(+)	58	57	52	62	0	0	36	73	0	81	0	50	56	50	59	62	50	72	50	47	68	0	0	66	76	58	0	44	52	58	228	CP GC SF
- + + + -	(-)	34	42	40	37	0	0	63	26	0	13	0	50	43	43	54	57	0	27	50	47	68	100	27	100	33	20	0	55	47	39	154	O OJ S SM SU

Figure 8.4: Continued

BO	BP	C	CC	CD	CL	CO	CP	FC	GC	HO	JY	LB	LC	LH	NY	O	OJ	PB	PL	S	SF	SV	SM	SP	SU	TB	IR	W	T%	T#	------ 65% ------ BP C GC JY PH S SF
50	71	69	58	0	0	54	46	0	73	0	0	100	20	53	46	57	41	80	52	67	100	0	0	0	0	0	40	55	54	199	BP C GC JY PH S SF
45	28	30	41	0	0	45	42	0	26	0	44	70	39	40	53	42	58	20	44	32	0	0	22	0	55	0	60	44	41	154	LB
54	55	28	44	0	0	60	65	0	45	0	73	73	52	46	59	37	37	50	68	50	60	0	40	0	57	0	55	41	52	238	LB PL
43	44	66	55	0	0	60	34	0	45	0	55	26	50	50	60	50	43	54	56	50	60	0	60	0	42	0	44	23	45	207	C
46	42	56	37	0	0	62	51	0	37	0	62	31	50	38	60	50	50	56	43	50	50	0	50	0	57	0	46	69	49	218	
53	47	37	62	0	0	37	44	0	52	0	37	56	42	59	39	50	45	45	50	50	33	0	42	0	57	0	46	59	54	229	W
61	58	59	50	0	0	66	52	0	61	0	56	65	52	56	55	22	63	57	73	54	25	0	33	0	40	0	50	59	41	215	CO PL
30	41	37	41	0	0	33	47	0	38	0	25	35	42	38	55	66	36	42	26	45	75	0	66	0	42	0	50	66	40	164	O SF SM
56	58	48	31	0	0	50	65	0	74	0	75	75	69	54	62	62	66	60	47	59	100	0	46	0	54	0	40	66	55	306	GC LB LC OJ SF W
41	33	48	68	0	0	50	35	0	22	0	20	20	30	38	40	37	37	26	52	40	40	0	53	0	47	0	60	33	40	212	CC JY
53	56	50	58	0	0	46	52	0	84	0	37	42	50	57	55	33	33	57	80	54	66	0	56	0	54	0	53	50	55	287	GC PL SF
44	43	45	41	0	0	46	40	0	15	0	62	47	44	48	44	66	71	42	19	45	43	0	37	0	47	0	38	50	41	213	OJ
51	52	50	45	0	0	46	53	0	38	0	50	53	58	41	58	81	62	42	45	56	33	0	46	0	52	0	50	36	42	288	OJ
46	47	41	54	0	0	36	46	0	61	0	57	41	41	29	44	18	21	40	45	51	66	0	53	0	60	0	50	59	45	221	SF
55	64	43	27	0	0	53	75	0	80	0	57	46	48	41	58	54	61	54	57	59	66	0	23	0	37	0	70	55	60	281	CP GC SF TR
38	35	47	72	0	0	40	25	0	19	0	28	46	45	35	58	61	38	87	61	40	33	0	52	0	64	0	30	38	37	205	CC
54	36	45	50	0	0	55	38	0	59	0	71	48	47	47	50	42	56	12	45	45	40	0	54	0	57	0	42	32	49	310	JY SF
47	58	51	46	0	0	44	55	0	36	0	18	40	46	40	49	39	50	65	42	62	80	0	45	0	50	0	14	47	46	276	
50	25	67	53	0	0	50	44	0	33	0	41	41	54	55	50	50	63	45	41	34	20	0	36	0	50	0	71	38	52	247	C NY SF TR
56	51	58	41	0	0	50	39	0	61	0	50	66	42	42	60	60	44	61	61	50	0	0	38	0	57	0	57	35	44	210	LB
56	40	35	50	0	0	57	60	0	47	0	42	34	50	56	50	57	57	54	56	45	40	0	37	0	36	0	55	35	46	196	
42	51	58	41	0	0	57	60	0	52	0	42	65	39	42	66	20	42	40	54	40	50	0	62	0	50	0	44	50	49	208	O
40	75	55	63	0	0	27	75	0	100	0	100	61	60	55	66	42	100	40	54	80	0	0	62	0	37	0	80	61	60	156	BP CP GC JY NY OJ
60	25	44	36	0	0	72	25	0	0	0	0	30	44	33	57	47	38	45	45	20	100	0	9	0	37	0	20	38	37	97	CO SF
38	28	60	38	0	0	60	65	0	18	0	28	50	45	50	57	42	60	87	58	40	0	0	50	0	28	0	69	48	48	182	PB TH
58	71	40	61	0	0	60	31	0	81	0	71	44	56	44	50	57	57	12	61	45	60	0	33	0	64	0	30	32	49	184	BP GC JY
42	53	50	63	0	0	54	39	0	52	0	36	41	46	50	53	16	42	50	45	38	0	0	63	0	50	0	14	47	46	188	
51	38	45	36	0	0	45	57	0	47	0	63	52	46	55	46	40	50	57	41	46	100	0	36	0	57	0	71	38	49	197	TR
52	45	28	30	0	0	36	57	0	56	0	55	37	54	42	42	60	56	26	61	54	33	0	38	0	57	0	60	68	47	220	PB SF W
38	50	71	69	0	0	36	42	0	30	0	63	58	45	59	31	60	71	60	56	53	0	0	46	0	85	0	31	60	50	235	C CC
71	50	61	66	0	0	47	50	0	38	0	71	60	50	50	68	14	42	40	43	55	0	0	54	0	14	0	62	50	57	221	BO CC JY O SU
28	37	38	33	0	0	47	50	0	42	0	28	39	47	50	40	57	57	57	55	55	50	0	45	0	36	0	37	50	40	158	
52	50	44	61	0	0	58	56	0	62	0	62	47	51	43	50	50	53	40	35	48	50	0	45	0	45	0	63	56	45	223	PB
43	50	48	38	0	0	60	43	0	33	0	33	58	38	51	54	37	50	47	71	60	66	0	47	0	47	0	36	43	51	201	BP SF
41	68	59	57	0	0	56	56	0	48	0	66	37	58	43	42	57	62	43	57	48	50	0	52	0	45	0	60	58	46	290	BP SF
55	31	40	35	0	0	60	31	0	45	0	50	26	37	39	34	50	50	56	44	29	66	0	45	0	47	0	40	34	42	259	JY
37	59	57	50	0	0	66	57	0	52	0	50	67	50	51	34	37	53	25	50	33	100	0	54	0	52	0	25	50	54	247	CO
62	40	50	31	0	0	33	57	0	44	0	85	66	45	44	57	78	46	46	30	66	25	0	57	0	63	0	75	57	59	317	LB O PB S SF TR
60	73	64	66	0	0	27	65	0	66	0	50	67	50	71	44	50	77	75	78	63	0	0	76	0	25	0	61	50	41	229	BP CO GC JY LH NY
39	21	35	33	0	0	50	38	0	33	0	44	44	56	33	34	50	50	60	63	25	50	0	42	0	42	0	36	57	38	147	CC LB S SM W
57	45	56	61	0	0	55	59	0	37	0	50	66	53	65	47	33	62	22	30	50	33	100	23	0	63	0	38	38	56	275	SF
39	45	37	38	0	0	46	39	0	62	0	37	28	43	42	33	62	55	55	57	52	66	0	44	0	36	0	44	31	41	202	SF O
39	41	56	33	0	0	33	50	0	41	0	56	52	44	55	31	66	31	33	39	47	33	0	76	0	50	0	60	28	45	195	CO JY NY PB SF
60	11	50	66	0	0	47	50	0	48	0	50	37	66	68	68	16	66	66	57	52	100	0	23	0	47	0	50	64	50	213	JY NY BP CC SM
38	80	50	22	0	0	46	58	0	51	0	37	42	62	59	40	33	53	39	52	66	28	0	44	0	47	0	22	49	49	245	BP CC SM
58	20	50	33	0	0	63	68	0	51	0	66	46	56	50	38	40	43	43	46	45	71	0	66	0	59	0	50	77	48	239	SF W
55	53	35	56	0	0	36	24	0	48	0	33	55	56	60	48	55	57	56	57	60	66	0	33	0	68	0	55	40	56	253	CP PB SF SU
44	30	53	43	0	0	51	45	0	35	0	50	38	38	34	39	33	50	37	52	52	37	0	60	0	35	0	44	44	40	183	O OJ
54	56	31	53	0	0	48	52	0	57	0	70	62	55	48	26	62	38	25	38	41	62	0	38	0	64	0	45	44	48	264	JY
47	37	61	75	0	0	25	46	0	61	0	43	46	37	39	26	55	25	40	40	54	38	0	40	0	50	0	54	44	47	259	CO CC NY TH
47	61	38	25	0	0	54	58	0	35	0	37	42	34	49	55	40	33	44	61	41	40	0	66	0	73	0	73	38	54	304	CC CO NY TH
47	47	26	40	0	0	50	60	0	29	0	60	71	37	45	73	33	58	45	57	60	66	0	41	0	26	0	66	57	42	233	BP LB SF TH
45	70	65	53	0	0	46	39	0	0	0	60	28	60	73	46	58	54	54	60	60	33	0	45	0	40	0	33	28	44	210	BP LB SF
54	29	65	53	0	0	46	39	0	0	0	60	28	60	73	45	58	58	54	60	60	33	0	45	0	60	0	33	71	52	245	W

Figure 8.4: Continued

Figure 8.4: Continued

Figure 8.4: Continued

Sign	BO	BP	C	CC	CD	CL	CO	CP	FC	GC	HO	JY	LB	LC	LH	NY	O	OJ	PB	PL	S	SF	SV	SM	SP	SU	TB	TR	W	T%	T#	65%
(+)	34	83	61	57	0	0	60	73	0	77	0	28	46	63	45	37	50	40	25	60	64	100	0	0	0	31	0	40	58	51	125	BP CP GC SF SM
(-)	58	16	38	28	0	0	40	26	0	22	0	71	46	31	45	62	50	60	75	40	28	0	0	33	0	68	0	60	33	44	108	JY PB SU
(-)	31	71	30	37	0	0	66	26	0	83	0	57	22	43	45	42	50	0	75	40	25	0	0	66	0	52	0	0	15	48	98	BP CO GC SM
(-)	68	28	70	62	0	0	33	73	0	16	0	42	72	56	54	54	37	100	60	60	42	0	0	33	0	47	0	61	0	58	148	BO C CP LB O PB
(+)	40	100	44	33	0	0	85	12	0	66	0	75	42	50	70	63	62	100	66	63	66	0	0	0	0	80	0	80	50	58	89	BP CO GC JY LH OJ
(-)	60	0	44	66	0	0	14	87	0	33	0	25	72	56	30	36	0	0	33	83	83	33	0	100	0	20	0	20	37	38	59	CC CP SM
(+)	64	37	46	66	0	0	50	45	0	66	0	50	55	50	82	0	50	75	0	27	16	33	0	50	0	73	0	50	33	56	129	CC LH O OJ PB S
(+)	36	37	53	20	0	0	50	54	0	66	0	25	44	43	11	25	28	100	0	0	33	0	0	50	0	26	0	50	33	39	91	GC NY
(-)	38	50	50	60	0	0	90	63	0	50	0	50	61	63	35	66	66	0	0	63	66	0	0	50	0	53	0	50	75	44	77	CO O S
(-)	61	50	50	40	0	0	10	36	0	16	0	42	36	64	14	85	28	42	100	36	33	0	0	50	0	40	0	50	0	44	68	NY PB W
(+)	50	60	33	71	0	0	25	33	0	41	0	0	0	36	63	66	50	60	50	46	57	23	0	60	0	50	0	50	0	49	98	C CC JY NY
(+)	50	40	66	28	0	0	66	58	0	58	0	100	50	35	31	33	42	50	50	38	42	66	0	66	0	50	0	50	100	47	95	C CO SF W
(-)	62	50	21	50	0	0	60	41	0	41	0	40	80	50	36	55	25	42	66	33	46	0	0	33	0	76	0	25	63	51	106	LB PB PL SM SU
(+)	37	60	64	50	0	0	66	33	0	66	0	60	20	50	44	50	57	60	50	30	35	0	0	33	0	23	0	75	55	45	95	SF TR
(+)	55	40	33	50	0	0	53	57	0	75	0	33	64	54	47	66	66	0	33	53	21	66	0	50	0	36	0	50	53	49	117	NY O OJ
(-)	45	60	50	50	0	0	46	30	0	76	0	20	66	36	30	55	66	66	33	41	66	0	0	16	0	63	0	80	71	47	113	GC OJ JY LB LC
(-)	52	44	50	80	0	0	66	33	0	66	0	33	66	68	48	28	60	60	60	50	35	0	0	33	0	54	0	83	44	55	126	CC CO GC JY LB LC TR
(+)	38	75	11	66	0	0	53	57	0	26	0	20	22	47	40	44	60	20	50	53	46	0	0	28	0	37	0	16	55	41	93	CP SF
(+)	61	25	77	16	0	0	60	42	0	76	0	80	40	47	40	71	80	80	50	46	50	64	0	57	0	62	0	66	66	42	116	C JY NY OJ S W
(-)	33	80	40	60	0	0	22	75	0	75	0	60	66	11	40	28	50	55	0	40	78	33	0	66	0	66	0	33	33	53	99	BP CP GC SM W
(+)	41	71	50	50	0	0	40	42	0	60	0	33	40	36	50	44	80	28	50	45	50	0	0	33	0	50	0	20	66	47	102	BP CP GC W
(-)	58	14	43	50	0	0	80	22	0	23	0	66	46	63	54	55	50	90	66	41	55	66	0	66	0	40	0	80	33	49	105	CO JY SF SM TR
(-)	59	50	41	61	0	0	63	42	0	50	0	44	50	27	36	53	50	22	33	27	27	0	0	25	0	35	0	33	50	46	105	LC OJ
(-)	40	71	58	83	0	0	56	70	0	50	0	66	60	75	66	36	33	10	0	58	72	75	0	50	0	50	0	75	37	54	160	BP CC OJ TR
(-)	56	28	41	16	0	0	34	29	0	42	0	66	53	61	33	36	40	75	77	41	50	72	0	38	0	55	0	25	12	46	141	JY PB SF
(+)	65	71	44	28	0	0	58	70	0	50	0	60	40	43	66	62	66	66	25	58	41	0	0	44	0	44	0	60	37	54	117	BP CP LH OJ SF SM
(-)	34	28	55	71	0	0	41	29	0	37	0	40	60	61	38	50	33	50	33	57	50	0	0	38	0	38	0	14	75	44	94	CC O PL
(-)	35	44	40	60	0	0	58	59	0	59	0	33	55	55	50	40	50	0	66	70	52	75	0	55	0	55	0	12	25	51	129	OJ PB SF
(+)	64	55	50	40	0	0	41	59	0	38	0	25	64	47	67	63	77	50	45	40	41	25	0	72	0	72	0	40	23	40	148	JY PL TR W
(-)	26	33	33	66	0	0	75	18	0	38	0	75	61	38	50	35	40	100	66	45	50	0	0	18	0	23	0	60	76	44	127	LH O PB
(+)	62	40	66	50	0	0	57	60	0	83	0	25	63	50	59	57	60	40	33	50	50	100	0	85	0	61	0	80	42	53	155	CP JY SF SM
(+)	37	50	72	37	0	0	57	60	0	16	0	66	63	73	59	42	71	28	20	45	50	100	0	66	0	76	0	66	57	57	118	C GC JY LC OJ PB
(-)	72	50	18	62	0	0	42	40	0	48	0	33	38	26	64	42	80	54	33	33	40	0	0	33	0	23	0	33	60	41	84	BO SM
(+)	57	72	20	66	0	0	42	54	0	52	0	50	28	63	70	50	83	54	16	40	50	0	0	65	0	65	0	57	42	55	156	BO CC LH O OJ PB
(-)	42	27	80	33	0	0	37	42	0	52	0	50	64	35	29	50	36	36	62	62	50	0	0	25	0	35	0	42	43	43	121	C LB
(+)	40	42	31	50	0	0	61	55	0	75	0	100	40	59	56	52	66	66	57	44	60	0	0	60	0	55	0	50	52	52	143	GC JY OJ SF
(+)	56	37	56	61	0	0	38	40	0	25	0	0	60	43	37	35	33	33	42	55	60	100	0	40	0	44	0	66	71	45	125	W
(+)	59	57	56	41	0	0	75	55	0	33	0	100	41	52	50	58	50	38	50	55	55	0	0	33	0	58	0	50	66	48	139	PB
(-)	40	62	50	38	0	0	60	64	0	69	0	62	58	47	46	58	50	61	33	61	43	0	0	50	0	41	0	44	60	45	164	GC SF
(+)	56	66	44	57	0	0	60	35	0	54	0	66	80	52	57	57	50	62	25	37	55	0	0	20	0	62	0	55	38	53	119	JY LB LC
(-)	34	33	55	42	0	0	53	37	0	45	0	33	20	58	61	35	25	37	62	37	43	0	0	60	0	37	0	50	53	41	86	O PB S
(-)	52	28	47	25	0	0	46	61	0	69	0	60	80	44	40	50	60	55	42	44	40	50	0	66	0	23	0	12	87	47	118	GC LB SM
(+)	47	71	47	75	0	0	53	38	0	30	0	100	64	50	40	38	44	44	42	55	60	50	0	33	0	61	0	20	50	46	115	BP CC TR
(+)	67	54	50	50	0	0	68	57	0	37	0	50	63	31	37	62	57	50	50	50	50	100	0	40	0	57	0	80	28	53	111	BO CO JY SF
(-)	32	45	50	50	0	0	31	42	0	70	0	50	35	36	62	28	50	37	50	62	41	0	0	60	0	42	0	75	71	45	94	GC TH W
(-)	60	50	40	0	0	0	25	88	0	33	0	0	33	56	56	62	50	37	16	15	37	50	0	66	0	71	0	40	60	48	125	CO CP SM SU
(-)	30	50	60	80	0	0	75	11	0	66	0	0	66	50	37	50	50	83	100	50	62	50	0	33	0	28	0	60	60	59	95	CC GC JY LB PB PL
(+)	56	66	100	33	0	0	0	100	0	0	0	0	50	50	44	0	50	50	0	100	0	0	0	0	0	50	0	0	40	59	38	BP C CO CP NY O
(-)	43	33	0	33	0	0	0	0	0	0	0	0	0	50	33	0	33	50	0	0	50	0	0	0	0	50	0	0	0	35	23	

Figure 8.4: Continued

	BO	BP	C	CC	CD	CL	CO	CP	FC	GC	HO	JY	LB	LC	LH	NY	O	OJ	PB	PL	S	SF	SV	SM	SP	SU	TB	TR	W	T%	T#				65%		

Figure 8.4: Continued

Figure 8.4: Concluded

		BO	BP	C	CC	CD	CL	CO	CP	FC	GC	HO	JY	LB	LC	LH	NY	O	OJ	PB	PL	S	SF	SV	SM	SP	SU	TB	TR	W	T%	T#	------- 65% -------
+++-+++	(+)	62	40	33	40	0	0	57	18	0	38	0	25	36	50	67	35	77	40	66	45	50	0	0	14	0	33	0	20	23	44	127	LH O PB
+++-+++	(-)	37	50	66	60	0	0	42	81	0	52	0	75	63	50	32	64	22	40	33	45	50	100	0	85	0	66	0	80	76	53	155	C CP JY SF SM SU
++++---	(+)	27	50	72	37	0	0	57	60	0	83	0	66	53	73	59	57	60	71	80	66	50	100	0	33	0	76	0	66	42	57	118	C GC JY LC OJ PB
++++---	(-)	72	50	18	62	0	0	42	40	0	16	0	33	38	26	40	42	40	28	20	33	40	0	0	66	0	23	0	33	57	41	84	BO SM
++++--+	(+)	57	72	20	66	0	0	62	54	0	48	0	25	28	64	70	50	83	54	83	37	50	50	0	75	0	65	0	57	60	55	156	BP CC LH O PB SM
++++--+	(-)	42	27	80	33	0	0	37	42	0	52	0	50	71	35	29	50	16	36	16	62	50	0	0	25	0	35	0	42	40	43	121	C LB
+++++--	(+)	40	42	31	50	0	0	61	55	0	75	0	100	40	59	56	52	40	66	57	44	60	100	0	40	0	55	0	50	33	52	143	GC JY OJ SF
+++++--	(-)	59	57	56	41	0	0	38	40	0	25	0	0	60	36	37	47	60	33	42	55	40	0	0	60	0	44	0	50	66	45	125	W
+++++-+	(+)	56	37	50	61	0	0	40	35	0	30	0	37	41	52	50	35	50	38	66	38	55	0	0	33	0	58	0	44	38	45	139	PB
+++++-+	(-)	40	62	50	38	0	0	60	64	0	69	0	62	58	47	46	58	50	61	33	61	45	100	0	50	0	41	0	55	53	53	164	GC SF
++++-++	(+)	56	66	44	57	0	0	46	62	0	54	0	66	80	71	57	62	0	62	25	62	33	0	0	20	0	62	0	50	87	56	119	BP JY LB LC W
++++-++	(-)	34	33	55	42	0	0	53	37	0	45	0	33	20	28	42	42	37	100	75	57	66	0	0	60	0	37	0	50	12	41	86	O PB S
++++++-	(+)	52	28	47	25	0	0	46	61	0	69	0	60	80	44	40	50	60	55	42	55	40	50	0	66	0	23	0	20	50	47	118	GC LH SM
++++++-	(-)	47	71	47	75	0	0	53	38	0	30	0	40	20	33	44	38	44	44	42	44	60	50	0	33	0	61	0	80	50	46	115	BP CC TR
+++++++	(+)	67	54	50	50	0	0	68	57	0	30	0	100	64	63	31	37	57	50	50	37	50	100	0	40	0	57	0	25	28	55	111	BO CO JY SF
+++++++	(-)	32	45	50	50	0	0	31	42	0	70	0	0	35	46	62	62	28	50	50	62	41	0	0	60	0	42	0	75	71	45	94	GC TR W
+++++++	(+)	60	50	40	0	0	0	75	88	0	33	0	0	33	50	56	62	50	50	16	15	37	50	0	66	0	71	0	40	60	48	95	CO CP SM SU
+++++++	(-)	30	50	60	80	0	0	25	11	0	66	0	100	66	50	43	37	50	37	83	76	62	50	0	33	0	28	0	60	40	48	95	GC GC JY LB PB PL

Figure 8.5: Daily Closing Patterns: Choppy Bear Markets

Pattern	BO	BP	±	C	CC	CD	CL	CO	CP	FC	GC	HO	JY	LB	LC	LH	NY	O	OJ	PB	PL	S	SF	SV	SM	SP	SU	TB	TR	W	T%	T#
– –	46	48	(+)	44	0	0	0	54	56	0	50	0	0	43	45	46	46	50	43	50	51	49	43	0	49	0	50	0	43	51	48	2746
– +	49	43	(+)	48	0	0	0	46	41	0	41	0	0	47	50	52	52	51	51	46	47	45	47	0	50	0	49	0	42	45	47	2670
+ –	45	31	(+)	48	0	0	0	52	48	0	39	0	0	41	47	51	46	51	47	48	43	45	42	0	50	0	47	0	45	45	46	2535
+ +	50	63	(+)	46	0	0	0	46	49	0	58	0	0	54	49	45	52	45	44	48	54	50	55	0	44	0	50	0	43	51	50	2716
+ +	41	39	(+)	42	0	0	0	46	56	0	56	0	0	45	39	45	49	49	45	48	49	50	45	0	49	0	42	0	39	46	46	2504
+ –	55	50	(+)	54	0	0	0	52	47	0	42	0	0	49	56	55	49	50	49	55	45	50	52	0	45	0	54	0	52	48	50	2766
+ +	43	44	(+)	40	0	0	0	43	41	0	41	0	0	39	46	53	44	39	47	44	40	41	45	0	41	0	39	0	41	44	42	2033
+ –	54	51	(+)	55	0	0	0	55	55	0	58	0	0	54	49	56	51	53	57	54	53	57	52	0	56	0	58	0	53	53	54	2561
– +	46	52	(-)	44	0	0	0	43	47	0	41	0	0	46	49	53	51	40	39	44	40	41	48	0	45	0	51	0	47	54	49	1321
– –	50	36	(+)	48	0	0	0	54	55	0	48	0	0	52	45	48	48	51	59	58	55	47	43	0	54	0	48	0	41	43	47	1258
+ +	46	21	(+)	47	0	0	0	44	47	0	40	0	0	41	44	51	44	43	39	40	42	47	43	0	45	0	50	0	41	45	46	1271
– –	49	67	(+)	49	0	0	0	44	50	0	57	0	0	55	50	48	51	45	43	48	54	49	62	0	45	0	46	0	43	50	50	1373 BP
– + +	42	44	(+)	42	0	0	0	50	49	0	58	0	0	47	40	37	46	52	35	39	52	42	49	0	45	0	46	0	32	47	46	1253
+ – +	54	50	(+)	52	0	0	0	47	48	0	40	0	0	60	56	53	51	56	49	52	52	49	52	0	42	0	51	0	55	43	50	1367
– + –	40	44	(+)	39	0	0	0	53	41	0	40	0	0	50	43	46	49	48	40	42	44	36	49	0	37	0	43	0	40	43	42	1079
+ + +	58	50	(+)	52	0	0	0	54	59	0	53	0	0	47	51	53	40	46	56	50	53	62	50	0	59	0	52	0	55	55	54	1378
– + +	47	48	(+)	44	0	0	0	54	36	0	44	0	0	45	51	59	57	40	40	51	46	45	57	0	54	0	49	0	48	48	48	1342
+ + –	45	41	(-)	48	0	0	0	50	49	0	39	0	0	53	51	53	56	53	52	55	43	47	50	0	45	0	50	0	41	51	47	1311
+ – +	51	58	(-)	52	0	0	0	49	50	0	44	0	0	41	51	45	46	39	53	48	50	50	57	0	52	0	44	0	45	45	50	1178
– – +	41	36	(+)	42	0	0	0	50	49	0	39	0	0	45	40	46	53	41	40	44	49	46	43	0	44	0	55	0	52	52	50	1255
+ – –	55	50	(-)	41	0	0	0	43	50	0	52	0	0	41	40	46	44	52	43	52	45	46	50	0	50	0	38	0	43	50	45	1174
+ + +	48	42	(+)	40	0	0	0	56	47	0	46	0	0	27	57	52	41	29	45	47	48	38	45	0	46	0	57	0	54	46	51	1316
– – –	49	52	(+)	40	0	0	0	53	40	0	41	0	0	48	48	38	44	38	38	45	45	43	45	0	43	0	34	0	36	43	43	881
+ + + +	48	66	(+)	55	0	0	0	54	55	0	58	0	0	66	47	56	62	60	49	50	61	52	52	0	53	0	65	0	55	62	53	1090 LB
– + + +	48	33	(+)	44	0	0	0	47	46	0	47	0	0	46	38	50	56	36	54	54	50	51	40	0	47	0	48	0	62	60	50	629 BP
+ – + +	47	23	(+)	52	0	0	0	46	47	0	51	0	0	30	45	50	47	45	60	50	46	39	33	0	52	0	51	0	34	47	47	594
+ + – +	49	76	(+)	41	0	0	0	53	50	0	43	0	0	66	48	54	55	44	40	50	55	48	33	0	43	0	41	0	42	47	48	627
+ + + +	40	42	(+)	45	0	0	0	54	36	0	56	0	0	66	47	45	46	53	39	47	50	49	66	0	43	0	54	0	45	45	48	645 BP LB SF
– + + –	55	57	(-)	52	0	0	0	50	49	0	34	0	0	47	46	60	48	38	53	60	46	52	52	0	33	0	41	0	45	40	48	664
– – + +	38	33	(-)	43	0	0	0	42	40	0	42	0	0	47	50	60	55	44	56	35	43	35	44	0	46	0	55	0	45	48	41	523
+ + – –	60	66	(+)	44	0	0	0	59	59	0	34	0	0	42	51	57	50	51	45	45	50	53	47	0	26	0	46	0	25	34	41	713 BP SM
+ – + –	45	33	(+)	49	0	0	0	39	59	0	42	0	0	39	46	37	34	64	42	46	46	41	34	0	50	0	44	0	53	50	48	668
– + + +	50	61	(+)	44	0	0	0	59	52	0	45	0	0	37	51	62	65	30	50	53	50	58	58	0	50	0	55	0	43	49	47	649
+ + – +	50	37	(-)	52	0	0	0	47	47	0	40	0	0	34	48	50	34	50	59	46	46	41	48	0	42	0	30	0	47	46	44	581
– + + +	45	62	(+)	41	0	0	0	51	50	0	58	0	0	52	48	55	61	61	40	45	55	48	51	0	43	0	69	0	36	44	50	633 SU
+ – – +	43	44	(-)	41	0	0	0	46	49	0	55	0	0	32	38	44	47	44	51	38	50	42	26	0	40	0	33	0	40	46	44	611
+ + + +	52	44	(+)	55	0	0	0	57	49	0	42	0	0	52	58	58	43	55	50	51	58	51	73	0	59	0	59	0	60	62	52	722 SF
– + + –	55	37	(-)	44	0	0	0	44	42	0	48	0	0	26	52	66	56	28	43	50	47	47	40	0	35	0	36	0	41	55	45	493 LH
+ – + +	42	62	(+)	52	0	0	0	62	54	0	51	0	0	54	52	33	58	60	50	50	52	50	54	0	64	0	63	0	55	42	51	557 LB
– + – +	43	42	(-)	43	0	0	0	57	47	0	47	0	0	45	39	55	48	73	53	40	42	50	54	0	40	0	53	0	39	51	48	641
+ – + –	54	35	(-)	52	0	0	0	41	50	0	39	0	0	51	43	34	48	26	53	57	56	49	42	0	52	0	46	0	48	40	47	627
+ + + +	44	20	(+)	49	0	0	0	53	59	0	59	0	0	57	53	40	39	46	42	47	49	48	59	0	47	0	58	0	48	60	45	603
– + + +	50	60	(-)	49	0	0	0	44	59	0	57	0	0	50	55	40	57	45	57	47	54	40	59	0	54	0	37	0	45	54	45	688
– – + +	44	35	(-)	39	0	0	0	48	42	0	55	0	0	53	33	28	48	52	31	41	49	45	45	0	56	0	53	0	17	36	44	558
+ + + +	54	50	(+)	55	0	0	0	48	55	0	43	0	0	42	61	66	66	39	60	56	47	54	54	0	43	0	46	0	69	62	52	653 LH TR
– + + –	42	60	(-)	41	0	0	0	55	56	0	42	0	0	44	58	50	43	51	54	42	50	36	60	0	42	0	60	0	60	43	43	511
+ + + +	56	30	(+)	44	0	0	0	51	52	0	57	0	0	50	53	56	56	40	43	51	52	63	52	0	52	0	61	0	39	50	53	630
– + + –	50	63	(-)	55	0	0	0	49	54	0	55	0	0	54	42	41	53	53	50	42	51	47	40	0	57	0	51	0	47	45	48	634
– + + +	43	27	(-)	48	0	0	0	50	47	0	39	0	0	54	54	54	47	50	50	57	44	54	48	0	42	0	48	0	41	54	47	627
+ + + +	41	50	(+)	50	0	0	0	50	50	0	59	0	0	45	53	34	73	26	53	40	42	50	52	0	52	0	60	0	48	40	48	563 O
+ + + +	57	50	(+)	45	0	0	0	50	46	0	46	0	0	51	43	53	40	40	58	57	56	49	42	0	52	0	40	0	48	60	49	583
+ + + –	39	40	(+)	43	0	0	0	46	53	0	53	0	0	49	43	34	53	58	59	51	49	39	59	0	66	0	47	0	44	53	47	522 SM
+ + + –	58	40	(-)	55	0	0	0	53	45	0	46	0	0	53	54	37	51	60	37	45	47	59	40	0	33	0	52	0	51	41	50	546

-------- 65% --------

Figure 8.5: Continued

	(+/-)	BO	BP	C	CC	CD	CL	CO	CP	FC	GC	HO	JY	LB	LC	LH	NY	O	OJ	PB	PL	S	SF	SV	SM	SP	SU	TB	TR	W	T%	T#	codes
+-+-+++	(+)	38	100	64	0	0	0	35	23	0	36	0	0	50	50	66	60	50	62	33	80	42	50	0	33	0	16	0	40	57	44	69	BP PL
+-+-++-	(-)	61	0	35	0	0	0	64	69	0	36	0	0	50	70	50	66	50	37	50	20	42	0	100	66	100	25	0	60	42	52	81	CP LC NY SM SU
+-+-+-+	(-)	60	0	30	0	0	0	57	50	0	30	0	0	28	50	50	60	33	50	66	38	42	0	0	0	0	0	0	50	25	44	58	PB SM
+-+-+--	(+)	40	100	60	0	0	0	42	50	0	70	0	0	71	60	100	40	66	25	66	84	80	50	100	0	75	75	0	33	66	53	69	BP GC LB LH O SU
+-+--++	(-)	57	50	33	0	0	0	53	78	0	47	0	0	75	36	20	33	50	42	50	15	20	16	0	0	0	60	0	66	33	53	86	CP LB PL S W
+-+--+-	(+)	35	50	66	0	0	0	46	14	0	52	0	0	25	63	80	50	42	50	75	20	38	50	0	40	0	40	0	66	33	43	71	C LH NY SM TR
+-+---+	(+)	73	0	12	0	0	0	62	50	0	35	0	0	57	28	0	75	100	75	44	50	53	50	0	0	0	33	0	0	100	48	81	BO NY O OJ PB TR
+-+----	(+)	26	50	75	0	0	0	37	46	0	58	0	0	28	71	100	25	0	25	25	55	53	50	50	0	66	66	0	0	0	47	79	C LC LH SU W
+-++++	(-)	52	0	36	0	0	0	33	17	0	56	0	0	55	33	0	58	50	33	50	40	25	33	0	50	16	16	0	0	71	41	60	SM
+-+++-	(+)	47	50	63	0	0	0	66	76	0	56	0	0	44	33	100	41	50	66	50	75	66	33	0	0	83	0	50	66	0	54	80	CO CP LH OJ S SF
+-++-+	(-)	50	0	33	0	0	0	53	23	0	37	0	0	16	83	100	42	66	66	58	58	50	66	0	0	0	75	0	0	75	46	54	LC LH O PB SU W
+-++--	(+)	58	0	66	0	0	0	38	69	0	75	0	0	66	43	0	57	33	100	66	41	50	33	0	0	25	0	33	0	25	52	50	C CP LB OJ SF SM
+-+-++	(+)	41	0	58	0	0	0	56	56	0	25	0	0	14	57	0	77	0	28	50	50	37	33	0	66	66	66	0	66	33	45	78	GC LB LH NY SM SU
+-+-+-	(+)	44	100	46	0	0	0	70	80	0	23	0	0	66	75	0	11	100	57	66	50	50	66	0	33	0	33	0	100	70	50	68	O PB SF TR
+-+--+	(-)	55	0	53	0	0	0	30	19	0	76	0	0	33	25	100	30	0	75	33	14	57	0	33	33	0	0	100	0	62	49	74	BP CO CP LB LC NY
+--++++	(-)	71	33	50	0	0	0	70	64	0	50	0	0	50	20	0	28	0	66	72	22	46	80	0	66	0	66	0	66	50	53	72	GC LH PB PL SM TR
+--+++-	(+)	28	33	50	0	0	0	50	38	0	30	0	0	50	50	100	57	33	50	27	77	75	33	100	0	33	0	25	50	83	48	62	BO OJ S SM SU W
+--++-+	(-)	52	100	33	0	0	0	50	46	0	70	0	0	50	33	0	40	50	66	50	47	46	60	0	50	0	50	0	50	16	51	58	CO LC LH NY O TR
+--++--	(+)	47	0	66	0	0	0	50	40	0	70	0	0	50	66	0	40	0	66	50	70	50	40	0	20	0	50	0	50	40	45	55	BP LH OJ PB
+--+-++	(+)	53	100	50	0	0	0	50	60	0	66	0	0	37	66	75	66	25	33	66	14	44	0	33	33	33	33	0	50	42	37	67	C GC LC O PL SF
+--+-+-	(-)	44	0	55	0	0	0	56	33	0	50	0	0	62	50	25	33	50	57	66	55	46	100	0	66	0	0	0	50	40	53	80	LH TR
+--+--+	(+)	59	0	44	0	0	0	43	66	0	80	0	0	66	40	0	42	33	50	72	44	46	20	0	33	0	66	0	37	50	48	95	BP GC O PB SF SM SU
+--+---	(-)	50	0	55	0	0	0	56	33	0	66	0	0	66	66	100	66	50	33	50	46	33	80	100	33	100	66	0	66	50	48	79	GC LB PB SM SU TR
+---+++	(+)	39	100	44	0	0	0	72	41	0	50	0	0	33	40	0	38	25	50	27	53	46	33	0	0	0	0	0	66	83	51	78	CP LH PL SF
+---++-	(-)	46	0	26	0	0	0	27	54	0	50	0	0	75	33	60	61	75	16	50	46	50	0	0	50	0	50	0	50	16	45	94	BP C CO LB LC SF
+---+-+	(-)	7	0	35	0	0	0	50	29	0	50	0	0	60	25	50	50	60	66	50	70	50	50	0	33	0	33	0	50	40	37	83	O PL
+---+--	(+)	92	50	52	0	0	0	50	64	0	56	0	0	20	57	50	66	50	50	0	14	55	50	0	66	0	66	0	50	66	59	55	
+----++	(-)	41	100	33	0	0	0	81	71	0	66	0	0	0	57	50	33	0	0	100	44	44	46	0	33	0	0	0	33	42	47	87	BO NY OJ PL SM SU
+----+-	(+)	52	100	50	0	0	0	18	28	0	43	0	0	100	42	66	66	0	50	66	50	46	46	0	0	100	50	0	66	80	50	69	CO CP PB
+-----+	(-)	50	0	87	0	0	0	36	44	0	66	0	0	60	36	25	40	100	100	72	53	57	0	0	50	0	0	0	66	20	57	74	BP C LB NY OJ SM
+------	(-)	37	100	12	0	0	0	63	55	0	50	0	0	40	50	71	71	75	16	27	46	0	50	0	33	0	0	0	33	28	46	71	CP LH OJ PB SF
-+++++	(+)	61	0	31	0	0	0	62	75	0	60	0	0	37	50	50	60	60	25	50	53	44	50	100	50	100	33	0	50	57	55	78	BP GC LB O SU
-++++-	(-)	38	0	59	0	0	0	62	25	0	40	0	0	62	12	0	66	25	66	50	22	56	100	0	50	0	50	0	66	25	42	67	LB PL SU W
-+++-+	(-)	66	0	50	0	0	0	45	16	0	50	0	0	66	50	100	37	50	50	0	57	50	0	0	0	33	0	50	66	80	54	87	CP NY OJ SF TR
-+++--	(+)	53	0	38	0	0	0	54	75	0	33	0	0	33	87	100	50	66	50	42	50	57	50	0	50	0	0	0	66	20	48	53	BO LC TR O PB
-++-++	(-)	46	0	53	0	0	0	46	44	0	66	0	0	20	20	75	66	33	50	66	55	57	0	0	0	0	100	0	66	66	49	68	BP CP LB O PH
-++-+-	(+)	38	0	44	0	0	0	53	59	0	66	0	0	71	62	0	50	0	75	66	44	42	100	0	50	0	0	0	66	33	51	61	LB NY SU TR W
-++--+	(-)	46	100	55	0	0	0	38	40	0	50	0	0	60	60	100	40	28	28	33	53	44	50	0	66	0	66	0	50	50	45	63	GC PB SF SM
-++---	(+)	50	0	33	0	0	0	64	31	0	83	0	0	37	16	37	40	33	57	25	46	70	50	100	14	0	85	0	50	83	56	67	LH OJ PB PL SU
-+-++++	(+)	40	0	66	0	0	0	35	68	0	66	0	0	40	50	75	33	62	20	25	16	54	0	50	0	66	66	0	33	33	45	59	NY TR
-+-+++-	(-)	50	100	46	0	0	0	35	68	0	44	0	0	33	25	16	36	37	33	80	55	20	0	25	50	85	0	0	83	33	56	56	O S SM
-+-++-+	(+)	50	100	46	0	0	0	80	71	0	66	0	0	71	54	0	12	0	50	75	44	20	0	50	66	66	0	0	33	66	45	67	C GC LC LH OJ PB SU
-+-++--	(-)	50	0	33	0	0	0	40	64	0	33	0	0	40	83	25	50	50	50	20	16	50	0	0	33	0	33	0	50	50	51	60	LB CP LC LH O S
-+-+-++	(-)	45	0	33	0	0	0	60	50	0	33	0	0	25	25	40	36	40	37	33	40	80	0	0	0	0	0	0	66	40	43	84	BP CP LH PB PL SU
-+-+-+-	(+)	54	0	66	0	0	0	50	63	0	66	0	0	75	16	12	60	33	62	75	83	50	0	33	0	66	0	0	33	33	56	67	GC LH PB PL SM TR
-+-+--+	(-)	50	0	16	0	0	0	63	31	0	62	0	0	62	62	83	37	62	60	62	16	60	0	0	0	100	0	0	66	66	49	75	NY OJ SF SM TR
-+-+---	(+)	50	100	83	0	0	0	55	36	0	37	0	0	33	25	16	50	40	40	16	40	70	0	0	33	0	0	0	33	0	50	50	O S SM TR
-+--+++	(-)	44	0	62	0	0	0	44	71	0	50	0	0	0	57	28	60	37	42	37	83	70	0	0	0	0	0	0	33	0	49	61	LH C SF TR W
-+--++-	(+)	50	100	16	0	0	0	57	28	0	62	0	0	66	62	83	60	40	57	62	16	60	100	0	0	100	0	0	75	0	49	59	BP C LB PL S SM
-+--+-+	(+)	55	100	37	0	0	0	42	71	0	28	0	0	66	0	16	37	42	20	50	0	25	0	0	0	0	0	0	0	100	61	37	NY S SM SU W
-+--+--	(-)	45	0	30	0	0	0	40	16	0	28	0	0	33	0	50	54	33	80	0	37	37	0	0	0	25	75	0	0	28	36	35	OJ SU

Figure 8.5: Continued

		BO	BP	C	CC	CD	CL	CO	CP	FC	GC	HO	JY	LB	LC	LH	NY	O	OJ	PB	PL	S	SF	SV	SM	SP	SU	TB	TR	W	T%	T#	-------- 65% -------
---+-++	(+)	46	100	20	0	0	0	45	46	0	30	0	0	66	42	100	27	50	60	25	66	40	20	0	100	0	33	0	40	50	42	56	BP LB LH PL SM
---+-++	(-)	53	0	73	0	0	0	54	53	0	50	0	0	33	57	0	72	50	40	75	33	60	60	0	0	0	66	0	60	50	54	73	C NY PB SU
---++--	(+)	47	0	43	0	0	0	63	47	0	50	0	0	20	45	28	37	100	30	38	63	66	50	0	75	0	25	0	62	37	47	90	O S SM
---++--	(-)	38	0	56	0	0	0	31	52	0	40	0	0	80	36	71	62	0	70	61	36	33	50	0	25	0	75	0	37	62	48	93	LB LH OJ SU
---++-+	(+)	41	0	63	0	0	0	69	65	0	30	0	0	0	54	40	33	100	66	66	44	75	0	0	0	0	0	0	33	37	50	79	CO O OJ PB S
---++-+	(-)	58	100	36	0	0	0	30	34	0	69	0	0	100	45	40	66	0	33	33	55	25	0	0	100	0	100	0	66	62	48	75	BP GC LB NY SM SU TR
---+++-	(+)	27	0	45	0	0	0	58	22	0	20	0	0	0	66	50	37	0	55	50	25	33	50	0	100	0	40	0	0	100	39	50	LC SM W
---+++-	(-)	66	0	54	0	0	.0	41	77	0	80	0	0	80	33	50	62	100	33	50	50	66	50	0	0	0	60	0	100	0	57	74	BO CP GC LB O S TR
---++++	(+)	35	100	20	0	0	0	33	30	0	25	0	0	0	63	50	44	50	20	50	11	33	66	0	0	0	0	0	100	0	34	40	BP SF TR
---++++	(-)	57	0	66	0	0	0	66	70	0	75	0	0	100	36	50	44	0	80	50	88	66	33	0	0	0	100	0	0	100	60	70	C CO CP GC LB OJ
--+----	(+)	51	100	58	0	0	0	83	72	0	50	0	0	75	47	25	60	0	0	0	50	36	0	0	0	0	100	0	50	50	53	81	BP CO CP LB SU
--+----	(-)	48	0	41	0	0	0	16	27	0	50	0	0	25	52	75	40	100	100	100	50	54	100	0	100	0	0	0	50	50	46	70	LH O OJ PB SF SM
--+---+	(+)	63	0	36	0	0	0	50	60	0	28	0	0	33	25	50	58	0	70	66	27	28	50	0	100	0	50	0	33	50	48	74	OJ PB SM
--+---+	(-)	36	100	63	0	0	0	50	30	0	71	0	0	50	75	50	35	0	20	33	72	71	50	0	0	0	50	0	66	50	49	75	BP GC LC PL S TR
--+--+-	(+)	55	0	35	0	0	0	56	76	0	77	0	0	60	63	33	22	60	57	25	66	45	20	0	0	0	33	0	50	60	53	90	CP GC PL
--+--+-	(-)	45	0	57	0	0	0	43	20	0	22	0	0	40	36	66	77	40	42	75	33	54	80	0	0	0	33	0	50	40	44	74	LH NY PB SF
--+--++	(+)	44	50	46	0	0	0	50	66	0	37	0	0	66	0	0	60	66	16	57	77	36	0	0	33	0	40	0	0	25	43	60	CP LB O PL
--+--++	(-)	55	50	53	0	0	0	50	33	0	62	0	0	33	100	100	40	33	83	42	22	63	0	0	66	0	20	0	60	75	53	75	LC LH OJ SM W
--+-+--	(+)	53	66	44	0	0	0	44	54	0	40	0	0	80	33	60	66	40	14	60	58	71	33	0	0	0	0	0	25	71	49	85	BP LB NY S W
--+-+--	(-)	40	0	55	0	0	0	55	40	0	60	0	0	20	60	40	33	40	85	40	35	28	50	0	0	0	100	0	75	28	46	80	OJ SU TR
--+-+-+	(+)	36	33	9	0	0	0	62	36	0	50	0	0	30	42	66	37	66	50	66	66	33	25	0	100	0	42	0	0	50	42	61	LH O PB PL SM
--+-+-+	(-)	63	66	90	0	0	0	37	63	0	50	0	0	60	42	33	62	33	50	33	33	55	75	0	0	0	57	0	100	50	55	80	BP C SF TR
--+-++-	(+)	52	0	36	0	0	0	37	65	0	68	0	0	60	44	50	46	100	50	50	83	69	50	0	0	0	33	0	33	28	52	91	GC O PL S
--+-++-	(-)	42	0	63	0	0	0	62	35	0	31	0	0	40	55	50	53	0	50	50	16	23	50	0	100	0	66	0	66	71	46	81	SM SU TR W
--+-+++	(+)	73	50	25	0	0	0	25	55	0	44	0	0	50	80	100	75	50	71	25	27	80	33	0	66	0	0	0	25	66	53	73	BO LC LH NY OJ S
--+-+++	(-)	26	50	50	0	0	0	66	40	0	55	0	0	50	20	0	25	50	28	75	72	20	66	0	33	0	100	0	75	33	43	60	CO PB PL SF SU TR
--++---	(+)	40	0	47	0	0	0	68	47	0	12	0	0	33	40	14	75	50	22	50	50	38	33	0	0	0	0	0	66	62	43	79	CO NY TR
--++---	(-)	55	0	47	0	0	0	26	52	0	87	0	0	66	50	85	25	50	77	50	50	61	33	0	100	0	100	0	33	37	53	98	GC LB LH OJ SM SU
--++--+	(+)	35	0	46	0	0	0	63	33	0	33	0	0	100	36	20	44	57	20	50	30	42	75	0	0	0	66	0	37	75	42	74	LB SF SU W
--++--+	(-)	60	0	53	0	0	0	31	66	0	66	0	0	0	54	80	55	42	60	50	70	42	25	0	75	0	33	0	62	25	53	93	CP GC LH PL SM
--++-+-	(+)	68	66	36	0	0	0	57	62	0	46	0	0	33	37	33	55	100	20	33	75	46	100	0	25	0	50	0	0	42	50	78	BO BP O PL SF
--++-+-	(-)	31	33	54	0	0	0	42	37	0	53	0	0	50	62	66	44	0	60	66	25	53	0	0	75	0	50	0	100	57	48	75	LH PB SM TR
--++-++	(+)	58	0	25	0	0	0	38	45	0	33	0	0	0	44	25	42	50	45	40	42	28	0	0	0	0	50	0	40	62	40	61	
--++-++	(-)	41	0	68	0	0	0	46	45	0	66	0	0	100	55	75	57	50	45	40	57	71	0	0	0	0	50	0	60	37	54	83	C GC LB LH S
--+++--	(+)	50	0	42	0	0	0	50	81	0	30	0	0	50	28	33	30	50	20	50	50	45	100	0	0	0	66	0	33	50	47	66	CP SF SU
--+++--	(-)	50	0	35	0	0	0	42	18	0	70	0	0	50	71	66	70	50	60	50	50	54	0	0	0	0	33	0	66	50	48	67	GC LC LH NY TR
--+++-+	(+)	62	100	50	0	0	0	50	42	0	50	0	0	40	53	0	60	50	44	50	16	71	0	0	0	0	66	0	0	75	49	61	BP S SU W
--+++-+	(-)	37	0	50	0	0	0	50	28	0	50	0	0	60	38	100	40	50	44	50	83	28	100	0	100	0	33	0	100	25	47	58	LH PL SF SM TR
--++++-	(+)	26	0	57	0	0	0	54	43	0	50	0	0	16	16	42	80	50	50	33	73	0	100	0	0	0	0	0	0	50	43	60	NY PL SF
--++++-	(-)	73	0	42	0	0	0	45	56	0	50	0	0	83	83	57	20	50	50	66	26	100	0	0	0	0	100	0	100	50	56	79	BO LB LC PB S SU TR
--+++++	(+)	30	0	62	0	0	0	42	30	0	0	0	0	0	25	75	28	100	50	25	33	20	40	0	0	0	100	0	0	100	36	35	LH O SU W
--+++++	(-)	60	100	25	0	0	0	57	70	0	100	0	0	100	62	25	71	0	25	75	33	80	40	0	100	0	0	0	100	0	56	54	BP CP GC LB NY PB
-+-----	(+)	55	0	40	0	0	0	80	60	0	25	0	0	60	61	42	50	100	80	66	14	33	50	0	0	0	0	0	60	66	49	64	CO O OJ PB W
-+-----	(-)	40	0	40	0	0	0	20	40	0	75	0	0	40	38	57	50	0	20	33	85	55	50	0	100	0	100	0	40	33	46	61	GC PL SM SU
-+----+	(+)	48	0	31	0	0	0	60	57	0	36	0	0	42	55	100	62	100	50	40	50	40	0	0	0	0	40	0	75	33	47	79	LH O TR
-+----+	(-)	44	100	62	0	0	0	30	42	0	63	0	0	57	44	0	37	0	50	40	50	60	0	0	0	0	60	0	25	66	48	80	BP W
-+---+-	(+)	28	33	50	0	0	0	27	80	0	68	0	0	60	36	50	50	50	0	33	57	44	40	0	100	0	60	0	75	50	47	76	CP GC SM TR
-+---+-	(-)	71	66	42	0	0	0	72	20	0	25	0	0	40	63	50	50	50	100	66	42	44	60	0	0	0	40	0	25	50	50	81	BO BP CO OJ PB
-+---++	(+)	50	50	50	0	0	0	30	29	0	33	0	0	40	0	42	35	0	30	22	50	71	40	0	33	0	25	0	0	33	37	60	S
-+---++	(-)	50	50	50	0	0	0	69	70	0	66	0	0	60	75	57	64	0	69	77	50	28	60	0	66	0	75	0	100	66	61	98	CO CP GC LC OJ PB
-+--+--	(+)	37	0	46	0	0	0	80	76	0	33	0	0	0	45	25	27	100	40	28	18	30	20	0	0	0	66	0	50	55	44	74	CO CP O SU
-+--+--	(-)	56	100	40	0	0	0	13	23	0	66	0	0	75	54	75	72	0	60	71	81	61	80	0	100	0	33	0	50	44	51	85	BP GC LB LH NY PB
-+--+-+	(+)	57	0	44	0	0	0	53	39	0	55	0	0	75	41	33	75	25	33	80	50	54	0	0	100	0	0	0	50	66	49	86	LB NY PB SM W
-+--+-+	(-)	42	0	44	0	0	0	46	57	0	44	0	0	25	50	66	25	50	66	20	50	36	100	0	0	0	100	0	50	16	47	82	LH OJ SF SU

Figure 8.5: Continued

		BO	BP	C	CC	CD	CL	CO	CP	FC	GC	HO	JY	LB	LC	LH	NY	O	OJ	PB	PL	S	SF	SV	SM	SP	SU	TB	TR	W	T%	T#	------- 65% -------
++++	(+)	42	50	37	0	0	0	43	35	0	31	0	0	25	44	55	40	33	50	47	23	47	47	0	61	0	33	0	31	41	41	363	
++++	(-)	55	37	57	0	0	0	56	57	0	68	0	0	68	52	55	55	46	40	64	53	50	47	0	37	0	66	0	63	58	55	489	GC LB PL SU
----	(+)	53	100	44	0	0	0	55	54	0	53	0	0	50	50	55	48	46	60	53	46	47	40	0	50	0	46	0	60	53	52	311	BP
----	(-)	42	0	46	0	0	0	42	45	0	46	0	0	43	42	45	51	46	40	35	46	47	53	0	50	0	53	0	30	46	44	263	
---+	(+)	45	0	49	0	0	0	54	60	0	47	0	0	25	36	55	51	41	50	55	41	36	27	0	55	0	42	0	50	39	47	298	O
---+	(-)	50	100	47	0	0	0	43	36	0	52	0	0	71	40	55	48	50	32	55	40	51	72	0	14	0	41	0	44	61	48	303	BP LB SF
--+-	(+)	35	30	47	0	0	0	50	61	0	66	0	0	48	40	55	48	33	50	34	55	60	60	0	55	0	58	0	50	30	46	296	GC
--+-	(-)	62	70	47	0	0	0	47	36	0	30	0	0	45	55	57	51	66	32	65	35	60	40	0	14	0	58	0	42	61	50	324	BP SM
--++	(+)	42	33	40	0	0	0	38	30	0	27	0	0	47	43	45	58	66	45	25	35	38	50	0	14	0	53	0	21	30	39	247	O
--++	(-)	56	66	54	0	0	0	61	68	0	72	0	0	52	50	41	41	22	51	74	62	58	50	0	85	0	46	0	78	69	58	365	BP CP GC PB SM TR W
-+--	(+)	45	36	48	0	0	0	60	35	0	61	0	0	40	33	34	34	51	46	51	50	50	33	0	42	0	56	0	57	47	48	324	O
-+--	(-)	51	63	43	0	0	0	34	35	0	51	0	0	51	52	66	65	10	51	48	51	43	66	0	80	0	43	0	35	52	47	315	LH SF
-+-+	(+)	56	25	55	0	0	0	50	47	0	48	0	0	32	57	57	51	35	55	52	36	45	44	0	36	0	66	0	50	57	49	318	SM
-+-+	(-)	41	75	37	0	0	0	48	48	0	54	0	0	57	52	57	45	47	51	35	38	45	57	0	63	0	28	0	42	55	49	325	BP SU
-++-	(+)	38	75	40	0	0	0	38	48	0	57	0	0	50	41	60	50	35	51	55	53	55	77	0	36	0	57	0	42	44	43	312	BP
-++-	(-)	57	25	57	0	0	0	60	53	0	37	0	0	38	55	55	50	64	63	58	40	40	0	0	63	0	50	0	57	55	52	373	SF
-+++	(+)	46	50	46	0	0	0	48	53	0	44	0	0	34	41	73	38	30	37	34	41	34	40	0	75	0	50	0	50	40	46	244	LH
-+++	(-)	39	45	51	0	0	0	51	46	0	55	0	0	50	58	26	61	61	55	37	41	62	58	0	75	0	64	0	50	53	51	270	SM
+---	(+)	58	27	40	0	0	0	38	43	0	52	0	0	57	61	63	49	33	63	64	63	51	58	0	57	0	56	0	35	60	50	327	LC
+---	(-)	49	33	44	0	0	0	47	32	0	42	0	0	42	68	36	50	46	46	50	40	44	20	0	43	0	61	0	64	42	46	302	
+--+	(+)	47	16	50	0	0	0	47	32	0	55	0	0	55	34	38	48	46	54	50	40	44	80	0	42	0	38	0	29	57	52	293	SF
+--+	(-)	44	30	41	0	0	0	40	40	0	53	0	0	40	55	38	51	46	26	31	40	50	40	0	42	0	55	0	33	42	52	349	SF
+-+-	(+)	53	50	51	0	0	0	56	56	0	45	0	0	39	59	72	50	53	73	62	58	48	60	0	50	0	44	0	57	61	53	339	LH OJ
+-+-	(-)	39	66	31	0	0	0	44	56	0	36	0	0	35	60	81	38	44	45	36	52	36	44	0	83	0	50	0	55	62	44	257	BP LH
+-++	(+)	60	16	60	0	0	0	52	52	0	60	0	0	55	37	61	61	66	35	47	51	63	42	0	55	0	50	0	44	37	52	303	
+-++	(-)	55	50	44	0	0	0	46	51	0	64	0	0	45	42	38	56	53	35	31	47	29	29	0	69	0	43	0	55	44	47	341	SM
++--	(+)	40	25	49	0	0	0	51	44	0	33	0	0	55	44	56	41	40	68	47	60	68	70	0	60	0	56	0	38	56	48	350	PB SF
++--	(-)	37	25	50	0	0	0	42	57	0	31	0	0	46	54	53	47	83	69	36	38	48	60	0	22	0	55	0	39	40	47	292	OJ
++-+	(+)	61	75	43	0	0	0	45	42	0	66	0	0	53	41	33	52	16	26	63	59	51	33	0	77	0	44	0	41	60	50	308	BP GC SM
++-+	(-)	35	40	50	0	0	0	50	46	0	35	0	0	50	33	80	52	35	63	47	46	46	61	0	88	0	71	0	62	50	50	280	SM SU
+++-	(+)	62	40	50	0	0	0	49	46	0	54	0	0	46	43	60	47	64	33	44	50	53	38	0	11	0	28	0	50	37	48	269	LH
+++-	(-)	41	100	34	0	0	0	54	34	0	32	0	0	36	44	60	40	37	53	55	25	50	55	0	60	0	12	0	30	38	41	207	BP
++++	(+)	56	0	59	0	0	0	45	34	0	67	0	0	63	50	75	51	80	55	45	46	46	44	0	40	0	61	0	57	34	54	269	GC PL SU
++++	(-)	44	60	46	0	0	0	48	51	0	42	0	0	44	47	45	57	20	45	45	54	54	18	0	44	0	50	0	42	65	47	299	
+-+-	(+)	53	40	47	0	0	0	51	48	0	57	0	0	55	49	55	42	80	55	38	53	38	81	0	55	0	50	0	42	34	50	516	O SF
+-+-	(-)	50	50	53	0	0	0	52	56	0	37	0	0	38	34	61	52	22	57	42	40	61	61	0	16	0	37	0	45	48	48	310	SM
+-++	(+)	46	50	46	0	0	0	45	46	0	62	0	0	57	60	38	45	66	35	56	51	47	46	0	50	0	62	0	36	52	48	312	O
+-++	(-)	48	44	45	0	0	0	42	47	0	54	0	0	43	41	36	60	37	48	52	52	36	55	0	37	0	45	0	46	56	46	350	
+---	(+)	31	33	45	0	0	0	46	47	0	54	0	0	65	40	36	37	31	69	47	52	36	55	0	57	0	37	0	26	40	43	319	
+--+	(+)	67	66	50	0	0	0	52	67	0	45	0	0	30	57	63	62	63	50	52	47	44	44	0	62	0	33	0	53	55	54	260	BO BP
+--+	(-)	44	28	39	0	0	0	57	67	0	50	0	0	45	42	37	52	42	63	42	42	53	38	0	42	0	54	0	50	49	49	325	BP
+-+-	(+)	50	57	58	0	0	0	57	27	0	50	0	0	55	57	60	37	44	57	59	41	53	53	0	57	0	66	0	50	54	49	322	CP
+-+-	(-)	38	20	52	0	0	0	42	27	0	36	0	0	55	51	57	60	44	44	59	44	41	53	0	57	0	28	0	33	45	47	311	SU
++--	(+)	52	80	44	0	0	0	54	48	0	36	0	0	48	66	35	64	50	33	56	51	47	54	0	44	0	71	0	25	44	44	248	LH
++--	(-)	50	33	40	0	0	0	42	48	0	52	0	0	31	35	53	55	50	39	42	42	36	30	0	40	0	38	0	33	36	44	283	
+-++	(+)	45	33	53	0	0	0	57	48	0	57	0	0	63	59	66	55	56	56	57	54	53	69	0	60	0	61	0	66	59	52	331	SF TR
+-++	(-)	57	33	44	0	0	0	43	31	0	56	0	0	17	66	60	63	33	64	56	58	58	27	0	50	0	50	0	28	68	45	230	LC W
++--	(+)	38	66	50	0	0	0	50	63	0	52	0	0	66	26	40	55	50	57	64	42	41	72	0	50	0	62	0	57	31	51	261	BP LB SF
++-+	(+)	44	33	53	0	0	0	57	47	0	57	0	0	41	48	42	53	50	45	55	53	54	50	0	25	0	50	0	42	43	46	292	BP SM
++-+	(-)	53	66	44	0	0	0	43	58	0	59	0	0	58	35	66	46	28	45	64	43	51	63	0	40	0	50	0	35	56	50	313	LB
+++-	(+)	38	0	47	0	0	0	59	47	0	34	0	0	76	45	42	31	57	50	45	51	51	63	0	40	0	60	0	31	47	46	293	BP
+++-	(-)	56	100	49	0	0	0	37	52	0	60	0	0	33	51	57	65	35	45	45	56	43	36	0	50	0	40	0	62	47	50	319	BP

Figure 8.5: Continued

		BO	BP	C	CC	CD	CL	CO	CP	FC	GC	HO	JY	LB	LC	LH	NY	O	OJ	PB	PL	S	SF	SV	SM	SP	SU	TH	TR	W	T%	T#	
(+)	+‑‑+‑	45	50	37	0	0	0	0	58	43	58	0	0	44	34	30	50	66	30	47	61	55	55	60	0	50	50	0	7	40	46	270	O
(−)	+‑‑+‑	53	50	58	0	0	0	0	58	60	58	0	0	50	66	60	50	16	57	37	39	41	52	40	0	25	50	0	76	59	50	295	TR
(+)	+‑‑+‑	46	50	27	0	0	0	0	42	42	45	0	0	50	31	37	48	58	58	56	60	37	36	47	0	25	25	0	61	38	42	238	
(+)	+‑‑++‑	51	50	66	0	0	0	0	52	51	54	0	0	50	68	62	51	41	35	56	60	63	50	75	0	75	75	0	38	61	55	310	C LC SU
(+)	+‑‑++‑	45	75	43	0	0	0	0	54	56	45	0	0	35	41	60	41	60	45	54	60	62	20	63	0	36	63	0	33	43	49	266	BP
(−)	+‑‑++‑	48	25	43	0	0	0	0	43	43	48	0	0	60	55	60	58	40	50	35	42	39	80	60	0	36	36	0	46	56	47	257	SM
(−)	+‑‑++‑	51	75	50	0	0	0	0	54	53	51	0	0	43	50	61	47	60	50	57	45	60	46	30	0	63	36	0	46	45	48	252	BP
(+)	+‑‑‑+‑	48	25	47	0	0	0	0	54	53	50	0	0	56	46	38	66	57	54	52	53	28	40	0	0	12	46	0	50	47	49	255	
(+)	+‑‑‑+‑	44	66	39	0	0	0	0	41	57	50	0	0	18	33	63	25	66	54	47	43	71	60	30	0	87	12	0	50	47	46	227	BP NY
(−)	+‑‑‑+‑	54	33	58	0	0	0	0	54	42	50	0	0	72	66	36	41	25	41	52	10	55	60	40	0	87	50	0	50	47	51	252	LB LC s SU
(+)	+‑‑‑++‑	42	25	46	0	0	0	0	30	33	26	0	0	75	41	52	55	75	46	35	80	57	62	0	0	25	75	0	46	53	39	141	SU
(−)	+‑‑‑++‑	55	50	50	0	0	0	0	69	66	73	0	0	75	55	44	42	75	46	64	85	50	37	62	0	25	25	0	100	53	58	210	CO CP LB O PL TR
(+)	+‑‑‑++‑	64	0	53	0	0	0	0	70	72	63	0	0	83	16	55	42	42	62	66	68	50	80	0	0	50	50	0	33	85	61	161	CO LC PB PL SM w
(−)	+‑‑‑‑+‑	32	0	43	0	0	0	0	29	27	36	0	0	20	64	54	44	57	33	45	68	31	14	0	0	42	42	0	33	14	36	95	
(+)	+‑‑‑‑+‑	38	0	62	0	0	0	0	45	61	59	0	0	80	36	45	55	42	50	54	31	62	75	80	0	42	42	0	66	37	46	145	PL
(−)	+‑‑‑‑+‑	59	100	37	0	0	0	0	54	38	40	0	0	42	26	63	50	58	33	90	68	57	25	80	0	57	42	0	37	66	50	157	BP LB SF SM TR
(+)	+‑‑‑‑++‑	42	33	48	0	0	0	0	36	40	70	0	0	31	50	55	71	66	70	37	50	26	0	0	0	66	57	0	22	27	46	159	GC SF w
(+)	+‑‑‑‑++‑	57	66	48	0	0	0	0	36	30	30	0	0	57	43	63	50	83	58	58	61	25	33	0	0	60	33	0	77	72	50	153	BP O PB SM
(−)	+‑‑‑‑++‑	31	0	40	0	0	0	0	33	33	27	0	0	47	48	28	35	66	47	41	25	37	41	0	0	60	60	0	83	37	56	121	NY O OJ SF SU
(+)	+‑‑‑‑+++‑	65	0	50	0	0	0	0	66	66	72	0	0	57	43	65	57	66	30	58	33	62	25	90	0	60	33	0	16	62	56	168	CO CP GC PL s SM
(−)	+‑‑‑‑‑+‑	51	42	50	0	0	0	0	59	56	61	0	0	47	48	36	35	33	55	41	47	25	40	0	100	42	42	0	71	61	45	168	O TR
(−)	+‑‑‑‑‑+‑	46	57	46	0	0	0	0	47	43	38	0	0	16	63	37	57	60	44	55	71	47	58	0	0	57	57	0	14	38	51	148	SF
(+)	+‑‑‑‑‑++‑	53	33	53	0	0	0	0	47	48	35	0	0	66	38	62	50	44	55	33	39	54	40	33	0	28	57	0	27	50	45	133	SM TR
(−)	+‑‑‑‑‑++‑	46	66	39	0	0	0	0	47	51	60	0	0	55	61	41	36	50	58	30	69	25	66	66	0	71	28	0	72	50	51	153	BP LB PL
(−)	+‑‑‑‑‑+‑	41	50	31	0	0	0	0	57	39	60	0	0	25	47	58	36	50	58	65	47	35	0	0	0	37	66	0	33	42	42	156	s
(+)	‑+‑‑+‑	51	50	65	0	0	0	0	42	52	44	0	0	55	55	80	36	33	33	66	69	75	60	66	0	71	42	0	66	60	52	191	SF SM SU TR
(−)	‑+‑‑+‑	43	100	57	0	0	0	0	42	47	44	0	0	25	55	20	64	66	60	33	30	51	50	66	0	28	66	0	25	44	46	115	BP LH PB PL
(+)	‑+‑‑+‑	56	0	42	0	0	0	0	47	52	55	0	0	42	45	37	62	77	31	45	47	48	30	0	0	57	46	0	55	40	48	128	O s SM SU TH
(−)	‑+‑‑+‑	24	28	39	0	0	0	0	37	47	43	0	0	57	36	64	35	90	9	14	38	55	60	0	75	42	42	0	40	40	43	154	LH OJ PB SM
(−)	‑+‑‑+‑	45	0	60	0	0	0	0	37	52	50	0	0	55	36	42	53	100	33	40	47	55	30	0	25	42	66	0	25	40	51	152	BO LC O
(+)	‑+‑‑++‑	50	0	45	0	0	0	0	57	69	52	0	0	62	30	37	37	33	37	33	41	56	40	0	0	87	20	0	20	36	44	140	SM SU
(−)	‑+‑‑++‑	55	50	40	0	0	0	0	29	46	52	0	0	44	65	58	40	40	55	55	58	43	40	0	33	12	66	0	80	63	52	168	CP SF
(+)	‑+‑‑++‑	40	50	41	0	0	0	0	42	50	44	0	0	41	56	62	64	77	22	33	41	56	75	0	66	28	28	0	57	50	44	144	SM SU
(−)	‑+‑‑++‑	41	100	25	0	0	0	0	66	50	44	0	0	55	47	40	64	77	77	55	47	50	40	0	0	75	12	0	80	63	52	172	CO OJ TR
(+)	‑+‑‑++‑	58	0	68	0	0	0	0	57	50	59	0	0	14	58	33	76	60	40	60	35	72	50	75	0	57	25	0	57	56	54	138	BP LH SM
(+)	‑+‑‑++‑	54	0	40	0	0	0	0	51	48	40	0	0	85	41	41	47	77	36	33	47	50	0	0	57	25	75	0	42	43	46	174	C NY s SU
(−)	‑+‑‑++‑	39	0	51	0	0	0	0	45	58	53	0	0	33	50	50	43	22	64	45	46	51	0	0	0	66	37	0	66	33	48	173	O TR
(+)	‑+‑‑‑+‑	64	100	40	0	0	0	0	51	58	39	0	0	50	44	37	43	64	68	54	53	48	50	0	0	62	66	0	25	66	48	182	LB PB w
(−)	‑+‑‑‑+‑	30	100	50	0	0	0	0	50	52	56	0	0	38	37	50	47	80	20	60	48	48	66	0	0	50	44	0	55	53	50	152	OJ
(+)	‑+‑‑‑+‑	65	0	50	0	0	0	0	50	66	62	0	0	53	66	75	52	31	31	60	46	61	50	0	0	33	50	0	44	46	52	156	BP LB SM
(−)	‑+‑‑‑+‑	33	100	32	0	0	0	0	46	57	23	0	0	36	36	36	47	25	33	46	16	50	16	0	0	20	20	0	16	33	38	125	BP LC PB SM SU
(+)	‑+‑‑‑+‑	63	0	56	0	0	0	0	57	73	76	0	0	58	56	75	61	33	66	62	46	50	0	0	0	71	46	0	55	66	57	141	CP LH O TR
(−)	‑+‑‑‑+‑	56	100	47	0	0	0	0	46	57	57	0	0	75	12	87	38	33	33	40	83	50	16	0	0	20	71	0	44	66	54	95	BP SF SM
(+)	‑+‑‑‑++‑	41	40	44	0	0	0	0	33	42	42	0	0	41	40	87	61	66	66	62	16	50	45	0	0	28	28	0	55	66	43	140	GC LB PL SU w
(+)	‑+‑‑‑++‑	56	40	41	0	0	0	0	41	56	41	0	0	31	26	57	40	38	66	46	53	50	66	0	0	44	20	0	40	40	49	165	BP CO CP SU w
(−)	‑+‑‑‑++‑	41	60	58	0	0	0	0	45	70	50	0	0	62	57	56	35	33	33	50	52	44	52	0	0	55	57	0	20	40	49	130	LH O SF SM
(+)	‑+‑‑‑++‑	43	60	58	0	0	0	0	50	56	72	0	0	63	73	42	35	50	30	50	72	52	52	0	0	57	55	0	40	36	44	160	CP OJ SM
(−)	‑+‑‑‑++‑	54	0	33	0	0	0	0	50	58	47	0	0	33	66	80	50	33	50	50	27	44	62	0	75	14	20	0	50	63	53	174	GC LC O TR
(+)	‑+‑‑‑++‑	45	100	55	0	0	0	0	50	66	47	0	0	36	36	90	64	50	61	37	53	37	66	0	0	57	57	0	37	36	48	165	BP NY
(+)	‑+‑‑‑++‑	41	50	41	0	0	0	0	51	58	47	0	0	36	57	20	35	50	50	50	27	31	0	0	0	14	40	0	40	36	44	130	PL
(+)	‑+‑‑‑++‑	58	50	58	0	0	0	0	51	61	52	0	0	36	57	52	64	33	61	50	72	68	100	75	0	37	50	0	25	63	53	155	LC LH s SF SM
(−)	‑+‑‑‑++‑	50	40	38	0	0	0	0	51	61	47	0	0	36	80	52	60	50	36	40	22	68	66	0	0	62	37	0	22	53	48	166	s SM
(−)	‑+‑‑‑‑+‑	46	40	57	0	0	0	0	48	33	47	0	0	36	57	52	52	50	63	60	56	27	56	33	0	62	37	0	75	46	47	162	SF TR

Figure 8.5:   Continued

		BO	BP	C	CC	CD	CL	CO	CP	FC	GC	HO	JY	LB	LC	LH	NY	O	OJ	PB	PL	S	SF	SV	SM	SP	SU	TB	TR	W	T%	T#	65%
-+++	(+)	24	33	35	0	0	0	59	43	0	38	0	0	37	60	66	36	50	25	60	54	44	50	0	66	0	40	0	0	57	42	116	LH SM
-+++	(-)	68	66	64	0	0	0	40	56	0	61	0	0	56	30	33	63	40	75	40	45	44	50	0	33	0	60	0	100	42	54	148	BO BP OJ TR
-+++	(-)	48	100	41	0	0	0	38	56	0	51	0	0	27	33	50	52	38	36	66	45	44	50	0	40	0	75	0	25	66	48	146	BP O PL
-+++	(-)	45	0	54	0	0	0	61	43	0	48	0	0	63	58	50	47	25	63	66	26	34	50	0	60	0	75	0	75	66	49	151	PB SU TR W
-+++	(+)	70	25	37	0	0	0	45	46	0	50	0	0	28	63	66	41	50	60	20	26	69	28	0	75	0	50	0	20	66	48	125	BO LH S SM W
-+++	(-)	29	75	50	0	0	0	45	50	0	50	0	0	57	26	33	58	30	30	55	52	46	71	0	25	0	50	0	80	42	47	122	BP PL SF TR
-+++	(+)	56	0	48	0	0	0	60	42	0	23	0	0	27	41	20	43	50	50	55	47	53	50	0	25	0	43	0	42	42	46	162	
-++-	(+)	40	100	43	0	0	0	36	57	0	76	0	0	72	50	80	56	50	50	46	47	53	41	0	75	0	66	0	28	57	50	177	BP GC LB LH SM SU
-++-	(-)	34	0	51	0	0	0	64	41	0	32	0	0	55	35	28	54	40	40	44	44	46	50	0	25	0	42	0	40	45	43	148	SF
-++-	(+)	63	100	45	0	0	0	32	58	0	64	0	0	44	60	71	59	60	50	44	58	53	80	0	62	0	57	0	60	54	53	183	BP LH
-++-	(-)	58	66	32	0	0	0	50	56	0	52	0	0	37	46	60	52	40	42	50	60	44	20	0	57	0	75	0	60	50	50	154	BP SF SU
-++-	(-)	41	33	60	0	0	0	45	43	0	47	0	0	50	50	60	47	0	42	50	60	40	100	0	0	0	25	0	100	50	47	146	TR
-++-	(+)	48	100	20	0	0	0	37	57	0	37	0	0	42	29	50	47	60	55	28	43	33	66	0	0	0	40	0	50	55	42	125	BP SF
-++-	(+)	52	0	75	0	0	0	55	38	0	62	0	0	57	70	50	52	40	33	57	56	66	33	0	80	0	60	0	50	44	54	158	C LC S SM
-++-	(-)	48	100	34	0	0	0	48	70	0	33	0	0	41	38	12	40	50	47	56	45	47	63	0	75	0	75	0	50	50	49	131	BP CP PH SF SU
-++-	(-)	48	0	50	0	0	0	48	29	0	66	0	0	58	61	87	52	36	50	25	50	43	20	0	0	0	25	0	50	50	47	127	GC LH SM
-++-	(+)	62	100	52	0	0	0	50	47	0	60	0	0	42	50	50	50	50	42	44	47	71	50	0	70	0	70	0	40	60	53	148	BP S SU
-++-	(+)	37	0	48	0	0	0	50	47	0	40	0	0	57	43	50	50	50	50	55	47	53	80	0	37	0	40	0	40	40	44	124	
-++--	(+)	33	0	38	0	0	0	50	50	0	42	0	0	28	22	50	78	50	33	66	66	15	50	0	37	0	70	0	50	46	44	118	NY OJ PL
-++--	(+)	66	0	57	0	0	0	50	67	0	57	0	0	77	77	66	21	27	50	37	29	84	50	0	50	0	42	0	50	46	54	147	BO LB LC S SU
-++--	(-)	37	33	53	0	0	0	28	38	0	20	0	0	0	40	41	27	33	20	62	84	20	40	100	66	100	0	0	62	35	—	73	SM SU
-++--	(+)	58	33	40	0	0	0	72	61	0	80	0	0	75	53	50	72	66	35	80	75	71	40	0	33	0	0	0	100	57	59	123	CO GC LB NY O PB
+++--	(+)	46	100	38	0	0	0	50	61	0	45	0	0	40	37	54	47	50	37	63	25	41	55	0	20	42	0	0	66	25	44	141	BP OJ TR
+++--	(+)	51	0	45	0	0	0	50	57	0	54	0	0	46	57	47	50	27	36	46	75	47	44	0	50	57	33	0	62	60	51	163	PL SM W
+++--	(+)	56	0	40	0	0	0	61	57	0	31	0	0	33	57	33	54	75	50	80	63	37	50	0	25	42	75	0	60	48	—	146	O
+++--	(+)	37	100	56	0	0	0	33	35	0	68	0	0	58	38	66	43	44	50	44	37	45	50	0	60	57	60	0	40	45	45	137	BP GC LH
+++--	(-)	29	33	48	0	0	0	48	55	0	61	0	0	46	43	50	50	47	60	28	45	56	54	100	0	40	75	0	75	37	46	145	O SM TR
+++--	(+)	70	66	48	0	0	0	55	40	0	33	0	0	53	52	50	52	16	71	42	40	63	45	0	60	60	25	0	41	50	—	157	BO BP OJ
+++--	(-)	52	33	38	0	0	0	43	28	0	30	0	0	50	23	33	45	31	22	36	36	46	42	0	20	33	20	0	33	37	—	116	
+++--	(-)	47	0	61	0	0	0	60	67	0	42	0	0	50	69	66	50	63	77	41	34	57	57	0	80	80	80	0	66	61	61	188	BP CP GC LC LH PB
+++--	(+)	39	25	46	0	0	0	30	62	0	57	0	0	42	46	22	36	36	45	58	34	36	57	0	50	60	42	0	54	54	45	145	O
+++--	(+)	55	75	40	0	0	0	45	45	0	40	0	0	66	63	77	57	42	50	66	65	52	66	0	75	40	57	0	45	45	49	158	BP LH NY SF
+++--	(-)	61	20	55	0	0	0	59	57	0	51	0	0	72	50	50	66	50	42	50	54	52	50	0	50	80	80	0	65	57	50	178	LB PB SM
+++--	(+)	36	80	37	0	0	0	48	49	0	42	0	0	33	46	50	65	33	53	33	34	42	50	0	25	37	66	0	35	46	46	162	BP SU TR
+++--	(-)	37	100	53	0	0	0	36	38	0	62	0	0	57	35	42	60	66	33	66	37	44	25	0	40	37	50	0	63	53	53	143	BP OJ
+++--	(+)	62	0	46	0	0	0	50	58	0	58	0	0	57	57	60	25	50	55	45	58	47	75	0	60	37	50	0	36	36	46	173	O SF
+++--	(-)	66	0	32	0	0	0	50	53	0	47	0	0	28	64	16	57	60	57	36	45	47	60	0	66	50	75	0	37	58	52	122	BO LH TR
+++--	(+)	33	100	64	0	0	0	45	26	0	52	0	0	40	21	75	44	38	72	45	45	38	40	0	33	50	64	0	58	62	51	133	BP LC SM
+++--	(+)	52	75	40	0	0	0	59	63	0	57	0	0	72	78	25	55	16	45	30	52	55	50	0	66	50	50	0	51	45	45	160	BP LB PL
+++--	(+)	44	25	53	0	0	0	40	31	0	42	0	0	27	68	50	65	33	53	53	25	44	14	0	50	60	75	0	35	35	45	142	LC TR
+++--	(-)	53	0	35	0	0	0	36	40	0	37	0	0	55	35	33	60	25	63	55	36	47	60	0	33	50	50	0	41	58	52	144	
+++--	(+)	46	50	60	0	0	0	50	58	0	58	0	0	33	36	0	44	42	36	28	41	47	60	0	66	30	70	0	50	33	42	170	LH SM
+++--	(-)	48	0	37	0	0	0	45	32	0	53	0	0	50	37	100	56	44	42	71	41	38	40	0	40	70	100	0	50	55	54	123	
+++--	(+)	51	50	62	0	0	0	45	64	0	59	0	0	54	27	0	42	25	66	33	52	55	66	0	25	25	0	0	25	25	45	158	LH PB SU
+++--	(-)	38	0	42	0	0	0	45	26	0	40	0	0	27	72	100	0	25	60	48	34	55	0	100	75	0	66	0	33	53	48	114	LC LH PB SF SU TR
+++--	(+)	61	0	47	0	0	0	45	56	0	59	0	0	54	27	0	42	25	66	33	40	40	11	0	75	25	33	0	0	25	48	121	OJ SM
+++++	(+)	57	100	45	0	0	0	36	51	0	79	0	0	66	36	33	37	16	38	27	46	40	11	0	83	50	33	0	53	53	47	158	BP GC LB SM
+++++	(-)	39	0	48	0	0	0	45	45	0	20	0	0	33	36	57	58	38	46	55	55	55	88	0	16	50	66	0	46	46	48	160	O PB SF TR
+++++	(+)	41	100	39	0	0	0	63	55	0	22	0	0	66	61	57	58	83	77	25	30	45	75	0	50	60	33	0	33	12	46	133	BP LB O OJ SF
+++++	(+)	54	0	50	0	0	0	36	44	0	77	0	0	33	38	28	41	16	22	75	65	54	25	0	50	40	66	0	66	87	50	144	GC PB TR W
+++++	(+)	44	25	50	0	0	0	66	66	0	85	0	0	61	37	16	37	16	64	45	52	47	62	0	75	80	20	0	50	85	54	141	CP SM SU W
+++++	(+)	55	50	50	0	0	0	54	30	0	47	0	0	38	62	83	43	37	45	28	41	38	37	0	25	20	50	0	37	14	44	116	LH
+++++	(-)	48	100	37	0	0	0	52	42	0	38	0	0	66	35	88	30	50	60	83	52	41	0	0	50	80	20	0	40	40	45	104	BP LB LH PB
+++++	(-)	51	0	62	0	0	0	52	36	0	61	0	0	33	60	11	61	50	40	16	61	47	47	100	50	0	100	0	75	60	51	118	SF SU TR W

Figure 8.5: Continued

BO	BP	C	CC	CD	CL	CO	CP	FC	GC	HO	JY	LB	LC	LH	NY	O	OJ	PB	PL	S	SF	SV	SM	SP	SU	TB	TR	W	T%	T#		------ 65% ------

Figure 8.5: Continued

Figure 8.5: Continued

Figure 8.5: Continued

	BO	BP	C	CC	CD	CL	CO	CP	FC	GC	HO	JY	LB	LC	LH	NV	O	OJ	PB	PL	S	SF	SV	SM	SP	SU	TB	TR	W	T%	T#	------ 65% ------
+-++---	50	50	42	0	0	0	50	81	0	30	0	0	50	28	33	30	50	20	50	50	45	100	0	0	0	66	0	33	50	47	66	CP SF SU LH - - -
+-++---	50	0	35	0	0	0	42	18	0	70	0	0	40	71	66	70	60	60	50	50	54	0	0	0	0	33	0	66	50	48	67	GC LC LH NY TR
+-++---	62	100	0	0	0	0	50	42	0	0	0	0	40	53	0	60	50	60	50	50	16	0	0	0	0	33	0	66	75	49	61	BP S SU W
+-++-+-	37	0	50	0	0	0	54	28	0	50	0	0	16	38	100	40	50	44	50	83	28	100	0	100	0	33	0	100	25	47	58	LH PL SF SM TR
+-++-+-	26	0	57	0	0	0	54	43	0	50	0	0	16	16	42	80	50	50	50	26	100	0	0	0	0	33	0	100	50	43	60	NY PL SF
+-++-+-	73	0	42	0	0	0	45	56	0	0	0	0	83	83	57	20	50	50	66	73	20	40	0	0	0	100	0	0	50	56	79	BO LB LC PB S SU TH
+-++-+-	30	0	62	0	0	0	42	30	0	0	0	0	25	25	75	20	25	25	25	33	33	0	0	0	0	100	0	100	100	36	35	LH O SU W
+-++-+-	60	100	25	0	0	0	57	70	100	25	0	0	100	42	42	71	0	80	75	23	20	40	0	0	100	0	0	0	0	56	54	BP CP GC LB NY PB
+-++-+-	55	0	40	0	0	0	80	40	0	0	0	0	60	61	42	50	80	66	14	33	33	50	0	0	0	60	0	60	66	49	64	CO OJ PB W
+-++-+-	40	0	40	0	0	0	20	40	0	75	0	0	40	38	57	50	20	50	85	55	55	50	100	0	0	0	0	33	43	46	61	GC PL SM SU
+-++-+-	48	0	31	0	0	0	80	57	0	36	0	0	57	55	100	37	50	40	50	50	50	50	0	100	0	100	0	25	33	47	79	LH O TR
+-++-+-	44	100	62	0	0	0	30	42	0	63	0	0	40	44	0	37	0	50	40	60	60	0	0	0	40	0	0	75	50	48	80	BP W
+-++-+-	28	33	50	0	0	0	27	80	0	68	0	0	60	36	50	50	50	28	33	57	44	40	0	33	60	60	0	75	50	47	76	CP GC SM TR
+-++-+-	71	66	42	0	0	0	72	43	0	25	0	0	25	53	50	35	50	50	22	42	60	60	0	66	0	0	0	25	66	50	81	BO BP CO OJ PB
+-++-+-	50	50	50	0	0	0	30	29	0	33	0	0	40	44	42	64	50	30	77	50	71	40	66	0	0	25	0	75	66	37	60	S
+-++-+-	50	50	50	0	0	0	69	70	0	66	0	0	60	75	57	0	0	69	50	50	28	60	0	66	75	75	0	0	66	61	74	CO CP GC LC OJ PB
+-++-+-	37	0	46	0	0	0	80	19	0	66	0	0	75	45	25	27	100	60	28	18	30	20	0	0	0	0	0	50	44	44	85	BP NY PB SM
+-++-+-	56	100	44	0	0	0	13	23	0	55	0	0	75	41	33	75	0	71	81	50	71	0	0	0	0	33	0	66	16	51	82	LB LH OJ SF SU
+-++-+-	57	0	44	0	0	0	53	39	0	44	0	0	25	50	66	33	0	33	80	50	54	0	0	0	100	0	0	50	57	49	69	BP PL
+-++-+-	42	0	44	0	0	0	46	57	0	63	0	0	50	50	71	50	0	62	33	20	36	100	33	0	0	0	0	40	57	47	81	CP LC NY SM SU
+-++-+-	38	100	64	0	0	0	35	17	0	36	0	0	30	30	50	33	50	37	50	50	42	50	0	0	0	0	0	60	42	52	58	PB SM
+-++-+-	61	0	35	0	0	0	64	69	0	36	0	0	28	70	50	66	66	50	50	40	42	0	33	66	0	25	0	25	25	44	69	CO LH O SU
+-++-+-	60	0	30	0	0	0	42	50	0	30	0	0	71	40	100	40	66	25	33	61	42	0	0	0	0	75	0	50	42	54	58	BP GC LB LH O SU
+-++-+-	40	100	60	0	0	0	53	78	0	47	0	0	75	36	20	33	66	42	50	84	80	50	0	0	0	60	0	33	66	53	86	BP GC LB PL S W
+-++-+-	57	50	33	0	0	0	46	14	0	52	0	0	25	53	80	20	50	50	66	15	16	16	0	66	0	60	0	66	83	43	71	C LH NY SM TR
+-++-+-	35	50	66	0	0	0	62	50	0	35	0	0	57	28	0	75	100	42	75	50	71	40	0	33	0	33	0	0	60	48	81	BO NY O OJ PB TR
+-++-+-	73	0	12	0	0	0	62	50	0	0	0	0	14	71	100	0	70	66	50	14	28	50	50	66	0	33	0	66	71	47	79	C LC LH SU
+-++-+-	26	50	75	0	0	0	37	46	0	58	0	0	66	75	0	25	100	66	50	50	53	53	0	0	0	66	100	0	0	41	80	CO LH OJ S SF
+-++-+-	55	0	53	0	0	0	66	19	0	76	0	0	33	43	100	30	0	66	50	55	57	0	0	66	0	85	0	75	0	54	54	LH O PB SU W
+-++-+-	71	33	50	0	0	0	66	76	0	50	0	0	16	20	41	42	0	66	50	52	75	66	0	0	0	75	0	0	66	53	58	CP LB OJ SF SM
+-++-+-	50	0	33	0	0	0	53	23	0	62	0	0	83	100	42	0	0	33	37	47	25	33	0	0	100	25	0	50	25	50	78	GC LB LH NY SU
+-++-+-	58	0	35	0	0	0	38	69	0	75	0	0	66	16	0	57	33	42	50	41	33	66	0	66	0	33	0	66	33	52	68	BP SF TR
+-++-+-	41	0	58	0	0	0	56	56	0	25	0	0	14	57	0	11	100	57	66	50	37	33	0	33	0	100	0	66	71	45	74	BP CO CP LB SU
+-++-+-	55	0	53	0	0	0	30	19	0	76	0	0	66	75	0	70	100	75	53	14	42	100	0	0	0	100	100	0	62	49	72	GC LH PB PL SM TR
+-++-+-	71	33	50	0	0	0	30	64	0	50	0	0	50	20	25	66	0	66	50	52	85	57	0	0	0	66	0	0	50	53	62	BO OJ S SM SU W
+-++-+-	28	33	50	0	0	0	66	76	0	52	0	0	33	83	100	42	33	33	37	47	66	33	0	0	0	66	0	75	0	48	58	CO LH NY O TR
+-++-+-	52	100	33	0	0	0	38	23	0	30	0	0	66	16	0	57	0	42	66	33	25	40	33	66	0	33	0	50	30	44	55	BP LH OJ PB
+-++-+-	47	0	66	0	0	0	50	46	0	70	0	0	50	57	0	40	0	33	66	50	44	100	0	66	100	66	0	66	50	53	67	C GC LC O PL SF
+-++-+-	53	100	50	0	0	0	50	60	0	80	0	0	62	80	25	55	0	66	50	26	80	0	0	0	0	33	0	66	60	48	95	BP GC O PB SF SM SU
+-++-+-	44	0	55	0	0	0	56	33	0	50	0	0	66	20	40	42	33	50	72	47	85	0	0	0	60	66	0	50	16	53	79	GC LB PB SM SU TH
+-++-+-	39	100	44	0	0	0	72	66	0	73	0	0	75	33	50	57	50	30	27	77	44	50	0	0	0	50	0	83	0	51	78	CP LH PL SF
+-++-+-	46	0	26	0	0	0	27	54	0	20	0	0	60	50	60	61	75	60	50	70	46	0	0	0	0	50	0	50	50	45	94	BP C CO LB LC SF
+-++-+-	7	0	35	0	0	0	50	29	0	36	0	0	57	28	50	33	50	25	14	50	55	50	0	0	0	33	0	50	60	37	83	O PL
+-++-+-	92	0	52	0	0	0	81	71	0	56	0	0	57	57	50	64	60	75	85	44	55	50	0	0	0	66	0	40	57	59	87	BO NY OJ PL SM SU
+-++-+-	41	0	33	0	0	0	18	28	0	43	0	0	42	42	50	60	0	66	44	44	46	0	0	0	0	50	0	66	0	47	69	CO CP PB
+-++-+-	52	100	66	0	0	0	36	44	0	33	0	0	50	0	66	40	100	33	50	66	0	50	100	0	0	0	0	66	28	46	74	BP C LB OJ SM
+-++-+-	50	0	87	0	0	0	44	55	0	66	0	0	50	66	33	46	100	0	53	50	71	0	0	0	0	50	0	57	0	50	71	C LH OJ PB SF
+-++-+-	37	100	12	0	0	0	63	25	0	60	0	0	50	33	60	22	66	16	50	66	43	0	0	0	0	66	0	33	75	42	78	BP GC LB PL SU W
+-++-+-	61	0	31	0	0	0	37	25	0	40	0	0	75	50	50	77	100	66	50	22	56	100	0	50	0	33	0	66	25	50	67	LB LH OJ SU
+-++-+-	38	0	59	0	0	0	62	75	0	40	0	0	25	50	50	77	100	66	50	22	56	100	0	50	0	33	0	66	25	55	87	CP NY O OJ SF TH

Figure 8.5: Concluded

		BO	BP	C	CC	CD	CL	CO	CP	FC	GC	HO	JY	LB	LC	LH	NY	O	OJ	PB	PL	S	SF	SV	SM	SP	SU	TB	TR	W	T%	T#	------ 65% ------
+++-+++	(+)	66	0	50	0	0	0	45	16	0	50	0	0	0	80	50	37	0	50	0	57	50	50	0	0	0	50	0	66	80	42	53	BO LC TR W
+++-++-	(−)	25	100	50	0	0	0	54	75	0	50	0	0	100	20	50	62	100	50	100	42	50	50	0	0	0	50	0	0	20	54	68	BP CP LB O PB
+++-+--	(+)	53	0	38	0	0	0	46	44	0	33	0	0	71	37	42	66	25	60	0	55	57	0	0	0	0	100	0	66	66	48	61	LB NY SU TR W
++++---	(−)	46	0	53	0	0	0	53	44	0	66	0	0	28	62	57	33	50	40	100	44	42	100	0	0	0	0	0	33	33	49	63	GC PB SF SM
++++--+	(−)	38	0	44	0	0	0	53	59	0	50	0	0	60	60	0	12	71	75	50	37	55	50	0	0	0	0	0	66	66	51	67	LH O OJ SU W
++++-+-	(−)	46	100	55	0	0	0	38	40	0	50	0	0	40	40	75	0	28	33	62	50	44	50	0	66	0	0	0	50	43	45	59	BP NY TR
++++-+-	(+)	50	0	33	0	0	0	64	31	0	83	0	0	37	28	0	60	66	25	20	50	75	50	0	0	0	0	0	50	50	45	56	GC O S SM
+++++--	(−)	50	0	66	0	0	0	35	68	0	16	0	0	62	71	100	33	25	80	37	25	25	50	0	33	0	100	0	50	50	54	67	C CP LC LH OJ PB SU
+++++-+	(+)	40	0	46	0	0	0	57	31	0	55	0	0	66	12	0	50	33	75	44	20	20	0	0	25	0	14	0	50	16	40	60	LB OJ PB
+++++--	(−)	50	100	46	0	0	0	35	68	0	44	0	0	33	87	100	66	20	25	55	55	80	100	0	50	0	85	0	50	83	56	84	BP CP LC LH O S
+++++-+	(−)	40	0	46	0	0	0	60	35	0	66	0	0	40	28	75	0	50	0	80	71	54	0	0	0	0	66	0	33	33	45	67	GC LH PB PL SU
+++++++	(−)	50	0	46	0	0	0	40	64	0	33	0	0	60	64	25	100	0	50	20	28	45	100	0	100	0	33	0	66	66	51	75	NY OJ SF SM TR W
++++++-	(+)	45	0	33	0	0	0	40	50	0	33	0	0	50	25	50	36	100	37	33	40	100	50	0	100	0	0	0	66	40	43	50	O S SM TR
+++++++	(−)	54	0	66	0	0	0	60	50	0	66	0	0	50	75	50	63	0	62	66	60	0	50	0	100	0	0	0	33	60	56	65	C GC LC PB
+++++++	(+)	50	0	16	0	0	0	44	63	0	62	0	0	0	62	83	37	100	60	62	16	30	100	0	0	0	0	0	66	66	49	61	LH O SF TR W
+++++++	(−)	50	100	83	0	0	0	55	36	0	37	0	0	62	37	16	37	0	40	37	83	30	0	0	0	0	0	0	66	66	47	59	BP C LB PL S SM
+++++++	(+)	44	0	62	0	0	0	57	28	0	50	0	0	0	50	0	0	57	0	50	0	75	0	0	100	0	100	0	0	20	50	37	NY S SM SU
+++++++	(−)	55	100	37	0	0	0	42	71	0	50	0	0	0	50	40	0	42	50	100	71	25	100	0	0	0	0	0	0	80	49	36	BP CP O PL SF W

Figure 8.6: Daily Closing Patterns: Bear/Bull Markets

Pred	Pattern	BO	BP	C	CC	CD	CL	CO	CP	FC	GC	HO	JY	LB	LC	LH	NY	O	OJ	PB	PL	S	SF	SV	SM	SP	SU	TB	TH	W	T%	T#
(+ -)	- - -	46	43	46	50	0	0	54	58	0	54	0	48	44	52	50	49	48	46	54	54	53	45	0	49	0	48	45	50	50	49	4548
(+ -)	- - +	49	52	47	46	0	0	43	39	0	44	0	46	43	44	48	46	44	44	44	44	47	42	0	43	0	46	41	47	45	45	4126
(+ -)	- + -	48	44	52	53	0	0	46	48	0	43	0	46	51	49	46	46	48	52	49	50	49	43	0	50	0	46	53	44	51	48	4651
(- +)	- + +	47	52	42	46	0	0	51	47	0	54	0	48	44	44	48	50	45	41	48	47	47	48	0	45	0	52	42	49	45	47	4537
(+ -)	+ - -	53	45	47	48	0	0	49	48	0	55	0	43	46	52	46	50	48	46	50	46	44	46	0	45	0	53	43	47	45	45	4657
(- +)	+ - +	43	51	47	50	0	0	48	48	0	42	0	51	46	43	47	43	48	47	47	46	45	52	0	47	0	41	50	46	50	47	4553
(+ +)	+ + -	38	43	40	50	0	0	46	45	0	43	0	46	52	46	52	50	49	52	46	46	45	45	0	46	0	54	45	45	44	45	4241
(+ -)	+ + +	58	52	54	48	0	0	52	50	0	54	0	50	52	50	50	52	49	46	49	52	51	52	0	52	0	54	43	53	53	50	4674
(- -)	- - - -	46	47	48	50	0	0	54	55	0	52	0	51	45	49	52	52	50	49	55	54	51	45	0	52	0	52	44	46	49	49	2055
(- +)	- - - +	48	49	43	45	0	0	45	42	0	46	0	40	50	45	42	45	47	43	43	45	45	47	0	41	0	42	48	46	47	45	1862
(+ -)	- - + -	46	49	55	61	0	0	47	47	0	44	0	48	48	48	47	44	50	40	48	51	51	44	0	51	0	47	55	46	52	46	2236
(+ +)	- - + +	49	46	39	38	0	0	49	48	0	55	0	49	50	45	49	52	44	40	49	48	54	48	0	43	0	51	39	47	45	46	2117
(- +)	- + - -	52	39	50	50	0	0	54	51	0	57	0	42	42	52	47	50	48	50	51	53	51	47	0	42	0	38	44	47	43	48	2210
(+ -)	- + - +	44	55	43	49	0	0	43	47	0	41	0	52	52	41	47	46	45	57	53	49	51	45	0	49	0	57	48	47	51	46	2109
(- -)	- + + -	38	43	37	54	0	0	45	45	0	42	0	46	43	43	46	50	43	39	46	49	45	47	0	45	0	41	52	43	44	44	2085
(+ +)	- + + +	59	52	56	43	0	0	53	52	0	55	0	50	50	53	48	50	48	47	53	48	51	47	0	49	0	55	40	49	53	51	2372
(+ -)	+ - - -	47	36	46	51	0	0	52	61	0	56	0	45	40	55	45	47	44	43	47	52	40	45	0	48	0	43	47	52	43	45	2283
(+ -)	+ - - +	48	58	50	47	0	0	44	36	0	41	0	45	55	42	50	50	45	50	45	45	46	45	0	44	0	49	45	50	43	47	2047
(+ +)	+ - + -	49	60	48	45	0	0	52	49	0	42	0	41	55	45	46	47	47	43	51	50	46	45	0	49	0	44	51	41	51	48	2205
(+ +)	+ - + +	47	60	45	53	0	0	48	48	0	53	0	51	51	47	48	47	47	48	49	50	50	48	0	46	0	55	44	53	49	47	2259
(+ +)	+ + - -	54	53	44	45	0	0	44	48	0	43	0	45	40	53	45	47	42	48	49	54	43	48	0	47	0	48	43	48	47	48	2253
(- -)	+ + - +	41	45	51	52	0	0	53	48	0	53	0	50	53	47	47	51	51	46	48	46	43	45	0	47	0	48	50	47	50	47	2231
(- +)	+ + + -	38	41	42	47	0	0	46	45	0	44	0	47	42	50	44	42	46	43	46	43	45	58	0	46	0	38	48	46	48	46	1971
(+ +)	+ + + +	57	55	52	52	0	0	51	48	0	53	0	50	53	47	46	53	51	50	57	53	49	46	0	51	0	55	43	52	54	49	2093
(+ +)	- - - - -	52	46	44	51	0	0	55	48	0	65	0	48	52	43	44	51	45	57	45	52	55	46	0	61	0	56	43	52	54	51	948
(- -)	- - - - +	43	51	47	45	0	0	44	48	0	35	0	46	36	48	56	37	37	57	52	36	53	46	0	48	0	42	48	44	47	48	820
(+ -)	- - - + -	46	46	55	56	0	0	44	49	0	48	0	53	38	52	43	44	48	50	48	47	44	40	0	46	0	55	37	44	47	48	990
(+ -)	- - - + +	45	51	39	43	0	0	53	42	0	51	0	46	59	43	54	56	48	38	49	51	50	40	0	46	0	39	48	49	50	47	980
(+ -)	- - + - -	50	51	51	57	0	0	50	53	0	63	0	46	56	51	51	38	53	42	52	59	44	40	0	52	0	45	39	48	39	49	1053
(- -)	- - + - +	45	46	40	42	0	0	39	45	0	35	0	48	45	40	41	44	44	54	45	40	48	54	0	44	0	51	57	43	49	45	963
(- +)	- - + + -	42	51	40	63	0	0	49	47	0	42	0	53	36	51	48	51	47	47	38	50	46	38	0	52	0	40	42	56	39	50	1009
(+ +)	- - + + +	53	51	51	36	0	0	54	50	0	56	0	43	48	56	51	53	44	47	57	61	52	45	0	44	0	57	50	50	58	49	1124
(+ -)	- + - - -	46	46	49	46	0	0	54	48	0	53	0	52	36	51	52	45	43	50	45	49	53	47	0	47	0	45	42	56	50	50	1045
(- -)	- + - - +	50	35	44	53	0	0	43	41	0	45	0	52	60	40	39	57	49	56	52	43	46	43	0	42	0	47	47	36	46	46	969
(- +)	- + - + -	43	58	44	40	0	0	58	58	0	47	0	56	44	46	53	41	47	51	47	38	45	40	0	47	0	47	40	54	45	47	1039
(+ +)	- + - + +	46	55	45	57	0	0	45	52	0	50	0	58	52	40	44	47	48	43	40	48	49	50	0	48	0	57	50	54	45	48	1077
(+ -)	- + + - -	53	52	52	45	0	0	48	45	0	55	0	41	55	48	45	41	41	40	48	48	52	42	0	45	0	50	45	51	48	47	1113
(+ -)	- + + - +	52	45	56	55	0	0	55	51	0	42	0	39	36	48	44	52	48	48	51	53	53	53	0	50	0	44	43	43	54	49	1180
(- -)	- + + + -	42	37	42	42	0	0	44	46	0	41	0	39	38	47	41	41	41	48	52	44	45	58	0	45	0	37	47	50	44	45	949
(+ -)	- + + + +	53	56	52	51	0	0	53	47	0	54	0	58	61	52	50	52	45	52	46	52	53	36	0	50	0	55	41	41	54	50	1043
(+ +)	+ - - - -	41	48	53	48	0	0	54	58	0	43	0	58	53	55	60	46	52	41	57	48	46	52	0	46	0	49	53	46	51	49	1008
(+ +)	+ - - - +	54	48	40	43	0	0	45	39	0	54	0	36	40	44	36	45	42	50	41	44	51	49	0	46	0	42	50	50	52	46	948
(+ -)	+ - - + -	46	51	55	65	0	0	50	45	0	42	0	44	62	46	52	52	50	30	53	53	42	46	0	53	0	55	55	42	54	50	1146
(- +)	+ - - + +	52	41	40	34	0	0	41	52	0	52	0	35	46	35	38	41	39	30	48	41	40	43	0	41	0	44	41	48	43	43	1047
(+ -)	+ - + - -	54	28	49	46	0	0	49	49	0	45	0	36	28	44	46	53	56	47	45	49	53	46	0	45	0	28	53	46	48	48	1084
(+ +)	+ - + - +	42	64	47	53	0	0	48	48	0	50	0	56	65	41	43	52	47	40	48	48	46	41	0	48	0	66	36	47	47	47	1070 SU
(- +)	+ - + + -	52	52	45	56	0	0	55	41	0	45	0	41	51	46	52	41	41	47	48	46	45	57	0	45	0	41	53	43	52	45	982
(- -)	+ - + + +	42	37	42	51	0	0	44	46	0	41	0	39	38	44	46	41	42	36	48	44	45	40	0	50	0	37	47	50	47	44	953
(+ -)	+ + - - -	53	56	52	48	0	0	53	47	0	54	0	59	61	55	50	52	52	52	46	52	53	36	0	50	0	55	38	41	54	50	1153
(+ -)	+ + - - +	41	46	53	53	0	0	49	58	0	43	0	58	40	54	58	52	50	41	57	48	46	45	0	46	0	41	53	46	51	51	1137
(+ +)	+ + - + -	51	59	53	40	0	0	42	39	0	34	0	39	58	42	38	45	42	46	39	44	39	49	0	47	0	54	54	41	43	44	992
(+ +)	+ + - + +	54	28	50	50	0	0	57	44	0	56	0	46	51	51	49	46	48	45	51	51	44	46	0	45	0	52	39	52	52	47	1068
(+ +)	+ + + - -	40	71	46	50	0	0	46	51	0	52	0	48	38	58	49	46	48	45	56	53	51	46	0	45	0	52	53	43	44	48	1099 BP
(+ +)	+ + + - +	58	53	46	42	0	0	46	51	0	52	0	48	42	51	50	54	54	52	52	52	54	53	0	48	0	45	42	43	44	49	1032
(- -)	+ + + + -	34	46	47	54	0	0	51	46	0	52	0	48	47	38	43	39	47	36	44	47	47	38	0	44	0	52	46	53	52	46	964

```
-------- 65% --------
```

Figure 8.6: Continued

		BO	BP	C	CC	CD	CL	CO	CP	FC	GC	HO	JY	LB	LC	LH	NY	O	OJ	PB	PL	S	SF	SV	SM	SP	SU	TB	TR	W	T%	T#	
++++	(+)	27	50	42	44	0	0	48	44	0	48	0	57	51	51	53	45	41	45	55	43	43	59	0	47	0	39	51	47	47	48	946	
++++	(+)	66	50	54	55	0	0	48	49	0	51	0	40	42	44	43	54	52	54	43	55	56	38	0	51	0	57	40	47	48	48	952	BO
-–-+	(+)	50	52	49	62	0	0	56	53	0	61	0	50	42	44	45	59	52	43	51	54	61	45	0	60	0	38	44	27	36	52	428	
-–-+	(-)	47	48	45	37	0	0	43	46	0	38	0	50	51	45	47	40	27	43	48	45	35	42	0	30	0	61	44	47	36	42	346	
-–-+	(-)	42	47	62	38	0	0	44	46	0	46	0	52	37	47	45	51	48	54	42	50	61	42	0	43	0	53	52	47	47	48	459	
-–-+	(-)	51	47	32	61	0	0	55	57	0	53	0	47	58	53	51	46	37	52	52	52	48	46	0	56	0	46	57	46	50	47	452	
-–-+	(-)	58	54	54	64	0	0	66	57	0	65	0	54	51	40	39	58	61	24	53	42	51	51	0	41	0	45	55	43	48	56	506	CO
++-+	(+)	35	41	35	35	0	0	32	42	0	34	0	40	44	53	39	39	37	72	44	57	51	51	0	48	0	48	44	51	51	44	433	OJ
-–-+	(-)	37	50	34	59	0	0	52	31	0	36	0	36	57	40	56	46	50	47	40	40	51	28	0	36	0	29	40	43	28	43	427	
-–-+	(-)	62	45	58	40	0	0	47	60	0	60	0	60	31	46	47	45	43	50	56	41	46	69	0	58	0	70	41	53	63	52	519	SF SU
++-+	(+)	56	22	44	71	0	0	59	68	0	32	0	37	35	62	52	38	42	38	57	52	41	48	0	44	0	42	42	59	53	48	466	CC CP
-–-+	(+)	35	66	48	28	0	0	38	49	0	64	0	54	60	49	45	52	50	40	58	54	52	54	0	39	0	37	56	38	55	47	444	BP
-–-+	(+)	46	55	45	31	0	0	50	49	0	47	0	20	52	44	46	46	41	50	43	42	40	56	0	44	0	37	40	42	46	48	501	
+–-+	(+)	53	45	49	68	0	0	52	49	0	52	0	75	46	52	48	48	51	45	39	34	45	43	0	48	0	62	46	53	42	48	511	CC JY
-–-+	(-)	48	52	46	47	0	0	42	43	0	47	0	30	62	42	47	39	39	37	61	54	56	38	0	45	0	51	48	46	50	45	537	LB
-–-+	(-)	46	42	52	52	0	0	52	52	0	50	0	61	33	43	49	58	57	56	43	42	40	56	0	47	0	39	48	42	46	48	542	
+–-+	(+)	44	35	39	43	0	0	54	48	0	56	0	35	42	46	48	42	41	37	52	32	50	50	0	52	0	33	56	46	44	44	448	
-–-+	(-)	52	58	53	56	0	0	45	45	0	50	0	60	63	55	48	48	53	46	51	50	45	46	0	58	0	44	46	36	42	51	515	
++-+	(+)	43	50	54	61	0	0	57	56	0	47	0	70	35	52	67	56	46	48	50	45	34	48	0	50	0	44	47	49	42	52	505	JY LH
-–-+	(-)	56	39	43	38	0	0	45	41	0	52	0	22	60	45	32	43	48	48	51	62	53	46	0	50	0	44	45	44	55	44	432	
-–-+	(-)	41	64	56	55	0	0	56	60	0	36	0	59	41	48	41	47	39	40	52	45	44	53	0	36	0	61	42	42	61	51	535	LB
-–-+	(+)	58	29	37	44	0	0	53	59	0	65	0	31	23	46	41	41	39	40	44	42	43	52	0	31	0	38	32	47	36	44	465	
++-+	(+)	26	26	45	52	0	0	46	55	0	44	0	41	35	47	52	49	54	48	44	42	55	57	0	45	0	23	53	48	47	47	515	
-–-+	(-)	43	60	52	47	0	0	53	60	0	52	0	54	58	47	33	58	50	50	48	48	40	48	0	48	0	69	44	44	62	47	511	SU
-–-+	(+)	23	52	36	31	0	0	33	43	0	34	0	57	47	57	64	47	34	52	45	54	44	58	0	37	0	40	59	44	53	44	457	
-–-+	(-)	76	47	58	62	0	0	64	60	0	57	0	42	47	59	54	50	53	47	54	45	53	38	0	56	0	55	36	52	46	53	554	BO
++-+	(+)	41	41	43	63	0	0	50	50	0	42	0	54	31	55	41	46	52	43	52	41	56	48	0	40	0	34	46	36	49	48	571	
-–-+	(-)	52	58	52	31	0	0	44	44	0	40	0	45	57	43	48	51	46	50	45	50	37	48	0	54	0	46	51	52	45	47	560	
+–-+	(+)	53	25	49	61	0	0	56	40	0	40	0	42	58	50	46	51	52	51	51	50	45	39	0	50	0	61	53	40	56	48	539	
++-+	(+)	40	75	44	38	0	0	55	35	0	55	0	52	41	59	45	52	43	66	58	43	53	55	0	36	0	56	53	56	42	47	530	BP
-–-+	(-)	58	55	56	41	0	0	47	46	0	51	0	44	44	48	50	42	50	30	41	55	40	29	0	36	0	35	38	34	48	48	506	OJ
-–-+	(-)	31	44	37	54	0	0	50	42	0	45	0	56	44	57	60	41	43	59	56	56	59	55	0	53	0	64	55	60	46	46	489	
+–-+	(+)	25	66	38	44	0	0	53	56	0	64	0	52	29	36	34	58	52	36	58	48	43	29	0	51	0	35	36	54	47	49	464	BP SF
-–-+	(-)	67	33	55	56	0	0	51	52	0	71	0	47	48	57	45	42	59	45	54	60	50	55	0	61	0	64	40	40	47	47	449	BO
+–-+	(+)	58	41	41	44	0	0	56	50	0	28	0	41	35	38	51	50	51	33	53	53	43	50	0	36	0	33	36	43	50	50	480	GC OJ SU
-–-+	(-)	39	54	47	50	0	0	43	41	0	50	0	47	39	59	54	39	43	50	41	42	45	42	0	50	0	32	58	51	45	48	429	
++-+	(+)	54	43	52	71	0	0	42	46	0	60	0	57	39	59	57	50	50	50	53	54	55	45	0	50	0	44	38	43	52	48	488	CC
-–-+	(-)	40	56	50	28	0	0	50	55	0	38	0	42	46	39	44	48	48	38	36	50	53	42	0	40	0	29	54	51	45	47	480	
+–-+	(+)	41	46	41	50	0	0	45	40	0	51	0	45	65	55	46	56	44	47	60	71	46	56	0	57	0	48	41	45	40	48	503	PL
-–-+	(-)	55	53	49	38	0	0	49	41	0	66	0	50	36	43	37	37	53	44	50	28	43	57	0	52	0	56	54	54	47	46	489	
++-+	(+)	44	50	54	61	0	0	54	41	0	34	0	53	36	50	42	40	45	47	51	53	44	44	0	44	0	54	55	48	48	48	539	GC PL
-–-+	(-)	50	50	42	66	0	0	56	48	0	34	0	52	41	47	40	53	50	50	50	61	34	34	0	52	0	50	45	45	51	45	557	
++-+	(+)	45	44	54	33	0	0	46	48	0	46	0	46	36	53	42	40	46	53	53	54	38	62	0	40	0	54	56	54	47	48	548	GC PL
-–-+	(-)	53	53	42	66	0	0	57	41	0	63	0	64	72	53	47	53	43	50	36	37	60	32	0	56	0	41	39	39	45	45	488	CC
+–-+	(+)	63	37	60	57	0	0	49	52	0	37	0	57	53	53	52	54	44	40	53	52	52	47	0	50	0	58	58	37	48	46	504	LB
-–-+	(-)	36	54	54	42	0	0	54	48	0	40	0	34	33	44	44	49	46	44	44	44	47	54	0	38	0	36	49	54	48	47	536	
+–-+	(+)	53	51	51	31	0	0	55	54	0	54	0	47	57	52	51	51	42	40	53	60	47	48	0	52	0	45	52	41	47	50	531	
++-+	(+)	55	38	39	71	0	0	50	62	0	48	0	52	33	44	42	42	46	57	50	50	54	48	0	46	0	45	47	47	50	50	594	CC
+–-+	(+)	41	53	39	28	0	0	48	46	0	48	0	61	43	44	58	53	41	41	50	45	45	48	0	48	0	54	47	50	49	46	570	CC

Figure 8.6: Continued

		BO	BP	C	CC	CD	CL	CO	CP	FC	GC	HO	JY	LB	LC	LH	NY	O	OJ	PB	PL	S	SF	SV	SM	SP	SU	TB	TR	W	T%	T#	
+ + - + -	(+)	55	33	51	38	0	0	51	42	0	62	0	30	26	58	56	40	63	59	47	51	37	0	44	0	35	46	46	52	48	536	
+ + + + +	(+)	41	62	34	61	0	0	43	54	0	37	0	60	37	35	42	57	57	36	40	50	48	0	47	0	60	32	40	48	46	513	LB
+ + - + +	(+)	42	45	43	52	0	0	55	34	0	56	0	50	37	35	50	42	41	50	49	36	44	0	50	0	44	52	40	46	44	477	
+ + + + +	(+)	57	54	60	47	0	0	41	65	0	40	0	55	55	56	39	57	50	49	63	54	58	0	55	0	48	52	53	48	51	551	
+ + + + +	(+)	56	40	55	48	0	0	49	69	0	66	0	54	55	62	55	57	47	54	58	63	54	0	55	0	54	57	54	54	53	519	CP GC
+ + + - -	(-)	44	60	55	48	0	0	49	25	0	26	0	31	50	39	39	41	38	34	35	57	38	0	42	0	25	35	36	41	41	395	
+ + + - +	(-)	57	29	53	42	0	0	43	46	0	31	0	59	50	54	46	48	54	34	47	39	45	0	56	0	28	57	44	48	46	482	
+ + + + -	(-)	40	70	42	57	0	0	56	51	0	60	0	58	40	56	54	58	47	47	48	51	55	0	43	0	71	39	48	46	49	512	BP SU
+ + + + +	(-)	58	50	39	44	0	0	41	53	0	55	0	41	53	56	38	46	47	51	45	63	53	0	61	0	44	46	48	47	50	483	
+ + + + +	(+)	38	50	42	57	0	0	56	46	0	41	0	41	53	38	35	35	37	52	45	36	46	0	35	0	55	40	50	52	44	426	
+ + + + +	(+)	23	33	50	52	0	0	50	45	0	59	0	58	38	45	46	48	52	55	34	50	42	0	53	0	38	51	36	48	47	446	
+ + + + +	(+)	76	66	50	55	0	0	47	45	0	40	0	37	55	52	52	48	54	47	43	61	50	0	46	0	53	42	59	48	49	470	BO BP
- - + + +	(-)	44	25	44	66	0	0	41	60	0	62	0	55	58	36	50	52	60	36	80	72	44	0	33	0	41	50	65	64	52	181	CC PL S
- - + + +	(+)	55	75	56	33	0	0	58	33	0	37	0	50	53	45	47	30	40	40	56	20	18	0	50	0	58	36	30	28	43	148	BP
- - + + +	(-)	42	46	74	50	0	0	54	58	0	53	0	55	41	35	47	56	43	63	53	53	68	0	33	0	62	48	51	63	52	223	C S
- - + + -	(+)	66	36	22	50	0	0	62	41	0	46	0	44	58	56	57	44	56	36	46	31	54	0	47	0	37	34	36	31	43	186	SM
- - + + -	(+)	25	54	29	36	0	0	37	46	0	28	0	50	43	43	52	50	33	76	30	42	41	0	42	0	69	57	54	46	46	221	BO GC PB
- - + - +	(+)	30	54	23	57	0	0	50	30	0	22	0	44	44	60	58	45	70	37	42	42	50	0	18	0	13	29	40	16	42	209	OJ S SU
- - + - +	(+)	70	54	51	42	0	0	50	69	0	77	0	55	33	41	41	40	36	56	57	50	72	0	75	0	86	25	51	79	53	193	LB
- - + - +	(+)	71	30	52	50	0	0	61	71	0	58	0	11	25	57	54	36	50	38	45	47	40	0	41	0	47	47	70	60	50	246	BO CP GC SF SM SU W
- - + - -	(+)	21	70	57	75	0	0	38	50	0	41	0	77	66	57	44	57	47	61	55	52	55	0	47	0	52	17	28	45	45	216	BO CP TR
- - + - -	(-)	43	76	44	27	0	0	40	57	0	43	0	25	66	62	56	57	39	85	66	42	52	0	46	0	31	61	57	54	51	196	BP JY LB
- - - + +	(+)	56	23	51	72	0	0	59	42	0	56	0	75	33	27	43	39	48	14	29	57	42	0	40	0	68	34	33	41	44	262	BP LB OJ PB
- - - + +	(+)	40	45	45	44	0	0	45	69	0	40	0	26	16	36	31	63	56	57	48	56	36	0	52	0	52	32	51	48	47	224	CC JY SU
- - - + -	(-)	60	60	23	55	0	0	50	50	0	70	0	73	54	50	41	36	41	40	48	34	55	0	42	0	35	50	67	51	50	248	CP LB
- - - + -	(+)	33	27	23	53	0	0	50	41	0	33	0	33	45	38	47	43	26	44	41	23	31	0	38	0	37	40	62	43	39	262	JY TB
- - - + -	(-)	66	63	52	46	0	0	61	71	0	66	0	55	54	56	54	52	50	38	58	69	68	0	53	0	50	56	28	60	53	170	
- - - - +	(+)	28	75	57	75	0	0	55	50	0	45	0	69	41	57	74	45	57	57	65	64	45	0	66	0	38	48	56	55	55	238	BO C GC O PL S
- - - - +	(-)	71	16	38	25	0	0	44	42	0	55	0	23	66	42	25	50	52	36	34	35	50	0	33	0	44	41	58	45	43	235	BP CC JY LH SM
- - - - +	(-)	50	50	63	50	0	0	64	54	0	70	0	55	71	59	41	50	57	43	50	40	36	0	70	0	64	59	43	57	49	194	BO LB
- - - - -	(+)	50	50	21	50	0	0	38	47	0	58	0	44	35	65	44	31	36	40	52	34	43	0	52	0	35	22	47	44	45	231	LB SM
- - - - -	(+)	43	33	57	53	0	0	37	61	0	44	0	50	54	44	35	36	73	40	45	58	68	0	71	0	22	50	46	26	49	209	GC OJ
- - - - -	(-)	52	55	42	46	0	0	62	38	0	42	0	40	45	55	34	29	36	45	53	41	45	0	23	0	72	38	50	47	46	254	O SF SM
- + - - +	(+)	70	45	54	16	0	0	50	46	0	53	0	60	41	44	55	53	54	54	46	52	64	0	61	0	63	72	52	64	50	236	OJ
- + - - +	(-)	70	55	38	70	0	0	50	53	0	55	0	50	14	58	52	45	43	42	50	52	47	0	61	0	38	53	42	36	48	233	TB
- + - - -	(-)	45	45	56	30	0	0	35	61	0	45	0	50	64	45	48	42	42	66	66	47	44	0	42	0	61	46	40	51	47	254	BO CC
- + - + +	(+)	66	9	45	66	0	0	36	31	0	31	0	62	64	50	54	68	63	43	50	63	50	0	30	0	58	53	45	48	49	257	LB PB
- + - + -	(-)	28	90	48	33	0	0	48	57	0	57	0	37	35	45	41	31	36	43	38	36	41	0	58	0	41	31	47	48	45	268	BO CC NV
- + - - +	(+)	50	60	58	33	0	0	38	47	0	58	0	44	47	65	44	50	34	59	62	34	48	0	17	0	42	33	47	44	48	245	BP
- + - - -	(-)	43	33	57	53	0	0	37	52	0	41	0	50	58	34	56	39	36	40	37	65	52	0	70	0	57	64	50	52	48	248	SF
- + - - -	(+)	38	40	38	61	0	0	52	50	0	50	0	58	58	55	50	36	40	36	52	25	52	0	70	0	57	64	50	52	48	252	SM
- + - + +	(+)	35	83	40	42	0	0	45	45	0	41	0	42	42	34	56	39	46	55	25	58	66	0	66	0	37	67	42	30	48	214	BP LH SF TB
- + - + +	(-)	57	16	56	57	0	0	54	50	0	50	0	57	42	45	28	35	57	44	53	41	53	0	65	0	62	22	50	42	47	213	PL
- + - + +	(+)	61	36	35	50	0	0	36	56	0	70	0	50	52	47	33	40	66	57	41	63	44	0	46	0	46	50	27	30	48	207	GC O OJ
- + - + -	(+)	38	54	60	37	0	0	45	39	0	30	0	33	47	59	42	52	25	33	36	36	52	0	46	0	53	50	64	57	48	207	
- + - + -	(-)	62	42	40	69	0	0	60	59	0	38	0	42	40	40	46	46	36	56	50	47	51	0	64	0	44	41	50	45	46	234	CC
- + - - +	(+)	31	57	52	30	0	0	29	59	0	61	0	28	41	43	35	44	33	36	44	76	45	0	41	0	64	52	44	56	50	253	LB SU
- + - - +	(-)	44	40	42	37	0	0	40	53	0	37	0	53	31	31	35	50	43	43	45	23	54	0	54	0	42	54	50	47	47	220	LB PL
- + - - +	(+)	52	42	60	62	0	0	40	61	0	60	0	53	41	31	42	52	30	43	62	52	51	0	45	0	42	54	43	40	46	246	JY
- + - - -	(+)	61	18	46	60	0	0	44	38	0	61	0	38	58	65	50	50	65	56	68	47	48	0	50	0	52	41	45	56	50	267	PB
- + - - -	(-)	39	33	53	27	0	0	50	47	0	67	0	38	60	40	40	42	53	53	62	60	65	0	62	0	61	50	44	44	51	264	GC
- + - + -	(-)	52	55	46	72	0	0	50	47	0	32	0	38	60	40	55	30	38	37	37	30	30	0	37	0	27	56	51	56	45	229	CC

Figure 8.6: Continued

	+/−	BO	BP	C	CC	CD	CL	CO	CP	FC	GC	HO	JY	LB	LC	LH	NY	O	OJ	PB	PL	S	SF	SV	SM	SP	SU	TB	TR	W	T%	T#	65%
−+−+−+	(+)	48	100	50	50	0	0	0	51	43	0	50	0	70	83	53	44	34	60	42	36	50	30	0	46	0	83	39	45	25	47	246	BP JY LB PL SU
−+−+−+	(−)	51	42	50		0	48	53			50	0	20	16	40	52	65	36	57	63	31	50	60	0	53	0	16	60	54	75	50	257	W
−+−+−+	(+)	54	44	40	60	0	39	56			57	0	50	30	38	58	42	31	31	60	55	40	39	0	44	0	60	31	54	47	47	263	
−+−+−+	(−)	45	55	56	60	0	60	40			40	0	50	30	58	47	42	50	62	54	54	40	61	0	50	0	45	55	44	52	50	280	PB
−+−+−+	(+)	63	50	45	80	0	39	45			36	0	62	30	47	44	45	55	47	54	54	40	75	0	33	0	62	51	57	45	49	227	CC SF
−+−+−+	(−)	36	40	55	20	0	56	50			57	0	37	70	52	50	52	48	45	45	45	55	50	0	66	0	37	48	28	54	47	218	LB SM
−+−+−+	(−)	44	50	53	28	0	50	54			31	0	54	81	52	52	52	41	40	60	47	40	50	0	37	0	62	43	33	48	49	274	LB
−+−+−+	(−)	48	50	36	57	0	50	45			68	0	45	18	44	43	33	40	36	47	50	40	47	0	50	0	37	46	52	48	45	253	GC
−+−−+−	(+)	54	28	52	71	0	59	48			72	0	30	50	58	41	46	66	37	50	50	40	47	0	50	0	44	48	48	44	50	288	CC GC OJ
−+−−+−	(−)	40	71	45	28	0	48	48			27	0	61	50	37	54	66	46	33	62	56	39	54	0	38	0	55	51	37	48	45	262	BP NY
−+−−+−	(+)	68	40	48	42	0	44	41			66	0	30	33	64	52	40	46	71	60	56	45	44	0	36	0	7	55	50	37	49	259	BO GC OJ
−+−−+−	(−)	32	60	48	57	0	48	58			33	0	37	50	30	50	55	59	28	40	58	43	44	0	57	0	84	40	43	58	47	249	SU
−+−−+−	(+)	51	20	29	36	0	45	41			60	0	37	47	35	52	40	44	58	44	38	43	53	0	44	0	52	58	41	40	45	243	
−+−−+−	(+)	48	80	61	63	0	50	58			35	0	62	47	59	30	40	48	35	51	61	56	46	0	55	0	41	52	50	50	49	207	BP
−+−−+−	(−)	61	37	40	53	0	59	71			70	0	64	50	53	57	53	41	47	47	58	41	62	0	63	0	30	52	57	64	55	272	CP GC
−+−−+−	(+)	38	62	54	46	0	40	19			17	0	14	41	40	38	52	39	42	47	54	37	37	0	31	0	38	38	30	32	37	185	
−+−−+−	(−)	58	20	51	70	0	32	50			31	0	63	41	36	56	40	37	42	62	41	45	46	0	66	0	51	50	56	56	46	233	CC SM
−+−+++	(−)	37	80	45	30	0	0	67	45	57	0	62	58	57	59	52	45	46	69	43	58	45	0	33	0	100	44	32	39	49	249	BP CO SU
−+−+++	(+)	66	25	50	42	0	41	59			44	0	62	60	72	50	69	44	52	38	55	44	61	0	68	0	45	59	56	42	54	243	BO LC NY SM
−+−+++	(−)	28	75	42	57	0	54	40			50	0	37	45	24	50	26	38	40	57	43	44	38	0	26	0	54	29	43	57	41	188	BP
−+−+++	(+)	25	37	55	36	0	31	33			70	0	77	45	52	48	37	47	60	56	35	50	63	0	58	0	33	50	43	47	52	207	GC
−+−+++	(+)	75	62	44	63	0	68	83			30	0	22	54	52	48	50	66	38	40	30	55	44	0	41	0	66	42	66	54	51	242	BO CO SU TR
−+−+++	(−)	52	76	48	55	0	71	16			60	0	37	33	39	50	66	38	31	56	30	55	62	0	62	0	60	36	60	50	51	220	BP CO NY O SM
−+−+++	(−)	41	23	44	44	0	28	83			40	0	62	35	61	55	34	23	46	43	69	45	44	0	15	0	66	23	34	41	43	183	CP PL SU
−+−+++	(+)	44	50	52	25	0	59	70			42	0	57	41	43	45	40	50	50	40	46	52	36	0	45	0	55	45	41	50	46	221	
−+−+++	(−)	48	50	39	75	0	62	50			60	0	42	58	38	56	48	66	38	55	53	50	63	0	54	0	44	55	55	58	50	243	CC
−+−+++	(+)	42	69	56	66	0	67	57			57	0	58	64	50	58	65	38	40	58	41	42	57	0	33	0	60	76	60	50	54	259	BP CC CO TB
−+−+++	(+)	57	30	40	33	0	28	42			42	0	33	35	42	55	34	41	76	54	57	50	62	0	53	0	35	23	34	50	43	206	OJ
−+−+++	(−)	42	70	28	60	0	54	30			57	0	31	55	46	50	50	42	31	42	42	50	20	0	52	0	50	53	36	54	44	216	BP
−+−+++	(−)	57	30	63	40	0	45	55			35	0	62	22	50	55	34	60	68	57	42	61	44	0	41	0	50	46	60	60	51	250	OJ SF
−+−+++	(+)	50	14	40	87	0	59	70			15	0	58	50	73	33	36	34	40	37	60	40	59	0	50	0	42	41	52	45	48	236	CC CP LC
−+−+++	(−)	50	57	55	12	0	37	30			78	0	41	50	26	62	63	43	60	62	40	52	36	0	30	0	50	47	41	54	46	225	GC
−+−+++	(+)	50	16	45	37	0	64	42			53	0	50	50	38	55	58	55	69	48	36	48	50	0	42	0	45	56	20	55	42	214	BP
−+−+++	(+)	50	83	45	62	0	35	54			46	0	81	83	55	43	58	55	69	48	53	48	50	0	57	0	54	71	45	47	53	269	JY LB OJ TR
−+−+++	(−)	58	75	50	50	0	40	17			52	0	40	60	46	50	42	31	31	60	58	54	37	0	40	0	28	54	53	47	47	264	BP
−+−+++	(−)	29	25	50	50	0	54	73			42	0	50	60	50	37	52	65	68	40	37	54	60	0	50	0	38	36	47	32	47	260	CP OJ
−+−+++	(+)	52	50	45	36	0	51	50			44	0	30	14	40	48	39	51	27	63	37	62	57	0	58	0	33	53	41	40	46	251	
−+−+++	(+)	42	50	48	63	0	51	46			50	0	70	85	48	56	47	41	72	62	58	34	42	0	41	0	60	41	50	55	48	263	JY LB OJ
−+−+++	(−)	54	54	45	37	0	58	59			47	0	71	66	43	46	56	37	36	31	58	48	45	0	56	0	53	39	38	32	51	250	JY
−+−+++	(+)	45	60	45	43	0	41	40			52	0	21	56	46	50	37	46	63	47	54	58	60	0	37	0	40	50	36	64	45	223	
−+−+++	(+)	30	69	54	62	0	51	36			36	0	66	66	48	64	63	46	80	62	62	63	50	0	57	0	60	57	45	65	52	290	BP JY LB OJ
−+−+++	(−)	70	33	45	37	0	45	45			63	0	20	44	46	56	31	20	37	36	38	60	48	0	31	0	40	48	30	38	43	240	BO CP
−+−+++	(+)	58	20	33	50	0	60	40			44	0	16	56	50	64	37	34	58	47	42	58	45	0	29	0	28	54	50	33	47	252	
−+−+++	(+)	37	80	32	40	0	51	48			55	0	83	100	48	32	68	56	41	50	57	36	50	0	58	0	57	39	38	61	48	258	BP JY LB NY
−+−+++	(−)	16	50	32	40	0	16	40			29	0	66	37	57	38	47	34	47	34	45	43	48	0	47	0	50	45	38	41	42	214	JY
−+−+++	(−)	84	60	60	50	0	80	55			70	0	33	50	42	61	47	56	36	65	38	54	31	0	52	0	37	50	61	58	55	280	BO CO GC
−+−+++	(+)	40	28	45	58	0	44	58			58	0	62	41	44	58	61	39	56	57	56	41	40	0	63	0	33	42	29	60	49	291	
−+−+++	(−)	56	71	50	33	0	52	41			41	0	37	41	44	37	43	31	43	42	43	41	60	0	36	0	66	53	64	36	49	279	BP SU
−+−+++	(+)	46	50	42	55	0	50	59			48	0	22	53	60	43	37	46	18	45	50	50	40	0	63	0	44	52	23	66	48	254	W
−+−+++	(+)	50	50	53	44	0	50	33			51	0	66	46	34	52	58	56	43	45	50	56	60	0	36	0	50	47	62	33	48	257	JY
−+−+++	(−)	70	50	60	60	0	60	47			50	0	55	50	55	44	48	31	54	50	43	42	44	0	42	0	44	42	23	38	49	236	BO OJ
−+−+++	(+)	20	50	36	45	0	52	44			26	0	60	87	44	61	50	68	42	53	65	33	64	0	66	0	33	45	73	45	49	215	O TR
−+−+++	(+)	12	50	54	55	0	43	50			73	0	40	12	30	50	50	46	42	53	46	66	33	0	33	0	56	34	66	54	47	229	LB SF SM TR
−+−+++	(−)	81	50	54	54	0	43	50			73	0	60	12	30	50	50	40	12	46	46	66	33	0	33	0	80	56	61	54	47	219	BO GC S SU

Figure 8.6: Continued

		BO	BP	C	CC	CD	CL	CO	CP	FC	GC	HO	JY	LB	LC	LH	NY	O	OJ	PB	PL	S	SF	SV	SM	SP	SU	TB	TR	W	T%	T#	
+ + — — — — — +	(+)	59	41	48	40	0	0	57	50	0	78	0	40	42	50	47	47	56	47	30	61	60	61	0	68	0	44	44	56	47	54	253	GC OJ SM SU
+ + — — — +	(−)	36	58	38	60	0	0	42	50	0	21	0	50	57	50	43	29	57	30	30	52	35	38	0	27	0	11	51	39	37	41	194	
+ + — — — +	(−)	43	42	57	75	0	0	51	35	0	77	0	55	50	55	47	29	56	37	58	25	45	40	0	37	0	37	70	45	70	50	236	CC GC TB W
+ + — — — +	(−)	56	57	40	25	0	0	41	50	0	22	0	44	50	41	52	70	40	57	44	66	57	38	0	56	0	50	24	50	34	45	216	NY PL
+ + — — — + +	(+)	46	42	56	62	0	0	44	51	0	61	0	50	28	48	42	55	44	28	52	33	42	55	0	30	0	50	67	46	48	46	246	PL
+ + — — — + +	(+)	53	57	32	37	0	0	56	48	0	38	0	33	57	43	57	37	51	42	52	42	39	44	0	65	0	50	56	46	50	48	253	TB
+ + — — — + +	(+)	40	80	52	70	0	0	41	51	0	40	0	11	27	54	57	60	72	39	47	54	54	47	0	63	0	56	45	50	50	48	278	BP CC PL
+ + — — — + +	(+)	50	20	44	30	0	0	58	48	0	59	0	55	77	65	41	33	33	40	50	22	54	47	0	36	0	40	39	47	50	46	265	LB
+ + — — — + +	(−)	50	47	53	38	0	0	48	47	0	61	0	25	23	47	54	42	32	32	50	75	58	44	0	38	0	41	62	62	54	50	257	PL
+ + — — — + +	(−)	50	52	38	61	0	0	52	47	0	61	0	75	60	53	53	42	35	41	50	52	41	50	0	55	0	58	37	31	45	47	244	JY LB
+ + — — — + +	(+)	41	44	41	50	0	0	46	38	0	43	0	33	60	53	53	66	36	54	51	36	42	35	0	47	0	30	50	30	56	45	244	NY SU
+ + — — — + +	(+)	58	55	48	37	0	0	50	61	0	75	0	66	40	38	55	27	63	37	48	47	36	57	0	52	0	70	46	62	44	49	266	JY SU
+ + — — — + +	(+)	60	66	38	30	0	0	50	40	0	75	0	45	45	50	44	52	50	63	33	36	36	48	0	45	0	32	46	48	45	45	248	BP GC
+ + — — — + +	(+)	39	33	61	70	0	0	50	59	0	25	0	45	50	52	44	57	46	42	50	66	63	43	0	54	0	50	64	52	51	52	289	CC PL
+ + — — — + +	(+)	33	20	50	63	0	0	29	47	0	44	0	54	45	50	34	33	45	50	50	40	52	52	0	47	0	36	47	50	48	44	213	
+ + — — — + +	(+)	62	80	45	36	0	0	66	47	0	50	0	54	54	50	52	57	41	62	39	47	41	52	0	47	0	58	44	52	50	50	242	BP CO
+ + — — — + +	(−)	36	22	61	50	0	0	51	80	0	50	0	42	30	52	52	53	50	35	42	55	33	38	0	56	0	83	50	45	45	47	188	CP SU
+ + — — — + +	(+)	54	77	32	50	0	0	48	20	0	37	0	57	50	47	35	47	45	58	57	40	46	61	0	56	0	16	46	45	45	47	187	BP
+ + — — — + +	(+)	57	50	31	28	0	0	37	44	0	30	0	33	62	38	43	42	33	55	27	66	53	56	0	45	0	33	42	58	48	48	253	CC
+ + — — — + +	(+)	42	33	31	33	0	0	36	57	0	70	0	66	44	54	39	52	41	50	39	53	53	33	0	55	0	53	42	39	51	48	249	GC JY
+ + — — — + +	(+)	41	25	36	33	0	0	55	45	0	62	0	50	16	54	56	45	45	61	52	68	57	50	0	53	0	60	38	55	61	48	247	
+ + — — — + +	(−)	52	60	39	66	0	0	55	45	0	42	0	33	30	41	39	58	60	49	44	43	40	50	0	38	0	49	48	39	50	47	243	BP CC JY LB
+ + — — — + +	(−)	29	60	34	66	0	0	66	25	0	45	0	66	83	33	47	29	41	45	50	33	56	38	0	44	0	16	51	40	50	43	212	CC CO
+ + — — — + +	(−)	50	40	65	33	0	0	33	75	0	54	0	38	61	33	47	57	58	54	68	56	46	57	0	44	0	90	62	55	50	52	260	BO CP LC NY PL SU
+ + — — — + +	(+)	50	50	29	46	0	0	38	66	0	66	0	42	37	61	50	42	61	50	33	33	40	42	0	40	0	62	33	40	48	52	223	CP GC PB SU
+ + — — — + +	(+)	50	62	62	53	0	0	57	33	0	33	0	57	62	38	43	42	33	55	27	66	40	52	0	60	0	0	33	38	54	44	188	PL
+ + — — — + +	(+)	50	55	55	18	0	0	63	42	0	31	0	50	83	45	39	56	59	47	57	61	48	44	0	46	0	75	64	43	40	47	230	LB SU
+ + — — — + +	(+)	44	50	40	81	0	0	36	57	0	62	0	50	30	44	56	43	45	37	52	68	57	51	0	53	0	25	35	56	55	50	242	CC
+ + — — — + +	(+)	44	62	30	45	0	0	40	50	0	72	0	55	16	54	32	50	55	33	44	31	47	63	0	55	0	33	36	44	45	47	222	GC PL
+ + — — — + +	(−)	33	25	60	55	0	0	59	56	0	27	0	44	60	44	56	35	44	44	44	66	52	36	0	44	0	66	52	53	45	51	224	SU
+ — — — — — +	(+)	66	75	50	44	0	0	30	37	0	43	0	50	57	52	57	64	35	38	43	66	52	36	0	52	0	40	44	41	50	46	227	
— + — — — — +	(+)	50	33	42	50	0	0	50	60	0	33	0	42	42	66	55	62	66	75	44	31	36	28	0	33	0	57	36	83	75	52	205	BO BP PL
— + — — — — +	(−)	50	66	52	50	0	0	50	40	0	33	0	50	37	66	55	37	66	16	0	0	0	42	0	33	0	36	16	0	0	42	77	LC O OJ PL S TR W
— + — — — — +	(−)	37	0	81	50	0	0	50	55	0	66	0	40	71	40	50	66	33	66	28	87	75	55	0	50	0	60	43	46	66	55	63	BP GC
— + — — — — +	(+)	70	33	66	50	0	0	36	100	0	40	0	28	28	53	55	34	66	33	57	12	25	44	0	50	0	60	33	38	33	39	100	BP C CO LB NY OJ
— + — — — — +	(+)	20	6	18	60	0	0	60	40	0	50	0	50	68	69	44	69	25	75	25	50	33	66	0	50	0	33	30	11	42	51	71	O
— + — — — — +	(−)	25	33	16	60	0	0	40	40	0	14	0	60	57	31	44	36	69	25	55	33	50	33	0	50	0	66	57	57	21	51	95	BO C LC O PB PL SF
— + — — — — +	(+)	75	33	25	40	0	0	41	42	0	85	0	60	44	70	33	42	75	66	25	71	69	33	0	50	0	80	28	70	57	43	83	OJ SU TB TR
— + — — — — +	(+)	83	50	40	50	0	0	58	57	0	66	0	30	30	70	39	37	36	33	33	33	50	70	0	33	0	20	57	45	21	50	97	LC OJ PL S
— + — — — — +	(+)	50	40	50	40	0	0	70	83	0	66	0	60	30	40	56	27	55	40	52	62	63	60	0	60	0	44	41	87	94	55	112	BO BP C GC SF SM
— + — — — — +	(+)	50	60	40	50	0	0	70	16	0	62	0	25	85	61	32	36	33	36	66	37	30	30	100	33	0	55	50	4	35	54	116	BO CO CP GC LH SF TR
— + — — — — +	(+)	50	50	60	14	0	0	47	71	0	53	0	75	20	23	25	36	58	33	42	33	20	30	0	44	0	64	58	28	41	40	83	LB NY PB
— + — — — — +	(+)	50	0	33	85	0	0	52	28	0	46	0	60	66	60	36	57	54	42	50	66	37	30	50	30	0	33	44	39	68	47	90	CC JY
— — — — — — +	(−)	16	41	33	33	0	0	36	55	0	42	0	33	66	40	71	63	36	57	22	62	23	60	25	0	0	0	30	66	50	50	117	LB PB SM W
— — — — — — +	(−)	83	58	66	85	0	0	63	44	0	57	0	40	33	40	55	36	14	41	66	33	25	60	0	50	0	60	31	66	50	37	125	BP CC LH TB
— — — — — +	(+)	33	75	21	75	0	0	63	0	0	25	0	75	66	78	20	57	78	53	66	66	75	60	0	66	0	0	30	66	50	51	72	BP CC JY PB TR
— — — +	(+)	6	25	71	25	0	0	75	75	0	60	0	25	66	25	57	53	50	33	80	50	33	80	0	62	0	50	40	22	50	57	111	BO C CP GC LB LC
— — — +	(−)	0	85	62	60	0	0	81	42	0	85	0	57	72	27	20	53	53	53	37	71	50	40	0	42	0	33	40	28	21	51	101	BP CC CO CP LC LH
— — +	(+)	100	14	33	33	0	0	66	25	0	40	0	28	75	27	57	62	36	38	33	50	60	60	37	71	0	44	40	57	57	44	88	BO LB
— — +	(+)	40	33	70	66	0	0	18	16	0	14	0	66	66	40	61	37	50	50	44	44	37	30	71	62	0	62	30	42	60	46	100	C CC LB SM
— + +	(+)	60	66	10	33	0	0	81	60	0	30	0	55	60	40	30	30	62	30	60	55	62	60	28	0	0	37	30	39	60	46	101	BP CO GC JY
— + —	(−)	38	0	53	62	0	0	27	75	0	30	0	55	60	12	53	68	0	0	57	25	50	71	0100	0	0	27	55	21	20	43	98	CP O SF SM
— + — +	(−)	53	66	46	37	0	0	72	25	0	61	0	33	40	87	60	38	25100	25	14	75	50	14	0	0	0	72	33	78	80	51	116	BP CO LC OJ PL SU

`------- 65% -------`

Figure 8.6:   Continued

		BO	BP	C	CC	CD	CL	CO	CP	FC	GC	HO	JY	LB	LC	LH	NY	O	OJ	PB	PL	S	SF	SV	SM	SP	SU	TB	TR	W	T%	T#	------- 65% -------
- + + +	(+)	20	60	15	0	0	0	53	27	0	0	0	66	61	23	38	38	66	38	66	62	40	54	0	28	0	20	87	61	50	50	132	JY OJ PL TB
- - + -	(-)	80	40	76	100	0	0	46	85	0	30	0	33	50	38	76	38	53	33	37	33	60	36	42	44	0	80	12	33	38	46	122	C CC CP LH SU
- + + +	(+)	53	50	39	60	0	0	63	85	0	66	0	54	45	45	71	42	30	50	25	71	57	46	44	44	0	44	57	38	46	50	131	CP GC LH PL
- - + -	(-)	46	50	52	40	0	0	27	14	0	33	0	75	40	52	57	62	70	28	28	57	50	54	55	55	0	55	42	42	42	46	121	LB O PB
- + + +	(+)	50	25	40	50	0	0	50	62	0	25	0	75	60	52	42	37	61	70	66	44	50	54	27	27	0	60	44	27	42	48	121	JY OJ PB
- + + +	(+)	40	75	60	50	0	0	50	37	0	62	0	25	60	47	42	37	38	30	33	33	50	27	63	63	0	40	55	50	50	47	118	BP TR
- + + +	(+)	50	57	66	33	0	0	50	33	0	62	0	40	33	71	42	37	55	66	33	33	50	26	0	0	0	40	55	55	33	50	119	C LC OJ PB SF
- - - -	(-)	40	42	33	50	0	0	58	66	0	37	0	60	50	28	36	41	38	33	30	66	80	0	71	71	100	33	66	44	33	46	111	CP LB S SM SU TB
- - + +	(-)	40	100	16	42	0	0	58	20	0	50	0	66	50	46	63	10	28	50	33	66	57	50	0	0	0	33	66	57	57	47	81	BP JY LB TB
- - - -	(-)	0	0	83	57	0	0	41	61	0	50	0	33	20	36	91	50	71	90	61	100	42	25	80	80	0	0	66	25	28	47	80	C CP NY O PB PL
- + + +	(+)	60	0	25	0	0	0	75	50	0	81	0	33	50	62	28	30	90	85	11	40	33	58	60	60	0	50	46	27	22	47	92	CO GC O OJ
- + + +	(+)	40	100	62	100	0	0	60	14	0	66	0	33	50	37	71	69	10	14	88	60	60	41	40	40	0	40	53	55	66	48	94	BP CC LH NY PB
- + + +	(+)	50	44	25	33	0	0	20	69	0	33	0	55	45	39	53	55	33	55	50	66	25	33	0	0	0	14	40	45	36	45	106	CP PL TH
- + + +	(+)	50	55	66	66	0	0	85	14	0	66	0	44	100	60	60	38	44	46	45	33	58	33	30	30	0	85	53	33	54	49	116	C CC GC LB SU
- - - -	(-)	54	100	25	40	0	0	27	30	0	42	0	25	40	26	46	50	50	50	50	77	54	50	40	40	0	40	12	48	45	50	106	CO CP LB PL
- - - -	(-)	36	0	25	40	0	0	60	64	0	57	0	20	40	36	50	25	27	75	14	50	14	60	41	41	0	33	50	26	41	41	94	BP JY TB
- + + +	(+)	45	60	45	45	0	0	40	35	0	18	0	20	60	37	75	63	63	25	85	36	85	30	58	58	0	55	66	60	73	54	125	GC LC NY PB S
- - + -	(-)	35	20	61	16	0	0	50	50	0	64	0	62	64	66	54	75	85	36	64	56	31	75	0	50	0	61	57	56	50	53	126	C O PB S
- + + +	(+)	50	80	36	83	0	0	38	18	0	35	0	77	60	35	70	70	14	80	33	42	72	25	50	50	0	30	42	36	43	47	103	BP CC NY OJ
- + + +	(+)	50	100	0	0	0	0	55	72	0	53	0	83	57	31	57	42	59	75	62	54	66	27	100	0	0	75	44	13	40	51	132	BP JY LB OJ PL S SU
- - - -	(-)	50	0	26	57	0	0	61	56	0	46	0	11	16	30	33	37	36	31	62	54	66	69	44	55	0	87	60	38	50	44	114	PB
- + + +	(+)	64	60	38	80	0	0	50	50	0	64	0	66	40	26	46	53	61	33	66	68	25	0	50	50	0	57	33	52	55	50	128	CC JY PL S
- + + +	(+)	25	45	45	33	0	0	36	44	0	77	0	62	83	56	41	41	50	66	50	36	54	69	0	55	20	0	66	47	44	49	124	LC LH OJ SF TB
- - - -	(-)	75	75	33	0	0	0	36	60	0	22	0	16	0	84	53	27	50	31	62	46	45	30	44	44	0	33	0	13	43	46	115	BO CC LC SF SU TR
- + + +	(+)	70	20	45	33	0	0	55	72	0	63	0	25	45	31	37	61	71	0	31	42	62	31	0	55	0	87	12	43	30	49	110	CP JY O SM
- - + -	(-)	75	75	45	33	0	0	36	44	0	22	0	62	83	56	46	72	22	66	31	54	54	69	55	0	20	66	60	36	30	46	126	LB SF SU
- + + +	(+)	70	20	50	33	0	0	62	75	0	63	0	33	66	0	46	57	68	57	75	0	54	50	0	33	0	0	60	61	68	47	120	BO BP GC OJ
- - - -	(-)	30	50	0	50	0	0	38	18	0	45	0	0	33	36	11	60	25	42	25	28	18	0	36	0	85	85	40	57	50	47	129	BO LC PB
- + + +	(+)	66	50	6	50	0	0	62	61	0	54	0	57	57	0	60	75	57	66	46	44	50	25	50	63	0	40	76	48	68	49	121	BP LB NY O
- - - -	(-)	33	64	100	50	0	0	77	61	0	66	0	20	55	36	38	0	35	42	53	60	35	42	16	0	40	40	76	48	30	43	115	BO CC LH PL
- + + +	(+)	57	50	87	45	0	0	43	75	0	71	0	57	57	64	35	57	57	44	46	37	37	42	83	0	0	11	52	31	69	50	119	CP JY O SU
- + + +	(+)	42	50	38	54	0	0	56	16	0	14	0	14	28	35	55	55	43	44	50	60	69	100	75	25	0	25	63	36	30	58	117	GC TB W
- + + +	(+)	55	0	45	0	0	0	30	45	0	30	0	60	66	27	35	42	44	25	40	30	50	66	66	0	0	37	36	36	30	45	135	BP C CO JY SM
- + + +	(+)	44	100	50	33	0	0	70	45	100	60	0	40	66	71	27	57	50	46	60	62	50	75	61	0	20	20	66	55	54	51	148	CP GC LC O S SF
- - - -	(-)	62	100	63	0	0	0	52	54	0	50	0	75	66	63	71	76	41	50	37	55	42	25	0	61	0	0	66	75	75	55	93	CC SF SM TB TR
- - - -	(-)	37	0	42	62	0	0	41	27	0	50	0	25	50	27	61	42	25	62	42	33	27	0	30	30	0	66	11	45	44	42	114	BP CO LC SU
- + + +	(+)	20	40	60	16	0	0	35	40	0	66	0	60	50	50	61	25	44	16	70	50	50	30	0	50	0	33	48	47	44	54	127	BP JY LB LH NY SF
- - - -	(-)	80	80	40	83	0	0	64	60	0	43	0	33	63	38	57	69	58	83	30	44	44	80	50	0	33	75	48	52	55	54	85	SU
- + + +	(+)	50	66	63	66	0	0	64	60	0	83	0	50	18	71	30	30	83	20	40	50	53	0	100	0	0	0	66	25	33	41	91	GC JY PB SU
- + + +	(+)	53	50	27	33	0	0	45	44	0	16	0	50	42	81	50	60	16	40	57	52	46	50	0	50	0	50	58	60	50	47	116	BO BP CC OJ PL
- + + +	(+)	38	50	42	25	0	0	44	42	57	42	0	66	33	63	50	73	66	57	47	50	50	20	0	0	0	42	41	62	53	54	112	BP CC GC NY O
- - - -	(-)	53	50	61	50	0	0	68	66	0	63	0	33	66	39	73	61	38	80	46	60	45	37	33	0	72	18	69	53	46	57	85	CP LC PL SU
- + + +	(+)	20	87	50	42	0	0	66	15	0	71	0	37	57	36	39	66	38	55	55	40	55	22	0	50	0	30	30	43	46	39	98	JY SM
- + + +	(+)	80	12	30	50	0	0	62	35	0	0	0	36	66	28	46	46	55	33	57	66	53	45	0	33	0	75	54	37	33	46	102	CC LB O SF
- + + +	(+)	40	83	66	44	0	0	15	69	0	90	0	54	33	53	52	53	33	66	42	33	44	77	42	45	0	37	45	56	44	50	146	BP CO CP NY SU TB
- + + +	(+)	60	16	80	44	0	0	69	64	0	14	0	54	33	53	33	18	33	0	50	75	33	0	57	42	0	62	54	61	44	49	100	BO BP OJ
- - - -	(-)	53	33	30	100	0	0	69	69	0	64	0	69	66	50	56	61	66	50	30	75	58	44	0	57	0	37	27	61	44	46	108	BP GC LB PL W
- + + +	(+)	39	33	30	100	0	0	64	64	0	90	0	64	0	28	18	85	55	50	50	45	33	38	0	0	37	62	54	14	55	49	117	C CP OJ SF SU
- - - -	(-)	53	33	70	0	0	0	30	35	0	64	0	50	66	53	52	33	62	0	50	46	46	44	60	60	0	60	33	38	55	44	103	CC CO PL
- + + +	(+)	54	0	0	0	0	0	55	52	0	35	0	50	66	40	50	66	37	100	50	46	53	55	0	40	0	40	66	77	44	52	108	C GC LB LH NY PB
- - - -	(-)	45	100	50	66	0	0	44	47	0	35	0	50	66	40	50	66	37	100	50	46	55	55	0	40	0	40	66	77	44	52	101	BP CC LB NY OJ TB TR

Figure 8.6: Continued

		BO	BP	C	CC	CD	CL	CO	CP	FC	GC	HO	JY	LB	LC	LH	NY	O	OJ	PB	PL	S	SF	SV	SM	SP	SU	TB	TR	W	Tr%		T#	
- + - + + +	(+)	57	85	42	100	0	0	52	41	0	16	0	60	57	52	36	20	11	70	70	66	80	0	50	0	0	60	53	36	52	51		137	BP CC GC LH PB PL S
- + - + + +	(-)	14	14	57	0	0	0	58	87	0	16	0	40	42	38	28	80	70	88	29	30	33	0	41	0	0	30	38	36	38	43		114	CP O OJ
- + - + + +	(+)	63	100	61	50	0	0	40	46	0	33	0	28	20	40	75	45	80	14	66	45	62	0	63	0	0	22	35	25	38	45		111	BP LH PB
- + - + + +	(-)	36	0	38	50	0	0	60	53	0	66	0	71	80	60	25	57	50	85	44	50	42	0	36	0	0	64	64	58	61	55		127	GC JY LB OJ SU
- + - + + +	(+)	58	40	57	75	0	0	62	72	0	70	0	80	50	41	54	71	50	20	55	50	42	0	83	0	0	40	66	60	14	51		126	CC CP GC JY NY SM TB
- + - + + +	(+)	41	60	42	25	0	0	37	27	0	30	0	20	50	58	45	28	50	80	55	50	57	0	16	0	0	40	33	33	85	43		99	OJ W
- + - + + +	(-)	22	33	68	66	0	0	41	18	0	33	0	62	66	70	62	45	57	57	53	50	57	0	60	0	0	54	60	72	53	53		141	C CC LB LC PL W
- + - + + +	(+)	77	33	31	33	0	0	52	81	0	66	0	25	33	29	37	36	38	42	46	22	53	0	30	0	0	45	30	38	27	43		114	BO CP GC
- + - + + +	(-)	85	0	36	66	0	0	66	75	0	61	0	50	50	50	58	35	36	36	35	60	62	0	37	0	0	45	41	55	33	53		136	BO CC CO CP SU
- + - + - - -	(-)	14	0	54	33	0	0	33	25	0	38	0	100	100	68	41	64	54	57	57	40	57	0	32	0	0	54	52	62	55	41		107	JY LB
- + - + - - -	(+)	15	25	30	33	0	0	18	46	0	30	0	57	20	31	72	22	33	66	12	72	62	0	57	0	0	60	54	39	66	41		102	LC OJ PL W
- + - + - - -	(+)	84	75	61	66	0	0	52	53	0	69	0	42	60	50	27	77	66	33	87	27	37	0	42	0	0	40	45	60	33	57		141	BO BP CC CO GC LH
- + - + - - -	(-)	31	20	44	25	0	0	52	30	0	57	0	66	100	68	72	22	33	66	12	45	62	0	0	0	0	20	27	45	43	43		121	JY LB
- + - + - - -	(+)	62	80	50	75	0	0	48	70	0	42	0	33	16	50	35	40	71	50	50	55	38	0	77	0	0	80	70	59	45	52		145	BP CC CP O SM SU TB
- + - + - - -	(+)	36	75	50	66	0	0	52	61	0	40	0	33	83	46	61	40	40	20	55	27	40	0	62	0	0	50	75	40	70	46		121	BP CC TB W
- + - + - - -	(-)	52	25	50	33	0	0	47	30	0	60	0	33	53	53	53	37	46	66	45	44	60	0	37	0	0	50	25	16	38	49		130	LB PL
- + - + - - -	(+)	100	25	63	0	0	0	69	60	0	45	0	33	57	41	44	38	42	22	54	45	46	0	12	0	0	80	50	20	54	47		103	BO CO OJ SU
- + - + - - -	(-)	0	75	27	100	0	0	30	30	0	45	0	40	100	58	44	53	57	57	45	54	53	0	87	0	0	20	42	83	53	48		105	BP CC JY SM TR
- + - + - - -	(+)	85	60	55	75	0	0	66	55	0	0	0	60	0	27	37	40	37	40	53	54	46	0	50	0	0	75	60	75	45	46		106	LB LC TR
- + - + - - -	(+)	61	40	38	50	0	0	53	40	0	0	0	40	100	35	44	60	60	62	53	46	60	0	50	0	0	80	60	20	54	51		117	BO CO GC SU
- + - + - - -	(-)	30	60	44	50	0	0	46	60	0	18	0	60	0	47	40	36	61	50	36	62	44	0	33	0	0	10	43	48	84	43		132	GC LB SF SM SU
- + - + + - -	(+)	50	60	53	100	0	0	53	50	0	60	0	50	33	55	41	30	60	55	44	33	46	0	33	0	0	90	71	52	15	50		138	CC TB W
- + - + + - -	(+)	50	40	46	0	0	0	33	33	0	40	0	60	66	45	58	69	33	33	55	28	50	0	55	0	0	80	28	23	28	45		124	LB NY PL SU
- + - + + - -	(+)	55	60	50	50	0	0	53	50	0	66	0	37	33	50	28	44	35	41	62	41	60	0	28	0	0	20	37	15	57	45		118	GC PL
- + - + + - -	(+)	44	40	38	50	0	0	46	50	0	33	0	62	66	38	70	50	64	12	52	70	50	0	57	0	0	40	60	76	57	50		131	LB LH TR
- + - + + - -	(-)	41	50	57	80	0	0	38	50	0	31	0	50	50	33	46	22	78	31	30	60	33	0	55	0	0	25	57	41	53	44		129	CC O
- + - + + - -	(+)	41	50	38	20	0	0	61	50	0	68	0	50	100	62	53	56	21	56	60	30	60	0	44	0	0	36	42	52	46	50		146	GC LB NY SU
- + - + + - -	(+)	62	22	50	50	0	0	57	50	0	44	0	33	28	25	30	18	46	50	60	71	52	0	50	0	0	36	50	53	57	45		114	PL
- + - + + + -	(-)	37	77	37	50	0	0	42	50	0	55	0	66	71	75	70	72	53	50	40	28	47	0	53	0	0	63	60	42	42	52		130	BP JY LB LC LH NY
- + - + + + -	(-)	58	33	37	66	0	0	68	50	0	44	0	33	50	68	41	15	66	50	60	35	25	0	42	0	0	0	27	62	66	44		116	CC NY O W
- + - + + + -	(+)	41	83	43	33	0	0	38	71	0	55	0	66	66	24	25	33	30	66	40	66	68	0	37	0	0	83	12	75	33	50		130	BP CP JY PL S SU
- + - + + + -	(+)	56	75	21	28	0	0	54	35	0	83	0	40	50	56	71	60	36	33	35	42	29	0	50	0	0	42	62	37	56	44		118	BP GC LH OJ
- + - + + + -	(-)	43	25	78	71	0	0	46	64	0	16	0	50	50	44	28	66	63	64	63	70	50	0	50	0	0	54	38	66	77	55		148	C CC NY S
- + - + + + -	(+)	29	100	55	50	0	0	40	50	0	41	0	33	37	40	25	38	33	40	42	42	85	0	30	0	0	45	47	52	53	44		107	BP PB SF
- + - + + + -	(+)	64	0	44	50	0	0	50	50	0	58	0	66	66	60	66	46	58	55	25	57	61	0	50	0	0	55	52	47	46	51		126	JY LH
- + - + + + -	(-)	40	0	41	50	0	0	36	50	0	66	0	66	20	50	40	33	54	41	33	37	33	0	42	0	0	80	56	33	33	45		85	CP GC NY SU
- + - + + + -	(+)	40	100	50	50	0	0	63	33	0	66	0	33	33	50	40	33	36	44	62	50	55	0	57	0	0	20	37	46	66	49		91	BP OJ SF W
- + - + + + -	(+)	87	33	55	57	0	0	50	53	0	33	0	50	66	31	26	25	75	12	87	50	55	0	50	0	0	75	50	32	55	46		127	BO LB PB SU
- + - + + + -	(-)	12	66	33	42	0	0	33	40	0	75	0	62	33	61	62	57	53	22	66	12	60	0	60	0	0	54	60	60	77	52		136	BP GC NY S
- + - + + + -	(-)	44	37	46	33	0	0	52	55	0	63	0	50	16	61	62	57	23	69	66	40	55	0	71	0	0	54	38	66	77	52		131	BP OJ PB TR W
- + - + - + -	(+)	44	50	40	66	0	0	42	44	0	36	0	50	83	30	37	42	76	30	33	60	44	0	20	0	0	45	46	33	22	44		107	CC LB O
- + - + - + -	(+)	28	50	35	57	0	0	42	30	0	66	0	71	20	68	30	44	60	60	60	60	62	0	60	0	0	46	42	53	44	44		104	CO GC JY
- + - + - + -	(-)	71	50	64	42	0	0	33	70	0	33	0	28	60	68	61	80	55	54	53	71	33	0	30	0	0	46	57	46	53	53		125	BO CP LC NY PL
- + - + - + -	(-)	33	33	27	50	0	0	46	77	0	66	0	33	50	66	75	66	30	22	54	57	30	0	20	0	0	83	41	58	41	50		94	CP GC JY LC SU TB
- + - + - + -	(-)	66	66	63	65	0	0	46	22	0	33	0	50	33	50	50	50	66	80	45	42	50	0	80	0	0	0	12	41	58	45		86	BO BP LH OJ SM
- + - + - + -	(+)	50	0	46	16	0	0	70	46	0	50	0	60	66	38	50	50	36	70	37	44	50	0	30	0	0	80	62	40	55	47		116	CO LB SU
- + - + - + +	(+)	50	100	53	83	0	0	30	53	0	50	0	40	33	50	45	66	54	36	62	55	37	0	69	0	0	20	37	59	44	49		121	BP CC SM
- + - + - + +	(+)	60	60	12	57	0	0	33	40	0	57	0	50	50	52	22	77	30	22	33	70	55	0	50	0	0	25	29	34	50	45		108	GC PB PL SF
+ - + - - +	(-)	40	40	75	28	0	0	66	60	0	33	0	50	50	52	45	20	60	80	42	16	44	0	71	0	0	75	64	62	50	51		124	C CO OJ SM SU
+ - + - - +	(+)	50	33	60	50	0	0	71	50	0	57	0	42	40	40	54	66	12	50	60	40	45	0	50	0	0	50	65	38	30	49		100	CO NY SF
+ - + - - +	(+)	50	66	40	50	0	0	33	33	0	42	0	50	66	52	40	50	66	25	57	54	37	0	50	0	0	50	35	83	70	48		99	BP OJ PL W
+ - + - - +	(-)	50	33	42	50	0	0	50	60	0	57	0	50	42	46	52	37	0	25	55	28	28	0	33	0	0	57	36	83	75	52		77	LC OJ PL S TR W
+ - + - - -	(-)	50	66	57	50	0	0	50	40	0	66	0	50	57	33	44	37	0	0	55	42	42	0	33	0	0	42	36	16	0	42		63	BP GC

Figure 8.6: Continued

	BO	BP	C	CC	CD	CL	CO	CP	FC	GC	HO	JY	LB	LC	LH	NY	O	OJ	PB	PL	S	SF	SV	SM	SP	SU	TB	TR	W	T%	T#		
(+)	50	66	81	50	0	0	71	55	0	40	0	40	71	53	50	33	66	33	28	87	75	55	0	50	0	60	33	46	66	55	100	BP C CO LB NY OJ	
(-)	37	0	18	50	0	0	28	44	0	60	0	60	28	50	33	50	0	57	12	25	50		0	40	0	40	38	39			71	O	
(-)	95	70	66	40	0	0	66	60	0	50	0	50	28	68	55	54	69	25	75	66	50	44	0	50	0	40	30	11	42	51	95	BO C LC O PB PL SF	
(-)	20	50	16	60	0	0	40	40	0	50	0	50	57	31	44	36	30	33	75	66	33	66	0	0	0	66	70	57		44	83	OJ SU TB TR	
(+)	25	33	25	60	0	0	41	42	0	14	0	40	60	70	33	50	60	66	50	71	69	33	0	0	0	20	57	45	21	43	97	LC OJ PL S	
(+)	75	66	70	40	0	0	58	57	0	85	0	60	40	30	55	42	30	33	37	28	23	66	0	100	0	80	28	37	71	50	112	BO BP C GC SF SM	
(-)	83	50	40	50	0	0	70	83	0	66	0	25	40	40	50	72	55	55	62	63	70	0	33	0	0	44	41	87	64	55	116	BO CO CP GC LH SF	
(-)	0	50	60	50	0	0	30	16	0	33	0	50	85	60	27	40	33	60	66	37	36	30	0	44	0	55	50	4	35	39	83	LB NY PB	
(-)	50	100	55	14	0	0	47	71	0	53	0	25	80	61	75	35	66	66	66	66	80	61	0	50	0	55	64	58		54	121	BP CP LB LH OJ PL	
(-)	50	0	33	85	0	0	52	28	0	46	0	75	20	23	25	58	33	42	33	42	33	20	0	30	0	33	44	28	41	40	90	CC JY	
(+)	50	16	41	33	0	0	36	55	0	42	0	60	66	60	28	36	54	42	66	37	61	38	0	75	0	53	0	39	68	47	117	LB PB SM W	
(+)	50	83	58	66	0	0	58	44	0	57	0	75	33	21	71	63	36	14	22	62	23	61	0	25	0	46	100	60	31	50	125	BP CC LH TB	
(-)	33	75	21	75	0	0	63	0	0	25	0	33	50	75	33	50	41	66	66	33	25		0	66	0	50	70	22	50	37	72	BP CC JY PB TR	
(-)	66	25	71	25	0	0	36	100	0	75	0	25	66	78	54	14	78	50	33	66	75	80	0	66	0	50	40	28	42	57	111	BO C CP GC LB LC	
(-)	0	85	37	66	0	0	71	75	0	60	0	57	25	72	80	57	62	37	53	63	36	40	0	62	0	33	40	57		44	101	BP CO CP LC LH	
(+)	100	14	62	33	0	0	18	40	0	14	0	28	66	40	61	38	50	37	44	55	62	60	0	28	0	62	60	42	60	46	88	LB	
(-)	40	33	70	66	0	0	81	60	0	85	0	55	60	38	62	30	62	30	57	28	28	0	37	0	0	37	30	39	40	46	100	C CC LB SM	
(-)	60	66	10	33	0	0	27	75	0	30	0	33	12	61	23	61	25	100	38	75	50	71	0	100	0	37	55	21	20	43	98	CP O SF SM	
(+)	38	0	53	62	0	0	72	25	0	61	0	50	40	87	60	36	38	53	66	66	40	36	0	42	0	72	33	78	80	51	116	BP CO LC OJ PL SU	
(-)	80	40	76	100	0	0	46	72	0	30	0	33	50	0	38	53	25	100	28	44	37	57	0	28	0	20	87	62	61	50	132	JY OJ PL TB	
(-)	53	50	39	60	0	0	63	85	0	66	0	54	45	45	71	42	30	50	25	71	57	46	0	42	0	44	57	38	46	50	122	BO CC CP LH PL	
(-)	46	50	52	40	0	0	50	14	0	25	0	45	28	54	28	50	70	61	70	28	28	53	0	44	0	55	42	46		48	121	LB OJ PB	
(-)	50	25	40	50	0	0	50	62	0	25	0	75	40	60	62	61	70	62	33	33	50	27	0	62	0	40	44	62	48	47	121	JY OJ PB	
(+)	40	75	60	66	0	0	63	85	0	66	0	25	66	47	42	47	38	50	60	33	33	50	0	63	0	40	55	68	50	47	118	BP TR	
(+)	50	57	66	33	0	0	41	33	0	33	0	60	40	54	63	50	55	66	75	28	28	80	0	71	0	33	55	55	50	50	119	C LC OJ PB SF	
(-)	50	42	33	66	0	0	58	14	0	37	0	60	80	66	36	41	38	66	44	40	33	73	0	0	0	33	66	65	57	46	111	CP PL S SM SU TB	
(+)	40	100	16	42	0	0	58	20	0	50	0	33	60	46	63	10	28	50	66	100	57	50	0	0	0	33	20	25	28	47	81	BP JY LB SU TB PL	
(-)	60	0	0	25	0	0	41	80	0	50	0	60	20	0	36	90	71	85	66	60	50	58	0	60	0	50	30	40	22	47	80	C CP NY O OJ	
(+)	40	100	62	100	0	0	58	16	0	42	0	33	80	30	57	42	59	10	88	60	66	41	0	40	0	75	44	44	48	48	94	BP CC LH NY PB W	
(-)	50	44	25	33	0	0	50	50	0	18	0	50	66	45	39	53	36	14	64	66	25	33	0	60	0	14	55	66	36	45	106	CP PL TR	
(-)	50	55	66	40	0	0	60	14	0	66	0	44	100	54	53	41	61	50	60	25	58	58	0	30	0	85	53	33	54	49	116	C CC GC LB SU	
(-)	36	0	25	66	0	0	66	69	0	57	0	25	100	58	45	57	50	50	50	77	54	50	0	40	0	40	12	48	54	50	106	CO CP LB PL	
(+)	54	100	50	60	0	0	27	37	0	42	0	75	25	35	36	36	33	26	22	45	50	14	0	60	0	33	50	28	26	41	96	JY OJ	
(+)	54	50	54	60	0	0	60	64	0	100	0	80	46	66	37	75	63	25	85	66	57	14	0	58	0	55	50	60	73	54	125	GC LC NY PB S	
(-)	45	50	45	60	0	0	40	35	0	66	0	62	60	66	30	26	20	75	85	57	85	77	0	50	0	55	57	56	50	53	126	O PB S	
(-)	50	80	63	16	0	0	50	50	0	35	0	37	83	35	54	30	85	14	80	42	22	30	0	50	0	30	44	22	25	43	103	BP CC NY OJ	
(+)	50	100	60	83	0	0	38	43	0	53	0	77	16	53	57	42	59	75	33	70	66	27	0	40	0	75	44	44	40	51	132	BP JY LB OJ PL S SU	
(-)	50	100	26	42	0	0	61	56	0	46	0	11	16	30	42	57	36	30	16	53	66	54	0	60	0	12	55	44	40	44	114	PB	
(-)	64	60	38	52	0	0	61	55	0	64	0	66	83	53	46	61	33	52	35	75	68	54	0	50	0	57	33	55	60	50	128	CC JY PL S	
(-)	64	40	61	100	0	0	50	44	0	66	0	33	40	66	66	53	38	66	64	25	31	72	0	50	0	42	66	47	44	48	124	LC LH OJ SF TB	
(+)	35	60	38	20	0	0	55	30	0	20	0	57	42	56	41	41	71	60	50	57	54	45	0	33	0	66	42	68	56	49	115	BO CC LC SF SU TR	
(-)	66	33	60	100	0	0	38	18	0	27	0	62	83	56	66	37	71	40	50	44	13	30	0	36	0	44	42	30	47	47	110	CP JY O SM	
(-)	33	50	50	33	0	0	55	72	0	63	0	37	16	36	53	27	60	25	84	42	54	54	0	55	0	87	33	38	43	49	126	LB SF SU GC OJ	
(-)	75	75	20	45	0	0	25	25	0	45	0	62	100	36	18	31	68	42	50	62	45	36	0	60	0	57	42	55	30	46	129	BO LC PB	
(+)	30	80	53	42	0	0	44	43	0	36	0	33	57	68	46	72	68	25	57	57	50	0	0	33	0	40	52	31	61	47	121	BP LB NY O	
(-)	66	50	50	66	0	0	55	25	0	54	0	11	60	11	53	60	40	57	46	42	54	45	0	36	0	60	57	42	25	46	115	BO CC LH PL	
(-)	33	50	50	33	0	0	72	25	0	45	0	66	60	36	77	40	75	31	46	28	50	63	0	0	0	85	40	57	49	49	119	CP JY O SU W	
(+)	35	0	6	50	0	0	22	38	0	66	0	20	33	42	38	54	35	55	44	62	37	42	0	16	0	40	76	48	43	43	117	GC TB	
(-)	64	100	87	50	0	0	77	61	0	33	0	80	55	52	30	45	57	33	53	55	37	42	0	83	0	50	11	48	31	50	135	BP C CO JY SM	

Figure 8.6: Continued

		BO	BP	C	CC	CD	CL	CO	CP	FC	GC	HO	JY	LB	LC	LH	NY	O	OJ	PB	PL	S	SF	SV	SM	SP	SU	TB	TR	W	T%	T#	65%
+ - + + + | -	(+)	57	50	53	45	0	0	43	75	0	71	0	57	57	72	64	44	66	44	50	60	69	100	0	75	0	25	52	63	69	58	148	CP GC LC O S SF
+ - + + + | -	(-)	42	50	38	54	0	0	56	16	0	14	0	14	28	27	35	55	33	44	50	40	30	0	0	25	0	37	44	36	30	36	93	
+ - + + + | -	(+)	55	0	45	66	0	0	30	45	0	60	0	40	50	63	27	57	44	46	60	50	66	0	0	33	0	50	69	50	45	45	114	CC SF SM TB TR
+ - + + + | -	(-)	44	100	50	33	0	0	70	45	0	50	0	40	50	71	71	76	50	46	60	37	30	66	0	61	0	30	66	27	54	51	127	BP CO LC SU
+ - + + + | +	(+)	62	100	50	37	0	0	52	54	0	50	0	75	66	63	71	85	41	50	37	55	42	75	0	30	0	20	66	55	75	55	119	BP JY LB LH NY SF
+ - + + + | -	(-)	37	0	42	62	0	0	41	40	0	50	0	25	33	27	28	15	25	16	45	25	50	25	0	61	0	80	11	25	44	39	85	SU
+ - + + + + -	(+)	20	20	60	16	0	0	35	40	0	66	0	66	50	27	61	42	41	25	70	0	50	30	0	50	0	66	40	47	44	42	91	GC JY PB SU
+ - + + + + +	(+)	80	80	40	83	0	0	64	60	0	33	0	33	50	63	38	57	58	83	30	100	50	60	0	50	0	33	48	52	55	54	116	BO BP CC OJ PL
+ - + + + + +	(+)	50	66	63	66	0	0	77	0	0	83	0	50	57	18	50	69	83	20	60	0	46	44	0	66	0	25	33	66	66	54	112	BP CC CO GC NY
+ - + - - + +	(-)	50	33	27	33	0	0	22	100	0	16	0	50	42	81	50	30	16	40	40	75	53	0	0	0	0	75	50	25	33	41	85	CP LC PL SU O
+ - + - - + +	(+)	38	50	42	25	0	0	54	44	0	42	0	66	33	63	50	60	33	50	57	42	50	20	0	66	0	57	58	60	50	47	98	JY SM
+ - + - - + -	(-)	53	50	42	75	0	0	45	44	0	57	0	33	66	28	57	85	66	28	46	57	50	80	0	33	0	42	41	40	50	49	102	CC LB O SF
+ - + - - - +	(+)	20	87	61	50	0	0	68	66	0	63	0	62	57	63	39	73	61	40	75	60	45	37	0	0	0	72	69	62	53	57	146	BP CO CP NY SU TB
+ - + - - - +	(+)	80	12	30	50	0	0	25	33	0	36	0	37	42	36	50	26	38	80	46	46	50	54	0	33	0	18	30	33	46	39	100	BO OJ
+ - + - - - +	(+)	40	83	50	75	0	0	62	15	0	71	0	36	66	36	47	55	55	57	66	66	57	22	0	45	0	54	42	56	33	46	108	BP GC LB PL W
+ - + - - - -	(-)	60	16	80	44	0	0	37	69	0	14	0	54	33	50	52	53	33	20	42	33	44	77	0	45	0	75	45	56	33	50	117	C CP OJ SF SU
+ - + - + + +	(+)	38	33	30	100	0	0	30	64	0	90	0	60	100	64	50	14	50	80	30	75	58	45	0	42	0	37	27	61	44	46	103	CC CO PL
+ - + - + + +	(+)	53	33	70	0	0	0	30	35	0	70	0	0	35	71	71	85	25	50	50	0	45	45	0	57	0	62	54	38	55	49	108	C GC LB LH NY PB
+ - + - + + +	(+)	54	0	37	33	0	0	55	52	0	64	0	0	33	53	50	43	62	0	50	50	46	46	0	60	0	60	33	14	55	44	101	
+ - + - + + +	(+)	45	100	50	66	0	0	44	47	0	35	0	33	66	40	50	36	37	100	46	46	53	55	0	40	0	40	66	77	44	52	119	BP CC LB NY OJ TB TR
+ - + - + + +	(+)	57	85	42	100	0	0	41	53	0	66	0	60	57	50	71	36	36	11	70	70	66	52	0	50	0	53	53	52	41	51	137	BP CC GC LH PB PL S
+ - + - + + -	(-)	14	14	57	0	0	0	58	87	0	16	0	40	42	38	28	54	80	88	29	30	33	40	0	41	0	30	38	36	52	43	114	CP O OJ
+ - + - + + -	(+)	63	100	61	50	0	0	40	46	0	33	0	28	20	40	75	45	28	14	66	45	62	63	0	63	0	22	35	25	38	45	111	BP LH PB
+ - + - + - +	(+)	36	0	38	50	0	0	53	53	0	66	0	71	80	41	54	71	57	85	54	54	37	36	0	36	0	77	64	58	61	51	126	GC JY LB OJ SU
+ - + - + - +	(-)	58	40	57	75	0	0	62	72	0	70	0	80	50	58	45	28	50	20	55	72	57	42	0	83	0	40	66	60	14	55	126	GC CP JY NY SM TB
+ - + - + - +	(+)	41	60	42	25	0	0	37	27	0	30	0	62	66	70	45	53	50	80	55	53	58	57	0	16	0	40	33	33	85	43	99	OJ W
+ - + - + - +	(-)	22	33	68	66	0	0	41	18	0	33	0	62	33	60	53	57	36	57	22	53	57	57	0	60	0	45	60	38	72	53	141	C CC LB LC PL W
+ - + - + - -	(-)	77	33	31	33	0	0	52	81	0	61	0	25	33	29	37	36	63	42	46	22	53	42	0	30	0	45	30	55	27	43	136	BO CP GC
+ - + + - + +	(+)	85	0	36	66	0	0	52	75	0	66	0	33	50	50	58	35	38	36	35	60	62	57	0	37	0	100	41	33	33	53	107	JY LB OJ PL
+ - + + - + +	(+)	15	0	54	33	0	0	18	25	0	38	0	0	66	31	42	64	54	54	0	37	31	42	0	37	0	0	52	32	55	41	102	LC OJ PL W
+ - + + - + -	(-)	84	75	61	66	0	0	75	53	0	69	0	57	60	72	72	77	66	66	12	72	37	57	0	42	0	60	45	60	33	57	141	BO BP CC CO GC LH
+ - + + - + -	(+)	31	20	44	25	0	0	48	30	0	57	0	66	42	60	65	40	21	50	50	27	42	58	0	57	0	40	20	27	45	43	121	JY LB
+ - + + - - +	(-)	62	80	50	66	0	0	52	61	0	40	0	33	16	46	30	71	50	50	44	44	58	40	0	77	0	80	70	59	45	52	145	BP CC CP O SM SU TB
+ - + + - - +	(+)	36	75	50	33	0	0	52	61	0	40	0	33	83	46	30	61	61	20	55	55	44	40	0	62	0	50	75	40	70	46	121	BP CC TB W
+ - + + + + +	(+)	52	25	50	33	0	0	47	30	0	60	0	33	57	41	44	38	42	66	44	72	55	60	0	37	0	50	25	55	30	49	130	LB PL
+ - + + + + +	(+)	100	25	63	0	0	0	69	30	0	45	0	33	50	58	41	53	42	66	44	44	55	40	0	12	100	15	50	19	38	47	103	BO CO OJ SU
+ - + + + + +	(-)	0	75	27	100	0	0	30	30	0	45	0	40	57	44	44	38	57	22	45	54	53	40	0	87	0	20	42	83	53	48	105	BP CC JY SM TR
+ - + + + + +	(+)	40	33	33	25	0	0	33	44	0	25	0	40	28	58	45	40	45	37	45	53	53	37	0	50	0	40	75	45	45	46	106	LB LC TR
+ - + + + + +	(-)	85	60	55	50	0	0	66	50	0	100	0	60	66	38	62	22	40	12	52	60	60	60	0	50	0	80	60	76	57	51	117	BP CC CO GC SU
+ - + + + + -	(+)	61	60	38	50	0	0	53	40	0	81	0	40	0	35	60	54	30	50	63	37	44	70	0	66	0	40	51	53	52	52	132	GC LB SF SM SU
+ - + + + + -	(+)	30	60	44	50	0	0	46	60	0	18	0	40	50	47	41	30	61	50	30	36	46	30	0	33	0	53	48	46	46	43	110	W
+ - + + + + -	(-)	50	60	53	100	0	0	53	60	0	40	0	50	33	55	58	69	33	33	55	44	46	50	0	55	0	10	71	52	84	50	138	CC LB NY PL SU
+ - + + + - +	(+)	50	66	46	0	0	0	33	33	0	40	0	37	33	45	29	35	66	66	41	33	46	44	0	28	0	90	28	23	15	45	124	CC LC NY O W
+ - + + + - +	(+)	55	60	38	50	0	0	53	50	0	33	0	62	66	38	58	50	50	40	66	66	50	50	0	55	0	40	15	76	28	45	118	GC PL
+ - + + + - +	(-)	44	40	38	50	0	0	46	50	0	31	0	50	50	33	46	22	64	12	52	41	40	50	0	57	0	60	57	41	53	50	131	LB LH TR
+ - + + + - +	(+)	41	50	57	80	0	0	38	50	0	68	0	50	0	68	41	78	33	56	63	52	44	44	0	44	0	25	57	52	46	50	146	GC LB NY SU
+ - + + + - -	(+)	41	0	38	50	0	0	61	50	0	44	0	50	50	75	70	75	66	60	60	60	53	50	0	36	0	36	42	50	50	45	114	PL
+ - + + + - -	(-)	37	77	37	50	0	0	42	50	0	55	0	66	71	68	41	72	53	50	40	28	47	50	0	54	0	63	12	42	42	52	130	BP JY LB LC LH NY
+ - + + + - -	(+)	58	16	37	66	0	0	61	28	0	44	0	66	50	40	58	33	66	60	33	25	46	42	0	42	0	27	12	66	44	44	116	CC LC NY O W
+ - + + + + +	(+)	41	83	43	33	0	0	38	35	0	83	0	66	71	56	71	33	33	60	35	36	29	37	0	40	0100	72	73	33	56	44	130	BP CP JY PL S SU
+ - + + + + -	(-)	56	75	21	28	0	0	54	35	0	16	0	40	50	44	28	66	53	33	64	63	70	50	0	60	0	57	62	62	43	55	148	C CC NY S SU

Figure 8.6: Concluded

		BO	BP	C	CC	CD	CL	CO	CP	FC	GC	HO	JY	LB	LC	LH	NY	O	OJ	PB	PL	S	SF	SV	SM	SP	SU	TB	TR	W	T%	T#	------- 65% -------
+++-+++	(+)	29	100	55	50	0	0	40	50	0	41	0	33	37	40	25	38	33	40	75	42	30	85	0	37	0	33	47	52	53	44	107	BP PB SF
+++-+++	(-)	64	0	44	50	0	0	50	50	0	58	0	66	62	60	46	66	58	50	25	57	61	14	0	50	0	55	52	47	46	51	126	JY LH
+++-+--+	(+)	40	0	41	50	0	0	36	100	0	33	0	50	20	50	40	33	54	33	37	41	22	33	0	42	0	80	56	53	33	45	85	CP GC NY SU
+++-+--+	(-)	40	100	50	50	0	0	63	0	0	33	0	50	60	50	40	36	36	66	62	50	55	66	0	57	0	20	37	46	66	49	91	BP OJ SF W
+++--++	(+)	87	33	55	57	0	0	50	53	0	25	0	33	66	31	60	46	46	40	87	50	33	20	0	50	0	75	50	32	55	46	127	BO LB PB SU
+++--+-	(-)	12	66	33	42	0	0	50	40	0	75	0	66	33	62	26	75	53	40	12	50	66	60	0	50	0	25	50	60	44	50	136	BP GC JY NY S
+++--+-	(+)	44	37	46	33	0	0	52	55	0	63	0	50	16	61	62	23	69	30	66	40	55	42	0	60	0	54	38	66	77	52	131	OJ PB TR W
+++--+-	(-)	44	62	40	66	0	0	42	44	0	36	0	50	83	30	37	76	30	33	33	60	44	42	0	20	0	45	38	33	22	42	107	CC LB O
+++-+-+	(+)	28	50	35	57	0	0	66	30	0	66	0	71	20	31	38	44	45	46	46	28	60	62	0	60	0	0	46	42	53	44	104	CO GC JY
+++-+--	(-)	71	50	64	42	0	0	33	70	0	33	0	28	31	38	20	55	54	53	53	71	33	37	0	30	0	0	46	57	46	53	125	BO CP LC NY PL
+++-+--	(+)	33	33	27	50	0	0	46	77	0	66	0	66	60	68	61	80	60	22	54	57	30	60	0	20	0	83	87	58	41	50	94	CP GC JY LC SU TB
+++-+--	(-)	66	66	63	50	0	0	46	22	0	33	0	33	50	66	25	50	30	66	36	42	61	40	0	80	0	0	12	41	58	45	86	BO BP LH OJ SM
++++-++	(+)	50	0	46	16	0	0	70	46	0	50	0	60	66	38	50	36	63	37	44	50	50	37	0	30	0	80	62	40	55	47	116	CO LB SU
++++-+-	(-)	50	100	53	83	0	0	30	53	0	50	0	40	0	50	50	54	36	62	55	37	66	62	0	69	0	20	37	59	44	49	121	BP CC SM
++++-+-	(+)	60	60	12	57	0	0	33	60	0	66	0	50	33	52	50	30	22	80	70	55	44	26	0	28	0	75	29	34	50	45	108	GC PB PL SF
++++-+-	(-)	40	40	75	28	0	0	66	40	0	33	0	50	50	38	60	60	77	20	30	44	16	71	0	71	0	75	64	62	50	51	124	C CO OJ SM SU
+++++++	(+)	50	33	60	50	0	0	71	50	0	57	0	42	40	52	45	66	12	50	42	16	45	71	0	50	0	50	65	38	30	49	100	CO NY SF
+++++++	(-)	50	66	40	50	0	0	28	33	0	42	0	42	40	47	33	33	87	50	57	83	54	28	0	50	0	50	35	50	70	48	99	BP O PL W

Figure 8.7: Daily Closing Patterns: Bull/Bear Markets

Pat	(±)	BO	BP	C	CC	CD	CL	CO	CP	FC	GC	HO	JY	LB	LC	LH	NY	O	OJ	PB	PL	S	SF	SV	SM	SP	SU	TB	TR	W	T*	T#	
- -	(+)	52	52	47	46	0	0	43	55	0	44	0	49	44	48	45	47	45	45	50	42	48	48	0	54	0	44	49	41	51	51	5114	
- -	(-)	44	43	48	51	0	0	43	42	0	48	0	47	48	48	49	53	48	45	47	42	42	42	0	42	0	49	47	49	44	45	4505	
- +	(+)	48	37	51	55	0	0	50	45	0	48	0	51	51	49	45	53	45	43	50	48	51	48	0	51	0	45	46	49	50	49	5246	
- +	(-)	48	57	42	42	0	0	48	51	0	51	0	45	49	49	46	47	48	41	48	50	52	44	0	46	0	51	45	49	47	47	5037	
+ +	(+)	48	42	43	42	0	0	48	48	0	59	0	46	45	46	55	44	44	49	51	52	52	42	0	44	0	46	45	49	48	48	5179	
+ +	(-)	47	54	52	54	0	0	50	48	0	39	0	50	51	51	41	50	49	46	47	46	46	52	0	51	0	49	48	46	50	48	5129	
+ +	(+)	48	36	42	60	0	0	47	43	0	54	0	52	47	48	46	48	48	48	48	46	44	46	0	46	0	42	51	45	45	47	4971	
+ +	(-)	48	63	54	39	0	0	51	53	0	54	0	45	50	45	48	52	45	53	51	49	52	48	0	49	0	53	43	49	52	50	5301	
- - -	(+)	53	58	49	48	0	0	54	52	0	53	0	51	51	45	62	48	56	50	51	56	54	48	0	58	0	52	46	51	53	52	2341	
- - -	(-)	44	33	48	50	0	0	43	36	0	45	0	44	36	35	52	36	43	48	45	44	41	41	0	38	0	45	48	48	45	45	2026	
- - +	(+)	51	35	55	55	0	0	50	41	0	45	0	41	48	41	48	41	42	41	48	48	55	40	0	54	0	51	44	50	49	49	2515	
- - +	(-)	42	38	41	41	0	0	47	57	0	62	0	48	48	57	47	56	49	52	51	56	48	53	0	43	0	47	43	45	48	48	2441	
- + -	(+)	54	58	52	53	0	0	50	49	0	36	0	50	50	50	50	41	49	48	46	46	47	50	0	52	0	48	50	46	53	48	2431	
- + -	(-)	46	40	42	59	0	0	48	41	0	44	0	50	50	42	48	51	51	43	46	49	46	52	0	42	0	44	47	47	46	46	2455	
- + +	(+)	48	60	55	39	0	0	49	56	0	54	0	45	47	54	49	47	52	52	51	52	47	48	0	52	0	52	45	46	50	50	2628	
- + +	(-)	50	45	44	43	0	0	54	58	0	53	0	46	53	44	46	49	41	48	50	54	54	47	0	49	0	54	45	53	49	50	2599	
+ - -	(+)	44	51	50	53	0	0	43	39	0	44	0	50	50	43	43	46	50	49	49	43	43	48	0	47	0	43	50	38	45	45	2344	
+ - -	(-)	45	47	47	56	0	0	51	49	0	48	0	61	57	54	51	48	48	42	50	48	48	49	0	52	0	45	49	48	47	47	2560	
+ - +	(+)	51	45	49	41	0	0	47	47	0	50	0	46	53	44	47	45	51	51	48	51	48	49	0	47	0	51	43	50	49	50	2464	
+ - +	(-)	53	50	45	43	0	0	49	49	0	44	0	50	45	43	51	46	44	50	51	46	54	39	0	45	0	47	48	51	45	49	2597	
+ + -	(+)	43	50	51	54	0	0	49	47	0	42	0	49	51	53	52	47	49	42	50	47	46	43	0	51	0	49	44	45	47	48	2540	
+ + -	(-)	50	28	41	61	0	0	44	47	0	44	0	52	43	52	44	40	45	46	48	48	46	49	0	49	0	41	54	43	42	47	2348	
+ + +	(+)	48	71	53	38	0	0	54	50	0	54	0	46	46	37	55	56	52	51	48	52	52	50	0	47	0	55	41	54	54	50	2500	BP
+ + +	(-)	54	50	44	44	0	0	54	47	0	59	0	54	52	31	51	47	51	50	47	46	48	43	0	60	0	46	58	50	50	51	1035	LC
- - - -	(+)	43	50	46	53	0	0	45	51	0	39	0	42	44	66	48	36	42	45	47	43	42	45	0	37	0	46	47	34	43	45	924	
- - - -	(-)	47	28	55	56	0	0	50	40	0	41	0	45	41	48	44	51	53	53	52	56	53	50	0	52	0	40	45	54	55	48	1141	
- - - +	(+)	51	71	40	43	0	0	48	55	0	58	0	47	55	51	54	40	41	40	47	43	45	41	0	45	0	55	49	54	56	48	1133	BP
- - - +	(-)	41	50	37	38	0	0	51	50	0	66	0	45	49	48	52	49	48	53	46	60	55	46	0	38	0	45	41	46	43	48	1189	GC
- - + -	(+)	54	44	55	58	0	0	47	48	0	32	0	52	50	35	36	41	46	47	42	45	45	49	0	57	0	53	44	49	46	48	1184	
- - + -	(-)	47	50	45	59	0	0	44	39	0	50	0	41	50	35	53	58	50	53	41	53	44	42	0	42	0	43	50	44	52	46	1163	
- - + +	(+)	48	50	50	40	0	0	54	60	0	51	0	56	46	61	58	39	48	44	54	45	53	53	0	52	0	54	49	49	50	50	1278	
- - + +	(-)	50	50	44	47	0	0	61	61	0	51	0	42	42	46	42	47	47	46	51	42	47	45	0	48	0	53	51	51	50	50	1211	
- + - -	(+)	43	50	48	49	0	0	36	43	0	60	0	53	52	62	43	48	48	48	46	51	47	56	0	50	0	45	56	42	46	46	1131	
- + - -	(-)	55	72	51	50	0	0	55	53	0	38	0	45	51	55	50	55	52	48	50	43	48	47	0	48	0	47	44	49	52	50	1202	BP
- + - +	(+)	46	30	37	59	0	0	51	49	0	41	0	59	48	42	50	44	55	52	43	46	39	57	0	43	0	45	43	50	47	47	1203	
- + - +	(-)	47	70	57	38	0	0	46	55	0	56	0	38	54	61	47	54	56	44	56	49	50	42	0	51	0	51	47	45	50	50	1284	BP
- + + -	(+)	50	44	44	41	0	0	47	55	0	55	0	49	61	58	54	48	48	49	51	51	52	58	0	50	0	54	54	60	54	51	1314	
- + + -	(-)	45	50	55	50	0	0	55	42	0	43	0	47	36	37	53	52	50	50	46	42	36	44	0	44	0	45	45	37	46	45	1142	
- + + +	(+)	39	36	42	59	0	0	43	49	0	49	0	77	59	61	69	48	52	44	48	49	49	52	0	44	0	52	47	40	49	49	1279	JY
- + + +	(+)	57	45	52	39	0	0	55	48	0	49	0	18	35	35	38	39	44	43	36	47	49	47	0	52	0	50	38	51	56	47	1238	
+ + + +	(+)	47	45	50	46	0	0	52	53	0	50	0	49	48	44	62	47	47	48	55	50	36	44	0	46	0	48	47	50	54	49	1230	
+ + + -	(-)	48	40	55	51	0	0	46	44	0	47	0	47	51	37	42	52	52	46	44	45	45	48	0	48	0	50	47	46	45	48	1198	

Figure 8.7: Continued

Code	±	BO	BP	C	CC	CD	CL	CO	CP	FC	GC	HO	JY	LB	LC	LH	NY	O	OJ	PB	PL	S	SF	SV	SM	SP	SU	TB	TR	W	T%	T#
++++	(+)	52	50	32	65	0	0	40	51	0	43	0	54	45	54	45	42	45	47	50	46	43	52	0	49	0	46	60	44	41	49	1158 BP GC
++++	(-)	45	50	57	34	0	0	57	46	0	46	0	41	50	54	50	50	54	47	50	48	54	47	0	47	0	50	34	52	48	48	1134
----	(+)	58	100	56	42	0	0	63	40	0	68	0	50	54	36	42	50	62	54	59	59	43	53	0	57	0	47	43	63	40	51	472 BP GC
----	(-)	41	0	43	54	0	0	36	58	0	28	0	44	42	60	57	46	33	36	37	37	56	43	0	42	0	52	50	30	55	46	425
		41	25	55	44	0	0	41	45	0	54	0	34	26	36	40	52	56	52	51	48	41	44	0	40	0	39	43	65	73	47	489 W
		56	75	42	45	0	0	56	55	0	55	0	60	70	71	56	46	33	53	48	41	47	56	0	59	0	54	48	38	26	49	514 BP LB LC
		34	30	38	42	0	0	53	41	0	64	0	39	40	50	56	47	42	50	47	50	42	43	0	37	0	48	50	38	26	45	518
		63	60	58	55	0	0	46	45	0	34	0	56	65	50	44	52	50	55	50	55	55	44	0	56	0	49	50	57	53	51	584
		47	75	43	57	0	0	45	27	0	45	0	45	51	31	63	49	45	33	46	46	42	44	0	37	0	45	51	37	51	44	509 BP
		50	25	54	42	0	0	52	72	0	54	0	54	48	63	27	45	45	60	51	51	55	55	0	58	0	53	44	56	48	52	600 CP
		45	62	45	41	0	0	57	50	0	50	0	57	60	48	41	42	44	55	48	44	44	54	0	51	0	52	34	55	51	49	580
		50	37	54	56	0	0	40	38	0	50	0	39	48	58	58	53	52	38	53	48	53	42	0	45	0	45	60	38	48	48	506
		57	55	56	60	0	0	58	55	0	51	0	37	56	52	52	50	37	41	38	36	48	54	0	52	0	47	46	52	48	50	599
		37	44	40	39	0	0	42	46	0	41	0	62	41	41	43	45	44	43	36	41	48	48	0	42	0	51	48	45	52	47	502
		57	60	43	42	0	0	44	46	0	60	0	47	45	36	55	60	51	47	55	58	53	48	0	53	0	47	50	49	51	48	615
		40	40	50	58	0	0	53	51	0	50	0	41	49	59	44	32	48	40	36	36	48	46	0	59	0	48	45	45	36	45	616
		43	80	45	43	0	0	52	55	0	47	0	58	60	46	52	64	46	53	59	41	52	52	0	36	0	55	50	36	36	52	528 BP
		51	55	42	55	0	0	62	62	0	53	0	45	43	57	61	54	45	51	65	59	59	42	0	54	0	56	41	55	64	53	604
		48	44	44	44	0	0	41	34	0	60	0	45	65	20	66	52	29	42	30	48	42	48	0	43	0	43	55	46	29	43	607
		51	44	68	60	0	0	50	35	0	45	0	36	48	46	47	61	54	52	48	41	59	57	0	60	0	53	50	43	53	48	495
		44	55	25	39	0	0	47	63	0	53	0	63	43	75	52	36	45	43	52	41	39	42	0	40	0	51	45	52	43	49	581 C
		42	0	40	31	0	0	36	47	0	60	0	54	48	57	66	32	50	50	48	50	42	48	0	54	0	52	42	46	36	46	598 LC SF
		51	100	48	62	0	0	60	51	0	39	0	41	47	52	33	50	48	53	55	48	56	48	0	43	0	44	46	42	64	50	541 LH
		47	33	36	54	0	0	44	40	0	42	0	68	50	36	53	65	53	48	50	48	56	51	0	41	0	47	60	49	42	46	580 BP
		43	66	63	42	0	0	55	58	0	54	0	36	31	46	56	60	42	48	50	50	46	45	0	58	0	50	36	46	57	51	570 JY
		42	42	37	40	0	0	47	51	0	32	0	49	52	66	41	49	37	45	42	44	40	41	0	56	0	53	53	50	45	51	622 BP
		48	42	55	60	0	0	52	47	0	53	0	47	36	30	54	50	54	53	53	42	53	48	0	37	0	44	42	40	51	45	647 LC
		45	40	41	61	0	0	34	50	0	44	0	75	65	54	56	44	55	42	44	31	45	45	0	37	0	44	65	40	36	49	574
		49	40	53	38	0	0	63	48	0	49	0	14	32	40	52	52	50	40	50	50	47	55	0	49	0	49	29	48	60	47	637 JY
		56	66	51	47	0	0	54	48	0	51	0	34	39	57	55	43	38	49	53	51	42	42	0	54	0	54	37	51	52	49	605
		40	33	45	50	0	0	45	48	0	43	0	58	60	80	46	55	44	38	46	55	47	66	0	51	0	47	43	43	47	47	635 BP LC
		59	100	27	58	0	0	40	48	0	36	0	56	40	50	34	48	39	45	44	45	46	48	0	44	0	43	66	52	50	49	609
		38	0	63	41	0	0	57	51	0	63	0	39	57	33	65	42	55	54	51	44	46	56	0	51	0	53	28	46	65	47	527 BP TB
		53	0	47	47	0	0	52	57	0	54	0	54	54	45	57	40	37	37	54	45	65	51	0	61	0	52	50	50	56	50	560
		43	100	50	52	0	0	55	44	0	48	0	45	46	78	42	54	37	44	45	54	29	45	0	33	0	42	44	40	36	45	534
		52	30	56	56	0	0	59	36	0	39	0	56	53	62	56	52	48	60	57	57	50	40	0	62	0	41	46	43	47	49	473 BP LC
		47	70	39	43	0	0	40	56	0	54	0	36	37	46	56	52	39	42	48	53	50	53	0	35	0	48	48	54	50	47	619
		48	75	32	30	0	0	49	56	0	67	0	46	58	50	50	47	53	57	48	46	58	50	0	37	0	43	36	47	50	50	587 BP
		45	25	53	64	0	0	42	42	0	32	0	35	37	46	38	49	46	42	44	38	44	44	0	60	0	41	44	51	46	45	629 BP GC
		46	66	50	37	0	0	57	54	0	46	0	52	46	56	54	50	41	55	31	43	53	52	0	46	0	50	52	51	54	47	566
		54	37	44	57	0	0	65	66	0	52	0	58	41	57	50	49	44	39	46	37	48	48	0	44	0	55	46	44	45	50	609
		38	62	41	39	0	0	32	42	0	42	0	73	20	57	50	37	51	44	50	57	50	47	0	47	0	47	52	46	47	51	644 BP
		54	33	46	52	0	0	58	46	0	57	0	55	41	46	42	58	44	57	53	66	47	66	0	55	0	45	48	50	50	45	610 CP
		54	66	53	47	0	0	41	50	0	45	0	44	50	46	42	47	43	42	52	43	52	38	0	52	0	45	43	45	59	49	548 JY SF
		58	28	51	35	0	0	46	57	0	54	0	40	40	30	55	47	42	55	45	49	47	64	0	48	0	44	44	51	40	48	594
		36	71	48	65	0	0	53	42	0	39	0	54	56	69	53	49	53	49	60	54	34	39	0	48	0	42	55	55	65	49	565 BP
		33	33	45	59	0	0	59	48	0	50	0	47	42	53	41	50	41	48	49	50	50	56	0	45	0	55	52	42	36	46	623
		56	66	50	37	0	0	54	54	0	46	0	52	56	58	38	50	46	41	57	37	53	51	0	62	0	45	46	51	45	51	629 BP LC
		54	37	41	39	0	0	50	53	0	59	0	58	57	57	50	50	44	55	48	50	50	47	0	50	0	37	52	48	52	52	556
		55	83	57	50	0	0	54	46	0	59	0	59	42	68	76	49	41	39	37	55	50	48	0	51	0	46	52	53	41	45	622 BP
		0	0	42	47	0	0	53	46	0	48	0	37	31	31	24	55	38	45	55	41	61	48	0	62	0	50	46	42	55	52	596 BP LC LH
		61	40	48	48	0	0	51	46	0	50	0	36	42	52	38	41	38	54	45	43	48	54	0	36	0	53	48	53	51	45	516
		35	60	48	43	0	0	46	53	0	48	0	60	40	52	45	38	45	47	45	47	47	45	0	45	0	44	49	42	45	46	677 / 607

Figure 8.7: Continued

		BO	BP	C	CC	CD	CL	CO	CP	FC	GC	HO	JY	LB	LC	LH	NY	O	OJ	PB	PL	S	SF	SV	SM	SP	SU	TB	TR	W	T%	T#	Notes
++−+−	(+)	41	60	42	58	0	0	45	42	0	58	0	55	50	48	60	56	33	46	54	49	53	47	0	46	0	55	44	50	47	50	618	
++−+−	(−)	58	40	55	39	0	0	52	56	0	38	0	44	47	57	40	41	61	49	45	50	45	47	0	45	0	41	51	46	52	47	589	
++−+−	(+)	48	25	38	61	0	0	57	43	0	40	0	54	55	50	40	55	37	51	55	62	37	47	0	50	0	43	32	52	34	47	602	BP
++−+−	(−)	48	75	54	35	0	0	37	50	0	59	0	43	47	45	53	49	38	51	44	50	44	44	0	50	0	53	55	44	61	49	637	BP
++−++	(+)	56	50	51	43	0	0	48	65	0	53	0	42	63	33	47	48	37	53	50	50	55	58	0	44	0	60	45	57	57	52	628	
++−++	(−)	43	50	48	54	0	0	48	33	0	45	0	52	48	58	52	50	56	43	46	50	48	60	0	53	0	37	36	45	44	44	535	JY
++−++	(+)	34	20	42	60	0	0	51	46	0	50	0	77	54	60	58	50	48	52	46	49	51	39	0	40	0	43	41	45	45	49	603	JY
++−++	(−)	65	60	50	38	0	0	48	49	0	48	0	22	40	40	37	46	45	43	53	49	51	39	0	57	0	42	58	48	53	49	593	
++++−	(+)	38	0	33	46	0	0	52	61	0	48	0	34	41	50	45	50	46	49	46	50	47	50	0	45	0	57	37	51	46	48	554	
++++−	(−)	54	100	63	51	0	0	45	38	0	48	0	47	58	60	55	34	50	46	48	43	41	51	0	50	0	51	55	35	53	49	546	BP
++++−	(+)	46	0	47	68	0	0	41	54	0	52	0	48	61	40	55	50	47	50	45	48	41	51	0	54	0	50	51	45	55	51	591	CC
++++−	(−)	52	100	41	31	0	0	58	47	0	84	0	37	61	44	50	34	47	50	54	50	62	23	0	44	0	50	41	62	27	51	543	BP
+++++	(+)	38	0	58	48	0	0	50	44	0	7	0	33	26	55	33	63	62	70	45	66	25	47	0	63	0	50	45	65	72	45	219	GC OJ PL
+++++	(−)	61	0	41	48	0	0	42	57	0	41	0	44	27	72	83	59	37	29	48	25	37	69	0	36	0	39	44	100	0	50	195	SF W
−−−−+	(+)	44	25	57	62	0	0	52	57	0	58	0	55	65	72	16	40	33	56	48	55	50	56	0	53	0	56	41	17	50	50	238	LH W
−−−−+	(−)	50	75	38	37	0	0	52	42	0	47	0	35	37	60	66	46	43	44	37	50	53	43	0	46	0	47	37	37	0	45	216	BP LC
−−−−+	(+)	22	66	41	42	0	0	50	39	0	50	0	50	56	50	33	50	50	50	52	52	50	50	0	60	0	50	62	50	50	42	218	BP LH
−−−−+	(−)	72	33	58	53	0	0	50	60	0	52	0	62	43	57	55	53	47	34	42	40	52	53	0	29	0	48	37	56	55	55	284	BO
−−−−−	(+)	31	100	54	51	0	0	26	33	0	33	0	64	61	75	33	43	42	60	52	47	55	46	0	70	0	51	28	66	61	44	216	BP LC
−−−−−	(−)	62	0	45	48	0	0	73	66	0	66	0	53	38	25	43	45	64	77	60	52	47	55	0	51	0	43	51	47	49	53	261	CO CP GC SM TR
−−−+−	(+)	39	66	55	46	0	0	45	52	0	62	0	57	42	57	33	53	43	60	46	60	55	35	0	46	0	54	58	66	61	49	285	BP
−−−+−	(−)	57	33	66	47	0	0	45	43	0	37	0	38	42	44	44	44	53	32	52	52	55	35	0	51	0	43	64	33	38	48	279	
−−−+−	(+)	53	66	46	47	0	0	56	63	0	52	0	55	41	44	35	55	31	50	57	20	48	44	0	48	0	40	33	40	60	50	259	BP TR
−−−+−	(−)	45	100	53	52	0	0	39	33	0	47	0	33	37	57	66	48	37	68	42	59	59	35	0	50	0	56	55	77	60	48	249	O PL
−−−++	(+)	55	0	48	60	0	0	58	58	0	38	0	58	42	58	33	48	52	46	48	37	59	20	0	54	0	42	43	22	50	47	285	BP LH
−−−++	(−)	63	33	50	62	0	0	39	39	0	50	0	50	56	42	50	56	47	52	51	48	47	56	0	39	0	51	52	50	43	48	292	SF
−−−++	(+)	36	66	45	37	0	0	65	31	0	44	0	50	43	50	57	60	39	56	53	46	61	41	0	66	0	40	44	41	50	50	259	SM
−−−++	(−)	52	33	40	51	0	0	57	54	0	44	0	54	50	57	70	30	50	36	49	76	47	58	0	33	0	55	43	44	69	53	243	BP
−−+−−	(+)	47	66	55	48	0	0	66	43	0	55	0	66	50	42	60	40	77	40	46	30	52	80	0	65	0	44	51	56	30	45	299	LH O PL
−−+−−	(−)	42	20	58	75	0	0	37	40	0	37	0	37	42	46	66	37	60	16	40	45	55	57	0	30	0	51	61	30	45	48	256	BP SF
−−+−−	(+)	52	80	35	25	0	0	62	60	0	56	0	62	44	48	42	66	33	40	62	45	52	26	0	55	0	45	38	50	50	50	278	CC NY
−−+−−	(−)	53	0	40	66	0	0	42	57	0	52	0	69	41	60	57	33	54	37	47	45	45	73	0	44	0	51	43	37	53	48	293	LH SM
−−+−+	(+)	38	100	30	66	0	0	57	53	0	36	0	46	48	41	30	35	51	68	48	52	47	46	0	18	0	38	39	62	53	48	271	LH SM
−−+−+	(−)	60	20	28	47	0	0	39	60	0	64	0	22	52	66	27	72	42	50	42	47	48	55	0	30	0	56	59	53	41	45	274	BP CC NY
−−+−+	(+)	30	80	71	52	0	0	60	60	0	31	0	10	52	41	72	39	57	57	48	39	69	38	0	70	0	47	76	43	58	53	271	JY LH PL
−−+−+	(−)	47	50	54	44	0	0	43	51	0	56	0	45	64	61	62	58	40	46	53	46	63	47	0	62	0	52	38	57	43	52	317	BP C SM
−−++−	(+)	52	50	41	55	0	0	56	46	0	44	0	54	32	38	37	41	50	47	44	41	31	52	0	28	0	46	57	33	56	44	326	
−−++−	(−)	29	66	38	61	0	0	56	48	0	47	0	66	55	43	60	50	42	51	51	49	51	42	0	39	0	69	50	47	49	49	274	
−−++−	(+)	63	0	36	47	0	0	56	56	0	52	0	37	51	33	30	57	47	51	45	44	50	42	0	53	0	42	60	50	47	47	306	BP JY LH TB
−−++−	(−)	36	100	57	52	0	0	53	51	0	45	0	36	51	37	50	35	46	42	45	50	44	52	0	26	0	50	26	47	50	49	291	BP GC LC
−−+++	(+)	56	20	46	53	0	0	68	60	0	22	0	63	44	66	30	54	27	54	54	42	70	35	0	62	0	41	56	46	49	51	297	BP CC NY
−−+++	(−)	62	33	57	38	0	0	53	51	0	36	0	36	66	33	37	35	34	37	45	39	57	42	0	36	0	40	36	40	42	48	291	JY LB
−−+++	(+)	55	75	53	46	0	0	50	64	0	66	0	33	48	46	40	51	57	30	54	61	42	50	0	40	0	38	63	50	51	48	248	BP TB
−−+++	(−)	40	25	44	50	0	0	64	30	0	33	0	62	50	60	66	47	43	52	48	51	39	46	0	57	0	39	36	50	30	48	268	C CP LH W
−+−−−	(+)	60	100	23	60	0	0	40	30	0	47	0	66	50	57	10	50	40	42	55	36	51	58	0	48	0	52	23	45	69	50	261	S
−+−−−	(−)	36	0	66	39	0	0	55	69	0	52	0	39	63	28	90	59	59	57	48	56	77	42	0	65	0	46	63	64	52	52	217	BP LC
−+−−−	(+)	63	0	36	47	0	0	53	57	0	54	0	51	51	45	33	50	41	50	44	41	35	42	0	41	0	53	57	46	44	43	294	CO LC PL
−+−−−	(−)	36	100	57	52	0	0	41	41	0	77	0	57	54	44	37	30	42	52	46	70	57	35	0	34	0	57	56	46	50	49	300	BP CP GC
−+−−+	(+)	56	20	46	53	0	0	41	64	0	57	0	33	60	62	46	47	52	60	52	61	62	50	0	40	0	36	36	40	42	51	306	BP GC
−+−−+	(−)	52	80	12	33	0	0	58	34	0	22	0	66	50	46	40	58	45	48	52	38	33	50	0	55	0	33	45	56	57	46	278	C JY
−+−+−	(+)	43	20	75	61	0	0	48	45	0	22	0	57	54	25	44	54	40	40	48	38	48	57	0	36	0	63	41	51	64	48	280	
−+−+−	(−)	51	50	54	60	0	0	69	62	0	47	0	75	54	60	50	58	60	60	52	34	48	37	0	41	0	36	36	40	43	50	285	LC
−+−+−	(+)	40	53	45	39	0	0	48	62	0	52	0	9	40	60	50	58	47	60	50	56	58	37	0	56	0	52	45	40	50	50	292	CO
−+−+−	(−)	55	33	25	60	0	0	30	34	0	40	0	81	60	40	50	31	47	60	50	43	41	62	0	43	0	45	55	56	56	46	270	BP JY

Figure 8.7: Continued

		BO	BP	C	CC	CD	CL	CO	CP	FC	GC	HO	JY	LB	LC	LH	NY	O	OJ	PB	PL	S	SF	SV	SM	SP	SU	TB	TR	W	T%	T#	------- 65% -------
-+-+-+	(+)	66	66	40	40	0	0	35	55	0	47	0	61	52	66	55	73	45	72	53	46	55	33	0	52	0	43	57	54	55	52	281	BO LC NY OJ
-+-+--	(-)	33	0	60	60	0	0	64	41	0	52	0	38	47	33	40	20	50	28	43	50	80	66	0	47	0	50	33	40	44	45	245	SF
-+-++-	(-)	61	50	52	38	0	0	60	54	0	50	0	16	46	41	40	25	66	59	52	48	16	66	0	52	0	50	33	40	54	48	300	S
-+-++-	(-)	33	50	47	61	0	0	60	43	0	48	0	83	53	83	58	52	37	45	48	51	58	29	0	48	0	52	46	45	62	49	308	JY LC O SF
-+-+++	(+)	57	50	81	43	0	0	54	50	0	35	0	38	42	57	33	50	46	65	54	51	58	66	0	50	0	34	48	71	58	49	281	C TR
-+--+-	(-)	42	50	18	56	0	0	45	50	0	62	0	61	57	28	66	53	53	31	45	52	53	38	0	50	0	63	48	25	41	49	280	LH SF
-+--++	(+)	52	100	50	50	0	0	62	54	0	57	0	54	68	55	69	60	52	53	46	50	54	60	0	56	0	46	47	44	62	54	311	BP LB LH
-+----	(-)	41	0	50	45	0	0	37	45	0	39	0	36	31	44	30	40	47	35	48	44	40	40	0	39	0	51	47	56	37	43	247	
-+-+-+	(+)	66	66	43	45	0	0	57	46	0	47	0	57	48	57	50	57	69	51	51	42	52	50	0	54	0	48	42	51	50	49	321	BO BP O
-+-+--	(-)	33	33	50	50	0	0	42	53	0	50	0	83	48	73	50	42	23	42	55	48	47	50	0	45	0	50	53	45	50	48	313	JY
-+-++-	(-)	48	50	43	64	0	0	37	33	0	49	0	66	44	50	53	65	35	38	61	55	54	40	0	50	0	60	35	54	65	50	305	JY
-+-++-	(-)	52	50	52	28	0	0	62	64	0	45	0	34	55	46	46	58	38	58	53	44	42	35	0	41	0	38	57	43	35	46	282	
-+-+++	(+)	50	50	44	59	0	0	56	51	0	31	0	40	50	77	60	58	57	48	53	48	48	37	0	40	0	45	32	51	16	46	298	LC
-+-+++	(+)	50	100	44	36	0	0	37	41	0	68	0	52	50	11	40	41	35	48	46	55	51	62	0	60	0	52	61	43	75	50	322	BP GC W
-+--+-	(-)	38	50	60	44	0	0	41	71	0	39	0	52	57	25	48	50	52	50	52	52	57	68	0	61	0	57	51	48	56	51	315	CP SF
-+--++	(+)	61	50	40	55	0	0	58	28	0	58	0	35	40	100	75	46	56	44	40	47	40	31	0	38	0	39	38	40	37	44	272	LC LH
-+---+	(+)	36	25	47	67	0	0	48	52	0	55	0	70	51	58	66	40	43	41	38	42	57	57	0	42	0	34	30	39	50	46	293	CC JY LH
-+----	(-)	64	50	47	32	0	0	52	44	0	42	0	50	44	44	33	55	55	61	45	57	45	42	0	52	0	62	45	60	44	50	323	
+--+-+	(+)	31	0	42	39	0	0	44	66	0	45	0	44	46	46	60	51	55	50	51	57	54	54	0	40	0	43	71	62	64	50	280	CP TB
+--+--	(-)	56	0	52	54	0	0	51	33	0	50	0	55	61	66	40	46	35	47	48	42	45	36	0	56	0	56	28	37	35	46	260	LC
+--++-	(-)	50	0	55	59	0	0	53	53	0	50	0	60	61	55	75	30	47	51	52	40	48	35	0	50	0	44	36	30	11	49	262	LH W
+--++-	(-)	50	100	44	40	0	0	52	39	0	62	0	30	38	44	25	69	57	52	48	47	56	64	0	50	0	44	36	69	55	52	253	BP NY TR
+--+++	(+)	70	100	50	35	0	0	71	34	0	37	0	60	52	27	33	59	66	52	52	55	35	81	0	57	0	45	53	26	33	52	246	BO BP CO O SF TR
+---+-	(-)	29	0	50	61	0	0	28	61	0	37	0	60	43	63	37	45	52	36	54	46	54	18	0	42	0	41	43	64	64	45	215	LH
+---++	(+)	38	0	52	46	0	0	34	44	0	55	0	41	26	66	45	52	47	64	45	36	54	33	0	34	0	48	43	75	45	45	241	TR
+----+	(+)	61	0	47	53	0	0	64	65	0	55	0	58	73	66	62	54	64	53	45	61	41	50	0	65	0	53	53	20	35	52	279	LB LC
+-----	(-)	42	14	37	42	0	0	40	44	0	80	0	46	44	55	46	46	53	53	46	53	52	56	0	36	0	48	62	41	58	48	284	GC
+-++-+	(+)	57	71	56	57	0	0	40	51	0	17	0	44	56	55	44	53	52	40	46	52	56	56	0	54	0	44	65	54	50	48	287	BP
+-++--	(-)	60	66	34	61	0	0	55	24	0	57	0	35	46	20	69	47	40	33	39	41	42	33	0	41	0	44	65	37	35	45	279	BP LH
+-+++-	(-)	39	33	60	38	0	0	38	36	0	62	0	61	53	73	23	69	57	60	56	56	47	66	0	53	0	56	34	37	66	52	322	CP LC SF
+-+++-	(-)	58	50	33	33	0	0	57	62	0	37	0	60	38	26	28	42	40	50	48	56	47	41	0	51	0	58	44	58	46	49	278	
+-++++	(+)	35	50	66	62	0	0	38	36	0	62	0	40	57	66	71	53	66	37	45	40	52	52	0	44	0	38	51	41	53	47	270	C LC LH
+-++++	(+)	61	50	77	84	0	0	41	71	0	50	0	66	61	53	33	46	37	47	46	52	52	33	0	58	0	54	34	30	42	54	316	C CC CO
+-+-+-	(-)	38	50	11	15	0	0	30	43	0	47	0	69	38	63	66	53	42	56	50	51	41	52	0	35	0	44	44	69	57	47	295	JY LH TR
+-+-++	(+)	68	50	50	45	0	0	48	35	0	66	0	70	44	46	50	51	68	45	54	61	52	33	0	31	0	51	56	52	40	49	317	BO GC JY
+-+--+	(+)	28	50	57	54	0	0	54	36	0	52	0	33	31	57	57	32	50	37	34	51	50	53	0	55	0	25	57	39	33	42	256	SM
+-+-+-	(-)	50	0	42	50	0	0	45	61	0	45	0	66	68	42	42	64	64	62	65	44	46	46	0	41	0	67	42	66	66	55	336	BP JY LB SU TR
+-+-++	(+)	52	100	42	64	0	0	47	71	0	50	0	66	68	63	45	57	52	45	53	36	60	61	0	44	0	38	63	61	27	54	295	CP NY
+---+-	(-)	47	40	57	35	0	0	47	25	0	47	0	54	57	42	45	27	42	54	46	36	31	38	0	56	0	42	61	36	27	43	236	
+--++-	(-)	56	66	80	45	0	0	61	31	0	48	0	33	36	18	45	57	68	46	50	38	62	22	0	70	0	42	25	37	58	47	291	BP C O SM
+--+++	(+)	40	33	13	54	0	0	35	66	0	59	0	62	57	54	63	46	46	41	47	48	55	77	0	30	0	55	35	53	70	48	296	CP JY LC SF
+---+-	(-)	36	0	35	25	0	0	31	45	0	59	0	62	35	50	36	40	28	46	45	48	42	40	0	33	0	48	47	46	27	45	255	
+---++	(+)	57	100	64	62	0	0	62	48	0	40	0	37	60	50	36	55	31	71	47	48	57	60	0	61	0	45	63	47	72	50	287	BP OJ W
+----+	(+)	34	100	53	61	0	0	47	41	0	50	0	60	55	58	53	59	35	47	48	51	35	70	0	52	0	45	63	47	43	48	286	BP SF
+-----	(-)	56	0	46	33	0	0	52	55	0	46	0	40	45	71	53	40	28	45	48	48	48	30	0	52	0	49	36	45	56	49	292	LC
+-++-+	(+)	40	40	16	34	0	0	52	50	0	59	0	58	40	68	26	40	40	28	51	63	65	53	0	47	0	53	65	41	46	46	312	LC
+-++--	(-)	40	40	72	65	0	0	41	50	0	52	0	41	40	25	66	45	30	34	48	46	31	38	0	47	0	45	30	48	46	46	290	C LH
+-+++-	(-)	58	0	52	57	0	0	22	51	0	56	0	55	57	57	25	48	36	57	40	54	52	44	0	36	0	47	59	52	29	47	311	LB LH
+-++++	(+)	37	50	47	42	0	0	59	46	0	47	0	33	42	42	75	45	63	82	43	40	45	55	0	47	0	49	36	47	70	47	296	CO LH W
+-+-++	(+)	56	50	53	44	0	0	59	41	0	56	0	55	51	28	37	46	45	54	51	42	45	17	0	63	0	60	25	53	70	50	290	C LH
+-+--+	(+)	43	50	46	56	0	0	40	52	0	56	0	56	34	33	50	46	55	43	37	54	51	52	0	31	0	36	66	43	30	47	294	O TB
+-++++	(+)	61	100	63	43	0	0	57	38	0	70	0	37	65	44	50	50	50	52	45	50	55	50	0	55	0	48	33	48	72	50	280	BP GC W

Figure 8.7: Continued

	BO	BP	C	CC	CD	CL	CO	CP	FC	GC	HO	JY	LB	LC	LH	NY	O	OJ	PB	PL	S	SF	SV	SM	SP	SU	TB	TR	W	T%	T#	
+ - | - | - |	43	0	61	42	0	0	43	53	0	48	0	44	55	0	66	40	57	38	52	33	58	57	0	55	0	55	37	53	62	49	254	LH
+ - | - | - |	50	0	38	57	0	0	56	43	0	51	0	50	62	45	47	51	54	39	58	44	37	42	0	61	0	56	39	31	41	47	244	LC PL
+ - | - | - |	47	40	58	56	0	0	51	43	0	54	0	50	54	100	52	45	42	57	41	58	40	40	0	61	0	41	56	41	58	50	302	
+ - | - | - |	52	60	33	43	0	0	48	40	0	45	0	60	33	45	47	42	35	35	51	58	58	60	0	38	0	58	39	63	58	46	278	BP O
+ - | - | - |	42	66	38	30	0	0	58	54	0	58	0	60	57	85	62	51	66	64	51	40	50	50	0	33	0	53	33	57	50	50	305	BP
+ - | - | - |	50	33	44	65	0	0	39	43	0	41	0	40	39	14	12	48	33	35	31	41	41	37	0	66	0	41	51	43	35	45	274	SM
+ - | - | - |	46	0	47	62	0	0	32	42	0	54	0	33	47	50	25	53	46	46	31	60	44	52	0	41	0	45	38	60	43	46	313	
+ - | + - | - |	53	100	52	37	0	0	68	54	0	54	0	66	50	37	58	43	51	56	63	60	55	47	0	51	0	57	57	51	47	50	343	BP CO JY
+ - | + - | - |	52	50	52	56	0	0	62	68	0	52	0	50	40	50	40	55	41	48	51	29	43	20	0	34	0	53	50	43	47	50	297	CP
+ - | + - | - |	38	50	38	37	0	0	34	28	0	45	0	50	55	37	40	44	36	55	48	29	54	80	0	65	0	53	36	43	47	45	269	SF
+ - | + - | - |	50	33	50	58	0	0	72	54	0	52	0	40	47	16	26	57	59	41	51	39	55	45	0	50	0	46	36	37	61	48	304	CO
+ - | + - | - |	50	66	50	41	0	0	28	61	0	56	0	60	52	83	73	50	42	57	40	40	51	45	0	50	0	51	57	60	38	49	307	BP LC LH
+ - | + - | + |	55	0	52	31	0	0	58	29	0	63	0	43	42	50	46	53	52	52	43	47	53	54	0	45	0	46	46	51	68	49	312	W
+ - | + - | + |	40	100	47	68	0	0	41	65	0	36	0	57	57	45	50	51	38	62	50	52	58	45	0	50	0	57	53	42	31	48	310	BP CC
+ - | + - | + |	30	0	16	68	0	0	38	47	0	45	0	43	42	14	16	55	36	52	47	40	41	50	0	64	0	37	42	30	44	43	272	BP C LC LH
+ - | + - | + |	70	100	83	31	0	0	61	50	0	54	0	55	54	45	50	50	47	60	49	52	58	53	0	50	0	59	57	69	55	54	261	CC
+ - | + - | + |	57	100	66	48	0	0	47	40	0	44	0	61	63	85	72	44	29	52	46	42	55	44	0	64	0	37	44	30	72	51	326	BO BP C TR
+ - | + + | + |	42	0	33	46	0	0	47	40	0	55	0	38	54	14	16	55	70	34	47	40	55	53	0	36	0	46	48	50	56	46	250	O W
+ - | + + | + |	56	0	52	61	0	0	43	46	0	52	0	63	63	50	50	61	44	61	46	42	58	54	0	57	0	59	41	56	56	54	343	LH
+ - | + + | + |	40	100	47	38	0	0	52	52	0	47	0	36	36	37	36	50	31	50	45	42	50	44	0	42	0	40	40	39	37	43	271	BP
+ - | + + | + |	35	66	42	56	0	0	56	52	0	70	0	50	54	37	63	48	54	54	50	42	54	44	0	46	0	50	54	45	29	50	299	BP GC
+ + | + + | + |	64	33	57	44	0	0	44	47	0	29	0	66	41	62	36	51	55	41	50	57	45	45	0	53	0	45	41	50	70	48	284	W
+ + | + + | + |	46	100	33	61	0	0	57	52	0	52	0	66	50	50	38	38	43	60	36	54	38	64	0	55	0	30	54	50	48	48	289	BP JY
+ + | + + | + |	46	66	66	35	0	0	39	64	0	47	0	28	43	75	58	55	35	54	40	66	58	54	0	38	0	47	45	45	50	48	293	C LC PL
+ + | + + | + |	69	50	47	43	0	0	59	56	0	68	0	22	78	60	42	42	33	56	46	42	54	46	0	37	0	62	60	66	58	54	295	BO GC LB LH TR
+ + | + + | + |	30	50	52	53	0	0	40	39	0	31	0	77	18	62	27	53	50	52	54	51	42	53	0	62	0	35	60	33	41	43	240	JY
+ + | + + | + |	31	0	40	54	0	0	56	41	0	42	0	82	55	62	58	62	58	62	54	57	57	69	0	36	0	64	45	48	35	52	289	JY SF
+ + | + + | + |	68	0	50	43	0	0	44	52	0	57	0	17	37	37	41	33	41	34	45	42	57	30	0	63	0	35	45	51	64	45	252	BO
+ + | + + | + |	42	0	14	51	0	0	65	60	0	51	0	76	62	33	55	31	50	53	50	50	36	62	0	40	0	52	38	42	48	48	261	JY
+ + | + + | + |	53	100	85	48	0	0	35	44	0	48	0	23	39	69	45	56	56	46	46	60	51	56	0	40	0	60	42	61	57	49	269	BP C
+ + | + + | + |	39	0	37	72	0	0	35	55	0	53	0	37	37	25	26	55	41	50	36	54	34	41	0	59	0	52	43	42	45	52	308	CC LC
- + | + + | + |	56	0	37	27	0	0	64	42	0	46	0	62	42	40	75	38	60	38	46	54	41	41	0	37	0	43	52	54	50	46	271	
- - | - - | - |	37	0	42	55	0	0	35	42	0	53	0	25	42	40	70	70	66	80	66	33	30	33	0	25	0	60	41	80	37	50	99	CO GC LH NY O OJ
- - | - - | - |	62	0	57	38	0	0	33	57	0	45	0	33	57	60	25	30	33	20	20	66	70	66	0	75	0	40	58	0	62	46	91	PL S SF SM
- - | - - | - |	60	0	66	77	0	0	16	39	0	54	0	18	62	62	8	57	60	58	42	81	66	66	0	42	0	81	50	80	0	52	114	C CC LH S SF TR W
- - | - - | - |	40	0	33	27	0	0	66	47	0	54	0	66	72	62	25	42	40	41	50	57	50	18	0	57	0	60	35	20	0	45	98	CO JY LB
- - | - - | - |	33	66	37	36	0	0	36	36	0	44	0	60	33	50	100	53	40	36	43	50	50	57	0	28	0	51	30	0	0	42	91	BP LH
- - | - - | - |	66	33	62	63	0	0	63	63	0	55	0	60	66	37	75	60	60	63	50	12	50	42	0	71	0	44	70	75	0	56	121	BO LB SM TB TR
- - | - - | - |	37	100	41	38	0	0	37	40	0	23	0	66	33	25	40	42	55	37	37	53	50	50	0	25	0	36	36	93	50	40	96	BP JY LC SF
- - | - - | + |	62	0	58	61	0	0	62	60	0	76	0	33	66	33	40	50	44	56	56	75	36	62	0	75	0	58	63	50	50	57	137	GC LB SM TR
- - | - - | + |	37	100	58	61	0	0	36	55	0	65	0	55	40	50	50	50	50	64	46	37	62	53	0	53	0	48	41	100	0	51	145	BP CC W
- - | - - | + |	56	0	40	28	0	0	63	55	0	35	0	44	47	50	42	37	28	28	55	75	63	37	0	46	0	51	58	33	0	46	131	PL
- - | + - | + |	60	50	28	54	0	0	45	84	0	55	0	40	53	75	75	66	42	46	46	12	50	50	0	55	0	51	30	66	66	52	113	CP LC LH NY TR
- - | + - | + |	60	50	71	45	0	0	54	15	0	44	0	60	46	25	33	57	53	55	36	53	50	50	0	33	0	48	70	33	33	47	103	C PL TB
- - | + - | + |	50	0	40	28	0	0	27	44	0	55	0	33	40	40	30	30	60	35	47	50	57	28	0	75	0	28	50	50	62	45	118	SM
- + | + - | + |	50	0	50	71	0	0	72	44	0	30	0	33	60	100	66	69	40	64	52	50	42	57	0	60	0	66	50	50	37	51	134	CC CO LC LH NY SU
- + | + - | + |	60	100	50	31	0	0	75	55	0	68	0	40	62	33	80	50	36	50	58	55	50	25	0	65	0	35	33	81	44	47	111	BP CC TR
- + | + - | + |	40	0	50	31	0	0	66	47	0	40	0	60	40	00	80	63	37	38	37	44	72	75	0	18	0	55	18	55	55	53	103	CO LC LH S SF TB
- + | + - | + |	50	50	40	50	0	0	66	57	0	40	0	40	40	25	100	31	100	47	56	33	50	16	0	76	0	58	50	33	0	53	148	CO LH O PL SM W
- + | + + | + |	36	25	60	92	0	0	33	42	0	17	0	40	53	75	40	40	56	62	52	33	63	83	0	23	0	41	44	66	50	45	126	LC NY SF TR
- + | + + | + |	54	75	40	7	0	0	54	65	0	82	0	28	70	40	84	37	56	43	66	37	58	18	0	50	0	46	50	42	50	48	137	CC LB NY
- - | + + | + |	60	0	0	33	0	0	53	45	0	58	0	60	70	25	15	60	54	30	50	53	53	60	0	88	0	50	40	50	75	49	124	LB LH SM W
- - | + + | + |	40	100	28	66	0	0	46	54	0	41	0	40	30	75	20	45	69	50	50	62	46	40	0	11	0	47	40	50	25	46	117	BP CC LC OJ

Figure 8.7: Continued

		BO	BP	C	CC	CD	CL	CO	CP	FC	GC	HO	JY	LB	LC	LH	NY	O	OJ	PB	PL	S	SF	SV	SM	SP	SU	TB	TR	W	T%	T#		65%
---+---+	(+)	50	0	33	18	0	0	30	52	0	25	0	0	46	50	66	26	40	38	40	88	55	0	37	0	53	45	50	16	44	115		JY LH PL S
---+---+	(-)	50	100	66	81	0	0	70	47	0	66	0	100	53	50	22	73	60	61	59	100	11	44	62	0	46	54	42	83	54	140		BP C CC CO GC NY W
---+---+	(+)	45	0	58	29	0	0	57	47	0	66	0	28	33	50	50	68	30	60	47	60	64	54	53	0	62	41	41	57	51	151		GC LB NY
---+--+-	(-)	54	0	33	70	0	0	42	47	0	33	0	71	57	60	75	31	60	55	52	40	35	45	30	0	33	50	44	57	45	132		CC JY
---+---+	(+)	22	100	36	63	0	0	55	52	0	43	0	100	75	25	57	37	45	52	59	62	43	33	33	0	36	80	44	37	49	141		BP JY LB LH TB
---+---+	(-)	77	0	54	36	0	0	44	48	0	56	0	0	16	75	75	62	45	40	40	37	56	60	38	0	59	20	55	50	48	138		BO LC SF
---+---+	(+)	42	100	55	42	0	0	53	60	0	61	0	20	70	25	25	40	50	44	57	60	56	14	42	0	38	40	72	50	49	116		BP LC TR
---+---+	(-)	58	100	33	50	0	0	46	60	0	38	0	30	70	100	37	60	50	55	42	40	43	57	57	0	61	60	27	50	49	119		LB
---+---+	(+)	41	0	70	52	0	0	42	30	0	61	0	0	46	33	66	50	18	50	50	50	50	60	57	0	40	83	61	28	45	134		C CP LH O W
---+--+-	(-)	54	0	36	43	0	0	42	70	0	38	0	60	53	0	33	81	61	50	65	50	40	0	50	0	60	16	30	71	51	138		LH O S W
---+---+	(+)	45	100	54	56	0	0	42	43	0	60	0	40	35	50	66	50	66	50	35	60	27	33	62	0	39	47	21	0	43	111		BP
---+---+	(-)	66	100	37	52	0	0	63	25	0	25	0	83	30	75	28	33	57	66	50	72	50	50	70	0	45	37	72	44	49	149		BO BP JY LC OJ SM TH
---+---+	(+)	33	0	62	47	0	0	36	75	0	75	0	16	69	25	57	66	28	33	52	37	50	33	23	0	54	56	27	55	48	144		CP GC LB NY
---+---+	(-)	63	75	16	33	0	0	41	63	0	88	0	40	25	50	25	62	45	57	57	50	54	60	38	0	29	75	55	50	50	147		BP GC LB LH PL
---+---+	(+)	27	0	66	66	0	0	58	33	0	11	0	60	25	50	25	37	55	45	42	30	36	57	53	0	64	75	55	85	47	137		C CC TB W
---+---+	(-)	66	100	60	55	0	0	40	50	0	40	0	16	43	0	33	43	60	33	64	60	54	40	53	0	41	53	33	57	47	130		BO BP
---+---+	(+)	33	0	40	44	0	0	60	50	0	40	0	66	33	56	66	44	50	35	47	50	45	45	40	0	55	38	55	42	50	138		C LC LH OJ
---+---+	(-)	40	50	66	60	0	0	75	71	0	57	0	14	33	66	33	44	41	57	52	47	50	14	66	0	52	60	36	28	49	135		C CO CP LC LH SM
---+---+	(+)	40	50	33	40	0	0	25	28	0	42	0	85	66	33	33	44	57	25	47	50	60	37	33	0	53	55	77	71	48	132		JY LB SF W
---+---+	(-)	57	0	50	40	0	0	33	37	0	42	0	50	50	60	25	57	72	50	50	50	50	40	33	0	42	16	66	57	51	140		LC OJ TR W
---+---+	(+)	42	0	50	60	0	0	66	37	0	57	0	50	44	25	25	28	44	27	45	47	41	40	66	0	46	33	22	33	44	121		CO LB SM
---+---+	(-)	33	50	50	33	0	0	47	51	0	62	0	50	44	56	33	58	42	75	42	71	78	25	42	0	46	37	64	42	50	159		OJ PL S
---+---+	(+)	50	50	50	66	0	0	52	45	0	37	0	57	57	55	57	41	57	25	57	28	14	57	57	0	50	38	35	40	51	151		C LC LH SF
---+--+-	(-)	41	100	75	45	0	0	63	40	0	22	0	42	62	60	25	45	66	33	56	50	50	30	16	0	31	61	64	60	46	126		BP C
---+---+	(+)	58	0	25	54	0	0	36	59	0	77	0	33	37	50	75	45	62	41	43	58	58	44	83	0	65	50	57	60	50	139		GC LH O SF SM
---+---+	(-)	50	50	63	66	0	0	70	61	0	45	0	50	50	80	100	73	60	42	55	47	41	55	70	0	58	36	77	60	56	155		BP C CO LC LH NY
---+---+	(+)	30	0	30	50	0	0	29	38	0	22	0	50	50	60	0	26	60	42	40	37	40	50	30	0	48	33	63	22	40	111		BP C
---+---+	(-)	55	0	38	46	0	0	61	43	0	50	0	20	37	50	40	76	62	47	40	37	58	44	63	0	55	50	57	28	50	166		NY
---+---+	(+)	44	100	61	53	0	0	38	56	0	63	0	28	66	66	33	23	47	38	22	37	41	55	36	0	45	37	36	71	47	155		BP LH PL
---+---+	(-)	37	0	33	73	0	0	66	33	0	63	0	50	44	33	66	55	62	35	55	83	60	47	46	0	56	16	47	57	49	143		CC LH PL
---+---+	(+)	62	100	44	66	0	0	57	66	0	50	0	30	55	66	33	50	33	44	40	16	35	75	46	0	40	66	47	42	48	137		BP CP LC O SF TB
---+--+-	(-)	62	0	37	53	0	0	45	45	0	35	0	70	35	25	50	29	33	35	50	64	55	60	45	0	33	56	38	83	48	148		SU
---+---+	(+)	37	100	37	38	0	0	57	50	0	65	0	70	64	20	42	70	41	42	50	37	45	50	54	0	48	33	42	45	48	149		BP JY W
---+---+	(-)	37	0	62	26	0	0	33	60	0	36	0	42	50	50	33	58	25	43	60	50	57	33	40	0	51	65	47	60	49	143		PL
---+---+	(+)	62	100	37	73	0	0	66	60	0	63	0	28	50	0	66	45	44	47	61	77	37	38	36	0	56	50	41	30	46	135		BP CC CO LH W
---+---+	(-)	27	0	44	66	0	0	33	33	0	63	0	50	66	0	33	55	50	35	50	54	60	40	36	0	39	16	41	70	49	134		CC JY LC LH
---+---+	(+)	62	100	58	25	0	0	57	66	0	50	0	30	66	66	20	41	66	33	39	28	65	57	42	0	60	66	57	55	45	154		BO BP NY PL
---+--+-	(-)	37	100	37	60	0	0	53	50	0	47	0	57	64	12	44	50	42	35	50	71	45	40	53	0	33	42	38	83	48	132		CP TB TR
---+---+	(+)	40	0	60	46	0	0	75	57	0	47	0	75	58	50	100	50	25	45	45	56	56	14	40	0	48	65	58	9	46	124		JY LC
---+---+	(-)	40	0	60	46	0	0	52	62	0	52	0	62	50	50	0	25	72	47	36	36	56	43	40	0	57	41	58	75	49	162		CO JY LH W
---+---+	(+)	50	0	16	38	0	0	52	62	0	52	0	50	25	33	33	36	25	43	57	52	62	54	44	0	57	42	52	54	48	123		CO JY LH
---+---+	(-)	75	100	54	36	0	0	41	37	0	40	0	75	53	66	25	38	66	53	50	54	60	42	45	0	43	28	66	80	54	118		BO BP CO JY O SF
---+---+	(+)	25	0	45	63	0	0	100	0	0100	36	0	25	46	50	75	51	33	60	42	50	60	0	20	0	56	57	22	0	42	92		LH
---+---+	(-)	35	0	57	40	0	0	42	38	0	63	0	28	50	0	50	50	41	33	50	50	60	35	20	0	62	52	91	50	46	122		TR
---+--+-	(+)	64	0	42	60	0	0	57	61	0	50	0	57	66	66	50	50	42	57	52	60	52	62	80	0	37	42	8	50	51	135		LB LC SM
---+---+	(-)	40	100	62	33	0	0	36	43	0	79	0	33	25	50	50	55	44	77	56	52	60	28	60	0	56	50	33	30	50	151		CO GC OJ PL
---+---+	(+)	60	100	37	66	0	0	36	57	0	16	0	41	62	80	44	53	55	57	42	33	43	50	50	0	41	42	60	70	47	141		BP CC LB LC W
---+---+	(-)	69	100	28	71	0	0	53	18	0	42	0	28	44	12	100	60	18	15	22	47	40	40	50	0	39	80	52	50	42	124		BO BP CC LH TH
---+---+	(+)	30	0	71	28	0	0	38	81	0	57	0	71	55	87	0	62	72	78	72	52	59	60	44	0	57	20	41	50	55	162		C CP JY LC O OJ PB
---+---+	(-)	50	0	16	33	0	0	52	37	0	33	0	50	28	33	33	36	33	33	57	41	52	50	54	0	57	41	52	50	48	135		LB LC O
---+---+	(+)	40	100	83	63	0	0	41	37	0	45	0	50	73	71	25	63	66	50	42	50	37	36	50	0	42	58	47	33	53	136		BP CO OJ SF
---+---+	(-)	75	50	0	16	0	0	41	40	0	51	0	50	26	28	75	60	46	46	45	33	45	50	37	0	50	42	42	66	44	133		LH W

Figure 8.7: Continued

		BO	BP	C	CC	CD	CL	CO	CP	FC	GC	HO	JY	LB	LC	LH	NY	O	OJ	PB	PL	S	SF	SV	SM	SP	SU	TB	TR	W	T%	T#	-------- 65% --------
-+--++-	(+)	54	50	60	45	0	0	56	36	0	87	0	75	46	33	75	57	25	38	52	75	58	25	0	25	0	53	85	37	33	51	147	GC JY LH PL TB
-+--++-	(-)	36	50	40	54	0	0	43	63	0	12	0	25	38	66	25	31	75	50	47	25	41	75	0	75	0	41	14	50	66	44	127	LC O SF SM W
-+--+++	(+)	21	0	63	35	0	0	53	38	0	50	0	0	20	100	50	35	66	50	23	57	38	33	0	50	0	33	50	0	18	38	107	LC O
-+--+++	(-)	78	100	36	64	0	0	46	61	0	44	0	100	80	0	50	64	33	50	76	42	55	66	0	43	0	58	50	84	81	58	162	BO BP JY LB PB SF
-+-+---	(+)	62	75	50	71	0	0	57	80	0	45	0	33	46	75	80	77	66	35	52	61	60	70	0	57	0	53	27	64	44	55	150	BP CC CP LC LH NY
-+-+---	(-)	37	25	50	28	0	0	42	13	0	50	0	66	46	25	20	22	33	64	47	38	20	30	0	42	0	46	72	35	44	41	111	JY TB
-+-+--+	(+)	50	50	100	50	0	0	81	37	0	53	0	0	30	16	40	58	66	45	73	35	61	16	0	55	0	35	33	33	57	48	142	C CO O PB
-+-+--+	(-)	40	50	0	50	0	0	18	62	0	46	0	100	70	83	60	41	33	45	26	64	33	83	0	44	0	59	55	50	42	48	142	JY LB LC SF
-+-+-+-	(+)	60	0	66	33	0	0	33	53	0	68	0	60	22	33	87	0	70	28	64	43	36	40	0	33	0	37	42	46	25	49	121	C GC LH O
-+-+-+-	(-)	40	0	33	50	0	0	55	40	0	31	0	40	66	65	12	66	30	71	23	56	63	60	0	66	0	55	57	53	75	46	115	LB LC NY OJ SM W
-+-+-++	(+)	40	0	75	100	0	0	40	35	0	48	0	75	70	33	36	54	55	50	47	40	46	60	0	40	0	36	66	45	20	47	134	C CC JY LB TB
-+-+-++	(-)	50	0	25	0	0	0	60	65	0	45	0	25	30	66	63	45	33	50	52	60	46	40	0	60	0	60	33	45	80	49	139	LC W
-+-++--	(+)	16	100	22	36	0	0	55	43	0	59	0	60	80	80	28	36	25	33	58	61	60	37	0	66	0	53	57	33	40	50	154	BP LB LC SM
-+-++--	(-)	50	0	66	63	0	0	44	56	0	40	0	40	20	20	71	57	75	58	37	38	40	50	0	33	0	46	42	46	50	46	141	C LH O
-+-++-+	(+)	54	0	60	57	0	0	25	58	0	54	0	0	61	50	0	52	50	42	48	21	41	66	0	66	0	55	66	72	20	50	150	SF SM TB TR
-+-++-+	(-)	45	50	40	42	0	0	66	41	0	45	0	100	38	50	100	41	50	52	52	78	54	33	0	33	0	44	33	27	80	48	144	CO JY LH PL W
-+-+++-	(+)	77	100	0	38	0	0	54	27	0	50	0	50	43	100	55	63	12	60	80	53	41	33	0	62	0	67	16	66	80	52	146	BO BP LC PB SU TR W
-+-+++-	(-)	22	0	100	61	0	0	45	66	0	50	0	50	56	0	44	36	87	40	20	46	50	58	0	37	0	27	75	33	20	45	126	C CP O TB
-+-++++	(+)	41	100	33	40	0	0	38	66	0	33	0	60	41	25	20	41	28	55	45	64	44	40	0	44	0	30	66	44	28	44	125	BP CP TB
-+-++++	(-)	58	0	55	60	0	0	61	33	0	66	0	20	58	50	80	58	57	45	54	35	55	60	0	44	0	70	25	56	71	53	149	GC LH SU W
-++----	(+)	42	0	66	46	0	0	45	47	0	46	0	75	71	0	75	57	66	21	61	12	44	66	0	44	0	51	40	57	66	50	124	C JY LB LH O SF W
-++----	(-)	42	0	33	53	0	0	54	47	0	53	0	25	28	100	25	42	33	64	38	87	44	33	0	55	0	41	50	42	33	46	115	LC PL
-++---+	(+)	55	33	66	55	0	0	55	52	0	63	0	50	73	100	55	42	60	71	60	44	16	44	0	61	0	53	60	18	50	54	170	C LB LC OJ
-++---+	(-)	44	66	25	44	0	0	44	36	0	36	0	50	20	0	44	52	30	23	40	55	83	55	0	38	0	46	30	72	50	42	131	BP S TR
-++--+-	(+)	60	100	25	27	0	0	63	42	0	47	0	70	52	40	80	53	66	64	44	46	57	75	0	28	0	52	21	21	57	47	149	BP JY LH O SF
-++--+-	(-)	40	0	50	63	0	0	27	53	0	52	0	30	41	60	20	46	33	35	51	53	42	25	0	71	0	38	71	71	28	47	149	SM TB TR
-++--++	(+)	60	0	50	70	0	0	46	34	0	45	0	0	27	50	0	55	37	52	30	64	52	50	0	52	0	36	45	62	57	45	146	CC
-++--++	(-)	40	100	50	30	0	0	53	60	0	54	0	100	66	50	75	40	50	47	60	35	47	50	0	36	0	57	45	37	42	50	161	BP JY LB LH
-++-+--	(+)	69	100	50	75	0	0	66	66	0	48	0	100	30	66	50	66	60	42	41	53	50	25	0	40	0	52	37	37	28	51	145	BO BP CC CO CP JY
-++-+--	(-)	23	0	41	0	0	0	27	29	0	48	0	0	70	33	50	33	40	52	58	46	44	75	0	60	0	47	50	56	57	44	125	LB SF
-++-+-+	(+)	66	0	50	77	0	0	72	28	0	34	0	0	75	33	14	56	66	35	66	62	43	75	0	41	0	55	0	20	61	49	150	BO CC CO LB O PB SF
-++-+-+	(-)	33	100	50	22	0	0	27	71	0	65	0	100	25	66	85	39	33	64	33	37	52	25	0	58	0	44	100	75	38	49	152	BP CP JY LC LH TB TR
-++-++-	(+)	50	0	62	25	0	0	66	33	0	56	0	33	50	100	0	46	60	41	40	53	39	60	0	26	0	50	36	47	88	45	148	CO LC W
-++-++-	(-)	50	100	37	75	0	0	33	55	0	43	0	66	50	0	75	53	20	54	59	40	60	40	0	66	0	42	63	41	11	50	163	BP CC JY LH SM
-++-+++	(+)	25	0	12	61	0	0	44	40	0	63	0	66	33	57	40	33	25	41	48	58	40	33	0	40	0	33	40	35	0	41	123	JY
-++-+++	(-)	75	0	87	38	0	0	55	59	0	36	0	33	61	42	60	66	62	58	52	41	59	66	0	40	0	58	60	65	100	56	168	BO C NY SF W
-+++---	(+)	45	100	66	43	0	0	42	70	0	45	0	50	52	66	77	42	28	60	57	63	46	60	0	57	0	54	33	42	33	50	135	BP C CP LC LH
-+++---	(-)	54	0	33	56	0	0	50	30	0	54	0	50	47	33	22	57	71	40	42	36	53	40	0	42	0	45	66	50	66	49	132	O TB W
-+++--+	(+)	57	0	55	61	0	0	40	52	0	50	0	66	61	0	66	50	45	50	45	33	55	54	0	54	0	71	50	52	44	53	169	JY LH SU
-+++--+	(-)	42	100	44	38	0	0	50	48	0	50	0	33	34	0	33	45	45	43	55	66	44	45	0	45	0	25	50	41	55	43	138	BP PL
-+++-+-	(+)	37	100	25	44	0	0	64	56	0	68	0	33	53	40	40	60	28	60	46	40	57	50	0	45	0	52	66	52	12	50	163	BP GC TB
-+++-+-	(-)	62	0	75	55	0	0	35	43	0	31	0	66	46	60	60	40	57	35	53	60	42	50	0	54	0	45	22	40	87	47	152	C JY W
-+++-++	(+)	33	100	25	63	0	0	35	31	0	60	0	71	60	0	40	35	57	40	80	27	35	62	0	44	0	33	33	50	62	46	135	BP JY PB
-+++-++	(-)	55	0	75	36	0	0	57	68	0	40	0	14	40	100	60	64	42	53	20	72	65	37	0	55	0	62	66	50	37	52	152	C CP LC PL TB
-++++--	(+)	77	0	72	50	0	0	71	60	0	83	0	0	71	25	83	41	28	37	38	58	37	50	0	28	0	64	25	54	33	53	140	BO C CO GC LB LH
-++++--	(-)	22	0	27	50	0	0	28	40	0	16	0	100	21	50	16	58	57	62	55	41	62	50	0	71	0	36	75	45	66	44	116	JY SM TB W
-++++-+	(+)	20	0	44	53	0	0	41	40	0	50	0	75	35	100	55	50	63	70	42	56	50	33	0	40	0	50	70	38	27	48	135	JY LC OJ TB
-++++-+	(-)	80	0	55	46	0	0	58	55	0	50	0	25	50	0	44	50	36	29	57	43	50	66	0	60	0	50	30	61	72	50	140	BO SF W
-+++++-	(+)	38	0	0	47	0	0	70	54	0	71	0	100	37	50	0	44	50	57	47	28	40	55	0	63	0	37	41	26	100	45	116	CO GC JY W
-+++++-	(-)	61	100	100	52	0	0	30	45	0	28	0	0	50	50	100	55	37	35	52	71	60	44	0	36	0	62	50	73	0	52	133	BP C LH PL TR
-++++++	(+)	53	0	40	67	0	0	44	71	0	64	0	50	30	100	50	12	66	53	43	70	40	60	0	54	0	50	68	30	50	53	139	CC CP LC O PL TB
-++++++	(-)	46	0	40	32	0	0	55	28	0	35	0	50	69	0	50	62	16	46	56	30	60	40	0	36	0	50	31	60	50	44	115	LB
+------	(+)	37	0	42	55	0	0	66	42	0	100	0	25	42	40	75	70	66	80	66	33	30	33	0	25	0	60	41	80	37	50	99	CO GC LH NY O OJ
+------	(-)	62	0	57	38	0	0	33	57	0	0	0	50	57	60	25	30	33	20	20	66	70	66	0	75	0	40	58	0	62	46	91	PL S SF SM

Figure 8.7: Continued

Sign	BO	BP	C	CC	CD	CL	CO	CP	FC	GC	HO	JY	LB	LC	LH	NY	O	OJ	PB	PL	S	SF	SV	SM	SP	SU	TB	TR	W	T%	T#	65%
(+)	60	0	66	72	0	0	16	52	0	45	0	33	18	37	75	57	60	58	42	42	81	66	0	42	0	40	50	80	100	52	114	C CC LH S SF TR W
(−)	40	50	33	27	0	0	66	47	0	54	0	66	72	62	25	42	40	41	50	57	18	33	57	57	0	60	35	20	0	45	98	CO JY LB
(+)	33	66	37	36	0	0	36	36	0	54	0	40	72	62	25	42	40	36	50	50	50	0	28	28	0	30	30	0	0	42	91	BP LH
(−)	66	33	62	63	0	0	63	63	0	55	0	60	66	37	0	46	60	63	37	50	42	42	0	71	0	44	70	75	0	56	121	BO LB SM TB TR
(+)	37	100	41	38	0	0	37	40	0	76	0	66	33	66	40	42	55	42	37	56	50	0	25	0	0	50	36	0	50	40	96	BP JY LC SF
(−)	62	0	58	61	0	0	62	60	0	65	0	33	66	37	40	52	44	57	56	37	50	33	75	75	0	50	63	93	50	57	137	GC LB SM TR
(+)	37	100	60	71	0	0	36	55	0	65	0	55	52	50	50	50	50	64	40	25	36	62	0	53	0	48	41	44	100	51	145	BP CC W
(+)	56	0	40	28	0	0	36	40	0	35	0	44	47	50	50	42	37	28	55	75	63	37	46	46	0	51	58	33	0	46	131	PL
(−)	60	50	28	54	0	0	45	84	0	65	0	40	53	75	75	75	66	66	42	46	12	50	55	55	0	30	66	66	0	52	113	CP LC LH NY TR W
(+)	40	50	71	45	0	0	54	15	0	44	0	60	46	25	25	33	57	53	53	87	63	50	33	33	0	48	70	33	33	47	103	C PL TB
(−)	50	50	40	28	0	0	27	55	0	55	0	33	53	30	30	30	60	35	47	50	50	57	75	75	0	28	50	50	62	45	118	SM
(+)	50	50	50	71	0	0	72	47	0	55	0	33	60	75	20	40	64	52	52	42	57	28	25	25	0	66	50	50	37	51	134	CC CO LC LH NY SU
(−)	60	100	71	68	0	0	25	55	0	40	0	40	62	33	50	50	69	61	55	27	42	72	60	60	0	65	33	81	44	51	111	BP CC TR
(+)	40	0	50	31	0	0	75	33	0	40	0	60	37	57	75	40	36	37	38	44	50	0	40	40	0	35	66	18	55	47	103	CO LC LH
(−)	50	50	40	50	0	0	66	42	0	60	0	60	40	25	80	64	63	50	52	33	50	16	76	76	0	58	50	33	100	53	148	CO LH O PL SM W
(+)	50	50	50	50	0	0	33	34	0	60	0	40	53	75	0	68	0	62	33	37	58	83	23	23	0	41	44	18	0	45	126	LC NY SF TR
(−)	36	25	60	92	0	0	45	45	0	58	0	71	70	40	60	0	37	56	52	47	58	18	50	50	0	46	50	57	50	48	137	CC LB NY
(+)	60	0	28	33	0	0	53	45	0	41	0	60	30	25	80	15	56	30	50	50	43	81	50	50	0	47	50	42	75	49	142	BP GC JY PB SF
(+)	40	100	28	66	0	0	53	54	0	66	0	40	70	75	40	40	54	69	42	100	60	60	88	88	0	47	40	50	25	49	124	LB LH SM W
(−)	50	0	33	18	0	0	30	52	0	38	0	60	30	75	66	66	30	60	50	0	86	40	11	11	0	47	45	50	16	46	117	BP CC LC OJ
(+)	50	100	0	0	0	0	46	43	0	66	0	100	46	50	22	26	60	61	59	0	0	55	37	37	0	46	50	16	71	44	115	JY LH PL S
(−)	50	100	66	81	0	0	70	47	0	66	0	28	53	50	73	73	60	61	20	59	0	0	62	62	0	54	54	42	83	54	140	BP C CC CO GC NY W
(+)	45	0	58	29	0	0	57	47	0	66	0	71	66	66	50	68	30	45	45	50	64	64	53	53	0	62	41	44	42	51	151	GC LB NY
(−)	54	0	33	70	0	0	57	47	0	33	0	33	33	57	30	30	60	55	47	50	64	54	30	30	0	44	50	44	57	45	132	GC JY
(+)	22	100	36	63	0	0	54	52	0	43	0	71	75	25	75	37	55	52	59	62	43	43	70	70	0	36	80	72	44	49	141	BP JY LB LH TB
(−)	77	0	54	36	0	0	55	48	0	56	0	16	30	75	28	33	45	47	35	37	50	56	23	23	0	59	37	55	37	48	138	BO LC SF
(+)	42	100	55	42	0	0	53	40	0	61	0	20	75	50	57	62	44	54	52	40	54	14	61	61	0	38	40	25	50	50	116	BP LC TR
(+)	42	0	33	50	0	0	46	60	0	38	0	60	70	40	25	60	50	57	42	50	50	57	0	0	0	61	60	27	50	49	119	LB
(+)	58	100	20	48	0	0	42	30	0	61	0	60	46	33	80	50	18	38	50	42	50	60	57	57	0	40	83	61	28	45	119	BP TB
(−)	41	0	70	52	0	0	42	70	0	38	0	40	30	75	66	50	81	61	35	42	45	45	50	50	0	83	16	30	71	51	134	C CP LH O W
(+)	54	0	36	43	0	0	42	43	0	60	0	40	53	50	44	44	60	50	65	60	40	40	16	16	0	60	52	57	100	53	138	LH O S
(−)	45	100	54	52	0	0	57	56	0	40	0	40	35	33	33	33	66	50	60	40	50	14	62	62	0	39	47	21	0	43	111	BP
(+)	66	100	37	52	0	0	63	75	0	25	0	83	57	28	33	57	33	37	35	50	27	27	70	70	0	54	37	72	44	49	149	BO BP JY LC OJ SM TR
(−)	33	0	62	47	0	0	36	28	0	75	0	16	30	57	66	66	28	43	52	37	50	50	44	44	0	56	56	27	55	48	144	CP GC LB NY
(+)	63	75	16	33	0	0	41	63	0	88	0	50	69	25	57	66	44	54	45	45	41	85	66	66	0	25	44	14	66	51	147	BP GC LB LH PL
(−)	27	25	66	66	0	0	58	33	0	11	0	50	25	75	25	37	55	42	42	27	54	15	53	53	0	75	33	57	42	47	137	C CC TB
(+)	66	100	60	55	0	0	40	50	0	40	0	66	43	50	50	60	60	33	64	60	54	54	0	0	0	41	53	33	57	47	130	BO BP
(+)	33	0	40	44	0	0	40	30	0	61	0	66	53	33	66	66	60	66	35	40	45	45	57	57	0	40	38	55	42	50	138	JY LC LH OJ
(−)	60	50	66	60	0	0	42	70	0	38	0	14	33	66	44	44	50	35	57	40	45	45	40	40	0	54	40	54	28	49	135	C CO CP LC LH SM
(+)	40	50	33	40	0	0	42	43	0	60	0	85	50	20	75	41	57	52	52	50	50	50	66	66	0	52	58	36	49	48	132	JY LB OJ TR W
(+)	57	0	50	40	0	0	36	56	0	42	0	16	69	50	28	57	44	72	37	37	47	47	33	33	0	53	33	71	66	51	140	LC OJ TR
(−)	42	50	50	60	0	0	58	37	0	57	0	60	75	50	57	66	54	45	45	57	70	78	0	0	0	46	42	64	47	44	121	CO LB OJ PL S
(+)	33	50	50	33	0	0	47	51	0	62	0	50	44	50	25	37	60	42	42	28	54	25	42	42	0	37	35	42	50	50	159	OJ PL S
(+)	50	50	50	45	0	0	47	45	0	37	0	50	55	60	25	58	33	75	57	71	41	14	57	57	0	35	61	35	42	47	151	CC LC LH SF
(+)	41	100	75	45	0	0	63	40	0	22	0	57	62	60	25	41	60	25	28	50	78	75	16	16	0	31	64	64	60	46	126	BP C LH O SM
(+)	58	0	25	54	0	0	70	59	0	77	0	42	37	20	75	64	60	33	57	43	50	30	83	83	0	65	30	35	46	51	139	GC LH O SF SM
(+)	30	30	50	50	0	0	70	61	0	45	0	37	50	75	28	60	60	58	58	60	42	70	70	70	0	48	36	40	77	56	155	BP C CO LC LH NY
(+)	55	0	38	46	0	0	29	38	0	50	0	50	37	50	40	60	60	47	40	37	58	44	63	63	0	55	33	63	28	40	111	BP
(+)	44	100	61	53	0	0	61	43	0	50	0	80	62	50	76	62	62	47	40	37	41	55	36	36	0	55	50	57	50	50	166	NY JY
(−)	37	0	33	75	0	0	38	56	0	50	0	0	30	66	23	25	62	60	45	78	60	25	46	46	0	56	16	47	71	47	155	CC LH PL
(+)	62	100	58	25	0	0	57	66	0	50	0	0	35	33	66	44	25	44	27	14	35	75	47	47	0	56	47	47	57	49	143	CC LH PL
(+)	62	0	37	53	0	0	57	66	0	50	0	30	64	20	42	50	66	44	40	16	35	55	40	40	0	40	66	47	42	47	137	BP CP LC O SF TB
(+)	62	0	37	53	0	0	45	45	0	35	0	30	55	60	50	55	35	35	50	50	55	55	45	45	0	33	37	61	0	48	148	SU O SF TB
(−)	37	100	37	38	0	0	45	50	0	65	0	70	64	20	42	33	35	35	50	64	50	50	54	54	0	33	56	38	83	48	149	JY W

Figure 8.7: Continued

	(+/-)	BO	BP	C	CC	CD	CL	CO	CP	FC	GC	HO	JY	LB	LC	LH	LY	NY	O	OJ	PB	PL	S	SF	SV	SM	SP	SU	TB	TR	W	T%	T#	
+−++−−	(+)	37	0	62	26	0	0	33	60	0	36	0	42	50	0	33	51		44	43	61	77	57	33	0	63	0	51	50	47	60	49	143	PL
+−++−−	(−)	62	100	37	73	0	0	66	40	0	36	0	28	50	0	66	45		55	43	38	22	35	66	0	36	0	45	35	41	30	46	135	BP CC CO LH SF
+−++−+	(−)	'27	0	44	66	0	0	41	50	0	63	0	50	40	66	80	45		33	35	50	22	35	60	0	42	0	45	35	45	45	45	134	CC JY LC LH
+−++−+	(−)	72	66	55	33	0	0	58	45	0	36	0	50	50	33	20	70		50	57	60	71	35	40	0	57	0	60	50	55	45	51	154	BO BP NY PL
+−++++	(+)	25	0	42	41	0	0	36	68	0	52	0	33	41	0	55	41		41	57	50	62	42	40	0	40	0	52	66	90	55	50	132	CP TB TR
+−++++	(+)	62	0	50	52	0	0	34	57	0	47	0	66	58	50	44	50		41	57	50	37	57	14	0	53	0	48	33	9	44	46	124	JY LC
+−++++	(+)	40	0	60	46	0	0	75	57	0	52	0	75	58	100	44	50		25	45	46	36	56	40	0	40	0	43	65	41	0	49	122	CO JY LH W
+−+++−	(+)	60	100	40	53	0	0	25	42	0	52	0	25	41	50	50	50		75	54	53	63	43	85	0	60	0	56	30	0	75	49	123	BP O SF
+−+++−	(+)	75	100	54	36	0	0	25	30	0	40	0	75	53	33	25	61		33	33	58	50	56	90	0	0	0	43	28	66	0	54	118	BO BP CO JY O SF
+−+−−−	(−)	25	0	45	63	0	0	60	60	0	60	0	25	46	50	75	50		57	30	42	50	60	10	0	0	0	56	57	22	0	42	92	LH
+−−−−−	(−)	35	0	57	40	0	0	42	38	0	50	0	57	33	33	50	53		57	35	47	50	47	25	0	20	0	37	52	91	50	46	122	TR
+−−−−+	(−)	64	0	42	60	0	0	57	61	0	50	0	66	66	50	50	46		52	50	52	56	52	62	0	80	0	56	42	8	50	51	135	LC SM
+−−−−+	(+)	40	0	62	33	0	0	53	43	0	79	0	50	25	75	50	44		44	77	56	66	56	28	0	60	0	50	50	33	30	47	151	CO GC OJ PL
+−−−−+	(−)	69	100	37	66	0	0	53	18	0	16	0	28	44	12	100	53		33	22	44	33	43	57	0	30	0	41	42	60	70	42	141	BP CC LB LC
+−−−−+	(+)	69	100	28	71	0	0	53	81	0	42	0	71	100	87	0	47		18	15	72	52	59	40	0	80	0	39	80	41	50	47	124	BP CC LH TB
+−−−++	(+)	30	0	71	28	0	0	38	62	0	57	0	71	55	87	0	62		72	78	72	52	60	54	0	44	0	57	20	52	50	55	162	C CP JY LC O OJ PB
+−−−++	(−)	50	0	16	36	0	100	52	62	0	50	0	50	71	37	33	36		33	50	57	50	62	54	0	54	0	57	41	52	50	48	135	LB
+−−+−−	(+)	40	100	83	63	0	0	48	53	0	45	0	28	62	33	42	66		66	62	64	50	36	36	0	45	0	42	58	47	66	49	136	C GC LH O
+−−+−−	(−)	75	50	100	83	0	0	58	40	0	31	0	50	73	71	75	40		71	23	50	42	60	60	0	50	0	50	57	40	63	53	163	BO C CC LB LC
+−−+−−	(−)	54	50	60	45	0	0	56	36	0	48	0	50	26	28	36	31		28	46	45	57	33	45	0	37	0	50	85	60	66	44	135	LH W
+−−+−−	(+)	36	50	40	54	0	0	43	63	0	12	0	75	38	66	25	40		71	53	47	25	41	75	0	25	0	50	37	33	18	51	147	GC JY LH PL TB
+−−+−+	(+)	21	0	63	35	0	0	46	38	0	50	0	25	20	66	50	35		66	50	52	57	33	33	0	75	0	41	14	50	66	44	127	O SF SM W
+−−++−	(−)	78	100	36	64	0	0	46	61	0	44	0	80	80	0	50	35		33	42	50	23	57	66	0	50	0	58	50	81	18	38	107	LC
+−−++−	(−)	62	75	50	71	0	0	57	80	0	45	0	33	46	75	80	77		66	35	52	61	55	66	0	43	0	53	84	84	58	55	162	BO BP JY LB PB SF
+−−++−	(+)	37	25	50	28	0	0	81	13	0	50	0	66	20	25	0	22		33	64	47	38	61	60	0	57	0	27	33	35	44	41	150	BP CC CP LC LH NY
+−−+++	(+)	50	50	100	50	0	0	54	37	0	53	0	20	30	16	40	52		36	77	48	21	51	30	0	55	0	46	72	35	44	48	111	C O PB
+−−+++	(+)	40	50	0	50	0	0	52	62	0	46	0	70	70	83	58	41		33	45	26	64	44	83	0	44	0	59	16	66	80	48	142	JY LC SF
+−−+++	(+)	60	0	66	33	0	0	55	53	0	68	0	40	22	33	87	66		66	28	64	43	36	60	0	33	0	37	46	25	66	49	121	C GC LH O
+−−+++	(−)	60	0	33	50	0	0	55	40	0	31	0	66	66	71	23	54		30	71	61	58	16	60	0	66	0	55	53	75	63	47	115	LB LC NY OJ SM
+−−+++	(+)	40	0	75	100	0	0	40	35	0	48	0	75	70	33	36	55		55	50	47	40	46	60	0	40	0	36	66	45	20	44	134	C CC JY LB TB
+−++−−	(+)	16	100	22	36	0	0	46	61	0	44	0	100	80	66	63	45		32	50	52	61	60	40	0	55	0	60	33	45	80	49	139	LC W
+−++−+	(−)	50	0	66	63	0	0	57	80	0	45	0	33	80	75	28	57		75	64	48	38	60	55	0	66	0	57	21	33	50	46	154	BP LB LC SM
+−++−+	(+)	54	0	40	57	0	0	44	56	0	40	0	40	20	20	71	52		50	58	37	21	41	50	0	33	0	46	42	46	50	46	141	C LH O
+−++−+	(+)	45	50	42	40	0	0	25	58	0	54	0	61	61	50	75	52		50	42	48	41	50	33	0	33	0	55	66	72	20	50	150	SF SM TB TR
+−+++−	(−)	77	100	0	38	0	0	54	27	0	45	0	38	43	100	55	63		50	60	80	53	41	33	0	62	0	67	16	66	80	48	144	CO JY LH PL
+−++++	(+)	22	0	100	61	0	0	38	66	0	50	0	50	56	50	44	41		87	40	20	46	50	58	0	37	0	27	75	33	20	52	146	BO BP LC PB SU TR
+−++++	(+)	41	100	33	40	0	0	30	66	0	33	0	60	41	25	44	28		28	35	54	43	55	40	0	44	0	30	44	28	20	45	126	C CP TB
+−++++	(−)	58	0	55	60	0	0	61	33	0	66	0	20	58	50	80	58		57	45	54	35	55	60	0	44	0	70	25	56	71	53	125	BP CP TB
+−++−−	(+)	42	0	33	53	0	0	54	47	0	46	0	0	71	12	75	57		66	21	61	12	44	66	0	55	0	41	40	57	66	46	149	GC LH SU W
+−++−−	(−)	42	0	33	53	0	0	55	47	0	53	0	25	28	100	55	42		33	64	60	44	16	44	0	61	0	53	42	57	66	44	124	JY LB LH O SF
+−++−+	(+)	55	33	66	55	0	0	54	36	0	63	0	50	73	100	75	42		60	33	44	44	83	33	0	61	0	64	30	18	50	54	115	LC OJ
+−++−+	(−)	44	66	25	44	0	0	63	42	0	36	0	50	20	0	44	57		23	60	60	38	16	55	0	38	0	46	72	72	50	42	170	C LB LC OJ
+−+++−	(−)	60	100	50	27	0	0	63	53	0	42	0	52	52	40	60	42		25	64	44	46	60	75	0	28	0	57	21	71	50	47	131	BP S TR
+−+++−	(+)	40	0	50	63	0	0	27	53	0	52	0	30	41	60	20	46		35	35	51	53	42	25	0	71	0	38	71	71	28	47	149	BP JY LH O SF
+−++++	(+)	60	0	46	70	0	0	66	34	0	45	0	27	41	50	75	55		37	52	30	46	52	50	0	52	0	36	45	62	57	45	146	SM TB TR
+−++++	(+)	40	100	50	30	0	0	66	66	0	48	0	66	66	66	50	33		60	35	47	60	52	25	0	36	0	52	45	37	42	50	161	CC CO LB LH
+−−+−−	(−)	69	100	30	75	0	0	52	66	0	65	0	30	70	14	85	39		33	64	54	41	44	75	0	60	0	47	37	56	57	44	145	BO CO CO CP JY
+−−+−+	(+)	23	0	41	17	0	0	72	28	0	34	0	0	70	33	0	46		66	52	58	44	52	50	0	60	0	55	50	20	61	49	125	LB SF
+−−++−	(+)	66	0	50	77	0	0	27	71	0	56	0	75	25	66	50	53		33	41	40	53	39	52	0	58	0	44	100	75	38	49	150	BP CP JY LC LH TB
+−−++−	(−)	33	100	62	25	0	0	66	33	0	56	0	33	50	66	85	46		60	41	40	40	60	60	0	26	0	50	36	47	88	45	152	CO LC W
+−−++−	(+)	50	0	62	25	0	0	33	55	0	43	0	66	50	0	75	53		20	54	59	40	60	40	0	66	0	42	63	41	11	50	163	BP CC JY LH SM

------ 65% ------

Figure 8.7: Concluded

		BO	BP	C	CC	CD	CL	CO	CP	FC	GC	HO	JY	LB	LC	LH	NY	O	OJ	PB	PL	S	SF	SV	SM	SP	SU	TB	TR	W	T%	T#	------- 65% -------
+++-++	(+)	25	0	12	61	0	0	44	40	0	63	0	66	33	57	40	33	25	41	48	58	40	33	0	40	0	33	40	35	0	41	123	JY
+++-++	(-)	75	0	87	38	0	0	55	59	0	36	0	33	61	42	60	66	62	58	52	41	59	66	0	40	0	58	60	65	100	56	168	BO C NY SF W
+++---	(+)	45	100	66	43	0	0	42	70	0	45	0	50	52	66	77	42	28	60	57	63	46	60	0	57	0	54	33	42	33	50	135	BP C CP LC LH
+++---	(-)	54	0	33	56	0	0	50	30	0	54	0	50	47	33	22	57	71	40	42	36	53	40	0	42	0	45	66	50	66	49	132	O TB W
+++-+-	(+)	57	0	55	61	0	0	40	52	0	50	0	66	61	0	66	50	45	50	45	33	55	54	0	54	0	71	50	52	44	53	169	JY LH SU
+++-+-	(-)	42	100	44	38	0	0	50	48	0	50	0	33	34	0	33	45	45	43	55	66	44	45	0	45	0	25	50	41	55	43	138	BP PL
+++-+-	(+)	37	100	25	44	0	0	64	56	0	68	0	33	53	40	40	60	28	60	46	40	57	50	0	45	0	52	66	52	12	50	163	BP GC TB
+++-+-	(-)	62	0	75	55	0	0	35	43	0	31	0	66	46	60	60	40	57	35	53	60	42	50	0	54	0	45	22	40	87	47	152	C JY W
++++-+	(+)	33	100	25	63	0	0	35	31	0	60	0	71	60	0	40	35	57	40	80	27	35	62	0	44	0	33	33	50	62	46	135	BP JY PB
++++-+	(-)	55	0	75	36	0	0	57	68	0	40	0	14	40	100	60	64	42	53	20	72	65	37	0	55	0	62	66	50	37	52	152	C CP LC PL TB
++++--	(+)	77	0	72	50	0	0	71	60	0	83	0	0	71	25	83	41	28	37	38	58	37	50	0	28	0	64	25	54	33	53	140	BO C CO GC LB LH
++++--	(-)	22	0	27	50	0	0	28	40	0	16	0	100	21	50	16	58	57	62	55	41	62	50	0	71	0	36	75	45	66	44	116	JY SM TB W
++++-+	(+)	20	0	44	53	0	0	41	40	0	50	0	75	35	100	55	50	63	70	42	36	50	33	0	40	0	50	70	38	27	48	135	JY LC OJ TB
++++-+	(-)	80	0	55	46	0	0	58	55	0	50	0	25	50	0	44	50	36	29	57	43	50	66	0	60	0	50	40	61	72	50	140	BO SF W
++++++	(+)	38	0	0	47	0	0	70	54	0	71	0	100	37	50	0	44	50	57	47	28	40	55	0	63	0	37	41	26	100	45	116	CO GC JY W
++++++	(-)	61	100	100	52	0	0	30	45	0	28	0	0	0	50	100	55	37	35	52	71	60	44	0	36	0	62	50	73	0	52	133	BP C LH PL TR
++++++	(+)	53	0	40	67	0	0	44	71	0	64	0	50	30	100	50	66	53	43	70	40	60	0	54	0	50	68	30	50	53	139	CC CP LC O PL TB
++++++	(-)	46	0	40	32	0	0	55	28	0	35	0	50	69	0	50	62	16	46	56	30	60	40	0	36	0	50	31	60	50	44	115	LB

Figure 8.8: Daily Closing Patterns: Bull/Bear/Bull Markets

`-------- 65% --------`

Pattern	Dir	BO	BP	C	CC	CD	CL	CO	CP	FC	GC	HO	JY	LB	LC	LH	NY	O	OJ	PB	PL	S	SF	SV	SM	SP	SU	TB	TR	W	T%	T#	Notes
- -	(-)	52	52	57	54	0	0	0	0	0	0	0	0	0	57	56	59	57	54	0	55	55	50	0	46	0	58	47	0	49	54	830	
- -	(-)	47	47	40	44	0	0	0	0	0	0	0	0	0	41	42	36	42	39	0	42	42	42	0	46	0	39	41	0	44	42	645	
- +	(-)	52	62	54	48	0	0	0	0	0	0	0	0	0	51	43	41	59	51	0	55	46	42	0	64	0	52	55	0	45	51	919	
- +	(-)	47	36	41	50	0	0	0	0	0	0	0	0	0	43	50	52	40	41	0	44	51	56	0	36	0	43	37	0	50	45	804	
+ -	(+)	52	48	38	59	0	0	0	0	0	0	0	0	0	51	51	49	48	53	0	53	49	50	0	50	0	50	48	0	40	50	889	
+ -	(-)	46	50	58	40	0	0	0	0	0	0	0	0	0	43	46	50	44	46	0	45	49	50	0	44	0	46	45	0	54	46	828	
+ +	(+)	47	48	43	44	0	0	0	0	0	0	0	0	0	48	43	46	43	45	0	52	48	40	0	44	0	48	44	0	35	46	836	
+ +	(+)	52	50	56	53	0	0	0	0	0	0	0	0	0	46	51	48	53	46	0	47	50	50	0	52	0	50	52	0	57	50	913	
- - -	(+)	45	54	66	61	0	0	0	0	0	0	0	0	0	56	58	72	54	66	0	51	54	50	0	46	0	45	51	0	58	54	354	C NY OJ
- - -	(-)	54	45	30	38	0	0	0	0	0	0	0	0	0	42	39	24	45	22	0	44	43	45	0	42	0	50	40	0	35	41	267	
- - +	(+)	50	59	48	44	0	0	0	0	0	0	0	0	0	54	39	39	50	56	0	54	41	32	0	64	0	51	51	0	55	50	414	
- - +	(-)	50	38	48	52	0	0	0	0	0	0	0	0	0	42	51	58	50	40	0	45	58	60	0	35	0	42	41	0	42	46	385	
- + -	(+)	51	43	44	54	0	0	0	0	0	0	0	0	0	50	51	44	41	50	0	67	49	50	0	46	0	52	37	0	51	49	399	PL
- + -	(-)	48	56	55	45	0	0	0	0	0	0	0	0	0	43	48	53	58	50	0	32	50	50	0	46	0	41	56	0	45	47	384	
- + +	(+)	50	54	47	57	0	0	0	0	0	0	0	0	0	45	37	46	54	46	0	52	50	30	0	42	0	49	47	0	41	46	430	
- + +	(-)	50	42	52	42	0	0	0	0	0	0	0	0	0	49	60	48	40	43	0	47	50	56	0	55	0	48	49	0	62	49	458	SU
+ - -	(+)	58	52	48	48	0	0	0	0	0	0	0	0	0	40	43	42	41	56	0	60	56	53	0	46	0	66	50	0	46	54	452	SU
+ - -	(-)	41	47	48	48	0	0	0	0	0	0	0	0	0	42	47	46	71	48	0	40	41	42	0	50	0	31	39	0	46	42	352	
+ - +	(+)	54	65	64	51	0	0	0	0	0	0	0	0	0	50	47	46	48	50	0	56	50	48	0	64	0	51	60	0	34	53	473	O
+ - +	(-)	45	34	35	48	0	0	0	0	0	0	0	0	0	42	48	48	28	44	0	43	45	48	0	35	0	46	29	0	58	43	385	
+ + -	(+)	51	52	35	63	0	0	0	0	0	0	0	0	0	51	43	43	41	56	0	41	50	47	0	53	0	48	52	0	32	50	456	
+ + -	(-)	45	46	60	36	0	0	0	0	0	0	0	0	0	52	43	41	44	40	0	55	48	52	0	41	0	50	40	0	50	46	418	
+ + +	(+)	46	42	38	30	0	0	0	0	0	0	0	0	0	53	52	45	28	48	0	54	47	50	0	47	0	44	41	0	61	46	387	
+ + +	(-)	53	57	61	64	0	0	0	0	0	0	0	0	0	43	39	48	71	48	0	45	49	43	0	49	0	54	56	0	36	50	424	O
- - - -	(+)	30	45	50	50	0	0	0	0	0	0	0	0	0	65	65	100	50	75	0	58	69	63	0	62	0	54	56	0	52	50	156	NY OJ S
- - - -	(-)	69	54	40	50	0	0	0	0	0	0	0	0	0	35	34	50	64	0	0	41	30	36	0	25	0	50	46	0	75	58	103	BO
- - - +	(+)	45	69	45	47	0	0	0	0	0	0	0	0	0	53	35	50	41	66	0	64	34	27	0	69	0	51	63	0	25	52	185	BP OJ SM
- - - +	(-)	54	30	50	47	0	0	0	0	0	0	0	0	0	46	55	44	58	33	0	35	58	63	0	30	0	40	31	0	70	44	156	
- - + -	(+)	64	40	47	55	0	0	0	0	0	0	0	0	0	58	60	40	40	50	0	75	53	41	0	50	0	54	11	0	25	51	197	PL
- - + -	(-)	35	60	52	45	0	0	0	0	0	0	0	0	0	41	40	50	60	50	0	25	46	58	0	40	0	37	83	0	43	47	181	TB
- - + +	(+)	50	58	52	47	0	0	0	0	0	0	0	0	0	42	25	50	33	50	0	52	41	44	0	36	0	51	40	0	28	44	185	
- - + +	(-)	50	38	47	52	0	0	0	0	0	0	0	0	0	53	74	50	60	35	0	47	41	55	0	61	0	44	54	0	71	52	217	LH W
- + - -	(+)	64	42	42	54	0	0	0	0	0	0	0	0	0	58	60	46	64	50	0	63	60	47	0	47	0	67	38	0	43	54	209	SU
- + - -	(-)	35	57	52	45	0	0	0	0	0	0	0	0	0	41	36	46	35	41	0	36	36	47	0	47	0	29	47	0	37	41	159	
- + - +	(+)	46	62	73	42	0	0	0	0	0	0	0	0	0	53	43	45	80	41	0	56	54	41	0	66	0	44	76	0	33	51	205	C O SM TB
- + - +	(-)	53	37	26	57	0	0	0	0	0	0	0	0	0	39	52	54	20	50	0	43	45	52	0	33	0	53	15	0	55	45	180	
- + + -	(+)	56	29	34	75	0	0	0	0	0	0	0	0	0	50	48	52	61	53	0	45	50	58	0	56	0	42	59	0	45	50	228	CC
- + + -	(-)	43	66	56	25	0	0	0	0	0	0	0	0	0	46	48	47	38	38	0	55	47	41	0	36	0	53	37	0	50	46	212	BP
- + + +	(+)	43	42	28	25	0	0	0	0	0	0	0	0	0	60	57	61	31	50	0	54	61	42	0	44	0	46	50	0	50	47	206	
- + + +	(-)	56	57	71	70	0	0	0	0	0	0	0	0	0	36	42	38	68	50	0	45	41	42	0	52	0	52	50	0	40	50	215	C CC O
+ - - -	(+)	63	66	73	68	0	0	0	0	0	0	0	0	0	54	56	66	58	64	0	50	43	33	0	39	0	40	55	0	50	54	192	BP C CC NY
+ - - -	(-)	36	33	26	31	0	0	0	0	0	0	0	0	0	45	43	27	41	28	0	42	53	50	0	50	0	55	44	0	38	41	147	
+ - - +	(+)	52	50	52	42	0	0	0	0	0	0	0	0	0	54	43	31	52	40	0	47	46	33	0	65	0	51	39	0	61	48	217	
+ - - +	(-)	47	46	47	57	0	0	0	0	0	0	0	0	0	41	46	68	47	60	0	52	53	60	0	34	0	43	52	0	48	48	219	NY
+ - + -	(+)	40	47	36	53	0	0	0	0	0	0	0	0	0	46	53	45	45	46	0	61	42	57	0	39	0	51	57	0	64	48	186	
+ - + -	(-)	60	52	63	46	0	0	0	0	0	0	0	0	0	44	53	54	50	53	0	38	57	42	0	56	0	44	35	0	35	48	188	
+ - + +	(+)	50	53	45	63	0	0	0	0	0	0	0	0	0	49	42	38	70	35	0	52	44	21	0	48	0	47	51	0	30	48	228	O
+ - + +	(-)	50	43	55	41	0	0	0	0	0	0	0	0	0	44	52	52	25	57	0	47	55	57	0	45	0	52	44	0	50	47	226	
+ + - -	(+)	53	58	51	41	0	0	0	0	0	0	0	0	0	54	50	62	53	33	0	58	51	60	0	51	0	66	63	0	47	54	227	SU
+ + - -	(-)	46	41	48	52	0	0	0	0	0	0	0	0	0	42	50	37	46	66	0	41	48	40	0	62	0	32	31	0	52	44	184	OJ
+ + - +	(+)	66	66	56	63	0	0	0	0	0	0	0	0	0	48	53	50	65	56	0	50	54	55	0	37	0	54	55	0	40	55	251	BP
+ + - +	(-)	35	33	43	36	0	0	0	0	0	0	0	0	0	48	43	50	33	37	0	44	48	44	0	54	0	43	37	0	60	42	192	O
+ + + -	(+)	43	68	38	56	0	0	0	0	0	0	0	0	0	50	56	55	50	50	0	36	50	28	0	37	0	52	46	0	10	50	211	BP
+ + + -	(-)	50	31	61	44	0	0	0	0	0	0	0	0	0	43	40	38	45	50	0	59	50	71	0	42	0	47	42	0	80	46	196	SF W

Figure 8.8: Continued

		BO	BP	C	CC	CD	CL	CO	CP	FC	GC	HO	JY	LB	LC	LH	NY	O	OJ	PB	PL	S	SF	SV	SM	SP	SU	TB	TR	W	T%	T#	
++++	(+)	50	42	53	41	0	0	0	0	0	0	0	0	0	48	48	23	12	42	0	53	41	50	0	51	0	45	26	0	28	44	171	
++++	(−)	50	57	46	50	0	0	0	0	0	0	0	0	0	58	39	64	50	50	0	40	85	50	0	66	0	71	68	0	57	52	201	O TB
−−−−	(+)	33	25	25	50	0	0	0	0	0	0	0	0	0	71	87	0	40	0	0	40	14	50	0	16	0	28	50	0	0	57	59	LC LH S SM SU W
−−−−	(−)	66	75	60	33	0	0	0	0	0	0	0	0	0	28	12	50	60	100	0	71	37	57	0	73	0	60	42	0	77	41	43	BO BP C
−−−+	(+)	50	40	40	50	0	0	0	0	0	0	0	0	0	50	46	50	80	0	0	28	56	28	0	26	0	40	0	0	11	53	83	OJ PL SM
−−−+	(−)	50	37	27	55	0	0	0	0	0	0	0	0	0	50	53	50	14	50	0	40	52	57	0	37	0	63	100	0	40	43	68	O
−−+−	(+)	50	62	50	44	0	0	0	0	0	0	0	0	0	52	42	85	50	85	0	47	71	71	0	62	0	36	41	0	60	44	70	
−−+−	(−)	40	66	50	55	0	0	0	0	0	0	0	0	0	46	25	44	20	37	0	44	80	66	0	22	0	42	0	0	21	55	86	C O SF TB
−−++	(+)	60	27	50	44	0	0	0	0	0	0	0	0	0	53	75	55	80	50	0	55	20	33	0	77	0	57	58	0	78	43	80	BP S SF
−−++	(−)	80	41	33	66	0	0	0	0	0	0	0	0	0	65	50	46	33	50	0	75	66	20	0	50	0	71	46	0	37	55	102	LH O SM
−+−−	(+)	20	58	58	33	0	0	0	0	0	0	0	0	0	34	50	46	66	40	0	25	33	20	0	50	0	21	46	0	50	39	102	BO CC O PL S SF SU
−+−−	(−)	66	50	72	45	0	0	0	0	0	0	0	0	0	60	50	54	33	20	0	60	66	28	0	50	0	50	53	0	28	52	72	
−+−+	(+)	33	50	27	54	0	0	0	0	0	0	0	0	0	36	50	45	66	57	0	58	58	60	0	63	0	39	16	0	57	45	103	BO C O S
−+−+	(−)	57	83	54	77	0	0	0	0	0	0	0	0	0	48	39	50	50	20	0	55	41	40	0	27	0	60	75	0	40	48	90	OJ SF TB
−++−	(+)	71	61	66	75	0	0	0	0	0	0	0	0	0	66	50	50	75	42	0	50	52	50	0	61	0	55	16	0	53	48	104	CC TB
−++−	(−)	28	66	90	80	0	0	0	0	0	0	0	0	0	30	43	33	40	40	0	50	35	25	0	30	0	80	60	0	66	49	104	BP
−+++	(+)	50	33	10	20	0	0	0	0	0	0	0	0	0	50	25	25	80	57	0	50	42	57	0	70	0	52	33	0	33	43	89	LC NY TB
−+++	(−)	50	50	62	41	0	0	0	0	0	0	0	0	0	51	32	41	55	16	0	57	56	62	0	40	0	43	50	0	42	48	91	BO C CC O W
+−−−	(+)	44	37	37	58	0	0	0	0	0	0	0	0	0	45	56	58	44	83	0	44	43	43	0	60	0	55	37	0	57	48	86	BP C CC NY
+−−−	(−)	12	33	25	53	0	0	0	0	0	0	0	0	0	30	43	25	50	33	0	60	41	66	0	33	0	44	0	0	70	40	68	SU
+−−+	(+)	57	66	75	46	0	0	0	0	0	0	0	0	0	50	56	75	50	66	0	40	58	44	0	53	0	40	30	0	30	56	100	SM
+−−+	(−)	57	60	36	54	0	0	0	0	0	0	0	0	0	57	47	10	62	60	0	53	45	42	0	45	0	42	40	0	16	47	100	OJ
+−+−	(+)	25	87	66	50	0	0	0	0	0	0	0	0	0	56	57	100	0	75	0	66	62	66	0	64	0	26	50	0	57	58	72	TB W
+−+−	(−)	42	30	63	45	0	0	0	0	0	0	0	0	0	34	47	90	40	0	0	90	50	60	0	28	0	66	37	0	42	38	101	BO BP C NY OJ SM
+−++	(+)	57	55	53	40	0	0	0	0	0	0	0	0	0	52	54	55	55	20	0	50	50	60	0	66	0	45	30	0	66	51	97	
+−++	(−)	42	44	46	60	0	0	0	0	0	0	0	0	0	47	45	44	80	50	0	9	52	42	0	36	0	23	68	0	33	45	98	NY
++−−	(+)	88	50	75	60	0	0	0	0	0	0	0	0	0	51	45	40	37	50	0	55	52	42	0	60	0	52	25	0	45	54	120	PL SU
++−−	(−)	11	50	25	40	0	0	0	0	0	0	0	0	0	43	54	60	62	50	0	44	41	57	0	40	0	56	44	0	55	43	89	BP TB W
++−+	(+)	44	70	33	57	0	0	0	0	0	0	0	0	0	54	60	28	46	42	0	50	57	33	0	61	0	47	53	0	0	49	124	BO C TB
++−+	(−)	55	30	66	42	0	0	0	0	0	0	0	0	0	44	41	57	16	57	0	50	42	66	0	33	0	44	30	0	40	46	99	
+++−	(+)	42	53	50	28	0	0	0	0	0	0	0	0	0	54	56	36	36	42	0	33	52	80	0	53	0	40	30	0	57	44	105	BP
+++−	(−)	57	46	50	71	0	0	0	0	0	0	0	0	0	56	57	63	50	50	0	66	55	100	0	46	0	59	69	0	40	52	100	C SF W
++−+	(+)	25	36	16	53	0	0	0	0	0	0	0	0	0	43	42	100	40	0	0	33	37	33	0	28	0	26	37	0	42	58	92	
+−−−	(−)	42	41	63	54	0	0	0	0	0	0	0	0	0	42	61	50	42	44	0	42	61	75	0	36	0	45	50	0	66	51	107	CC O PL SF TB
+−−+	(+)	57	25	52	46	0	0	0	0	0	0	0	0	0	66	57	46	62	50	0	81	54	44	0	66	0	48	16	0	45	54	86	BO C NY OJ PL SF
+−+−	(−)	75	41	63	54	0	0	0	0	0	0	0	0	0	40	22	53	44	75	0	60	45	55	0	47	0	40	44	0	42	42	56	BO SU
+−++	(+)	25	58	36	45	0	0	0	0	0	0	0	0	0	52	77	42	44	25	0	40	52	80	0	47	0	56	44	0	57	46	99	BP TB W
+−++	(−)	55	46	58	37	0	0	0	0	0	0	0	0	0	33	42	53	50	37	0	51	55	0	0	63	0	36	60	0	30	50	87	SF
++−−	(+)	44	53	41	62	0	0	0	0	0	0	0	0	0	51	66	41	57	57	0	42	40	100	0	46	0	36	87	0	36	52	120	BO LC PL SM
++−−	(−)	55	44	57	46	0	0	0	0	0	0	0	0	0	48	28	50	25	42	0	42	40	100	0	46	0	36	60	0	33	44	93	TB
++−+	(+)	44	55	42	53	0	0	0	0	0	0	0	0	0	50	42	40	100	66	0	72	40	50	0	88	0	54	87	0	36	52	100	LH O
++−+	(−)	16	75	75	40	0	0	0	0	0	0	0	0	0	40	52	60	0	33	0	36	60	57	0	55	0	11	46	0	54	44	109	LH SF
+++−	(+)	83	25	36	72	0	0	0	0	0	0	0	0	0	55	57	54	80	75	0	45	57	42	0	40	0	54	12	0	60	52	96	LH O
+++−	(−)	66	35	54	27	0	0	0	0	0	0	0	0	0	41	38	45	20	25	0	63	45	57	0	55	0	52	53	0	40	52	84	SF
+++−	(+)	33	57	22	26	0	0	0	0	0	0	0	0	0	42	35	50	35	60	0	36	50	42	0	40	0	47	60	0	40	44	97	BP C O OJ PL SM TB
+++−	(−)	55	47	77	68	0	0	0	0	0	0	0	0	0	55	37	16	42	12	0	41	50	33	0	29	0	56	42	0	0	46	83	BO
++−+	(+)	44	52	61	55	0	0	0	0	0	0	0	0	0	44	62	57	44	75	0	40	53	25	0	60	0	37	60	0	60	55	118	BO CC O OJ
++−−	(−)	71	66	61	55	0	0	0	0	0	0	0	0	0	62	20	50	57	87	0	50	25	33	0	37	0	54	60	0	30	40	106	W
++−+	(+)	28	33	38	44	0	0	0	0	0	0	0	0	0	61	62	20	50	75	0	42	35	33	0	54	0	54	35	0	33	49	102	BO BP NY OJ
++−+	(−)	50	47	57	57	0	0	0	0	0	0	0	0	0	38	31	80	50	25	0	57	64	66	0	40	0	39	57	0	66	49	111	OJ NY SF W

Figure 8.8: Continued

Pat	+/−	BO	BP	C	CC	CD	CL	CO	CP	FC	GC	HO	JY	LB	LC	LH	NY	O	OJ	PB	PL	S	SF	SV	SM	SP	SU	TB	TR	W	T%	T#	------ 65% ------
++++-+	(+)	66	54	42	54	0	0	0	0	0	0	0	0	0	55	52	30	50	66	0	62	43	75	0	43	0	71	54	0	50	56	108	BO NY OJ SF SU
++++-+	(−)	33	45	57	45	0	0	0	0	0	0	0	0	0	41	47	50	50	33	0	37	56	25	0	50	0	23	36	0	50	41	80	
++++-+	(+)	45	50	55	68	0	0	0	0	0	0	0	0	0	36	38	75	50	66	0	50	43	80	0	48	0	53	68	0	50	49	124	CC NY O TB
++++-+	(−)	54	50	44	31	0	0	0	0	0	0	0	0	0	58	57	25	25	66	0	50	56	60	0	48	0	46	31	0	50	48	121	OJ SF
++++-+	(+)	50	63	53	45	0	0	0	0	0	0	0	0	0	58	40	71	44	42	0	30	56	60	0	42	0	58	72	0	50	53	104	NY TB
++++−−	(−)	50	36	46	45	0	0	0	0	0	0	0	0	0	34	28	40	55	57	0	69	37	40	0	57	0	41	27	0	50	44	88	PL
++++++	(+)	28	70	37	71	0	0	0	0	0	0	0	0	0	45	71	40	90	71	0	62	40	40	0	66	0	55	41	0	100	57	120	BP CC LH O OJ SF SM
+++++−	(−)	71	29	62	28	0	0	0	0	0	0	0	0	0	51	28	40	10	28	0	37	60	25	0	33	0	40	50	0	100	40	85	BO W
+++++−	(+)	42	66	50	50	0	0	0	0	0	0	0	0	0	48	61	72	57	57	0	33	44	25	0	42	0	47	61	0	25	50	101	BP NY
+++++−	(−)	42	33	50	50	0	0	0	0	0	0	0	0	0	46	38	27	42	42	0	66	55	75	0	57	0	52	30	0	50	46	93	PL SF
++++++	(+)	57	27	57	60	0	0	0	0	0	0	0	0	0	40	43	0	50	50	0	71	30	75	0	47	0	47	20	0	50	43	75	PL SF
−−−−+	(+)	42	72	42	20	0	0	0	0	0	0	0	0	0	55	50	75	100	50	0	28	69	25	0	47	0	52	60	0	0	52	89	BP NY O S W
−−−−+	(−)	50	33	33	66	0	0	0	0	0	0	0	0	0	50	100	0	66	33	0	0	66	100	0	0	0	60	33	0	0	51	22	CC LH O PL S SU
−−−−+	(+)	50	66	66	33	0	0	0	0	0	0	0	0	0	50	0	0	33	0	0	33	50	50	0	75	0	25	66	0	100	46	20	BP C TB
−−−−+	(−)	33	33	100	66	0	0	0	0	0	0	0	0	0	30	28	0	100	0	0	100	50	50	0	25	0	30	33	0	100	61	36	CC LC LH PL SM SU
−−−−+	(+)	66	66	100	33	0	0	0	0	0	0	0	0	0	46	62	66	0	0	0	50	55	25	0	50	0	50	66	0	0	38	23	BO BP C O TB
−−−−+	(+)	100	50	0	33	0	0	0	0	0	0	0	0	0	50	37	33	33	100	0	50	44	75	0	50	0	50	50	0	100	44	30	BO NY
−−−+−	(+)	0	0	50	66	0	0	0	0	0	0	0	0	0	50	14	33	0	33	0	60	66	100	0	18	0	33	71	0	28	55	38	C CC O SF TB W
−−−+−	(−)	33	33	50	50	0	0	0	0	0	0	0	0	0	50	85	66	50	28	0	0	83	100	0	81	0	66	100	0	71	62	29	S SF
−−−+−	(+)	100	40	66	50	0	0	0	0	0	0	0	0	0	53	22	60	50	25	0	33	50	50	0	25	0	75	50	0	33	52	51	BO C LH NY O SM
−−−+−	(−)	0	25	50	75	0	0	0	0	0	0	0	0	0	41	45	25	20	50	0	66	50	71	0	25	0	70	42	0	66	52	45	BO O PL SU
−−−+−	(+)	50	20	40	75	0	0	0	0	0	0	0	0	0	22	60	50	75	0	0	40	33	100	0	33	0	30	0	0	50	44	38	OJ W
−−−+−	(−)	33	40	75	25	0	0	0	0	0	0	0	0	0	84	33	75	100	0	0	60	50	100	0	64	0	37	85	0	54	51	36	BO C NY O S SM
−−+−+	(+)	50	60	60	25	0	0	0	0	0	0	0	0	0	7	66	50	100	0	0	75	50	50	0	25	0	33	14	0	63	45	32	BP CC PL SF
−−+−+	(−)	50	60	40	80	0	0	0	0	0	0	0	0	0	33	44	50	50	100	0	25	57	66	0	50	0	66	20	0	66	49	48	CC TB
−−+−+	(+)	100	71	85	66	0	0	0	0	0	0	0	0	0	62	37	66	33	0	0	40	16	0	0	50	0	33	71	0	75	55	40	BO BP LH OJ SF
−−+−+	(−)	0	28	14	33	0	0	0	0	0	0	0	0	0	37	62	33	0	50	0	33	83	100	0	75	0	66	0	0	25	43	40	LC NY O PL TB
−−+−−	(+)	50	75	66	66	0	0	0	0	0	0	0	0	0	46	37	66	33	66	0	66	50	71	0	25	0	30	57	0	33	45	36	BP CC LH OJ SU W
−−++−	(−)	50	25	50	50	0	0	0	0	0	0	0	0	0	46	50	66	50	50	0	33	16	0	0	75	0	66	25	0	75	43	40	BO BP C CC NY PL
−−++−	(+)	50	25	50	50	0	0	0	0	0	0	0	0	0	37	62	33	66	0	0	85	28	0	0	75	0	30	57	0	25	45	31	O S SF SU
−−++−	(−)	50	25	50	33	0	0	0	0	0	0	0	0	0	46	50	66	100	50	0	14	50	60	0	25	0	70	42	0	66	45	46	BP O SM
−−++−	(+)	100	75	100	66	0	0	0	0	0	0	0	0	0	25	66	100	75	100	0	80	71	60	0	20	0	30	100	0	75	52	53	NY OJ PL SF SU
−−++−	(−)	33	20	40	60	0	0	0	0	0	0	0	0	0	55	45	25	0	50	0	20	57	50	0	40	0	30	0	0	25	37	34	PL TB W
−+−−+	(+)	66	50	37	40	0	0	0	0	0	0	0	0	0	45	37	50	75	100	0	80	50	50	0	83	0	70	0	0	50	57	52	BO BP C CC LH NY
−+−−+	(−)	75	25	62	60	0	0	0	0	0	0	0	0	0	52	50	25	75	25	0	40	40	100	0	60	0	72	50	0	37	48	48	BO O OJ PL
−+−−+	(+)	25	40	16	50	0	0	0	0	0	0	0	0	0	47	57	25	56	66	0	42	33	33	0	16	0	18	55	0	62	37	49	BO NY SU
−+−−+	(−)	100	75	50	57	0	0	0	0	0	0	0	0	0	55	57	75	75	40	0	80	57	66	0	42	0	37	55	0	33	60	63	BO C O PL SF SM SU
−+−−−	(+)	60	72	25	42	0	0	0	0	0	0	0	0	0	33	44	50	50	50	0	20	50	50	0	57	0	62	44	0	66	37	39	NY OJ
−+−+−	(−)	0	27	75	50	0	0	0	0	0	0	0	0	0	50	50	50	50	50	0	60	50	50	0	50	0	64	33	0	66	54	57	BO BP C LC PL
−+−+−	(+)	0	42	75	50	0	0	0	0	0	0	0	0	0	75	33	33	0	100	0	60	33	0	0	50	0	35	33	0	100	45	47	OJ SF W
−+−+−	(−)	100	57	75	50	0	0	0	0	0	0	0	0	0	25	62	66	100	0	0	40	33	0	0	50	0	62	66	0	0	49	45	BP
−+−+−	(+)	0	42	50	50	0	0	0	0	0	0	0	0	0	33	25	66	50	100	0	100	66	100	0	50	0	37	33	0	50	47	43	C W
−+−+−	(−)	50	100	100	50	0	0	0	0	0	0	0	0	0	62	100	50	100	50	0	100	62	66	0	50	0	50	50	0	0	48	43	BO LH OJ W
−+−+−	(+)	50	50	37	40	0	0	0	0	0	0	0	0	0	45	37	50	0	0	0	0	37	40	0	0	0	50	50	0	50	50	44	NY O S SF TB
−++−+	(+)	66	50	62	60	0	0	0	0	0	0	0	0	0	58	42	50	66	100	0	80	60	40	0	83	0	50	66	0	100	64	44	BP C NY OJ PL SM
−++−+	(−)	25	40	83	50	0	0	0	0	0	0	0	0	0	41	57	75	25	66	0	0	40	0	0	16	0	60	0	0	33	33	23	BP O OJ PL SM SU
−++−+	(+)	75	83	16	50	0	0	0	0	0	0	0	0	0	57	37	25	56	40	0	0	50	50	0	66	0	60	66	0	100	59	51	BO C O PL SM
−++−−	(−)	25	16	50	42	0	0	0	0	0	0	0	0	0	50	55	50	50	50	0	40	53	50	0	50	0	35	33	0	33	37	32	S SF
−++−−	(+)	60	72	25	50	0	0	0	0	0	0	0	0	0	33	42	40	25	50	0	60	57	50	0	57	0	64	44	0	66	54	57	BO BP C LC O PL SM
−+++−	(−)	60	50	40	40	0	0	0	0	0	0	0	0	0	12	40	40	100	0	0	75	53	50	0	28	0	75	25	0	50	41	45	OJ PL SU
−+++−	(+)	40	60	60	60	0	0	0	0	0	0	0	0	0	87	60	40	40	0	0	25	46	50	0	71	0	16	75	0	100	53	53	LH SM TB W
−+++−	(−)	42	50	66	57	0	0	0	0	0	0	0	0	0	61	61	44	0	50	0	75	46	50	0	40	0	57	0	0	66	53	54	C PL
−+++−	(−)	57	50	33	42	0	0	0	0	0	0	0	0	0	38	38	55	100	50	0	25	40	100	0	60	0	42	0	0	33	46	47	O SF

Figure 8.8:   Continued

	sign	BO	BP	C	CC	CD	CL	CO	CP	FC	GC	HO	JY	LB	LC	LH	NY	O	OJ	PB	PL	S	SF	SM	SP	SU	TB	TR	W	T%	T#	
-+-+-+	(+)	0	50	100	25	0	0	0	0	0	0	0	0	0	50	40	33	100	50	0	83	28	40	0	42	100	0	0	42	47	34	C O PL SM TB
-+-+-+	(-)	100	50	0	75	0	0	0	0	0	0	0	0	0	25	66	50	50	50	0	16	71	60	42	57	60	0	0	42	47	34	BO CC NY S
-+-+-+	(+)	66	33	57	80	0	0	0	0	0	0	0	0	0	50	77	66	50	50	0	50	63	50	57	54	60	0	100	0	59	58	BO CC LH NY W
-+-+-+	(-)	33	66	28	20	0	0	0	0	0	0	0	0	0	50	22	33	50	50	0	50	36	33	0	36	40	0	100	0	38	37	BP
-+-+-+	(+)	25	50	25	16	0	0	0	0	0	0	0	0	0	60	44	0	40	66	0	42	66	33	42	37	50	0	0	0	49	48	OJ S W
-+-+-+	(-)	75	50	75	83	0	0	0	0	0	0	0	0	0	35	55	100	60	33	0	57	33	66	57	50	62	0	0	60	48	47	BO C CC NY
-+-+-+	(+)	66	62	50	66	0	0	0	0	0	0	0	0	0	68	50	25	33	66	0	50	50	14	0	66	50	0	0	60	56	50	BO LC OJ PL SU
-+-+-+	(-)	33	37	50	33	0	0	0	0	0	0	0	0	0	31	50	25	62	33	100	37	50	71	0	33	50	0	0	40	41	37	SM
-+-+-+	(+)	75	60	57	0	0	0	0	0	0	0	0	0	0	66	66	20	33	100	0	60	33	50	50	47	40	0	0	60	54	65	BO LC LH OJ
-+-+-+	(-)	25	40	42	100	0	0	0	0	0	0	0	0	0	33	58	66	66	0	0	40	66	66	50	42	60	0	0	40	43	52	CC NY O SF
-+-+-+	(+)	0	50	50	33	0	0	0	0	0	0	0	0	0	56	58	83	60	66	0	50	28	75	50	70	25	0	0	40	53	53	NY OJ SF SU
-+-+-+	(-)	100	50	50	66	0	0	0	0	0	0	0	0	0	37	41	16	40	33	0	60	71	25	40	30	75	0	0	60	45	45	BO CC S TB
-+-+-+	(+)	50	25	33	22	0	0	0	0	0	0	0	0	0	63	50	25	33	50	0	55	55	66	53	45	45	0	0	50	46	58	CC NY O OJ
-+-+-+	(-)	40	66	60	50	0	0	0	0	0	0	0	0	0	54	20	75	50	66	0	20	44	42	66	54	71	0	25	0	50	58	SF
-+-+-+	(+)	60	33	50	50	0	0	0	0	0	0	0	0	0	45	80	25	33	33	0	80	50	0	33	45	28	0	75	0	50	50	BP NY SM TB
-+-+-+	(-)	25	71	66	77	0	0	0	0	0	0	0	0	0	58	83	50	83	100	0	75	50	100	63	50	50	0	0	0	62	66	LH PL SF W
-+-+-+	(+)	75	28	25	40	0	0	0	0	0	0	0	0	0	41	16	85	16	0	0	25	50	42	36	46	50	0	50	0	36	38	BP CC LH O OJ PL SF
-+-+-+	(-)	50	71	66	60	0	0	0	0	0	0	0	0	0	52	50	14	40	66	0	75	33	75	25	77	50	0	50	0	55	59	BO
-+-+-+	(+)	25	28	33	60	0	0	0	0	0	0	0	0	0	41	50	50	14	43	0	75	33	66	57	53	11	0	50	0	41	44	PL SF W
-+-+-+	(-)	100	37	66	50	0	0	0	0	0	0	0	0	0	34	44	50	40	33	0	25	33	0	37	55	25	0	0	0	41	38	BO C PL W
-+-+-+	(+)	0	62	33	0	0	0	0	0	0	0	0	0	0	66	66	75	100	66	0	0	66	0	50	44	75	0	100	0	54	50	NY O OJ S TB W
-+-+-+	(-)	0	0	33	33	0	0	0	0	0	0	0	0	0	55	100	25	33	100	0	0	83	50	0	70	66	0	100	0	66	37	LC LH SM SU TB
-+-+-+	(+)	100	100	100	66	0	0	0	0	0	0	0	0	0	20	0	60	66	66	0	100	16	66	100	30	33	0	0	0	33	19	BO BP C OJ PL SM
-+-+-+	(-)	100	71	25	75	0	0	0	0	0	0	0	0	0	30	25	40	33	0	0	75	30	33	66	25	50	0	75	0	47	41	CC LC LH O SU
-+-+-+	(+)	0	28	66	66	0	0	0	0	0	0	0	0	0	69	75	66	50	50	0	25	60	42	33	75	25	0	0	0	46	40	CC PL SU W
-+-+-+	(-)	25	25	33	66	0	0	0	0	0	0	0	0	0	50	54	40	33	66	0	66	50	25	25	80	0	0	66	0	45	40	BO BP C O SF SM TB
-+-+-+	(+)	75	75	66	33	0	0	0	0	0	0	0	0	0	45	45	50	50	0	0	33	50	75	75	16	100	0	0	33	54	47	BO BP S
-+-+-+	(-)	33	83	33	57	0	0	0	0	0	0	0	0	0	43	40	50	25	40	0	25	36	0	28	60	42	0	0	0	48	48	O PL SF SM W
-+-+-+	(+)	50	16	42	42	0	0	0	0	0	0	0	0	0	56	60	50	75	60	100	0	0	0	71	40	57	0	100	0	51	51	CC LC OJ S SF SU
-+-+-+	(-)	50	42	50	80	0	0	0	0	0	0	0	0	0	80	60	50	60	0	0	50	66	100	50	70	44	0	0	25	60	56	CC S
-+-+-+	(+)	50	57	50	20	0	0	0	0	0	0	0	0	0	20	50	50	25	0	0	50	20	0	50	20	0	0	40	0	36	34	OJ SF TB
-+-+-+	(-)	50	42	66	33	0	0	0	0	0	0	0	0	0	65	36	42	66	66	0	55	66	66	62	58	55	0	0	40	53	64	CC PL SF
-+-+-+	(+)	50	60	71	66	0	0	0	0	0	0	0	0	0	35	54	57	42	0	0	44	33	25	37	41	14	0	50	0	45	54	BP NY O
-+-+-+	(-)	50	40	40	80	0	0	0	0	0	0	0	0	0	42	50	33	33	33	0	33	62	50	50	54	100	0	0	50	49	53	BO C CC NY O PL SF
-+-+-+	(+)	50	14	25	66	0	0	0	0	0	0	0	0	0	57	35	40	66	25	0	75	60	62	0	45	50	0	50	0	54	45	BO CC NY OJ SM
-+-+-+	(-)	85	85	37	20	0	0	0	0	0	0	0	0	0	56	57	75	66	75	0	25	36	37	33	54	25	0	0	0	49	54	C PL SU TB
-+-+-+	(+)	20	50	66	33	0	0	0	0	0	0	0	0	0	43	50	25	33	0	0	33	44	75	75	41	58	0	66	0	54	44	BO PL SM SU W
-+-+-+	(-)	33	60	42	66	0	0	0	0	0	0	0	0	0	50	40	66	100	100	0	66	55	33	25	50	14	0	33	0	53	36	CC C OJ
-+-+-+	(+)	66	50	61	75	0	0	0	0	0	0	0	0	0	25	50	33	50	0	100	37	33	25	62	63	33	0	0	33	43	50	BO LC NY OJ PL SM
-+-+-+	(-)	40	50	42	62	0	0	0	0	0	0	0	0	0	75	62	66	50	50	0	85	50	37	37	55	42	0	0	0	44	43	BP CC
-+-+-+	(+)	100	50	66	33	0	0	0	0	0	0	0	0	0	33	80	0	0	0	0	62	66	0	37	44	71	0	50	0	56	45	BO BO CC NY PL SU
-+-+-+	(-)	33	66	33	66	0	0	0	0	0	0	0	0	0	57	62	80	0	0	0	14	50	66	0	71	57	0	100	0	43	43	CC BO C
-+-+-+	(+)	83	40	75	62	0	0	0	0	0	0	0	0	0	36	42	37	33	0	0	85	55	16	81	23	42	0	0	66	42	64	BO SM TB W
-+-+-+	(+)	16	60	25	37	0	0	0	0	0	0	0	0	0	52	58	66	75	100	0	75	33	0	18	54	45	0	0	0	49	50	BO NY O PL
-+-+-+	(+)	25	42	61	0	0	0	0	0	0	0	0	0	0	43	50	25	44	0	0	40	62	0	64	50	55	0	33	0	49	58	BP
-+-+-+	(-)	75	33	57	38	0	0	0	0	0	0	0	0	0	50	54	50	50	0	0	28	37	0	28	54	33	0	0	33	43	54	NY SF
-+-+-+	(+)	80	50	50	80	0	0	0	0	0	0	0	0	0	47	27	50	80	66	0	71	37	100	50	45	66	0	33	0	52	56	BO CC O OJ PL SF TB

Figure 8.8: Continued

Figure 8.8: Continued

		BO	BP	C	CC	CD	CL	CO	CP	FC	GC	HO	JY	LB	LC	LH	NY	O	OJ	PB	PL	S	SF	SV	SM	SP	SU	TB	TR	W	T%	T#			65%			
--+++	(+)	100	0	33	100	0	0	0	0	0	0	0	0	0	83	50	0	0	100	0	0	66	0	0	0	0	33	0	0	0	52	19	BO	CC	LC	OJ	S	
--++-	(-)	0	100	66	0	0	0	0	0	0	0	0	0	0	16	50	100	0	0	0	0	33	0	0	100	0	33	0	0	0	44	16	BP	C	NY	SM	O	
--++++	(+)	100	50	100	100	0	0	0	0	0	0	0	0	0	42	57	0	100	33	0	100	0	100	100	0	0	50	100	0	50	64	32	BO	C	CC	O	PL	S
--++--	(-)	0	50	0	0	0	0	0	0	0	0	0	0	0	57	42	100	0	66	0	0	0	0	0	0	0	25	0	0	50	34	17	NY	OJ				
--+++	(+)	100	100	50	66	0	0	0	0	0	0	0	0	0	87	100	66	50	0	0	0	0	0	44	55	0	66	66	0	0	60	29	BO	BP	CC	LC	LH	NY
--++-	(-)	0	50	33	50	0	0	0	0	0	0	0	0	0	12	0	33	50	100	0	0	0	0	0	55	0	33	33	0	100	39	19	OJ	W				
--+-++	(+)	0	75	33	50	0	0	0	0	0	0	0	0	0	33	0	100	0	33	0	0	100	0	55	50	0	33	33	0	0	44	19	BP	PL	TB			
--+---	(-)	100	25	66	50	0	0	0	0	0	0	0	0	0	100	100	100	0	66	0	0	50	100	0	0	0	50	100	0	0	55	20	BO	CC	LC	LH	NY	OJ
--+--	(-)	100	75	0	0	0	0	0	0	0	0	0	0	0	45	100	33	0	0	0	33	25	0	0	50	0	25	25	0	0	40	16	BO	BP	LH	W		
--+-+	(+)	0	25	100	100	0	0	0	0	0	0	0	0	0	0	0	66	0	66	0	66	75	0	0	50	0	50	75	0	0	57	23	C	CC	NY	O	PL	S
--+--	(-)	0	100	100	0	0	0	0	0	0	0	0	0	0	33	60	100	50	100	0	66	0	0	100	0	0	50	50	0	100	70	22	BP	C	CC	NY	OJ	SM
--+++	(+)	0	60	50	100	0	0	0	0	0	0	0	0	0	66	40	50	100	50	0	100	40	0	0	0	0	0	0	0	0	29	9	LC	O	PL	S	SM	
--+--	(-)	0	40	33	0	0	0	0	0	0	0	0	0	0	40	100	0	0	50	0	0	0	0	100	0	0	100	60	0	100	65	26	BO	CC	O	PL	S	SM
--+++	(+)	100	100	100	0	0	0	0	0	0	0	0	0	0	85	75	25	0	50	0	16	16	0	0	0	0	71	0	0	0	58	31	BO	BP	LC	LH	PL	SM
--+--	(-)	0	0	33	66	0	0	0	0	0	0	0	0	0	14	25	75	50	50	0	83	83	0	0	33	0	14	100	0	0	39	21	CC	NY	S	TB		
--+++	(+)	100	66	0	33	0	0	0	0	0	0	0	0	0	28	0	0	25	50	0	0	0	0	33	0	0	25	0	40	60	34	16	BO	BP	SU			
--+-+	(+)	0	33	100	66	0	0	0	0	0	0	0	0	0	71	100	100	0	50	0	100	75	0	66	0	0	33	75	0	60	63	29	C	CC	LH	NY	PL	
--+--	(-)	0	66	66	50	0	0	0	0	0	0	0	0	0	66	50	0	0	0	0	0	0	0	50	0	0	42	0	40	0	41	16	BP	C	LC	OJ	S	W
--+-+	(+)	66	33	33	50	0	0	0	0	0	0	0	0	0	33	50	60	100	0	0	100	25	100	0	50	0	57	0	0	0	50	26	BO	O	PL	SF		
--+--	(-)	0	100	0	100	0	0	0	0	0	0	0	0	0	40	50	0	0	100	0	0	25	100	0	0	0	33	100	0	66	52	18	O	PL	SF	SM	TB	W
--+++	(+)	50	100	60	66	0	0	0	0	0	0	0	0	0	57	60	66	0	50	0	100	71	0	66	33	0	66	0	0	100	63	31	BP	CC	NY	PL	S	SM
--+--	(-)	50	0	20	33	0	0	0	0	0	0	0	0	0	42	40	33	0	0	0	0	0	0	33	0	0	42	0	0	0	34	17	SF					
--+-+	(+)	25	50	33	0	0	0	0	0	0	0	0	0	0	54	80	0	66	100	0	28	100	57	100	50	0	33	0	0	0	47	23	LH	O	OJ	SF	SU	
--+--	(-)	75	50	66	100	0	0	0	0	0	0	0	0	0	36	20	33	0	33	0	42	0	100	50	50	0	66	0	0	0	50	24	BO	C	CC	PL	SU	
--+++	(+)	100	75	0	0	0	0	0	0	0	0	0	0	0	66	42	33	0	100	0	100	0	0	0	0	0	0	60	0	60	53	21	BO	BP	LC	OJ	PL	SU
--+--	(-)	0	25	100	100	0	0	0	0	0	0	0	0	0	33	57	0	100	0	0	0	0	0	0	0	0	0	0	40	0	41	16	C	CC	O	S		
--+-+	(+)	66	66	40	0	0	0	0	0	0	0	0	0	0	90	71	0	0	33	0	75	33	50	20	0	0	37	100	0	33	55	35	BO	BP	LH	OJ	PL	TB
--+--	(-)	33	33	60	100	0	0	0	0	0	0	0	0	0	10	14	100	66	66	0	25	66	50	80	66	0	50	0	66	0	41	26	CC	NY	O	SM	W	
--+-+	(+)	0	0	0	33	0	0	0	0	0	0	0	0	0	66	50	100	0	100	100	100	100	0	50	50	0	60	25	0	25	53	25	LC	NY	O	OJ	PL	SF
--+--	(-)	0	100	66	0	0	0	0	0	0	0	0	0	0	16	50	0	0	0	0	0	75	0	50	0	0	40	75	0	0	44	21	C	CC	S	TB		
--+++	(+)	66	50	100	75	0	0	0	0	0	0	0	0	0	25	20	0	0	0	0	50	33	0	33	33	0	33	60	0	0	45	26	BO	C	CC	NY	O	S
--+--	(-)	33	50	0	25	0	0	0	0	0	0	0	0	0	66	80	50	0	0	0	33	50	0	50	66	0	86	40	0	100	50	29	LC	LH	S	SF	SU	W
--+++	(+)	50	100	66	33	0	0	0	0	0	0	0	0	0	100	50	0	0	100	0	66	66	0	50	50	0	60	100	0	25	60	26	BO	BP	CC	LC	O	S
--+--	(-)	50	0	33	66	0	0	0	0	0	0	0	0	0	0	50	100	0	50	100	33	33	0	0	0	0	40	0	0	75	39	17	CC	NY	PL	SF	W	
--++-	(+)	33	87	50	100	0	0	0	0	0	0	0	0	0	60	0	100	0	50	100	0	66	0	0	0	0	55	0	0	0	71	32	BP	CC	LH	OJ	PL	S
--++-	(-)	66	12	50	0	0	0	0	0	0	0	0	0	0	40	0	0	0	50	0	0	33	0	0	0	0	44	100	0	100	28	13	BO	TB				
--+++	(+)	0	66	100	0	0	0	0	0	0	0	0	0	0	28	100	100	100	0	0	0	83	50	0	50	0	60	75	0	75	60	26	BP	C	LH	NY	O	S
--+--	(-)	0	33	0	100	0	0	0	0	0	0	0	0	0	57	0	0	0	0	0	100	16	50	50	50	0	40	0	0	0	34	15	CC	PL	SF	SU	W	
--+++	(+)	100	50	100	100	0	0	0	0	0	0	0	0	0	72	33	50	0	66	0	33	33	0	25	0	0	33	50	0	0	44	19	BO	C	CC	LH	S	SM
--+--	(-)	0	50	0	0	0	0	0	0	0	0	0	0	0	80	100	0	0	0	0	0	66	0	75	50	0	66	66	0	100	53	23	LC	LH	S	SU	TB	
--+++	(+)	0	0	0	0	0	0	0	0	0	0	0	0	0	80	50	33	100	0	0	0	50	0	75	50	0	50	0	0	0	82	19	LC	LH	NY			
--+--	(-)	100	0	0	0	0	0	0	0	0	0	0	0	0	20	50	66	0	100	0	50	50	0	0	0	0	0	50	0	0	17	4	BO					
--+-+	(+)	0	75	100	0	0	0	0	0	0	0	0	0	0	33	20	50	0	0	0	50	33	33	0	0	0	33	100	0	50	47	21	BO	BP	OJ	SM	TB	
--+--	(-)	100	25	0	100	0	0	0	0	0	0	0	0	0	66	80	50	0	100	0	50	80	50	0	0	0	66	0	0	0	47	21	CC	LC	LH	O	S	SU
--+-+	(+)	0	33	50	0	0	0	0	0	0	0	0	0	0	80	50	33	0	66	0	75	50	0	0	0	0	0	0	0	0	46	15	LC	O				
--+--	(-)	100	83	66	0	0	0	0	0	0	0	0	0	0	57	66	66	0	0	0	25	50	0	40	60	0	0	100	0	0	53	17	BO	BP	CC	NY	SM	TB
--++-	(+)	100	100	100	75	0	0	0	0	0	0	0	0	0	60	33	33	0	66	0	0	0	0	0	0	0	33	66	0	50	68	28	BO	BP	C	OJ	SM	TB
--+--	(-)	0	0	0	0	0	0	0	0	0	0	0	0	0	40	66	66	0	0	0	0	0	0	0	0	0	0	33	0	0	26	11	LH	NY	O			
--+++	(+)	66	50	50	33	0	0	0	0	0	0	0	0	0	60	37	50	0	100	0	66	33	0	0	0	0	66	0	0	0	54	31	BO	CC	O	PL	S	SU
--+--	(-)	33	50	50	66	0	0	0	0	0	0	0	0	0	40	50	50	0	0	0	33	66	0	50	50	0	33	0	0	100	43	25	CC	OJ	SF	W		

Figure 8.8: Continued

		BO	BP	C	CC	CD	CL	CO	CP	FC	GC	HO	JY	LB	LC	LH	NY	O	OJ	PB	PL	S	SF	SV	SM	SP	SU	TB	TR	W	T%	T#	65%
+--++-	(+)	50	0	33	66	0	0	0	0	0	0	0	0	0	40	71	33	50	0	0	100	66	100	0	40	0	50	0	0	33	49	26	CC LH PL S SF
+--++-	(+)	50	100	66	33	0	0	0	0	0	0	0	0	0	60	28	66	50	0	0	33	0	0	0	50	0	33	0	0	0	49	26	BP C NY W
+--++-	(+)	33	0	50	0	0	0	0	0	0	0	0	0	0	57	0	50	0	0	33	57	33	0	0	0	0	0	0	0	0	35	16	
+--++-	(+)	66	100	50	100	0	0	0	0	0	0	0	0	0	42	100	50	100	100	66	42	100	0	0	50	0	66	0	100	0	64	29	BO BP CC LH O OJ
+--++|	(-)	33	50	100	100	0	0	0	0	0	0	0	0	0	40	60	60	100	0	0	66	42	100	100	0	0	16	0	0	0	52	24	C CC O S SM
+--+|-	(-)	66	50	0	0	0	0	0	0	0	0	0	0	0	60	40	40	0	50	0	100	25	75	0	0	0	83	0	50	0	47	22	BO PL SF SU W
+--+|-	(-)	66	50	0	0	0	0	0	0	0	0	0	0	0	37	37	50	0	50	0	0	0	0	0	0	0	75	0	0	50	59	32	BO C PL S SM SU
+--+|-	(-)	33	50	0	50	0	0	0	0	0	0	0	0	0	62	62	50	0	50	0	66	40	66	0	0	0	12	0	50	0	38	21	
+--+|-	(+)	0	100	0	66	0	0	0	0	0	0	0	0	0	0	60	0	0	0	0	100	40	66	0	0	0	33	0	0	0	48	16	BP CC SF W
+--|+-	(+)	100	0	0	33	0	0	0	0	0	0	0	0	0	0	40	100	0	100	0	100	60	33	0	0	0	33	0	0	0	51	17	BO LC NY OJ PL SU
+--|+-	(+)	0	0	0	50	0	0	0	0	0	0	0	0	0	75	25	0	0	100	60	50	25	0	0	75	0	33	0	0	33	47	16	C LC CC OJ SM
+--|+|	(+)	0	100	0	50	0	0	0	0	0	0	0	0	0	25	75	100	0	0	40	50	50	50	0	66	0	66	0	33	0	47	16	BP LH NY O SU
+--|+|	(-)	100	50	0	100	0	0	0	0	0	0	0	0	0	33	50	86	33	100	33	50	50	100	75	66	0	100	0	33	0	56	21	C LC NY PL SF SU TB
+--||-	(-)	100	0	75	50	0	0	0	0	0	0	0	0	0	66	57	43	0	100	33	50	0	100	66	33	0	66	0	66	0	40	15	BO CC LC OJ SM SU
+--||-	(-)	100	25	50	0	0	0	0	0	0	0	0	0	0	66	57	43	0	100	33	57	28	100	33	33	0	33	0	66	66	58	34	BO C LH O PL SM SU
+--|||	(+)	33	66	33	0	0	0	0	0	0	0	0	0	0	28	42	66	100	0	25	33	28	100	33	0	0	66	0	33	0	39	23	BP NY O PL SF
+-+++-	(+)	66	33	66	40	0	0	0	0	0	0	0	0	0	28	60	0	0	0	50	0	0	0	66	0	0	66	0	0	0	42	20	BP O SU
+-+++-	(+)	100	0	66	0	0	0	0	0	0	0	0	0	100	0	40	100	0	100	50	50	66	100	66	0	0	33	100	0	0	55	26	BO C LC NY OJ S
+-++|-	(+)	0	100	0	66	0	0	0	0	0	0	0	0	0	50	75	0	0	0	100	0	0	100	25	0	0	0	0	0	0	41	26	BP CC LH SF
+-++||	(-)	100	33	66	0	0	0	0	0	0	0	0	0	0	80	60	100	0	100	0	0	66	100	40	0	0	40	100	0	0	54	22	BP C LC OJ PL SF
+-+|+-	(+)	100	33	0	0	0	0	0	0	0	0	0	0	0	20	40	60	100	100	0	0	60	100	60	0	0	0	50	0	0	59	14	BO CC NY O SF
+-+|+|	(-)	100	33	0	0	0	0	0	0	0	0	0	0	0	45	20	0	100	50	0	100	0	100	40	0	0	50	50	66	66	37	24	BP O PL SF SU W
+-+||-	(+)	50	80	33	50	0	0	0	0	0	0	0	0	0	54	60	100	0	0	75	75	50	0	0	25	0	25	50	33	66	48	25	C NY S SM
+-+|||	(-)	50	20	66	50	0	0	0	0	0	0	0	0	0	83	33	50	0	0	25	25	50	50	0	50	0	33	33	50	33	55	29	BO C CC LC PL S
+-|++-	(-)	100	50	100	100	0	0	0	0	0	0	0	0	0	16	66	0	0	0	66	40	50	0	0	66	0	20	66	50	0	44	23	LH O SU TB
+-|++|	(-)	33	66	100	0	0	0	0	0	0	0	0	0	0	25	25	100	100	100	50	50	50	50	25	0	0	60	66	33	66	46	30	BP C NY O OJ TB W
+-|+|-	(+)	66	33	0	0	0	0	0	0	0	0	0	0	0	66	75	0	0	0	50	50	40	0	60	0	0	66	0	33	0	50	33	BO LC LH SF SU
+-|+||	(-)	100	50	0	25	0	0	0	0	0	0	0	0	0	50	75	100	0	0	50	0	40	0	60	0	0	66	0	33	0	47	22	BO C LC NY O SU
+-||+-	(-)	0	50	100	75	0	0	0	0	0	0	0	0	0	32	25	0	0	100	50	50	60	100	40	0	0	33	100	0	0	49	21	C CC OJ SF TB
+-||+|	(+)	0	100	0	50	0	0	0	0	0	0	0	0	0	33	57	20	100	50	50	50	50	66	80	0	0	42	0	0	0	50	26	BP O SF SM
+-|||-	(+)	0	0	100	50	0	0	0	0	0	0	0	0	0	66	42	80	0	0	50	50	50	33	20	0	0	14	0	0	0	41	27	C LC NY TB W
+-||||	(+)	75	0	0	0	0	0	0	0	0	0	0	0	0	58	20	0	100	100	50	50	33	60	0	37	0	33	60	0	0	51	24	BO O OJ SU
++++-	(-)	25	0	0	50	0	0	0	0	0	0	0	0	0	33	60	100	0	0	50	50	50	0	50	0	0	20	40	0	100	46	29	BO BP LH NY O PL
+++|-	(-)	75	66	25	14	0	0	0	0	0	0	0	0	0	50	80	66	100	50	66	60	40	0	16	0	0	20	42	0	66	50	32	C CC SM TB W
+++||-	(-)	25	33	75	71	0	0	0	0	0	0	0	0	0	20	33	0	0	50	33	60	33	0	83	0	0	60	66	0	0	56	28	BO BP C LH NY OJ
+++|||	(+)	100	0	100	80	0	0	0	0	0	0	0	0	0	40	100	100	33	100	25	33	33	50	50	0	0	80	100	0	33	38	19	O SU TB
++|+-	(+)	33	66	0	0	0	0	0	0	0	0	0	0	0	60	0	0	66	0	25	33	50	50	0	75	0	50	60	0	0	48	24	CC O OJ SM
++|+|-	(+)	66	33	0	25	0	0	0	0	0	0	0	0	0	50	0	33	100	100	100	75	0	100	75	25	0	40	0	0	0	52	26	BO C LH NY PL S
++||+|	(-)	33	30	50	50	0	0	0	0	0	0	0	0	0	60	60	0	0	0	50	25	25	0	50	0	0	71	100	0	0	57	22	BO CC PL S SU TB
++||-	(+)	100	70	50	50	0	0	0	0	0	0	0	0	0	71	40	80	0	80	33	50	50	0	28	0	0	85	0	0	0	39	15	LC O SM SU
++||-	(-)	0	50	33	50	0	0	0	0	0	0	0	0	0	28	40	20	100	0	66	50	50	100	50	0	0	14	0	0	0	53	35	LC O SM NY OJ PL SF
+++++-	(+)	100	50	50	33	0	0	0	0	0	0	0	0	0	57	50	100	0	0	50	66	66	100	50	0	0	42	100	0	0	45	30	BO BP NY OJ PL SF
+++++-	(+)	0	50	50	33	0	0	0	0	0	0	0	0	0	42	50	0	100	0	50	33	50	0	50	0	0	57	0	0	0	50	22	NY S SF TB W
++++|-	(+)	50	60	50100	33	0	0	0	0	0	0	0	0	0	33	50	50	100	0	50	20	33	100	100	0	0	66	42	0	0	47	21	BO C CC O OJ
+++|+-	(-)	50	40	50	0	0	0	0	0	0	0	0	0	0	66	80	33	0	0	50	80	80	0	0	33	0	33	42	0	100	44	30	LC CC O SF SM OJ
+++||-	(-)	0	40100	0	0	0	0	0	0	0	0	0	0	0	42	66	66	0	50	0	0	16	0	33	0	0	83	0	100	0	38	26	LC OJ S W
++|+++-	(-)	33	0	50100	0	0	0	0	0	0	0	0	0	0	50	50	33	100	0	75	33	33	0	66	0	0	60	0	50	0	57	28	CC O S SM SU TB
+++++|-	(-)	66	100	50	100	0	0	0	0	0	0	0	0	0	50	0	0	0	100	25	66	0	0	0	0	0	40	0	0	0	52	20	CC OJ PL SM
++++++-	(+)	66	50	50100	0	0	0	0	0	0	0	0	0	0	50	0	0	0	0	100	0	0	0	0	0	0	60	0	0	0	42	16	BO BP S
+--|---|-	(-)	33	50	50	50	0	0	0	0	0	0	0	0	0	50	0	0	0	0	0	0	0	0	0	0	0	50	0	0	0	35	13	BO CC O PL SF SU
																																7	

Figure 8.8: Continued

Figure 8.8: Continued

		BO	BP	C	CC	CD	CL	CO	CP	FC	GC	HO	JY	LB	LC	LH	NY	O	OJ	PB	PL	S	SF	SV	SM	SP	SU	TB	TR	W	T%	T#	----- 65% -----
+-+++-|	(+)	50	100	66	33	0	0	0	0	0	0	0	0	0	100	50	0	100	50	0	33	66	33	0	100	0	60	100	0	25	60	26	BP C LC O S SM TB
+-++-|	(-)	50	0	33	66	0	0	0	0	0	0	0	0	0	100	0	100	0	50	0	66	33	100	0	100	0	40	0	0	75	39	17	CC NY PL SF W
+-++-+|	(+)	33	87	50	100	0	0	0	0	0	0	0	0	0	60	100	0	50	100	0	100	66	100	0	100	0	55	0	0	0	71	32	BP CC LH OJ PL S
+-++-|	(-)	66	12	50	0	0	0	0	0	0	0	0	0	0	40	0	50	0	0	0	0	33	0	0	0	0	44	100	0	0	28	13	BO TB
+-+++-|	(+)	0	0	0	0	0	0	0	0	0	0	0	0	0	28	100	100	100	0	0	0	83	50	0	0	0	60	75	0	0	60	26	BP C LH NY O S TB
+-+++-|	(-)	0	33	0	100	0	0	0	0	0	0	0	0	0	57	0	0	0	0	0	0	16	50	0	50	0	40	0	0	0	34	15	CC PL
+-++-|	(+)	100	50	100	100	0	0	0	0	0	0	0	0	0	27	66	0	33	33	0	100	33	0	0	25	0	33	50	0	0	44	19	BO C LH PL
+-+++-		(-)	0	50	0	0	0	0	0	0	0	0	0	0	0	72	33	50	0	66	0	66	0	0	0	75	0	33	0	0100	53	23	LC OJ S SM W
+-+++-		(+)	0	0	0	100	0	0	0	0	0	0	0	0	0	80	100	0	0	0	0	0	100	0	0	0	0100	100	0	0100	82	19	CC LC LH S SU TB W
+-+-		(-)	100	0	0	0	0	0	0	0	0	0	0	0	0	20	0	0	100	0	0	0	0	50	0	0	0100	0	0	0100	17	4	BO C OJ SM TB
+-+++-		(+)	100	75	100	0	0	0	0	0	0	0	0	0	0	33	20	0	0100	0	50	50	0	33	0	0	0	33	100	0100	47	21	BO BP C OJ SM TB
+-++-		(-)	0	25	0	100	0	0	0	0	0	0	0	0	0	66	80	50	100	0	50	50	80	33	0	0	0	66	0	0	47	21	CC LC LH O S SU
+-+-		(-)	0	33	50	0	0	0	0	0	0	0	0	0	0	20	50	0	0	0	0	0	75	50	0	0	0	75	0	0	46	15	LC O S
+-+-+-		(+)	100	100	66	50	0	0	0	0	0	0	0	0	0	66	50	33	0	50	50	0	25	0	0	0	0	0	0	0	53	17	BO BP C NY SM TB
+-+++-		(+)	100	83	60	75	0	0	0	0	0	0	0	0	0	42	33	50	50	0	50	50	0	100	0	40	0	50	0	0	52	27	BO BP CC S SU
+-+-		(-)	0	16	40	25	0	0	0	0	0	0	0	0	0	57	66	50	50	0	0	50	100	0	0	0	0	0	0	0	47	24	LH O W
+-+++-		(+)	100	100	100	75	0	0	0	0	0	0	0	0	0	60	33	23	0	66	0	66	0	33	0	0	0	33	0	0	68	28	BO BP C CC OJ S
+-+-		(-)	0	0	0	25	0	0	0	0	0	0	0	0	0	40	66	0	100	0	0	0	100	33	0	66	0	33	0	0	26	11	LH NY O
+-++-		(+)	66	50	50	33	0	0	0	0	0	0	0	0	0	60	37	50	100	0	66	66	100	0	0	50	0	66	0	0	54	31	BO O PL S SU
+-+-		(-)	33	50	50	66	0	0	0	0	0	0	0	0	0	40	25	75	0	100	33	0	33	33	0	50	0	33	0	0 34	43	25	CC LH PL W SF
+-++-		(+)	50	0	33	66	0	0	0	0	0	0	0	0	0	40	71	33	50	0	40	50	50	0	0	40	0	50	33	0 34	49	26	BP C NY
+-++-		(+)	50	100	66	33	0	0	0	0	0	0	0	0	0	60	28	66	50	0	66	66	66	0	0	60	0	50	33	0 66	49	26	BO BP CC LH O OJ
++-++-		(+)	33	50	0	50	0	0	0	0	0	0	0	0	0	57	0	0	50	0	0	33	57	0	0	50	0	33	0	0	35	16	C C O S SM
+-+-+-		(-)	66	100	50	100	0	0	0	0	0	0	0	0	0	42	100	50	100	100	0	66	42	100	0	50	0	66	100	0	64	29	BO CC O OJ SM
+-+-+-		(-)	33	50	100	100	0	0	0	0	0	0	0	0	0	40	60	100	50	0	66	0	75	25	0	0	0	16	0	0	52	24	C C O SM
+-+-+-		(+)	66	50	100	0	0	0	0	0	0	0	0	0	0	60	40	40	0	50	0	100	66	75	0	75	0	25	33	0	58	22	BO PL SF SU W
+-++-		(-)	66	50	100	50	0	0	0	0	0	0	0	0	0	37	37	50	50	0	0	66	66	0	0	33	0	75	0	0	59	32	BO C PL S SM SU
+-+-+-		(+)	33	50	0	0	0	0	0	0	0	0	0	0	0	62	62	50	50	0	0	0	33	0	0	0	0	12	0	0	38	21	BP CC SF W
+-+++-		(+)	0	100	0	66	0	0	0	0	0	0	0	0	0	0	60	0	100	0	0	0	0	66	0	66	0	66	0	0 66	48	16	BP LC NY OJ PL SU
+-+++-		(+)	100	0	0	33	0	0	0	0	0	0	0	0	0	71	40	100	0100	0	0	50	60	33	0	0	0	33	0	0 66	51	17	C NY S SM
+-++-		(-)	50	20	66	50	0	0	0	0	0	0	0	0	0	54	20	75	100	0	0	0	50	0	0	25	0	25	50	0 33	47	16	BP LH NY O SU
+-++-		(+)	100	50	100	100	0	0	0	0	0	0	0	0	0	83	33	50	0	0100	40	50	50	50	0	50	0	75	33	0 50	56	21	C LC NY PL SF SU TB
+-+-+-		(-)	0	50	0	0	0	0	0	0	0	0	0	0	0	16	66	50	100100100	0	66	33	57	25	0	50	0	75	66	0 66	40	15	BO C NY O PL SM
+-++-+-		(+)	100	0	75	50	0	0	0	0	0	0	0	0	0	50	25	100100100	0100	0	33	57	75	0	50	0	66	100	0 33	58	34	BP O PL SF SU
+-++-+-		(-)	0	100	25	50	0	0	0	0	0	0	0	0	0	33	42	66	100	0	25	66	66	0	0	40	0	33	0	0	39	23	BO LC LH NY O SU
+-+-+-		(-)	0	100	0	66	0	0	0	0	0	0	0	0	0	28	60	0	0	0	0	25	33	0	0	0	0	66	0	0	42	20	C LC OJ SM
+-+-+-		(+)	0100	0	66	0	0	0	0	0	0	0	0	0	0	71	40100	0100	0	50	66	66	0	0	66	0	33100	0 66	55	26	BP O SU
+-+-+-		(-)	50	20	66	50	0	0	0	0	0	0	0	0	0	54	20	75	0	0	0	75	66	0	0	25	0	50	33	0 33	41	20	C NY S SM
+-+-+-		(+)	100	50	100100	0	0	0	0	0	0	0	0	0	83	33	50	0	0	50	50	50	0	0	50	0	75	66	0 50	54	26	BO C CC LC PL S
+-++-+-		(-)	0	50	0	0	0	0	0	0	0	0	0	0	0	16	66	50100	0	0	0	50	40	0	50	0	66	33	0 33	59	22	LH O SU TB
+-+-+-		(+)	100	33	0100	0	0	0	0	0	0	0	0	0	20	40	0	0100	0	0	0	40	0	0	60	0	66	0	0	37	14	BP C NY O OJ TB
+-++-+-		(+)	50	0	33	50	0	0	0	0	0	0	0	0	0	45	20	0100	0	50	0100	0	100	0	0	0	75	50	0 66	48	24	BO LC LH SF SU W
+-+-+-		(+)	50	20	66	50	0	0	0	0	0	0	0	0	0	54	60100	0	0	0100	0	66	0	0	50	0	25	50	0 33	55	25	C NY S SM
+-++-+-		(+)	100	50100100	0	0	0	0	0	0	0	0	0	0	83	33	50	0	0	0	75	75	50	0	50	0	75	66	0 50	50	29	BO LC NY OJ PL SU
+-+-+-		(-)	0	0100	0	0	0	0	0	0	0	0	0	0	16	66	50	0	0	0	25	25	50	0	50	0	25	33100	0 50	44	23	LH O SU TB
+-++-+-		(+)	33	66100	0	0	0	0	0	0	0	0	0	0	25100100100	0100	50	25	25	0	0	66	0	50	0	0	46	30	BP C NY O OJ TB
+-++-+-		(+)	66	33	0	0	0	0	0	0	0	0	0	0	0	66	75100100100	0	0	50	50100	0	0	60	0	66	0	0 33	50	33	BO LC LH SF SU W
+-++-+-		(+)	100	33	0	0	0	0	0	0	0	0	0	0	0	33	25	0	0100	0	50	40	0	0	60	0	66	0	0 33	47	22	BO LC LH NY O SU
+-+-++-		(+)	0	0100	50	0	0	0	0	0	0	0	0	0	33	57	20100	0	50	0100	0	0	0100	0	33100	0100	49	21	C CC OJ SF TB
+-+-++-		(+)	0	100	50	0	0	0	0	0	0	0	0	0	0	33	57	20100	0100	50	50	0	0	80	0	42	0	0100	50	26	BO BP C O SF SM
+-+-++-		(+)	0	50	0	50	0	0	0	0	0	0	0	0	0	66	80	0	0100	0	50	50	33	0	0	20	0	57100	0100	41	27	C LC NY TB W
+-++-++-		(+)	75	0	0	0	0	0	0	0	0	0	0	0	0	58	20	0100100	0	50	50	50	0	0	37	0	33	60	0100	50	26	BP O OJ
+-++-+++-		(-)	25	0100	50	0	0	0	0	0	0	0	0	0	0	33	60100	0	0	0	50100	50	0	50	0	66	40	0100	51	30	C NY S SU W

Figure 8.8: Concluded

		BO	BP	C	CC	CD	CL	CO	CP	FC	GC	HO	JY	LB	LC	LH	NY	O	OJ	PB	PL	S	SF	SV	SM	SP	SU	TB	TR	W	T%	T#	------- 65% -------
+++-+++	(+)	75	66	25	14	0	0	0	0	0	0	0	0	0	0	50	66	100	50	0	66	40	0	0	16	0	20	33	0	100	46	29	BO BP LH NY O PL W
+++-+++	(-)	25	33	75	71	0	0	0	0	0	0	0	0	0	0	20	33	0	50	0	33	60	0	0	83	0	60	66	0	0	50	32	C CC SM TB
+++-+++	(-)	100	100	80	50	0	0	0	0	0	0	0	0	0	0	100	0	33	100	0	25	33	50	0	50	0	20	0	0	66	56	28	BO BP C LH NY OJ W
+++++---	(+)	0	0	20	50	0	0	0	0	0	0	0	0	0	0	60	0	66	0	0	50	33	0	0	50	0	80	100	0	33	38	19	O SU TB
+++++---	(-)	0	0	20	75	0	0	0	0	0	0	0	0	0	0	50	0	100	100	0	0	0	0	0	75	0	50	60	0	0	48	24	CC O OJ SM
+++++--+	(+)	100	50	80	25	0	0	0	0	0	0	0	0	0	0	50	100	66	0	0	100	100	0	0	25	0	50	40	0	100	52	26	BO C LH NY PL S
+++++--+	(-)	66	50	33	66	0	0	0	0	0	0	0	0	0	0	60	0	0	0	0	100	75	0	0	25	0	71	100	0	0	57	22	BO CC PL S SU TB
+++++-+-	(+)	33	50	66	33	0	0	0	0	0	0	0	0	0	0	40	100	0	100	0	0	25	0	0	50	0	28	0	0	0	39	15	C LH O
+++++-+-	(-)	0	30	50	50	0	0	0	0	0	0	0	0	0	0	71	40	0	80	0	33	50	0	0	71	0	85	100	0	0	53	35	LC O SM SU TB
+++++-++	(+)	100	70	50	50	0	0	0	0	0	0	0	0	0	0	28	40	100	20	0	66	50	100	0	28	0	14	0	0	0	45	30	BO BP NY OJ PL SF
+++++-++	(-)	0	50	0	33	0	0	0	0	0	0	0	0	0	0	57	50	100	0	0	50	66	100	0	50	0	42	100	0	0	50	22	NY S SF TB W
+++++++-	(+)	100	50	50	100	0	0	0	0	0	0	0	0	0	0	42	50	0	100	0	50	33	0	0	57	0	57	0	0	0	47	21	BO C O OJ
+++++++-	(-)	50	60	50	0	0	0	0	0	0	0	0	0	0	0	33	50	50	100	0	50	20	100	0	0	0	66	42	0	100	51	30	CC O SF SM SU
+++++++-	(-)	50	40	50	0	0	0	0	0	0	0	0	0	0	0	66	50	33	0	0	50	80	0	0	33	0	33	42	0	0	44	26	LC OJ S W
+++++++-	(+)	0	60	0	0	0	0	0	0	0	0	0	0	0	0	50	80	66	0	0	0	16	0	0	66	0	0	0	0	50	38	19	LH NY S
+++++++-	(-)	0	40	100	0	0	0	0	0	0	0	0	0	0	0	42	20	33	100	0	0	83	0	0	0	0	100	100	0	0	57	28	C O S SM SU TB
+++++++++	(+)	33	0	50	100	0	0	0	0	0	0	0	0	0	0	50	50	0	0	0	75	33	0	0	100	0	60	0	0	0	52	20	CC OJ PL SM
+++++++++	(-)	66	100	50	0	0	0	0	0	0	0	0	0	0	0	50	25	0	0	0	25	66	0	0	0	0	40	0	0	0	42	16	BO BP S

Figure 8.9: Daily Closing Patterns: Bear/Bull/Bear Markets

		BO	BP	C	CC	CD	CL	CO	CP	FC	GC	HO	JY	LB	LC	LH	NY	OJ	PB	PL	S	SF	SV	SM	SP	SU	IB	TR	W	T%	T#	
– –	(+)	0	51	0	0	0	0	56	56	0	54	0	0	0	0	50	60	53	49	0	54	48	0	46	0	57	46	0	52	51	1041	
– –	(–)	0	46	0	0	0	0	42	41	0	43	0	0	0	0	48	39	39	47	0	40	50	0	50	0	38	50	0	46	45	913	
– +	(+)	0	43	0	0	0	0	54	45	0	37	0	0	0	0	46	42	52	49	0	50	46	0	46	0	45	45	0	47	47	1007	
– +	(–)	0	50	0	0	0	0	45	50	0	61	0	0	0	0	50	54	45	49	0	48	56	0	50	0	51	50	0	47	50	1071	
+ –	(+)	0	49	0	0	0	0	40	47	0	57	0	0	0	0	60	51	53	56	0	49	32	0	50	0	43	44	0	51	48	1045	
+ –	(–)	0	43	0	0	0	0	59	46	0	40	0	0	0	0	36	46	42	46	0	47	67	0	47	0	54	51	0	45	48	1030	SF
+ +	(+)	0	49	0	0	0	0	45	37	0	43	0	0	0	0	45	38	40	45	0	48	38	0	36	0	49	38	0	34	42	787	
+ +	(–)	0	46	0	0	0	0	52	59	0	55	0	0	0	0	49	55	57	53	0	49	56	0	60	0	55	44	0	62	54	1012	
– – –	(+)	0	61	0	0	0	0	45	53	0	44	0	0	0	0	53	38	62	44	0	48	36	0	49	0	44	49	0	54	51	472	NY
– – –	(–)	0	35	0	0	0	0	52	44	0	43	0	0	0	0	46	32	32	45	0	35	38	0	48	0	33	50	0	41	42	412	
– – +	(+)	0	51	0	0	0	0	45	50	0	40	0	0	0	0	41	42	53	53	0	50	40	0	51	0	42	42	0	57	45	492	
– – +	(–)	0	50	0	0	0	0	50	55	0	58	0	0	0	0	51	53	45	53	0	49	57	0	47	0	55	53	0	42	50	525	
– + –	(+)	0	52	0	0	0	0	36	45	0	52	0	0	0	0	60	56	58	59	0	42	32	0	52	0	41	45	0	54	49	531	
– + –	(–)	0	41	0	0	0	0	63	50	0	53	0	0	0	0	36	41	40	40	0	51	67	0	45	0	53	50	0	43	47	511	SF
– + +	(+)	0	38	0	0	0	0	48	38	0	44	0	0	0	0	55	44	44	48	0	48	36	0	36	0	55	39	0	36	42	429	
– + +	(–)	0	57	0	0	0	0	50	60	0	58	0	0	0	0	39	57	52	54	0	50	54	0	61	0	44	55	0	60	54	544	
+ – –	(+)	0	42	0	0	0	0	57	56	0	53	0	0	0	0	48	56	56	51	0	52	61	0	43	0	54	47	0	48	51	533	
+ – –	(–)	0	55	0	0	0	0	42	49	0	44	0	0	0	0	48	43	43	46	0	50	57	0	52	0	43	49	0	51	47	476	
+ – +	(+)	0	37	0	0	0	0	58	49	0	36	0	0	0	0	50	44	50	46	0	50	47	0	43	0	47	49	0	51	46	496	
+ – +	(–)	0	59	0	0	0	0	42	44	0	63	0	0	0	0	50	54	48	52	0	46	52	0	50	0	46	46	0	48	49	518	
+ + –	(+)	0	48	0	0	0	0	42	50	0	54	0	0	0	0	50	54	48	52	0	43	31	0	48	0	52	46	0	48	48	493	
+ + –	(–)	0	42	0	0	0	0	57	43	0	41	0	0	0	0	37	53	45	47	0	47	68	0	48	0	52	50	0	48	48	489	SF
+ + +	(+)	0	57	0	0	0	0	42	41	0	40	0	0	0	0	37	43	35	47	0	47	40	0	37	0	47	35	0	34	42	333	
+ + +	(–)	0	38	0	0	0	0	54	52	0	59	0	0	0	0	59	60	61	51	0	49	60	0	56	0	50	57	0	60	54	424	
– – – –	(+)	0	52	0	0	0	0	54	60	0	36	0	0	0	0	42	60	71	44	0	52	54	0	46	0	80	51	0	53	52	215	OJ SU
– – – –	(–)	0	47	0	0	0	0	45	36	0	41	0	0	0	0	57	40	28	55	0	41	58	0	50	0	20	44	0	46	45	188	
– – – +	(+)	0	27	0	0	0	0	49	50	0	44	0	0	0	0	31	42	66	51	0	51	57	0	50	0	42	41	0	58	49	232	BP OJ
– – – +	(–)	0	54	0	0	0	0	50	50	0	54	0	0	0	0	62	52	33	48	0	51	42	0	50	0	52	55	0	41	48	230	
– – + –	(+)	0	41	0	0	0	0	39	50	0	71	0	0	0	0	43	60	57	65	0	34	27	0	57	0	48	48	0	66	50	267	GC W
– – + –	(–)	0	35	0	0	0	0	44	39	0	28	0	0	0	0	50	34	39	34	0	56	72	0	40	0	44	49	0	33	46	246	GC SF
– – + +	(+)	0	61	0	0	0	0	44	59	0	40	0	0	0	0	53	30	36	39	0	54	33	0	28	0	52	38	0	50	40	197	
– – + +	(–)	0	46	0	0	0	0	52	48	0	59	0	0	0	0	38	55	60	58	0	45	56	0	70	0	47	55	0	45	55	274	SM
– + – –	(+)	0	53	0	0	0	0	32	43	0	54	0	0	0	0	33	77	48	54	0	51	61	0	42	0	59	52	0	43	51	261	NY
– + – –	(–)	0	30	0	0	0	0	67	46	0	42	0	0	0	0	60	22	51	52	0	45	38	0	51	0	36	45	0	56	46	240	
– + – +	(+)	0	63	0	0	0	0	46	51	0	50	0	0	0	0	33	46	51	45	0	51	50	0	50	0	52	43	0	40	46	244	
– + – +	(–)	0	48	0	0	0	0	62	47	0	38	0	0	0	0	66	53	48	59	0	48	53	0	48	0	43	47	0	52	49	274	LH
– + + –	(+)	0	45	0	0	0	0	56	44	0	39	0	0	0	0	28	37	35	54	0	55	44	0	28	0	55	54	0	33	39	259	LH
– + + –	(–)	0	57	0	0	0	0	54	59	0	60	0	0	0	0	71	57	58	54	0	44	44	0	68	0	45	61	0	60	57	267	
– + + +	(+)	0	42	0	0	0	0	56	48	0	50	0	0	0	0	60	75	60	51	0	51	28	0	50	0	45	35	0	55	51	171	LH SM
– + + +	(–)	0	63	0	0	0	0	54	51	0	45	0	0	0	0	53	25	35	56	0	32	71	0	47	0	36	58	0	38	44	245	LH
+ – – –	(+)	0	30	0	0	0	0	51	37	0	37	0	0	0	0	53	42	44	56	0	55	21	0	53	0	45	47	0	52	46	244	NY
+ – – –	(–)	0	60	0	0	0	0	60	58	0	62	0	0	0	0	40	53	55	54	0	44	68	0	44	0	51	49	0	47	51	213	SF
+ – – +	(+)	0	44	0	0	0	0	32	43	0	47	0	0	0	0	72	40	60	52	0	51	44	0	47	0	31	41	0	45	48	249	
+ – + –	(+)	0	43	0	0	0	0	46	51	0	50	0	0	0	0	56	36	53	49	0	41	50	0	43	0	50	40	0	23	44	272	SF
+ – + –	(–)	0	52	0	0	0	0	39	37	0	46	0	0	0	0	40	59	43	54	0	58	59	0	35	0	43	55	0	76	53	251	LH
+ – + +	(+)	0	60	0	0	0	0	32	43	0	52	0	0	0	0	60	39	62	53	0	58	60	0	50	0	45	41	0	52	52	252	CO SU
+ – + +	(–)	0	34	0	0	0	0	67	46	0	47	0	0	0	0	40	60	37	42	0	38	40	0	54	0	50	54	0	47	45	221	
+ + – +	(+)	0	43	0	0	0	0	46	39	0	50	0	0	0	0	56	36	53	49	0	41	50	0	43	0	56	40	0	60	49	262	W
+ + – –	(–)	0	52	0	0	0	0	59	60	0	46	0	0	0	0	40	59	59	54	0	59	57	0	35	0	55	55	0	52	52	256	CO
+ + + –	(+)	0	34	0	0	0	0	30	34	0	32	0	0	0	0	37	52	37	42	0	38	57	0	54	0	50	41	0	47	45	242	
+ + + +	(+)	0	60	0	0	0	0	66	63	0	50	0	0	0	0	59	43	42	64	0	58	57	0	45	0	56	45	0	57	49	233	GC
+ + + –	(–)	0	53	0	0	0	0	30	60	0	50	0	0	0	0	59	52	51	35	0	58	11	0	45	0	47	37	0	40	47	210	
+ + + +	(–)	0	45	0	0	0	0	47	57	0	50	0	0	0	0	40	56	48	35	0	41	68	0	51	0	63	53	0	42	48	204	SF

---------- 65% ----------

Figure 8.9: Continued

		BO	BP	C	CC	CD	CL	CO	CP	FC	GC	HO	JY	LB	LC	LH	NY	O	OJ	PB	PL	S	SF	SV	SM	SP	SU	TB	TR	W	T%	T#	65%
++++	(+)	0	57	0	0	0	0	47	47	0	37	0	0	0	0	50	53	0	36	51	0	43	16	0	52	0	38	41	0	37	46	153	
++++	(−)	0	36	0	0	0	0	52	43	0	62	0	0	0	0	42	46	0	63	46	0	56	83	0	38	0	55	46	0	62	49	164	SF
----	(+)	0	33	0	0	0	0	52	72	0	71	0	0	0	0	37	50	0	75	36	0	57	42	0	46	0	100	56	0	83	52	98	CP GC OJ SU W
----	(−)	0	66	0	0	0	0	47	27	0	28	0	0	0	0	37	16	0	25	64	0	14	57	0	45	0	0	43	0	16	46	87	BP
---+	(+)	0	50	0	0	0	0	40	55	0	58	0	0	0	0	33	16	0	50	50	0	37	60	0	54	0	25	52	0	71	46	99	W
---+	(−)	0	30	0	0	0	0	60	44	0	33	0	0	0	0	40	66	0	50	50	0	62	40	0	54	0	62	52	0	28	50	109	LH NY
--+-	(+)	0	44	0	0	0	0	39	69	0	69	0	0	0	0	40	36	0	50	50	0	21	40	0	65	0	40	57	0	57	48	112	GC PB
--+-	(−)	0	44	0	0	0	0	60	44	0	30	0	0	0	0	50	63	0	66	23	0	64	100	0	34	0	50	47	0	42	48	111	OJ SF
--++	(+)	0	36	0	0	0	0	44	33	0	10	0	0	0	0	40	33	0	41	50	0	38	37	0	34	0	62	36	0	60	39	91	
--++	(−)	0	59	0	0	0	0	51	60	0	90	0	0	0	0	40	55	0	58	55	0	61	50	0	65	0	37	60	0	60	56	131	GC
-+--	(+)	0	70	0	0	0	0	48	40	0	33	0	0	0	0	25	80	0	72	46	0	44	81	0	31	0	63	60	0	60	55	137	BP NY OJ SF
-+--	(−)	0	30	0	0	0	0	59	48	0	66	0	0	0	0	62	20	0	27	53	0	55	18	0	63	0	58	35	0	40	42	105	GC
-+-+	(+)	0	23	0	0	0	0	40	44	0	47	0	0	0	0	28	48	0	43	53	0	36	33	0	55	0	58	48	0	47	47	127	
-+-+	(−)	0	76	0	0	0	0	37	36	0	52	0	0	0	0	71	53	0	56	42	0	63	66	0	33	0	41	51	0	60	49	132	BP LH SF
-++-	(+)	0	52	0	0	0	0	62	40	0	46	0	0	0	0	80	36	0	55	23	0	66	37	0	57	0	44	53	0	55	46	127	LH S
-++-	(−)	0	36	0	0	0	0	40	40	0	44	0	0	0	0	20	36	0	40	76	0	33	42	0	42	0	55	44	0	44	50	139	PB
-+++	(+)	0	63	0	0	0	0	40	40	0	44	0	0	0	0	28	0	0	41	45	0	44	60	0	35	0	40	33	0	30	39	78	
-+++	(−)	0	36	0	0	0	0	50	53	0	55	0	0	0	0	71	100	0	50	52	0	50	12	0	57	0	60	63	0	70	56	111	LH NY
+---	(+)	0	64	0	0	0	0	52	52	0	52	0	0	0	0	55	80	0	57	52	0	68	12	0	54	0	62	29	0	63	50	120	NY S
+---	(−)	0	21	0	0	0	0	44	47	0	42	0	0	0	0	44	20	0	35	39	0	25	87	0	41	0	37	63	0	43	45	108	SF
+--+	(+)	0	33	0	0	0	0	46	41	0	57	0	0	0	0	80	47	0	46	57	0	61	38	0	55	0	46	52	0	42	50	131	CO LH
+--+	(−)	0	50	0	0	0	0	53	55	0	27	0	0	0	0	75	56	0	63	41	0	61	40	0	56	0	53	61	0	57	47	121	GC
+-+-	(+)	0	42	0	0	0	0	46	35	0	57	0	0	0	0	25	37	0	36	58	0	38	60	0	43	0	12	36	0	33	49	130	LH
+-+-	(−)	0	47	0	0	0	0	45	30	0	42	0	0	0	0	50	35	0	50	48	0	40	40	0	34	0	87	59	0	58	53	136	SU
+-++	(+)	0	50	0	0	0	0	54	70	0	50	0	0	0	0	33	57	0	76	45	0	70	40	0	53	0	55	51	0	75	50	107	CP W
+-++	(−)	0	57	0	0	0	0	64	68	0	77	0	0	0	0	66	56	0	23	48	0	29	57	0	65	0	28	43	0	61	47	131	CP OJ
++--	(+)	0	28	0	0	0	0	43	44	0	63	0	0	0	0	45	27	0	68	47	0	57	33	0	30	0	71	53	0	25	52	136	LH SU
++--	(−)	0	71	0	0	0	0	43	60	0	36	0	0	0	0	42	54	0	62	28	0	33	66	0	66	0	44	60	0	44	40	126	BP SF SM
++-+	(+)	0	31	0	0	0	0	56	36	0	62	0	0	0	0	81	55	0	26	56	0	35	33	0	37	0	54	34	0	54	55	121	LH PB W
++-+	(−)	0	68	0	0	0	0	47	61	0	69	0	0	0	0	57	18	0	73	48	0	66	100	0	40	0	36	38	0	77	48	118	SF
+++-	(+)	0	27	0	0	0	0	66	47	0	30	0	0	0	0	35	46	0	56	51	0	58	75	0	62	0	22	58	0	22	48	75	CP NY
+++-	(−)	0	61	0	0	0	0	33	44	0	64	0	0	0	0	64	38	0	50	40	0	40	25	0	44	0	25	61	0	61	41	88	GC LH OJ SF
++++	(+)	0	41	0	0	0	0	62	53	0	69	0	0	0	0	70	53	0	44	57	0	60	57	0	40	0	71	41	0	37	48	110	BP OJ SU
++++	(−)	0	58	0	0	0	0	37	57	0	30	0	0	0	0	28	56	0	31	56	0	60	28	0	56	0	28	56	0	56	56	127	CP NY
+-+-+	(+)	0	50	0	0	0	0	54	50	0	64	0	0	0	0	71	25	0	63	46	0	60	25	0	25	0	77	32	0	40	41	91	NY SU
+-+-+	(−)	0	64	0	0	0	0	58	38	0	64	0	0	0	0	66	78	0	69	50	0	33	50	0	75	0	22	61	0	55	52	125	LH SM
+-+--	(+)	0	35	0	0	0	0	42	33	0	30	0	0	0	0	33	25	0	30	45	0	41	50	0	53	0	54	37	0	44	44	117	LH NY OJ
+-+--	(−)	0	25	0	0	0	0	40	33	0	54	0	0	0	0	44	33	0	45	53	0	50	22	0	52	0	44	33	0	60	42	99	
+-+--	(−)	0	75	0	0	0	0	60	66	0	45	0	0	0	0	44	66	0	54	42	0	50	77	0	42	0	55	66	0	40	56	144	BP CP NY SF TB

Figure 8.9: Continued

		BO	BP	C	CC	CD	CL	CO	CP	FC	GC	HO	JY	LB	LC	LH	NY	O	OJ	PB	PL	S	SF	SV	SM	SP	SU	TB	TR	W	T%	T#	------ 65% ------
+ + + -	(+)	0	64	0	0	0	0	19	27	0	52	0	0	0	0	66	60	0	58	68	0	47	50	0	41	0	50	51	0	62	50	116	LH PB
+ + + -	(-)	0	35	0	0	0	0	80	61	0	42	0	0	0	0	33	40	0	41	31	0	47	50	0	55	0	50	44	0	37	47	110	CO
+ + + -	(+)	0	41	0	0	0	0	46	47	0	66	0	0	0	0	60	37	0	61	51	0	40	33	0	35	0	71	36	0	25	45	110	GC SU
+ + + +	(-)	0	58	0	0	0	0	53	52	0	33	0	0	0	0	33	62	0	38	48	0	55	66	0	58	0	28	58	0	75	52	125	SF W
+ + + +	(+)	0	33	0	0	0	0	68	66	0	54	0	0	0	0	66	44	0	56	70	0	42	75	0	58	0	58	38	0	40	55	112	CO CP LH PB SF
+ + + -	(-)	0	66	0	0	0	0	27	33	0	45	0	0	0	0	33	55	0	43	29	0	50	25	0	35	0	41	61	0	60	43	87	BP
+ + + +	(+)	0	60	0	0	0	0	70	37	0	25	0	0	0	0	76	28	0	28	35	0	55	100	0	46	0	33	46	0	75	48	101	CO LH SF W
+ + + +	(-)	0	40	0	0	0	0	25	56	0	75	0	0	0	0	23	57	0	71	64	0	40	0	0	46	0	50	46	0	25	47	99	GC OJ
+ + + +	(+)	0	58	0	0	0	0	47	50	0	50	0	0	0	0	33	33	0	58	52	0	55	20	0	62	0	30	55	0	20	48	80	LH NY SF SU
+ + + +	(-)	0	33	0	0	0	0	52	50	0	40	0	0	0	0	66	66	0	33	47	0	44	80	0	25	0	70	44	0	80	48	75	GC W
+ + + +	(+)	0	63	0	0	0	0	42	27	0	66	0	0	0	0	57	28	0	42	60	0	46	0	0	54	0	28	56	0	33	49	71	NY SF SU W
+ + + +	(-)	0	31	0	0	0	0	57	54	0	33	0	0	0	0	28	71	0	57	34	0	53	37	0	45	0	71	68	0	66	46	56	CO CP GC OJ S TB W
+ + + +	(+)	0	50	0	0	0	0	90	100	0	100	0	0	0	0	60	50	0	100	43	0	100	62	0	53	0	37	87	0	100	64	30	
- - - +	(-)	0	50	0	0	0	0	10	0	0	0	0	0	0	0	40	50	0	56	44	0	0	37	0	38	0	0	31	0	0	34	56	
- - - +	(+)	0	66	0	0	0	0	45	62	0	40	0	0	0	0	25	25	0	66	44	0	25	83	0	58	0	50	48	0	80	51	50	BP OJ SF W
- - - +	(-)	0	33	0	0	0	0	54	37	0	40	0	0	0	0	75	75	0	33	55	0	75	16	0	41	0	20	52	0	20	46	46	LH S
- - - +	(+)	0	100	0	0	0	0	26	50	0	50	0	0	0	0	25	25	0	40	80	0	20	100	0	84	0	100	66	0	100	44	49	BP PB SM W
- - - +	(-)	0	0	0	0	0	0	73	40	0	50	0	0	0	0	75	75	0	60	20	0	60	0	0	15	100	60	51	0	60	51	56	CO LH NY SF
- - - +	(+)	0	60	0	0	0	0	20	40	0	14	0	0	0	0	0	0	0	40	40	0	0	33	0	27	0	60	31	0	0	34	34	NY SU
- - - +	(-)	0	40	0	0	0	0	80	60	0	85	0	0	0	0	50	50	0	83	60	0	50	50	0	72	0	80	54	0	40	60	60	CO GC S SM
- - - +	(+)	0	75	0	0	0	0	58	62	0	75	0	0	0	0	20	85	0	16	60	0	40	100	0	33	0	47	70	0	60	57	64	BP GC NY OJ SF SU
- - - +	(-)	0	25	0	0	0	0	41	37	0	25	0	0	0	0	50	14	0	40	40	0	55	33	0	66	0	20	47	0	33	40	45	SM
- - - +	(+)	0	50	0	0	0	0	63	60	0	44	0	0	0	0	0	50	0	33	56	0	33	0	0	52	0	25	47	0	75	50	56	W
- - - +	(-)	0	50	0	0	0	0	36	54	0	55	0	0	0	0	100	50	0	60	37	0	66	25	0	37	0	75	52	0	25	47	53	LH OJ S SU
- - - +	(+)	0	53	0	0	0	0	42	36	0	44	0	0	0	0	0	40	0	18	58	0	50	50	0	58	0	0	50	0	75	48	64	LH W
- - - +	(-)	0	38	0	0	0	0	57	36	0	55	0	0	0	0	0	60	0	81	41	0	50	50	0	41	100	28	50	0	25	48	64	PB SU
- - - +	(+)	0	62	0	0	0	0	41	33	0	55	0	0	0	0	50	0	0	30	60	0	40	0	0	33	0	40	23	0	0	37	34	SF
- - - +	(-)	0	37	0	0	0	0	58	50	0	100	0	0	0	0	50	100	0	57	45	0	60	33	0	55	0	60	76	0	100	60	55	GC NY TB W
- - + +	(+)	0	33	0	0	0	0	55	50	0	33	0	0	0	0	30	57	0	66	37	0	60	0	0	58	0	75	23	0	50	48	51	LH NY OJ SU
- - + +	(-)	0	33	0	0	0	0	40	25	0	66	0	0	0	0	20	50	0	50	42	0	40	66	0	60	0	25	70	0	66	47	50	GC SF TB
- - + +	(+)	0	57	0	0	0	0	66	53	0	0	0	0	0	0	60	62	0	50	85	0	75	38	0	66	0	57	50	0	66	57	78	CO LH PB S SM W
- - + +	(-)	0	28	0	0	0	0	33	40	0	41	0	0	0	0	40	37	0	50	14	0	25	61	0	33	0	42	39	0	33	38	53	GC
- - + +	(+)	0	40	0	0	0	0	54	60	0	58	0	0	0	0	80	50	0	22	57	0	57	0	0	44	0	66	44	0	43	48	64	CP LH OJ
- - + +	(-)	0	71	0	0	0	0	56	9	0	45	0	0	0	0	20	50	0	77	58	0	25	25	0	50	0	50	60	0	66	47	63	SF SU W
- - + +	(+)	0	28	0	0	0	0	56	33	0	45	0	0	0	0	50	28	0	71	25	0	42	0	0	46	0	28	50	0	33	45	60	LH OJ
- - + +	(-)	0	33	0	0	0	0	43	66	0	45	0	0	0	0	50	71	0	28	60	0	25	75	0	53	0	71	45	0	0	49	63	CP NY S SF SU
- - + +	(+)	0	57	0	0	0	0	59	69	0	66	0	0	0	0	42	57	0	47	33	0	75	100	0	40	0	20	45	0	50	49	71	CP GC LH OJ S
- - + +	(-)	0	57	0	0	0	0	36	30	0	33	0	0	0	0	25	57	0	25	43	0	0	40	0	60	0	80	66	0	50	45	63	SU TB
- - + +	(+)	0	30	0	0	0	0	46	75	0	33	0	0	0	0	50	50	0	27	57	0	50	33	0	35	0	25	68	0	50	49	63	CP TB
- - + +	(-)	0	70	0	0	0	0	53	25	0	66	0	0	0	0	75	50	0	42	42	0	66	66	0	60	0	22	22	0	40	46	59	BP GC LH SF
- - + +	(+)	0	25	0	0	0	0	60	62	0	60	0	0	0	0	60	50	0	33	81	0	66	0	0	62	0	33	36	0	71	54	60	PB S W
- - + +	(-)	0	50	0	0	0	0	40	37	0	40	0	0	0	0	40	50	0	50	18	0	33	100	0	37	0	66	57	0	28	43	48	SF SU
- + - +	(+)	0	50	0	0	0	0	40	66	0	60	0	0	0	0	50	50	0	60	55	0	37	33	0	50	0	50	30	0	66	48	37	BP CP
- + - +	(-)	0	71	0	0	0	0	50	66	0	33	0	0	0	0	50	0	0	40	44	0	62	66	0	25	0	33	40	0	33	45	35	GC SF
- + - +	(+)	0	28	0	0	0	0	53	33	0	50	0	0	0	0	50	0	0	66	66	0	50	42	0	50	0	66	53	0	0	50	55	BP CP NY PB
- + - +	(-)	0	66	0	0	0	0	46	30	0	50	0	0	0	0	50	100	0	33	33	0	50	57	0	40	0	66	53	0	100	47	51	SU W
- + - +	(+)	0	33	0	0	0	0	50	36	0	0	0	0	0	0	20	50	0	40	58	0	45	100	0	53	0	60	33	0	60	48	58	OJ SF
- + - +	(-)	0	55	0	0	0	0	50	63	0	100	0	0	0	0	80	87	0	12	41	0	54	0	0	46	0	40	66	0	40	51	62	GC LH TB
- + - +	(+)	0	44	0	0	0	0	54	50	0	69	0	0	0	0	71	0	0	71	66	0	28	37	0	55	0	42	42	0	75	53	65	GC LH NY OJ PB W
- + - +	(-)	0	50	0	0	0	0	45	41	0	30	0	0	0	0	0	12	0	33	50	0	71	62	0	36	0	57	57	0	25	46	56	S
- + - +	(+)	0	25	0	0	0	0	40	50	0	20	0	0	0	0	25	25	0	33	50	0	63	40	0	54	0	50	29	0	33	42	56	GC LH
- + - +	(-)	0	75	0	0	0	0	54	28	0	80	0	0	0	0	50	83	0	66	65	0	36	0	0	66	0	50	66	0	66	53	68	BP TB W
- + - +	(+)	0	30	0	0	0	0	37	28	0	56	0	0	0	0	50	83	0	28	28	0	0	0	0	80	0	57	46	0	28	51	70	NY S SM
- + - +	(-)	0	70	0	0	0	0	62	57	0	37	0	0	0	0	50	16	0	71	35	0	100	0	0	20	0	28	53	0	71	46	63	BP OJ SF W

Figure 8.9: Continued

Figure 8.9: Continued

		BO	BP	C	CC	CD	CL	CO	CP	FC	GC	HO	JY	LB	LC	LH	NY	OJ	PB	PL	S	SF	SV	SM	SP	SU	TB	TH	W	T%	T#		65%
+ + – – – +	(+)	0	80	0	0	0	0	55	25	0	100	0	0	0	0	50	33	75	50	0	20	33	0	35	0	100	56	0	50	51	51	BP GC OJ SU	
+ + – – – –	(–)	0	20	0	0	0	0	44	40	0	50	0	0	0	0	50	66	25	50	0	80	66	0	64	0	50	36	0	50	45	45	NY S SF	
+ + – – + +	(+)	0	88	0	0	0	0	66	40	0	0	0	0	0	0	50	54	66	45	0	71	33	0	54	0	50	47	0	40	56	65	BP CO OJ S	
+ + – – + –	(–)	0	11	0	0	0	0	33	43	0	100	0	0	0	0	25	45	33	41	0	44	66	0	45	0	60	52	0	75	51	50	SF	
+ + – + – +	(+)	0	66	0	0	0	0	37	56	0	100	0	0	0	0	75	33	72	58	0	44	42	0	44	0	20	45	0	25	46	73	BP GC NY OJ W	
+ + – + – –	(–)	0	33	0	0	0	0	62	56	0	0	0	0	0	0	75	33	18	58	0	66	57	0	55	0	25	45	0	25	46	67	LH	
+ + – + + +	(+)	0	50	0	0	0	0	47	37	0	0	0	0	0	0	50	33	30	80	0	66	0	0	90	0	75	54	0	50	36	39	S	
+ + – + + –	(–)	0	50	0	0	0	0	52	62	0	50	0	0	0	0	50	66	70	80	0	33	100	0	37	0	50	54	0	33	62	67	NY OJ PB SF SM SU	
+ + + – – +	(+)	0	20	0	0	0	0	47	63	0	75	0	0	0	0	33	75	28	11	0	44	0	0	50	0	50	50	0	66	44	49	GC NY W	
+ + + – – –	(–)	0	80	0	0	0	0	52	36	0	25	0	0	0	0	66	25	71	88	0	55	50	0	50	0	50	50	0	33	53	59	BP LH OJ PB SF	
+ + + – + +	(+)	0	22	0	0	0	0	75	20	0	40	0	0	0	0	16	33	50	35	0	66	50	0	58	0	50	50	0	60	43	51	CO S	
+ + + – + –	(–)	0	55	0	0	0	0	25	80	0	60	0	0	0	0	83	66	50	65	0	33	50	0	41	0	50	47	0	40	54	63	CP LH NY	
+ + + + – +	(+)	0	42	0	0	0	0	46	41	0	100	0	0	0	0	80	40	57	53	0	18	100	0	50	0	50	47	0	22	47	59	GC LH SF SU	
+ + + + – –	(–)	0	57	0	0	0	0	53	58	0	0	0	0	0	0	20	40	42	46	0	81	0	0	50	0	80	40	0	66	50	62	S W	
+ + + + + +	(+)	0	20	0	0	0	0	53	18	0	33	0	0	0	0	33	33	9	50	0	62	100	0	16	0	33	40	0	33	38	42	SF SU	
+ + + + + –	(–)	0	80	0	0	0	0	46	81	0	66	0	0	0	0	66	66	81	50	0	0	0	0	83	0	80	53	0	66	60	66	BP CP GC LH NY OJ	
– – – – – +	(+)	0	83	0	0	0	0	50	50	0	80	0	0	0	0	100	100	57	40	0	57	50	0	33	0	60	48	0	66	56	49	BP GC LH NY	
– – – – – –	(–)	0	16	0	0	0	0	25	50	0	20	0	0	0	0	0	0	42	40	0	36	0	0	66	0	40	23	0	33	41	36	SM PB	
– – – – + +	(+)	0	33	0	0	0	0	35	12	0	50	0	0	0	0	50	75	55	70	0	33	33	0	50	0	71	76	0	50	58	47	NY PB	
– – – – + –	(–)	0	66	0	0	0	0	65	87	0	80	0	0	0	0	50	50	44	25	0	66	66	0	42	0	66	53	0	83	47	65	BP CP S SF SU TB	
– – – + – +	(+)	0	50	0	0	0	0	14	22	0	66	0	0	0	0	33	50	60	30	0	37	0	0	57	0	100	37	0	50	59	50	GC PB SU	
– – – + – –	(–)	0	25	0	0	0	0	85	66	0	33	0	0	0	0	66	50	40	70	0	50	0	0	57	0	33	37	0	50	47	47	CO CP LH	
– – – + + +	(+)	0	66	0	0	0	0	42	33	0	66	0	0	0	0	60	50	25	70	0	66	0	0	28	0	28	23	0	16	40	40	BP GC PB	
– – – + + –	(–)	0	33	0	0	0	0	57	66	0	33	0	0	0	0	40	100	75	30	0	63	100	0	57	0	100	76	0	83	59	59	CP NY OJ SF SU TH	
– – + – – +	(+)	0	25	0	0	0	0	72	60	0	50	0	0	0	0	75	75	25	25	0	70	75	0	28	0	33	37	0	50	41	45	CO LH NY PB SF SU	
– – + – – –	(–)	0	75	0	0	0	0	18	40	0	0	0	0	0	0	25	25	75	30	0	50	25	0	71	0	50	62	0	50	46	33	BP OJ SM	
– – + – + +	(+)	0	57	0	0	0	0	63	20	0	0	0	0	0	0	100	50	28	18	0	80	0	0	40	0	33	50	0	100	48	37	LH S SF GC OJ	
– – + – + –	(–)	0	42	0	0	0	0	27	33	0	100	0	0	0	0	0	0	71	81	0	10	0	0	60	0	33	50	0	100	45	39	CP GC OJ PH	
– – + + – +	(+)	0	66	0	0	0	0	58	33	0	50	0	0	0	0	0	20	75	50	0	28	0	0	60	0	40	50	0	50		32	BP OJ	
– – + + – –	(–)	0	33	0	0	0	0	41	66	0	0	0	0	0	0	100	80	25	50	0	71	100	0	20	0	60	55	0	100	52	37	CP LH NY S SF W	
– – + + + +	(+)	0	83	0	0	0	0	22	33	0	75	0	0	0	0	25	0	33	57	0	20	33	0	50	0	50	55	0	0	52	39	BP GC S	
– – + + + –	(–)	0	16	0	0	0	0	77	50	0	0	0	0	0	50	100	0	66	35	0	80	33	0	50	0	50	33	0	100	43	32	CO LH NY SM TB	
– + – – – +	(+)	0	33	0	0	0	0	0	0	0	0	0	0	0	0	0	0	100	55	0	0	80	0	80	0	0	83	0	0	66	20	CO LH NY SM TB	
– + – – – –	(–)	0	33	0	0	0	0	55	0	0	0	0	0	0	0	33	0	100	44	0	43	20	0	20	0	0	16	0	100	33	10	BP SF	
– + – – + +	(+)	0	66	0	0	0	0	44	66	0	50	0	0	0	0	0	100	0	57	0	0	0	0	57	0	50	46	0	0	53	30	BP CP OJ SF W	
– + – – + –	(–)	100	33	0	0	0	0	0	0	0	0	0	0	0	0	66	100	100	42	0	100	20	0	42	0	0	53	0	100	44	25	LH NY S W	
– + – + – +	(+)	0	0	0	0	0	0	100	66	0	0	0	0	0	0	33	0	100	80	0	43	0	0	28	0	50	46	0	100	47	22	BP CP PB SM SU	
– + – + – –	(–)	0	50	0	0	0	0	40	40	0	100	0	0	0	0	0	0	100	20	0	0	66	0	28	0	66	16	0	50	52	24	CO GC LH NY OJ S	
– + – + + +	(+)	0	50	0	0	0	0	60	60	0	100	0	0	0	0	0	0	100	25	0	100	0	0	71	0	66	75	0	50	30	15	NY OJ PB S SM TB	
– + – + + –	(–)	0	0	0	0	0	0	63	75	0	50	0	0	0	0	66	66	0	50	0	66	75	0	71	0	42	57	0	100	57	32	GC OJ PB S SF SU	
– + + – – +	(+)	0	66	0	0	0	0	36	25	0	0	0	0	0	0	66	33	66	50	0	33	25	0	63	0	33	50	0	0	39	22	CP NY OJ SF SU	
– + + – – –	(–)	0	33	0	0	0	0	50	100	0	0	0	0	0	0	0	0	0	50	0	0	0	0	63	0	33	63	0	0	59	29	LH SM	
– + + – + +	(+)	0	50	0	0	0	0	37	33	0	50	0	0	0	0	0	0	50	37	0	100	0	0	36	0	100	36	0	100	38	19	BP CP NY SU	
– + + – + –	(–)	0	50	0	0	0	0	62	50	0	66	0	0	0	0	0	0	66	16	0	66	66	0	62	0	0	66	0	0	51	31	LH S OJ	
– + + + – +	(+)	0	0	0	0	0	0	0	0	0	0	0	0	0	0	0	0	0	0	0	0	0	0	0	0	0	33	0	0	32	28	GC LH OJ S SF TB	
– + + + – –	(–)	0	66	0	0	0	0	0	0	0	0	0	0	0	0	0	0	100	0	0	0	0	0	0	0	0	42	0	0	46	28	PB CO W	
– + + + + +	(+)	0100	0	0	0	0	0100	55	100	0	0	0	0	0	0	0	0	0	0	0	43	0	0	0	0	0	0	0	0	32	11	BP CO	
– + + + + –	(–)	0	33	0	0	0	0	44	0	0	50	0	0	0	0	33	0	0	20	0100	0	80	0	28	0	50	46	0	0	64	22	CP GC NY OJ PB SM	
+ – – – – +	(+)	0	0	0	0	0	0	100	66	0	0	0	0	0	0	66	0	100	25	0	100	20	0	71	0	16	16	0	100	48	22	CO CP GC LH NY SM	
+ – – – – –	(–)	0	50	0	0	0	0	40	40	0	100	0	0	0	0	0	0	100	75	0	66	40	0	71	0	66	75	0	50	52	22	BP OJ SF TB	
+ – – – + +	(+)	0	66	0	0	0	0	63	75	0	50	0	0	0	0	33	33	0	50	0	33	75	0	33	0	50	57	0	50	44	33	GC SF SM	
+ – – – + –	(–)	0	50	0	0	0	0	30	60	0	0	0	0	0	0	0	0	60	33	0	25	0	0	66	0	50	40	0	50	52	28	CP LH OJ PB S	
+ – – + – +	(+)	0	0	0	0	0	0	50	0	0	60	0	0	0	0	50	0	33	0	0	0	0	0	57	0	100	50	0	0	41	22	SU W	

Figure 8.9: Continued

		BO	BP	C	CC	CD	CL	CO	CP	FC	GC	HO	JY	LB	LC	LH	NY	O	OJ	PB	PL	S	SF	SV	SM	SP	SU	TB	TR	W	T%	T#		------ 65% ------
--+++	(+)	0	50	0	0	0	0	28	16	0	75	0	0	0	0	0	0	0	100	55	0	0	0	0	44	0	0	54	0	33	42	24		GC OJ S SU W
--+-++	(-)	0	50	0	0	0	0	71	83	0	0	0	0	0	0	0	0	0	0	44	0	0	0	0	55	100	33	36	0	66	53	30		CO CP NY S SU W
--+++	(+)	0	20	0	0	0	0	62	75	0	80	0	0	0	0	100	100	0	100	55	0	100	0	28	0	33	10	0	0	0	53	34		CP GC NY OJ S SF
--+-++	(-)	0	60	0	0	0	0	37	25	0	20	0	0	0	0	0	0	0	100	44	0	100	0	71	0	66	80	0	100	0	43	28		SM SU TB W
--+-++	(-)	0	42	0	0	0	0	66	83	0	50	0	0	0	0	50	50	0	83	100	0	0	50	10	66	0	70	0	33	0	53	34		CO CP OJ PB TB
--+-++	(-)	0	57	0	0	0	0	33	16	0	0	0	0	0	0	50	50	0	16	0	0	25	50	80	0	33	30	0	66	0	45	29		S SM
--+++	(+)	0	33	0	0	0	0	57	33	0	0	0	0	0	0	100	33	0	50	80	0	75	50	60	0	0	20	50	0	66	49	27		GC LH PB S W
--+-+++	(+)	0	66	0	0	0	0	40	66	0	0	0	0	0	0	66	66	0	50	66	0	50	0	40	50	0	20	0	33	0	50	28		BP CP NY SF SU TB
--+++	(+)	0	80	0	0	0	0	40	100	0	0	0	0	0	0	0	0	0	33	33	0	50	50	50	0	100	80	50	0	0	57	19		BP CP LH OJ PB
--+-+++	(-)	0	20	0	0	0	0	60	0	0	0	0	0	0	0	0	0	0	66	0	0	50	0	50	0	50	66	0	66	0	33	11		TB
--+++	(+)	0	0	0	0	0	0	0	0	0	0	0	0	0	0	0	0	0	33	75	0	50	33	0	60	50	25	66	0	0	44	22		LH PB
--+-++	(-)	0	100	0	0	0	0	62	60	0	25	0	0	0	0	0	0	0	100	33	0	50	66	20	0	33	25	0	0	0	52	26		BP GC OJ SF SU TB
--+++	(+)	0	0	0	0	0	0	37	40	0	75	0	0	0	0	50	0	0	25	75	0	66	0	28	0	66	66	100	0	0	41	21		OJ S W
--+-++	(-)	0	100	0	0	0	0	63	40	0	0	0	0	0	0	0	0	0	0	0	0	0	37	71	0	66	75	0	100	0	58	60		BP GC LH PB SM SU
--+++	(+)	0	100	0	0	0	0	36	60	0	100	0	0	0	0	100	50	0	50	100	0	33	0	50	50	33	27	0	50	0	47	25		BP NY SU
--+-++	(-)	0	0	0	0	0	0	57	33	0	33	0	0	0	0	0	0	0	50	0	0	50	62	50	0	66	72	50	0	100	52	28		CP GC TB W
--+++	(+)	0	25	0	0	0	0	42	66	0	66	0	0	0	0	50	0	0	50	33	0	66	40	0	0	33	21	50	50	0	33	29		S
--+-+++	(+)	0	75	0	0	0	0	64	62	0	0	0	0	0	0	50	60	0	50	66	0	33	40	50	0	50	78	50	0	50	60	47		BP PB TB
--+-+++	(-)	0	25	0	0	0	0	20	100	0	57	0	0	0	0	100	100	0	100	80	0	100	0	20	0	40	35	0	25	0	50	30		CP NY PB S SM
--+++	(+)	0	75	0	0	0	0	80	0	0	42	0	0	0	0	33	0	0	100	0	0	0	0	0	0	50	64	0	75	0	46	32		BP CO LH OJ SF
--+++	(+)	0	50	0	0	0	0	50	55	0	60	0	0	0	0	0	0	0	57	42	0	50	0	50	0	0	37	0	0	0	52	29		SF W
--+-++	(-)	0	100	0	0	0	0	50	44	0	40	0	0	0	0	66	20	0	42	57	0	50	0	25	50	60	62	100	0	100	48	33		LH NY W
--+-++	(-)	0	0	0	0	0	0	0	75	0	80	0	0	0	0	0	80	0	50	60	0	40	50	50	50	60	30	100	0	50	48	30		BP CP GC S
--+++	(+)	0	28	0	0	0	0	71	100	0	20	0	0	0	0	0	0	0	33	0	0	33	0	58	0	40	70	50	0	33	48	30		CO NY TB
--+++	(+)	0	33	0	0	0	0	33	33	0	40	0	0	0	0	50	0	0	42	44	0	100	0	42	0	50	53	33	0	66	49	31		GC LH S SU
--+-++	(-)	0	66	0	0	0	0	66	66	0	60	0	0	0	0	0	0	0	57	55	0	20	0	57	0	100	33	66	0	0	47	30		BP CO CP PB W
--+-++	(-)	0	50	0	0	0	0	33	50	0	50	0	0	0	0	100	0	0	33	100	0	66	50	0	75	50	36	0	0	100	51	24		CO CP LH PB SM
--+++	(+)	0	0	0	0	0	0	77	40	0	66	0	0	0	0	0	100	0	66	33	0	66	0	20	0	50	63	0	100	0	48	23		NY OJ S
--+-++	(-)	0	0	0	0	0	0	22	40	0	33	0	0	0	0	33	0	0	33	66	0	50	0	40	0	25	50	50	0	80	50	30		CO LH W
--+-++	(-)	0	100	0	0	0	0	33	100	0	0	0	0	0	0	0	0	0	55	44	0	50	50	0	0	0	27	20	0	0	45	27		BP CP NY OJ
--+++	(+)	0	71	0	0	0	0	28	0	0	80	0	0	0	0	66	0	0	66	50	0	40	0	50	0	50	60	50	0	50	54	16		BP CP OJ W
--+++	(+)	0	28	0	0	0	0	71	100	0	0	0	0	0	0	0	0	0	33	0	0	33	0	33	0	100	66	0	50	0	48	19		CO LH SM SU TB
--+-++	(-)	0	33	0	0	0	0	50	25	0	75	0	0	0	0	50	0	0	42	25	0	50	0	50	0	100	33	0	50	0	49	18		LH OJ PB TB
--+++	(+)	0	40	0	0	0	0	50	75	0	25	0	0	0	0	0	0	0	42	80	0	80	100	0	0	0	62	100	0	50	48	18		CP S SF SU
--+-++	(-)	0	66	0	0	0	0	66	66	0	0	0	0	0	0	0	0	0	57	75	0	20	0	57	0	100	33	66	0	66	43	22		GC SU W
--+++	(+)	0	50	0	0	0	0	28	33	0	0	0	0	0	0	50	0	0	71	0	0	50	75	75	0	100	25	0	33	0	54	28		BP CO CP LH PB SF SM
--+++	(+)	0	0	0	0	0	0	37	42	0	0	0	0	0	0	0	0	0	57	33	0	100	0	20	0	100	63	0	0	0	45	25		GC OJ S
--+-++	(-)	0	50	0	0	0	0	62	57	0	0	0	0	0	0	50	0	0	33	66	0	0	100	80	0	0	50	27	0	100	52	29		NY PB SF SM SU
--+++	(+)	0	25	0	0	0	0	55	85	0	0	0	0	0	0	0	0	0	71	57	0	33	0	33	0	0	37	0	100	0	51	32		CP GC PB W
--+++	(+)	0	75	0	0	0	0	44	14	0	16	0	0	0	0	0	0	0	0	80	0	50	0	14	0	100	62	0	0	0	45	28		BP NY OJ SM SU
--+-++	(-)	0	40	0	0	0	0	44	25	0	0	0	0	0	0	0	0	0	33	42	0	40	0	85	0	66	75	33	0	33	37	22		SU TB
--+++	(+)	0	0	0	0	0	0	28	33	0	0	0	0	0	0	50	50	0	28	0	0	60	100	0	66	50	25	66	0	66	62	36		CP LH OJ SF SM W
--+-++	(-)	0	60	0	0	0	0	71	66	0	0	0	0	0	0	0	0	0	57	57	0	100	0	0	0	50	27	66	0	57	57	32		BP CP NY OJ SF TB
--+++	(+)	0	100	0	0	0	0	20	85	0	0	0	0	0	0	50	0	0	100	50	0	60	0	0	80	50	72	0	0	0	41	23		CO GC PB SM
--+++	(+)	0	0	0	0	0	0	50	40	0	66	0	0	0	0	100	57	0	60	50	0	50	66	75	0	33	27	0	0	0	52	34		GC LH SF SM SU
--+-++	(-)	0	100	0	0	0	0	50	60	0	33	0	0	0	0	0	42	0	40	50	0	50	33	25	0	33	50	66	0	0	47	31		BP W

Figure 8.9: Continued

Figure 8.9: Continued

	BO	BP	C	CC	CD	CL	CO	CP	FC	GC	HO	JY	LB	LC	LH	NY	O	OJ	PB	PL	S	SF	SV	SM	SP	SU	TB	TR	W	T%	T#						65%

Figure 8.9: Continued

Figure 8.9: Concluded

		BO	BP	C	CC	CD	CL	CO	CP	FC	GC	HO	JY	LB	LC	LH	NY	O	OJ	PB	PL	S	SF	SV	SM	SP	SU	TB	IR	W	T%	T#	65%
+++++++	(+)	0	0	0	0	0	0	60	14	0	50	0	0	0	0	0	0	0	11	25	0	50	100	0	25	0	100	54	0	50	38	23	SF SU
+++++++	(−)	0	100	0	0	0	0	40	85	0	50	0	0	0	0	100	100	0	77	75	0	50	0	0	75	0	0	36	0	50	58	35	BP CP LH NY OJ PB SM
+++++++	(+)	0	66	0	0	0	0	50	50	0	66	0	0	0	0	100	100	0	50	50	0	66	100	0	25	0	66	28	0	100	52	27	BP GC LH NY S SF
+++++−−−	(−)	0	0	0	0	0	0	50	50	0	33	0	0	0	0	0	0	0	50	50	0	33	0	0	75	0	33	64	0	0	45	23	SM
+++++−−	(+)	0	33	0	0	0	0	25	20	0	50	0	0	0	0	33	0	0	50	60	0	0	66	0	50	0	50	22	0	0	37	24	SF
+++++−−−+	(−)	0	0	0	0	0	0	75	80	0	50	0	0	0	0	66	0	0	50	40	0	100	33	0	60	0	50	77	0	0	62	40	BP CO CP LH S TB
+++++−+−	(+)	0	100	0	0	0	0	25	60	0	75	0	0	0	0	33	33	0	50	70	0	50	0	0	50	0	50	83	0	50	52	29	GC PB TB
+++++−+−	(−)	0	0	0	0	0	0	75	60	0	25	0	0	0	0	66	66	0	50	30	0	50	0	0	40	0	50	16	0	50	45	25	BP CO LH NY
+++++−++	(+)	0	100	0	0	0	0	33	40	0	66	0	0	0	0	57	0	0	50	75	0	66	0	0	25	0	0	83	0	20	44	26	BP GC PB S
+++++++	(−)	0	0	0	0	0	0	66	60	0	33	0	0	0	0	42	100	0	50	25	0	33	0	0	50	0	50	25	0	80	54	32	CO NY TB W
+++++++	(+)	0	0	0	0	0	0	71	0	0	50	0	0	0	0	0	0	0	50	50	0	66	33	0	50	0	50	75	0	0	46	19	BP CO LH SF
+++++−−	(−)	0	66	0	0	0	0	28	100	0	0	0	0	0	0	100	0	0	100	50	0	66	33	0	100	0	100	50	0	100	53	22	CP OJ S SM TB W
+++++−+	(+)	0	33	0	0	0	0	75	33	0	0	0	0	0	0	0	100	0	25	14	0	71	100	0	50	0	100	50	0	100	48	22	BP CO LH S SF SU
+++++++	(−)	0	75	0	0	0	0	66	25	0	0	0	0	0	0	0	33	0	75	85	0	14	0	0	100	0	50	66	0	0	44	17	BP SM TB
+++++++	(+)	0	25	0	0	0	0	60	25	0	0	0	0	0	0	0	66	0	50	100	0	40	0	0	0	0	50	33	0	100	52	20	CP NY PB SF W
+++++++	(+)	0	100	0	0	0	0	40	75	0	0	0	0	0	0	50	0	0	50	66	0	60	100	0	0	0	100	50	0	0	52	18	BP GC PB S SU
+++++++	(−)	0	0	0	0	0	0	71	50	0	0	0	0	0	0	50	100	0	50	16	0	0	0	0	50	0	0	50	0	0	44	15	CO NY W

Figure 8.10: Daily Closing Patterns: Whipsaw Markets

		BO	BP	C	CC	CD	CL	CO	CP	FC	CP	GC	HO	JY	LB	LC	LH	NY	O	OJ	PB	PL	S	SF	SV	SM	SP	SU	TB	TR	W	T%	T#	
- - -	(+)	48	0	53	49	0	0	42	56	41	56	56	0	42	52	55	42	49	55	59	55	55	0	0	0	50	0	62	47	54	50	53	3320	
- - +	(-)	50	0	49	49	0	0	42	41	46	41	41	0	45	45	55	45	56	47	44	40	40	0	0	0	42	0	37	50	51	49	43	2692	
- + -	(+)	46	0	48	50	0	0	49	48	46	44	44	0	50	48	48	45	56	47	43	41	41	0	0	0	48	0	43	50	51	49	48	3302	
- + +	(-)	50	0	48	47	0	0	51	46	46	53	53	0	41	50	49	38	50	56	43	43	43	0	0	0	47	0	52	44	53	46	48	3312	
+ - -	(+)	48	0	48	47	0	0	51	46	46	48	48	0	41	51	47	54	38	43	47	48	48	0	0	0	48	0	57	44	53	41	48	3303	
+ - +	(+)	48	0	46	48	0	0	45	48	46	46	46	0	53	47	43	43	57	49	50	46	46	0	0	0	45	0	40	49	45	55	48	3307	
+ + -	(+)	47	0	46	48	0	0	41	41	46	34	34	0	50	52	50	52	52	41	43	43	43	0	0	0	42	0	44	49	43	55	43	2749	
+ + +	(-)	52	0	56	49	0	0	56	54	34	65	65	0	49	52	50	50	45	52	53	54	54	0	0	0	52	0	53	48	54	53	52	3312	
- - - -	(+)	55	0	60	53	0	0	58	63	57	57	57	0	47	51	53	51	50	56	61	61	50	0	0	0	53	0	60	53	60	49	55	1487	
- - - +	(-)	44	0	36	45	0	0	39	35	38	38	38	0	34	46	44	44	54	41	43	43	44	0	0	0	41	0	39	56	43	36	41	1119	
- - + -	(+)	50	0	49	47	0	0	54	49	50	50	50	0	47	44	47	50	54	49	49	54	42	0	0	0	49	0	50	51	55	49	48	1628	
- - + +	(-)	47	0	46	51	0	0	43	45	49	49	49	0	54	54	50	50	50	38	47	54	53	0	0	0	45	0	39	45	45	44	47	1595	
- + - -	(+)	45	0	45	47	0	0	50	45	47	47	47	0	38	52	58	58	44	54	47	54	51	0	0	0	47	0	51	48	51	60	47	1580	
- + - +	(+)	54	0	48	49	0	0	46	50	48	48	48	0	56	56	44	39	50	49	49	49	42	0	0	0	45	0	48	46	45	60	48	1603	
- + + -	(-)	53	0	42	51	0	0	42	40	31	31	31	0	46	47	40	40	52	40	37	40	53	0	0	0	40	0	58	53	44	43	43	1431	
- + + +	(+)	46	0	45	53	0	0	46	45	39	68	68	0	50	51	54	49	40	54	46	58	39	0	0	0	53	0	59	49	49	53	53	1759	GC
- + + +	(-)	41	0	50	44	0	0	50	47	57	54	54	0	56	52	58	50	48	41	51	57	60	0	0	0	48	0	62	42	50	51	52	1719	
+ - - -	(+)	54	0	50	44	0	0	50	47	57	57	57	0	42	46	50	50	33	40	49	49	42	0	0	0	44	0	60	43	49	60	44	1470	
+ - - +	(-)	53	0	52	48	0	0	53	47	52	52	52	0	45	50	39	48	43	43	47	48	44	0	0	0	49	0	37	53	55	45	48	1572	
+ - + -	(+)	41	0	44	48	0	0	45	47	39	39	39	0	50	50	46	62	50	49	50	48	52	0	0	0	49	0	49	50	48	45	47	1618	
+ - + +	(+)	54	0	50	44	0	0	50	47	57	57	57	0	42	46	48	48	33	42	49	45	46	0	0	0	44	0	58	43	49	60	45	1612	
+ + - -	(+)	41	0	44	48	0	0	45	47	44	44	44	0	50	50	49	49	50	49	50	48	52	0	0	0	49	0	30	50	41	50	47	1576	
+ + - +	(+)	38	0	38	46	0	0	40	41	40	40	40	0	46	46	50	50	50	42	49	45	46	0	0	0	44	0	28	43	39	45	44	1215	
+ + + -	(-)	61	0	58	52	0	0	56	52	59	59	59	0	48	51	45	51	50	53	48	52	52	0	0	0	50	0	71	51	57	51	52	1445	SU
+ + + +	(+)	61	0	56	53	0	0	60	57	71	71	71	0	48	57	57	57	27	53	53	61	41	0	0	0	53	0	66	51	57	51	56	627	GC SU TR
- - - - -	(+)	38	0	41	45	0	0	39	42	28	28	28	0	49	48	40	30	41	43	42	35	52	0	0	0	31	0	33	38	30	45	41	459	
- - - - +	(-)	50	0	41	46	0	0	56	54	61	61	61	0	47	47	52	60	60	52	50	35	41	0	0	0	50	0	42	50	56	55	48	725	
- - - + -	(+)	47	0	56	52	0	0	40	39	38	38	38	0	44	45	44	47	30	40	40	35	58	0	0	0	50	0	44	43	44	55	48	725	
- - - + +	(-)	45	0	42	50	0	0	53	44	50	50	50	0	37	54	55	55	41	44	54	47	52	0	0	0	51	0	46	42	44	57	48	764	
- - + - -	(+)	54	0	52	47	0	0	42	52	40	40	40	0	56	50	41	29	50	43	43	51	43	0	0	0	39	0	53	54	55	60	48	766	
- - + - +	(-)	64	0	44	51	0	0	49	40	30	30	30	0	44	41	41	38	50	41	38	50	94	0	0	0	45	0	52	50	43	45	45	731	NY
- - + + -	(+)	35	0	53	46	0	0	50	55	69	69	69	0	49	51	62	30	27	52	56	58	33	0	0	0	48	0	42	46	56	57	52	851	GC
- - + + +	(-)	39	0	52	44	0	0	50	53	57	57	57	0	43	50	30	56	53	53	60	55	50	0	0	0	43	0	62	38	53	55	52	836	
- + - - -	(+)	58	0	45	53	0	0	45	53	40	40	40	0	43	42	43	42	27	42	34	47	47	0	0	0	43	0	37	56	43	42	44	713	
- + - - +	(+)	47	0	44	50	0	0	48	45	46	46	46	0	43	51	43	40	40	58	39	45	48	0	0	0	46	0	44	43	56	48	46	742	
- + - + -	(-)	53	0	52	47	0	0	49	50	50	50	50	0	40	40	54	54	37	50	58	53	46	0	0	0	49	0	56	43	40	48	50	790	
- + - + +	(+)	37	0	45	45	0	0	46	47	39	39	39	0	56	56	45	11	52	41	50	41	48	0	0	0	49	0	41	54	40	47	47	838	
- + + - -	(+)	37	0	47	50	0	0	47	47	38	38	38	0	48	45	52	52	77	50	46	53	43	0	0	0	49	0	37	54	40	47	49	862	NY
- + + - +	(-)	62	0	55	45	0	0	39	44	61	61	61	0	56	45	41	63	63	54	52	44	58	0	0	0	51	0	79	43	60	46	44	633	
- + + + -	(+)	62	0	55	53	0	0	57	48	61	61	61	0	60	36	37	46	46	36	43	47	40	0	0	0	51	0	54	52	59	53	53	765	SU
- + + + +	(+)	47	0	64	53	0	0	60	67	49	49	49	0	48	44	48	52	48	48	59	61	57	0	0	0	47	0	57	52	52	51	55	811	CP
+ - - - -	(+)	52	0	31	45	0	0	37	31	45	45	45	0	46	37	50	29	29	50	53	36	39	0	0	0	56	0	47	45	45	45	41	611	
+ - - - +	(-)	51	0	56	50	0	0	45	45	41	41	41	0	54	37	43	36	53	50	53	48	41	0	0	0	36	0	39	50	46	49	49	847	
+ - - + -	(+)	48	0	38	48	0	0	45	50	56	56	56	0	40	62	53	50	50	43	50	50	52	0	0	0	36	0	39	47	46	36	47	813	
+ - - + +	(-)	45	0	49	45	0	0	50	48	43	43	43	0	39	50	59	44	44	40	43	47	38	0	0	0	48	0	44	54	59	36	47	772	
+ - + - -	(+)	55	0	46	51	0	0	47	47	55	55	55	0	38	48	55	28	28	36	40	47	38	0	0	0	48	0	51	51	43	47	48	789	
+ - + - +	(-)	38	0	39	51	0	0	34	43	31	31	31	0	43	48	45	71	71	50	36	41	45	0	0	0	34	0	65	51	52	47	42	662	
+ - + + -	(+)	61	0	55	47	0	0	62	55	68	68	68	0	55	56	60	50	50	50	58	58	45	0	0	0	61	0	35	45	52	48	54	853	GC NY
+ - + + +	(-)	50	0	47	52	0	0	54	51	50	50	50	0	43	42	45	43	43	52	47	61	68	0	0	0	52	0	61	43	43	51	51	829	PL
+ + - - -	(+)	46	0	49	52	0	0	42	45	48	48	48	0	40	45	37	50	50	48	43	37	26	0	0	0	38	0	38	52	56	46	44	694	
+ + - - +	(+)	38	0	49	55	0	0	42	49	34	34	34	0	56	37	41	52	52	52	41	41	27	0	0	0	48	0	34	40	40	47	47	770	
+ + - + -	(-)	58	0	49	42	0	0	53	45	62	62	62	0	58	54	41	50	43	46	50	58	65	0	0	0	50	0	65	40	58	50	48	784	SU
+ + + - +	(+)	52	0	57	52	0	0	54	47	43	43	43	0	47	54	58	42	42	36	46	56	43	0	0	0	50	0	68	39	55	43	50	726	SU
+ + + + -	(-)	45	0	40	44	0	0	44	46	51	51	51	0	47	47	37	57	57	55	50	40	56	0	0	0	45	0	28	54	42	52	46	663	

-------- 65% --------

Figure 8.10: Continued

		BO	BP	C	CC	CD	CL	CO	CP	FC	GC	HO	JY	LB	LC	LH	NY	O	OJ	PB	PL	S	SF	SV	SM	SP	SU	TB	TR	W	T%	T#	
++++	(+)	36	0	32	46	0	0	41	37	0	40	0	0	44	48	61	35	38	51	46	35	0	0	0	42	0	50	41	34	45	44	535	
++++	(−)	64	0	62	51	0	0	54	57	0	60	0	0	50	50	35	64	53	46	51	64	0	0	0	50	0	50	48	57	54	52	631	
----	(+)	69	0	60	50	0	0	50	65	0	40	0	0	42	55	60	66	47	53	67	50	0	0	0	50	0	66	66	75	57	55	256	BO NY PB SU TB TR
----	(−)	30	0	39	47	0	0	50	34	0	60	0	0	55	44	39	33	47	39	29	50	0	0	0	46	0	33	29	25	33	41	192	
-+-+	(+)	38	0	45	50	0	0	67	65	0	56	0	0	56	55	54	66	51	40	35	35	0	0	0	48	0	50	48	72	61	51	324	CO NY TR
-+-+	(−)	57	0	54	50	0	0	32	35	0	44	0	0	43	45	45	33	35	57	63	64	0	0	0	46	0	50	42	27	32	45	288	
--++	(+)	46	0	42	55	0	0	58	45	0	60	0	0	35	46	62	20	53	50	50	56	0	0	0	57	0	50	44	52	42	49	357	
--++	(−)	60	0	52	42	0	0	41	52	0	25	0	0	61	53	34	60	38	50	49	39	0	0	0	35	0	83	52	47	57	47	341	SU
-+++	(+)	57	0	44	56	0	0	42	37	0	40	0	0	50	38	33	77	39	31	54	68	0	0	0	38	0	42	43	36	39	44	318	NY PL
-+++	(−)	42	0	55	43	0	0	57	59	0	59	0	0	47	61	63	22	57	50	45	25	0	0	0	54	0	57	48	63	55	53	386	
--+-	(+)	42	0	56	52	0	0	54	51	0	52	0	0	56	50	57	33	54	64	56	48	0	0	0	42	0	62	45	60	45	52	404	
--+-	(−)	52	0	39	44	0	0	45	46	0	48	0	0	40	50	42	66	41	27	38	52	0	0	0	50	0	37	54	35	52	43	335	NY
-++-	(+)	56	0	48	40	0	0	44	45	0	40	0	0	36	50	45	45	53	43	40	40	0	0	0	38	0	42	51	44	44	44	341	
-++-	(−)	43	0	48	54	0	0	55	52	0	51	0	0	60	47	57	40	33	61	53	60	0	0	0	58	0	57	41	31	46	52	402	
-+++	(+)	61	0	56	41	0	0	58	49	0	58	0	0	51	43	44	25	53	39	40	46	0	0	0	50	0	50	28	56	58	47	406	
-+-+	(−)	38	0	42	54	0	0	36	42	0	37	0	0	46	46	43	57	43	50	45	53	0	0	0	38	0	42	51	44	34	44	414	NY
-+-+	(+)	33	0	42	37	0	0	42	50	0	21	0	0	52	43	50	28	35	35	53	60	0	0	0	58	0	20	39	36	51	44	328	
-+-+	(−)	66	0	57	62	0	0	54	43	0	78	0	0	41	56	46	44	51	47	50	41	0	0	0	48	0	80	57	63	48	53	387	BO GC SU
-+-+	(+)	37	0	61	57	0	0	58	68	0	51	0	0	46	43	53	71	43	56	50	54	0	0	0	42	0	66	58	64	50	54	385	CP NY SU
-+-+	(−)	62	0	33	40	0	0	39	31	0	44	0	0	43	51	56	28	35	65	45	45	0	0	0	51	0	33	41	35	44	43	306	
-+++	(+)	50	0	60	56	0	0	60	46	0	44	0	0	56	33	35	33	62	47	50	34	0	0	0	56	0	53	65	47	40	49	390	LC NY
-+-+	(−)	50	0	34	39	0	0	40	49	0	52	0	0	39	66	61	66	31	51	50	57	0	0	0	32	0	33	34	52	52	46	374	TR
-+-+	(+)	37	0	57	37	0	0	54	42	0	43	0	0	34	46	60	40	55	38	46	58	0	0	0	42	0	50	57	66	42	47	385	
-+-+	(−)	62	0	36	59	0	0	43	50	0	53	0	0	59	52	38	60	38	58	51	31	0	0	0	53	0	50	39	22	57	48	327	
-+++	(+)	18	0	45	46	0	0	42	41	0	23	0	0	48	45	45	50	50	41	53	40	0	0	0	41	0	63	56	48	60	44	387	BO GC
-+-+	(−)	81	0	52	50	0	0	54	56	0	76	0	0	51	48	56	50	46	65	54	46	0	0	0	50	0	36	37	48	35	52	440	SU
-+++	(+)	58	0	43	48	0	0	60	44	0	45	0	0	47	54	55	14	44	48	60	46	0	0	0	53	0	66	50	35	56	51	396	NY
-+-+	(−)	41	0	49	51	0	0	39	52	0	51	0	0	43	47	42	71	48	50	42	27	0	0	0	40	0	33	50	65	43	46	411	LB
-+++	(+)	52	0	41	55	0	0	43	52	0	37	0	0	72	47	57	0	48	55	42	66	0	0	0	42	0	55	62	46	55	49	398	NY PL
-+-+	(−)	47	0	54	40	0	0	55	44	0	62	0	0	25	45	42	100	44	42	56	66	0	0	0	46	0	44	34	50	45	47	385	
-++-	(+)	56	0	61	66	0	0	53	55	0	54	0	0	40	60	60	35	57	39	58	40	0	0	0	53	0	68	30	56	50	50	386	SU
-+-+	(−)	39	0	36	50	0	0	46	54	0	40	0	0	55	40	40	50	42	39	38	60	0	0	0	40	0	26	65	40	50	46	353	
-++--	(+)	28	0	19	44	0	0	46	38	0	28	0	0	48	43	63	28	37	56	41	34	0	0	0	40	0	60	43	40	46	42	267	
-+-+-	(−)	71	0	77	52	0	0	51	53	0	71	0	0	46	53	46	35	59	41	53	65	0	0	0	51	0	40	40	46	53	53	335	BO C GC NY
-++-+	(+)	57	0	48	53	0	0	66	55	0	84	0	0	55	46	53	60	55	52	59	33	0	0	0	67	0	66	45	66	35	55	338	CO GC SM SU TR
-+--+	(−)	42	0	48	46	0	0	33	44	0	16	0	0	44	53	43	20	41	47	37	53	0	0	0	28	0	33	42	33	59	41	254	
++-++	(+)	63	0	40	44	0	0	48	42	0	66	0	0	38	43	51	44	43	50	63	63	0	0	0	44	0	37	50	45	50	46	375	GC
+-+-+	(−)	36	0	56	53	0	0	46	46	0	33	0	0	55	48	35	50	55	58	47	50	0	0	0	53	0	66	66	33	34	50	412	
+-++-	(+)	53	0	40	40	0	0	43	54	0	44	0	0	36	43	50	50	30	47	50	37	0	0	0	48	0	66	35	66	34	46	376	SU
+-+-+	(−)	36	0	57	55	0	0	52	47	0	50	0	0	54	31	46	50	50	52	52	55	0	0	0	41	0	33	56	22	49	49	401	TR
+-+-+	(+)	75	0	44	46	0	0	55	46	0	21	0	0	49	60	36	50	42	41	34	56	0	0	0	51	0	63	56	47	43	46	391	BO
+-+-+	(−)	25	0	51	50	0	0	44	48	0	78	0	0	61	36	60	50	45	55	64	40	0	0	0	63	0	27	43	52	56	51	434	GC
+-++-+	(+)	36	0	48	35	0	0	52	55	0	60	0	0	50	52	60	20	55	50	40	40	0	0	0	45	0	53	46	53	45	51	406	
+-+-+-	(−)	63	0	44	64	0	0	44	44	0	36	0	0	30	49	43	50	39	39	56	54	0	0	0	43	0	37	43	46	49	45	358	
++-++	(+)	38	0	43	61	0	0	51	46	0	50	0	0	58	52	49	60	50	45	39	39	0	0	0	52	0	56	46	58	47	47	363	
+--+-+	(−)	47	0	43	47	0	0	43	43	0	57	0	0	33	50	46	0	47	59	48	54	0	0	0	57	0	54	43	37	31	47	401	W
++-++-	(+)	36	0	52	47	0	0	55	55	0	42	0	0	41	47	52	80	40	40	51	38	0	0	0	49	0	28	41	37	68	49	425	NY
+-+-++	(−)	41	0	42	53	0	0	37	37	0	62	0	0	48	48	62	35	41	40	48	65	0	0	0	50	0	15	45	35	40	43	290	NY
++--++	(+)	58	0	55	43	0	0	60	54	0	37	0	0	58	52	62	100	49	48	56	35	0	0	0	50	0	84	51	65	50	53	354	SU
++-+-+	(−)	57	0	42	56	0	0	61	70	0	44	0	0	48	40	53	44	40	55	69	69	0	0	0	46	0	40	47	42	56	55	388	C CP PB PL
++--+-	(+)	53	0	52	43	0	0	49	43	0	38	0	0	54	40	50	22	30	59	46	23	0	0	0	46	0	37	57	43	40	40	282	TR
++-++-	(−)	46	0	42	56	0	0	50	51	0	61	0	0	39	54	47	40	44	35	52	41	0	0	0	54	0	50	51	31	43	47	395	

Figure 8.10: Continued

	BO	BP	C	CC	CD	CL	CO	CP	FC	GC	HO	JY	LB	LC	LH	NY	O	OJ	PB	PL	S	SF	SV	SM	SP	SU	TB	TR	W	T%	T#		65%
+ + – + –	47	0	40	52	0	0	44	50	0	42	0	0	43	58	55	50	36	42	53	42	0	0	0	51	0	47	52	55	29	47	373		
+ + – + –	52	0	55	44	0	0	51	47	0	57	0	0	56	41	44	50	63	55	42	50	0	0	0	40	0	52	36	44	67	49	386		W
+ + – + +	60	0	36	55	0	0	27	40	0	40	0	0	43	46	45	100	40	36	36	50	0	0	0	27	0	66	47	47	40	40	311		SU
+ + – + +	44	0	47	44	0	0	70	58	0	57	0	0	52	51	52	50	57	58	62	41	0	0	0	70	0	33	52	52	37	56	433		CO NY SM
+ + + + +	50	0	52	55	0	0	47	59	0	52	0	0	66	58	73	50	45	61	60	77	0	0	0	57	0	57	37	68	57	54	362		LB LH PL
+ + + + –	23	0	54	56	0	0	45	45	0	47	0	0	30	41	26	33	60	38	38	29	0	0	0	34	0	42	55	31	43	41	278		
+ + + + +	71	0	45	43	0	0	52	45	0	25	0	0	53	53	56	50	40	50	59	62	0	0	0	55	0	18	37	53	63	46	335		BO SU TR
+ + + + +	43	0	54	59	0	0	57	39	0	62	0	0	45	55	33	50	42	54	56	45	0	0	0	38	0	81	68	53	37	50	363		
+ + + + +	56	0	42	36	0	0	40	33	0	26	0	0	41	52	37	66	68	42	39	54	0	0	0	48	0	60	53	46	53	45	314		GC NY O
+ + + + +	44	0	50	50	0	0	35	90	0	66	0	0	52	53	60	60	47	45	48	35	0	0	0	44	0	40	36	33	46	46	285		
+ + + + +	55	0	55	44	0	0	35	10	0	60	0	0	54	46	34	40	36	54	51	55	0	0	0	50	0	40	46	50	53	50	250		
– + – + +	50	0	38	50	0	0	64	36	0	33	0	0	38	70	33	100	54	36	90	44	0	0	0	41	0	60	50	83	54	55	271		CP TR
– – – + –	50	0	44	51	0	0	21	10	0	66	0	0	61	29	33	100	54	60	10	44	0	0	0	41	0	14	85	50	36	42	106		CP LC LH NY PB SU TB
– – – – +	33	0	50	41	0	0	35	36	0	50	0	0	43	42	35	0	46	45	43	52	0	0	0	46	0	50	50	80	36	43	81		GC
– – – – +	66	0	47	51	0	0	35	57	0	63	0	0	31	44	53	100	54	60	55	66	0	0	0	62	0	37	37	16	26	43	143		CO NY TR W
– – – – –	33	0	35	48	0	0	34	34	0	18	0	0	47	40	44	75	46	42	42	20	0	0	0	32	0	50	50	80	36	49	111		BO
– + – + +	66	0	64	36	0	0	65	57	0	21	0	0	50	59	55	46	42	55	45	22	0	0	0	60	0	37	37	76	66	48	142		PL TR
– + – + +	62	0	58	60	0	0	58	60	0	78	0	0	57	55	63	33	53	53	80	66	0	0	0	31	0	66	50	38	33	43	138		BO LB NY SU
– + + + +	37	0	61	48	0	0	44	35	0	80	0	0	45	42	36	66	50	68	99	53	0	0	0	54	0	33	61	37	52	53	139		NY PL SU
– + + + +	41	0	35	41	0	0	55	44	0	20	0	0	64	50	35	50	24	28	28	53	0	0	0	51	0	60	37	77	66	54	173		GC TR W
– + + + –	50	0	34	43	0	0	36	52	0	16	0	0	41	21	65	66	64	56	42	46	0	0	0	48	0	40	77	57	42	41	184		GC OJ PB
– + – + +	62	0	52	45	0	0	64	39	0	83	0	0	72	51	42	100	64	56	56	53	0	0	0	38	0	100	11	50	57	44	141		NY PL
– + + + +	37	0	47	50	0	0	64	50	0	89	0	0	22	72	66	50	52	40	46	46	0	0	0	55	0	25	30	50	58	44	157		SU TR
– + + + +	55	0	52	41	0	0	29	50	0	10	0	0	45	36	53	50	42	45	46	0	0	0	0	28	0	75	65	64	33	53	192		GC NY
– + + + –	44	0	47	39	0	0	32	41	0	30	0	0	50	59	50	25	38	55	51	54	0	0	0	66	0	33	50	50	64	51	199		C GC
– + + + +	16	0	41	39	0	0	68	51	0	69	0	0	46	44	40	50	30	51	58	45	0	0	0	83	0	66	72	71	60	45	175		PL SU
– + + + +	83	0	58	52	0	0	75	41	0	25	0	0	68	57	44	50	38	50	30	25	0	0	0	11	0	33	63	50	35	56	135		LB
+ + + + –	70	0	61	38	0	0	25	58	0	75	0	0	41	39	25	50	30	52	56	72	0	0	0	56	0	60	28	57	31	52	178		BO CO GC LC LH SU TB
+ + – + –	30	0	33	51	0	0	75	59	0	46	0	0	32	48	42	50	38	38	38	58	0	0	0	43	0	40	75	66	60	52	176		BO CO SU TR
+ + – + +	50	0	50	37	0	0	25	37	0	53	0	0	72	52	46	40	30	48	47	25	0	0	0	19	0	75	25	0	50	44	151		GC PL SM
+ + + + +	50	0	50	58	0	0	41	39	0	31	0	0	27	42	53	100	70	47	52	58	0	0	0	66	0	25	41	40	54	44	213		CO SM TB
+ + + + –	57	0	33	52	0	0	52	50	0	62	0	0	30	78	48	33	30	55	52	42	0	0	0	60	0	50	20	40	66	47	178		OJ
+ + – + +	42	0	50	47	0	0	50	50	0	28	0	0	54	60	53	50	70	52	48	22	0	0	0	50	0	37	80	36	47	48	206		LH PL SU TR
+ + + + +	33	0	29	46	0	0	45	27	0	71	0	0	42	44	50	80	30	52	36	25	0	0	0	51	0	50	35	54	63	44	179		LB NY
+ – + + +	66	0	11	42	0	0	46	51	0	25	0	0	57	55	57	50	70	48	47	58	0	0	0	37	0	50	47	45	48	41	161		SU TB W
+ – + + +	20	0	88	57	0	0	50	62	0	68	0	0	26	45	57	50	30	47	52	42	0	0	0	50	0	0	57	36	52	53	167		BO GC SM
+ – + + –	80	0	53	50	0	0	50	72	0	36	0	0	73	65	38	60	41	38	46	30	0	0	0	46	0	50	54	63	60	56	199		SU
+ – + + +	37	0	57	38	0	0	50	51	0	64	0	0	28	60	57	50	58	48	58	50	0	0	0	32	0	60	50	50	40	40	200		BO GC NY
+ – + + –	62	0	38	39	0	0	60	40	0	60	0	0	50	26	50	33	33	56	50	50	0	0	0	56	0	40	33	63	35	44	203		LB TB
– + – + –	50	0	41	39	0	0	44	60	0	33	0	0	57	35	41	46	70	57	33	53	0	0	0	66	0	62	42	46	65	51	191		NY SU
– + + + +	43	0	57	52	0	0	52	62	0	50	0	0	60	61	52	0	33	59	40	35	0	0	0	50	0	71	50	25	62	43	201		C LC TR
– + – + –	37	0	29	46	0	0	50	41	0	41	0	0	47	34	47	41	41	30	32	22	0	0	0	42	0	28	18	75	31	53	172		
– + + + +	62	0	88	57	0	0	44	53	0	82	0	0	42	61	52	54	60	62	62	44	0	0	0	50	0	71	63	75	62	49	135		
– + + + +	60	0	53	38	0	0	52	46	0	41	0	0	57	34	47	33	36	37	37	55	0	0	0	51	0	28	18	31	31	47	175		C NY W
– + + + –	60	0	57	50	0	0	50	41	0	58	0	0	42	60	52	100	41	30	62	22	0	0	0	42	0	71	63	75	62	53	172		CP GC O SM SU
– + – + –	40	0	38	50	0	0	45	46	0	16	0	0	57	45	50	50	28	41	28	30	0	0	0	25	0	35	35	54	63	44	123		
– + – + +	55	0	33	50	0	0	46	51	0	64	0	0	26	65	57	57	41	59	59	50	0	0	0	47	0	50	35	54	63	51	173		
– + – + –	50	0	47	39	0	0	50	54	0	35	0	0	73	60	57	50	60	63	46	50	0	0	0	46	0	60	50	45	40	51	200		LB O PB PL
– + + + +	50	0	58	52	0	0	50	54	0	50	0	0	28	57	50	50	55	59	58	50	0	0	0	40	0	37	50	36	60	43	199		
– + – + +	75	0	41	39	0	0	52	36	0	40	0	0	57	26	38	20	33	30	30	53	0	0	0	42	0	37	50	63	35	43	171		
– – + + –	25	0	53	54	0	0	44	41	0	17	0	0	47	53	41	50	47	39	32	58	0	0	0	50	0	25	46	50	60	53	180		BO
– – + + +	60	0	53	46	0	0	50	53	0	82	0	0	60	46	52	54	39	54	53	46	0	0	0	48	0	25	46	50	65	53	223		GC NY PB PL
– – + + –	40	0	47	28	0	0	50	53	0	41	0	0	47	50	46	33	60	60	62	44	0	0	0	48	0	71	18	63	62	49	190		SU
– + – + +	60	0	47	71	0	0	46	46	0	58	0	0	42	34	47	100	36	37	37	55	0	0	0	51	0	28	63	75	31	47	183		CC O TR

Figure 8.10: Continued

	BO	BP	C	CC	CD	CL	CO	CP	FC	GC	HO	JY	LB	LC	LH	NY	O	OJ	PB	PL	S	SF	SV	SM	SP	SU	TB	TR	W	T%	T#	------ 65% ------
(+)	33	0	48	63	0	0	50	45	0	50	0	0	54	56	41	0	60	36	33	52	0	0	0	69	0	71	37	41	75	48	181	SM SU W
(-)	66	0	48	36	0	0	47	50	0	42	0	0	45	43	55	100	40	56	62	41	0	0	0	21	28	50	58	25	66	47	179	BO NY
(+)	38	0	57	46	0	0	45	34	0	56	0	0	23	50	50	100	61	62	47	50	0	0	0	42	75	50	75	33	48	187	SU TR
(-)	46	0	42	43	0	0	54	62	0	43	0	0	50	76	50	100	62	52	52	58	0	0	0	57	14	33	58	47	49	192	LB NY W
(+)	66	0	44	44	0	0	42	28	0	42	0	0	30	51	31	100	28	38	44	58	0	0	0	28	14	33	58	66	40	134	BO NY
(-)	33	0	56	51	0	0	57	52	0	57	0	0	54	65	68	0	64	53	51	41	0	0	0	71	85	61	41	47	55	181	LB LH SM SU
(+)	60	0	56	45	0	0	62	66	0	50	0	0	54	65	45	40	41	66	72	57	0	0	0	51	50	42	38	52	56	223	CP OJ PB
(-)	40	0	40	54	0	0	37	30	0	43	0	0	45	30	50	20	47	33	27	28	0	0	0	40	50	52	61	47	40	160	
(+)	57	0	50	42	0	0	43	48	0	35	0	0	69	48	44	100	52	57	42	85	0	0	0	47	25	47	57	50	47	207	NY PL
	42	0	45	57	0	0	56	51	0	64	0	0	54	51	51	0	41	39	55	14	0	0	0	50	50	47	42	45	50	221	
(+)	62	0	27	48	0	0	46	53	0	42	0	0	55	63	63	0	42	40	62	25	0	0	0	47	75	50	50	33	47	190	SU
(-)	37	0	65	52	0	0	48	43	0	57	0	0	54	36	36	100	59	31	58	0	0	0	0	43	25	50	50	61	48	191	NY
(+)	66	0	36	61	0	0	36	41	0	0	0	0	52	40	48	0	55	57	66	40	0	0	0	20	80	38	36	36	39	163	BO SU
(-)	33	0	59	38	0	0	75	58	0	58	0	0	48	54	48	0	57	58	69	63	0	0	0	79	38	38	38	39	57	234	CO PB SM
(+)	44	0	47	46	0	0	41	60	0	66	0	0	31	60	62	50	29	30	33	91	0	0	0	50	40	61	53	59	54	194	GC OJ PL
	52	0	52	53	0	0	58	39	0	33	0	0	60	37	50	0	30	33	0	0	0	0	0	40	60	57	50	47	42	150	
(+)	23	0	65	63	0	0	30	40	0	16	0	0	50	46	52	50	60	46	37	37	0	0	0	55	15	41	21	35	44	169	
(-)	69	0	34	36	0	0	60	44	0	66	0	0	50	40	47	20	58	57	62	62	0	0	0	34	84	58	78	58	52	202	BO GC SU TR
(+)	30	0	57	58	0	0	59	44	0	30	0	0	50	45	45	20	31	52	50	36	0	0	0	62	50	53	71	31	48	161	TR
(-)	70	0	39	38	0	0	36	44	0	70	0	0	50	54	45	80	56	41	44	63	0	0	0	37	50	30	28	56	46	154	BO GC NY
	50	0	42	37	0	0	20	38	0	47	0	0	31	33	57	100	47	51	60	60	0	0	0	36	33	35	16	40	44	119	GC LC NY
	50	0	42	62	0	0	70	61	0	0	0	0	63	36	36	0	30	52	48	40	0	0	0	57	66	64	83	60	52	141	CO SU TR
	77	0	69	56	0	0	61	56	0	50	0	0	46	42	57	50	58	60	56	50	0	0	0	50	50	66	83	59	57	145	BO C TB TR
	22	0	30	43	0	0	38	43	0	50	0	0	57	55	42	20	41	37	39	50	0	0	0	51	50	31	16	31	40	104	NY
(+)	41	0	38	57	0	0	57	65	0	42	0	0	52	44	52	66	31	61	67	80	0	0	0	45	50	66	46	46	48	163	TR
(-)	50	0	61	42	0	0	42	35	0	55	0	0	47	68	68	33	66	61	39	20	0	0	0	53	38	45	47	38	49	163	NY PB PL
(+)	57	0	36	56	0	0	68	42	0	33	0	0	30	45	33	50	50	33	29	50	0	0	0	45	57	54	52	52	45	201	CO LH
(-)	42	0	53	39	0	0	31	54	0	55	0	0	65	55	31	80	35	41	53	75	0	0	0	38	100	54	66	55	42	194	SU
(+)	58	0	50	50	0	0	50	42	0	44	0	0	53	36	26	80	35	25	51	75	0	0	0	45	25	45	44	47	45	171	NY PL
(-)	41	0	55	47	0	0	64	52	0	47	0	0	64	64	73	20	46	63	50	56	0	0	0	33	75	52	66	52	52	197	LH OJ SU
(+)	42	0	45	40	0	0	36	47	0	52	0	0	62	60	52	50	35	27	45	43	0	0	0	66	33	47	33	51	45	211	SU TR
(-)	57	0	35	40	0	0	51	48	0	64	0	0	37	60	47	50	37	57	50	56	0	0	0	28	66	41	33	53	45	183	SM
(+)	50	0	57	56	0	0	48	48	0	35	0	0	56	46	48	0	56	39	39	63	0	0	0	71	66	66	40	52	45	170	PL SM SU TR
(-)	75	0	44	43	0	0	50	34	0	36	0	0	51	57	40	0	56	39	57	36	0	0	0	50	66	21	63	60	45	196	BO SU
(+)	25	0	51	53	0	0	46	58	0	54	0	0	44	42	56	100	43	42	33	22	0	0	0	55	33	36	39	51	41	225	NY TB
(-)	50	0	43	34	0	0	47	57	0	0	0	0	37	56	66	100	40	53	50	62	0	0	0	50	14	55	30	38	47	185	LH NY
(+)	50	0	56	65	0	0	56	35	0	0	0	0	55	43	33	0	60	46	60	31	0	0	0	44	85	38	70	61	50	196	GC SU TR
(-)	14	0	60	65	0	0	75	75	0	73	0	0	78	64	35	100	43	61	51	77	0	0	0	58	66	61	60	30	55	198	CP GC NY PL SU
(+)	85	0	35	32	0	0	25	20	0	20	0	0	27	42	64	100	53	34	46	22	0	0	0	34	33	38	40	61	40	146	BO
(+)	50	0	65	50	0	0	51	33	0	44	0	0	63	21	31	0	50	60	49	38	0	0	0	41	50	42	42	44	47	191	
(-)	50	0	26	50	0	0	48	60	0	52	0	0	78	68	68	100	57	57	57	61	0	0	0	41	30	57	48	44	49	199	LC LH NY
(+)	22	0	59	35	0	0	51	29	0	60	0	0	50	39	48	50	44	30	44	36	0	0	0	23	28	57	41	36	43	156	
(-)	77	0	33	60	0	0	45	66	0	18	0	0	50	60	51	0	44	69	53	45	0	0	0	66	71	42	30	58	53	194	BO CP OJ SM SU
(+)	100	0	54	61	0	0	62	61	0	81	0	0	56	65	41	50	38	50	62	50	0	0	0	48	37	53	46	45	55	212	BO GC OJ
(-)	85	0	46	42	0	0	46	50	0	66	0	0	65	57	57	0	50	41	62	50	0	0	0	43	50	46	66	33	53	226	BO GC W
(+)	14	0	53	57	0	0	54	37	0	33	0	0	36	42	38	75	54	59	37	44	0	0	0	48	50	54	33	44	44	189	NY TR
(+)	66	0	43	48	0	0	32	57	0	40	0	0	76	56	56	0	46	37	20	47	0	0	0	36	75	58	50	60	47	189	BO LB SU
(-)	33	0	52	43	0	0	64	42	0	60	0	0	15	50	43	0	53	40	60	70	0	0	0	50	25	35	42	40	49	196	PL
(+)	71	0	43	46	0	0	46	42	0	33	0	0	50	42	59	0	43	44	60	14	0	0	0	42	72	16	46	50	48	170	BO SU
(-)	28	0	42	56	0	0	53	50	0	66	0	0	50	57	37	50	56	55	37	85	0	0	0	42	18	77	46	50	49	175	GC PL TB
(+)	20	0	31	46	0	0	37	52	0	20	0	0	35	43	73	50	20	50	55	0	0	0	0	47	50	37	28	69	43	124	LH W
(+)	80	0	62	48	0	0	62	42	0	80	0	0	64	52	26	50	80	44	44	100	0	0	0	47	50	50	71	30	53	155	BO GC O PL TR

Figure 8.10: Continued

	BO	BP	C	CC	CD	CL	CO	CP	FC	GC	HO	JY	LB	LC	LH	NY	O	OJ	PB	FL	S	SF	SV	SM	SP	SU	TB	TR	W	T%	T#
(+)	50	0	46	55	0	0	83	28	0	83	0	0	61	35	61	50	47	55	55	33	0	0	0	68	0	33	47	75	25	54	152 CO GC SM TR
(−)	50	0	53	44	0	0	16	71	0	16	0	0	38	64	38	45	45	45	55	44	0	0	0	31	0	66	47	25	68	43	123 CP SU W
(−)	50	0	48	37	0	0	46	46	0	63	0	0	44	43	75	57	57	48	63	55	0	0	0	33	0	60	60	33	61	45	178 NY
(−)	62	0	48	62	0	0	43	48	0	36	0	0	50	47	56	25	36	50	35	42	0	0	0	66	0	50	35	66	61	51	200 SM TR
(+)	57	0	35	43	0	0	50	29	0	37	0	0	45	62	43	50	18	35	35	50	0	0	0	50	0	75	38	20	27	41	165 SU
(+)	42	0	58	56	0	0	37	70	0	62	0	0	50	37	52	68	50	52	80	77	0	0	0	42	0	55	80	45	55	54	215 CP O TR W
(+)	75	0	42	53	0	0	58	37	0	20	0	0	57	63	25	56	35	44	60	22	0	0	0	57	0	66	62	45	55	49	201 BO NY PL SU
(−)	25	0	47	46	0	0	41	55	0	80	0	0	39	36	70	33	52	55	60	64	0	0	0	42	0	33	37	54	45	48	197 GC LH
(−)	33	0	51	42	0	0	54	57	0	77	0	0	76	33	62	0	63	51	46	64	0	0	0	40	0	55	44	46	68	53	207 GC LB W
(−)	66	0	41	57	0	0	43	42	0	18	0	0	17	61	37	100	31	44	51	28	0	0	0	54	0	33	44	53	32	43	167 BO NY
(+)	45	0	42	61	0	0	53	42	0	56	0	0	61	48	60	54	54	42	57	50	0	0	0	46	0	37	61	62	18	51	193 NY
(−)	45	0	57	38	0	0	43	43	0	43	0	0	38	52	40	45	45	57	42	33	0	0	0	50	0	62	30	37	72	46	172 W
(+)	66	0	35	50	0	0	41	48	0	58	0	0	40	52	44	35	35	56	51	60	0	0	0	52	0	33	61	36	25	46	201 BO
(+)	16	0	57	50	0	0	58	51	0	41	0	0	56	48	56	66	45	43	46	66	0	0	0	43	0	33	38	54	75	49	215 NY W
(+)	33	0	36	59	0	0	31	45	0	77	0	0	47	45	46	45	45	50	50	66	0	0	0	70	0	16	50	44	61	46	143 GC PL SM
(−)	66	0	57	38	0	0	62	54	0	22	0	0	52	56	59	50	54	50	65	23	0	0	0	29	0	83	100	77	61	52	163 BO SU TR
(−)	55	0	82	50	0	0	61	76	0	33	0	0	41	41	85	50	58	31	65	80	0	0	0	31	0	33	54	50	61	55	153 C CP LH PL
(+)	44	0	17	47	0	0	33	35	0	55	0	0	50	58	14	25	35	56	52	45	0	0	0	62	0	66	46	77	47	41	114 SU
(+)	50	0	56	44	0	0	59	43	0	50	0	0	69	33	57	50	35	61	47	45	0	0	0	62	0	50	46	22	41	51	186 LB TR
(+)	50	0	37	55	0	0	40	57	0	50	0	0	26	66	42	66	52	30	54	45	0	0	0	33	0	38	53	22	47	44	162 LC
(+)	40	0	54	57	0	0	43	40	0	50	0	0	41	59	47	30	30	47	60	26	0	0	0	65	0	54	44	60	26	47	174 NY
(+)	60	0	45	36	0	0	53	59	0	60	0	0	58	40	52	33	70	50	53	40	0	0	0	35	0	61	27	40	73	50	182 O W
(+)	40	0	34	51	0	0	30	36	0	50	0	0	30	50	43	33	33	42	42	42	0	0	0	34	0	66	56	42	30	40	136 SU
(+)	40	0	53	48	0	0	65	63	0	50	0	0	65	56	30	56	57	50	42	42	0	0	0	62	0	33	43	57	70	56	189 NY W
(−)	44	0	46	41	0	0	62	61	0	40	0	0	75	57	40	60	35	61	57	64	0	0	0	68	0	100	45	57	47	56	160 LB LH SM SU
(+)	55	0	53	58	0	0	18	33	0	60	0	0	25	42	10	50	60	33	42	29	0	0	0	22	0	33	36	42	47	39	113 LC
(+)	28	0	36	48	0	0	56	47	0	50	0	0	57	60	33	25	60	47	52	28	0	0	0	59	0	62	50	50	66	49	155 LC
(+)	71	0	63	51	0	0	39	43	0	25	0	0	38	29	33	33	57	54	61	57	0	0	0	40	0	66	25	50	20	46	147 BO SU W
(−)	60	0	42	60	0	0	55	60	0	33	0	0	57	50	62	50	58	58	54	54	0	0	0	38	0	66	50	33	40	52	141 SU
(−)	40	0	57	33	0	0	44	35	0	66	0	0	36	50	42	50	41	42	61	45	0	0	0	33	0	33	41	35	45	44	119 O TR
(+)	75	0	33	40	0	0	63	30	0	66	0	0	40	57	33	66	33	41	41	41	0	0	0	34	0	66	56	53	46	49	123 TR
(−)	25	0	50	51	0	0	36	70	0	66	0	0	60	57	33	40	33	52	41	42	0	0	0	43	0	50	41	33	46	48	121 BO CP GC NY PL
(−)	75	0	100	57	0	0	44	100	0	25	0	0	23	80	80	66	66	58	58	100	0	0	0	20	0	100	100	33	30	53	43 C CP LC LH PB PL
(−)	50	0	0	35	0	0	55	0	0	75	0	0	76	20	0	0	66	25	0	0	0	0	0	60	0	100	100	50	57	43	35 GC LB O
(−)	50	0	40	58	0	0	20	77	0	100	0	0	50	83	50	100	75	50	33	20	0	0	0	33	0	50	50	0	50	58	62 CO CP GC LC NY O
(+)	50	0	60	41	0	0	20	22	0	0	0	0	50	20	50	50	25	50	66	16	0	0	0	60	0	100	50	0	83	40	43 PB PL SU
(+)	33	0	28	35	0	0	0	42	0	0	0	0	28	66	100	75	66	57	69	80	0	0	0	66	0	100	66	0	20	50	56 LC LH O PB PL SM
(−)	66	0	71	64	0	0	100	57	0	0	0	0	71	33	0	25	42	42	30	0	0	0	0	33	0	100	33	0	80	46	52 BO C CO LB SU W
(−)	66	0	66	62	0	0	36	75	0	100	0	0	55	41	22	60	60	55	55	75	0	0	0	41	0	0	0	35	45	42	60 BO CC NY PL SU
(−)	33	0	100	100	0	0	63	0	0	100	0	0	44	58	77	50	37	44	44	25	0	0	0	50	0	100	30	100	64	55	78 C CP LH TR
(+)	37	0	55	62	0	0	55	33	0	0	0	0	45	50	66	33	20	58	81	100	0	0	0	71	0	50	57	100	28	54	75 GC LH PB PL SM TR
(+)	62	0	44	37	0	0	44	0	0	0	0	0	54	87	37	100	60	37	52	33	0	0	0	57	0	66	42	25	50	48	58 NY TB W
(−)	50	0	50	41	0	0	20	62	0	0	0	0	20	12	62	33	33	42	42	66	0	0	0	60	0	33	80	71	50	53	71 LC O SU TR
(+)	33	0	50	52	0	0	73	37	0	28	0	0	80	50	50	50	50	37	42	0	0	0	0	60	0	33	30	71	14	43	68 CO GC PL
(+)	66	0	44	33	0	0	30	80	0	71	0	0	70	61	50	50	33	33	45	75	0	0	0	42	0	100	66	70	14	43	93 CC CO CP GC NY W
(−)	20	0	40	42	0	0	44	13	0	18	0	0	30	33	12	33	71	45	45	75	0	0	0	60	0	66	25	100	57	71	75 BO LB PB PL SU TB TR
(−)	80	0	60	57	0	0	70	44	0	33	0	0	66	33	12	71	33	33	45	75	0	0	0	42	0	25	25	100	42	43	60 LB O PL TR
(+)	80	0	60	57	0	0	70	44	0	66	0	0	66	66	66	66	28	66	54	25	0	0	0	57	0	75	66	33	50	55	76 BO CO GC LC LH NY
(+)	83	0	88	61	0	0	80	75	0	100	0	0	45	55	75	66	66	44	54	33	0	0	0	50	0	50	54	66	66	61	86 BO C CO CP O OJ TR
(+)	16	0	11	38	0	0	20	25	0	0	0	0	33	44	50	100	0	16	42	66	0	0	0	50	0	33	45	33	12	37	52 GC NY PL
(−)	80	0	66	38	0	0	75	58	0	66	0	0	58	55	71	75	75	58	58	33	0	0	0	80	0	66	85	75	75	53	98 BO C CO LH O SM
(−)	20	0	26	61	0	0	25	41	0	41	0	0	58	44	28	29	29	42	42	66	0	0	0	0	0	14	41	41	66	44	82 GC NY OJ PL SU W
(−)	33	0	60	38	0	0	62	50	0	10	0	0	11	44	69	50	75	31	55	100	0	0	0	64	0	66	33	100	50	49	94 LH O PL TR
(−)	66	0	30	61	0	0	37	42	0	80	0	0	77	44	30	100	25	68	40	0	0	0	0	35	0	0	66	0	50	47	91 BO GC LB NY OJ TB

Figure 8.10: Continued

	±	BO	BP	C	CC	CD	CL	CO	CP	FC	GC	HO	JY	LB	LC	LH	NY	O	OJ	PB	PL	S	SF	SV	SM	SP	SU	TB	TR	W	T%	T#	65%
--|--+|+	(+)	20	0	45	36	0	0	44	37	0	0	0	0	60	55	42	0	66	33	47	42	0	0	0	7	0	100	77	28	100	44	70	O SU TB W
--|-++|-	(-)	80	0	54	57	0	0	44	62	0	100	0	0	40	44	57	0	33	55	52	28	0	0	0	69	0	0	22	57	0	49	78	BO GC SM
--|-+-|+	(+)	25	0	14	43	0	0	60	35	0	100	0	0	30	50	63	0	37	61	69	25	0	0	0	69	0	66	61	42	50	49	87	GC NY PB SM SU
--|-+-|-	(-)	75	0	71	56	0	0	40	57	0	0	0	0	60	50	58	0	62	48	23	25	0	0	0	23	0	33	38	57	50	46	82	BO C
--|+--|+	(+)	40	0	28	66	0	0	50	54	23	0	0	0	57	45	58	0	40	60	50	0	0	0	0	50	0	0	66	28	42	46	93	CC TB
--|+-+|-	(-)	60	0	64	33	0	0	50	37	76	0	0	0	42	45	41	100	50	40	60	0	0	0	0	40	0	100	33	71	57	50	101	GC NY SU TR
--|++-|+	(+)	60	0	80	47	0	0	64	53	66	0	0	0	50	84	37	50	42	60	40	60	0	0	0	50	0	50	75	25	33	56	101	C GC LC TR W
--|++-|-	(+)	30	0	10	47	0	0	35	46	33	0	0	0	50	15	62	50	57	40	40	40	0	0	0	60	0	50	61	25	33	41	74	
--|+++|+	(+)	0	0	14	40	0	0	50	18	0	0	0	0	58	60	33	33	50	33	18	50	0	0	0	14	0	0	60	18	0	35	47	
--|+++|-	(+)	0	0	50	60	0	0	50	81	50	0	0	0	33	40	66	66	37	66	62	50	0	0	0	57	0	33	60	25	81	58	78	BO C CP LH NY OJ
--|---|+	(+)	100	0	50	60	0	0	60	66	88	0	0	0	66	61	42	50	66	80	52	44	0	0	0	53	0	42	100	33	33	56	84	CP GC O OJ SU TR
--|---|-	(-)	0	0	50	40	0	0	40	33	0	0	0	0	50	38	30	0	33	20	50	55	0	0	0	30	0	0	14	0	66	40	60	BO W
--|--+|+	(+)	100	0	36	35	0	0	53	47	66	0	0	0	22	62	62	0	33	57	28	50	0	0	0	66	0	100	25	40	66	44	79	GC SM SU W
--|--+|-	(-)	57	0	54	64	0	0	50	35	33	0	0	0	77	37	62	0	42	68	68	50	0	0	0	16	0	0	75	60	33	51	90	LB NY O PB TB
--|-+-|+	(+)	42	0	50	25	0	0	83	58	28	0	0	0	15	53	63	100	50	52	42	0	0	0	0	50	0	0	50	66	0	50	90	CO NY OJ W
--|-+-|-	(-)	50	0	50	58	0	0	16	25	71	0	0	0	69	33	27	0	50	33	44	57	0	0	0	50	0	100	50	50	33	43	78	GC LB SU
--|+--|+	(+)	75	0	46	47	0	0	55	57	0	0	0	0	21	60	50	0	40	20	29	66	0	0	0	26	0	0	50	33	42	41	88	BO PL SU
--|+-+|-	(-)	25	0	53	47	0	0	44	62	100	0	0	0	78	40	50	100	40	70	70	33	0	0	0	60	0	33	50	66	57	55	119	GC LB NY OJ PB TR
--|++-|+	(+)	33	0	50	21	0	0	61	60	70	0	0	0	53	83	57	50	61	59	0	33	0	0	0	60	0	0	20	0	71	51	91	GC LC W
--|++-|-	(-)	66	0	50	78	0	0	38	40	30	0	0	0	30	16	42	50	100	38	40	55	0	0	0	57	0	66	80	14	0	47	84	BO CC O PL SU TB
--|+++|+	(+)	66	0	54	66	0	0	20	40	60	0	0	0	50	64	42	0	80	35	28	46	0	0	0	66	0	66	33	71	28	48	100	CC O SM SU W
--|+++|-	(-)	75	0	45	33	0	0	50	53	20	0	0	0	50	35	52	0	20	58	64	50	0	0	0	27	0	33	50	50	28	46	96	BO
--|---|+	(+)	33	0	44	54	0	0	50	41	20	0	0	0	28	54	44	0	71	61	36	42	0	0	0	42	0	100	66	80	50	46	78	CO O SU TB TR
--|--+|-	(-)	50	0	55	27	0	0	30	58	0	0	0	0	71	45	45	60	28	38	64	57	0	0	0	57	0	66	33	25	50	51	85	GC LB NY
--|-+-|+	(+)	66	0	44	58	0	0	30	25	80	0	0	0	40	68	37	100	0	37	30	66	0	0	0	0	0	0	33	25	50	38	62	BO LC NY PL
--|-+-|-	(-)	33	0	70	43	0	0	70	84	45	0	0	0	60	31	62	0	85	62	60	33	0	0	0	70	0	100	66	75	40	55	90	CO GC O SM SU TB TR
--|+--|+	(+)	75	0	30	56	0	0	70	15	54	0	0	0	46	53	33	0	55	34	34	33	0	0	0	20	0	0	41	42	33	60	120	BO C CO CP PL SM W
--|+-+|-	(-)	25	0	57	44	0	0	50	56	0	0	0	0	62	58	50	100	71	60	54	66	0	0	0	50	100	33	50	75	37	37	75	SU O PL TR
--|++-|+	(+)	0	0	42	55	0	0	50	43	50	0	0	0	37	41	50	0	28	33	42	50	0	0	0	47	0	33	45	75	37	49	98	NY O PL TR
--|++-|-	(-)	100	0	25	60	0	0	42	62	0	0	0	0	66	57	66	28	36	41	52	33	0	0	0	63	66	33	45	25	66	47	94	BO
--|+++|+	(+)	60	0	75	40	0	0	57	31	37	0	0	0	33	41	66	0	41	58	42	50	0	0	0	18	33	66	50	28	50	46	88	LH SU TB
--|+++|-	(-)	66	0	36	50	0	0	10	38	44	0	0	0	46	50	30	0	63	50	42	50	0	0	0	13	100	42	50	75	64	51	97	C LB NY TR
--|---|+	(+)	33	0	54	50	0	0	89	61	55	0	0	0	53	40	61	0	42	50	66	0	0	0	0	86	0	57	42	50	46	58	76	BO PL SU
--|--+|-	(-)	28	0	57	50	0	0	42	57	40	0	0	0	41	60	83	50	62	58	53	83	0	0	0	58	0	33	57	50	50	52	118	CO PB SM
--|-+-|+	(+)	57	0	42	61	0	0	57	42	60	0	0	0	40	16	41	50	58	42	45	50	0	0	0	33	0	66	75	25	33	44	90	LH PL TR
--|-+-|-	(-)	12	0	68	61	0	0	38	22	11	0	0	0	66	55	71	50	20	57	42	50	0	0	0	69	0	20	55	25	33	46	77	SU TB
--|+--|+	(+)	75	0	31	38	0	0	52	55	88	0	0	0	33	44	28	50	80	42	57	50	0	0	0	23	0	80	40	75	66	50	93	C LB LH SM
--|+-+|-	(-)	20	0	62	60	0	0	22	50	0	0	0	0	33	20	50	50	33	16	34	16	0	0	0	71	100	0	100	25	66	45	101	BO GC O SU TR W
--|++-|+	(+)	80	0	37	33	0	0	8	41	0	0	0	0	55	80	42	42	16	34	20	20	0	0	0	35	100	0	28	0	16	44	80	CO TR
--|++-|-	(-)	66	0	50	45	0	0	21	50	45	0	0	0	30	60	33	75	57	83	65	80	0	0	0	54	0	38	61	20	57	47	82	BO GC LC NY PL SU
--|+++|+	(+)	66	0	50	54	0	0	64	42	60	0	0	0	25	55	41	85	38	14	62	44	0	0	0	36	0	33	57	50	58	42	61	GC NY SU
--|+++|-	(-)	33	0	80	57	0	0	77	40	62	0	0	0	61	37	55	0	66	50	50	75	0	0	0	54	0	66	42	57	53	56	70	TB TR
--|---|+	(+)	100	0	80	57	0	0	22	40	0	0	0	0	37	40	55	0	66	57	61	40	0	0	0	50	0	40	100	50	51	54	67	BO C CO O TR
--|--+|-	(-)	0	0	20	57	0	0	22	60	0	0	0	0	33	60	44	0	33	28	34	66	0	0	0	71	0	0	40	30	66	42	52	GC NY PL SM
--|-+-|+	(+)	33	0	28	92	0	0	81	61	50	0	0	0	66	50	33	42	16	34	34	20	0	0	0	66	0	66	50	50	53	53	92	CO CO LB NY SM SU
--|-+-|-	(-)	66	0	71	7	0	0	18	38	44	0	0	0	33	50	66	0	57	83	65	80	0	0	0	33	0	33	16	0	42	44	77	BO C LH OJ PL
--|+--|+	(+)	50	0	28	52	0	0	20	35	60	0	0	0	72	42	33	0	28	14	62	50	0	0	0	54	0	38	20	57	47	47	94	CO LH OJ
--|+-+|-	(-)	50	0	57	36	0	0	64	57	55	0	0	0	42	30	37	50	14	62	44	44	0	0	0	36	0	33	61	80	42	42	73	LB NY PL
--|++-|+	(+)	20	0	37	50	0	0	71	70	62	0	0	0	75	30	42	80	50	50	48	50	0	0	0	54	0	66	42	57	53	56	97	BO CO CP LC
--|++-|-	(-)	80	0	62	50	0	0	41	50	37	0	0	0	25	75	80	100	66	66	48	50	0	0	0	33	0	71	66	42	53	51	88	LB LH NY O OJ
--|+++|+	(+)	33	0	50	33	0	0	58	50	0	0	0	0	33	58	53	30	33	16	52	50	0	0	0	66	0	50	75	42	46	46	79	BO LC SM TB
--|+++|-	(+)	100	0	14	55	0	0	33	50	80	0	0	0	33	55	53	0	30	40	48	50	0	0	0	28	0	50	25	50	45	45	90	GC NY SU
--|---|-	(-)	50	0	85	44	0	0	66	44	20	0	0	0	50	44	44	40	40	65	52	71	0	0	0	71	33	33	25	75	40	51	102	GC C CO PL SM TR

Figure 8.10: Continued

		BO	BP	C	CC	CD	CL	CO	CP	FC	GC	HO	JY	LB	LC	LH	NY	O	OJ	PB	PL	S	SF	SV	SM	SP	SU	TB	TR	W	T%	T#	------- 65% -------
-+--+-+-	(+)	50	0	50	44	0	0	43	15	0	42	0	0	55	60	0	0	42	44	40	57	0	0	0	53	0	100	28	60	53	45	101	SU NY
-+--+-+-	(-)	50	0	50	50	0	0	50	76	0	42	0	0	38	40	42	100	57	55	57	42	0	0	0	46	0	100	57	40	46	50	113	CP NY
-+--+-+-	(-)	50	0	42	30	0	0	42	58	0	0	0	0	41	66	75	0	50	40	0	100	0	0	0	36	0	20	75	40	42	46	84	LC LH PL TB
-+--+-+-	(-)	50	0	57	69	0	0	47	41	0	100	0	0	50	33	25	0	53	53	60	0	0	0	0	63	0	80	25	60	57	51	93	CC GC SU
-+--+-+-	(+)	0	0	87	72	0	0	25	76	0	80	0	0	75	55	45	100	42	57	45	80	0	0	0	60	0	100	57	66	40	58	107	C CC CP LB NY
-+--+-+-	(-)	100	0	12	28	0	0	75	23	0	20	0	0	12	44	54	0	57	42	50	20	0	0	0	26	0	0	42	0	50	38	71	BO CO
-+--+-+-	(+)	25	0	50	40	0	0	46	20	0	14	0	0	66	18	41	0	65	65	52	50	0	0	0	35	0	40	50	0	50	42	81	LB
-+--+-+-	(+)	75	0	37	60	0	0	53	66	0	85	0	0	33	81	58	100	0	30	47	50	0	0	0	42	20	40	47	40	40	52	99	BO CP GC LC NY TB TR
-+--+-+-	(-)	25	0	53	50	0	0	56	25	0	0	0	0	40	30	0	0	75	21	45	28	0	0	0	20	0	20	62	0	50	43	77	O W
-+--+-+-	(+)	75	0	30	37	0	0	43	75	0	66	0	0	60	70	50	50	25	78	51	42	0	0	0	80	0	100	37	28	33	53	95	BO CP GC LC OJ SM SU
-+--+-+-	(-)	0	0	30	50	0	0	47	45	0	0	0	0	50	50	50	0	33	33	44	66	0	0	0	68	0	0	33	80	55	45	82	PL SM TR
-+--+-+-	(+)	100	0	69	42	0	0	52	33	0	0	0	0	50	52	40	0	66	60	55	33	0	0	0	25	0	60	50	0	44	51	93	BO C GC O OJ
-+--+-+-	(+)	83	0	55	42	0	0	55	66	0	100	0	0	20	69	54	0	60	45	64	42	0	0	0	53	0	0	60	0	83	55	107	BO GC LB LC W
-+--+-+-	(-)	16	0	44	57	0	0	44	66	0	30	0	0	23	46	63	50	40	54	35	57	0	0	0	46	0	100	40	100	16	42	82	CP SU TR
-+--+-+-	(+)	80	0	33	53	0	0	20	70	0	46	0	0	33	46	36	0	42	50	48	23	0	0	0	54	0	66	50	55	33	48	90	BO CP SU W
-+--+-+-	(-)	20	0	66	46	0	0	73	30	0	53	0	0	66	46	64	0	57	50	52	57	0	0	0	40	0	33	50	33	33	49	92	C CO LB
-+--+-+-	(+)	100	0	60	53	0	0	46	36	0	50	0	0	44	53	36	50	44	0	78	20	0	0	0	40	0	0	40	40	57	47	86	BO PB SU
-+--+-+-	(-)	0	0	40	46	0	0	53	63	0	0	0	0	55	53	28	0	55	55	100	21	0	0	0	53	0	16	100	40	42	50	90	OJ PL TB
-+--+-+-	(+)	50	0	37	30	0	0	27	50	0	0	0	0	61	66	33	50	25	60	60	0	0	0	0	50	0	0	33	28	75	43	57	LH SU W
-+--+-+-	(-)	0	0	62	53	0	0	72	33	0	36	0	100	30	57	63	50	37	25	60	0	0	0	0	33	0	0	33	71	16	51	68	CO JY PL TR
-+--+-+-	(+)	100	0	60	52	0	0	90	27	0	53	0	0	72	42	63	0	45	45	64	100	0	0	0	72	0	0	33	62	25	54	86	BO CO GC LB SM
-+--+-+-	(+)	0	0	40	47	0	0	10	72	0	0	0	0	27	36	36	0	50	54	50	0	0	0	0	27	0	100	66	37	62	42	68	CP SU TB
-+--+-+-	(-)	66	0	50	56	0	0	58	41	0	62	0	0	38	60	80	50	57	50	64	0	0	0	0	53	0	0	55	30	44	45	113	LH
-+--+-+-	(+)	33	0	42	52	0	0	47	18	0	44	0	0	53	40	46	0	28	45	31	0	0	0	0	46	0	0	37	60	55	50	93	SU
-+--+-+-	(+)	33	0	40	47	0	0	34	81	0	55	0	0	61	60	57	50	57	45	68	83	0	0	0	47	0	100	55	33	30	42	119	BO CP PB TR
-+--+-+-	(-)	75	0	54	42	0	0	72	40	0	20	0	0	50	64	69	23	22	25	48	63	0	0	0	64	0	0	77	50	54	53	106	BO CO NY PL SU TB
-+--+-+-	(-)	25	0	37	55	0	0	27	40	0	80	0	0	35	35	57	69	50	75	51	15	0	0	0	35	0	0	22	50	45	46	97	GC LH O OJ
-+--+-+-	(+)	33	0	60	69	0	0	55	69	0	81	0	0	50	28	57	0	57	62	37	57	0	0	0	42	0	0	40	28	63	53	102	CP GC LB SU
-+--+-+-	(+)	66	0	52	46	0	0	40	30	0	18	0	0	57	42	42	100	45	36	62	42	0	0	0	50	0	0	40	71	36	42	82	BO NY TH
-+--+-+-	(+)	40	0	37	58	0	0	52	37	0	41	0	0	80	33	58	0	31	46	100	0	0	0	0	57	0	66	60	57	16	48	93	LB PL SU
-+--+-+-	(-)	33	0	62	41	0	0	50	56	0	58	0	0	20	66	41	42	62	63	53	0	0	0	0	42	33	33	40	42	66	44	93	LC W
-+--+-+-	(+)	33	0	38	53	0	0	50	37	0	70	0	0	50	41	0	0	37	45	46	0	0	0	0	56	0	50	54	57	30	52	105	GC
-+--+-+-	(+)	33	0	61	53	0	0	37	35	0	28	0	0	50	50	66	0	18	55	50	0	0	0	0	43	0	100	45	42	69	41	122	LH SU W
-+--+-+-	(+)	66	0	25	60	0	0	50	61	0	71	0	0	46	33	0	0	33	35	50	16	100	0	0	83	0	0	42	37	37	52	67	GC PL SM
-+--+-+-	(+)	66	0	62	42	0	0	50	81	0	66	0	0	14	12	83	100	66	64	58	0	0	0	0	16	0	100	57	100	44	56	92	BO LC O PB SU TR
-+--+-+-	(-)	50	0	77	52	0	0	58	81	0	66	0	0	14	12	83	100	40	28	60	0	0	0	0	33	0	33	60	40	44	52	78	C CP GC LH NY
-+--+-+-	(-)	50	0	22	42	0	0	41	18	0	33	0	0	71	87	16	0	57	40	40	0	0	0	0	55	0	66	33	60	55	44	67	LB LC SU
-+--+-+-	(+)	75	0	50	44	0	0	50	70	0	50	0	0	78	41	70	0	40	62	52	54	0	0	0	54	0	50	50	37	52	52	102	BO LB LH TR
-+--+-+-	(+)	25	0	37	55	0	0	50	58	0	25	0	0	14	58	30	100	50	37	47	45	0	0	0	45	0	36	57	72	40	43	85	NY SU
-+--+-+-	(+)	66	0	60	38	0	0	40	27	0	75	0	0	25	40	54	100	50	40	35	80	0	0	0	30	0	63	40	27	60	50	103	NY PL SM TR
-+--+-+-	(-)	33	0	31	52	0	0	40	55	0	41	0	0	25	57	41	0	55	28	64	20	0	0	0	37	0	50	40	33	33	42	71	GC PL
-+--+-+-	(+)	66	0	52	47	0	0	50	44	0	58	0	0	75	42	58	0	33	71	76	0	0	0	0	62	0	50	66	66	66	55	94	BO LB NY OJ PB TH
-+--+-+-	(-)	57	0	63	38	0	0	75	45	0	28	0	0	87	66	100	75	1	57	46	58	0	0	0	55	0	50	50	66	66	55	86	CO LB LC LH NY SU
-+--+-+-	(+)	42	0	36	61	0	0	12	45	0	71	0	0	12	33	0	25	88	42	53	41	0	0	0	44	0	0	25	50	50	41	64	GC O
-+--+-+-	(-)	0	0	37	40	0	0	53	45	0	33	0	0	55	87	40	100	40	44	58	28	0	0	0	53	0	100	71	40	40	48	77	LC NY TB
-+--+-+-	(-)	100	0	62	60	0	0	38	45	0	66	0	0	44	12	60	0	60	60	47	42	0	0	0	46	0	0	14	60	60	48	78	BO GC SU
-+--+-+-	(+)	50	0	33	61	0	0	64	63	0	75	0	0	58	50	42	0	66	66	53	75	0	0	0	30	0	50	55	20	44	52	74	OJ PL
-+--+-+-	(+)	50	0	66	27	0	0	35	36	0	50	0	0	41	50	57	0	33	33	46	25	0	0	0	70	0	50	33	80	44	44	62	C O SM TR
-+--+-+-	(-)	50	0	66	72	0	0	75	42	0	50	0	0	83	41	63	50	36	36	42	0	0	0	0	57	0	100	63	42	0	49	59	C CC CO LB SU TR
-+--+-+-	(-)	100	0	33	27	0	0	25	57	0	25	0	0	16	58	27	50	50	50	63	57	100	0	0	42	0	0	60	0	50	48	58	BO PL
-+--+-+-	(+)	50	0	0	57	0	0	44	100	0	25	0	0	23	80	100	0	66	33	50	100	100	0	0	20	0	0	0	0	50	53	43	C CP LC LH PB PL
-+--+-+-	(-)	50	0	35	0	0	0	55	0	0	75	0	0	76	20	0	0	66	25	0	0	0	0	0	60	0	0	0	0	50	43	35	GC LB O

Figure 8.10: Continued

	+/-	BO	BP	C	CC	CD	CL	CO	CP	FC	GC	HO	JY	LB	LC	LH	NY	O	OJ	PB	PL	S	SF	SV	SM	SP	SU	TB	TR	W	T%	T#	65%
+-------	(+)	50	0	40	58	0	0	80	77	0	0	0	0	50	83	50	100	75	50	33	20	0	0	0	0	0	50	100	50	83	58	62	CO CP GC LC NY O
+-------	(-)	50	0	60	41	0	0	20	22	0	0	0	0	50	16	50	0	25	50	66	80	0	0	0	50	0	50	25	0	16	40	43	PB PL SU
+------+	(+)	33	0	28	35	0	0	0	42	0	0	0	0	28	66	100	0	75	57	69	80	0	0	0	66	0	66	33	0	20	50	56	LC LH O PB PL SM
+------+	(-)	66	0	71	64	0	0	100	57	0	0	0	0	71	33	0	0	25	42	30	0	0	0	0	33	100	33	66	100	80	46	52	BO C CO LB SU
+-----+-	(+)	66	0	0	66	0	0	36	25	0	100	0	0	55	41	22	100	60	62	55	75	0	0	0	33	0	33	0	0	35	42	60	BO CC NY PL SU
+-----+-	(-)	33	100	33	0	0	0	63	75	0	0	0	0	44	58	77	0	37	44	44	25	0	0	0	50	0	50	30	0	64	55	78	C CP GC LH TR
+-----++	(+)	37	0	55	62	0	0	55	50	0	0	0	0	45	50	66	0	20	58	81	100	0	0	0	71	0	71	33	100	28	54	75	GC LH PB PL SM TR
+-----++	(-)	62	0	44	37	0	0	44	50	0	0	0	0	54	50	33	100	60	25	18	0	0	0	0	28	0	28	50	0	71	42	58	NY TB W
+----+--	(+)	50	0	50	41	0	0	20	62	0	0	0	0	40	87	37	0	66	37	52	33	0	0	0	57	0	57	75	75	50	50	71	LC O SU TR
+----+--	(-)	50	0	50	52	0	0	80	37	0	28	0	0	60	12	62	0	33	62	42	66	0	0	0	42	0	42	25	0	50	48	68	CO GC PL
+----+-+	(+)	33	0	55	66	0	0	80	80	0	71	0	0	20	38	50	100	50	50	33	0	0	0	0	40	0	40	33	30	71	53	93	CC CO CP GC NY W
+----+-+	(-)	66	0	44	33	0	0	73	80	0	81	0	0	80	61	50	0	50	50	66	100	0	0	0	60	0	60	66	70	14	43	75	BO LB PB PL SU TB TR
+----++-	(+)	20	0	40	42	0	0	30	13	0	18	0	0	0	18	0	71	33	33	45	25	0	0	0	42	0	42	0	0	42	55	60	LB O PL TR
+----++-	(-)	80	0	60	57	0	0	70	44	0	33	0	0	30	66	75	66	66	66	54	75	0	0	0	57	0	75	25	100	57	61	76	BO CO GC LC LH NY
+----+++	(+)	83	0	88	61	0	0	100	75	0	66	0	0	45	55	50	0	16	42	57	33	0	0	0	50	0	54	66	66	50	37	86	BO C CO CP O OJ TR
+----+++	(-)	16	0	11	38	0	0	20	58	0	0	0	0	45	44	71	100	75	29	58	33	0	0	0	10	0	45	33	85	12	53	52	GC NY PL
+---+---	(+)	80	0	66	38	0	0	75	41	0	10	0	0	33	58	71	0	25	70	41	66	0	0	0	80	0	14	25	75	75	44	98	BO C CO LH O SM
+---+---	(-)	33	0	60	61	0	0	62	42	0	80	0	0	11	41	28	100	75	31	66	0	0	0	0	64	0	66	14	0	50	49	82	GC NY OJ PL SU W
+---+--+	(+)	66	0	30	36	0	0	37	42	0	0	0	0	40	44	0	100	25	44	40	0	0	0	0	35	0	33	100	0	50	47	94	LH O PL TR
+---+--+	(-)	20	0	45	36	0	0	44	37	0	80	0	0	77	44	30	0	66	33	47	42	0	0	0	7	0	66	77	28	100	44	91	BO GC LB NY OJ TB
+---+-+-	(+)	80	0	30	61	0	0	44	42	0	0	0	0	40	55	42	0	33	55	52	57	0	100	0	7	100	22	57	0	0	44	70	O SU TB W
+---+-+-	(-)	25	0	14	43	0	0	60	35	0	0	0	0	60	44	62	0	62	38	69	50	0	0	0	69	0	61	42	50	0	49	78	BO GC SM
+---+-++	(+)	75	0	71	56	0	0	50	57	0	100	0	0	57	45	58	0	40	50	23	25	0	0	0	23	33	38	57	0	50	46	87	GC NY PB SM SU
+---+-++	(-)	40	0	28	66	0	0	50	54	0	23	0	0	57	84	45	100	62	40	50	0	0	0	0	50	0	66	28	42	50	46	82	BO C
+---++--	(+)	60	0	64	33	0	0	64	37	0	76	0	0	42	37	41	0	40	42	60	60	0	0	0	40	0	33	71	57	66	50	93	CC TB
+---++--	(-)	60	0	80	47	0	0	83	53	0	66	0	0	50	50	37	50	57	68	52	42	0	0	0	60	0	38	75	66	33	50	101	GC NY SU TR
+---++-+	(+)	30	0	10	40	0	0	35	46	0	66	0	0	50	15	50	60	50	57	42	50	0	0	0	50	0	61	50	33	66	41	74	C GC LC TR W
+---++-+	(-)	100	0	14	40	0	0	55	47	0	0	0	0	58	60	33	0	66	33	18	50	0	0	0	14	0	60	50	50	18	35	47	
+---+++-	(+)	75	0	85	60	0	0	50	81	0	50	0	0	33	60	66	66	37	66	62	50	0	100	0	57	100	20	25	81	66	58	78	BO C CP LH NY OJ
+---+++-	(-)	25	0	50	47	0	0	60	66	0	88	0	0	50	61	42	66	66	80	62	44	0	0	0	53	100	42	100	33	33	56	84	CP GC O OJ SU TR
+--+----	(+)	100	0	50	40	0	0	40	33	0	11	0	0	30	38	57	50	33	42	70	55	0	0	0	30	0	14	40	0	66	40	60	BO W
+--+----	(-)	57	0	36	35	0	0	53	47	0	66	0	0	22	64	42	0	57	57	28	42	0	0	0	66	0	33	50	71	14	44	79	GC SM SU W
+--+---+	(+)	42	0	54	54	0	0	83	53	0	76	0	0	77	84	68	50	60	66	50	55	0	0	0	27	0	50	80	50	71	48	90	LB NY O PB TB
+--+---+	(-)	50	0	44	54	0	0	70	46	0	28	0	0	50	37	50	0	40	57	42	42	0	0	0	42	0	50	66	80	50	46	96	BO C CO NY OJ W
+--+--+-	(+)	50	0	55	27	0	0	16	58	0	28	0	0	15	50	27	50	60	66	57	57	0	100	0	57	0	33	20	50	33	51	90	CO NY OJ
+--+--+-	(-)	75	0	44	58	0	0	30	41	0	80	0	0	71	45	60	100	37	38	64	57	0	0	0	57	0	33	20	50	33	43	78	GC LB SU
+--+--++	(+)	66	0	48	47	0	0	30	42	0	50	0	0	40	60	80	0	37	66	60	66	0	0	100	0	0	33	25	50	40	41	88	BO PL SU
+--+--++	(-)	33	0	55	35	0	0	69	41	0	0	0	0	60	31	62	85	60	62	60	33	0	0	0	70	0	66	41	57	66	55	119	GC LB NY OJ PB TR
+--+-+--	(+)	75	0	70	43	0	0	30	84	0	45	0	0	53	58	58	55	55	65	65	66	0	0	0	42	0	41	57	66	37	60	91	GC LC W
+--+-+--	(-)	25	0	30	56	0	0	15	60	0	54	0	0	46	33	44	0	44	65	65	33	0	0	0	43	100	50	42	43	33	37	84	BO CC O PL SU TB
+--+-+-+	(+)	100	0	57	44	0	0	50	56	0	50	0	0	62	58	50	71	60	60	34	66	0	0	0	47	0	33	45	75	37	49	100	CC O SM SU W
+--+-+-+	(-)	60	0	25	55	0	0	42	42	0	37	0	0	37	41	50	50	28	33	65	33	0	0	0	41	100	45	25	25	50	47	96	BO
+--+-++-	(+)	60	0	60	28	0	0	42	42	0	0	0	0	33	58	36	0	33	38	64	57	0	0	63	0	100	66	57	28	46	38	78	CO O SU TB TR
+--+-++-	(-)	33	0	44	50	0	0	57	31	0	62	0	0	66	42	33	100	37	58	60	33	0	0	18	0	0	75	64	50	41	51	85	GC LB NY PL
+--++---	(+)	75	0	70	44	0	0	30	56	0	50	0	0	62	58	50	71	60	60	34	66	0	100	13	0	33	45	75	64	37	49	62	BO LC NY PL
+--++---	(-)	100	0	42	55	0	0	66	43	0	50	0	0	37	41	50	28	33	33	65	33	0	0	41	0	33	33	25	25	50	47	90	CO GC O SM SU TB TR
+--++--+	(+)	60	0	25	60	0	0	42	62	0	37	0	0	40	35	52	36	41	65	66	66	0	0	63	0	66	25	28	50	50	46	120	BO C CO CP PL SM W
+--++--+	(-)	40	0	75	40	0	0	57	31	0	62	0	0	66	42	33	44	60	58	34	33	0	0	18	0	33	75	64	50	46	51	75	SU
+--++-+-	(+)	100	0	36	50	0	0	10	38	0	44	0	0	46	50	30	63	28	33	65	66	0	0	0	13	100	42	50	46	37	49	98	NY O PL TR
+--++-+-	(-)	66	0	54	50	0	0	89	61	0	55	0	0	53	40	61	0	42	50	66	0	0	0	86	0	0	57	50	46	58	58	118	CO PB SM

Figure 8.10: Continued

		BO	BP	C	CC	CD	CL	CO	CP	FC	GC	HO	JY	LB	LC	LH	NY	O	OJ	PB	PL	S	SF	SV	SM	SP	SU	TB	TR	W	T%	T#	
+-++++--	(+)	28	0	57	50	0	0	42	57	0	40	0	0	50	40	50	60	62	58	53	83	0	0	0	58	0	33	25	75	50	52	90	LH PL TR
+-++++--	(-)	57	0	42	50	0	0	57	42	0	60	0	0	41	40	16	50	25	41	46	0	0	0	0	33	0	66	75	25	33	44	77	SU TB
+-++++-I	(+)	12	0	68	61	0	0	38	22	0	11	0	0	66	55	71	50	20	57	42	50	0	0	0	69	0	20	55	25	50	46	93	C LB LH SM
+-++++-I	(-)	75	0	31	38	0	0	52	55	0	88	0	0	33	44	28	50	80	33	45	16	0	0	0	23	0	44	75	66	33	50	101	BO GC O SU TR W
+-+++-++	(+)	20	0	62	60	0	0	83	47	0	100	0	0	33	20	42	25	50	55	50	83	0	0	0	64	0	0	40	100	25	45	80	CO TR
+-+++-++	(+)	80	0	37	33	0	0	8	41	0	100	0	0	55	80	28	75	55	55	50	16	0	0	0	35	0	100	20	0	58	47	82	BO GC LC NY PL SU
+-++++++	(+)	66	0	50	45	0	0	21	50	0	0	0	0	30	20	42	100	62	38	45	40	0	0	0	50	0	100	28	33	60	45	61	BO GC NY SU
+-++++++	(+)	33	0	50	54	0	0	64	50	0	0	0	0	61	37	57	0	25	61	54	40	0	0	0	50	0	100	0	71	60	51	70	TB TR
++++++++	(+)	100	0	80	57	0	0	77	40	0	0	0	0	37	40	55	66	57	57	61	33	0	0	0	28	0	0	71	66	50	54	67	C CO O TR
++--++++	(-)	0	0	20	42	0	0	22	60	0	100	0	0	62	69	69	42	66	57	61	66	0	0	0	71	0	0	28	33	30	42	52	GC NY PL SM
++--+--+	(+)	33	0	28	92	0	0	81	61	0	50	0	0	66	50	44	100	33	16	34	20	0	0	0	66	0	66	60	100	66	53	92	CC CO LB NY SM SU
++--+--+	(-)	66	0	71	7	0	0	80	35	0	50	0	0	33	50	33	0	57	83	65	80	0	0	0	33	0	33	16	0	16	44	77	BO C LH OJ PL
++--+-++	(+)	50	0	28	52	0	0	18	38	0	20	0	0	72	57	66	50	57	14	62	44	0	0	0	54	0	38	20	57	42	47	94	CO LH OJ
++--+-++	(-)	50	0	57	36	0	0	20	64	0	60	0	0	42	42	33	0	28	85	37	55	0	0	0	36	0	100	61	80	58	47	94	LB SU TR
++-++--+	(+)	80	0	37	50	0	0	28	30	0	55	0	0	75	30	0	100	33	20	50	75	0	0	0	33	0	0	57	50	53	42	73	LB NY PL
++-++--+	(+)	20	0	62	50	0	0	71	70	0	44	0	0	25	69	37	66	66	66	48	50	0	0	0	54	0	66	42	50	33	56	97	BO CO CP LC O OJ SU
++-+++-+	(-)	80	0	37	50	0	0	41	50	0	62	0	0	66	25	80	100	33	16	52	50	0	0	0	28	0	33	57	50	46	51	88	LB LH NY O OJ
++-+++-+	(+)	100	0	50	33	0	0	58	50	0	37	0	0	33	75	20	0	44	52	71	50	0	0	0	33	0	50	25	75	40	51	79	BO LC SM TB
++-+-+++	(+)	50	0	14	55	0	0	50	76	0	80	0	0	33	55	40	100	42	44	65	28	0	0	0	66	0	50	50	40	46	45	90	GC NY SU
++-+-+++	(+)	50	0	85	44	0	0	66	44	0	62	0	0	55	60	40	0	57	55	52	71	0	0	0	28	0	33	25	75	40	51	102	C CO PL SM TR
++-++-++	(+)	50	0	50	44	0	0	43	15	0	42	0	0	55	60	57	0	42	44	57	0	0	0	0	53	0	100	28	60	53	50	101	SU
++-++-++	(+)	50	0	42	30	0	0	42	58	0	0	0	0	38	66	75	42	57	55	57	42	0	0	0	46	0	0	57	40	46	46	113	CP NY LH PL TB
++-+++-+	(+)	50	0	57	69	0	0	57	41	0	100	0	0	41	66	25	0	50	50	40	60	0	0	0	36	0	20	75	40	42	46	84	LC LH PL TB
++-+++-+	(-)	50	0	87	42	0	0	25	76	0	80	0	0	75	55	45	100	42	57	60	C	0	0	0	63	0	80	25	60	57	51	93	CC GC SU
++-++-+-	(-)	100	0	12	28	0	0	75	23	0	20	0	0	12	44	54	0	57	42	50	20	0	0	0	26	0	100	57	66	40	58	107	C CC CP GC LB NY
++-++-+-	(+)	25	0	50	60	0	0	46	20	0	14	0	0	66	18	41	0	0	65	52	50	0	0	0	35	0	42	42	33	40	38	71	BO CO
++-++-++	(+)	75	0	37	60	0	0	53	60	0	85	0	0	33	81	58	100	65	30	50	50	0	0	0	42	0	40	33	40	50	42	81	LB
++-++-++	(+)	25	0	53	50	0	0	56	25	0	33	0	0	40	30	50	50	30	75	45	28	0	0	20	20	100	62	57	66	52	99	BO CP GC LC NY TB TR
++-+-+++	(+)	75	0	30	37	0	0	43	75	0	66	0	0	60	70	50	50	75	21	78	42	0	0	0	80	0	100	37	28	33	43	77	O W
++-+-+++	(+)	25	0	53	50	0	0	56	25	0	66	0	0	60	46	40	50	33	33	51	42	0	0	0	68	0	40	33	80	55	53	95	BO CP GC LC OJ SM SU
++-++-++	(-)	75	0	30	37	0	0	43	75	0	100	0	0	80	53	40	0	66	55	64	57	0	0	0	25	0	60	66	20	44	45	82	PL SM TR
++-++-++	(+)	100	0	55	42	0	0	44	58	0	30	0	0	20	69	54	54	45	45	64	42	0	0	0	54	0	100	40	10	16	42	93	BO C GC LB LC W
++-++-++	(-)	83	0	44	57	0	0	46	66	0	70	0	0	44	46	63	36	60	50	48	28	0	0	0	45	0	33	50	40	83	49	107	BO GC LB
++-+++++	(+)	16	0	33	53	0	0	20	70	0	46	0	0	66	53	28	66	44	54	55	57	0	0	0	53	0	16	50	40	42	47	82	CP SU TR
++-+++++	(+)	80	0	66	46	0	0	73	30	0	53	0	0	33	46	36	0	57	45	52	80	0	0	0	72	0	16	50	66	42	50	90	BO CP SU W
++-++-++	(+)	20	0	40	47	0	0	10	72	0	28	0	0	27	46	36	50	44	50	50	50	0	0	0	27	0	33	50	75	25	42	92	C CO LB
++-++-++	(+)	66	0	50	43	0	0	29	62	0	0	0	0	38	53	58	0	57	78	35	50	0	0	0	46	0	100	66	60	44	50	86	BO PB SU
++-++-++	(-)	33	0	42	56	0	0	58	41	0	37	0	0	45	40	0	50	42	54	31	0	0	0	0	47	0	55	33	30	42	42	90	OJ PL TB
++-++-++	(-)	66	0	60	47	0	0	34	81	0	55	0	0	61	66	41	0	57	45	68	0	0	0	0	47	0	44	66	60	53	53	57	LH SU W
++-++++-	(+)	75	0	36	57	0	0	72	46	0	20	0	0	50	64	23	100	22	25	48	83	0	0	0	64	0	100	77	50	54	51	68	BO CO GC LB O PL TR
++-++-++	(+)	25	0	54	42	0	0	27	40	0	80	0	0	75	35	69	0	77	75	51	16	0	0	0	35	0	22	50	45	45	46	86	BO CO GC LB SM
++-++-++	(-)	66	0	52	37	0	0	55	69	0	81	0	0	28	57	0	0	45	62	37	57	0	0	0	42	0	100	40	28	63	53	68	CP SU TB
++-++-+-	(+)	66	0	52	46	0	0	40	30	0	18	0	0	72	57	42	100	31	62	62	42	0	0	0	50	0	0	40	71	36	42	102	BO CP SU TB
++-++-+-	(+)	40	0	37	58	0	0	52	37	0	41	0	0	57	33	58	0	62	36	46	100	0	0	0	57	0	66	60	57	16	48	113	LH SU
++-+++++	(+)	66	0	50	58	0	0	60	18	0	41	0	0	80	33	58	42	36	63	53	46	100	0	0	57	0	33	40	42	66	48	93	BO CP PB TR
++-+++++	(+)	33	0	42	56	0	0	58	41	0	58	0	0	20	66	0	50	37	63	53	0	0	0	0	42	0	33	40	42	66	48	119	BO CO NY PL SU TB
++-++-++	(+)	66	0	60	47	0	0	34	18	0	58	0	0	50	50	41	0	57	50	31	0	0	0	0	56	0	100	55	30	54	44	106	BO CO NY PL O OJ
++-++-++	(+)	33	0	38	46	0	0	50	38	0	70	0	0	50	50	33	66	18	45	46	0	0	0	0	56	0	54	57	30	69	44	97	GC LH O OJ
++-++-++	(-)	66	0	61	53	0	0	50	61	0	30	0	0	50	50	66	0	54	55	50	0	0	0	0	43	0	100	45	42	69	52	122	LH SU W

Figure 8.10: Concluded

		BO	BP	C	CC	CD	CL	CO	CP	FC	GC	HO	JY	LB	LC	LH	NY	O	OJ	PB	PL	S	SF	SV	SM	SP	SU	TB	TR	W	T%	T#	------- 65% -------
+++-+++	(+)	33	0	25	60	0	0	37	35	0	71	0	0	46	33	50	0	33	35	16	100	0	0	0	83	0	0	42	0	37	41	67	GC PL SM
+++-+++	(-)	66	0	62	40	0	0	50	64	0	28	0	0	53	66	41	0	66	64	83	0	0	0	0	16	0	100	57	100	62	56	92	BO LC O PB SU TR
+++-+--	(+)	50	0	77	52	0	0	58	81	0	66	0	0	14	12	83	100	40	28	60	0	0	0	0	33	0	33	60	40	44	52	78	C CP GC LH NY
+++--++	(-)	50	0	22	42	0	0	41	18	0	33	0	0	71	87	16	0	60	57	40	0	0	0	0	55	0	66	33	60	55	44	67	LB LC SU
++++---	(+)	75	0	50	44	0	0	50	35	0	50	0	0	78	41	70	0	40	62	52	54	0	0	0	54	0	0	50	100	37	52	102	BO LB LH TR
++++--+	(-)	25	0	37	55	0	0	50	58	0	50	0	0	14	58	30	100	40	37	47	45	0	0	0	45	0	100	50	0	37	43	85	NY SU
++++-++	(+)	33	0	60	53	0	0	40	27	0	25	0	0	25	60	54	100	50	50	35	80	0	0	0	70	0	36	57	72	40	47	95	NY PL SM TR
++++-+-	(-)	66	0	40	38	0	0	55	72	0	75	0	0	75	40	45	0	50	37	64	20	0	0	0	30	0	63	28	27	60	50	103	BO CP GC LB
+++++-+	(+)	33	0	31	52	0	0	40	55	0	100	0	0	25	57	41	0	55	28	23	100	0	0	0	37	0	50	40	33	33	42	71	GC PL
+++++-+	(-)	66	0	52	47	0	0	60	44	0	0	0	0	75	42	58	100	33	71	76	0	0	0	0	62	0	50	60	66	66	55	94	BO LB NY OJ PB TR W
+++++--	(+)	57	0	63	38	0	0	75	45	0	28	0	0	87	66	100	75	11	57	46	58	0	0	0	55	0	100	50	50	66	55	86	CO LB LC LH NY SU W
+++++-+	(-)	42	0	36	61	0	0	12	45	0	71	0	0	12	33	0	25	88	42	53	41	0	0	0	44	0	0	25	50	22	41	64	GC O
+++++--	(+)	0	0	37	40	0	0	53	45	0	33	0	0	55	87	40	100	40	44	58	28	0	0	0	53	0	100	71	40	40	48	77	LC NY TB
+++++++	(+)	100	0	62	60	0	0	38	63	0	66	0	0	44	12	60	0	60	55	41	42	0	0	0	46	0	100	14	60	60	48	78	BO GC SU
+++++-+	(-)	50	0	33	61	0	0	64	63	0	0	0	0	58	50	42	0	0	66	53	75	0	0	0	30	0	50	55	20	44	52	74	OJ PL
+++++--	(+)	50	0	66	27	0	0	35	36	0	0	0	0	41	50	57	100	33	33	46	25	0	0	0	70	0	50	33	80	44	44	62	C O SM TR
+++++++	(-)	0	0	66	72	0	0	75	42	0	50	0	0	83	63	50	50	33	36	42	0	0	0	0	57	0	100	40	100	50	49	59	C CC CO LB SU TR
+++++++	(-)	100	0	33	27	0	0	25	57	0	50	0	0	16	58	27	50	50	63	57	100	0	0	0	42	0	60	60	0	50	48	58	BO PL

9

Island Tops and Bottoms

A chart pattern which has been popular with traders for many years is the "island." Island signals can come at any time, however, they occur most often at important tops and bottoms. Unfortunately, it is not possible to know that an island is an island until after it has become an island. If this sounds like a line from *Alice's Adventures in Wonderland,* to you, it will become clear if you think about it for a while. Let's first define our terminology.

An *island top* is defined as a price bar whose trading range falls entirely outside the range of the bar before it and the bar after it. An *island bottom* is defined as a price bar whose trading range falls entirely outside the range of the bar before it and the bar after it. Figure 9-1 illustrates *island top* and *island bottom* signals. Figures 9-2 through 9-4 illustrate island signals in several markets. It is possible for island signals to be formed over a period of two, three, four or five days. Consider Figure 9-5, which illustrates multiple-day islands. Also examine Figures 9-6 through 9-9, which show multiple-day islands tops in various markets.

My test results on multiple- and one-day island tops and bottoms were impressive. The test results are shown in Figure 9-10. The algorithms for island tops are as follows.

One-Day Island Top

$$L2 > H1 \text{ and } L2 > H3$$

Multiple-Day Island Top

$$L2, L3 \ldots Ln < H1 \text{ and } L2, L3 \ldots Ln > Hn$$

where:

L2 = low of day 2;
H1 = high of day 1;
H3 = high of day 3;
Ln = low of nth day; and
Hn = high of nth day

It should now be clear to you that it is not possible to know that an island top is being made until the last day has been formed. What may appear to be an island top day or a multiple island top could, in fact, prove to be nothing more than a breakaway gap. A breakaway gap is defined as a price bar surrounded by gaps before and after it, and which precedes a substantial price move in the direction of the gap.

Island bottoms have also been touted as reliable signals. Although island tops and bottoms are not very common price bar signals, they do seem to occur at critical market junctures. Single- and multiple-day island bottoms are defined as follows:

One-Day Island Bottom

$$H2 < L1 \text{ and } H2 < L3$$

Multiple-Day Island Bottom

$$H2, H3 \ldots Hn < L1 \text{ and } H2, H3 \ldots Hn < Ln$$

where:

H2 = high of day 2;
L1 = low of day 1;
L3 = low of day 3;
Hn = high of nth day; and
Ln = low of nth day

Again it should be clear that it is not possible to know that an island bottom is being made until the last day has been formed. What may appear to be an island bottom day or a multiple island bottom could, in fact, prove to be nothing more than a "break-away gap."

THE TEST

In order to test one- and multiple-day island top and bottom signals, I used the following rules:

1. A one-day island top was considered a sell signal. A short position was taken on the close of the day the island was completed. The position was considered stopped out when the low of the day before the last day of the island formation was penetrated on a closing basis. If this occurred the position was closed out at a loss.

2. A multiple-day island top formation follows the same rules. A close above the lowest low of the string of days which form the multiple day island top was used as the stop loss point.

3. A one-day island bottom was considered a buy signal. A long position is taken on the close of the day the island was completed. The position was considered stopped out when the high of the day before the last day of the island formation was penetrated on a closing basis. If this occurs the position was closed out at a loss.

4. A multiple-day island bottom formation follows the same rules. A close below the highest high of the string of days which form the multiple-day island bottom was used as the stop loss point.

Figure 9.1: Island Top and Island Bottom Signals

Island Top

Island Bottom

Figure 9.2: 1-Day Island Top—July 1986 Corn

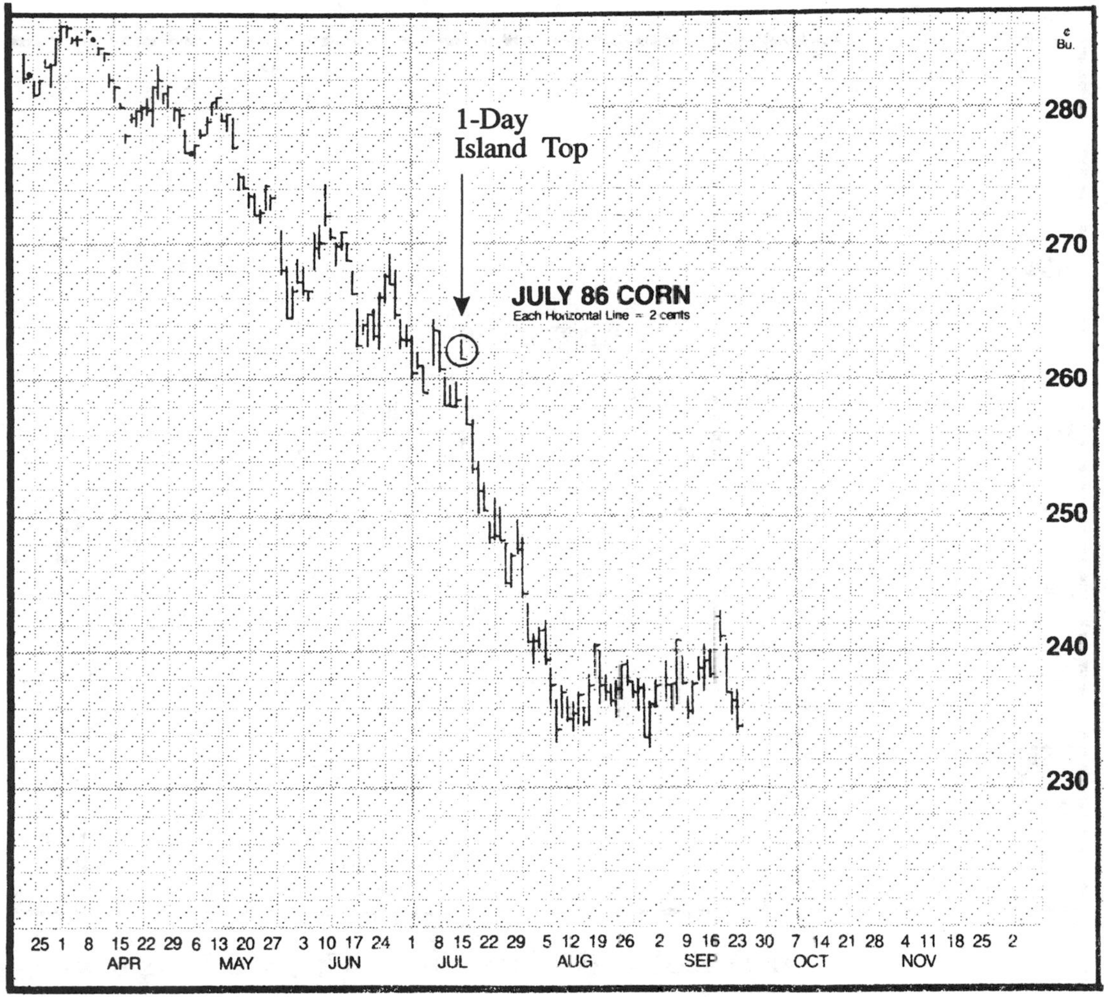

Figure 9.3: 1-Day Island Top—December 1986 Oats

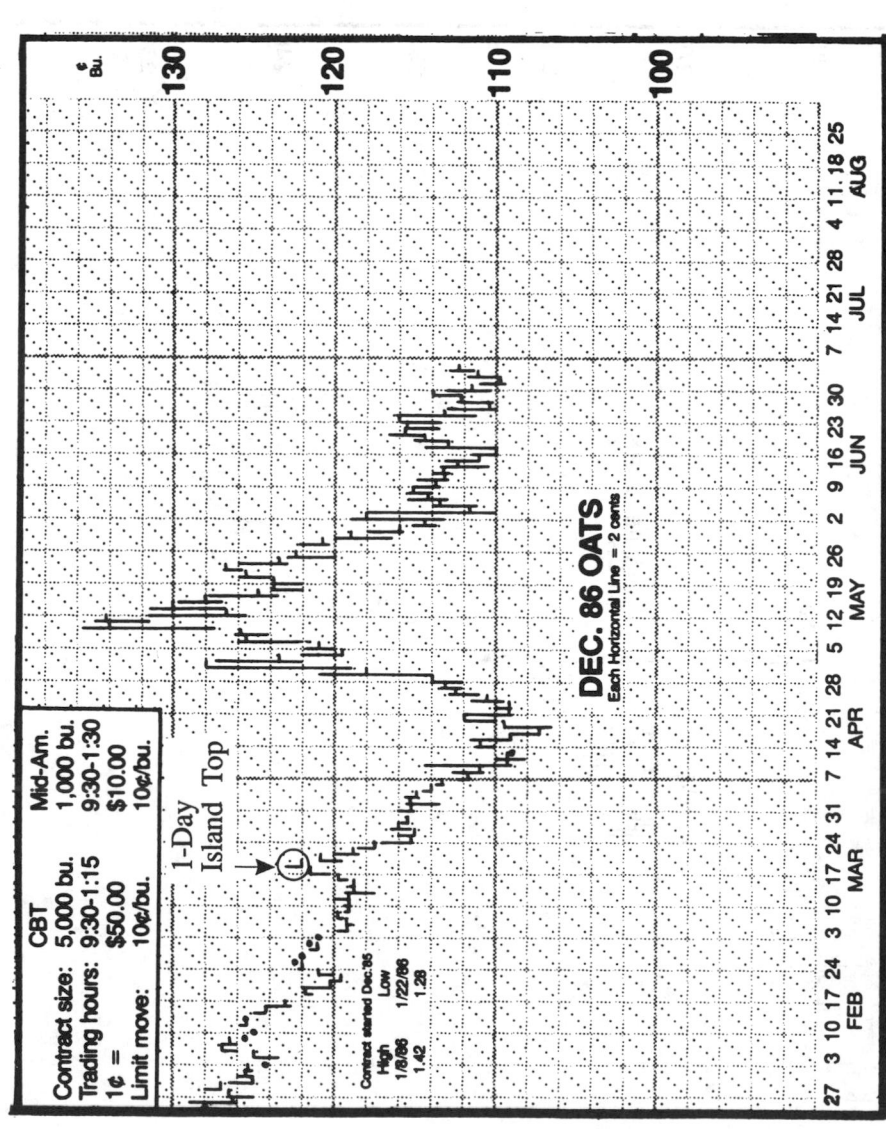

Figure 9.4: 1-Day Island Top—May 1984 Corn

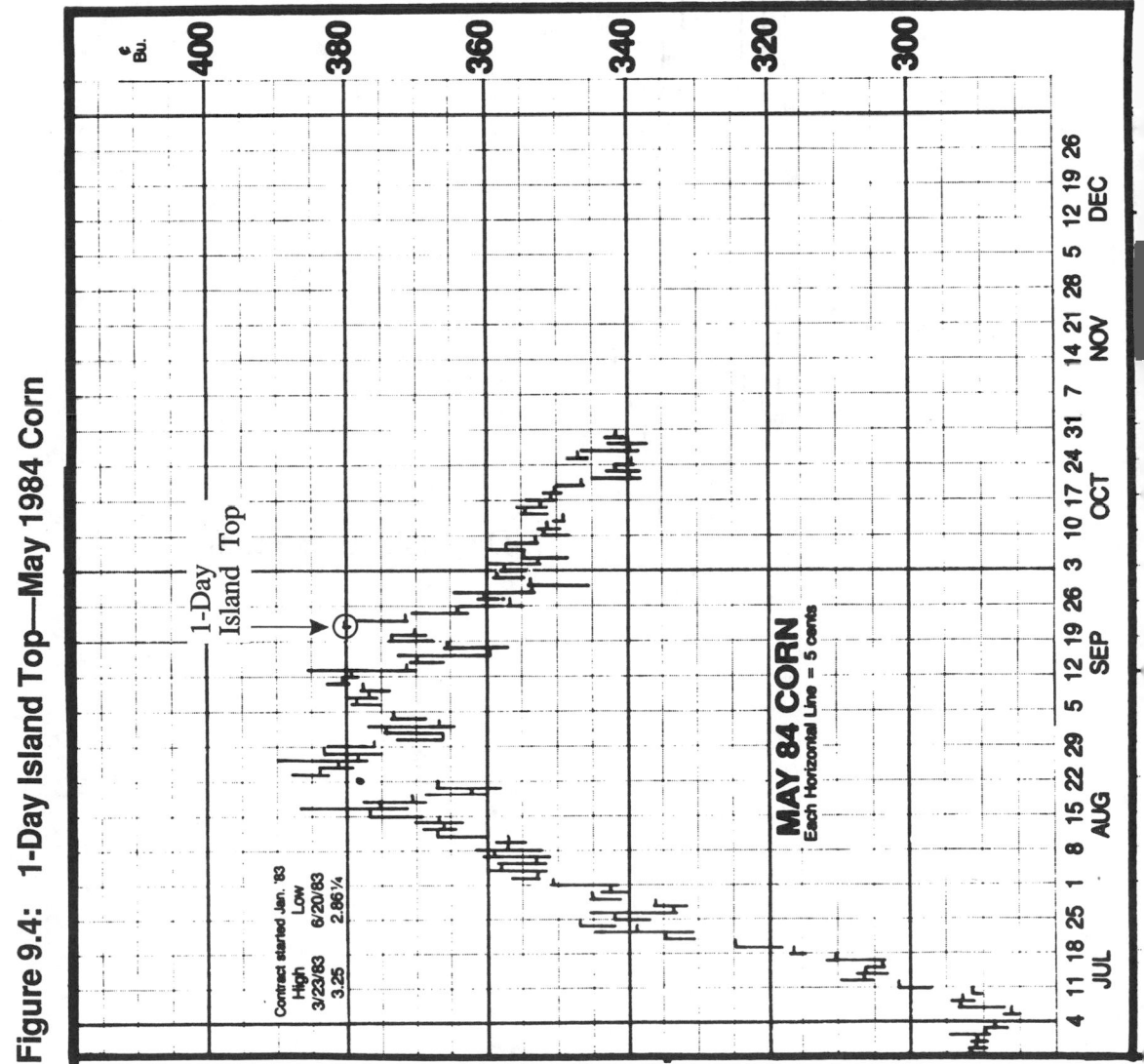

Figure 9.5: 2-Day Island Top and Bottom

Figure 9.6: 2-Day Island Bottom—December 1988 Wheat

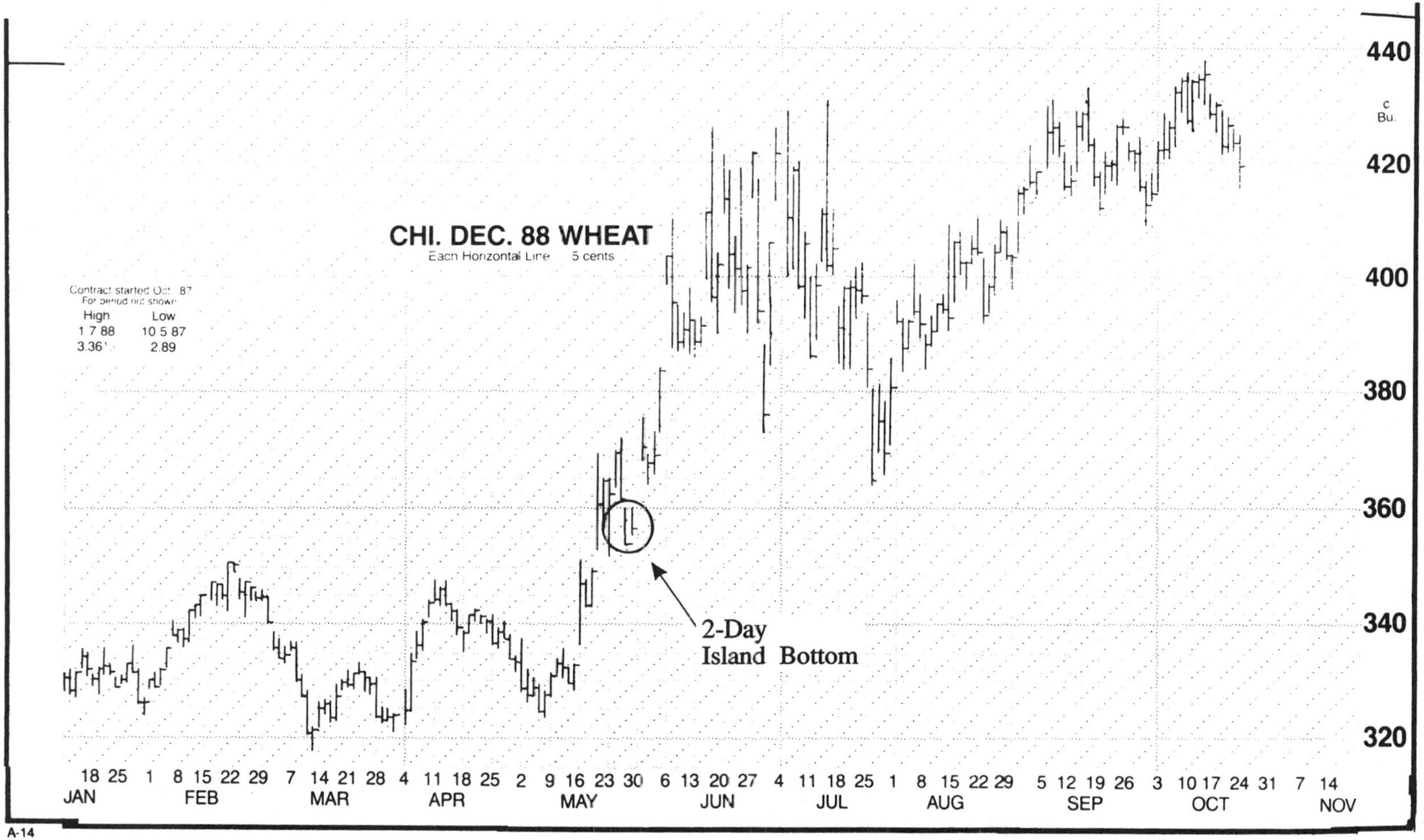

CHI. DEC. 88 WHEAT
Each Horizontal Line = 5 cents

Contract started Oct. 87
For period not shown
High   Low
17 88   10 5 87
3.36¹   2.89

2-Day
Island Bottom

A-14

Figure 9.7: 2-Day Island Top—July 1988 Soybean Oil

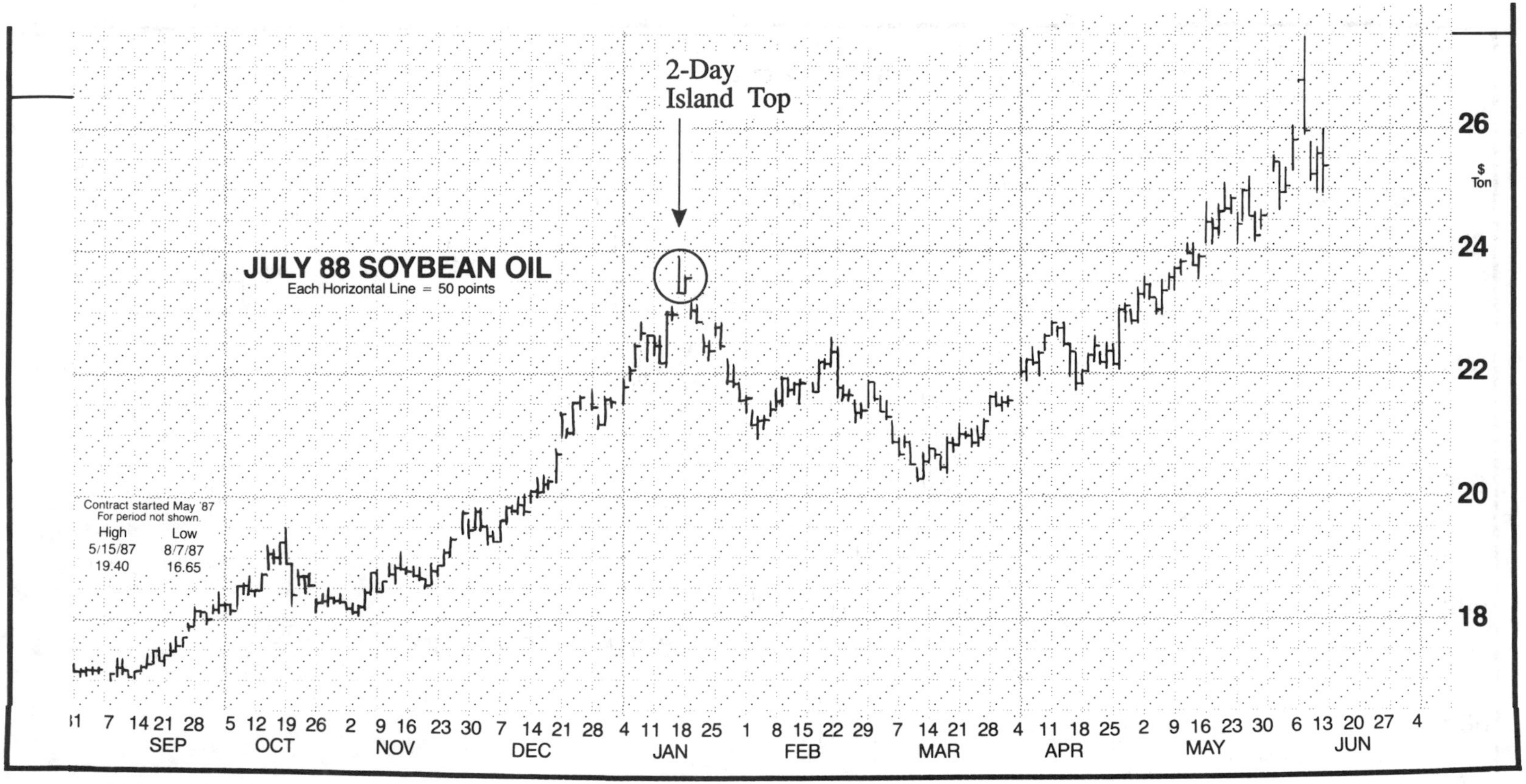

Figure 9.8: Multiple Day Island Tops and Bottoms—June 1980 Gold

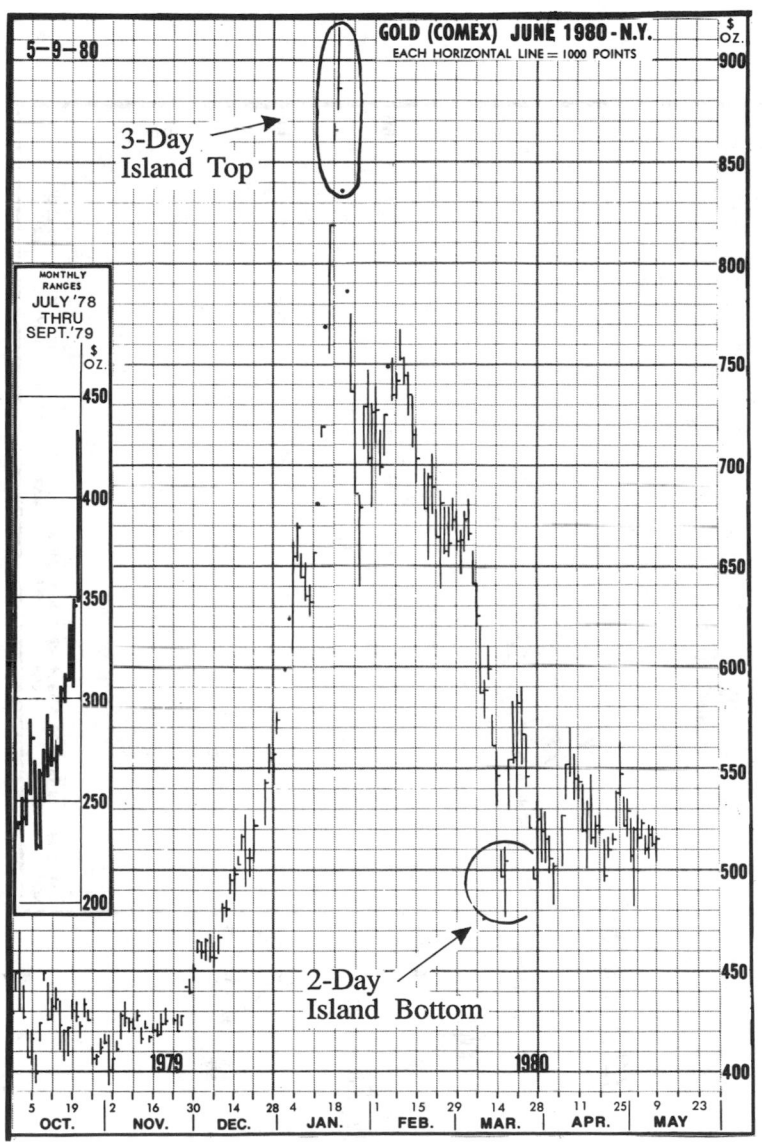

Chart reprinted with permission of Commodity Research Bureau
30 S. Wacker Drive #1820 Chicago, IL 60606

Figure 9.9: 2-Day Island Top—July 1986 Pork Bellies

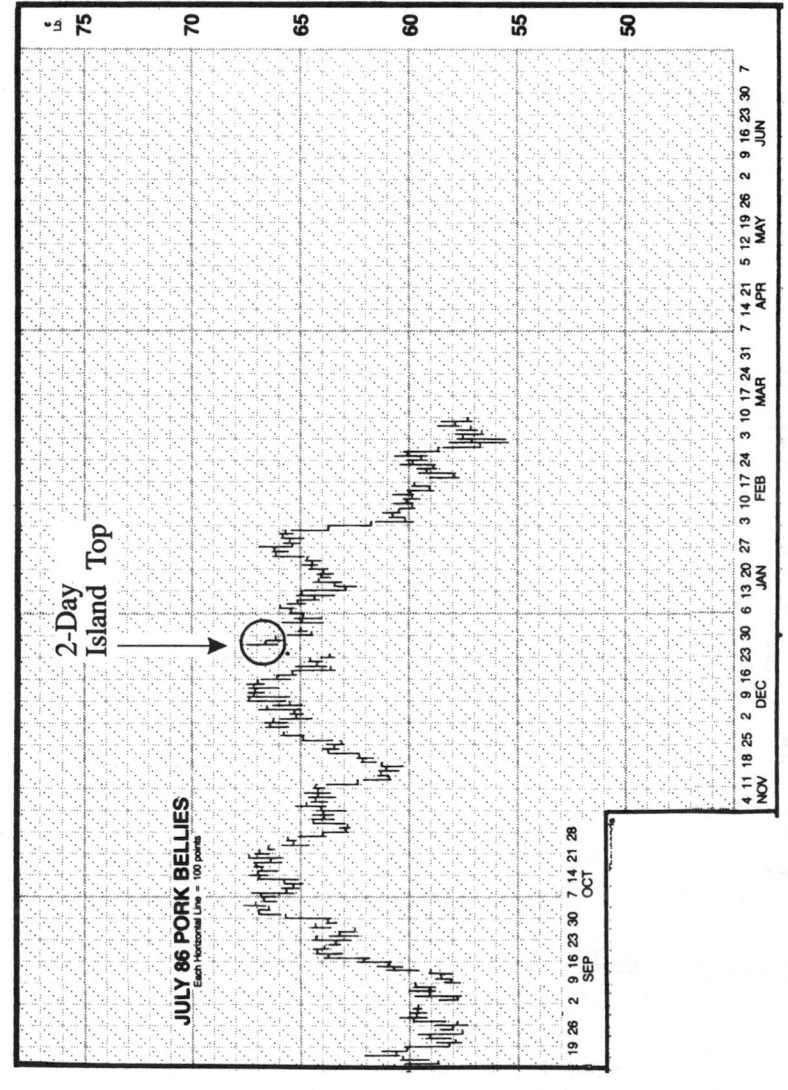

Figure 9.10: Summary of 1-, 2-, 3-, 4-, and 5-Day Island Signals

Market	1 DAY COUNT	1 DAY AVG +/-	2 DAY COUNT	2 DAY AVG +/-	3 DAY COUNT	3 DAY AVG +/-	4 DAY COUNT	4 DAY AVG +/-	5 DAY COUNT	5 DAY AVG +/-	TOTAL COUNT	TOTAL AVG +/-
BO	21	-.43	8	2.07	7	1.42	3	-.74	2	-1.64	41	.29
BP	100	.16	37	1.63	8	-.73	3	-3.13	0	.00	148	.42
C	32	-.84	12	7.36	4	-5.19	0	.00	3	7.67	51	1.25
CC	54	2.23	20	7.59	9	13.23	4	-6.65	4	-5.50	91	3.76
CD	213	9.05	52	22.00	23	-1.15	8	-11.97	5	38.27	301	10.43
CO	91	1.35	37	-1.40	10	1.93	5	3.09	3	-6.02	146	.60
CP	122	.83	38	.66	13	1.93	2	12.70	4	14.10	179	1.31
GC	75	7.08	23	8.30	7	-9.89	1	-13.90	1	11.00	107	6.07
JY	139	.27	36	.46	13	-.04	4	1.27	0	.00	192	.30
LB	37	1.25	16	-2.58	8	-3.01	4	-3.37	2	21.05	67	.14
LC	21	.75	15	-.22	2	2.57	0	.00	0	.00	38	.46
LH	59	.66	18	.54	8	-.04	7	.04	2	.00	94	.50
NY	38	2.38	16	-.90	11	.58	3	-.71	2	-.67	70	1.10
O	51	-2.09	24	18.45	10	-.25	5	-10.32	3	7.75	93	3.28
OJ	87	.89	39	1.61	8	-4.17	1	-2.75	1	-1.30	136	.76
PB	19	.93	13	-1.39	4	9.72	3	-3.92	0	.00	39	.68
PL	99	-3.92	25	-8.18	7	-6.51	4	-13.70	5	34.66	140	-3.71
S	26	8.80	21	15.41	5	98.02	3	148.75	1	18.12	56	26.91
SF	172	.10	51	-.01	15	-.29	7	1.58	2	6.70	247	.15
SM	36	1.89	19	-1.31	3	4.60	3	-5.70	0	.00	61	.66
SU	69	.68	31	1.28	6	-.12	3	1.03	0	.00	109	.81
TB	16	-.17	8	-.25	1	-1.48	3	-.53	5	1.14	33	-.06
TR	15	1.36	8	-1.29	6	-.60	1	-2.94	4	2.22	34	.37
W	9	24.19	9	1.08	4	-8.31	0	.00	1	-25.00	23	7.36

--------- GRAND TOTALS ---------

	#	AVG $	TOT $
1 DAY ISLAND	1601	253.60	406012.06
2 DAY ISLAND	576	320.66	184697.81
3 DAY ISLAND	192	300.48	57692.39
4 DAY ISLAND	77	76.02	5853.66
5 DAY ISLAND	50	1566.90	78345.19

IntraDay Timing Signals

Advances in computer technology and software development which began in 1980's have opened a vast new area of research to futures traders in the 1990's. The ability to test systems using daily price data is now standard procedure, and the ability to develop and thoroughly test trading systems using intraday data is rapidly gaining in popularity. In testing systems and trading signals on daily and intraday data, I've discovered that there are some signals and indicators which do not perform well on daily data but which have shown impressive historical results on intraday data.

This Appendix will discuss some of my findings in the area of intraday timing signals. While I do not intend it to serve as a thorough evaluation and examination of such signals, I do believe that it will serve as an excellent starting point. Remember that the amount of historical data which has been evaluated in preparing the tests discussed in this Appendix is limited. It covers about one year of tic-by-tic data. Given the large number of price tics each day and the number of trades examined, the test can be considered valid; however, I advise those who are seriously interested in pursuing these indicators to subject them to more scrutiny.

Opening Price Gap Signals

For many years traders have been fascinated with opening price gaps. The feeling among traders has been that price gaps provide important information about a market. Before examining some of these ideas, let's first define the term "opening price gap" as follows:

An opening price which is below the previous day's low price is defined as a "gap lower open" (GLO).

An opening price which is above the previous day's high price is defined as a "gap higher open" (GHO).

Figure 1 shows GLO and GHO signals. As you can see, I've shown the GLO signal following a downtrend and the GHO signal following an uptrend. The general feeling among traders regarding price gaps is that a gap higher opening during a daily uptrend can turn into an important short-term sell signal if the gap is filled (i.e., if the market declines to within the gap or to below the high of the previous day). Conversely, a gap lower opening during a declining daily trend sets up a possible reversal to the upside if the gap is penetrated on the way back up.

While these conclusions seem reasonable, the only scientific way to validate their efficacy is to subject them to a thorough test using intraday data. There are several commercially available software packages available for this purpose, and by the time you read this book there may be several others. I prefer to use Omega TradeStation.

Figure A.1:   GHO and GLO

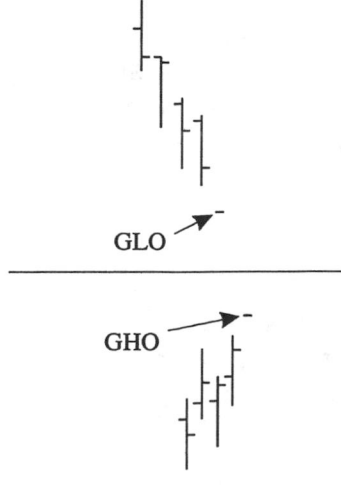

Opening Gap Penetration Signals

An intraday timing signal popularized by Larry Williams used gap openings as its primary parameter. The "OOPS" signal, as Larry called it, used the following rules:

1. If market open is greater than previous day's high (GHO), then sell short on a stop one tic below the previous day's high, (see Figure 2). Exit on the close of the day. Use either a money management stop loss or a stop loss above the high of the current day.

Figure A.2: OOPS Sell Signal

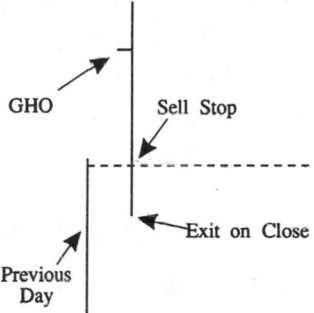

2. If market open is lower than previous day's low (GLO), then buy on a stop one tic above the previous day's low (see Figure 3). Exit on the close of the day. Use either a money management stop loss or a stop loss above the low of the current day.

Figure A.3: OOPS Buy Signal

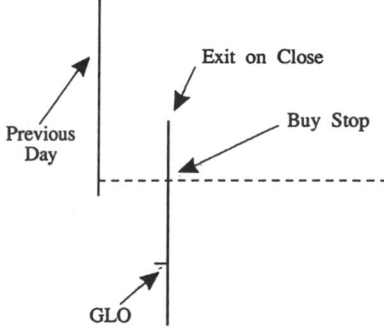

The OOPS signal sounds simple enough, but there are various parameters which may be tested in order to fully analyze its performance. Among these are:

1. Size of the opening gap.

2. Number of tics penetration through previous low or high.

3. Size of stop loss.

4. Trailing stop loss, if any.

5. Price target, if any.

The OOPS signal is easily tested using the advanced features of TradeStation since the parameters are objective and easily converted to mathematical algorithms. Based on an examination of OOPS parameters with the most active futures markets, I found that its best performance was in S&P futures. Figure 4 shows the system test using the following parameters:

1. Size of opening gap twenty-five points or more.

2. Size of low or high penetration ten points.

3. Stop loss $1500.

4. Trailing stop loss $1500.

Figure 4-1: Results of OOPS Trade System in S&P Using One Year of Data, 15 Point Opening Gap and 15 Point Penetration

Performance Summary: All Trades

Total net profit	$	11625.00	Open position P/L	$	0.00
Gross profit	$	20400.00	Gross loss	$	-8775.00

Total # of trades	30	Percent profitable	67%
Number winning trades	20	Number losing trades	10

Largest winning trade	$	2725.00	Largest losing trade	$	-1500.00
Average winning trade	$	1020.00	Average losing trade	$	-877.50
Ratio avg win/avg loss		1.16	Avg trade(win & loss)	$	387.50

Max consecutive winners	7	Max consecutive losers	3
Avg # bars in winners	4	Avg # bars in losers	3

Max intraday drawdown	$	-2925.00		
Profit factor		2.32	Max # contracts held	1
Account size required	$	2925.00	Return on account	397%

Performance Summary: Long Trades

Total net profit	$	9475.00	Open position P/L	$	0.00
Gross profit	$	10975.00	Gross loss	$	-1500.00

Total # of trades	9	Percent profitable	89%
Number winning trades	8	Number losing trades	1

Largest winning trade	$	2725.00	Largest losing trade	$	-1500.00
Average winning trade	$	1371.88	Average losing trade	$	-1500.00
Ratio avg win/avg loss		0.91	Avg trade(win & loss)	$	1052.78

Max consecutive winners	7	Max consecutive losers	1
Avg # bars in winners	4	Avg # bars in losers	4

Max intraday drawdown	$	-1500.00		
Profit factor		7.32	Max # contracts held	1
Account size required	$	1500.00	Return on account	632%

Performance Summary: Short Trades

Total net profit	$	2150.00	Open position P/L	$	0.00
Gross profit	$	9425.00	Gross loss	$	-7275.00

Total # of trades	21	Percent profitable	57%
Number winning trades	12	Number losing trades	9

Largest winning trade	$	1675.00	Largest losing trade	$	-1500.00
Average winning trade	$	785.42	Average losing trade	$	-808.33
Ratio avg win/avg loss		0.97	Avg trade(win & loss)	$	102.38

Max consecutive winners	4	Max consecutive losers	4
Avg # bars in winners	3	Avg # bars in losers	3

Max intraday drawdown	$	-3775.00		
Profit factor		1.30	Max # contracts held	1
Account size required	$	6775.00	Return on account	32%

As you can see, the results were impressive. Slippage and commission of $75 per trade were deducted from the average trade and positions were all closed out at the end of the day. (While the OOPS signal was also tested on currencies, crude oil and several other markets, I cannot as yet report results or parameters. I suggest, however, that you experiment on your own using various gap sizes and point penetrations.)

Variations on OOPS

In addition to the basic OOPS signal, I have also tested what I have called the gap on open price signal (GOOPS). The rules are as follows:

1. Market must gap higher or lower on open.

2. Wait one hour after open before entering any trades.

3. If market is above opening price at end of one hour after a GLO, then buy at market with stop loss below low of day or use money management stop loss.

4. If market is below open at end of one hour, then place buy stop X tics above opening price and use same stop loss procedure as in #3.

5. If market is below opening price at end of one hour after a GHO, then sell at market with stop loss above high of day or use a money management stop loss.

6. If market is above opening after one hour, then sell on stop X tics below opening price using same stop loss procedure as in #5.

As noted above, the GOOPS signal must be more thoroughly evaluated using various parameters.

Consecutive Closes

The Consecutive Closes (CC) indicator is simple to understand. The following abbreviations are used in my discussion of the CC indication:

CC = consecutive closes

CCU = consecutive closes up

CCD = consecutive closes down

CCU or CCD preceded by a number indicates the number of consecutive closes up or down (i.e. 4 CCU = 4 consecutive up closes).

I tested 3, 4, 5 and 6 CCU and CCD. The trading rules are as follows:

1. A buy or reverse to long signal occurs on the close of trading of the *nth* consecutive up close.

2. A sell or reverse to short position occurs on the close of the *nth* consecutive down close.

3. The unit of time varies according to test.

Sample Buy and Sell Signals

A buy signal using a 4CC system, therefore, might appear as follows:

Closing Price	Change	Count
4550	+25	+1
4545	−05	−1
4560	+15	+1
4565	+5	+2
4590	+25	+3
4600	+10	+4 Buy on Close of this time period

A sell signal occurs on the fourth consecutive lower close. The position would be entered on the close of trading and held until either stopped out or until reversed by a contrary CC signal.

As you can see, the system requires no computer or sophisticated mathematical formulae. It is easy to implement and monitor provided you have access to intraday data. Figure 4 illustrates sample buy, reverse to long, sell and reverse to short signals.

A hybrid CC system which enters the market on one CC combination and exits on another should be considered. We know that markets move up more slowly than they move down; hence, a 5CC entry signal and a 3CD exit/reverse combination might prove much more effective than a CC entry and exit system which uses the same CC units.

Figure 5:   Test #1 4cc, 60-Minute S&P; $75 Shippage and Commission; $3,000 Initial Stop Loss; $1,800 Trailing Stop Loss

Performance Summary: All Trades

Total net profit	$	40625.00	Open position P/L	$ 0.00
Gross profit	$	88400.00	Gross loss	$ -47775.00
Total # of trades		86	Percent profitable	44%
Number winning trades		38	Number losing trades	48
Largest winning trade	$	12725.00	Largest losing trade	$ -1875.00
Average winning trade	$	2326.32	Average losing trade	$ -995.31
Ratio avg win/avg loss		2.34	Avg trade(win & loss)	$ 472.38
Max consecutive winners		5	Max consecutive losers	7
Avg # bars in winners		15	Avg # bars in losers	6
Max intraday drawdown	$	-9725.00		
Profit factor		1.85	Max # contracts held	1
Account size required	$	9725.00	Return on account	418%

Performance Summary: Long Trades

Total net profit	$	32250.00	Open position P/L	$ 0.00
Gross profit	$	57275.00	Gross loss	$ -25025.00
Total # of trades		45	Percent profitable	47%
Number winning trades		21	Number losing trades	24
Largest winning trade	$	12725.00	Largest losing trade	$ -1875.00
Average winning trade	$	2727.38	Average losing trade	$ -1042.71
Ratio avg win/avg loss		2.62	Avg trade(win & loss)	$ 716.67
Max consecutive winners		5	Max consecutive losers	5
Avg # bars in winners		19	Avg # bars in losers	7
Max intraday drawdown	$	-9725.00		
Profit factor		2.29	Max # contracts held	1
Account size required	$	9275.00	Return on account	348%

Performance Summary: Short Trades

Total net profit	$	8375.00	Open position P/L	$ 0.00
Gross profit	$	31125.00	Gross loss	$ -22750.00
Total # of trades		41	Percent profitable	41%
Number winning trades		17	Number losing trades	24
Largest winning trade	$	5575.00	Largest losing trade	$ -1875.00
Average winning trade	$	1830.88	Average losing trade	$ -947.92
Ratio avg win/avg loss		1.93	Avg trade(win & loss)	$ 204.27
Max consecutive winners		8	Max consecutive losers	10
Avg # bars in winners		11	Avg # bars in losers	6
Max intraday drawdown	$	-12450.00		
Profit factor		1.37	Max # contracts held	1
Account size required	$	12450.00	Return on account	67%

Figure 6: Test #2 4cc, 60-Minute S&P with Same Parameters as Test #1

Performance Summary: All Trades

Total net profit	$	22550.00	Open position P/L	$ 0.00
Gross profit	$	48425.00	Gross loss	$ -25875.00
Total # of trades		37	Percent profitable	35%
Number winning trades		13	Number losing trades	24
Largest winning trade	$	12800.00	Largest losing trade	$ -1875.00
Average winning trade	$	3725.00	Average losing trade	$ -1078.13
Ratio avg win/avg loss		3.46	Avg trade(win & loss)	$ 609.46
Max consecutive winners		3	Max consecutive losers	5
Avg # bars in winners		37	Avg # bars in losers	11
Max intraday drawdown	$	-9975.00		
Profit factor		1.87	Max # contracts held	1
Account size required	$	12975.00	Return on account	174%

Performance Summary: Long Trades

Total net profit	$ 14150.00	Open position P/L	$ 0.00
Gross profit	$ 35425.00	Gross loss	$ -21275.00
Total # of trades	26	Percent profitable	31%
Number winning trades	8	Number losing trades	18
Largest winning trade	$ 12800.00	Largest losing trade	$ -1875.00
Average winning trade	$ 4428.13	Average losing trade	$ -1181.94
Ratio avg win/avg loss	3.75	Avg trade(win & loss)	$ 544.23
Max consecutive winners	2	Max consecutive losers	7
Avg # bars in winners	40	Avg # bars in losers	11
Max intraday drawdown	$ -10800.00		
Profit factor	1.67	Max # contracts held	1
Account size required	$ 13800.00	Return on account	103%

Performance Summary: Short Trades

Total net profit	$ 8400.00	Open position P/L	$ 0.00
Gross profit	$ 13000.00	Gross loss	$ -4600.00
Total # of trades	11	Percent profitable	45%
Number winning trades	5	Number losing trades	6
Largest winning trade	$ 4975.00	Largest losing trade	$ -1625.00
Average winning trade	$ 2600.00	Average losing trade	$ -766.67
Ratio avg win/avg loss	3.39	Avg trade(win & loss)	$ 763.64
Max consecutive winners	1	Max consecutive losers	2
Avg # bars in winners	31	Avg # bars in losers	11
Max intraday drawdown	$ -2525.00		
Profit factor	2.83	Max # contracts held	1
Account size required	$ 5525.00	Return on account	152%

Test #1: Sixty-Minute S&P Futures 4CC Performance Summary

Figure 5 shows the results of this test. I consider them impressive. The test covered about one year of tic-by-tic data and eighty-four trades. The accuracy rate was 46 percent, with seven maximum consecutive losers. It was necessary to use a rather wide initial stop loss as well as a large trailing stop loss given the volatile nature of S&P futures. Admittedly a large percentage of the net profit came from one large profit of over $12,000, but the system performance even without this trade is still very respectable at over $394 profit per trade.

Test #2: Thirty-Minute S&P Futures 6CC Performance Summary

Now examine the results of the thirty-minute S&P method using 6CC as the indicator. The results here are even more impressive than they were for the sixty-minute test on an average trade basis. Do note, however, that nearly half of the net profits were the result of one large winner of nearly $13,000. But even if we remove this winner from the total figure, the net profit per trade is still very high (see Figure 6).

Figure 7: 30-Minute S&P, 7cc, with Same Parameters as Test #1

Performance Summary: All Trades

Total net profit	$ 24275.00	Open position P/L	$ 0.00
Gross profit	$ 37100.00	Gross loss	$ -12825.00
Total # of trades	20	Percent profitable	45%
Number winning trades	9	Number losing trades	11
Largest winning trade	$ 12575.00	Largest losing trade	$ -1875.00
Average winning trade	$ 4122.22	Average losing trade	$ -1165.91
Ratio avg win/avg loss	3.54	Avg trade(win & loss)	$ 1213.75
Max consecutive winners	3	Max consecutive losers	4
Avg # bars in winners	42	Avg # bars in losers	9
Max intraday drawdown	$ -4200.00		
Profit factor	2.89	Max # contracts held	1
Account size required	$ 4200.00	Return on account	578%

Performance Summary: Long Trades

```
Total net profit          $   18325.00   Open position P/L      $        0.00
Gross profit              $   29725.00   Gross loss             $  -11400.00

Total # of trades              14        Percent profitable             43%
Number winning trades           6        Number losing trades            8

Largest winning trade     $   12575.00   Largest losing trade   $   -1875.00
Average winning trade     $    4954.17   Average losing trade   $   -1425.00
Ratio avg win/avg loss          3.48     Avg trade(win & loss)  $    1308.93

Max consecutive winners         3        Max consecutive losers          3
Avg # bars in winners          44        Avg # bars in losers           10

Max intraday drawdown     $   -4325.00
Profit factor                   2.61     Max # contracts held            1
Account size required     $    4325.00   Return on account             424%
```

Performance Summary: Short Trades

```
Total net profit          $    5950.00   Open position P/L      $        0.00
Gross profit              $    7375.00   Gross loss             $   -1425.00

Total # of trades               6        Percent profitable             50%
Number winning trades           3        Number losing trades            3

Largest winning trade     $    4525.00   Largest losing trade   $    -900.00
Average winning trade     $    2458.33   Average losing trade   $    -475.00
Ratio avg win/avg loss          5.18     Avg trade(win & loss)  $     991.67

Max consecutive winners         1        Max consecutive losers          2
Avg # bars in winners          39        Avg # bars in losers            6

Max intraday drawdown     $   -1150.00
Profit factor                   5.18     Max # contracts held            1
Account size required     $    1150.00   Return on account             517%
```

Figure 7 shows the performance summary of the 7CC indicator in thirty-minute S&P futures. The results are impressive even considering that more than one-half of the net profits were derived from only one trade. At $1,213.75 per trade after slippage and commission I think you'll find this approach well worthwhile. Note also that the maximum number of consecutive losers was only five. I have not tested too many other CC periods or time frames; I suggest you do so if you have an interest in this approach. The ideal situation, of course, would be to find a combination of timeframe and CC length which produces consistent profits without a high percentage of the net profit per trade being the result of only one or two trades.

Index

T
Thanksgiving, 198, 271
Timing
   see indicator, key date, pattern,
      signal
   market, 15
   signal, 15
     seasonal, 265-280
Track record, 10-11
TradeStation, *see* Omega
Trading systems, 199-200
   efficiency, 3
Treasury bonds (T-bonds), 131, 179,
   200
Trending market, 14, 69, 193
Trends, 10-12, 108
   see indicator, signal
Triple moving average, *see* indicator

V
Veterans Day, 198

W
Welles Wilder's Relative Strength
    Index (RSI), 282
Wheat, 131, 179, 236, 266
Whipsaw, 109, 118
   market, 14, 57, 123, 127, 150,
      155, 179, 287-288, 291-292
   results, 193
Williams and Noseworthy, 239
Williams, Lary, 282, 303-304, 423
World War II, 198